DAYS OF OUR YEARS

Sincerely
Pierre van Paassen

DAYS
OF OUR YEARS

by

Pierre van Paassen

1940

THE DIAL PRESS · NEW YORK

Printed in the United States of America

HADDON CRAFTSMEN, INC., CAMDEN, N. J.

Contents

DAYS OF OUR YEARS

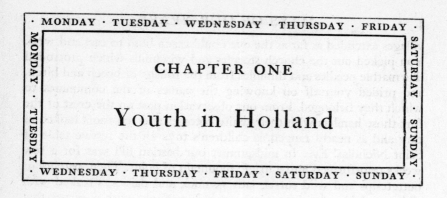

CHAPTER ONE

Youth in Holland

I

MY EARLIEST RECOLLECTIONS go back thirty-five years to a silent street in a small urban community of the Netherlands. One side of the street was deeply shaded in summertime by a row of mulberry trees whose branches projected from an adjacent orchard over the top of a crumbling stone wall. At one time men must have passed in and out of that garden through a low door cut in the wall under a sculptured arch, but in my days that door was never opened. The orchard lay abandoned and neglected, a desert of weeds and rank grass. Boys carved their initials and those of their sweethearts in the worm-eaten door and used the wall as a rampart in games and street battles. Everything inside the orchard, the summerhouse, the fountains, the ornamental benches, was given over to decay, but to us it was a world of miracles. No matter where you scratched the moss and creeping vine, you came upon myriads of spiders and ants and bugs rushing about on their mysterious business: weaving their webs, waging their wars and founding their colonies and empires amidst the accumulation of dust and saltpeter. At the end of the street, rising like a steep mountain from the plain, appeared the green earthworks of a dismantled military fort. Its moats had been dry a hundred years and the sharp pikes on its encircling palisades had been twisted into inoffensive rings, or entirely removed by successive generations of boys eager to climb to the bastion's summit for a view of the river with its endless procession of flat-bottomed ships, steamboats and fishing rafts. On the farther shore, under a blue sky dotted with disklike clouds, the immense panorama of Brabant's friendly

3

villages extended as far as the eye could reach both to east and west. You picked out the church steeples and windmills which protruded like marble needles and thimbles from the foliage of beech and birch, and prided yourself on knowing the names of the communes to which they belonged. From our observation post on the crest of the fort those hamlets with their white cottages and red roofs looked as tiny and as neatly ranged as children's toys on the festive table of Saint Nicholas' Eve. In midsummer our bastion hill was for a few weeks transformed into a magic mountain of color. Then, patches of buttercups and wild sorrel, lady's-smock and daisies, streaked with ribbons of blood-red poppies, covered its flanks with a carpet that rippled softly in the river breeze. But with the first days of August the feast of flowers came to an end. The silhouette of the mower could be seen from the street, swinging his implement against the southern horizon. After he had passed, the fairy mountain was an earth-brown knoll again, covered with stubbles, and waiting disconsolately for the rains and snow of winter. Facing the abandoned orchard, across the cobblestone roadway, stood a line of nine unpretentious houses of red brick, all alike in outer appearance, except that the windows of the structure in the middle of the row were devoid of curtains. In its shallow porch above the entrance hung a signboard with this inscription painted in vivid letters of black on white: HERE IS A SCHOOL WITH THE BIBLE. THE FEAR OF THE LORD IS THE BEGINNING OF WISDOM.

In that institution I spent seven of the most impressionable years of my life.

Not a single detail of the school's interior arrangement has faded from my memory. . . . I still see the long line of wooden shoes in the hallway and the austere whitewashed classrooms where our eyes smarted from the clouds of acrid smoke which poured from the potbellied stoves on winter mornings when the wind blew from the northwest. On such days, we boys were required to take turns in inducing the smoldering peat and coal fire to burst into flame by means of a pair of bellows. I do not recall anyone ever succeeding. And small wonder! For reasons of economy the coal was doused with water before being put into the stove! Back of the principal's desk hung a rack for his collection of long clay pipes which he used in rotation. Occasionally, when we judged that reprisals were in order for some measure of collective punishment the master had meted out, we secretly smeared the mouthpieces of his pipes with a certain invisible and unmentionable concoction. We then sat back to watch his grimaces of disgust when he placed the stem in his mouth. Another object of amusement in the classroom was a large-sized wood gravure of "Johannes Calvijn." Calvin was pictured in profile in a high-collared toga. The side of his face was almost covered by a long velvet flap which descended from a flat beret to his shoulders. Besides the tip of his nose, which had been daubed a violent purple by some youthful iconoclast, a deft touch of crayon had prolonged the reformer's black goatee into something that looked like a cross between a corkscrew and a rattlesnake. It bristled forth with so Mephistophelian an effect from the mass of pleats and ruffles around his neck that whenever the principal, pointing to Calvin's likeness, awesomely mentioned the name of "our beloved father in God," we had all we could do to keep from screaming. Above Calvin's portrait, but safe from the disfiguring pencils of would-be vandals, hung a row of yellowed prints representing the other reformers—Farel, Beza, John Knox—and a colored lithograph of William the Silent, Prince of Orange, the father of the fatherland.

Thinking of that now distant place and day, it is as if I feel a breeze from the Middle Ages blow into my face. That school was a model of authoritarianism: the pupils were considered and treated as little automatons without a will or inclination of their own. The discipline was ascetic, almost penitential; while the curriculum did not differ in essentials from that in use in Dutch schools a hundred or even two hundred years earlier. Before I had learned to read or write, the principal made me memorize long quotations from Holy Writ and from the Heidelberg Catechism. At the age of six I could reel off, without a single error, that whole list of Hebrew "begetters" from the first chapter of Matthew's Gospel which is supposed to be Christ's family tree. For this almost incredible feat of memory in a child of six, an uncle of mine, more in pity than in admiration, presented me with a leather-bound copy of Hans Andersen's *Fairy Tales*, from which he was good enough to read me a piece each night before I was put to bed.

The headmaster, a tight-lipped, sallow-complexioned old fundamentalist whose protruding blue eyes were enlarged to twice their natural size by a pair of enormously thick lenses, was a descendant of a Huguenot family which had settled in Holland after the revocation of the Edict of Nantes. Gaunt, his face a mask of deep wrinkles, his bony fingers tapering off into nails as long as those of a

Chinese mandarin, he inspired me with so much more terror than respect that I still see his ghost at times. There was not a spark of humor in that man. Not once in all those years did I see his face soften into a smile. He had come to the teaching profession much in the same spirit as an Inquisitor approaches a victim in the torture chamber. His conception of his task was not to guide and shepherd, but to correct a crowd of hopelessly bad children, who were inclined from birth—as that lovely Catechism specified—"to do evil and hate God." In fact, the whole system of "Schools with the Bible" in Holland was set up to counteract the rational mode of thought which swept over Europe in the wake of the French Revolution. Against the spirit of inquiry and free thought of the nineteenth century, which was deemed to have poisoned two or three generations of Dutchmen, these schools were to provide an antidote by instilling respect for the ancient verities.

The "instilling" was frequently done (in our case) with the aid of a brass-edged ruler of ebony wood, which the principal, in spite of his reputed shortsightedness, manipulated with uncanny precision. He never missed. Upon the slightest provocation: a mere whisper in the classroom or a giggle, he advanced upon you without a word, seized hold of your wrist, and brought down his stick on your knuckles, not in anger, but with calm deliberation. If you wept in pain and humiliation after one of these punitive ministrations, he locked you up for the rest of the day in a small dark room where the coal was kept and which swarmed with rats and mice.

The principal was assisted by three younger men, who constantly quarreled with him because of his merciless severity. Every term saw a new set of assistant masters, but rheumatic and asthmatic "Monsieur"—the title was a remnant from the Napoleonic era—seemed both immovable and immortal. He grew more inflexible and forbidding as time went on. I still see him suddenly jumping from his chair at his desk where he had been silently reading our compositions, and, in a blaze of anger, his lips curled in a tigerish leer that revealed his yellow stumps of teeth, pouncing upon a fellow pupil in whose copybook he had just discovered a sentence that displeased him. He went on beating until the boy sank fainting to his knees. The offending sentence, I happen to recall, dealt with "snowflakes fluttering from a pitilessly gray heavenly roof."

Heaven, it appeared, was never pitiless. . . .

In springtime, when the windows were opened, we could hear the carillon in St. John's cathedral tower sing out the passage of the hours with selections from the patriotic hymnology. Often, too, a wandering band of German musicians would stray into the street. If they played Luther's "A Safe Stronghold," or some such solemn chorale, we children were permitted to listen, the music being judged edifying by Monsieur. But upon hearing the umpah-band striking the first bars of so "worldly" a piece as "Oh, Susanna," the master would almost suffer an apoplectic fit. He turned purple with rage, the veins in his scrawny neck suddenly stood out like thick blue cords, and he slammed the windows shut with a loud bang. A kinder reception was accorded the local operator of an organ of Barbary, a bearded individual who was popularly known by the onomatopoetic name of Jan Rèteketè. A fellow Calvinist, Jan knew Monsieur's predilections on the subject of music. When he came near our school, he always changed the record he was playing to Sankey's well-known revival song, "Lord, I Hear of Showers of Blessing," in which we were allowed to join our voices, Monsieur leading off. But neither the master nor Jan Rèteketè suspected, I am sure, that there existed another set of words to this tune—far from edifying.

When I first came to his school, Monsieur was in the habit of including in his morning prayer a fervent appeal to the Lord God of Hosts for the support of our kinsmen, the Boers of the Transvaal, who were at that time defending the independence of their republic against British usurpation. He prayed in a harsh and rasping voice, speaking to God as to a fellow schoolmaster in a succession of short, staccato exclamations: "Go Thou to their aid. . . . Delay not. . . . For the water has come up to their lips. . . . Smite Thou the enemies of Thine elect. . . . Consume the perfidious foe with the fire of Thy nostrils. . . . Revenge Thy servants, our brothers, so that the earth may be filled with Thy terror and glory. . . ." Some mornings this went on for a quarter of an hour before a group of boys six years old, who had to keep their eyes closed, and their hands folded above their desks while Monsieur laid down the law to the Almighty. After prayer, we sang a stanza or two from a rhymed version of the Psalms, whereupon the master read a goodly portion from the "*Staten*"-Bible before passing on to the order of the day: spelling, arithmetic and the history of our fatherland. Upon the conclusion of the religious exercises we were allowed to unfold our hands and were given a minute to blow our noses, while Monsieur took a pinch of snuff. This made him sneeze so vehemently that he staggered on his feet. It was the only physical exercise he indulged in.

It soon became evident, however, that Monsieur's daily intercessions failed to have the desired effect on the course of hostilities at the other end of the world. The heroism of the Boers was of no avail against the overwhelming military pressure England was bringing to bear: Generals Buller and French crushed the farmer commandos one by one, President Kruger fled to Holland, and Botha signed the peace of Vereeniging. The war "for freedom and right" was over, and lost.

Britain's triumph in South Africa cut a deep impression in my youthful mind. After listening to Monsieur's solemn apostrophes, I could not understand how a God whose chief attribute was said to be justice could have permitted the forces of evil to overwhelm a people that had completely placed its trust in Him. The facile explanation advanced in the fundamentalist milieu in which I grew up, that "God's ways are inscrutable and past finding out," left me unsatisfied and ill at ease. I thought, but took good care not to voice a sentiment which might have seemed to cast doubt on the divine perfection, that the God, who had in the past stood steadfastly by Holland in its long struggle with Spain, had damaged His reputation irreparably by giving the victory to England in this case. I had never yet heard of Napoleon's theory that God is always on the side of the best artillery, nor had I come to the conviction (which I gained after fighting as a soldier in the Great War) that no cause, whatever its merits, warrants the closing of men's eyes to the goodness of the sun.

Some of the most intransigent Boers, who preferred exile to swearing the required oath of allegiance to Edward VII, settled in our community after the war. They became the heroes of my youth. It was from them, on long winter evenings at home, that I learned the details of that uneven struggle for the possession of the diamond fields and the gold mines of Kimberley and the Rand; the ghastly concentration camps wherein Boer women, separated from their husbands and children (Kitchener had said in one of his communiqués that he had found Dutch mothers to be totally bereft of a normal maternal instinct), were given over to the lust and the cruelty of a whisky-crazed soldiery. It was enough to make you boil with rage and vow, along with other little boys, to go forth some day and take revenge in that not distant city up the Thames.

Our elders, although less martially inclined (they knew Holland's weakness), deeply felt the shame and the humiliation inflicted on our race by England. And I vividly recall one Sunday morning in our church: an exiled South African dominie, choosing for his text the episode which deals with the Prophet's experiences in the lions' den, proceeded to compare the woes of the people of the Transvaal with the ordeal of the Hebrew seer in the midst of ferocious beasts. He so deeply stirred us all that one member of the congregation, suddenly rising in his seat, exclaimed with shaking fists: "But I say to you all: the God of Daniel still liveth!" Upon these words that entire congregation of undemonstrative Dutchmen, tears running down their grim faces and the organ crashing out the tune, burst into the Boer national anthem:

> The four-color of our dear Transvaal,
> Will surely fly over the veldt again!

It was an incident never to be forgotten. Whenever in later years, in Geneva or elsewhere, I heard a Haile Selassie or a Dr. Chaim Weizmann affirm their faith in England's high purposes, or I listened to Captain Eden or Lord Cecil repeat Woodrow Wilson's prophetic phrase about self-determination for small peoples, or heard Gandhi or Azaña talk of the British sense of fair play, the pathetic figure of Oom Paul Kruger going the round of Europe's chancelleries rose before my mind's eye, and his words, pronounced at a meeting in the city of Utrecht to which my father took me, came back to mind: "England told them to shut the door in my face and all of them obeyed."

2

The population of the community of Gorcum in which I was born had been stationary between twelve and thirteen thousand for fully three centuries, ever since the foundation of the Dutch Republic. Hemmed in by a ring of old-fashioned bastions, palisaded redoubts, and deep moats, the town was incapable of expansion. For the building of a doghouse or a cowshed outside the gates, permission from the War Department was necessary, and since that body invariably refused to sanction the erection of anything "that might offer a visible target to enemy guns," the burghers had long ago given up trying. We lived in a house that was built in 1644. The building next door was a hundred years older. It bore a sculptured inscription on the façade which read: PRAISE THE LORD. HONOR HIM. FOR THE DAY OF RECKONING IS BEARING DOWN UPON YOU! Cannonballs were embedded in its walls, and of one of these projectiles the story was told, that before coming to lodge between two windows, it had taken off the head of my maternal great-great-grandfather as he stood quietly smoking his pipe in the cool of the evening. The argument as to whether it was a Prussian or a French ball that had decapitated the old gentleman was occasionally revived in our family. Nobody could be quite sure, it seemed, inasmuch as the incident had occurred at a moment when two rival armies were contending for possession of one of the town's outer forts.

There were men living, when I was a boy, who remembered having seen Louis, the first King of Holland, and his brother the Emperor Napoleon. Half an hour from the city walls, near the village of Dalem, the spot was pointed out where Bonaparte had stood one winter morning, watching the river pile up immense blocks of ice against the dikes as he passed by in a carriage on his way from Paris to Amsterdam to make peace between Louis and Hortense. In order to save the dike, Napoleon, with his quick grasp of a dangerous situation, had ordered the batteries of the town wall to fire into the river to break up the buckling glacial pyramids.

Except for the Emperor's visit, the community's only claim to fame was that it was the birthplace of Jan van der Heyden, the inventor of the fire engine, and that it had harbored (albeit for a few short hours) one of Holland's greatest sons, Hugo Grotius, the jurist and father of the League of Nations. Grotius had been imprisoned for his political and religious beliefs in the castle of Loevesteyn, an early, medieval bastille which stands on Monks' Island at the confluence of the Meuse and an estuary of the Rhine a mile above Gorcum. He had managed to escape from that prison by hiding in a double-bottomed bookcase which his jailers carried out themselves. The famous bookcase stood in the Orphan House in our town, and many times I sat in it, breathing through the holes that the author of *The Right of War and Peace* had cut in the false bottom with his own penknife.

Nothing ever happened to disturb the peaceful flow of life in our community: children were born; the singing tower changed its tune once a year; old men sat on wooden benches by the river's edge watching the ships drift by; women gathered around the pumps to gossip; the young lieutenants of the garrison strolled about after four in the afternoon and let their sabers rattle a little on the cobblestones when they spotted a pretty girl; there was a fire occasionally, or the body of a drowned fisherman was washed up on the shore; and once a year, on the Queen's birthday, the troops held a parade and everybody, except a handful of Socialists, wore an orange-colored ribbon and drank lemonade. By seven in the evening, earlier in wintertime, the streets were deserted, and after ten, the night watch with his lantern went the rounds to see that all doors were locked. This man, Ary Struyck, a rheumatic cripple, lived in a small chamber in the clock tower and looked after the carillon, winding it up when it had run down. Many times I climbed to his loft to watch the bats swarm out of the belfry at sundown and to listen to his reminiscences. When he grew old and failing, I clambered the narrow spiral stairway on Sunday afternoons to read to him, at my mother's instigation, a chapter from a ponderous book of no less ponderous sermons by a divine named Kohlbrugge. The trouble with Ary in his later years was that he was worried about the hereafter. Not that he had been a spectacular sinner in his day—that would have been almost impossible in our community—but because the doctrine of predestination, in which he was a firm believer like everyone else, made eternal salvation uncertain for any man, no matter how righteous. The same problem troubled me not a little in my adolescent years, and when I was a student at the local gymnasium, I decided that when I should have become a pastor, I would compose a book of answers to questions of doubt and anguish that men and women might ask on their deathbeds. If I have not carried out that high resolve it is because I grew more interested in the way men live rather than in their last agony.

3

With my uncle Kees, a landscape painter, I roamed the neighboring countryside looking for picturesque sites: quaint bridges and old churches. In the long summer vacations I crossed the river with him and walked south into Brabant and Flanders. We often stayed away for weeks on these excursions, and when we finally returned home, sun-tanned and weather-beaten, he had a book full of sketches to work on during the winter months. In the evenings we lodged in the humble village hostelries and I listened to his talk with the peasants. If the hour grew late, he let me sleep in the mornings, while he went out with his palette and brushes. After the noon meal of black bread and beer, we invariably pushed on to the next place.

From Uncle Kees I learned more history than from all the school-books combined. His favorite subject was the Franco-Prussian War, the era of Napoleon III, and the Commune of Paris. That period, he used to say, was the turning point in the evolution of Europe. He described it as the beginning of the trustification of business which would, he predicted, cause the peoples, after a short time of com-parative well-being, a series of bloody nationalistic wars wherein rival states would seek to eliminate each other by the most ruthless means conceivable. I never asked him how he knew all this, but I must acknowledge after all these years, that my uncle Kees saw the future clearer than many a contemporary statesman who went on blandly holding forth the vision of poverty abolished and all classes of men enjoying the fruit of human ingenuity in a managed society.

I believe that the secret of Uncle Kees' knowledge of the world lay in the fact that he had spent several years at one of the art academies in Paris. There he had met all types of men: he had been the companion of painters, amongst them Vincent van Gogh; of poets, dreamers and ne'er-do-wells. He had seen the great Tolstoy on the banks of the Seine, and had heard Victor Hugo, Renan, Élisée Reclus and Bakunin in popular assemblies. The giants, he called them. Uncle Kees knew the story of the Commune's every barricade, and on our walks, he patiently explained to me the mean-ing of the decrees issued by the first Popular Government in Europe. Breathlessly, his eyes aflame, his fists clenched, he would suddenly come to a halt on one of those rural roads in Brabant and tell me again the story of the last butchery in the cemetery of Père Lachaise.

"On that day," he would burst out, "all the hyenas of Europe, all the crowned and uncrowned wolves thought they had squelched the voice of freedom for all eternity. They set about to re-create the world in their own petty image. What we see around us today is the result: pettiness in art, pettiness in economics, pettiness in love, pettiness in religion. But mark my words, *you* Pierre, *you* will live to see the day when the whole European kettle is going to explode and the debris will come tumbling down to bury this bourgeois world."

"Who will make the kettle explode, Uncle Kees?"

"They will do it themselves, my boy! They live by violence and they will perish by violence!"

The kilometers were shortened by his talent for storytelling. He spoke with passionate simplicity. He was a champion of every struggling cause in the world; he seemed to experience the joys and sorrows of others as if they were his own. He would grow as excited about Irish independence or about Macedonian nationalism as if he had been born in Cork or in the Balkans. I drank in his words with fervor, and till this day I remember whole sentences from his wayside conversation. But there were also days when we trudged along for miles in silence until, weary with his own thoughts, he would suddenly break into song: "China is a charming land which will surely please Your Highness," or would recite from Shelley, whom he knew in translation, or from Victor Hugo, his favorite. Often, too, we lightened our step by whistling in unison, while he took from his knapsack the tin provision box and drummed out a march with his fingers.

If ever there was a man of whom it could be said that he had two fatherlands, France and his own, Uncle Kees was that man. In the years of our constant companionship, he communicated to my spirit something of his boundless admiration for France and the French people. They represented, he would assert, the vanguard of humanity, and whatever was done in Paris was of importance to all of us Europeans. I do not mean to infer that he held Holland in low esteem: all the Dutch in him revolted against men who talked disparagingly, or even lightly, about our people and our country. He followed with almost religious passion the painful developments of the Dreyfus affair which had thrown not only France, but half of Europe, in turmoil. He would seize the newspapers and read the latest news from Paris with exclamations of joy, or, depending on the occasion, with snorts of indignation: "Ah, those Jesuits!" When he exclaimed thus, I knew that things had not gone so well for our hero on Devil's Island. A hundred times I heard from him what Zola had written, what Picquart had said, why an attempt had been made on the life of Maître Labori, and why Major Henri had committed suicide in the prison of Mont-Valérien. It was my uncle, too, who took me to see my first moving picture, which dealt precisely with the Dreyfus case. We went no less than four times to the local meeting house in Gorcum to see the same film, and that is why every detail of the scenes remains vividly engraved in my memory. I do not remember the names of the actors, but it seems to me that it was a more realistic portrayal than the American production in which Mr. Paul Muni later starred with so much éclat. For one thing, Zola's wife and mistress were shown in friendly relationship, something which is, of course, inconceivable in Hollywood. Clemenceau, who was not an advocate, did not wear a lawyer's gown in the court scene, while Anatole France, that man of taste and feeling, conveyed a more dignified impression in the Pantheon scene.

Although farm machinery had begun to make its appearance, we noticed on our roamings in the rural regions of Holland and Flanders that the peasants still cut their grain with a scythe. Children of orthodox parents in the outlying hamlets, where no "School with the Bible" existed, walked four or five miles to town and back in their wooden shoes every day. We sliced our long beans by hand in the late summer, and made apple cider in November; the wheat was ground to flour between flat stones turned by a windmill. But a change was in the air. I well remember the first automobile puffing up to the ferry, and the shower of stones with which the peasants pelted the occupants of the monster that frightened their horses. The sight of a motorcar was said to turn the milk in the cows' udders. For years, one of my schoolmates bore the humiliating nickname of "the liar" because, having been taken for an automobile ride in a southerly direction, he had returned a few hours later, declaring that he had been as far as where the signposts by the roadside were in the French language.

Uncle Kees was one of those men who looked upon industrialization with mingled feelings of pride in human achievement and fear for the future. He was not optimistic about the miracles of technique and the invention of more and more ingenious machinery for the production and distribution of goods. Unless the whole human race could benefit from this change, he saw in technical advance a limitation placed on human progress rather than a spur. "Some day," he would say, "the common people will pay dearly for these newfangled contraptions." He was not wrong in that prediction. For industry, as time went on, engaged armies of workers whom the countryside furnished, and then threw them into unemployment and poverty for ever longer periods of depression. Not till after the war did the blighting effect of the industrialization process become quite apparent to all—crowded cities and depopulated villages. In Holland, which escaped the war, the disaster was not so great, but I can take you through some of the most fertile districts of France which are today totally abandoned; wholly depopulated regions with thousands of uninhabited farmhouses, châteaux, municipal buildings, schools, monasteries and churches—all slowly crumbling. Yet, for fifteen hundred years, there lived in those same districts a dense and prosperous agricultural population. Somehow or other the cities seem to have grown in the past without taking the people from the farms.

When I was no longer a child, Uncle Kees would come to our house on autumn nights, when the wind blew a hurricane and the rain played with ghostly fingers on the windowpanes, to insist that we go for a walk. He preferred a place where we could let the full force of the storm lash our faces: the top of one of the old ramparts or the end of a pier, jutting into the groaning river. There he would laugh in a mocking, defiant way and light his pipe in the teeth of the yelling wind. He was never happier than on a rainy day, which meant that he was in good humor at least three hundred days of the year. To go walking and get drenched to the skin was a joy to him. That idiosyncrasy I shared with him all my life, even through the war in France, until Ethiopia finally cured me.

Our Uncle Kees was an inexhaustible mine of local lore. He knew all the haunted houses and their stories and the exact location of the long passageways under the city's streets, which our lords, the Seigneurs of Arkel, had caused to be dug in the course of their wars with Jacqueline of Bavaria, five hundred years ago. "Dig down here," he would tell us boys, "on the west side of the church, if you want to see Prussian skulls, or near the leaning clock tower, if you want a Frenchman's crossbones." The area around the church was indeed full of human remains and they rested so near to the surface that you often scraped a bone when you went digging a pot for your game of marbles. The soil pushed the bones up and the municipality was forced to dump loads of sand there each spring to keep all those old enemies decently under cover.

On our hikes Uncle Kees carried an enormous extensible telescope which we would train from time to time on a distant village tower or on the bowsprit of a barge sailing down the river. I used to borrow the cumbersome instrument from him later on when I grew interested in astronomy and went to study the nocturnal heavens from the roof of our house, but on these escapades between the chimney pots he would never join me.

"There is too much of interest here below to worry much about those distant planets," he would say, "and then," he added, "if your father is right, I expect we will have all eternity to study what goes on up there!"

On Sundays, all the year round, he came to our house at an early hour in the morning and took me to church, not to church in our town, but in some distant village. He always knew of a village to which the Synod had exiled some young pastor with modern ideas who could be counted upon to preach the Social Gospel. Many times we were away before dawn. Winter's sleet and cold made no difference. To guide our steps over the short cuts he knew through the snow-covered meadows, we carried a lantern which it was my job to polish and fill with oil on the preceding Saturday afternoon. "Forwards and no looking back," he would exclaim in the frosty dawn, crunching the snow under his shoes and stamping as if he were marching off to war. On such festive days, he wore a frock coat under his cloak and one of the big black felt hats, *flambards* they were called, that he imported from Monsieur Gibus in Paris. His pockets were stuffed with currant buns and other delicacies which we munched even during the service, not infrequently scandalizing the rural beadles with our unbecoming conduct. On the way home he smoked a cigar while we discussed the architecture and the history of the church we had just visited, or we commented on the sermon.

"Now Uncle Kees, was that dominie quite sound in his concept of the Trinitarian doctrine? I could not understand . . ."

"Do not try to understand," he would interrupt me, "only remember this: when the minister spoke of God he did not refer to the same divinity our own pastor has in mind. You must accustom yourself to the idea that every village in Holland has its own deity, sometimes two or three. One dominie preaches a joyful Christ, another compares Him to a tribal Jehovah who breathes fire like a terrible Chinese dragon, still another turns God into a notary public who spends eternity recording the most insignificant daily acts of Russian peasants, Dutch burghers and Dyak head-hunters."

Then to his house where dinner was served by Grietje, the old maid who had nursed him as a child and whom he had inherited from his parents along with the house. The meal was eaten in silence with Grietje hovering over us. After the cream pudding with currant juice he opened a bottle of wine and drank a glass with the reverent gestures of a connoisseur, while I took down the Bible from the shelf and read a chapter. Once, I remember, he chuckled when I read from Jeremiah about the prophets who interfered with the preparations of the captains of war.

"Why do you laugh?" I looked up, thinking that a mispronunciation of a Hebrew given name had perchance provoked his mirth.

"I laugh," he said, "because our present-day prophets seem to be inclined to do the very opposite!"

Most citizens in Gorcum took a nap on Sunday afternoons, but not Uncle Kees. Time was too precious; he wanted to be awake every minute of the day. He would seat himself before the harmonium and improvise, warming up before turning to the classics: Haydn, Gounod, Wagner, Bach and Beethoven. When he was in a particularly jovial mood he played a composition entitled *The Battle of Waterloo*. This piece necessitated at certain points an execution in duo; therefore I had to sit by his side on the bench before the instrument and bring down the basso keys at the appropriate moment—when Napoleon's artillery roared its dissonant bark at Wellington's charging cavalry. I liked that piece immensely, as did Uncle Kees. But later in life, I thought it a strange anomaly that so confirmed and uncompromising an antimilitarist as Uncle Kees should have been so fond of martial music. And not only of martial music, but of all manner of military displays and processions as well. We always went together to see the parades of the garrison, and more than once, witnessed the autumn maneuvers of the national army in the nearby provinces of Brabant and Gelderland. That habit, too, stuck with me all my life. On my brief periods of leave of absence from the firing line, I spent my mornings watching the guard change in front of Buckingham Palace. I cannot help it. I like to see a parade. I seldom miss the Fourteenth of July display on the Champs Élysées in Paris, and in my dreams I still see myself occasionally commanding a platoon.

Uncle Kees also played the flute but he could not sit still when he executed Mozart's *Zauberflöte* or a part from Tchaikovsky's *Casse-Noisette*. He paced the length and breadth of the house, marched off into the garden and timed himself with a curious shrug of the shoulders. Frequently, too, on those Sunday afternoons, he would give me a book to read while he buried himself in a volume. To watch him read was a curious spectacle. He was oblivious to what went on around him. But he did not really read: he engaged in conversation with the author. For a time everything would be silent in the room, and then there would be a sudden exclamation: "No, sir, no, sir, dammit all, sir, now you are going too far. That's nonsense!" That would be Uncle Kees addressing the author. Or else, in a mildly reproving tone, "Little brother, if you go on talking like that I'll throw you into the fire." Many times he roared with laughter and jumped up to stamp around, only to bury his nose in the pages again with a quick ferretlike gesture.

He was a man approaching fifty when I was sixteen. Tall, blue-eyed, always dressed in black, powerfully built, with a dark mustache and a goatee (the Parisian style of the seventies and eighties), he might have been taken for a retired military man. He had remained unmarried and was ill at ease and even shy in the presence of women. As soon as any woman came into the room, except my mother who was his sister, he was nervous and silent. He knew everybody in the community, but had only one bosom friend, a geometrist. This geometrist was a peculiar, taciturn individual, who went bareheaded winter and summer and who was suspected of being a Freemason. Theirs was the strangest friendship I ever came across: Uncle Kees possessed an enthusiastic and sensitive nature, while the geometrist was a short-spoken, dry-humored man. They seldom exchanged a word when they were in each other's company. What they did have in common was their contempt for politics and a detestation of the Catholic Church and all its works. Neither of them ever voted. Once, while strolling along together, we saw a certain Roman chaplain approach in the distance. The geometrist remarked bitterly, "Whenever I see that monk, I smell the fagots of the Inquisition!"

From Uncle Kees came the only liberal influence I experienced in my youth. On my sixteenth birthday he presented me with the keys to a set of mysterious, black-painted bookcases which stood in a low-ceilinged room upstairs. "Here," he said, as he opened the cupboards one after the other and ran his fingers over the backs of the soberly bound volumes, "here are the lamps that never go out!"

For the first time I held a book by Voltaire in my hands. And there were also Rousseau and Bayle, Proudhon and Lamennais, Saint-Simon, Goethe and Tolstoy, and, on another shelf, the modern Dutch and Flemish poets whose works were proscribed at the *Gymnasium* where I studied because the professor of Netherlandish literature was of the opinion that nothing worth reading had been produced in our language since the eighties. I entered a new world and felt like a man who, after having been locked in a cell, suddenly finds the door wide open and walks into a garden full of sunlight and flowers. At first the broadening of my horizon produced a sense of almost feverish exaltation, such as a prospector must experience when coming upon a vein of fine gold in the schist. Classes finished, I rushed to Uncle Kees' library to continue my reading. My blood ran faster. I began to see visions. The shades from the past took on flesh and blood. History, heretofore a dry recital of dates and facts, assumed new meaning. There was a deeper sense to our human existence than that of being a mere play ball of the blind forces of fate and predestination.

Of the company of humanists in my uncle's library, there were two, Ernest Renan and a French workingman named Anthime Corbon, who captivated me most with their religiously motivated social passion. The simplicity of Renan's style made me catch my breath. Throughout that vast work on the sources of Christianity, which was the first of his books I took in hand, I was swept along by his tranquil, classical grace and his unostentatious but enormous erudition. When he stripped the figure of Jesus of the accretions of dogma and superstition in which the Church had wrapped it, I felt that he demonstrated once and for all that truth is superior to all fictions. Renan might have been a defrocked priest, but he became my Pontifex Maximus. I have never tired of him, and although much of his criticism is antiquated today, and some of his conclusions may even appear naïve and even childish in the light of the enormous progress since made in the scientific reconstruction of the sources of Christianity, he remains the giant who calmly braved the obscurantists, and the first scholar to effect a definite breach in the wall of literal inspirationism. Not till many years later did I learn from his own daughter how he was vilified and calumniated by some of his Catholic contemporaries as the Devil's henchman and Antichrist, but this does not prevent me from believing that Renan brought the world more Christian philosophy than all his tenderly evangelic detractors combined.

The opening of Uncle Kees' treasure chest made me aware that beyond the somber forest of our Calvinist formalism there were wide open spaces and broad vistas. I had moved into the company of prophets who had seen man's destiny not in the fulfillment of a set of iron rules prescribed by the Church. There was another road to salvation than that inflexible system wherein heaven, hell, and earth were fixed for all eternity, and which had a ready-made answer for every conceivable question of doubt. "The ills to which man is subject: poverty, exploitation, war, do not derive from fatality," wrote Renan. "Misery is not a metaphysical substance. It is the reality into which millions of Europeans are sinking. It is in reshaping and transforming the conditions under which he lives that man answers to the most inexorable demands of the universe." "Brothers," said Corbon, "You say that winter stands before the door, but I have consulted the fig tree and have reached the conclusion that the human race is approaching its blossomtime. Everything is susceptible to change, everything has changed in the past, everything will change in the future! Nothing is permanent in history but the element of change itself!"

And then Voltaire: *"Ecrasez l'infâme!"* *L'infâme* that was the darkness which wanted to be darkness, that was the history which presented a monstrous comedy, instead of fulfillment; a procession of sanguinary and grotesque personages; kings, Caesars, popes, tyrants, executioners. *L'infâme* was brute force and prison walls behind which the souls of men melted in tears and suffering. *Ecrasez l'infâme!* Crush, wipe out that world of the oppressors and their clique of usurpers who bend the necks and the conscience of man— the priests who make man say, "I believe and I obey"! In the traditional caricatures of history, Voltaire is usually decried as a trail blazer for the materialist conception of human evolution, the cynical skeptic who was out to destroy the last hope of mankind. The truth is that Voltaire did not lead any movement of opposition to religion, or even to its confessional form consecrated by tradition and custom. He resisted the domination of the spirit by the letter, of life by formula, of tolerance by constraint. He sought to substitute individual initiative for the compulsion of collective belief.

In time, I must say, my exaltation in the presence of the new prophets wore off, and the old religion came back to the surface. I felt remorseful for having strayed from the narrow path and for having fallen into doubt. I went back to reading Thomas à Kempis and Saint Augustine. On such days I avoided Uncle Kees like the plague. Nothing could dispel the gloom that settled over my spirit. And all my life thereafter I have been subject to spells of the deepest spiritual anguish. The Jesuits are not wrong when they say, "Give us the child and the man will belong to us." I have carried Calvin on my back thirty-five years, and sometimes I still feel fragments of him adhering to my shoulders.

Uncle Kees might have helped me get rid of the burden entirely, and I am sure he would have been willing, but he remained behind in Holland when my parents moved to Canada. He accompanied us to the boat in Rotterdam when we sailed. He stood on the quay as the anchor was lifted and the ship slowly moved from the shore. His face was pale and drawn and suddenly I noticed that he had grown very old: his shoulders were sagging and his hair had turned gray. I kept looking at him till he became an indistinguishable black speck on the wharf. We were to remain in North America but five years and he wrote me a long letter every week, two hundred and sixty-two letters in all. When the five years had passed and he was notified that our family would not return at all, he extinguished the lamp in his library one stormy night in the autumn of 1919, locked his harmonium, and quietly walked to the river for the last time.

4

For weighty reasons of national interest, the denominational system of education sponsored by the Calvinistic middle classes in Holland stresses the principle of God's guiding hand in history. Providential preferment is deemed to have preserved the Dutch race and culture through the storm and stress of the ages. This exclusive character attributed to the nation led inevitably to comparisons with the early history of the Jewish people, whose sacred books had served as the foundation stone of the Dutch Republic. We were the spiritual successors of the Chosen Race. When the dominies invoked the divine blessing upon the nation and spoke to the Almighty of "thine own Israel," they did not refer to the remnants of the ancient Hebrew people scattered over the length and breadth of the earth, but to the descendants of the blond and blue-eyed Batavians, Frisians and Saxons who settled at the mouths of western European rivers before Caesar's day. Year in, year out, it was drummed into my head in school and catechism class that the Lord of Sabaoth with singular solicitude had preserved us from the Assyrians of Spain and from the Chaldeans across the Channel. Had He not raised William of Orange, brought up like Moses in the luxuries of a foreign court, to shatter the chains that bound our country to the yoke of the Hapsburg empire? We could point to many a David in our national history who had overcome the knavish plot of this or that Dagon of the Philistines. God's breath, not English sea power, had destroyed the Armada of Philip. None other than Jehovah had caused the thaw to set in when Louis XIV's armies advanced over the frozen rivers to crush the Dutch Republic. A pyramid of skulls and dry bones was still to be seen on the spot where the advance guard of the French armies, like Pharaoh's host, had perished by the action of the waters in 1672.

The everyday language of our people was so permeated with Biblical phrases and quotations that citizens from another, more "worldly" milieu, sometimes had difficulty in understanding us. If the elections in the provincial synod for instance went to the modernists (which happened more than once, for Holland, it should not be overlooked, besides being a stronghold of Calvinist fundamentalism, was also, and still is, the home of the most advanced and radical school of Biblical criticism in the world), our people deemed it a case of the Philistines invading Zion. With us news did not travel from Delfzijl to Terneuzen, the two extremities of the national territory, but from Dan to Beersheba. A man did not meet his Waterloo in a business failure but his Gilboa. Catholic clergymen were of course Baal's priests and their Pope and Church respectively Antichrist and Babylon, the great harlot of the Book of Revelations. The Catholics in our community were unimportant citizens who kept to themselves and suffered from a minority complex. Few of our people doubted that if ever they should regain power they would soon bring back the Inquisition and the torture chambers to wash their hands in the blood of the heretics.

I do not think I exaggerate when I say that our life was over-shadowed by a cloud of gloom. We moved in an atmosphere of joylessness, not unlike that which must have prevailed in the Geneva of Calvin's days, and of which contemporary writers have left a description in their chronicles. Always the dominies held before our eyes the fact that man was a worm, yea, lower than a worm, a miserable sinner, doomed to hell-fire. He lay under the curse of original sin and was once and for all unworthy of the slightest lovingkindness on God's part. Men and women went around with long faces to show that they were always conscious of their miserable estate. Often it drove them to suicide. Worry over religious questions was not always the cause, but it was that in the case of one old and humble citizen who never spoke a word to anyone and whom I saw quietly wade out into the river one afternoon. Some of us boys ran in after him and dragged him back to the shore. We then escorted him to the old people's home, of which he was an inmate. Coming down the street, we met one of the dominies who inquired what had happened. The would-be suicide explained.

"But how could you, how could you?" exclaimed the pastor. "Suicide, the sin for which there is no forgiveness!"

"Dominie," said the little man meekly, "I did it banking on the blood sacrifice of Jesus!"

I do not seek to detract from the merit of Calvinist principles, nor would I minimize the historic significance of those democratic Calvinist consistories, which, unlike Luther with his preaching of passive obedience to the state and his denial of the people's right to revolt, resolutely withdrew their allegiance from princes and governments when the cause of Christ was at issue. In Calvinism, the Protestant Reformation attained the highest evolution of its religio-political principles. Without the fire of Calvinism there would have been neither a Dutch Republic nor a Republic of Geneva, that other refuge of the human spirit through the times of autos-da-fé, inquisition, and political proscription. Calvinism is one of the forces which has moved the world and determined the course of Europe's evolution. It has also functioned politically. From the beginning the strength of Calvinism resided in the fact that it sought to make of the believer a conscious and active instrument in the service of God, a God-conscious militant who knew what he believed in and why he believed it: a man who did not hesitate to pit his convictions against the power of the state, the princes and the dictatorships. It was Calvinism which formed the hosts who resisted and overcame the wordly dictatorships of France, the Netherlands, and Great Britain. It was Calvinism which broke the chains in which the spiritual dictatorship of Rome and the Jesuits sought to enslave western Europe. To be an "elect of the Lord" was not a mere theological phrase with which the Inquisition had to reckon, but a political fact, a thousand times tested on the battlegrounds of freedom.

Today Calvinism has shrunk to a mere confessional organization to keep dogmas and doctrines intact and immovable, but, at one time it aimed at a theocracy, the rule of God, of absolute justice in every domain of human relationships. In that sense alone Calvinism was the heir of Judaism; not because the history of the Netherlands accidentally lends itself to analogies with certain happenings in Hebraic lore and mythology.

Our self-identification as a sort of spiritual Israel left the small group of Jews in our town in a curious position. They, too, were ultraorthodox, and I can still hear the voice of our neighbor, the doctor, coming across the silent garden at dawn, reciting with passionate sobs at times the age-old prayers of his people. There were occasions, sucn as the Day of Atonement, when the doctor could be heard to weep.

"This is because he is thinking of Jerusalem," said my mother, with whom, for many years, I spent the early hours of the day going over my lessons. "The Jews have an undying nostalgia for Jerusalem. They are not happy here, even if they are not persecuted in Holland as they are in Russia."

Indeed they were a people apart. They were different. They always seemed to be waiting for something to happen. What? They did not complain, but you felt that some secret was gnawing at their hearts. In spite of the fact that they were full and equal citizens before the law, and that they occupied prominent positions in the social life of the community, they were strangers. My mother attributed Jewish separateness to a certain stubborness of spirit. All their troubles, she thought, would cease the day (which she felt bound to come) they accepted Jesus Christ.

It would be a falsehood to say that some of our best friends were Jews. We children did not consort with theirs, except on the day when they went around with rattles in the streets in celebration of the foiling of Haman's plot by Queen Esther. Then we would join them and sing their songs of jubilation and help them carry and finally burn the effigy of that distant enemy of their people. On Passover we usually had matzoth on the table, the unleavened bread that the Jews eat in commemoration of their last hurried meal in Egypt. The matzoth came from the doctor's wife. My mother was very unhappy about the fact that she could never return the compliment by sending over some dainty cakes or dishes, for the doctor observed the dietary laws and did not eat food prepared in non-Jewish homes. But he frequently spent the evening with my parents. He had an inexhaustible store of knowledge relating to ancient Jewish practices and the history of his people. It was from him that I learned that the Crusades, which at school I had been led to think of as a beneficial event in the life of the peoples of Europe (because they had built a bridge between East and West), had cost tens of thousands of Jews their lives.

But more frequently the conversation turned to the persecutions that the Jews were undergoing in Russia. The Great War lay still in the future: humanity had not yet been poisoned with its own blood; we had not yet become inured to calamity and injustice. We were therefore appalled by the accounts of pogroms that reached us from Kishinev and Białystok. Prayer meetings were held in the ultra-Calvinist churches for the salvation of "the folk of Israel." Before long we had two emissaries from the Jewish community in Russia staying at our home. I vividly recall that Sunday evening when a Russian Jew with a long white beard, who kept his hat on, ascended the pulpit and in broken German told us the whole harrowing story of his people's persecution. What stirred me most was his recital of events after the massacre of which he had been an eyewitness. His own wife and children had perished in the bloody attack. Before her death, the woman had seen the mob throw her two children into a burning oven. At this point in his story, the Jew broke down and buried his head in his hands on the Bible.

When he recovered, he went on to say that thousands of young Jews all over Russia had begun to arm themselves with revolvers, determined to defend themselves if the attacks should be repeated. This decision on the part of the Jewish youth to resist had caused an even greater disturbance than the actual pogroms, if that were possible. For now the rabbis resisted. *"Kein Gewalt!"* no violence, they had cried in anger. "We must not shed blood! That is not Israel's way!" The counsel of the rabbis prevailed: no blood was shed by Jews. But vast numbers left for America.

We saw them passing through the ports of Antwerp and Rotterdam on their way to the new land of freedom. I was about ten years old when my mother took me to the water-front district where thousands of Russian Jews were waiting to board ships for the great unknown. It was evening when we arrived on the wharves. In the sheds, by the unsteady light of a few petrol lamps, we could see that mass of fugitives lying or sitting on their bales and sacks of baggage.

Infants wailed. Young girls shrieked in their sleep. Old men were sitting forlornly in the open doorways, staring with unseeing eyes at the river which at that hour was sprinkled with silver by the last rays of a sinking sun. Most of these people were in rags. Hunger and long years of destitution had left an ashen imprint on their faces. There was an air of hopeless impotence about their movements; a dumb defeatist resignation, almost unhuman. With their eyes they followed the visitors and the official who led us around. And into those eyes crept that same look of fearful alertness of the hunted animal which I was to notice in later years on the faces of natives in Somaliland, Nigeria and Ethiopia, where the approach of a white man, any white man, inspires the blacks with dire apprehension.

We learned that many of the Jewish emigrants had not eaten for days. Others had spent their last kopecks in buying bread in local Jewish bakeries. Naturally, certain Jewish charitable organizations had done their utmost to relieve the distress, but their resources had proved inadequate. Every train from the East brought new contingents of poverty-stricken starvelings who had invested their last resources in a steamship ticket. A Christian society, the official explained, had lately come to the rescue. At first the fugitives from the Czar's domains had accepted the gifts of food and warm clothing with alacrity. But now that was different. These wretched humans obstinately refused to be succored. They silently shook their heads when the Christian welfare workers came bearing gifts. Even milk for the babies was refused. Yes, there had been instances, we were told, when old Jews had interposed themselves between suckling mothers and the charity workers at the moment when these were persuading the women to take some of the nourishment proferred. What was the matter? What had happened? The Jews imagined, our guide explained, that the price for taking our charity involved the acceptance of a copy of the New Testament in the Yiddish language. Thousands of these books had been sent to the ports of Hamburg, Bremen, Rotterdam, and Antwerp when the flood of Jewish migration poured westward through Europe. In decency, the Jews felt, they could not accept bodily relief and at the same time turn down the accompanying spiritual consolation. Hundreds of the small volumes had been discovered neatly piled up in an out-of-the-way corner of the wharf building after the departure of the last boat for America.

I believe there was on the whole less indignation over the incident when it became known in our community, where some individuals, my parents included, had generously contributed towards the purchase of the New Testaments, than a sense of disappointment and amazement. We were abashed, some hurt, by what was called a sample of Jewish effrontery. So that was it! Even those hard-pressed Jews from Russia were as stubborn in their rejection of the Gospel as our own Jews! Did we not have an indication there, one pastor inquired, of one of the sources of the hatred for the Jew in Orthodox Russia? How long, another with a more gentle heart lamented, how long yet would the Jews continue hardening their hearts to the pleadings of the Good Shepherd? Did they still not realize that all their woe had come over them because their ancestors in Jerusalem had defiantly accepted responsibility for the Saviour's death with that terrible invocation: his blood be upon us and upon our children? Such were the remarks which followed the announcement of the waterside incident.

I do not think that the intervening years have brought much change in the general Christian approach to the Jewish problem. I have frequently observed a rather embarrassed reticence on the manner of Jesus' death, and on his personality in general, on the part of speakers in those meetings to foster good will between Christians and Jews in America, where Christians, incidentally, distinguish themselves by massive abstention. The contributions of individual Jews to science, charity, the arts, statesmanship and politics, if not Marxistic, are lauded to the skies, but on the fundamental issue which divides the Orthodox Christian believer from the Jew, an embarrassing silence is maintained. And how can it be otherwise? The majority of the Protestant Christians in America are still taught in church and Sunday school that Jesus was executed by order of Caiaphas and the Jewish Sanhedrin, and that the entire Jewish people to this day remains solidary with that decision. I do not, of course, intimate that anti-Semitism, which is now visibly on the increase in America, has its roots exclusively in religious ground. But it has a religious source too, and that is a source which the Church, or at least a section of it, pollutes. For it is not only in the backveld or amongst the benighted inhabitants of the Bible Belt that the culpability of the Jew in the tragedy of Golgotha still has currency today. If the Jews suffer, the hidebound fundamentalist sees in that a demonstration of God's wrath for the execution of His Son. From this assumption it is but natural to give God a helping hand and lash out when the opportunity presents itself.

I had never heard in my youth of *The Protocols of the Elders of Zion*, that vile forgery concocted in those peculiar mystico-sensuous circles of Orthodox Russia whose last and fairest blossom was the monk Rasputin. I made the acquaintance of this product of medieval obscurantism in enlightened America where Mr. Henry Ford gave it wide circulation in his periodical *The Dearborn Independent*. We knew of the blood-ritual libel, however, but that fabrication, to us at least, had no direct bearing on the Jews. The blood-ritual charge, we were taught, had first been leveled not at Jews, but at the early Christians by *indicateurs* of the imperial Roman police who sought a pretext and the approbation of the otherwise tolerant citizenry for the proscription of a religious cult of which many adepts refused to bear arms in Caesar's service. A suggestion that children were immolated on the Christian altars in the catacombs, where slaves and ex-convicts assembled in the dead of night, was calculated to excite the mob's bloodthirstiness and at the same time enhance the government's popularity amongst the upper classes when it decided to proceed against the sectaries with the utmost rigor. The government's *agents provocateurs* linked the agapes or love feasts of the Christians with the lascivious orgies in which the idle and degenerated Roman aristocracy indulged during the celebration of the Dionysian mysteries. It must be supposed that the rite of the Holy Eucharist lent some semblance of authenticity to the allegations, for it confused the Christian sacrament in the pagan mind with the practices of older religions which made sanctification of the individual contingent upon the eating of holy food, generally the sacrificed flesh of a divine bull or ram.

On the other hand, there was current among our people a vague belief which was always mentioned in mysterious tones. It attributed to the Jews some secret magic power which enabled them to suspend, or at least effectively intervene in, the normal processes of nature. This power was supposed to reside in their knowledge of the correct pronunciation of God's name. Everybody was aware that the Jews never uttered the name of the Master of the Universe. Only in exceptionally perilous circumstances, when the existence of the Jewish people as a whole was threatened, as in Russia, for instance, did the rabbis in a last desperate resort have recourse to a ceremony of which the purpose was to place Israel's enemies under a curse. This ceremony was known as the Malediction of the Name. In the course of it, the officiating rabbi extinguished the holy lamp before the scroll of the Law and reversed the candles in the seven-branched Menorah. Then, in an awesome silence, as every Jew wrapped his face in his prayer shawl, the rabbi slowly pronounced the name of God, the famous Tetragrammaton, first revealed to Moses at the burning bush. The effect was said to be immediate death of the tyrant who was at that particular moment making life miserable for the Jews.

It was an interesting story and I liked it. I confess that there were days in my life when I almost wished it were true. To be frank, I would not have felt the slightest pang of regret if that magic had been successfully tried out on a certain paperhanger from Vienna, and had sent him and a few of his associates to join the battle-weary Nordic warriors in their drinking bouts up in old Valhalla.

5

My father was a stranger in the town: he hailed from Flanders and never quite mastered the local dialect. But my mother's family was an indigenous old clan in whose original home, my grandfather's house, a structure dating from the fifteenth century, every article—the milk vat, the heavy oaken chairs, the window sills, the sagging walls, and the cupboards—had accumulated a polish from the touch of many generations. There was something friendly and almost human in these objects. When you stroked their surface you felt as if you were brushing the hands of one of those lace-capped women whose portraits hung in the hall and who had formerly lived in the house. But the women, beautiful as some of them were, interested me less at that age than the picture of a young man with ruddy cheeks and a laughing face. It was said of him that he had emigrated to Australia or to America, and had never been heard of thereafter. The story was told of him that one day— it was in the Napoleonic era—he had met the French military governor of Gorcum on a stroll near the drawbridge, just outside the Arkel Gate; in a flash of defiance he had refused to give that foreign dignitary the required salute. When this official, a certain Marquis de Saint-Cyran, had begun to insult the whole Dutch nation by screaming excitedly about *têtes de fromage* and *sales cochons*, and even had raised his cane to strike, the laughing young man of the portrait had lifted the silk-pantalooned Frenchman bodily over the railing of the drawbridge and pitched him into the Linge River where he was sucked under by the current.

Grandfather's house was said to be haunted, but I never saw the family ghost, perhaps because I kept my head steadily under the covers whenever I slept there. It was a good house nevertheless, with an open door to neighbors and friends from far and near. Every itinerant preacher, Bible seller or fund raiser for worthy and pious causes was welcome there. My grandfather not only set the fatted calf before these wanderers but also saw to it that they carried a few guilders away with them. At this fireside, I saw swarthy men wearing fezzes who were out to gather funds for some persecuted sect in Persia, followers of Bahaullah; Tolstoyan pacifists fleeing military service in the Czar's empire; Salvation Army officers bound for or returning from the leper colonies in Java; zealots who had been moved by the Spirit to go and sell the Bible in Spain; Hernhutters en route from Bohemia to Canada; and several priests who had left the Church of Rome. Once we entertained a gigantic Abyssinian monk who drank a whole crock of Schiedam gin before dinner and decamped the next day, taking along a silver alarm clock under the folds of his long black cloak. Once, too, we were hosts to a "brother" from faraway and fabulous America. He first puzzled and then amused us children a good deal by reason of the fact that, although a Protestant, he wore his collar backside-forward in the Roman style. He, I remember, brought us greetings from relatives in Grand Rapids, Michigan, whom I had never seen.

They were an odd assortment, these propagandists of the faith. Some installed themselves for weeks and gave orders as if they were lords of the manor. My grandfather treated them all with Christian forbearance, although I heard him sigh more than once with relief when a particularly intrusive pilgrim girded his loins to move to some other corner of the Lord's vineyard. One brother only was ever shown the door. He was a colporteur of religious tracts, who took it in his head to go knocking on the door of one of the servant girls in the middle of the night. My grandfather had an early breakfast laid for him and eyed him with one of those glacial Calvinist stares during the meal, until the man, in great discomfort, suddenly blurted out: "Yes, it is true . . . I have prayed a thousand times to be kept from trespassing on the commandment, 'Thou shalt not commit adultery,' but the Lord always puts new temptations in my path!"

That was passing the buck in quite a novel way and even my grandfather had to smile.

We had a relative on nearly every street in Gorcum. The degree of affinity was often quite remote, but we made no distinction and greeted each other as "cousins." One of these "cousins," a man named Dirk de Koster, lived all by himself in a big house whose shutters were perpetually bolted. We visited him only on New Year's Day when we went to wish him the compliments of the season and eat his cookies. He was a tall, somber man with drooping mustaches and bushy eyebrows. People thought him queer in our community, and it was said that he had lost his mind in South Africa where he had served in the commando of Piet Wessels against the British. The walls of the only room he occupied in his ancestral house were plastered with colored lithographs of Boer generals: Christiaan De Wet, Botha, Joubert, Jo Beyers; and with scenes from the battles of Magerfontein and Elandslaagte. He had cut the latter from *The Illustrated London Graphic*. On his table lay the open Bible and a map of South Africa.

Every New Year's morning we boys went to hear Cousin Dirk's one and only story. "We were in a mining camp in north Transvaal and had found gold," he would begin. "One morning we saw a troop of red-coated cavalry riding up. They were Englishmen. Soon these horsemen dismounted and three officers came over to

our mess hall where we served them brandy. As they were drinking, one young lieutenant's eye fell on the portrait of President
Kruger on the wall and he smashed the glass cover with his fist,
saying, 'Take that, you monkeyface!' "

"And what did you do then, Cousin Dirk?" came our ritual
question.

"I said to that Englishman, 'What would you say, sir, if I called
Queen Victoria a monkeyface?' "

" 'I'd lash you with my riding crop,' " replied the officer.

"And so?" we queried in chorus.

"And so," answered Cousin Dirk, "I whipped my own riding
crop from my boot and I let him have it right across the snout.
Once, twice, three times! The officer called for help, but his men
had found our supply house and were guzzling our whisky. When
he pulled his revolver I shot him down. Not one of those red-necks
escaped that day. No, not one. We picked them off one by one
as they staggered drunkenly around the kraal."

Cousin Dirk had come back to Holland after the war to look
for the girl who had promised to marry him after he should
have made a quick fortune abroad. She had been a poor man's
daughter, but beautiful as an angel, he was wont to say. His parents
had refused their consent and their support. That is why he had
gone to the gold fields.

But the girl had apparently wearied of waiting for him, and had
married another man. She had gone to live in Antwerp. Cousin
Dirk either could not, or would not, believe that he had been
jilted. His parents had died while he was in Africa, and he had
inherited their fortune, but he had lost all notion of time. Every
evening, rain or shine, this middle-aged man would walk to the
street where his boyhood sweetheart had once lived and would
stand on the corner like a lovesick yokel, a small bouquet of flowers
in his hand. In later years he began meeting the trains and scanning
the faces of the incoming passengers.

"Good evening, Cousin Dirk!" we said, when we happened to
pass by the station.

"Good evening," he would smile back. "Have you boys seen
Cornelia?"

Towards the end, his mind began to wander and he would come
to my mother to tell her that he no longer remembered whether
he had left Cornelia behind in Holland or in South Africa. He

would shake his head disconsolately and sit for long hours trying
to collect his thoughts. His was the first corpse I ever saw. By
the side of his head in the coffin lay the Transvaal flag. In his
hands was clasped the yellowed photograph of the girl.

6

Sports and athletics were frowned upon as a useless and unworthy
pastime when I was a lad. Children from Christian homes had more
important things to do than hopping around on the tennis court or
football field. Moreover, sports might in my case have interfered
with my studies at the *Gymnasium* with its overchanged curriculum
which included six languages: French, German, English, Latin,
Greek and Hebrew. You took a stroll to the river after school, and
returned to your homework which lasted until ten or eleven in the
evening. You then sang the evening hymn with Mother at the harmonium, ate a dish of oatmeal mush with sirup "to steady the
stomach," and went to bed only to rise early in the morning for a
hasty checkup on the lessons for the day. Of course, Sunday was a
day of absolute rest. To have taken a schoolbook in hand on that
day would have been akin to committing a sin against the Holy
Ghost.

Sin, sin, sin, everything was sin! When the kermis was held,
a joyous innocent pastime for the townfolk and the peasants from
the neighborhood, you were required, if you had to go out, to
turn your head away from the crowded merry-go-rounds, cake-
walks and good-smelling waffle booths. In the kermis-week, it is
true, counterattractions were offered for "God's people" in the
church or in the vestry hall: special Bible readings or recitations
from the "good" poets by demure and decorously gowned ladies,
or lantern slides of Biblical scenes would be shown with comment
by an *explicateur*. There was one particular serial for the magic
lantern which was trotted out every year around kermistime. It
was called *Jessica's First Prayer* and dealt with the spiritual evolution of a fallen woman in the slums of London. I saw the lanky,
peach-blonde Jessica stalk so often through the various stages that
led up to her conversion that the pictures had become mere ghosts

of their former selves. The lady's gaudy blue gown was full of blank streaks where the coloring had come off the slides.

Nevertheless, it must not be thought that we were unhappy. You did not envy the children whose parents prepared them for a more liberal view of life. On the contrary, you pitied them, for were they not like Dives in the parable enjoying the sweet in this lifetime while we had our good time in reserve in the hereafter?

An essentially fair and just arrangement!

But there was also another side to the picture of piety and conventionality in Gorcum.

There was one street in the town in which I did not set foot until I was seventeen and then only with a trembling heart. It was flanked on both sides by a row of low-ceilinged taverns and beer cellars wherein full-bosomed blonde women of the type painted by Rubens, "that most learned Calvinist of the Netherlands," stood behind the bars to serve drinks to soldiers of the garrison and to fishers and mariners from the freight ships plying between Rotterdam and the Rhine cities. In one café, it was whispered, the guests drank their beer while watching nude women play at billiards. That street was the surest short cut to hell. Individuals known as "midnight missionaries" were in the habit of taking turns in doing sentinel duty at its entrance to warn adolescents and strangers of the dangers that lurked behind the row of purple-curtained windows and the latticed swinging doors. On Saturday nights the street roared with the cymbalic clattering of hurdy-gurdies and the tingle-tangle of automatic music boxes. Those midnight missionaries, I must say, were valiant soldiers of the Lord, for not a few of them received the martyr's crown in the form of a thorough thrashing; not, to be sure, in the public streets, but when they went snooping at nights, armed with pocket torches, to break up amorous idyls under the walls and in the niches of the old bastions around the city, or in the shrubbery along the river's shore where there was more petting on one night, rain or shine, than in a whole week in the Bois de Boulogne of Paris, which is surnamed "*bois d'amour*." That may be saying a good deal, but I know whereof I speak.

If we boys of pious homes, who were chained to our books in the evenings, could not see a great deal of "the ways of the world" on that Street of the Broken Bottle, as it was called, there were other compensations. Among the young officers of the artillery regiment quartered in our town were wealthy lads free from family restraint, who could afford to let women from The Hague or Brussels come to visit them. This did not happen frequently, it is true, but whenever such damsels were to arrive by the only train that stopped at our station in the late afternoon, the news of it was bruited about in some mysterious way, and we "gymnasiasts" went in a body to the station to see the ladies come in and be welcomed by the officers. Since these women could not be taken to the quarters in the highly proper bourgeois homes where the officers resided, and since no hotel keeper dared to rent out a room for fear of scandal, the orgies were staged in the office of a certain merchant, a *bon vivant* and notorious libertine who enjoyed shocking the people of a puritan town with his I-don't-care-a-damn attitude. The office was located in the rear of his store in a lightless narrow alley which ran the length of his warehouses. Of course, the windows were covered with wooden shutters like all windows in our town, but there were several cracks in the shutters. The merchant bribed a certain night watchman named Willem van den Oever to keep an eye on the alley on the big nights, and Willem cheerfully executed this favor: he had a bench rigged up near one window of the office and charged ten cents for a peek through a good-sized crack halfway up the shutters.

What I saw there one night made me gasp!

7

All the ages through which a people has lived are leaves from the same book. Whatever we are is the result of the long travail of the centuries. I would be committing a grievous injury to my fatherland if I should convey the notion that the parochial Calvinism of our community was typical of Dutch life in general. In the large cities the doors stood wide open to all the free winds of the spirit, and the atmosphere was therefore far less stifling. When one considers the geographical position of Holland, it is evident that this could scarcely have been otherwise. History having placed them at the crossroads of three of the world's great cultures, the Dutch have silently, but with cautious discrimination, absorbed everything they came in contact with, without surrendering a single essential of their own national ethos. The greatest contribution the Dutch have made to the sum total of civilization, in my estimation, is that they accustomed themselves at an early date to look upon their own country without conceit, considering it merely as a complementary part of a single whole. Thus they have developed, perhaps to a higher degree than any other nation in Europe, a harmonious conception of citizenship and humanity, and thus did Holland also become a home for the European spirit at a time when the countenance of other nations was still distorted by what Nietzsche called "the great plague of European national pride."

Even so, of such towns as ours, where the Calvinist congregations formed a world apart as it were, hermetically closed to modern thought, there were hundreds in the Netherlands, and there still are. One needs but switch on one of the Dutch broadcasting stations to learn what interests the people most: if it is not a sermon, no matter what the time of day, it will be either a religious song service or scriptural reading. In the small communities the Dutch remain essentially a Bible people, and religion seems stuck in their bones. But, as always happens when large numbers of people accept a religious, or, for that matter, a political dogma from the past, interest has gradually concentrated not on the truth or error of the idea, but on the precise form of doctrine. For when the ideal lies in the past, defense of traditions, not the creation of new values, becomes the objective. But then also petrification sets in. In our church we still sang the hymns of the Protestant rebels with their frequent reference to a better world; we still heard sermons based on texts from the Prophets of Israel with their messianic fire, aflame with a hope for the liberation of all mankind, but the ministers preached that the existing social order was decreed and instituted by God and hence unchangeable and inviolate for all eternity. Therewith was restored, in principle at least, the fatalism of the *decretum horribile* of antiquity which weighed like a crushing burden on the ancient world before Christianity came to give a new orientation to socio-political relationships. Little remained of the old revolutionary impulse of Calvinism, and even less of the spiritual dynamite of primitive Christianity which was to have shattered the strongholds of "this world" of Mammon and Moloch.

Preparing as I was for the ministry of the Dutch Reformed Church, and growing up in a milieu where that church was the center of life, I could not help noticing that something was seriously wrong. If Christ's saying were true that the tree is known by its fruit, the Christian church's functional operation from which was to have come the impulse for a spiritual, and hence for an economic and social regeneration in our time, was clearly stagnating. Why did the masses turn away from Christianity? Why were the churches empty? The need of the times was great and growing constantly; there were weariness and sorrow and moral decay, and, on the other hand, a thirst to believe. Why, then, was the *solutio Christi* not accepted? These things I felt rather than expressed, but I felt them with a growing poignancy. Yet to whom could I go with my disquietude? I was still far from suspecting that our ministers, whom I venerated with filial devotion, were vaunting the excellence of the existing social system because they were of that class in society whose sun stood highest in it. I did not turn to the liberals, in spite of Uncle Kees' gentle influence, and must say that on the whole I am glad of it. For the liberals were not only the first to throw spiritual values overboard, thus planting in the masses (long before Marxism raised the banner of the class war) the seed of doubt and skepticism and robbing them of the strongest weapon in the struggle for a juster social order, but they drew back in their shell as soon as they became aware of religion's value as a stabilizing force in a society wherein contradictions of class and caste were growing constantly sharper. They had begun by compromising with the fundamentalists in declaring that religion was a matter of private concern, whereas religion "has always been a cultural and social question of the first magnitude in great moments of history." The result of this attitude was a double morality: one for private life and another for social, political and national conduct. Of Christian principles there was not, and there is not today, the slightest evidence in the policies pursued by the succession of Calvinistic governments in Holland who claim to "subject all their decisions to the Word of God." In its subordination of every phase of life to imperialist considerations, in its exploitation of tens of millions of human beings in the Indonesian colonies in the interest of a small coterie of regents who own the banks, the oil wells, the rubber plantations, and the means of production in general, Calvinist Holland does not differ one whit from "godless France" or from "heathen Japan." It is a capitalist imperialism.

I still believed that Christianity held the solution of all the world's ills and therefore expected everything from the church. That many pastors of my acquaintance, half a dozen of them relatives, carefully side-stepped any and every implication of the social question in their sermons, irritated but did not dismay me. I consoled myself with the thought that it was only a matter of time before the church would come out into the open and resolutely enter the social arena on the side of the weary and heavy-laden. I could not conceive of the church of Jesus, the proletarian carpenter and his twelve fisher-men-disciples, sponsoring a society of cutthroat competition, colonial exploitation and subhuman living conditions for the masses. A new generation of pastors was growing up and I would be one of the new phalanx. The day would come when the revolutionary ardor of the old *Militia Christi* would reassert itself, and the church, reinspired with the ideals of its founder, would engage in a struggle of life and death with the powers of "this world," whom it had been commanded to overcome. Socialist movements and labor unions would then become superfluous. In principle, the organization for the transformation of society was in existence: it was the church of Christ. If that church would only be true to its calling, there was nothing to fear. For we had the divine promise that not even the gates of hell would prevail against it. Thus I reasoned in my youthful optimism. . . .

Gradually the disconcerting reality dawned upon me. I began to see that the church deliberately shirked its responsibility by projecting the establishment of the Kingdom of God into the hereafter. I saw that it compromised with, and excused, every conceivable form of injustice and violence. I heard the ministers thunder against free thought, new ideas and godlessness, but never heard them say a word against the preparations for war, against the destruction of human life which is the greatest blasphemy conceivable.

And then it slowly began to dawn upon me why Marx had called religion the opium of the people, and why Socialism had to fight against the conception of a God who was said to will the existing order of things, and against a Christ who was made to cover with his name the injustice of a society in which one class enjoyed culture and well-being and the other toiled and slaved and yet sank deeper and deeper into misery.

I began to slip away in the evenings to the People's Hall on the Street of the Fishers. There, by the light of a couple of oil lamps suspended from the ceiling, I heard Domela Nieuwenhuis, Enka, Daan van der Zee, Schermerhorn, Henriette Roland-Holst and Barthélemy de Ligt—heretics, rebels, outcasts, poets, excommunicated pastors. With its corrugated iron roof, on which the rain clattered like muffled kettledrums, the place looked more like a freight shed than an assembly hall. But there I heard words I had never heard in the catechism class or in church gatherings. Men were called upon to be comrades, socii, brothers. I learned that there was a cosmic sense and not chaos in the struggle of classes and castes, that it meant growth, evolution, moving forward. The new teachers showed that even the egoism of individuals and classes led inevitably to a higher goal, that the most conscienceless capitalist in his wildest scramble for profits yet served the interests of future generations.

De Ligt, who was to become one of the great social philosophers of our time, was still a Protestant pastor. He was publishing a religio-socialist weekly which circulated *in petto* in the *Gymnasium*. I sat riveted to my seat one night, scarcely able to breathe, when I heard him decry our church as inhuman and therefore anti-Christian, because it functioned as a pillar in a social system which made of the most essential things to sustain human life—bread, water, milk, the soil and light—the object of speculation and profit. He called that society anti-Christian in which men were forced to dig treasures from the earth, turn them into manufactured articles, ship and transship them by boat and train, embellish the earth, always producing wealth and more wealth and yet living in the worst slums, dressed in the worst clothes, partaking of culture and art and education only to the extent of the crumbs which fall from their masters' table and then finally, in cruel irony, being asked and even being forced to defend with their lives that in which they had no share.

My disquietude increased almost to panic. What was the good of continuing my studies for the ministry? What would be the sense in preaching the good life to people who lacked the elementary essentials for a truly human existence? Was not our church betraying the nature and the social conscience of the Gospel in sanctioning—with its silence—these social and economic conditions under which it was impossible for man to attain his full human stature? Were not all sentiments of humanity being crushed and brutalized before our very eyes? How could men be asked to become followers of Jesus when our churches deliberately closed their eyes to their sordid destitution and misery, justifying these conditions as a natural consequence of the economic development wherein no one was allowed to interfere? I came to the conclusion that preaching the Gospel had no meaning without a simultaneous humanization of the material conditions under which the majority lives. My whole life suddenly became meaningless. My preparations for the ministry now appeared an empty gesture. And with my sense of frustration and disillusionment a deep sadness came over me. I was filled with a fundamental shame, for a Christian knows that he cannot live in opposition to the church without causing injury to himself, since something resembling pharisaism creeps in between his indignation and his personal conduct.

At school I encountered the same blank wall. When Italy suddenly seized Turkey's last province in north Africa and the Balkan War devastated the southeastern corner of Europe, my liberal teachers at the *Gymnasium*, which was not a denominational institution, casually dismissed these outbreaks of violence in the Continent's most backward areas as the last spasm of a dying medievalism. Western Europe, they argued with facile optimism, had grown too enlightened to have recourse to such barbaric practices. The dark ages lay behind. Democracy was breaking through in the most remote corners. Even Russia now had a parliament, and Bulgaria had just accorded its citizens equal franchise. Day was breaking at last, and the heavens would soon be all aglow. Man was about to reach the summit in his long and weary climb toward the human ideal. It was merely a question of time before the nations of the world would be walking hand in hand on the road of progress and prosperity. That was the optimistic interpretation given us of contemporary history. I suppose it does not differ in essentials from what adolescents in America were hearing about the same time. Only the conrector of the college, Dr. Jan Berlage, a brother of the world-famous architect, who was a Social Democrat, said to me one day as we walked home from school together that Europe and the world, instead of moving toward a greater era of well-being and happiness, were on the threshold of a period of violent readjustments. He thought that the period of upheaval that we faced might well last a century or more.

A few days after I heard that strange warning, which stuck in my memory, a fellow traveler in a train compartment, who happened to be an agent for the firm of Friedrich Herder in Solingen, informed my father that the factories he represented were working overtime on large orders for bayonets. It became noticeable, too, that the number of French and German buyers in the local horse market constantly increased. Uncle Kees began crumpling the Parisian newspapers in disgust after reading of vast scandals in the French financial world and of the subsidies paid by the German government to French journals and journalists for whipping up the war spirit. The Republic of Danton and Victor Hugo had allied itself with the Autocrat of Russia. England had a new fleet under construction on the wharves of the Tyne and Clyde. From Potsdam came the stamp of marching feet. Wilhelm's defiant speeches re-echoed in the smallest hamlets of the Continent. Without paying heed to the prophecies of old women who were seeing signs in the sky (swords crossed over the Milky Way, a blood-red hand on the moon—unmistakable warnings since time immemorial of dire things in the offing), indications of an impending disaster grew almost daily more plentiful.

The Pan-Teuton societies across the Rhine were publishing maps in which half of Europe, Holland included, was shaded in the German imperial colors. There came reports of Russia extending her railway net to the Galician borders of the Dual Empire. Austria had annexed Bosnia and Herzegovina to acquire a jumping-off-place for attack in the direction of Serbia. Wilhelm journeyed to Constantinople and Jerusalem and called himself the Sword of Islam. In France, the nationalist poets, Déroulède and Barrès, were exalting the spirit of war and announcing the day of revenge for the defeat at Sedan. The mobs tore the shrouds of mourning off the statue of Strasbourg in the Place de la Concorde. Poincaré raised the term of military service from two to three years, and returning visitors from Paris brought word that the old forts at Verdun and Metz and Belfort, dismantled forty years earlier by the orders of Bismarck, were now bristling with a brand-new type of artillery. There had been a demonstration on the boulevards when it was learned that a young German lieutenant in Zabern boasted of having substituted the tricolor of France for toilet paper. Military maneuvers took on unheard-of proportions in Holland.

Troops were moving through Gorcum bound for the outlying provinces of Brabant and Limburg. Everybody knew that these divisions were merely to be used as sacrifice units in the event of an invasion. They were supposed to give the general staff time to bring the defenses of the so-called water line in order. Our mayor was confidentially informed by the government that in the event

of war, the civilian population was to be evacuated to the islands of
Zeeland, for our community was certain to be bombarded, its forts
being in the first line of defense of Amsterdam, the capital.

It was going to happen, after all. The veneer of civilization was
wearing thin. After twenty centuries of Christianity and humanism,
Europe was preparing to plunge back into original sin, the sin of
Cain: brother was going to assassinate brother once more.

In later years I have never understood how statesmen and politicians on the Allied side could seriously maintain that they and the
whole world were completely taken unawares by Germany's ag-
gression in 1914. I heard Lloyd George in Geneva denounce the
Reich as the wantonly vicious tiger which sprang on a peaceful,
innocent France. Nobody was prepared, he exclaimed. Germany
struck when Europe was at peace—the blow came like a bolt from
the blue. André Tardieu wrote a whole book to prove German
treachery. How is it these statesmen, with intelligence services and
the armies of spies and informers at their elbows, did not know
when my father knew, and Uncle Kees and Ary Struyck and Dr.
Berlage and Barthélemy de Ligt and our washwoman?

Holland escaped the war by a miracle. It so happened that Germany, contrary to the calculations of her own general staff, found
that Belgium provided sufficient space to maneuver her armies for
the attack on France. But nobody could foresee this in 1913. Everybody fully expected that we would be drawn into the bloody
maelstrom. We could only hope for the best—and pray. And this
we did. The pastors implored God to spare the land which in the
past had so often been singled out by the divine solicitude, and to
let the chalice of war pass by our lips. That was all they did about
it. When I asked them, as I did more than once, quite naïvely, I
must admit, why they did not condemn the principle of war itself
and preach passive resistance, or urge that a Christian nation place
its trust in the Christian practice of spiritual defense, I was told that
war had always been one of God's instruments to bring the peoples
back to His service. The nations of Europe had trodden the divine
precepts underfoot in following the path of materialism and free
thought, consequently punishment was bound to follow. War was
frankly interpreted as an act of divine retribution, a sort of physical
and spiritual corrective in the life of the nations. The law of their
anthropomorphical God was operating like clockwork: you do this,
I do that. To appease a sulking deity who was deemed to share the

dominies' pet aversion to the theory of historical materialism, millions of young lives were to be blotted out in the subsequent holocaust.

To have ventured upon a critical examination of the operation of an economic order which produces catastrophes like war and cycles of unemployment, seemingly automatically, was far beyond my intellectual capacity and would, moreover, have been dismissed as an adolescent impertinence. Historical evolution and human emancipation were not merely hollow words in my environment, they were dangerous and even blasphemous things to mention. You were considered streaked with a queer mental twist if you as much as uttered a word of criticism on the way life was ordered for the mass of the people. That subject was as much a closed book at home and at school as was the sexual question. It was bad enough that those agitators and eccentrics from the big cities invaded our peaceful community to talk to fishermen, shipyard workers and the like about birth control, Socialism, and proletarian solidarity, stirring the people up, injecting the spirit of discontent and revolt. The first effect of those Sunday-night gatherings, which were held in a filthy hall in the worst slum quarter of the town, was that hitherto humble and law-abiding citizens decided to go strolling in the meadows, or to play games on the Lord's day, or even to go fishing in the canals and rivers, when they should have been filling up the seats marked for the poor in the rear of one of the side wings in the great cathedral church, as their fathers and fathers' fathers had done before them. The elders and supervisors (Uncle Kees, of course, called them the scribes and Pharisees) considered this decline in church attendance a bad omen. I remember how they had a sandwichman parade the streets for a time with a sign bearing a quotation from the poet Beets: "Who abandons God is abandoned by Him." But high pressure of that sort did not help any more than did a house-to-house canvass by the pastors.

The proletariat had enough of the church. It elected a Socialist to the municipal council, defeating an uncle of mine, who had held the seat for years by virtue of his unimpeachable orthodoxy and his prominence as a local merchant. What was the world coming to? Klaas Verhey, a brewery worker, who had never paid a cent of taxes in his life, sitting in with the honored city fathers! Where could a fellow like that have learned polite manners? The owner of a soap factory resigned in disgust from the council when Klaas came in, but the proletariat promptly voted another of its candidates into the vacant seat. Hitherto the council chamber had been more of a club where the gentlemen had repaired once a week after dinner to smoke a cigar and drink a bottle of port. But those two Socialists, instead of accepting a glass and being congenial, began to make sport of the old customs. They wanted water on the table, they said, to keep their fellow members from falling asleep. The impertinence of those rascals, as if the council had not always been awake to the interests of the community! And what else did they want? Klaas Verhey began to make speeches, standing up and rapping the table. He talked about slum clearance and a better sewer system, and he insisted that a doctor and a staff of nurses be appointed to take charge of the local hospital, which was still known by the medieval name of *Pest-Huis*, and where a half dozen military pensioners were now looking after the sick. The institution had acquired an evil reputation among the poor as a place from which nobody ever returned. Klaas thought it would also be a boon to the community, if some of the ill-famed pothouses and taverns on the Street of the Broken Bottle could be closed up. He cited cities in Germany and Sweden where such improvements had been made. Now where could he have learned all this? And the effrontery of the man: a brewery worker telling the bank president, the dominie, the baron, and the chairman of the board of trade how to conduct their business! Had anybody ever heard the like? And if the saloons were really to be closed, what would become of the brewery and of Klaas Verhey's own job? Ha, that was a good one! The reformer surely had not thought of that in his fanatical zeal! Why did he not go to Germany or Sweden or one of those foreign places if he liked it so well, instead of making a commotion in the council, turning the chamber into a theater, a showplace where dozens of his cronies and fellow workers dropped in to hear him talk and, *sakkerloot!* forget themselves so far as to applaud his extravagances.

A couple of miles out of town, down the river, lay a shipyard. It employed about three hundred people in season. These workers went out by way of the Chancellery Gate, past our house, at half past five in the morning. They were at their jobs at six, and did not return till shortly after seven in the evening when we were at dinner. You could hear the clatter of their clogs on the cobblestones outside. They were going home to those rows of one-roomed cottages on the other end of town near the Dalem Gate and the river, where the cookstove and the privy stood in one corner and the smallest children were already asleep in the *bedstee* (a sort of cupboard built in the wall) when the breadwinner came home. Many of the workers would stop on the Street of the Broken Bottle for a quick drink of Geneva at the counter. After washing up and eating supper most of them returned to the taverns to play cards and to drink. Then would ensue fights with knives or with wooden shoes used as knuckle dusters, and women screaming, and hasty calls for the doctor to sew up a wound and for the police to make an arrest.

I knew the quarter quite intimately, having visited nearly every one of the cottages at one time or another in the company of my mother. She went there to visit the sick or to call on parents of the hundreds of children who were pupils in the Sunday school she had founded. Tuberculosis was making frightful ravages in that neighborhood. In the semiobscurity of many an interior lay the emaciated form of some boy or girl, a father or a mother, patiently awaiting the hour of healing which never came. In summer they sat on the porch in the brief spells of sunlight, their tired eyes following the play of the crowds of ragged children in the street. Mother would sit down with them and gently seek to direct the conversation to the inevitable issue of their illness and the condition of their soul: a most difficult approach, for it is one of the psychological characteristics of consumption that the sufferer never loses hope in his ultimate recovery and hence will not hear of death. She did her best to cheer them by talking of the Father's house where there are no more tears or poverty or disease, but when she came home, she invariably burst into tears. About Christmastime we children were pressed into service to help carry the hampers of foodstuffs and knitted underwear that Mother and the ladies of a sewing circle manufactured in the course of the year. Once, too, I remember Mother taking charge of a cleanup campaign in a row of cottages located in an alley so narrow that, by standing in the middle and stretching out your hands in both directions, you could touch the houses on either side. The homes swarmed with vermin and nearly all the children were covered with scaly sores. Every day, for weeks, I came to the alley after school to take my mother home.

Verhey's election to the municipal council was the beginning of a new era in Gorcum. A new spirit invaded the community. For one thing, the shipyard workers no longer drifted home at nights in small groups or singles. They came marching home in a body, like a battalion of soldiers, stamping their clogs in rhythmic cadence, ten, twelve abreast: Nardus de Smet, the giant with the wooden leg in the lead, and Tinus Brandt, the fighting rascal, with his shirt wide open in front so that the red hairs on his chest were showing, waving his arms. All of them singing, singing as if they wanted to burst their lungs, and the apprentice boys beating small wooden clappers to the step of the tune, so that the windows rattled as the procession went by. What had come over those fellows? And what were they singing? All you could catch of the song were the words of the refrain about a sacred ideal and liberation. A sacred ideal? Who wanted to be liberated? And from what? What were they up to? Wasn't this disturbing the peace and a matter for the police to attend to? Something was afoot, surely! It was all the result of those meetings in the Fish Hall where freethinkers and atheists and busybodies from Amsterdam and Utrecht came to read poetry and explain history and economics to the rabble. What would happen next?

Next they were planning to open a night school, a popular university, they called it. That was another of Klaas Verhey's ideas. There were to be classes in literature, history, social science, and in economics, of course. Now what in the name of heaven was the good of that? What was the point of it? Evening classes, but no church attendance, eh? I still hear the Lutheran pastor fuming and raging one evening to my father and Uncle Kees on the subject of the popular university. Had a worker, he asked, the time to go listening to lectures after spending twelve hours on the job? Wouldn't the late hours make a man unfit for the next day's task? The school Verhey had in mind would be the opening wedge in disturbing the peace of the community. A laborer was worthy of his hire, no doubt, but must he not give something in return? Where was labor's sense of responsibility? Social peace depended on the close collaboration—the brotherly co-operation, the minister called it—between capital and labor. The capitalist supplied the means to earn a living. He was therefore in a sense the benefactor in society. He was entitled to service on the part of his employees. If business was good the worker fared well by it, did he not?

"No," interrupted Uncle Kees suddenly, and I noticed that there was an ugly scowl on his face, "no, that is not true! Business has been doing well for a hundred years and the workers of this town are still housed in stinking holes. And even now when they want a share in the culture which you, Dominie, have acquired at leisure and in comfort, and they are willing to sacrifice a few hours of sleep, you would deny them the opportunity."

"I deny them? God forbid!" the minister answered indignantly. "I am merely saying that this popular university will not provide the proper background for the re-education of the masses."

"What will provide the proper background then, your sermons about justification by faith?" shot back Uncle Kees.

"Sir," resumed the pastor icily, as he reached for his hat and rose to leave, "I am proud to be a citizen of a free country! Our fathers gave their lives that all citizens should have equality before the law. That is my fundamental tenet!"

"That may be true about the fathers," interrupted Uncle Kees again, who was in one of his contradictory moods that day, "but the fathers are dead. It is with their descendants that we are dealing."

"You deny, sir, that we enjoy equality in Holland?"

"We have equality in so far that both the pauper and the millionaire are forbidden to steal a loaf of bread!" stormed Uncle Kees.

"Are you aware that wherever these popular universities have been established, they have turned out to be breeding nests of materialism and godlessness?"

"Dominie," said Uncle Kees, "God is in many places where His name is not even mentioned."

"Well, sir," returned the dominie, his face livid with anger, "I am leaving you now, but I can tell you that there is not going to be an atheistic, Socialist, popular university in this town. We will not tolerate it. We will have nothing of it. It sounds innocent enough, I will admit, but a school like that would shake the morale of the common people and disturb their spirit of resignation. And moreover," he added, "where will the money come from to pay for a hall and for lectures and for books? Have you ever thought of that?"

"I have some books," replied Uncle Kees quietly. "I also have a house and I think I can give a lecture or two."

"You ought to stick to your paint and brushes, *mijnheer*," snapped the dominie, now thoroughly aroused.

"And you, *Nostradamus*," flung back Uncle Kees, "you go on about your soothsaying business!"

That was a quarrel. The whole town spoke of it and took sides. But Uncle Kees carried out his promise to lecture at the night school. His first subject was Rembrandt. I attended the meeting. At midnight, when I had to leave, he was still holding forth on the folly of the Communards of Paris in having neglected to seize the banks.

A young public-school teacher began to give readings from the modern poets at the popular university until the board of education discovered that he was an anarchist and therefore unfit to teach five-year-olds their ABC's. A minister from a neighboring hamlet stepped into the breach and taught social science. He lost his living after three months when his board of elders taxed him with something he could not deny: he had taken a certain blonde servant girl, a well-known figure, to one of the waffle booths at the kermis, and thereafter had gone bicycle-riding with her in the dark. That was called conduct unbecoming a servant of the Lord. The pastor moved away. The challenge was taken up by one of the top-class students at the *Gymnasium*. He failed to pass the baccalaureate examination, which meant in his case, since he studied at the expense of the town, that he could not repeat the last year and was forced to go and look for a job.

Klaas Verhey was not having much luck with his "professors." The local newspaper was poking fun at him and his "school of social philosophy." The reaction was trying to kill the scheme with ridicule before resorting to sterner measures. One day the journal would satirize the Socialist councilman in an article which bore the title: "From Beer Brewing to Biology." A week later the same publication asked whether men who set themselves up as teachers should not first submit their qualifications. Were individuals allowed to practice medicine without the proper schooling? Why then should those who aimed to cure the ills of society be exempt? Uncle Kees was never mentioned by name in those newspaper attacks, but our town weekly began to reproduce unfavorable criticisms from the metropolitan journals on the style of painting in vogue in the school he followed. Degenerate French art, it was called, lacking the finesse, the beauty, the sweep of imagination of the Dutch masters. Why were these sloppy moderns trying to force the monstrosities of the Montmartre school down our throats? An alien, degenerate art! Gutter slime! Products of the Parisian sewers! Chaotic emanations of an absinthe-crazed coterie of nihilists and loose women!

Ha, how that vituperation would make him laugh! He doubled up with mirth. "The grocers are on the warpath!" he would exclaim. "The penny pinchers are worried!" Everybody recognized, of course, at whom the editor's barbs were aimed. There was only one painter in town. Uncle Kees was the culprit. But Klaas Verhey lost his job. That was a stunning blow. He would be forced to seek work elsewhere. The man had a wife and five children to look after. He could not remain idle for long. Clearly the affairs of the popular cause had reached a crisis. For who was there to succeed Klaas? He had been the animator, the never-tiring champion, and he was about to leave town. . . .

Things were at this stage when our neighbor, the good doctor, stopped me on the street one day and asked me to come to his office the same evening. In itself, his request had nothing unusual. I frequently went to consult him when I had difficulty with a passage in Homer or Virgil. We sometimes sat talking till midnight. His house was so near my home that the gardens touched.

As usual, I found the old Jew that night in his library with a large Hebrew tome in front of him. His neatly trimmed white beard was almost touching the book and he was wearing his skullcap. When I entered, he kissed the yellowed page reverently and closed the heavy volume.

"Well, Doctor, here I am! I hope I am not disturbing?"

"Not at all, not at all, I wanted to see you," he said. "I wanted to ask you what you think of this rumpus about Verhey's popular university? Don't you think some of your boys in the top classes of the gymnasium ought to step in there? We cannot allow the reaction to have its own way in this case. They have gone far enough. There is a limit to forbearance and passivity. Economic pressure is being brought to bear on the workers now. The whole scheme will be ruined unless someone takes it seriously in hand. The workers alone cannot defend themselves against these unfair tactics. It is up to you and me to go to their aid. We have to fight if needs be. Why don't you call a meeting of the students and make the proposal? Tell them I will do what I can. I am an old man and have never taken a share in public affairs, but now we are faced with . . . *l'infâme!*"

"I am afraid," I said, "that your presence amongst the friends of the school might inject the Jewish question into the case. That would be worse. All your coreligionists in town might suffer in consequence."

"Quite possible," the doctor replied. "In fact, I know, from having spoken to them about the school, that our leading Jews will deeply resent anything that may disturb their tranquillity. In fact, that is their whole conception of Judaism: tranquillity. But it isn't mine. Nor is it yours of Christianity, is it?" he arched his eyebrows.

Our interview closed with my promise to take action at once. But nothing ever came of the desire to help Verhey's night school. We were suddenly faced with a crisis in our family. My father, who had suffered some severe financial setbacks, had decided to go abroad for a time, with the intention and hope of recouping his fortunes. He was hesitating between South Africa and Canada, and was in correspondence with various land agencies in both countries when my youngest brother died after two or three weeks of grievous suffering. The boy's death so affected my mother that we feared for her reason. The doctor advised an immediate change of environment, and it was therefore thought best that she accompany my father on his voyage abroad. But if she went, why not we, my brother and I? The university could wait in my case. My brother, who was about to enter a military academy, pleaded to be taken along. We would see the world, we would learn to speak English. The experience would stand us in good stead in later life.

And so, in the spring of 1914, the house was closed and we sailed away. . . .

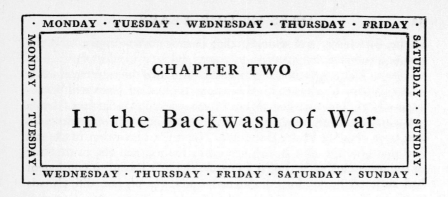

CHAPTER TWO

In the Backwash of War

I

WHILE MY FATHER and brother went exploring the Far West for a suitable ranch, I remained behind with my mother in Toronto, where I entered the University and began the study of theology. For a while I hesitated between Victoria College, a Methodist institution, and Wycliffe, the seminary of the evangelical branch of the Anglican Church. I finally decided for the Wesleyan school, since preparation for the Methodist ministry provided that the student divide his course of training, in alternate years, between the seminary and probation in the field as assistant to an established clergyman. The prospect of preaching delighted me, for whereas I would have had to wait at least six years in Holland before I would have been called to a pastorate, in Canada, it seemed that I could be in the pulpit as soon as I had acquired sufficient command of English to address a congregation. During my first year, therefore, I concentrated on the language; I read the English poets and classics and digested the sermons of the Reverend John Wesley, Hugh Latimer, John Henry Newman, Keble and other divines long dead. I was so immersed in this work that I had not noticed how a grave tension had developed in Europe following the murder in Sarajevo. The outbreak of the war took me completely by surprise. However, everyone agreed that this war would not last a year. Three months, was the general prognostication with regard to its duration. The Allies were simply going to walk to Berlin and bring the arrogant Hohenzollern to reason. The newspapers optimistically called it a mere promenade. I was happy that Holland had not become involved

51

at the first blow, and thought that Dutch native caution and the people's fundamental aversion to things military would take care of the rest. There was not much enthusiasm for the war in Canada either. Native Canadians, on the whole, took small interest in European affairs. The first contingent of troops which left from Canada was almost entirely made up of English and Scottish reservists who had been residing in the Dominion. Not till a succession of defeats had shattered the first British armies in France, and the full horror of the gas attack at St. Julien (wherein the first Canadian contingent had suffered heavy losses) dawned upon the people, did Canada bestir itself in earnest. Even so, it took a lot of high-pressure propaganda to make the citizens of a free country put on the strait jacket voluntarily. It was difficult to convince the average Canadian that his country was menaced while the British navy remained intact and the German army was fought to a standstill on the Marne. Moreover, Canada had no military tradition; the uniform was held in contempt; the soldier's profession had always been looked on as a last refuge for ne'er-do-wells. As the war lengthened and the existence of the British Empire itself appeared to be at stake, Canadians responded more readily to the call to arms. However, the French Canadians, who constitute nearly half the Dominion's population, showed so little inclination to rush to "Mother England's" assistance—and for good reason—that the government had recourse to compulsory service to fill the gaps in the overseas' army.

I felt that the war was no concern of mine. We were Hollanders, strangers in a strange land, without any obligation but to obey the laws and keep silent on the issues involved in Europe, even when the reports of atrocities committed by German soldiers in Belgium and France grew more and more fantastic. I went to school. I was having my first taste of higher criticism; that was more important than following the fortunes of the contending armies five thousand miles away. I had work to do and I liked it.

We must have been halfway through the winter semester when one morning I was summoned to the office of the Dean of Theology. I entered expecting nothing of more importance than a remark on my progress, or a suggestion for study. But I found the Dean in a serious mood. As soon as I was seated, he asked me if I had sufficient knowledge of the "Austrian" language to carry on an intelligent conversation in it, and perhaps even preach in it. The question startled me. I replied that since the official language of Austria was

German, I did not think I would have much difficulty in conversation, and that with some months of practice, I would perhaps even be ready to use it publicly. But what had the Dean in mind? Well, it was this way: the Alberta Conference of the Methodist Church was calling for missionaries to work in a large colony of Austrians who had settled near the city of Edmonton. A few ministers had already gone out there, but they were badly handicapped by their inability to speak the language. The work was not progressing satisfactorily. It was almost impossible to establish contact with the colonists.

Were the colonists originally Catholics or Protestants? The Dean did not know exactly. Some, he thought, belonged to the Moravian community, others, he had learned, claimed to be followers of Tolstoy. But if I knew the "Austrian" language I ought to heed the call. Clearly this was God's finger beckoning.

I went home to talk the matter over with my mother. At first, she thought that I was too young to assume a pastorate. But when it was explained to her that I would merely be assistant to a minister, in Sunday-school work probably, she was delighted that I should have an opportunity to meet with such excellent Christians as Hernhutters and Dukhobors. I notified the Dean that I was ready to leave at once.

Before setting out on the long journey, I found that I still had to undergo an examination as to my theological fitness. I dreaded this ordeal, not only because of my hesitant English speech, but also because in the Dutch *Gymnasium*, examinations had always been nerve-racking tortures. Still, once seated before the board of examiners in Toronto, I felt perfectly at ease. It was quite like a pleasant conversation. The Dean nodded to my answers in friendly fashion as the professor in patristics questioned me for an hour on Methodist discipline, justification by faith, and John Wesley's and my own conception of holiness.

Half an hour after reaching the Albertan village to which I had been directed, I was sitting dumfounded in the study of the minister in charge of the mission. This gentleman, who was to be my superintendent, began by informing me that our parishioners did not speak a word of German. They were Ruthenians! Former subjects of Austria, to be sure, but their language was a Slavonic idiom, akin to Russian and still more to Ukrainian. Moreover, they were as yet not even our parishioners. We had to win them away from the

Orthodox Church first. That was not going to be an easy matter: their own priests were on the spot to see that none of the sheep went astray. It was fortunate, the pastor said, that we lived in Canada where the law guaranteed freedom of worship; elsewhere we might be faring worse, for the Orthodox priests bitterly resented our ministry. It was a long, long story of struggle and opposition and heartbreaks and insults. I would soon see it all with my own eyes.

"But then I am useless in Alberta," I blurted out, after the superintendent concluded his tale of woe. "I do not know anything of the Russian language except the Greek letters in its alphabet."

"That is about as much as we know here," he replied, referring to himself and his associates.

"How then do you manage to preach?" I inquired.

"We have not begun to preach yet. We will probably have to wait until we can train some young Ruthenian converts as missionaries."

"In the meantime," he said, "a hospital has been built on the prairie; the most encouraging thing is that some of the Ruthenian farmers are beginning to call there to consult the doctor about their bodily ills."

"Does the doctor know Ruthenian?" I asked.

"Not yet. He is studying the language like the rest of us."

"Who are the others?"

There was Brother So-and-So and his wife, two fine Christian souls. They came from Battle Creek—formerly ran a hardware store there—until the Lord called them to this work. And there was a young Englishman, a university graduate, who had come to Alberta as a teacher. . . .

But nobody knew the Ruthenian language. Fortunately, in the house, there were a grammar, a dictionary, and New Testaments galore. All I could do for the present was to begin the study of Ruthenian. I am not sorry that I studied it, for it came in useful in Russia later on—my Ruthenian made the moujiks and the commissars of the USSR smile a little, but we understood each other.

The first morning, the superintendent and I rode out on horseback to inspect our far-flung parish. I had never as much as touched a horse in my life and the experience was a painful one. I slipped out of the saddle a dozen times until, in desperation, I grabbed the horse around the neck. Then the beast raced off like a streak of lightning. The superintendent, thinking that I had the animal under control at last, rode on behind, shouting: "Praise the Lord, brother, praise the Lord!" But I was saying something entirely different under my breath, and in order not to shock either the superintendent or the horse, I was saying it in good old fatherlandish Dutch.

An epidemic of typhus was raging amongst the Ruthenians. I had myself inoculated against the dread malady at the hospital. Here I met our coworker, the doctor. He was an American by birth, and a man of truly apostolic character. "We gotta cure 'em," he kept on saying as he busied himself about the laboratory. "We must not let 'em die. Talk and sermons are of no damn use here! We gotta get into those cottages of theirs and clean out the damned lice. That's what we gotta do. They're burning up in their own dirt. Are you with me?" he called at me. "Get into the buggy. I am running up to the creek today. Seven of 'em sick there. Can't let 'em die."

For six months I scrubbed Ruthenian cottages with the doctor. We carried out the vermin-swarming straw sacks on which the peasants slept, sprinkled them with gasoline, and set them on fire. "*Slawa Isousa Christoe!*" the doctor would call out to the groups of men, women and children who would crowd in the doorways of their isbas as soon as they heard the sound of our horses' hoofbeats stop in their front yard. *Slawa Isousa Christoe*, Glory be to Jesus Christ—that was the traditional greeting in rural Ruthenia. It was also the only Ruthenian phrase the doctor knew. Without preliminaries he went right down to business: "Who is sick here? Nobody sick? Since when haven't these kids been washed? Come on, boy, I'll show yeh! I got soap. I ain't gonna hurt yeh. Come on! What's yer name, Ivan, Piotr, Vladimir? *Slawa Isousa Christoe*, yer head is crawling with lice, boy! It's a damned shame. Get me the disinfectant, Pierre, and hand me the clippers, too, while ye'r at it. Might as well give this boy a haircut!"

And then to the next place. "Ah, atta boy, Fydor, that's fine work!" The doctor was slapping a farmer on the back for following his advice in whitewashing the walls of his cottage. "*Slawa Isousa Christoe!* That's the stuff! No more fever, eh, Fydor? You're feeling fine now! What's that, Fydor? Sick? Who's sick? Your boy sick? Been to Edmonton? Got a dose? Bring him out, Fydor! Tell him to come out. No, not here, over in the stable. His mother and sisters don't need to see this. What's the matter, boy? Show it to me, pull

it out! Don't be afraid! Tell your boy not to be afraid, Fydor.
Cripes, I mean, *Slawa Isousa Christoe*, that's syph what you got
there! That's syph your boy got there, Fydor! Gotta send him to
the hospital, Fydor, do you hear? That boy gotta take treatment,
yeh get me? Tell him not to be afraid. We're gonna fix him up.
Slawa Isousa Christoe! Everything'll be all right!"

In a few days I had memorized a set of Ruthenian phrases about
food and boiling water and "where is the pain?" and "stay in bed."
With the aid of signs and gesticulations I managed to get myself
understood. I could also recite the Lord's Prayer and, on leaving a
family, we would now stand in the yard for a moment and repeat
the words in unison. "That's fine," the doctor would say. "We're
getting together all right. If we can get those kids to learn baseball
now, *Slawa Isousa Christoe*, we'll be all set. Write for some bats
and gloves to the Missionary Board, will yeh, Pierre? Tell 'em to
send some more Testaments, too. We don't need 'em, the Testaments, I mean, but if yeh don't ask for Bibles, yeh won't get the
bats either. After all, it's a simple question out here. We gotta cure
'em first. Matter of hygiene. We gotta show 'em, convince 'em,
see, even if we gotta keep on washing those kids ourselves for a
year. They're as good as gold. Finest farmers on earth. They've
been spoiled by that Czar and his lords and kings over there in
Europe. The humanity's crushed out of them!"

The epidemic checked at last, we were summoned to a conference of the field workers in Edmonton. The doctor, who had attended previous assemblies of this sort, refused to go, pleaded an
overcharged list of patients, and said he pitied more than envied
me my holiday in the big city. In Edmonton, where the missionary
work amongst Ruthenian immigrants had made considerable advance, I met all my colleagues in the ministry for the first time.
There were twenty or twenty-one—all gathered in the home of
the former hardware merchant with whom I lodged the first night.

A prayer meeting opened the proceedings the next morning at
nine. Everyone present kneeled by the side of a chair in the parlor.
My superintendent, who fulfilled the function of presiding officer,
designated the persons who were to lead in prayer by calling their
names in turn. My host, the hardware man, came first. To my
amazement, he began telling God certain details of his own career
in the ministry. First, his hatred of religion and his ignorance of the
Bible, then his long period of doubt and striving with the spirit,

and finally his liberation from sin. He dramatically described his transfer from hardware to theology as a case of a firebrand having been plucked out of the fire. He spoke a full half hour and when he said amen at last, I felt ready for breakfast. But now his wife began speaking and continued at great length, furnishing several supplementary details to her reverend spouse's biography. She prayed for eighteen minutes.

I had heard about such Methodist exercises of self-contemplation, but, of course, had never witnessed one. When I say that I did not like what I saw and heard, I put it mildly. I did not undervalue the strength of the feelings which must have been at the root of such a show of piety, but I vaguely felt that it was a substitute for something that should have revealed itself in a more practical form. Moreover, since I was extremely uncomfortable kneeling by a rocking chair which wobbled each time I shifted from one painful knee to the other, I began to wish for the end of the exercises. How long was this going to last? Did nobody else have sore knees? When were we going to have breakfast? Those were the things that worried me. It soon became evident that we had only started. The superintendent next called on a certain Brother Chisholm, a lanky, elderly man, who wore a clerical collar and whose features bore an extraordinary resemblance to those of the late Eugene Debs. Speaking with meticulous precision, but with a strong nasal accent, this brother managed to weave the whole story of the miraculous fishing episode on the shore of Lake Tiberias into his prayer, winding up with calling us all fishers of men, and expressing the hope that our nets would soon be full to the bursting point. I must say that analogy was well done. If God had not read the King James version of the Galilean fish story, He ought to have been tolerably well informed when Brother Chisholm got through. But now I wanted to get up. My knees were aching. I had a cramp in the calf of my leg. I was experiencing excruciating pain. I could no longer concentrate my thoughts on the proceedings. I could smell coffee somewhere and I was beginning to feel faint. The perspiration trickled down my forehead. Should I get up and leave the room? The hardware man was intoning a song: "O Happy Day that Fixed My Choice." Maybe this was the moment to leave. I decided to stick it out just another minute. But after the first stanza one of the sisters went into action. In a high-pitched, sadly lamenting voice she was telling Jesus she had been a vile, contemptible, lascivious sinner. She had spit into the Master's face. She had done this, she had done that, the one thing worse than the other. I was frankly abashed, for she had seemed endowed with a rather pleasing personality. She had thick blond hair that she wore in the German Gretchen style, a lovely white skin, and, from what I could see of them, legs that were tastefully shaped. But her bosom heaved in anguish as she poured forth a stream of self-accusations. She had a life of iniquity behind her. Iniquity was the word she used, but she did not specify. I felt genuinely sorry for her, for she was in evident distress. I would have risen to wipe her tear-stained face with my handkerchief, but was afraid that my gesture might be taken amiss by the congregation. The Spirit had to have its course. The blonde sister was panting for breath. She could not find words to express her emotion and started to scream. She threw her head back so far that a button tore off her blouse and her breasts became visible. I thought the superintendent would cut her slobbering exhibitionism short, but he was encouraging her with loud and repeated amens to go on and on. I was writhing in agony. My knees seemed to be resting on needles, and I wanted a cup of coffee. What was the matter with these people? Where did they get all that energy so early in the morning—before breakfast, at that? The sister was now bellowing at the top of her voice about her being bound for Canaan's shore and about the blood, the blood, the precious blood! It almost nauseated me.

Suddenly she stopped on a high note and burst into hysterical sobs. This is the end, I thought, and was glad of it, for her sake and my own. Surely, I thought, we will have a little refreshment now. We had deserved it. I got up off my knees and hunched down. It was a great relief. I mopped my brow. I was suffering in body and spirit. I was sick with what I had witnessed. I wanted to get out into the fresh air. I quietly rose to leave.

"Back on your knees, Brother," came the stentorian voice of the superintendent, and unctuously he added: "Will you lead us next?"

That was too much. If I had spoken to God that moment I would have apologized for being present in a religious gathering where religion was turned into a mockery, into an outlet for suppressed sex emotions. I was furious at his asking me to pray.

"No, sir," I answered. "I have nothing to say. I don't know of anything to say. It seems to me everything worth saying has been said here this morning. I don't feel well."

I suddenly remembered the doctor telling me that he felt more pity than envy upon my leaving for Edmonton. I knew now what those words meant. But the superintendent had now also risen. He took me by the arm, as everyone stared at me with mingled looks of indignation, pity, and condescension. The superintendent was shaking with emotion. I had scandalized the assembly. Nothing like it had happened to him in the course of twenty-five years in the ministry. I had given offense to my brethren, nay, I had offended the Lord. He placed his hands on my shoulder, took me aside into the hardware man's bedroom where hung a strong marital night odor.

"We will kneel down together here," he said, "alone with Jesus."

"I prefer going out into the fresh air," I said, "and taking a walk. I want a cup of coffee. I haven't eaten since yesterday noon. We arrived too late for supper last night."

"Coffee?" he said. "Can you think of coffee, now? Remember, Brother, man shall not live by bread alone."

A few days later I was on my way back to the East.

Toronto was a changed city. It had caught the war fever thoroughly. Every second or third man you met on the streets wore a uniform of some sort. On the corners in the downtown district you saw crippled veterans leaning against the buildings or hopping about on their crutches. Recruiting posters carrying challenging inscriptions and pictures had been plastered over all the billboards. Flags were displayed in places where one should have least expected them: above the counters in cafeterias, on bulletin boards in front of churches, in butchershops, everywhere. In each shop window was a card asking for clothes or comforts for the troops abroad. Military bands were playing on the lawn in front of the City Hall, in the noontime business recess. There, prominent citizens—bankers, newspaper editors, clergymen, civic officials and the like—were making recruiting speeches. On the first occasion when I listened, I noticed that the Germans were no longer yellow dogs who ran at the sight of the first Canadian bayonet; they were now ruthless, unspeakable Huns who were using every means of terror to gain their ends. They had also become loathsome homosexuals. The Kaiser, I learned, had already appointed the official who was to be the first German Governor General of Canada. A cement floor, six feet thick, had been discovered somewhere up in the northern forests. There could be no doubt, of course, that this was intended as a gun emplacement by the Germans. In short, the menace was coming nearer home: the boys were being urged to go out and protect their own mothers and sisters.

It is, perhaps, unfair to speak flippantly of that time. True, the Canadian people were being misled like every other people, but they and most of the national leaders were in dead earnest. The soldiers leaving for the front did not march off in the expectation of loot or glory. They were aware of the immense risks they were about to face. There was no exaltation, nothing like the mass intoxication to which Hitler and Mussolini were to work up the German and Italian youth in later years. Nobody said that war was man's natural estate, and a healthy sport. The Canadian youth went to war in the full knowledge that they were marching into hell. This gave them a certain grandeur, a touch of gallant chivalry, and clothed their adventure with the dignity of a crusade.

Still believing that we would eventually return to Holland, I quietly resumed my studies. I had lost an entire year and did not intend to drop farther behind. I wanted to forget the episode in the missionary field as soon as possible. But I also began to follow the newspaper accounts of the struggle in Europe and the more and more insistent appeals to young Canadians to enlist in the army. It began to appear to me as if the war was really a struggle against barbarism. I read Viscount Bryce's summing up of atrocities said to have been committed by the German legions in occupied territory. I had not thought such wanton cruelty possible in our age. France was clearly bleeding to death. Hindenburg was evidently maneuvering to deliver a *coup de grâce* to Russia before turning his whole might against France. One day I received a letter from Uncle Kees in which he said that if they would have him, he would shoulder a rifle and march against the Prussians. That letter made me sit up. If Uncle Kees felt that way about it, there was indeed something to worry about. He had always held that whatever happened in France, or to France, concerned all of us Europeans. He was not likely to be influenced by propaganda, for Uncle Kees was free to see both sides of the case. Why should he then talk like a militarist? I grew disquieted.

One of my professors asked me point-blank one day why I did not join the forces. I explained that I was a Hollander. But this was not a question of nationality, he replied, it was a question of humanity. Every individual in the world had to make up his mind on what side he would take his stand. An exceptional situation had arisen which required exceptional and heroic measures. Christian civilization was threatened by the menace of German autocracy. In the first place, it was a Christian's duty to help set up a nobler and juster social order by slaying the Teutonic beast which respected neither age nor sex, universities nor churches. This was a war of defense, a holy war, a crusade for justice and righteousness. God willed it! Moreover, and this was frequently used as an argument by ecclesiastical recruiting sergeants, German scholars had been first and foremost in submitting the Bible to textual and historical criticism, thus sowing seeds of doubt as to the verbal inspiration and divine authority of the Scriptures, a crime than which there was nothing more heinous to the fundamentalist mind.

Discussions with my teachers on my own participation in the lamentable and bloody military sport became a daily preoccupation. They usually ended in violent disagreement. I still defended the conscientious objectors against the accusation of cowardice. I had an immense respect for these men who dared to row against the stream. As I see it now, they were the real heroes of the war period. Given over to the mob's opprobrium by the various Christian states, spending years in prison and concentration camps for the crime of having refused to assassinate, they were the real defenders of Christianity's own and fundamental principles. They, and not the churches, saw that it was high time to close that period which Constantine, a pagan emperor, in an unholy hour, had opened in the history of Christianity. The men of the church to whom I went with my doubts and misgivings were amongst the most vociferous in assuring the youth that the campaign against Germany was a war to save what was man's most precious possession in this world: freedom. The community of civilized nations from which Germany was excluded by reason of her unprovoked attack on "poor little Belgium," and by her proclamation of the principle that might is right, had to defend itself against the assault of the Hun. At the bottom was a certain barbarous instinct at the root of the German people.

It was always the same argument. It did not seem to occur to anyone that part of the guilt may have lain elsewhere. We knew nothing about the real causes of the war. And this was one lesson

I learned from the whole harrowing experience, a duty, namely, to point out to my fellow men what I have learned of the wheels within wheels which set such catastrophes in motion. The German people are not more barbarous than any other nation. War is not a consequence of animalistic instincts in man, but a result of profound social antagonisms which pitch vested interests against natural forces. Not only the war, but the ruin and decay which have come over every land after the war, are the outcome of the same fundamental maladjustment: the exploitation of a productive majority by a moneyed minority.

But of these things I had little knowledge in 1916. Theological seminaries, where boys are trained to be men's guides in life's most difficult moments, did not include sociology or the study of international relations in their curricula. The prescribed history books gave us an either partly or totally false picture, a caricature of the past. Had we but known of the intrigues of an Izvolsky and a Poincaré, who had for years been planning to have "their" war exactly in 1914; or of Britain's determination to crush her German rival as she had successively crushed Holland, Spain and the France of Napoleon for precisely the same reasons; or of Russia's plot to seize Constantinople; or of King Albert's betrayal of his country's neutrality by drawing up a joint plan of military action with the French and British general staffs—if we had known all this, the peoples might have shown less eagerness to throw themselves into the jaws of Moloch.

Added to my religious objections to war was a disgust for the way in which the Canadian newspapers dropped the last vestige of critical scrutiny with reference to events taking place in Europe. Their editors swallowed and reproduced the outrageous propaganda stories emanating from the Allied lie factories without the slightest compunction. To this day, hundreds of thousands of easygoing citizens of the Dominion are firmly persuaded that the Asquith cabinet in 1914 was something like the shadow of God on earth, that Belgian babies were currently carried on the point of German bayonets, that Bavarian yodelers took a particular delight in cutting off the breasts of Flemish nuns, that the Huns boiled enemy corpses in order to extract grease for the soap in the Kaiser's bath, and that Britain drew the sword solely to avenge the wrong done to Albert and Elisabeth of Saxe-Coburg-Gotha.

Inexperienced as I was, I could taste the vileness of the poison used to inflame the mind of an innocent people. But I dared not protest. I barely escaped with my life one Sunday afternoon when soldiers, who had returned from the front, invaded the Labor Temple in Toronto and insisted that the audience, which had assembled to hear a British left-wing Laborite, sing the national anthem. The Finnish Socialist band, which was present to enrich the program, struck up the "Marseillaise" instead. That was the signal for a brutal attack. The veterans in uniform rushed the platform. With crutches and sticks they battered down the speaker, the musicians, and the members of the audience who stood in their way. I staggered into the street, my face streaming blood, while a half dozen men yelled death and damnation to all pro-Germans, aliens, and spies. The next day at school, the professor of French took me aside and quietly warned me that I should always be on my guard in a country where the alien and the foreigner were regarded *a priori* as obnoxious intruders upon a preserve set aside for that section of the Anglo-Saxon population which sets the tone in Canada.

At home we merely smiled on days when the newspapers announced another thundering victory for the Belgian army or when, as happened once, the Toronto *Mail and Empire* blazoned forth the news that the River Meuse was flowing "red with blood of the Germans," and that the Cossacks were five days' marching distance from Berlin, or yet on another occasion when the same journal, which seemed vaguely aware that all had not been well in Belgium, coolly made the suggestion that the eight million Flemings and Walloons sink their silly differences, which were merely of a linguistic nature anyway, and adopt English as their common medium of speech. I do not believe that this precious advice was primarily intended as a circulation stunt. In the editorial offices in Toronto, they still settle the problems of Europe from time to time with the same keen sense of political realism.

It must be said to the credit of the French Canadians that on the whole they showed little enthusiasm for the noble sacrifice "Mother England" asked them to make. Those foresters and peasants along the St. Lawrence estuary had on an earlier historic occasion manifested a remarkable independence of judgment. That was in 1901, when they refused to join Great Britain in destroying the two Dutch republics in South Africa. The laxity of Quebec in sending its children to the shambles naturally evoked a burning indignation in Protestant Ontario. The Orangemen and the descendants of the United Empire Loyalists pretended to see, in Quebec's slackness in pushing the recruiting campaign, corroborative evidence of a long-suspected lack of loyalty to the Empire, and, what is perhaps more ludicrous, a sinister plot on the part of the Catholic clergy to bring about a French-speaking majority in the Dominion after the war by allowing only English-speaking boys to be killed off. It should be pointed out that amongst the fundamentalist brethren of Ontario French is pretty well synonymous with Roman Catholic.

I was still holding out against enlistment, but I felt myself weakening. The physical dangers did not perturb me, in fact I never gave them a moment's thought. Belgium's rape, which was by many deemed Germany's worst crime, did not rouse my indignation for a moment. I had always held the Belgian state, oppressor of the Flemish people, in abomination. If Germany had done nothing else but attack Belgium and Russia, I would not have thought of enlisting. It was the fate of France which filled me with anguish. An eventual defeat of France appeared to me the greatest disaster civilization could suffer. That would mean extinguishing the lamps for good. I was not so foolish as to think that my participation in the war was going to make any difference. But with that anxiety over France, I justified an act which was in reality the inability of the individual to resist the pressure of society.

An incident, insignificant in itself, finally led me to take the fateful step. One afternoon I was accosted on the rear platform of a streetcar by a woman, who was dressed in mourning. She told me that three of her sons had been killed at the front. She showed me their photographs. Suddenly she began to talk very loudly. "Why aren't you in khaki?" she demanded. "Why do you dare to stand there laughing at my misery? Why don't you go over and fight? Fight, avenge my boys!" she screamed. "Madam," I tried to calm her, "I am not a Canadian." That remark set her yelling at the top of her voice. She screamed that she, the mother of three heroes who had died for their king and country, had been insulted by a foreigner, a slacker, a German spy, a Red, and I don't know what else.

I pulled the cord to bring the street car to a halt. I alighted. But the woman followed me off and she kept up her screaming about spies and Germans. A crowd gathered. We were in front of the King

Edward Hotel. Somebody stopped me just at the moment when I thought of taking to my heels as the best way out of the predicament. I was immediately surrounded by a mob. A group of business men, who had managed to stay five thousand miles away from where the poppies grow, and who were at that moment emerging from the hotel, gallantly rushed to the woman's aid and forced me to submit, as she pinned a white feather through my coat into my flesh: the badge of white-livered cowardice. The last I saw of her was through a pair of badly battered eyes as she laughingly picked up some of the feathers which had dropped from her bag in the scuffle.

That same evening, after a mass meeting in the Metropolitan Methodist Church, where an appeal was made for recruits, Justice Ian McLaren and the Honorable Newton W. Rowell, the Liberal leader, promised to secure a position for me as interpreter with the army overseas. The following day I enlisted in the Corps of Guides.

Upon arrival in the training camp I was immediately transferred to another unit.

"Your interpretations," said the potbellied sergeant major to whom I protested, "will be carried out with a pick and shovel on the glorious field of honor in France and Flanders."

Indeed, all the use I could ever make of my knowledge of languages in the service was confined to composing billets-doux which my comrades desired to address to French demoiselles. For eighteen months, too, I carried on a correspondence for an illiterate French Acadian with his illiterate wife. He would bring me her letters, which were written for her by a parish priest somewhere in Nova Scotia, and have me read their contents. After four or five days of meditation, the soldier would come to me to dictate his reply. This usually consisted of advice on agricultural matters. One day I suggested putting a few words of affectionate greeting at the bottom of the letter, for by that time I knew that he loved her dearly, his *chère Thérèse* and the children. He consented with a nod of the head. The phrases I put in made him laugh in a shy, grateful way. Soon thereafter, the unknown priest in Canada began to reciprocate with a choice of endearing terms, until in the end something like a rivalry in the *terminologie d'amour* developed between the priest and myself.

In 1918, I was a member of the squad which fired a salvo of honor over the illiterate Acadian's open grave.

A boy, who was a piano teacher in civil life, taught me how to twist a long butcherknife, which was fastened to the end of my rifle, into the soft part of an adversary's body, while a gentleman who once sold postage stamps introduced me to the gentle art of crawling up stealthily behind an enemy sentinel and strangling him to death with bare hands before he could give the alarm. Little by little we learned the whole modern technique of serial murder. In less than three months, we were deemed sufficiently expert in assassination, theft, and arson to be sent over to France to save Christian civilization.

The first blood we saw was the coagulated, fly-infested chunks of human flesh that the Gurkhas from India carried fastened to their belts: trophies of war—ears, noses, sexual organs, and whole heads of German soldiers whom these valiant men from the East had massacred in a nocturnal raid. A few days later, in Abbeville, I saw the piano teacher's head completely severed from his body and his trousers stripped from his legs by an aerial bomb that the Richthofen circus aimed at the railway bridge. The postal employee later coughed up his lungs, filled with poison gas, in a hospital at Béthune.

I have never heard of a single case of chivalry or pity towards the enemy, either in the Great War, or in the subsequent campaigns in Syria, Ethiopia and Spain which I followed as a correspondent. The French took it for granted that any gray-clad creature that could still crawl or move a finger had to be finished without further ado. Wounded men, in fact, had less of a chance of life when discovered by so-called "mopping-up" patrols than prisoners of war, for a prisoner was considered somebody who had voluntarily thrown up the sponge, whereas of a wounded man one never knew if he would not recover and become a dangerous antagonist again at some time in the future.

Every army pillaged. My friend, Paul Vaillant-Couturier, formerly editor of *Humanité*, who served as a lieutenant in the tank corps, told me once that several of the men under his command managed to support their large families by going out at nights, at the risk of their lives, to extract money and valuables from the putrefied cadavers of friend and foe alike. I am not entirely without guilt in the matter myself, for I forcibly deprived a drunken Portuguese colonel of his bicycle one sunny spring day to go AWOL to Amiens, and by the time the Armistice was signed, I had acquired such a dexterity in raiding French wine cellars, in spite of the fact that my job towards the end was to work on the morale of the troops, that I had the reputation of being one of the best providers of liquid refreshment in the company. I always carried a few bottles for a friend in my knapsack. One of those bottles, I fear, cost an Algerian soldier his life, but saved a Canadian. It happened this way: Lawrence Scoville, a sergeant in the 26th Battalion, and I were coming along a lonely road one night in France. As we crossed a bridge we were challenged by a group of fez-wearing Algerians on the prowl. Between the Algerians and the Canadian troops there existed a latent state of hostility of which I do not know the origin. When the party of Africans stopped us, a short altercation followed, and they drew their knives. We were unarmed. But I had my bottles as usual. Pulling them from my knapsack I went into battle and struck the first man across the face, just at the moment when his long knife flashed near Scoville's throat. The Algerian bounded back, buckled over the railing of the bridge, and dropped into the river below. The others fled.

The notion that war brings out the best in man—not in the Mus-solinian sense, who repeats Bernhardi when he says that war has a regenerating effect upon the nations (something that is completely refuted by the survival of the sick and the weak after a modern war), but chivalry, camaraderie and self-sacrifice—that notion, it seems to me, rests largely upon the mythical accounts of war given by historians. I had my head stuffed full with stories of gallant and chivalrous incidents and encounters from the Boer War, the Napoleonic campaigns, the struggle of the Netherlands against Spain, the Franco-Prussian war, and the Russo-Japanese conflict. I know now that all that is literary history, historiographical gossip, general-staff fables, with not a single eyewitness account in the lot. Actually, war brings the basest instincts to the fore. The moment an apparently good-natured farm yokel received his first pair of stripes he turned into an arrogant brute. The war revealed char-acter and laid the souls of men bare. It is true that I have seen obscure fellows, silently plodding men, suddenly transformed at the approach of a great danger, rising to a genuine grandeur. But do we need war for that?

There is not an ex-soldier who, in going over his personal souvenirs of those years, has not asked himself that question. A ditch, four years wide, cuts across the lives of millions of men. In that ditch they crawled through mire and filth, physically and spiritually. When we glance back twenty years we can scarcely recognize ourselves as being those credulous and timid strangers who marched away, flowers on their rifles, blessed by the clergy and kissed by the loveliest women. What have we, what has the world gained by that immense trial? I must admit that I have personally benefited from the war in that it brought me into contact with humanity, not as a fabricator of theological formulae, or as a dreamer or as a mystic, but as a man. War showed me the dignity of looking events squarely in the face.

But that war is a crime, futile, loathsome, and all the rest of it, is universally recognized today. As far back as the close of the Napoleonic Wars, pacifist congresses condemned war as contrary to reason and morality. Towards the close of the nineteenth century, vast numbers of citizens had come to believe, in spite of the fact that socialist economists always predicted new conflicts, that civilized men had become too reasonable to indulge in such folly. In a burst of enthusiasm, Victor Hugo foresaw the abolition of armed conflicts when he exclaimed, "In the nineteenth century war will be dead, the scaffold will be dead, hatred will be dead, frontiers will be dead, royalty will be dead, dogmas will be dead, man will commence to live!"

Why is it that, far from having been abolished, a new and more frightful kind of warfare than any that has ever been waged in the past, seems to be facing humanity. In this hour too, when every statesman, Hitler and Mussolini included, warns us that a world conflict may well mean the end of civilization? In every country you find organizations to foster peace and international understanding. Every government does its utmost to prevent the outbreak of war. Diplomats fly to and fro in feverish alarm, whenever a conflict appears imminent. In nearly every capital you could, until a few years ago, see monster demonstrations against war in which hundreds of thousands shouted their horror of, and their opposition to war. And yet war is coming again. And yet it is almost here. . . . Any tolerably well-informed observer knows that Manchukuo, Ethiopia, the Rhineland's remilitarization, and Spain are but preludes to a finale of abysmal woe which is in store for the peoples.

What is the matter? Does Hitler not detest war in reality? Are men like Chamberlain and Eden not in earnest when they say that a new war would signify the greatest calamity that can befall the

British peoples? Can we not take Stalin and Mussolini, Daladier and Cecil, and all the others at their word when they affirm that they are occupied night and day in trying to save the world from the impending disaster? Or is there perhaps some hidden fatality, some irresistible superforce which frustrates the efforts of all these peacemakers, and which causes the nations, against their own wills, to pile up huge armaments at a rate never before witnessed in history? Who wants war, anyway? What is pushing us toward it?

For thirteen years I have wandered up and down the European continent inquiring and observing, talking with leaders in the social, religious, economic and political spheres in every country. I have lived in France and mixed in all classes of society in Germany, Italy, Rumania, Spain, Belgium, Russia, Morocco, Turkey, Palestine, Austria and Switzerland, but I have yet to meet the man or the woman who longs for war, or who thinks that war would be a benefit to anyone. Yet at best, they only hoped that it would be prevented. With so much good will in the world, with so general an awareness of the danger, and so universal an opposition to war, why is it that the highways of Europe resound again with the metallic step of heavy-shod legions? Why is the nocturnal sky lurid with the reflection of belching steel ovens? Why are millions of men under arms again ready for the slaughter?

To solve this puzzle became an anguishing preoccupation with me in the years when I saw the gradual return of every state to that old theory so often discredited in the past: if you want peace, prepare for war!

The League of Nations, the Kellogg Pact to outlaw war, the Disarmament Conference, Briand's eloquence, Cecil's zeal, Stresemann's pleading, Litvinov's arguments—all the ceaseless striving of the innumerable peace societies, all of it has been sterile, all of it has come to nought. Nobody has found a solution, not even the Neo-Marxists of Russia who were going to found a new world. They, too, fell back upon the old methods, and imitated the bourgeois governments in creating a formidable war machine of their own.

"Everything has been tried to set the world in the ways of peace," remarked Lord Cecil to me one day, as we crossed the Channel together on the way to Geneva.

Everything? Really everything? Yes, everything except the one thing that will make war truly impossible: *disarmament*.

But can that be done? Imagine what staggering proportions unemployment would reach in Germany, Italy, England, France, and Japan, if all the men now engaged in munition factories, armament plants, steel mills, clothing factories, chemical laboratories, ship-yards, mines, forests, and all the other auxiliaries of the war indus-try, not to speak of the legions in the armies, navies, and air forces of the world, should suddenly be thrown out of work? Wouldn't that be a disaster of the first magnitude? Where would America's precarious prosperity be on the day when that should come to pass?

No, rather than face an interruption of the profit system, the imperialist states prefer a universal armament race, even at a risk of plunging the nations into a second world war. There are things more precious to preserve than civilization and democracy. It is more important to assure the continuous flow of dividends into the coffers of a small international coterie which owns the banks and the land and the means of production, than to employ the earth's resources in the satisfaction of the physical, social and spiritual needs of all men, all peoples, and all races of the earth.

The modern states will never voluntarily disarm. They cherish their armament campaigns as the highest good. For they mean profits through the stimulation of the inner market, a safeguard against violation of a foreign market by rivals, and preparation for a redivision of the world's markets.

But war is not an act of God like an earthquake or a flood. It is not an inescapable fatality. War is inseparable from the capitalist system of production. Humanity will never get rid of the one till it gets rid of the other.

2

In August, 1871, when half of Paris lay in ruins and the blood of fifty thousand Communards was being washed off the pave-ments, the newly elected President of the Republic, Adolphe Thiers, promised the masters of Europe that the proletariat would never again disturb the peace of mind of the bourgeoisie, inasmuch as he, with his own hands, had smothered the revolutionary spirit for all time to come.

Less than half a century later, mankind was called to witness a resurrection of that spirit when a mortal blow was dealt to the colossus of imperial Russia, the most formidable bulwark of reaction on earth. That blow shook the world as it had not been shaken since Danton flung the head of a king into the face of the powdered *émigrés*. The ghost of the Commune was stalking through the corridors of history. Words that had been locked in unlit dungeons for a generation rose from their tomb. They became flesh and blood. They turned into axes and rifles, into cannons and barricades, into columns of partisans, into armies of workers and peasants.

They grew into the first Socialist Republic of history!

In 1917, millions of weary hearts thrilled with a new hope. The infinite patience of the martyred peoples, Rolland announced, had reached the point of exhaustion. The kettle was boiling at last. To prevent an explosion, the governments had closed up all the cracks beforehand and seated themselves on top. Despite these precautionary measures, the pent-up steam was beginning to escape with a snarling hiss. The conviction that the nations had been the victim of a colossal bloody swindle was gaining ground. Here and there the free spirit of human beings who had been imprisoned in the iron-bound cells of nationality during the four years of collective hysteria ventured to look across the borders again. In the suffering eyes of their neighbors they recognized their own features, distorted by the same murderous illusion. "Amongst the masses indignation was deepening over the incalculable treasure which had proved easily available for the frenzied game of war, whereas financial support for measures aiming at their own social amelioration had never been forthcoming without bitter struggle."

A vague, inarticulate movement, as that of a giant stirring in his sleep, became discernible. The peoples were waking up. The chains that bound them began to rattle. There was still talk in the press and in the propaganda bureaus about baby-murdering Huns and cannibalistic Senegalese, but not a few of those in the trenches clearly saw through the mystification. The four years of "righteous war had piled up more ruins and folly than had the feudal lords and the Church in the ten centuries of their undisputed almightiness."

From the distance came "the dull thud of Lenin's heavy ax-blows." The pamphlets of Romain Rolland, the only man who had kept himself free of hatred, were finding their way into the trenches. Rolland spoke the words of human pity and brotherly love which the Church should have spoken. He sought to pierce the icy crust

of hatred which covered the European Continent, and called on
the adversaries to stretch out their hands to each other in the name
of their common humanity. Rolland was followed by Henri Barbusse. Fresh from the fray with a pair of poisoned lungs, Barbusse
broke the spell of incantation about sacrifice, heroism, and the
fatherland, which had mesmerized the peoples for three years. His
Under Fire for the first time revealed the realism of war, and what
was going on, not in editorial offices or ministerial salons, but in the
consciousness of the people. He showed that men were beginning
to ask what sense there was in that war for justice and freedom, to
what extent the peoples were to benefit from the ghastly bloodletting, and who was the real enemy who should have been conquered before the peasant from across the Rhine. In the end, Barbusse and Rolland both demanded what was essentially human: an
immediate peace without sanctions or reparations, a moral peace,
not a military one.

The poilus of France began to debate whether or not to return
to their firesides before Clemenceau's "war to the bitter end" should
have reached that dismal climax. In the spring of 1918, André
Maginot admitted[1] in a secret session of the Chamber that there
remained but one single division between Paris and the battle line
on which the government could place absolute reliance. The red
flag had been hoisted on the ruined sugar refinery of Souchez. In
response, a German regiment had intoned the "Marseillaise" and
had walked across no man's land to fraternize. Letters tied to
clods of earth were being thrown from the one trench to the other.
Messages were exchanged. It became necessary to forbid British
troops to converse with German prisoners of war. The press curtailed publication of casualty lists. Divisions had to be shifted to
break up secret contacts established with the enemy across the
line of death.

Tens of thousands of men were still dying each day. But in the
châteaux, far from the crash of high explosives, and protected from
aerial raiders by an agreement with the German high command not
to bombard each other's headquarters,[2] the Allied generals and poli-

[1] Paul Allard, *Comptes-rendus sténographiques des séances secrètes de la
Chambre des deputés*, 1917-1918.

[2] The Crown Prince states in his memoirs that a French aviator dropped a
bomb in the neighborhood of German headquarters just once. "After retaliation
we were never bothered again," he adds.

ticians kept up their quarrels about precedence and prestige. Joffre, who had suggested putting Foch in an old ladies' home after the Somme, was himself pushed out by Nivelle. Pétain took up the succession for a time until Castelnau stepped into his shoes. The lack of accord amongst the gold-braided chiefs threatened to prolong the war eternally. A heavy subterranean rumble of discontent shook the army zones. Mutinies broke out. At one time, eighty-seven French regiments were affected, at another time, one hundred and fifteen. Courts-martial functioned night and day. For a mere whisper of discontent in a regiment, a company was decimated. Divisions were purposely sent into battle to be massacred, to kill the spirit of defeatism.

Strikes were being called in Paris and Lyons. In December, 1917, the metalworkers folded their arms and demonstrated on the boulevards. The sons of the Communards had recognized the futility of the blood bath into which the united front with the ruling class had tricked them. The repression increased. The bitter disillusion over "millions of lives sacrificed for a resulting zero turned the wrath of those morally responsible for the disaster against the men who had foreseen it." Spy hunts were organized. The censors redoubled their efforts to prevent the people from learning the extent of the horror. The billboards in the big cities were placarded with flaming posters, warning against the sinister intrigues of pacifists, against enemy agents and foreign gold, against emissaries from the dead International of labor. Crowds were enjoined to silence in public. Shut up—fight! Do not reason—kill! Since one lie which raises the morale of the troops and of the civilian population is worth a thousand truths in wartime, lie factories were set in operation. They supplanted the universities. Savants and intellectuals, authors and pulpiteers, those who prided themselves on stating the truth for its own sake, began howling with the pack. Men gave up their convictions as easily as their lives. Free investigation, independence of judgment, human pity—all were put in moth balls and laid in the storage room till after the war. Criticism was abolished, conscience proscribed. Christendom repudiated its name by adopting Mars. The Deity was split into a number of tribal Jehovahs. From a hundred thousand pulpits the voice of Antichrist roared hatred.

Every new retreat of the armies was interpreted as the result of defeatist propaganda; never were the quarreling old generals held responsible. Every diplomatic blunder was attributed to spies; not a single statesman would ever admit that a ghastly error had been made. Civil and military courts were working overtime. The medieval system of *lettres de cachet* was revived in France. Secret denunciation filled the jails. Men who showed too much zeal in laying bare the machinations of the international cannon trust and its press in seeking to prolong the war were enjoined to keep silent or railroaded to jail. One of the most outspoken pacifists, Almereyda, whose testimony on the witness stand would have revealed the extent of the corruption in high places, was found garroted in his cell. Seeing an opportunity to dispose of his political opponents, the old "Tiger of France" seized upon the frenzy against defeatism to try Joseph Caillaux for high treason. Malvy was banished. Briand escaped by a hairsbreadth. The sinister pair, Daudet and Maurras, licking their blood-dripping chops, boasted in their journal that they were delivering more "traitors" to the executioner than the intelligence services of France and Britain combined. Every morning the meadow behind the castle in Vincennes rang with the salvos of the firing squad.

Nor was the end in sight! Men were not yet tired of hatred. The battlefields were turning into abattoirs. At Verdun, on the Chemin des Dames, in Flanders, the holocaust to Moloch, the dance of death, was reaching an obscene climax. The armies had received new weapons from the laboratories. Poison gas had been used freely. Now experiments were being made with disease germs. Even if this diabolic device was not utilized in 1918, it will remain the eternal mark of shame of a dehumanized, debased generation which seriously pondered its employment. Boys who could scarcely support the weight of a rifle were being drafted and thrown into the gaping jaws of death as sacrifice units. The new German levies holding the Hindenburg line had hunger stamped on their face. Sanatoria and jail, venereal hospitals and insane asylums—all were being combed for more cannon fodder. The monster was insatiable. The Europe of Christianity and humanism was sinking into a miasma of gore and lies.

Then word came from Italy about factory occupations. There had been trouble amongst the submarine crews at the German naval base at Kiel. The "Kaiser's coolies" were refusing to go down below the waves to meet a certain death. Alsatians serving in the German army were flocking into France. French conscripts ran into Switzerland and Spain for safety. Bosnians deserted the double eagle of Habsburg to join their Serbian brothers. A Czech army was wandering aimlessly over the Muscovite plain. A famine was raging in Bulgaria, the black plague had broken out in Salonika, typhus was decimating the Turkish army. Over in France the imperial Russian troops who had been brought from Odessa to bolster up the Allied morale, and who had covered themselves with glory at Verdun, refused to fight the moment Russia was out of the war. They were disarmed and massacred, ten thousand of them, by order of Foch, to preserve the French army from the virus of revolutionism.[3] Then, soviets sprang from the ground in Hungary. Standing on foreign soil, the Belgian army was so torn by dissension over the growth of the movement for Flemish autonomy at home, that its best divisions were disarmed and consigned to the lumber camps in southern France. Here they were presently joined by the Russian volunteers in the Canadian army who had downed arms the moment Trotsky signed the peace of Brest-Litovsk. From Italy came word of regiments constituting themselves into a Division of Peace. Signs were multiplying on every hand that the peoples were growing tired of the dance that imperialism had called. The prospect of glory and victory had long since receded from view. It now appeared certain that the war, from whatever angle one looked at it, was going to be a bad bargain for everyone concerned. Neither ideals, ambitions, nor national interests were going to be satisfied. Only blood and tears. . . .

Germany had based all her calculations on a swiftly conducted war and an early victory. At the outset she had a supply of war stocks which could scarcely have carried her through a year of warfare on two fronts. The Allies, therefore, could have brought the Kaiser to his knees before the end of 1915, by instituting an economic blockade.[4] But that would have meant giving up the choicest profits of war: the contraband commerce. Throughout the first three years of the war the Reich received an uninterrupted stream of supplies through Holland, Switzerland, and the Scandinavian countries, especially cotton, without which she could not have continued to fight for a day. This went on until America

---

[3] The massacre of these Imperial Russian troops is mentioned by Winston Churchill in his history of the World War.

[4] *Enquête sur la situation de la métallurgie;* official government publication, substantiated in *Neueste Nachrichten* of Leipzig, Oct. 10, 1917.

angrily protested that England, Germany's chief adversary, was crowding her out of the European market.[5] German capitalism had not neglected its opportunities either: right up to the beginning of 1917, the Krupp Works of Essen shipped a quarter of a million tons of steel a month through Switzerland to the Comité des Forges in France.[6] In addition to payment in gold, one of the conditions in this deal was that French aviation was to refrain from bombarding the iron-ore mines, the blast furnaces and the rolling mills of the Longwy district which had been occupied by Germany early in the war.[7] Ships loaded with nickel from New Caledonia, destined for Germany, seized by French destroyers in open sea and brought to port at Brest and Cherbourg and there declared prizes of war by the maritime court, were ordered released by the French government and reached Bremen safely.[8] Representatives of the German chemical trust, of the Swiss copper interests, and of Vickers, Krupp, Schneider-Creusot, and the Comité des Forges met in Vienna at the moment when the armies were locked in a death struggle in the mud of Flanders. Their sole purpose was to devise ways and means of keeping the war going profitably. *"On croyait mourir pour la patrie, on mourait pour les industriels,"* said Anatole France when he learned the answer of Senator Bérenger as to why the metallurgical district of Thionville was not taken back at the outbreak of the war, when it was undefended by the Germans and the French army was within a stone's throw. The reason no attempt had been made to recapture Thionville was that it would have brought the war to a premature termination. "For the occupation of Thionville," declared the Senator, "would have reduced Germany to seven million tons of poor steel per year; all production would have been stopped. Seizure of Thionville would have put an end to the war immediately." The stoppage of the war was to be prevented at all costs. General Sarrail, commanding in Lorraine, worked out a plan of strategy in 1915 to capture, or else destroy, the Briey

[5] André Ribard, *La France, histoire d'un peuple,* Editions Internationales, Paris, 1938, p. 335.

[6] Jean Galtier-Boissière et René Lefebvre, *Crapouillot, numéro spécial,* article *"Les Marchands de canons contre la nation,"* Paris, 1933, pp. 40-46.

[7] Pierre Bruneau, *Le Rôle du haut commandement au point de vue économique de 1914 à 1921,* Paris, 1921, p. 55 *et seq.*; also report by M. Laurent Eynac in the Chamber of Deputies, *Journal officiel,* Feb. 14, 1921.

[8] Admiral Consett, *Les Triomphes des forces economiques,* Paris, 1927, p. 126.

district where Germany exploited the captured blast furnaces of the Comité des Forges. When the Commander in Chief, Joffre, got wind of the projected offensive, Sarrail was called to Paris, had an interview with Poincaré, President of the Republic, and the plan was shelved. Thanks to French ore, made available by the initial order to the French armies to withdraw twenty-two kilometers from the border before a single blow had been struck, Germany was able during four years to inundate the East and the West, on land and the high seas, with a torrent of steel. In return for magnetos for airplane motors, shipped by Germany, France gave bauxite, an indispensable ingredient in the manufacture of aluminum for Zeppelins. The dreadful barbed wire strung out by the British at Ypres and on the Somme, which became a deathtrap for the Prussian Guard, was manufactured by the Drahtwerke of Opel and Company, and had found its way through Holland to England. Australia shipped fat to Germany via Norway and Denmark; the Straits Settlements copra; Ceylon tea; Wales coke and coal, tar, ammoniac and glycerine for high explosives, all of it in British ships.

The Allied high command tranquilly figured on finishing the war with the fresh forces from America in the fall or winter of 1919. When Lenin repeated his call for peace over and over again, the Entente maintained an obstinate silence. The Allies were more than ever determined to gain the victory without jeopardizing the interests of the ruling classes. On the other hand, strikes increased, and the peasants who had once set châteaux aflame were growing restless. In alarm, the French government proposed to replace the men employed in munition plants with workers to be imported from America. They desired to send the entire French male population to the front. A violent wave of protest was the answer to this proposal. The Council of Labor threatened to call a general strike and the scheme was dropped. But now the government began to look for ways and means to disband the labor unions. Time was growing short. America's participation in the war had made a final victory in the field a virtual certainty. A new danger loomed on the horizon, and it was growing more and more precise: a further postponement of peace threatened to bring on a social revolution. Only when the upper classes recognized the imminence of what would have been a major disaster to the ruling cliques of bankers and merchants of death was a single high command for all fronts finally instituted, and, upon the urging of America, the economic blockade at last applied in earnest. Germany immediately realized that the end had come. She launched a last desperate offensive and collapsed.

Suddenly Wilhelm fled to Amerongen, Emperor Karl to Lausanne, the Crown Prince to Wieringen. The Turkish Sultan and his harem had earlier been packed off to an island in the Aegean. Ferdinand of Bulgaria, just in time, conceived a desire to go hunting butterflies in the forests of Liechtenstein. The generals took off their medals. Ludendorff disguised himself with a false beard and a pair of black glasses. The Russian nobility took up dishwashing in Constantinople. The pot was cracking. The Bank of England was bulging with the family jewels of archdukes, beaten generals, and panic-stricken international financiers. In Berlin the banners of the people were marching in the Sieges Allee. Crowds ripped the epaulets from the *Junkers'* shoulders. Bismarck's statue was crowned with a Phrygian bonnet. Bavaria abolished parliament and set up a council of people's commissars. Munich sang the "Carmagnole." In Berlin the Philharmonic Orchestra struck up the "Marseillaise" under the statue of Frederick the Great. At the front the butts of rifles went up in the air, cannons were spiked, machine guns beaten to smithereens. One hundred and thirty French regiments were on the point of leaving the line and marching on Paris.

Then the Armistice was signed!

It came not a day too early. Another three months and Soviet France would have been exchanging greetings with the liberated German people. The ruling classes of Europe had recognized the common danger. No tediously prolonged negotiations had been necessary to bring the war to a close. Instinct had spoken. Immediately after the meeting in the forest of Rethondes, Foch and Hindenburg agreed to leave a gap of fifty miles between the retreating Germans and the allied victors to prevent contact and fraternization. Prussia's Iron Division, entirely made up of *Junkers*, was summoned from the Baltic front to maintain order in Berlin. Clemenceau suggested distributing the American Expeditionary Force over the length and breadth of France "to hold a revolution in check." Before the retreating German army had quite crossed the Rhine, the press of France was clamoring to give Ludendorff, the most prominent exponent of the hated Prussian militarism, carte blanche to strangle the new freedom in Russia "which menaced a system of social injustice by which all the bourgeoisies live."

Without transition, the imperialist war turned into a war of the imperialisms against the peoples. With the approval of the Allied high command a German army was rushed to the aid of the White Guards of Finland and helped to exterminate the forty thousand Socialists of Helsingfors. Rumanian boyars, who had run like hares when Mackensen entered Transylvania, were encouraged by Franchet d'Esperey, who commanded the Salonika front, to seize the choicest Magyar estates after the Hungarian army had demobilized as a token of good faith. That was their recompense, not for winning victories, but for trampling working-class leaders to death in the streets of Budapest. Had not Woodrow Wilson vetoed the idea, the offer of the German high command to suspend operations in all theaters of war, and jointly march on Moscow to wipe out the Bolshevik regime, would have been accepted. Foch was favorably inclined. With Cardinal Mercier, who had pleaded for compassion early in the war, it remained an *idée fixe* until his dying day. The Allies thought they could handle Russia alone.

But now the German bourgeoisie began sending up alarm signals. Clemenceau knew his history. He remembered that in 1871, before peace was concluded between France and Germany, Bismarck had loaned Adolphe Thiers the necessary cannon to extinguish the Commune of Paris. In December, 1918, the "Tiger of France" returned the compliment by stipulating that 50,000 German machine guns were to be excepted from destruction to enable Ebert and Noske to shoot down the Spartacists in Berlin and the soviets in Bavaria. The German bourgeoisie was permitted to organize a civic guard of 400,000 men, the so-called *Reichswehr* (of which the world was to hear more), because England insisted that total disarmament would deliver the Reich up to Socialism.

Europe's bourgeoisies consented to every complicity in order to maintain the established social order. The essential fact of the history of 1919 which does not figure in official chronicles, consists in the singlemindedness of the ruling classes of every country to arrest the march of humanity towards Socialism. In this way a new problem was added to all the national and international problems of the world: the problem of class. Within a few years that problem dominated all others. It upset all the traditional national policies of the preceding century.

3

It was a gray afternoon in the autumn of 1917. A fine drizzle, more like a thin mist, had been falling since early morning. It had turned the pavement into a gleaming black mirror and had deepened the somber hue of the house fronts to the color of wet ashes. For a brief moment the sun had seemed on the point of breaking through the low-hanging clouds to dispel the gloom which hung over the great city. A wan, pale shaft of light had softly tipped the spires of the Sacré-Coeur. It had seemed as if the hill of Montmartre had tried to raise itself to meet the mystic glow. That was at noon. . . . Within an hour, sharp gusty blasts blew through the empty squares and the clustered chimney pots on the roofs, bringing up new and more massive rain bearers from the sea. The streets had darkened early, and an infinite sadness, the hopelessness of the worst year of the war, had settled over Paris.

Pedestrians were few, and the glass-sheltered sidewalk cafés along the Boulevard de Strasbourg deserted of their habitués. Here and there small groups of poilus, their earth-colored haversacks slung over their shoulders, were spending the last few hours of their leave from the front in the small taverns which dot the neighborhood of the Gare de l'Est. The men talked in monosyllables. Most of them were silent. Not, to be sure, because of the warning signs which had been hung up everywhere by a spy-crazed government, but because there was nothing to talk about. The days when their elders had gaily marched away, accompanied by the laughing *midinettes* to the bunting- and flag-draped station, lay now in the unreal distant past. The doors of that mournful depot at the end of the street had become a portal of death to tens of thousands of their comrades.

What was there to say? Vividly present in their minds was the outline of beloved faces, the memory of a last kiss and dear hands that would not let go. Ahead lay the journey back to the line, the gluey mudholes, the barbed wire, the whole godforsaken dreariness of shell-plowed fields, the nerve-racking bark of machine guns, perhaps the grave. . . . Would they ever come back? Above the portico of the church of Saint-Laurent, across the street from the

Gare de l'Est, its sculptured figures of saints and bishops now hidden behind piles of sandbags, hung a placard with the words: ENTER HERE PASSER-BY AND PRAY FOR THE SOULS OF THOSE WHO ARE IN THIS HOUR DYING FOR THE FATHERLAND. It was the darkest month of the war. Not because a national defeat seemed imminent. There are things worse than defeat and more murderous than cannon. The endlessness of the nightmare crushed men's spirits. It was the crime that suffocated the great city, the crime of being the accomplice in a perverted cause which murdered the nation's youth and turned youth into murderers. Children were now going to the front who could scarcely support the weight of the soldier's equipment. Men beyond middle age were being called up. A million French families had been plunged into mourning. A nameless sorrow, immense and inexpressible, held the life of France in a paralyzing grip.

And still the white-haired old men in the salons of the ministries talked of holding out "twenty years if needs be"!

Three priests, one of them a frail elderly man, who leaned heavily on a walking stick, were seen to alight from a taxicab in front of the Gare de l'Est shortly before five o'clock. Passing rapidly inside, they made their way through the vast waiting rooms filled with soldiers, to the platform of the Swiss Express. There, ushered in by a military stationmaster to whom they showed their passes, they entered a reserved compartment in the small first-class section. They had scarcely gained their seats when the train began to move and the locomotive, belching thick smoke, slowly picked up speed.

It was an ordinary leave train, one of the many carrying men to and from the area of operations up north. Most of the dilapidated coaches were without doors and windows or showed other evidence of having passed through the fighting zone. Even the first-class carriage, in one of which the priests were traveling, was without light.

Upon entering the compartment the oldest of the three had slumped down in a corner by the window and had opened his breviary. His lips moved in prayer, but the failing light soon compelled him to abandon his reading. With a sigh, he resigned himself, and stared out of the window at the last houses of the melancholy Parisian suburbs. The elderly prelate was extremely short of stature.

His feet, shod in the rough leather brogues with metal clasp of the simple Roman parish priest, scarcely touched the carriage floor. A startling pallor, the hue of yellow alabaster, overspread his fine symmetrical face. The blanched skin accentuated the expressiveness of his black luminous eyes. His hands lay quietly on the breviary in his lap, but from time to time, his thin transparent fingers would attempt to restore circulation in his hands, for the train was unheated and the chill dampness entered through the cracks of the ill-fitting doors and windows. The old man seemed to be suffering from a cold, for he coughed incessantly: a dry hacking cough that brought him but small relief. One of the younger priests, a tall man of athletic build, glanced over in the direction of his old companion whenever a new spasm seized him. He had placed a plaid over the aged man's knees and now wrapped another cloak over his shoulders. He was thanked for his attention with an almost imperceptible nod of the head.

The three men did not speak. As night descended they were sitting in complete darkness. Only when the train slowed up under the hood of a wayside station did the solitary lamp, carried by the stationmaster on the platform, illumine for a fleeting moment the face in the corner of the compartment. It could then be seen that the old man was leaning his head against the plush-upholstered wall and that he had closed his eyes. When the carriage moved forwards, the darkness rushed back.

In Troyes the train moved into a siding. Outside on the concrete platform could be heard the metallic clatter of soldiers' boots. Although the end of the voyage had not been reached, the men were leaving the carriages to refresh themselves at the open-air buffets, where on long tables stood steaming containers of coffee served by women in nurses' uniforms. When they had stood still for about an hour, one of the two younger priests left the compartment, saying that he would inquire as to the cause of the delay. He returned presently to announce that the right of way was being kept clear for a hospital train coming back from the battle front in Champagne. Having spoken these words, he readjusted the plaid on the old man's lap and pressed the ends gently around his body. Then the three men settled down to wait.

Soon a heavy rumble could be heard in the distance, the hissing hulk of an engine suddenly darkened the carriage window, and the reflection of the flames in a locomotive's open furnace threw fantastic dancing shapes of livid red on the compartment's wall. Other coaches, unlit, lumbered slowly by until, with a grating and creaking of brakes, the hospital train came to a standstill. The railway station and the animated scene in front of the canteens were now hidden completely from the view of the clerical travelers.

Except for the labored breathing of the old man, it was silent in the compartment. Suddenly a light was switched on in the train on the adjoining track. What the tall young priest saw in the illuminated compartment, which almost touched the one wherein they were traveling, caused him to rise hastily. He stepped on the seat and tried to disentangle the curtains from the rod in order to lower them. But the rusty rings would not slip freely and he fumbled with the green cloth. While the younger priest was thus occupied, the gaze of his aged companion turned slowly towards the lighted window. He sat up with a start and his breath stopped short as he bent forward, his covers falling from his knees.

Quite near, so that he could have touched him had not the two windows separated them, sat a young soldier. A white-uniformed orderly was placing a cigaret between the soldier's lips and held up a burning match. The old priest rose from his seat. He placed his hands on the pane. He saw that of the young man's arms but two short stumps remained, and these were wrapped in bandages which showed dark spots on the extremities.

"*Domine, Domine, miserere, miserere,*" he whispered. His voice was husky and choking with tears. But the spectacle held him spellbound with its silent horror. He pressed his forehead against the pane as if he wanted to break it. Slowly the young man's face in the other carriage turned towards the window. The old priest gasped and wanted to step back. But the wounded soldier had seen him. He peered at the shape he had discerned in the semiobscurity and brought his face still nearer. Then he smiled and nodded his head in friendly fashion at the old prelate. The two men looked straight into each other's eyes. At that moment the hospital train began to move imperceptibly and with every heartbeat the distance between them widened. The old priest made the sign of the cross in the direction of the receding face and sank back upon his seat, sobbing like a child.

In Chaumont the three clergymen alighted. It was pitch-dark by now. The steelshod toes of the soldiers stumbled against the rail, as they crossed the tracks, and clattered with a herdlike trample towards the exits where military police officials verified their papers by the light of small oil lamps which they carried suspended from a button on their greatcoats. The priests were met by a staff officer who saluted gravely as he held the door of a mud-bespattered limousine open for them. As soon as they had stepped inside, the car swerved into the cobbled street, sped through the old town, and in a few minutes was plowing through the mire of a rural road.

Far away to the right the travelers could see an occasional flash in the sky, as of a summer night's sheet lightning, and when the car was halted for the first time at a crossing by a patrol of helmeted men who demanded to see their *laissez-passer*, a sustained rumble as that of rolling thunder drifted over to them from the east. In an hour they passed through Domremy-la-Pucelle, the birthplace of Joan of Arc, and through the town of Vaucouleurs. Then turning to the right, the car entered a highway where progress was much slower because of a long procession of munition-laden trucks, endless files of men tramping up to the front and equally long caravans of ambulances moving back to the rear. Just outside the city of Conflans, the limousine came to a halt before a small château where the corps commander had his headquarters. Accompanied by his entire staff, the general had come outside in the *cour d'honneur* to welcome the three clerical visitors. But the old priest graciously declined to partake of the dinner which had been prepared for him and asked permission to retire to his room.

One of his companions remained downstairs to make arrangements for a visit to the front line. He was informed that there was a possibility of an enemy offensive in the morning. Raids carried out in the last few days had established the fact that the enemy had brought up a number of fresh divisions from the Russian front. Prisoners had talked of large-scale operations in the offing. In fact, the attack might now come any day. It might be launched at daybreak. In that event, a visit to the front would be out of the question for the three priests. On the other hand, if the offensive did not come off at dawn, there was a good chance that it would not materialize before another twenty-four hours at least. However, a decision could be made within a short time, for if an offensive were planned, the artillery would go into action long before dawn in an effort to batter the wire entanglements and the redoubts in preparation for the infantry waves which would then follow with the first streaks of daylight.

The priest carried this message upstairs to his elderly companion, whom he found kneeling on a *prie-dieu* with his eyes closed. He retired on tiptoe, but returned after an hour only to find the old man still in the attitude of prayer.

Dawn came crawling through the orchard at the château, a gray diffusion that lit up the grass and the shrubbery with tufts of white. The old priest watched the new day through the open window. He had wrapped a heavy woolen muffler around his neck and had buttoned his long black coat and now stood, his hands on his back, facing east. There was a sound of running motors in the court below, and as he stepped forward to look out of the window he could see officers and soldiers running about pell-mell. The low voice of the corps commander could be heard giving some brief instructions. In a few minutes they would all be moving towards the line where everything was calm after a short nervous cannonade at the crack of dawn.

The priest's face had lost its careworn lines of the day before. He looked strangely rested for a man who had spent the night alternately in prayer and pacing his room. It seemed as if the long hours of vigil had strengthened him: his mouth was tightly closed with determination and in his eyes burned a somber fire. He turned around sharply as his tall companion of the train journey entered the room and knelt before him. He blessed him and raised him up.

The small caravan of staff cars moved as near to the communication trenches as was safe. Then the officers and the priests alighted to enter a deep ditch in which men, with blanched and muddy faces, stood against the shored walls to afford them passage. Some of the soldiers took off their helmets at the sight of the cassocked priests and knelt on the "duckboards" to receive their blessing. Others were preparing food and carrying dixies with steaming liquids up the steps of the kitchen dugouts. The enemy must have been similarly occupied at that hour, for the front was silent. Through the communication trench the party reached the second-line defenses. Here the scene changed: the soldiers stood closely ranged against the wall, bayonets fixed. Officers were pacing to and fro in front of the ranks, their gas masks open and the revolvers protruding from their holsters. A colonel came forward to greet the corps commandant and the two men had a whispered conversation. No, the enemy's mass attack was not due that morning, the colonel said. Some prisoners brought in during the night had spoken of two days hence. Yet the opposite trenches and the subterranean concentration centers were known to be packed with reinforcements. The French troops were being held in a constant state of alert. One could never tell. The Boche might decide to attack at noon. That silence all along the line was ominously depressing. The enemy might be preparing a surprise.

Again the party of visitors moved forward into a zigzagging trench. In ten minutes' time they were in the midst of a crowd of poilus who stood closely packed, watching their officers who peered through the periscopes into no man's land. An oppressive tense atmosphere prevailed in the small "bay" where the post of command was located. Machine gunners had their hands on the trigger handles. Snipers stood looking steadily up into tiny mirrors which they had attached to the wooden stakes on the parapet. The only sound to be heard was the metal click of gunlocks being opened and shut for verification.

"Now you are in the front line," said the corps commander to the old priest in a low voice. "But I must warn you that we can stay here but a minute. . . . It is too dangerous." The prelate looked at the poilus all about them. Unable to kneel because of the lack of room, they were bowing their heads.

"These men are Bretons!" said the corps commander.

"Bretons, these? And in front of us, over there," the priest pointed to no man's land, "who are they?"

"We have a Bavarian division facing us," replied the corps commander.

The old ecclesiastic dropped his head on his breast: "Bavarians, Bretons," he murmured, "Christians both!" His eyes closed as if in pain. A tear ran down his cheek. Slowly he unfastened his muffler and then began to unbutton his black overcoat.

"Please," he said to the soldiers about him, "please, my children, let me pass."

The men stepped aside in amazement, their eyes wide open, their mouths agape as the little man walked over to the firing step and started to mount the ladder that stood against the parapet. Before he set foot on the lower rung, he flung off his overcoat.

"*C'est le Pape!*" cried the soldiers when they beheld the white papal soutane. "It's the Pope! *Le Pape!*"

"Yes, I am the Pope, my children. In the name of Christ, I call upon you, let there be peace. Peace!" His voice was pitched in a sharp tenor. "Peace!" Now he was on top of the parapet and tore the crucifix from his breast.

"*Friede, Friede,*" the old man called out in German. "Come to me! Come, have no fear! Christ calls you to love one another! Come! Here are your brothers, my children from Brittany! Come, let me embrace you!"

The French officers stood dumfounded. But the Pope went on speaking German as he began walking over toward the opposite trenches. His cassock caught on the barbed wire, but he tore himself free and he injured his hand in doing so. Drops of blood fell on his white cassock. He staggered as his feet sank into the mud.

But he held high the cross of the Redeemer.

The German soldiers were now running out of the trenches. "*Der Papst! Der heilige Vater!*" they were calling. The Bretons were climbing the parapets too, following the Pope into no man's land. All along the line men were lifting and pulling each other onto the parapets—into the open, into the free air of early morn.

"The war is over," cried the Pope in French and in German: "*La guerre est finie!*" "*Der Krieg ist beendigt!*" "I declare peace, peace on earth, for all, for everyone, in the name of Jesus Christ!"

Men were kneeling at his feet, Germans, Frenchmen, officers, soldiers. They sobbed and kissed the tatters of his torn cassock. The Pope stood in their midst, his face lifted to the sun.

"*Pater noster,*" intoned the Holy Father . . . and again: "*Pater Noster* . . . Hallowed be Thy Name . . . Thy Kingdom come. . . .*" A rumble of voices took up the prayer in French, in German, in Breton, in Flemish, in the Bavarian dialect, in Provençal. . . . "Thy will be done on earth as it is in heaven. . . ." Suddenly the Pope stopped speaking. His head had fallen on his breast. He clutched his throat with his bleeding hand and staggered backward. The tall priest, who had followed him into no man's land, caught him in his arms.

As they carried the unconscious Pope through the communication trench, machine guns were rattling and spitting death from both sides. A *Minenwerfer's* projectile exploded on the spot where the Pope had last stood, and buried the shoe that had fallen from his feet under a shower of brown mud.

For years I have tried to verify this story. I have looked into army records, both in France and in Germany, to find out which regiments were in the opposing lines on the Champagne front on the 27th of October, 1917. In both countries I have spoken with survivors of that month's struggle. They did not remember. In Rome I questioned men who might have heard about a short absence of Benedict XV from the Vatican. There was a dubious shaking of heads and a disturbed questioning look. Was it then merely a legend, a figment of the fertile imagination of Jean Richard Bloch, who first wrote of it in the monthly review *Europe*? Incidentally, he claimed to have heard the story from a priest. Was it a wish fulfillment of the Dutch pacifists of *Kerk en Vrede*, who seriously discussed the incident in their publication? Some Tolstoyan refugees from Soviet Russia in Geneva accepted the account of a visit of the Pope to the battlefields as Gospel truth. A famous Flemish priest, a papal prothonotary, said that he could well believe it to be true. He had seen the passionate prayer of the pontiff Benedict for peace. But I found no definite confirmation. I could not locate a single man who had been present on that day, anyone who had seen with his own eyes.

And yet, suppose it had been the Pope out there in no man's land!

4

I returned to Canada in February, 1919, on a troopship carrying six thousand men among whom were a few thousand minor casualties. We disembarked at Quebec, in a subzero temperature. Immediately upon stepping ashore, we were drawn up in parade formation on the landing quays because the Duke of Devonshire, who was Governor General of Canada that year, had made a special journey down from Ottawa to welcome us home. After letting us wait for two hours in a fierce cold, His Excellency and his aides finally drew up in a string of gleaming limousines. The officials were dressed in gorgeous blue uniforms with black fur collars. With this gala dress went astrakhan bonnets, polished riding boots and swords. We were called to "attention" and as the party of dignitaries slowly advanced toward us, their group presented such an unreal picture of Ruritanian movie splendor that the troops were struck speechless by the spectacle. The spell lasted but a moment. The next minute it exploded with a bang when someone in the rear ranks called out in a loud voice, "Look, boys, the soldiers are coming!" Then there was no controlling the laughter: our officers stormed up and down the lines fuming, raging, swearing, and finally pleading for silence in the ranks, all to no avail. The Duke, a florid-cheeked man with puffy eyelids, pretended not to notice the hilarity that his arrival had provoked, and quietly mounted a small wooden platform of the kind Caesar used in the schoolbook pictures to harangue the legions, and started to make a speech. The ranks grew silent at once. He began by telling us all about the war, the glory of it, the nobility of the services we had "so cheerfully rendered" and the reward that was now in store for us. That is about as far as he got. "Your King and country," he said feelingly, "thank you. And I say to you, from the bottom of my heart, henceforth nothing is going to be too good for you!" At this point in the Duke's address, a crippled veteran whose stump was freezing exclaimed in a stentorian voice: "B . . . . . !" The Duke looked abashed for a moment as a new roar of laughter greeted the veteran's exclamation, shrugged his shoulders, and stepped down from the platform. We were then each presented with a walking stick and a white envelope which contained a mimeographed letter of gratitude from the Empire, with King George's and Queen Mary's signatures rubber-stamped at the bottom.

In the course of our short stay in the city of Quebec, the troops grew restless and began rioting. They had previously sacked the French base camp of Etaples, bombing their way past the British guard detachments posted at the bridges leading across a railway culvert from the camp into the town of Etaples of which the taverns and brothels were "out of bounds" to all troops, which meant that they were reserved for officers only. The taverns were wrecked, the brothels invaded *en masse*, and the naked whores tossed high on the blankets found in the bedrooms. Thereafter they had raised a new rumpus in the camp of Rhyl, which was a concentration point for embarkation in Wales. In Rhyl as in Etaples many persons had been killed. It now looked as if Quebec in turn was about to have a taste of the *furor canadensis*. Dismissed from parade after the Duke's hasty departure, thousands of men marched into the city, tearing down street signs in the French language on the way. Streetcars were commandeered; local citizens found driving in sleighs were stopped, pushed out, and forced to surrender their conveyances to the veterans. The walking sticks, donated by the patriotic citizens of Quebec, were used to batter in their own shop windows.

Prohibition was in force at the time and bootleggers peddled their synthetic wares in the old city's dark alleys and at the back of the immigration buildings along the water front where we were quartered. The first day there were three dead from poison-liquor. Dozens of men found staggering around in pain or half blinded had been taken to hospitals or locked up in the local police stations. When word of these arrests reached the dock district, a mass invasion of the city was decided upon to release the imprisoned comrades. They were indeed set free, but not until all the policemen of Quebec had been bowled over and the interior of the police stations thoroughly wrecked. A second descent, on which smuggled hand grenades were to be carried along, was prevented by a hasty entrainment for the demobilization centers in the interior.

My city was Toronto. There I was given some money and a suit of civil clothes. I was informed by a medical board that I was entitled to a pension of five dollars a month and an unlimited period of vocational training with a view to my civil re-establishment. I could not at once make up my mind what to do. As a matter of fact, I cared very little as to what was going to happen. On the homeward journey, and during the first weeks in Canada, I walked around like a man in a daze, drifting aimlessly through the streets. The restaurants, clubs, hotels, and the buildings at the fair in Toronto were full of discharged soldiers. Most of them were from cities and villages further inland. Few of them appeared eager to go home. They clung together as if afraid to break up and face life individually. We had grown so accustomed to being treated as mere automatons, whose thinking was done for them by someone else, that we all seemed to be waiting for the next word of command.

At military headquarters, where one returned every day along with thousands of others as if drawn by some ineluctable urge, officials were assuring the men that they would be properly looked after. There was going to be a gratuity, a bonus; land was going to be made available for settlement; convalescent camps were to be established; even broken-up homes were going to be mended by marital relations boards. All that sounded fine, but I had a feeling, nevertheless, that I had been the victim of an enormous nonsense. And not only I, but thousands of young men who had been deprived of everything that makes for human dignity by their submission to an arbitrary fate; men who had thrown their lives into the scales on the supposition that they were helping to preserve something precious in this world. All they had done was to clear the road for the same bourgeois democracy which had unleashed the storm just stilled, to start all over again. While we were stepping on the troopship's gangplank in Liverpool, the statesmen had started in Paris and London to lay out the tinder for the next conflagration. On the other hand, I was happy to have escaped with only a minor bodily injury. I was going to forget the nightmare, burn my uniform as soon as I would be finally discharged, throw my badges and tokens into Lake Ontario, and efface every trace of my shame and humiliation. The thought of returning to my theological studies, interrupted three years earlier, flitted through my mind occasionally. The idea plunged me into a most somber mood. No doubt it would provide a tranquil existence after the tumult, but the war had implanted a restlessness in my spirit which filled me with an inexpressible contempt for the uneventful drudgery of everyday life. I did not crave adventure, but subconsciously, I suppose, I had expected something phenomenal to happen upon the return home, some great change, a new start. There had been a thunderstorm and the atmosphere had failed to clear. It was the same petty, monotonous, joyless, suffocating world of three years before, only now I was more intensely aware of it. Faces and voices of old acquaintances looked and sounded familiar, and yet we did not understand each other. Something had come between us. Friends wanted to hear stories of the battlefield, experiences, heroism, and you felt like vomiting when the subject was mentioned. There were still individuals who would get excited about the Kaiser, urging that he be hanged and the Crown Prince brought to trial. But their ravings only produced a snicker amongst the majority of the returned men. Why the Kaiser? Why Hindenburg? Those war lords had been victims of circumstances as much as the humblest privates in the ranks. The war had not been started because the Kaiser had decreed it. Germany had been maneuvered into a position where there was no other way out but war. The cause lay much deeper. There was something in the nature of the constituted order which produced wars as naturally as toadstools come to the surface after a spell of rain in the forest. Vaguely men had begun to feel that there was nothing gained in attributing the guilt of the war to certain individuals.

The Dean of Theology tapped me on the shoulder in a friendly way when I met him on the street one day. He said that everything was ready to pick up where I had let off. "Nothing has changed," he said. "It will be an honor to have you back with us."

An honor? An honor to take back an apostate? How could one like me—whose hands were stained with blood—ever approach the Lord's table . . . ?

The board of the Soldiers' Civil Re-establishment Commission summoned me one day and presented me with a list of trades and professions from which to choose. After some hesitation I decided to become a telegraph operator and was registered at one of the vocational schools. This gave me something to do. But it soon became evident that far too many had decided upon this vocation and that there would never be enough jobs in Canada to go around for the school's graduates. I therefore decided to look for my own job, and actually landed one in a department store, where I was set to wrap parcels for the suburban delivery with a supervisor behind my back. The employment agent, who hired me, said that I was fortunate in being privileged to work for so fine a Christian firm as the one whose services I was about to enter. He declared that opportunities for advancement from twelve dollars a week upward were practically unlimited. The president of the store himself, son of the founder, had also started at the bottom of the ladder and had worked himself up to a hundred thousand a year. That sounded encouraging, but I could not muster up sufficient enthusiasm to walk in the president's footsteps with the pile of parcels on the table before me. I lasted exactly one month. In that time I reached the conclusion that a man who can wrap a broom, a chamber pot, a clothes wringer and a picture frame into one neat, presentable parcel, is not only an artist, but a genius. I did not belong to that category and fell to daydreaming while the endless chain deposited an assortment of groceries, ladies' underwear, crockery, mousetraps, stovepipes and rolls of toilet paper on my table. One morning I sat down to watch the silly accumulation grow to mountainous heights and absentmindedly broke off pieces from a wedding cake which was to have gone out with the eleven o'clock delivery. That was the end of my career as an aspirant merchant prince. The supervisor suggested that I "get my time" and go still my hunger at the cafeteria around the corner.

It was a lovely day outside!

With the money earned I traveled up north to the gold mines and was engaged on a blasting gang in the Big Dome of Porcupine. I was assigned the job of crawling into an ore chute in which the loose rock had become jammed. I had to place a charge of dynamite, light the fuse, and retreat hastily out of that narrow tube in the roof to await the explosion down the drift or crosscut. It was a most perilous maneuver, involving infinitely more risk than cutting the barbed wire in no man's land. My partner, a Croatian peasant, piously made the sign of the cross each time his turn came to go up the chute where the tons of broken rock hung suspended above our heads.

The level on which we worked was flooded, and we waded and stumbled through the swirling water. But not quickly enough to suit the foreman, a Cousin-Jack, who called us a couple of damned, lazy bohunk sons-of-bitches every time he paid us a visit in that dank labyrinthine maze. That fellow had the vilest tongue of any man I ever knew. Still it was not the vituperation but the injustice of the mucker boss' criticism that made my Croatian partner boil over with anger. If I had not restrained him he would have attacked the foreman a dozen times with pick and shovel when he gave us one of his scorching lambastings. My companion swore he'd "get" the Cornishman, and one night, when we saw his carbide lamp come swinging down the drift just as we were about to blast an enormous chunk of rock that had fallen into the passageway, the Croat suggested that we withdraw, after placing our charge without giving the warning signal, and let the foreman walk straight into the explosion. The Cousin-Jack stopped to light his pipe and that saved his life, but he fired us both, for he realized full well what we had been up to. Our successors at the job, two Polish greenhorns, were killed the following night when the rock in the chute crashed down just as they were placing their charge. I never heard a man laugh so joyously and so long as my Croatian miner when he learned of the accident.

Then followed a spell as streetcar conductor, again in Toronto. This ended when an individual who rode back with me to the barns on the last run at midnight remarked, before jumping off, that he had forgotten to pay his fare. I had noticed his returned soldier's badge and had talked with him of the days in France and had deliberately neglected to present the fare box to a comrade. Next morning I learned that he had been an inspector.

I started wandering through the streets again, restless, haunted, took up peddling magazines from door to door, worked a few nights on a milk-delivery job in Buffalo, and as a locomotive fireman on the Grand Trunk, always getting fired or quitting in disgust.

Calling for my pension one day, I was informed that the Soldiers' Civil Re-establishment Commission had prepared a new list of vocational training opportunities. The choice ran all the way from accountant to piano tuner and sausage maker. The officials urged me to try again. I shut my eyes and let my finger run down the list. When I opened them I found that I had pointed out the word "journalism." My choice produced a little embarrassment amongst the members of the board, for there was no school of journalism in existence in Canada at the time. A solution was found, nevertheless: I was to go the rounds of the local newspaper offices and request the editors to let me sit around the local room long enough to learn the job. The government would pay me a salary until I could stand on my own feet.

The first man I approached was the editor of the *Telegram* of Toronto, a certain Mr. Robertson. "Sit down," he said. "Heroes are always welcome in this office!" When I had explained the object of my call, he remarked: "The first requirement of a newspaperman is that he have the 'seeing eye,' a keen sense of observation. Go out in the street, look around for an hour or two, and come back here and write me a story. I will let you know then whether or not you have any aptitude for the job." Before attempting to write a story, I strolled into the office of *The Toronto Daily Star*, another afternoon paper, and was ushered into the presence of the managing editor, a Mr. John R. Bohn. "What exactly could you do?" he asked kindly enough. "Well, perhaps you could use someone," I said, "to watch the foreign press. I have a working knowledge of several languages," and I named a whole string, adding one each time he raised his left eyebrow in feigned astonishment. "That's fine, that's extraordinary," said Mr. Bohn, "but what we really need here in this office is somebody who understands Bulgarian." That was the one European language, I think, I had failed to mention.

I had not dared to lift my eyes to *The Globe*, which was at that time Toronto's most distinguished newspaper, the "*Manchester Guardian* of Canada," it was called. *The Globe* had not been included in the list of offices to be visited because of the austerity of its pages and its superior reputation: only the foremost craftsmen were employed on its editorial staff. Yet, passing the *Globe* building a few minutes after Mr. Bohn's rejection of my services, I casually entered, climbed the stairs to the news department, and, seeing not a soul about, was on the point of leaving when a gentleman entered the hallway, and inquired what I wanted. Again I explained the situation. "In case you will permit me to sit around in this office," I repeated my little lesson.

"Not in case, not in case," corrected the gentleman. "In the event of." But he also told me to come back the same evening to start work. I had spoken to one of the foremost Canadian journalists, Thomas Stewart Lyon, Editor of *The Globe*.

The first weeks I accompanied regular staff men on their routine assignments: to the courts, to the morgue, to political meetings, to police headquarters, interviewing prominent visitors, and, on Sundays, to the churches to report sermons of the local divines. At the end of three months I was assigned to "hotels and rails." I had my own beat. But I was not bringing in many "stories," for whenever a visitor of prominence arrived—Sir Philip Gibbs, Chesterton, Margot Asquith, Colonel Repington, Marshal Fayolle or Cardinal Mercier— an experienced senior reporter came along.

This was the case when General Bramwell Booth of the Salvation Army came to conduct a special holiness service. The reporter whom I accompanied to the mass meeting was a man called Horace Bell, a quiet, dry-humored English journalist of the old school who took down the sermon in shorthand. We sat at the press table. As soon as the General concluded his exhortation, we quietly rose and tiptoed towards the exit. Another orator had taken up the conduct of the service and was inviting sinners to step forward to the mercy seat. Noticing us moving out, the speaker interrupted his talk and challenged us with the words: "Where are you two men going?"

"We are from the press, sir," replied Horace.

"That may be so," said the evangelist, "but you also need Christ!"

"That's true enough," came back my colleague, "but the first edition comes out at eleven. The city editor wants to see us!"

"God is more important than the city editor," warned the Salvationist.

"True again," admitted Horace, "but the city editor doesn't think so!"

About that time, I think it was in the fall of 1921, the government announced an agricultural settlement scheme for discharged soldiers in the far north: a farm, a house, and a loan of a thousand dollars for every able-bodied veteran who wished to take advantage of the offer. I was seriously considering the proposition when I dropped into the old Union Depot, which was part of my beat, and sat down among the crowds in the waiting room. Presently two priests entered and took a seat beside me. They spoke in French. This was nothing unusual in Canada, of course, but I soon noticed that theirs was not the quaint, almost medieval speech of Quebec. We entered into conversation, when one of the clerics asked me in broken English how much time they had for the Montreal train. I told them the hour, and I added: "But you are from France, *mon Père*, and not from Montreal!"

"*Ah, oui, oui, c'est bien vrai,*" came the answer. "But I have not seen France for twenty-two years."

"Twenty-two years? *Mon Dieu*, that is a long time. You will find the country greatly changed. The whole north is devastated, right down to St. Quentin and Arras."

"Yes, I know," sighed the priest, "but I learned all this but three months ago."

"Three months ago? You heard about the war but three months ago? How is that possible?" I asked. "The war has been over for three years!"

"We learned of the war three months ago, and, not that it had finished, but that it had just started," the priest said. "You see," he went on, "we are missionaries, this father and I." He pointed to his companion. "We have been stationed in the interior of Borneo for twenty-two years. Three months ago, a Dutch trading expedition came to our station in the uplands from points still farther inland. From its members we learned that a war had broken out in Europe in 1914. Belgium had been invaded, they told us, Louvain destroyed, Rheims bombarded, Paris threatened. What we heard was incredible, ghastly: the massacre of civilians at Namur, the deportation of thousands of Belgians to Germany. To say that we were thunderstruck would be using a mild expression. *Nous fûmes annihilés.* The thought of that war crushed us, each in his own way, for I am a Frenchman, but my colleague here," he pointed again to the other priest, "this father is a German. We were in a most painful situation. For long years we had worked together as brothers, with never a cross word or disagreement between us—and then suddenly that news.

"Yes," he continued, "it was more than painful. It was torture. We dared not look each other in the face. For even if I am a priest, I am a son of France, too. The thought of my country and my people being trod underfoot choked me. My companion was as badly disturbed as I was. Perhaps more so. We could not speak. We could not eat. We could not sleep. We walked around, each with his own thoughts, thoughts of murder at times. Horrible!" He was silent for awhile.

"Well," he looked up at the clock, "it is time. We must be going." They rose to leave.

"Permit me to help you down with your baggage," I offered, picking up a couple of their satchels.

As we walked down the stairs to the train, I asked: "And how long did that awful tension between you two last, Father?"

"For two weeks we could not bear the sight of each other. We avoided each other, each going his own way. It was dreadful. Yes, life was ebbing out of me, with sorrow and indignation. Then one day, as we met on the porch of our little church, both of us stretching out our hands to ring the bell for the Angelus, we burst into tears and wept on each other's shoulders."

When I returned to the office, the city editor asked me the usual question: "Anything?" I told him the story I had heard. His jaw dropped and he said, "Tell it to one of the rewrite men; he will fix it up for you!" But a moment later I was summoned to the chief's office. I told him of my meeting with the priests.

"Are you writing that story?" asked Stewart Lyon.

"No, sir. I am going to tell it to a rewrite man."

"Nothing of the sort," snapped the editor-in-chief. "You are going to write that story in your own words, just as you told it to me."

I did. But it took an hour and a half. I turned in my first article.

Stewart Lyon had stayed in the office till one in the morning to put the heading on it himself. Then he signed my name to it. The next day the reporters in Montreal caught the two priests as they were about to embark for Europe and the story was flashed over the length and breadth of the Dominion. Stewart Lyon told me to inform the Soldiers' Civil Re-establishment Commission that my course of training in journalism was over. I was a member of the staff of Canada's national newspaper.

A year later I was called from Toronto to Atlanta by the late Clark Howell, publisher of *The Atlanta Constitution*. For that journal I began writing a syndicated column that went out to twenty-nine important newspapers, including the New York *Evening World*. In 1924, *The Evening World*, at the suggestion of Arthur Krock, appointed me its roving correspondent in Europe, with headquarters in Paris.

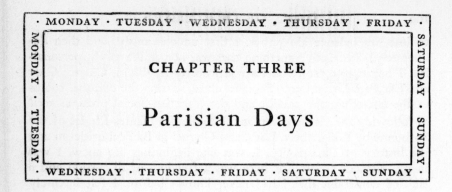

CHAPTER THREE

Parisian Days

IN A LITTLE MORE than a decade, of which two full years had been taken up with military service on the Continent, I found myself back in Europe, almost within hailing distance of the spot whence I had started in 1913. I could not deny that my life had been a strange odyssey. But the course it had taken was scarcely of my own choosing. I had been, as Luther once said, "like a blind horse that does not know where its master is leading." Detesting militarism and yet a nationalist, I had gone through the greatest war in history as a soldier in an alien army. After preparing for the ministry of the Gospel, I had landed in a profession to which I had never aspired and for which I felt little aptitude and not the least enthusiasm. I had never gone in search of adventure; no urge to see strange or unusual sights drove me on. I would have been perfectly content to live unobtrusively in a little corner with my own kind, not necessarily Dutchmen, but humble folk without any other ambition but to be at peace with each other. And now I was embarked on a period of wandering "to and fro in the earth" that would go on uninterruptedly for fifteen years. What would it bring me? Where was I heading? It was all very delightful to be the correspondent of a great American newspaper in Europe, but I also had my own life to live, independent of circumstances, time, birth, situation and all the other accidents of terrestrial existence. I felt an irrepressible, although still unavowed avidity to devote myself to some cause or an ideal. This is perhaps a bad quality in a newspaperman who is supposed to be detachment personified. At any rate, in that new world of Paris which I now entered, I was so violently torn between a loyalty to my own generation on the one hand, and the requirements of the position I filled on the other, that, in order not

99

to lose my balance altogether, I first unconsciously, and then deliberately, developed something that was not unlike a split personality. I began to attend courses and lectures by Blum, Charles Gide and Elie Faure, running to Socialist clubs, visiting the editorial rooms of the left-wing, the pacifist and the Christian-Social press, as well as following the classes given at the École des Hautes Études of the Sorbonne by Guignebert, Lods, and Goguel in Biblical criticism and the history of Christianity. It was like beginning life anew. I was in my element at last, for here was a freedom of discussion and a lack of constraint that I had never known before. I felt intensely for and with the youth of France whose organizations I began to frequent. Their aspirations were my own. Their ideals were those for which I myself had been groping. Their passion for discussion, their burning sense of justice, their universal interest captivated me and swept me along.

Like the young men and women whom I came to meet in the forward-looking movements, I was suspicious of the shibboleths of the past and of the prejudices of our elders, determined above all to breathe, to live and love and not to become, or help to prepare, fertilizer for a new crop of death on the so-called fields of honor. We had our eyes towards the sun, and were all catching signals of hope from the future; we even thought that we had seen the first outline of our messiah over there in the east on the Slavic horizon. We felt as if something precious lay within our grasp, and as if the miracle might be around the next bend in the road. We wanted to be hewers of wood and carriers of stone. With our faith and hands we desired to build a new house for humanity.

The exigencies of my job drove me in an entirely different direction, towards that milieu of tired intellectuals whose creativeness had narrowed down to a mere desire to entertain and please; men and women who considered poetry and love and devotion and even human pain as chiefly intended to feed syllogisms and wisecracks. They were the artists who had been born with silver spoons in their mouths; people who had created nothing, and yet set the tone in cosmopolitan circles of art and literature; authors of *bon ton* and of *bonne compagnie* who chose their words well, and oiled them well, so that they slipped easily into one ear and out the other without touching anything in passing; critics whose chief occupation was to manipulate a polishing brush; the *petits précieux* of Molière, eccentrically dressed, impeccably mannered, who wrote moralizations for the safe and sound papers owned by the munitions trusts and the steel kings; poets who pontificated, surrealized, supra-inspired and dished up their "tenderly admirable reticences" whenever they smelled Coty at ten thousand francs an ounce; women who hired broken down grandees to go slumming in Montmartre, to see a pimp and his girl fornicate in a coffin, or a Negro gigolo commit sodomy on a white woman;—what color scheme, *madame! quel rhythme, monsieur!*; journalists who prided themselves on their objectivity, their passionless neutrality, men who never lost their composure, who were always calm, never nettled, always astute, who never grew indignant or angry, and who never shed a tear or uttered a curse; financiers who exploited rubber plantations in Senegal, sugar fields in Cochin China, banana groves in Guinea, gold mines in the Cameroun and "blue" movies in Marseilles and Buenos Aires. All these distinguished people were always in search of new thrills, new frills, new emotions, new "kicks" in art and love and literature. Of authentic emotions, of real anguish and genuine joy of life, they shied away as from an electric current. They wanted synthetic art, mistook publicity for fame and imagined they could buy their peace of mind as one buys a pair of slippers at a bazaar. They distributed favors with lavish facility. Tea with the foreign minister of Mirabolia, an invitation to the boudoir of a celebrated danseuse, a tip for tomorrow's market, a voyage to Saïgon on a luxury steamer, a decoration for your friend from America. Tell him it's in the bag, *mon cher! Tout s'arrange!* Nothing was impossible. Theirs was the kingdom and the power and the glory!

One of my first assignments was to investigate the mysteries of the Bois de Boulogne, the delights of the bars of Montmartre, the joys of the night clubs on the hill, where tens of thousands of Americans were squandering millions of francs on doubtful pleasures. We were in the midst of that annual tourist migration which reached its height in the summer of 1929, and thereafter never returned. Like a cloud of mosquitoes they descended on Paris, male and female, round and lean, bespectacled men, short-skirted women, black and white, rich and poor. Everybody was in the swim. The franc was quoted at forty-five to the dollar and the stock market at home was skyrocketing. Every terrace café had its contingent of American sightseers, restless and ill at ease, sitting down and jumping up, unaccustomed to leisure in the afternoon, eating Thanksgiving dinners for luncheon, drinking liqueurs like water, and wondering after an hour what made the pavements behave like a trick mirror. The Folies Bergères were sold out weeks in advance, the dancing *mondaines* blotto at six in the evening. America wanted to dance? *Eh bien*, dance it should! Gaumont Palace, once a gigantic motion-picture house built over the cemetery of Montmartre, was turned into a ballroom. Every cubit space on the old hill where Saint Denis was beheaded became a night club, a hotsy-totsy, a gambling joint or a peep show. The Tabarin, where the specialty had been the cancan since the days of Napoleon the Little, had a hundred imitators in a month: here the stomach dance, there the shimmy, here the hips to the fore, there the navel. The Moulin Rouge, with six bars, two on every floor, revived the saturnalia of Caligula; lassies wearing the Salvation Army bonnet and a pair of silk stockings sold the cigarets; Cleopatra, in the costume of Saint Godiva, rode around on the shoulders of an ebony-black Nubian; Messalina, the nude empress, her long hair hanging loose, crowned with the golden oak leaves, stood in the imperial chariot drawn by sixty slave boys who were painted and powdered to resemble girls, and who were whipped by swarthy-hued slaves with excruciating leather straplets. In the loges and balconies *les Américains* drank champagne, threw *serpentins*, and encouraged the most audacious in the floor show to greater audacity. A procession of young girls, wriggling their haunches impatiently, carried silken banners with inscriptions that declared that they were tired of being virgins; an army of Dianas ready for the hunt, the kohl on their lashes their only garment, swarmed in and out of the crowd, rubbing shoulders, hips and stomachs. Outside the hall broken-down grand dukes with the star of St. Michael on a chauffeur's blouse, czarist officers, Cossack generals with waxed mustaches, the debris of the first deluge, waited to take the Americans back to their hotels. At dawn the charwoman swept up the *serpentins* and busted balloons, for there would be other Americans on the morrow. Six boat trains full due at the Gare St. Lazare at noon! *Vive l'Amérique! Vive l'amour! Vive le dollar!* The Golden Calf with the head of George Washington!

About this time there was a strike in Hainaut. Fifty thousand men and women who worked in the coal mines of Belgium had refused to go on crawling on their bellies through the perilously narrow galleries, dragging out the baskets of "black diamonds" for a dollar a day. They were in revolt. They burned the pit heads. They carried sticks of dynamite in their skirts and trousers. They threatened to march on Brussels. They wanted masks to protect them against the dust which made them spit up their lungs; rails around the shafts into which their comrades had plunged to death; the utilization of an explosive that would not go off prematurely and tear their bodies to shreds of meat and rags; a hot room on the surface in which to dry their clothes after a day or a night in subterranean downpour; baths to clean up in before they went home, so that their children might recognize them.

"There are thousands amongst them who speak only Flemish," said Auguste Habaru, the editor of *Monde* to me. "Why don't you go out there? See what they want, question them, encourage them, fight for them and tell us about it in an article or two. We have no money to send a reporter and you speak their language. Your compatriot Vincent van Gogh once fought for them in his awkward, stumbling way. He was a missionary there, took sick at the misery he saw. Things haven't improved since Vincent's days. Why don't you go?"

Aye, there I wanted to go. There was my place. But Jimmy Walker was on the way to Europe, and the American Legion convention was about to open in Paris, and Gloria Swanson might have something to say about the Marquis de la Falaise and their reportedly ruined romance. I had been caught wandering on my own hook around the ghettos of Lodz and Warsaw when Lindbergh arrived. There had been the devil to pay. I had not been on hand to ask Foreign Minister Briand, as instructed by cable, if an eventual success by Lindbergh would not arouse the envy and anger of the French people, since disaster had just befallen two French flyers who had failed to cross the ocean. No, I could not go to Hainaut. I had to remain in Paris.

A strike? What was *The Evening World* going to do with reports about a strike in Belgium? There was labor trouble in the mining districts of Kentucky and Pennsylvania, and they were not even reported, except when there was violence. Furthermore, I had just been instructed by John H. Tennant, the managing editor of *The Evening World*, to send "a daily picture of some phase of Parisian life." This meant that I was expected to paint a picture of Paris which conformed to the popular American notion of French mores: gay abandon and a riotous morality. *Midinettes* could never be anything but sunny creatures who filled the boulevards with laughter and song. To have pointed out the conditions under which the tens of thousands of women live who toil in the fashion sweat-shops where American society buys its finery would have landed the articles in the managing editor's wastepaper basket. To have shown that the average French family follows an almost puritan code of morals and is far more exclusive and inaccessible than a corresponding middle-class family in England, Germany or America, or that the Parisian puts up his shutters at seven and retires earlier than New England villagers, would have stamped you as an ignoramus or a fool. That was not the "gay Paree" the American newspaper reader had been led to imagine. Hollywood and the popular magazines had given him an entirely different idea, and that idea was not to be disturbed: the apache, long since vanished from the stage, had to be resuscitated; Orleanist and Bonapartist pretenders to the throne, whose names are scarcely known in Paris, assumed grotesque importance across the ocean through their interviews and statements; the students of the Sorbonne were always shown in the act of rioting, and American visitors endlessly astonishing the white-aproned waiters in the terrace cafés with the size of their tips. Monte Carlo, the beaches of the Côte d'Azur, and the salons of the Faubourg St. Germain, where an international leisure class disported itself, were the topics in which, I was more than once reminded, American newspaper readers interested themselves.

The doings of every fugitive king and politician, from Alfonso to Kerenski, whom the French press had the good taste to hide behind a merciful veil of silence, assumed grave importance to us who had to keep tagging at their heels. Kerenski published a regularly irregular weekly paper on the Rue Vineuse in Passy. You reached the editorial sanctum on the fifth floor by hoisting yourself up by a greasy rope which served as banister to a dilapidated stairway. The same building housed the headquarters of several Russian clubs and *émigré* organizations. On every floor you could hear another fine plan for the redemption of Holy Mother Russia. On the first landing, a middle-aged staff of gentlemen in shiny frock coats were eternally drafting and redrafting a liberal constitution which was to be submitted to a national assembly the moment Stalin should have vacated the Kremlin. On the floor above sat the exiled synod of the Orthodox Church. The aging, heavily whiskered and heavily robed popes and archimandrites experienced some difficulty in scaling the almost perpendicular stairs, but once arrived, they sat all day around the samovar, gulping down one glass of tea after another, in a room where the only adornment was a life-sized photograph of Nicholas Romanov and some pictures of several late lamented fathers in God with unpronounceable names. I would have dropped in more frequently, for I had a standing invitation to come back, and liked to listen to the arguments about the necessity of the Russian people to suffer and suffer and suffer à la Dostoevski, had it not been that I always developed a headache in the synodal chambers where the floor was never swept, no cuspidor ever provided, and never a window opened.

The various ideologies professed on different floors (on the third were the Ukrainian Fascists, who moved to Berlin when Hitler attained power) had necessitated the installation of iron-barred doors at the entrance to every suite of offices. Before entering, you had to submit to a close scrutiny by a watchman who eyed you through one of those spy holes with which the doors in lodge rooms of Elks and Moose are generally equipped. Curiously enough, if you wanted to learn something about the "association of loyal Cossack officers" you had to ask Muliekov. If you were curious about Kerenski, only the liberals could answer your queries. It was they who informed me that, of an issue of ten thousand copies of Kerenski's paper, *Oppressed Russia*, nine thousand nine hundred and ninety-five copies were purchased by the Soviet embassy to be burned in the furnace—five copies having been left for the files. In front of the building stood a French policeman who searched all those entering for arms. The cop was posted there after the regrettable incident of the demented Russian general who complained that he heard the troika bells on the snowy steppes of Russia in his head. This gentleman had decided to shoot up the whole place. After killing and wounding several persons, he had grown so furious at the sight of a wall map of the USSR in one of the rooms that he had taken his stand right in front of the chart, so that in blowing out his brains he had covered the entire Muscovite plain with blood.

I do not remember how many cables I received asking what Carol and Madame Lupescu were doing in their retreat at Neuilly-sur-Seine—the love-nest motif being good at any time in the American press, or what the bleary-eyed Prince of Wales was up to on his week ends in Cannes or Paris-Plage. We all helped to fabricate the ·
myth of the innocent Prince Charming because it was the expected thing to do, and therefore must be held at least partly responsible for the universal astonishment when later he made a vaudeville show

of the throne of England. I trailed the fatuous Amanullah all over Europe; camped on the doorstep of Nancy Miller's château after she had married a Hindu raja, who needed watching, according to the Scotland Yard detective who had been detailed to join us in those vigils solitary and monotonous in St. Germain-en-Laye; I pumped La Belle Otéro on her liaison with Peter of Serbia; Gaby Deslys on hers with Manuel of Portugal; bought perfume, at the expense of the Messrs. Pulitzer, from the Shah of Persia who preferred a shopkeeper's existence on the Rue Vivienne to the Peacock Throne in Teheran; stood my ground in a scrap with the Aga Khan's valet when that potentate married a country maiden; but was knocked down by a secret-service man—a Dutchman at that—who trailed in the wake of Wilhelm Hohenzollern on a rural lane near Doorn.

"The desk" in New York seemingly labored under the illusion that a reporter merely had to whisper the paper's name to become at once the recipient of Foch's or King Albert's confidences on the subject of postwar Germany's behavior, or for Gabriele d'Annunzio to dash off a crisp résumé of his latest *billets d'amour* to Madame Ida Rubinstein. You received a cablegram telling you "to find out from Zita" when she expected to put Otto on the Austrian throne, or to ask "Kemal Pasha personally" why he had divorced his wife.

Mr. Tennant's idiosyncrasies no doubt reached their height the day he learned that, upon the installation of a telephone system in the Vatican City, the Catholics of America had presented the Pope with a golden apparatus. "Go Rome," he cabled me. "Ask Pope to call this office on golden telephone."

At Harry's Bar on the Rue Daunou, over a glass of *pernod*, I pictured myself overcoming the endless obstacles of etiquette at the Vatican (which was more elaborate and strict than that in vogue at the Spanish court), and finally, dressed in evening clothes, placing my request, drawn up by a notary, before Monsignor Pizzardo, the Secretary of Extraordinary Ecclesiastical Affairs, and receiving the mocking stare of that lordly diplomat of the Church.

So I cabled back: "Please ask Coolidge" (who was President at the time) "to come to your office to make the call." I imagined that that would hold them in New York. Undaunted Jack Tennant replied: "Go Rome just the same and ask Pope about Americanization of the Vatican." As luck would have it, the Pope did say in the course of an audience, at which the interviewer must be silent, that an American firm had just fitted the Vatican's library with a new device to regulate the atmosphere. Achille Ratti could therefore be cited in a headline as "the American Pope."

After this, reverting from the fountain of truth to the source of joy, came the suggestion to make inquiries of Josephine Baker, the dusky banana-skirt dancer from Harlem who made good in Montmartre, if her relations with a certain Italian count were "a regular marriage or the other thing." Josephine told me, and rightly so, that it was none of my ding-dang-dong business and called over the bouncer, one of her fellow countrymen, a bozo of Jack Johnsonian frame, to pitch me out of her cabaret. I withdrew before any damage was done, except that I left the bill unpaid.

To give credit where credit is due, I must admit that the Russian nobility was the least snobbish. They were a joy forever. They had an uncanny foreknowledge of what was wanted of them, and never failed us on a blue Monday when spot news was scarce. You only had to telephone the adjutant of Cyril Romanov, "Czar before God and the conscience of humanity," to learn that a revolt in the Red Army had just been bloodily suppressed, or that Stalin and Trotsky had been belaboring each other again with empty vodka bottles at the windup of the last bacchanalian orgy in the Kremlin. I do not know what we would have done without General Eugene de Miller or his aides-de-camp—Prince Galitzine and General Koutiepov. They never failed to have a communiqué on tap, foreshadowing momentous events, such as "an immediate march" of the Cossack officers of Paris to liberate Holy Mother Russia, or setting forth details of the latest famine in the Soviet Union.

De Miller, who vanished mysteriously in 1937, like Koutiepov five years before him, always bragged about his underground connections with circles close to Stalin, and actually had half the foreign correspondents, the Germans especially, believing him. That legend was finally disturbed, a little rudely, by *Pravda*'s correspondent in Paris. He caused a letter to be addressed to the General from Moscow, wherein such a harrowing picture was drawn of conditions in the Soviet capital that the latter published it forthwith under an eight-column heading in *Resurrection*, the paper of the Russian monarchists in Paris, as emanating from "the usual reliable source close to the bloody oppressor." I was in the plot because I wanted to test De Miller's reliability, and had given the key of that letter to several left-wing papers in Paris. They sprang the hoax one morning by publishing the first two words of its every paragraph, thus making the following sentence: "General, you are a damn liar, this letter was written to show that you have no reliable information on what is going on in the Workers' Fatherland." One of the princes of the blood of Rurik thereupon challenged *Pravda*'s man and myself to settle the affair on the field of honor, an invitation which was prudently declined.

Whereas the "Americanization" of different phases of European life was a subject that never seemed to exhaust the curiosity of my managing editor, the glorification of man-made values, which is characteristic of contemporary America, filled the more sensitive amongst the French with an instinctive horror. They felt that the process of industrialization detracted from human dignity because it led to a disdain for those phases of human activity which cannot be made serviceable in the production of material things. To them, America was the symbol of capitalist production, its highest apex, and they looked upon it as a destructive, dehumanizing factor. Their attacks and warnings against the Americanization of life in France were weakened, it is true, by reason of the fact that they turned themselves against industrialization at a time when there was still a shortage of commodities, and the speeding up of productivity appeared the most important task of science. But unlike my managing editor, who seemed to imagine that all Europe was speechlessly marveling at the boundless prosperity of America, and envying us, the Americanization process was regarded in Paris as the starting point of a long and cruel crisis in human affairs.

Although that crisis was deemed inevitable as a transitory stage towards human emancipation, its approach and imminence filled men with apprehension and dread. They saw clearly that the struggle ahead would inevitably be accompanied by a contemptuous dismissal of every independent activity of the spirit as backwardness or egotistical intrigue and, on the other hand, by a psychological penetration of all classes in society with the spirit of competition, a hunger for profits, and a mentality of violence. This, they felt, would interrupt for generations humanity's striving for a world order based on a more brotherly basis. For they knew that capitalist industrialization, instead of bringing well-being, not only destroyed economic stability and undermined all exterior security of life, but also robbed millions of human beings of all inner support. It deprived them of the traditional values which could have helped them find their way in the confusion and chaos of a transitional period in history. The emphasis placed on material-technical relationships in America, and more and more also in France, was depriving man of much, perhaps of everything, that a few years earlier gave direction to life and filled it with content. All spiritual values seemed destined to be cast overboard or destroyed. Nothing was to be left but a transparent set of occupations which covered up the emptiness of life. Only a thin veneer remained of the beneficent cloak of humanist tradition which, in former days, enveloped man with its warmth.

Certain representatives in Paris of the German press, then already tainted with the "live dangerously" Fascist philosophy, like Friedrich Sieburg and Ernst Curtius, chided the Parisian intellectuals on their aversion to face realities, attributing French wariness to a desire for tranquillity and mental serenity. There was more envy than sincerity in these arguments. If there was not a people freer, happier and stronger in Europe than the French, they owed this to a circumstance which some may call a trifle, but which is nonetheless tenacious, a spirit of discussion. The French newspapers sincerely sought to keep their readers informed of the entire movement of ideas. They accorded space to a discussion of the actual problems of life, to questions of philosophy and esthetics. They ventured to draw conclusions from world events without always tacking on a label of interior politics. Their newspapers did not respond to the inertia of the reader with their own inertia. Their writers loved the audacious word. They were never neutral. With them impartiality did not mean the same thing as indifference. From time to time they were set on fire and they were never afraid of controversy. This love of the French for spiritual speculation, the enormous variety of reading matter, and the freedom of judgment and criticism were largely responsible for that cultural elite which placed France foremost in the world of ideas.

But the real worth-while things in French life, that passionate search for truth in the postwar generation, the currents and cross-currents in the intellectual sphere, the movements which occurred away from the surface, were not supposed to interest the American newspaper reader, who, in the words of Herbert Bayard Swope, then director of the *World* papers' editorial policy, is to be fed "in spoonfuls and damned small ones at that." What the sinister Raymond Poincaré said, as he unveiled monuments to the war dead every Sunday, was deemed important. The views of a Romain

Rolland, who, in an interview back in 1926, predicted with astonishing precision the tragic impasse from which the statesmen at the present moment vainly seek to extricate Europe, were rejected by the foreign editor of *The Chicago Tribune* with the remark: "Who is this fellow Rolland anyway?" No, when Mistinguette renewed the insurance on her precious legs, that was news! When an actress returned from Hollywood, then we were required to be on hand to collect the pearls of wisdom Madame might care to scatter concerning American movies, politics, economics, religion and literature. Usually Madame had been terribly impressed with the Manhattan skyline, with the number of speakeasies off Broadway, or with the sincerity of Adolphe Menjou. You could be certain that when the papers drifted back from America, you would see some blazing headline informing the American public that France, through the eyes of this or that mademoiselle, was seeing America as a great people. Lord Northcliffe's advice that a good article should contain either or all of three subjects—sex, the flag and murder—was in the main our guiding line.

Religion was a subject most scrupulously to be avoided, as the average American editor dreads nothing more than the business manager who informs him that some local pastor, priest or rabbi has taken objection to a certain report. Thus, an event like the Abbé Turmel's phenomenal battle with the Inquisition, which every Frenchman—Left, Right, Catholic or atheist—followed with fervid interest, or the resignation from the Curia of a French cardinal, something without precedence in the history of the Church, was passed over in absolute silence in America. A description of the harrowing condition of the Jews in Poland and Lithuania, which I had spent two months in investigating, was barred from publication in the New York *Evening World*, on the advice of the late Louis Marshall. It was thought that the solution of the problem, a Zionist one, envisaged by every intelligent Jew in Poland, did not harmonize with the policy of the American Joint Distribution Committee, which preferred to hide from the world, under a blanket of charity, the hopeless plight of its coreligionists in eastern Europe. It was even more difficult to narrate anything concerning the pioneer work in Palestine in a paper owned and operated by assimilated American Jews. Yet, this enterprise exercised a strong appeal in non-Jewish and especially liberal Protestant milieus. It disturbed the equanimity of the "Jews who are Americans," since they do not like to be reminded of the fact that there is such a thing as a Jewish people and a Jewish land. The same Mr. Marshall, in a ten-page brief, advised the editors of *The Evening World*, who had asked him for an opinion, against publishing the result of my first visit to the Holy Land. He claimed that his private sources of information did not confirm what I had ventured to say about the Palestinian orange industry. Mr. Marshall did not think that the industry would ever grow to a point where the Holy Land could export citrus fruit.

Today, Palestine is the second largest orange-exporting country in the world.

From time to time, I ventured to send a news letter or a longer article for the Sunday editions on a particular phase of the research carried on at the Sorbonne's theological school by some of the most eminent masters of the day; for instance, when Daniel Massé concluded that Jesus and Barabbas, the murderer released by Pontius Pilate in the Gospel narrative, were one and the same person, or when Arthur Drews came from Germany to expound his theory of the sun myth. I would have perished if the blasts that a multitude of divines, hot-gospelers and exhorters directed at my person, or at the newspapers which published the items, could have reached me. That I was an imp of the Devil and Antichrist, a faith-destroying Bolshevik, or the paid servant of a dechristianizing Judaism, for merely reporting something of the conclusions reached by scholars who had spent a lifetime in laying bare the sources of our faith, goes without saying. I used to repair the damage as best as I could by forthwith interviewing some depository of the simple verities and having him say that the old-time religion, which had been good enough for Paul and Silas, was good enough for me and him. That generally fixed up things.

"To what does Pola Negri attribute her lack of success in the American movies?" came the urgent cable from one Pacific coast newspaper, with an indication where the lady could be found. I could not locate her, not even with the aid of the Prefecture of Police, and therefore, when the demand from America grew more and more insistent, I cabled back in desperation: "Probably to the fact that a black cat ran across the gangplank when she first set foot on American soil."

"Worth five thousand words," came the reply. In a week I was inundated with cablegrams from newspapers and magazines from all over the country for more, and, in order to meet the demand, I had to go to the Quai St. Michel to procure a dozen volumes on occultist nonsense and superstitious practices. The subject was inexhaustible. I even attended a Black Mass in a mansard on the Rue Vavin where an individual in sacerdotal vestments celebrated the Eucharist on the naked abdomen of a woman who lay stretched out in all her glory on the altar beneath a reversed crucifix. I was put out of the joint when my turn came to spit on the cross, but not before I had watched the celebrant cover it with obscene gestures in honor of Satan. Another nonconformist, who had been escorted to the door by the ushers in none too angelic a fashion, explained over a glass of beer at the Rotonde that the sect of which we had just beheld the supreme rite was really a heretical offshoot of a mother church in the Etoile quarter. The celebrant we had seen, he said, was a bastard priest of a false religion; he volunteered to lead me to the fountain of truth uptown. But I had seen enough. Moreover I had to interview Maurice Chevalier, who was coming by a late boat train. *"Et les grattes-ciel, Monsieur Chevalier, et le cinéma-parlant, que pensez vous du nouveau modèle Ford, Maître?"*

Neither *"Maître"* Maurice nor Aimée Semple MacPherson nor the famous Jimmy Walker had anything to say. Yet we had to make these persons live up to their reputations. It was therefore agreed to have Aimée say that the colored balloons floating in the smoke and fume-laden atmosphere of Montmartre's dives of iniquity reminded her of a sinner's inflated existence, gay and impressive on the outside, hollow within. One pinprick by the dear Lord, and pfuit!— there was a tattered rubber rag. Tapped for wisecracks, the irrepressible Mayor of Gotham failed to produce. He simply could not think of anything worth cabling. He was worried, he explained, by a phantom from Washington which pursued him wherever he went, but this was not for publication. We compromised by having him say that although he did not know the French language, he understood the Parisians perfectly, inasmuch as he had a good ear for music. This was deemed a neat compliment when the local press learned of it.

Although *The World*'s bureau was located in the business quarter near the Opéra, we soon learned to leave the "grand" boulevards to the tourists, and spent most of our time across the river on the Montparnasse, and in the Latin Quarter. Here we rented an apartment on the Rue St. André-des-Arts, in a house of dilapidated exterior of which the concierge boasted that it had once housed

Danton and his family. The district frightened the opulent foreigners who want the picturesque with all modern comforts. We were left alone with our neighbors who were what the Parisians call *petits gens*: artisans, functionaries, medical students, struggling painters, political refugees and the like. After a week or so of suspicious glances at the newcomers, our neighbors began to nod a greeting, then passed on to commenting on the weather, and before a month was over were discussing politics with us, the best sign that we had been accepted.

Near our house were the Luxembourg Gardens, where the children sailed their ships on the pond, and students could be heard on summer evenings reciting poetry to their girl friends while waiting for the shadows to deepen. Although the fashion has passed when every Frenchman had his permanent seat in a café, you discovered that many of the coffeehouses in the neighborhood still catered to a special clientele. Upstairs in the Closerie des Lilas, where Svengali and Trilby are supposed to have met, was the gathering place of the impressionist painters, one of whom, the regretted Leopold Gottlieb, became a dear friend. Across the street was the headquarters of the surrealists. Here pontificated André Breton amidst a coterie of disciples from all over the world. The gentle Raymond Duncan, Isadora's gifted brother, was a habitué there, before he let his hair grow long and donned classic Grecian robes with sandals for ordinary street wear. I have never understood how the surrealists, who are mostly concerned with dreams and the subconscious, justify their claim to be the trail blazers of world revolution, but I did admire the fire with which they arranged demonstrations in favor of the imprisoned Gandhi, and plastered the hoardings of Paris with a denunciation of colonial rule, British and French alike. Henri Béraud was a habitué of Montparnasse at the time. He later went over to Fascism and published a volume in which he advocated an alliance of all the nations on earth against Britain. He thought it would do the English good to be reduced to slavery for about a thousand years and to be distributed over the length and breadth of Europe as valets and servants to more deserving gentlemen. The British ambassador made a *démarche* with the Quai d'Orsay to have Béraud's book withdrawn from circulation, but nothing was done about it.

In the Rotonde Café I sat in with Don Miguel de Unamuno, the great Spanish mystic, who had been exiled by Primo de Rivera to one of the Canary Islands whence a couple of enterprising French journalists had rescued him in a motor launch. He was a restless spirit and the center of Spanish republicanism. No other group in the cafés looked so much like a band of conspirators. For one thing, they always talked in whispers, even when the conversation dealt with purely literary subjects.

Around the corner, on the Rue Vavin opposite Les Vikings, the hangout of Scandinavian artists, was a small café where the militant atheists met twelve years ago. This group had no affiliation with the organization of the militant godless, which has its seat in the Soviet Union. All members had come to their views by "independent research." As a matter of fact, not Lenin, but Mussolini, was considered somewhat of a hero in this milieu. Not the Mussolini of the Lateran Pact, but the earlier, fiery anticlerical. A picture of the young Benito in the act of insulting a priest on a street in Bologna was prominently displayed on one of the walls of this tavern. The establishment has gone bankrupt since.

This was before the Grande Chaumière, which stands at the intersection of the Boulevards Montparnasse and Raspail, had been turned into a vulgar bar. In its poorly lighted taproom you could see many of the painters and sculptors of the Latin Quarter between five and six in the afternoon. Here they met and discussed terms with prospective models, both male and female. It was nothing unusual to see one of the demoiselles suddenly rise from the table and expose her upper body to the critical gaze of a master of the brush. It was done so naturally and frankly that no one was shocked. Before the old Chaumière had disappeared, it acquired an unsavory reputation, and was frequented by prostitutes and *souteneurs*, who played the roles of artists and models to whet the appetite of middle-aged gentlemen in search of adventure.

The Rotonde, now a renovated palace with glittering mirrors, was the gathering place of a group of independent painters; men and women who disdained to have their works hung in the official salons. They were a poverty-stricken lot who recruited their models from amongst the ladies of the evening. The services of the girls were paid for with a meal and a night's lodging in the artist's garret studio. The elders in this group later graduated into some form of respectability, and twice a year exhibited in a large wooden hut which they erected on the parkway of the Boulevard Raspail.

When this happened, the younger artists broke away and formed an association of their own known as "The Real Independents."

Friends from Holland and America dropped in. I saw Barthélemy de Ligt, back after more than ten years. Tall and distinguished as ever, his hair turned a little white at the temples, but the same flame of goodness in his blue eyes, he had come a long way since those early days when I had heard him speak as a young Protestant pastor in the People's Hall of Gorcum. On his shoulders had fallen the mantle of the great libertarian thinkers of the last century, and he had to his credit, amongst numerous philosophical books, that immense work on *La Paix créatrice*, whereby his name will live in history, and wherein is traced the evolution of the conception of the human ideal amongst the heretical trail blazers, from Isaiah to Gandhi. There are few men in this world to equal Barthélemy de Ligt in erudition and wisdom, but he had sacrificed every prospect of success or prominence by turning his back on all the official schools. He had cast his lot with the most persecuted and the most maligned people on earth: the anarchists. A living symbol of non-violence, incapable of the least ungenerous thought towards any creature, a man with a heart so great that it encompassed all humanity, De Ligt was nevertheless a person as closely watched by all the political police departments in Europe, including the G.P.U. of Russia, as if he had been the chief of a band of white slavers or a fiend in human guise. Why? Simply because he was a man with an idea: every chief of state, from the Calvinist Dr. Colijn in Holland to the Communist Joseph Stalin, had recognized in him the man of absolute peace, always the most dangerous adversary of the established order. What sessions we had together! Many times we walked around all night and were surprised by the dawn at the end of a boulevard. Sometimes our conversation drifted to Russia and the Bolshevik experiment. De Ligt felt that it had failed completely. Where there is domination, he would say, there can be no room for comradeship. "There new forms of oppression and exploitation inevitably make their appearance. There grows the tyrant, who is rooted in the slave. Wherever priests or leaders or dictators speak *pro vobis omnibus*, where ministers, bureaucrats, officers decide for you without consulting you, there Socialism cannot live—there its germ dies. Where group interests have precedence over the general interest, where humaneness and humanity are neglected, where only one's own nation counts and the interests of all others are ruthlessly subordinated, there grows no International that is going to liberate the earth of race wars, the class struggle and wars between states. Man's goal is revealed by the means he employs. Whatever the goal may be, the character of the means to reach it inexorably determines the nature of the goal. The political instruments of Bolshevism are those of Machiavelli and Loyola."

With Dean "Dick" Sheppard of St. Martin-in-the-Fields and Lord Ponsonby, De Ligt was one of the moving spirits in the Antimilitarist Bureau, the War Resisters' International, and the Peace Pledge Union, which together number two hundred thousand members in England alone, and to which Aldous Huxley also adheres. Huxley's latest book, *Ends and Means*, bears the unmistakable imprint of the close collaboration on which he and De Ligt have embarked.

It was curious to see De Ligt, the author of *The Conquest of Violence*, ask for the floor in the colossal assemblies called in Paris and Brussels by the International League against War and Fascism and the *Rassemblement Universel de la Paix*, the latter under the chairmanship of Lord Cecil. He was indignantly refused, as if he had been Alfred Rosenberg, or another one of the philosophers of the sharpened sword. They could not depart from the agenda, not even on a point of order. Pierre Cot, France's minister of aviation in the Blum cabinet, was scheduled to speak and did make a passionate plea for peace. We walked out when Cot got through, and took in a movie next door to the congress hall. By chance, the newsreel showed the same Pierre Cot in the company of a number of Soviet aviators, smilingly patting the gleaming flanks of a new type of bombing plane.

Peace the goal and bombing planes the means!

I could not follow De Ligt in his anarchist philosophy, but along with the Quakers, the War Resisters, the International of Antimilitarist clergymen, I helped prepare the summoning of a world congress, not against war and Fascism, but against militarism and imperialism the breeders of the real disease to which civilization may succumb. Events in Spain prevented me from attending the congress, which was held in Paris, in 1937, and which is the beginning of a saner approach to the question of war and peace than that of the *si-vis-pacem-para-bellum*-ists.

Then there was Leonhard Ragaz, the great apostle of the Social Gospel in Europe. Professor Ragaz had continued to live in Zurich, after he gave up his professorship in the university of that city. He had founded a Christian Socialist *Volkshochschule* and was publishing a monthly periodical devoted to the establishment of a synthesis of Christianity's and Socialism's essential task in a modern world. When he reproduced certain of my articles in his monthly *Neue Wege*, which had originally appeared in *Les Cahiers de réconciliation*, I decided to visit him. In one of those articles I had said, apropos of the Soviet government's antireligious activity, that probably all the outer organizational forms of Christianity would have to be swept aside before the world could again witness a revelation of Christ. Our friendship dated from the moment I walked into his study. "You are right," he said, as I entered, "Christianity is neither good nor divine, nor are our dogmas and doctrines the truth, but Christ is the truth! The whole of Christianity must go into the fire," he continued, "and it is going into the fire in order to be purified. For Christianity has to die in order that Christ may live. Men must be turned away from the established religions and be converted to the Kingdom of God. The greatest obstacle to the advent of the Kingdom in our day are the religious people with their *sacroegoismo* of individual spiritual salvation."

That was something entirely new. To Ragaz, the faith of the proletariat in its struggle for a new social order was identical with the belief in the Kingdom of God promised by Christ and the Prophets of Israel. He did not see the social struggle of the millions as an independent factor in society. It was a continuation of the striving of the Apostles. The effervescence amongst the peoples, the restlessness in the lowest strata of society, the cry for the right to live—all were to him a sign of God. "The higher the proletariat places its ideal," he would say, "the more must we see that they believe in what Jesus wanted, even if they themselves do not know it or do not acknowledge it."

"Leave the church," he would tell the multitudes who came to hear him, "leave the church, tear yourselves free from the official dogmas and creeds and go out into the world—to fight the battle of the weary and the heavy-laden!"

Ragaz was not a Bolshevik by any means—he was an orthodox Christian, but he considered the mighty things done in the Soviet Union a distinct advance of the Kingdom of God on earth.

It goes without saying that a man voicing these sentiments was the object of the concentrated hatred and attacks of that respectable, exteriorized Christianity, of which Switzerland is one of the strong-est bulwarks. When Signor Motta, the President of Switzerland, and Mussolini's personal friend, began agitating for a program of military preparedness and the Social Democrats of the country came to his support, Ragaz called mass meetings all over the country to protest against the prostitution of both the Socialist and the Christian ideal in the service of Mars. Alone, he began the struggle, publishing a weekly paper, speaking in mass meetings, and in open-air courses in the Alps. Soon he acquired a following, but he did not found a new sect. His disciples, scores of Protestant pastors in Switzerland, hundreds in Holland, many in France, remained where they were. They sought to bring the churches they represented into the social arena, not as mere rubber stamps for the state's every action of vio-lence and injustice, but as a new militia of Christ, determined to fight "the world"!

Today, Ragaz and his followers are about the only group seri-ously resisting the militarization and the Fascization (for militarism and Fascism are inseparable) of life in that ancient stronghold of freedom which was the Swiss Republic. But even five or six years ago, the Professor was so much the object of police chicanery and interference that it was not wise to communicate with him by mail—his correspondence was opened by order of Motta's political depart-ment. I therefore made frequent trips to Zurich, and occasionally he came to Paris.

This occurred about the same time that Romain Rolland, who had retired to Switzerland before the flood of patriotic hysteria in the last war, ceased to be molested. The author of *Above the Battle* had begun to advocate large armies for the European democracies and was no longer dangerous. When I visited Rolland in Villeneuve, in 1936, to ask him to intercede with his friends in the Soviet Union towards the alleviation of the woeful condition of the Tolstoyan Christians and Dukhobors, the old man, who at one time had been a spokesman for any and every struggling cause, looked out of the window and declared lamely that no sacrifice was too great to protect the hopeful beginnings made in Russia.

That was also the view of Litvinov, the shrewd diplomat, who occasionally could be seen wandering about in the Latin Quarter at nights with Ilya Ehrenbourg, the most versatile of Russian newspaper correspondents, and Louis Aragon, the poet. For a time I was naïve enough to believe that as an active member of the Friends of the

Soviet Union, I merely had to point out the damage that the Soviet State suffered in the eyes of forward-looking men and women all over the world, by its inhuman policy towards ideological minorities, to obtain a mitigation of the cruel treatment. I found Litvinov, with his impassive yellow mask, by far the most unsympathetic of the Soviet statesmen and leaders with whom I discussed the point, either in Geneva or Moscow. I have never been impressed with Litvinov's superiority as a diplomat or as an orator in Geneva. He was extremely cautious in his pronouncements and, when making a public appearance, read everything from carefully prepared statements. Disregarding political antecedents, a man like Nicholas Titulescu, in spite of an ugly face and eunuch's voice, was far more impressive, and so was the Spaniard, Señor de Madariaga. Litvinov never rose to an imaginative flight of thought, like Léon Blum, for example, or even Paul-Boncour. After Russia had entered the League, Litvinov played the role of social lion in international circles in Geneva and Paris. At the receptions in the Soviet embassy in Paris, or in the Hotel des Bergues on the Lake of Geneva, where an opportunity was afforded "to drink a cup of tea with His Excellency the Commissar of Foreign Affairs of the Union of Socialist Soviet Republics," standing room only was the rule. I remember one cocktail party at which Princess Starhemberg, the mother of Rudi, the aspirant dictator of Austria, presided, and where Litvinov, his face wreathed in smiles, was throned between the Princess Torlonia and the Countess Coudenhove-Kalergi, with a couple of princesses of the blood on tabourets at his feet.

"Go and look at Rasputin with his whiskers off," said Van Beek en Donk, the correspondent of the *Nieuwe Rotterdamsche Courant*, when I arrived. The conversation at the moment when I entered dealt with caviar, which, the great man said, was a regular item on the menu in the Red army. Someone, I think it was Robert Dell of *The Manchester Guardian*, asked him quietly what was the daily ration of champagne issued to the troops.

Litvinov was the great champion of the collective security idea in those days, concluding nonaggression pacts to left and right, and trying to convince the world that the Soviet Union no longer represented a danger to anybody; that, in other words, the historical phase of the USSR, acting as the spearhead and inspiration of the world's proletariat in its revolutionary struggle against capitalism and imperialism, had been brought to a close. On every successive visit to Geneva, the Commissar had some new feather in his cap. If it was not Latvia or Turkey he had succeeded in bringing into the fold of the family of peace-loving nations, it was China or Afghanistan. Beaming satisfaction, he received congratulations all around, beginning with Lord Robert Cecil, M. Barthou and Pierre Laval, who, as an ex-Communist, and therefore familiar with the Socialist interpretations of history from which Litvinov's policy departed on fundamental points, probably understood better than anyone else that the new system of collective security left the road wide open for a beautiful general race for collective violence.

For Litvinov's championship of the *status quo* in Europe, on which his whole peace policy was based, with the co-operation of France and all the victor nations of the last war, had no other practical effect but that of creating new alignments for and against the Treaty of Versailles, with all its glaring injustices and mistakes. After the rejection of his general and total disarmament proposal by the other great powers, Litvinov advanced no other solution for the problems confronting postwar Europe than to fall in line with the most grasping feudal and imperialist states by pursuing an intensely militarist and nationalist policy, instead of a revolutionary International Socialist one.

I believe that if Litvinov had spent half the effort he wasted in securing Russia a set of dubious alliances with imperialisms and bourgeoisies which remained fundamentally antagonistic to Socialism, if not its bitterest enemies, on educating the workers of the world for their historic task of overthrowing the capitalist system, his country would not be in its present position, where she faces a prospective alliance of all the great imperialisms.

He chose to cast to the wind the advice proffered in 1932 by the Total Disarmament Committee under the chairmanship of Donald Grant, and composed of the Quakers of the U. S. A., the Fellowship for Reconciliation, the International Antimilitarist Bureau, the International of Antimilitarist Clergymen, the War Resisters' International and the Women's International League for Peace and Freedom. All of these organizations urged immediate pressure by the masses in every country, those of Russia included, by methods of direct action, such as a refusal of military service, both individual and collective, opposition to budget credits for military purposes, the refusal to manufacture, transport or use any war machines or material, in order to force the different governments to accept

Russia's total disarmament proposals integrally and immediately. For that, it is true, the co-operation of the Second International and of the Trade Union International would also have been necessary. But Russia had given up her participation in revolutionary action abroad (this had been one of the principal conditions for diplomatic recognition of the USSR by different bourgeois governments), and could therefore not collaborate herself, with the result that the workers were lulled with false confidence in diplomatic intrigue, in parliamentary negotiations, in fruitless petitions which were nothing but scraps of paper. Bureaucratic commissions docilely followed the governments of their countries in a course of action which would ultimately lead, via Manchukuo, Ethiopia, Spain and Austria, to a concerted attack against the Soviet Union herself.

To the home of the esthetic Marvin Lowenthal, author of *A World Passed By*, on the tranquil Quai de Béthune came George Seldes, the author of *Sawdust Caesar*, the poet André Spire, Professor Félicien Challaye, on whose account the students rioted one day in the Latin Quarter, Sholom Asch, the novelist, and the distinguished playwright Edmond Fleg, of the Comédie Française. It was there that I also met young Francesco Nitti, son of one of Mussolini's predecessors in the Italian premiership, and Carlo Rosselli, who was assassinated with his brother in the forest of Ourly-sous-Bois in 1937. The name of Rosselli was familiar to me before I met him, as the editor of the valuable Paris Italian newspaper *Giustizia e Libertà*, the chief organ of the exiled Italian liberals. As far back as 1934 Rosselli predicted that Mussolini would inevitably be compelled to send a looting expedition to Africa in order to shift part of the huge and insupportable armament burden from the shoulders of his poverty-stricken agricultural country, which for years he had been forcing to play the role of a first-class power. Rosselli exposed the policy of bullying Britain the Duce ushered in after conquering Ethiopia, and showed that Mussolini never had the slightest intention of attacking England, but merely sought to make her disgorge something of her opulence and wealth, above all lend him money for exploiting the newly acquired empire in Africa.

A liberal of the old school, Carlo Rosselli was banished to the Lipari Islands shortly after the Black Shirts came to power. He had been rescued from this prison by Francesco Nitti, Jr., who took him in a motorboat to the coast of Tunis. Of a wealthy family, Rosselli thereafter spent his fortune in aiding anti-Fascist refugees and publishing the best-informed newspaper on the situation in Italy. He was in touch with the underground movement at home, and made several trips back into the lion's den at the risk of his life. But he always returned to Paris. The information he brought back was obtained in circles close to Mussolini, and was so accurate that Rosselli's newspaper became a thorn in the Dictator's flesh. His brother, a professor of history in the University of Florence, who took no part in politics, was visiting him when the two men were murdered. At the time of his death, Rosselli had begun to print details concerning the Italian army's "pacification" of Ethiopia. The last I saw him was in Madrid, in the midst of the Civil War. When I told him that I was flying to Paris the next day, he asked me to take along certain documents which "clearly established" responsibility in the murder of King Alexander of Jugoslavia. I had a deuce of a time getting those papers past the French police inspectors on the flying field near Marseilles.

Those were the days when *The World* counted amongst its contributors Joseph Caillaux, Anatole de Monzie, Victor Margueritte, and André Tardieu. *The World*'s Bureau was the last remaining link of an era during which correspondents were treated on a footing of equality by statesmen and diplomats, and not as lackeys who are summoned when someone has a statement to communicate which can as well be taken down by a stenographer. They were on the inside, as the saying goes, and did not need to stand about in an antechamber, kowtowing before the assistant third secretary. Nowadays, the political correspondent has to hunt high and low for snatches of information and fit them together like the pieces in a picture puzzle.

One of the strangest figures to come to *The World*'s office, where there was a daily flow of visitors, was Ignace Trebitsch-Lincoln. Said to be a son of Jewish parents, Trebitsch, when I knew him, had been a Catholic priest in Vienna, an Anglican clergyman in London, a Member of Parliament in Westminster, and was said to have been a secret agent for Germany in the U. S. A. and Canada during the World War. He had been secretary to Leon Trotsky, political adviser to one of the Chinese governments, and something or other at the court of Afghanistan. He always knew—sometimes months in advance—what was going to happen, but he never revealed his sources. This gave him an air of mystery, although there was nothing fundamentally mysterious about him. He was a restless soul, the Wandering Jew par excellence, who vainly sought for peace of mind in all the highways and byways of life. Personal success was the least of his concerns (he could have carved a brilliant career in half a dozen professions), and had more than once started out, only to break off suddenly, cut all his attachments and connections, and turn up on another road. He was a marvelous writer, but he seldom had the patience to sit down long enough to compose an article. He blew in, made some startling announcement that left everybody flabbergasted, and went out again. Once (coming from Italy, I think) he brought the news that the French government had decided to occupy the Ruhr. The Ruhr was occupied four months later. In 1929, he predicted Hitler's advent to power in the spring of 1933. Everybody smiled at that prophecy. He disappeared for long periods, but whenever he came back, the story of his experiences sounded more incredible.

Once he dropped in from India and began sending frantic telegrams to Lloyd George, asking the former Premier to intercede with the authorities for a landing permit in England. His only son, found guilty of murder, had been sentenced to die on the gallows. Trebitsch had rushed all the way from Indo-China to have a last word with his boy. Britain had deprived Trebitsch of his citizenship for his activities during the war. When Lloyd George did not reply, Trebitsch tried everyone of his former parliamentary colleagues. Without avail. I sat with him, waiting for the dawn, when his son would be hanged. Trebitsch kept his watch in his hand and paced the floor. When the first streaks of light appeared in the east the tension became unbearable. He rushed outside and clenched his fists at the rising sun. The blood streamed from his mouth and nostrils. Then he sat on the curb in a half swoon, moaning like a wounded animal. When he recovered his senses, the boy over in England was dead.

Thereafter, it was in 1930, Trebitsch disappeared. In the summer of 1935 he was back, but this time he was wearing the yellow robe of a Buddhist monk. I noticed him at the wicket in the Gare du Nord buying a ticket for Berlin.

"I see," I said to him, "that you have gone back to the *yarmakle*," pointing to his tight-fitting skullcap of a type that his Jewish ancestors must have worn in Hungary.

"I announce to you," replied Trebitsch gravely, "the doctrine that is glorious in the beginning, glorious in the middle, and glorious at the end—the Gospel of Our Lord Buddha."

Trebitsch said he was on his way to see the Führer and the leaders of the neopagan movement in the Reich. "Buddhism," he explained, "is a purely Aryan religion, and if the German people want to have done with that Jewish cult known as Christianity . . ."

I wished him the best of luck in his interview with Hitler, but never learned how he fared. Before boarding the train he gave me his new Chinese name and the address of the monastery in Ceylon of which he said he was the abbot. "If you ever want to say goodby to all this," said Trebitsch with a broad sweep of his yellow sleeve, "come and see me. I'll make a monk out of you."

One day Christian Rakovsky—with whom I searched the bookstalls along the Seine quays for data on Saint-Simon, the work on which he was engaged when Stalin had him imprisoned as a Trotskyist—took me into the back room of Lavenue's café near the Montparnasse station to see Panaït Istrati, the Rumanian storyteller. Panaït had just reached Paris from Nice where the police had found him one morning on the beach, his throat slashed and an unmailed letter to Romain Rolland in his pocket. Rolland had rushed down to the Mediterranean from his retreat in Villeneuve, and had revived a will to live in the wounded boy. Under Rolland's inspiration Panaït had begun to write in an amazingly fluent French. His books carried an echo from the peasant huts of Transylvania, the ghettos of Galicia and the quays of Constantinople. He told of the Anatolian girls who climb to the top of the hills to steel their breasts in the night winds that blow from the Aegean; of the filthy taverns in Smyrna where Circassian tribesmen make delivery of human flesh for the resorts of Salonika and Athens; of lone pilgrims who went to expiate unmentionable crimes on the Saviour's tomb in Jerusalem; of the lung disease of the pearl fishers off the Arabian coast. Panaït knew them all: he had slept in all the caravanserais of the Levant, and prowled in all the forbidden bazaars from Meknes to Medina. Son of a Wallachian peasant woman and a boyar, he had started out in life as a cook's devil on a tramp steamer that carried cocaine out of the Piraeus; and had successively served as towel boy in the smartest mirror house of Teheran, cotton checker in Brăila, valet to the Coptic Patriarch in Alexandria, interpreter in Baghdad, organizer of a tailors' union in Bucharest, croupier in a gambling casino in Damascus, and guide in the Cairo bazaar. He had seen bad days in Naples. He began to write of Koranic scholars in Alcázar University, prostitutes in Hodeida, millionaires in old Byzance—the dream of the camel driver, the hunger for sunshine in the pestilential *Judengassen*, the sorrow of the Galla mothers who see their children carried away to the harems of Arabia. And Panaït revealed the humanity of them all. . . .

We did not become friends till later. First Panaït was to undergo his Russian experience. He left with Rakovsky, who was hounded out of Paris by the reactionary press for having signed some left-wing manifesto against the terror in Indo-China. Christian had forgotten for a moment that he was Soviet ambassador. Panaït had decided to settle in Russia and write of his beggars and down-and-outers in a world where all values had been reversed. In three months' time he was the most popular writer in the Soviet Union and had millions of rubles in the bank. But when he found nameless woe below the Dnieper, where he had expected mounting joy, Panaït traveled back to Moscow to question the authorities. Then the doors in the commissariats began to close, and the official journalists, who had first gathered up his every word as pearls of wisdom, slunk away at his approach.

Istrati's return to Paris was the signal for a campaign of vilification, unimaginable on the part of his former comrades. A year or so before the literary idol of the Communist daily *Humanité*, he was now denounced as a mountebank, and a Rumanian Fascist gangster, as André Gide was to be called a Protestant Pharisee in later years. He wanted to speak of what he had seen, but the bark of the pack drowned out his words. Panaït resumed his wanderings, disillusioned, bitter. . . . Together we started out for Turkey and walked to Ankara, interviewed Kemal Pasha, slept in a grotto near the Ephesus of St. Paul, where whirling dervishes executed a forbidden dance for our benefit, and ate the heavily spiced meals in the Anatolian village inns while watching the girls dance in the primitive squares. We landed in Mount Athos, the republic of monks, after having been questioned on our arrival in Athens on the suspicion of being in league with a gang of dope peddlers with whom we played cards on the crossing from Antioch. Back in Paris, the Rumanian dropped from sight for a long time. Once he looked me up when I lived in Bourg-en-Forêt to inquire where he could buy red peppers. In the afternoon he brought a chance acquaintance to my home, some purple-nosed vagabond with a knapsack slung over his shoulder, whom he had encountered on his walk in the forest. According to Panaït, the man was inspired. The two of them sat drinking red wine in the back of the garden till the sun went down, and with nightfall, they set off in the direction of Marseilles. Each time I saw him thereafter he seemed to have grown thinner. When it began to rain he fled south, for he held the rain responsible for his coughing spells.

Panaït died before he could learn that the Communists were killing his last book wherein he had made the heretical assertion that some bourgeois individuals he had met were better human beings than some revolutionaries of his acquaintance. But for this the Rumanian government gave him a state funeral.

Thus the years rolled by. They were relatively uneventful years from the international point of view when compared with the days of anxiety that were to follow. There was not a cloud on the horizon large enough to inspire the least disquietude. The peace of Europe seemed secure. For a moment the specter of a "Red imperialism" had been conjured up on the eastern horizon, but the army of the new Russia had shown itself to such startling disadvantage in the war with Poland that no one could seriously envisage it as a potential threat to the established order in Europe. America was going through a wave of prosperity which had caused the depression of 1921 to be forgotten. Hitler's brown-shirted cohorts appeared mere bands of hoodlums, and still confined their activity to befouling synagogues and Jewish cemeteries. Democrats like Bruening, Stresemann and Mueller were still in control in the Reich, and behind them stood a powerful Social Democratic party as a guarantee of law and order at home and peace abroad. It is true that Mussolini made the welkin ring now and then with a flamboyant speech. His outbursts evoked little more than amused smiles and shrugs of the shoulders in the chancelleries; nobody paid any attention of what was said by the "Masquerade Ball Caesar," as Paul-Boncour called him once in a speech in the French parliament. Japan, recovering from the earthquake of 1923, and digesting the loot of previous conquests, was not yet prepared to launch her great robbing expeditions on the Asiatic mainland. The Labor party was in power in England, with the pacifist Ramsay MacDonald at the head of the cabinet. There was really little to disturb the hearts of men.

Even so, in Geneva, where I went whenever the League held a session, an undercurrent of uneasiness was becoming discernible; the idea of a universal disarmament was no longer thriving. Peace, to be sure, was still on everybody's lips in the public sessions where large delegations of schoolteachers, social workers and representatives from the Protestant churches of America, Britain and the Scandinavian countries followed the proceedings with something akin to religious enthusiasm. But behind the scenes, in the hotel rooms and in the quieter resorts along the shores of the Lake of Geneva, where the diplomats and statesmen withdrew to spend their week ends, resolutions and decisions were constantly being whittled down, made less formal, less committing, less exact, and less categorical, before being introduced on the floor of the Assembly or in the Council. The game of procrastinating, delaying and postponing the application of the clauses of the Versailles Treaty dealing with general disarmament was in full swing, but it was not yet played in the open. No one could point to a precise danger, some genuine potential threat to world peace serious enough to prevent the victor nations from carrying into effect their solemn, treaty-bound pledges to proceed with their own disarmament. And yet the statesmen spoke in a general way about the need of security, and of still more pacts of guarantee to implement the Versailles Treaty. What were they waiting for in that era of reconciliation and peaceful international collaboration of which Briand, the French Foreign Minister, who was called the guardian angel of the League, foreshadowed the early advent? Had he a plan to bring the dream to realization?

We flocked to Geneva every time he was scheduled to speak, for he incarnated the hope of humanity. After Wilson's eclipse he was the one man with a world-wide moral authority. He, we thought, was to be the mediator in the restoration of universal confidence. He had spoken of reconciliation. The world was hungry for his voice that leaped over the frontier of nations and classes. He was thought to possess the secret that would end the suspense and the latent crisis. When he rose his reputation exorcised the tumult, and a white silence rushed in. He cast a spell with his voice. "It is like hearing music," said Austen Chamberlain, who closed his eyes as he listened to the Frenchman, "the music of a violoncello." Briand's gestures were awkward. There was nothing appealing in his physique: a tousled head of hair, a drooping moustache shading a cynical leer, hunched shoulders on a crooked spine—almost a dwarf. But the fascination of his voice was overwhelming. It kept you nailed to your seat if you had found one. The multitude hung to his lips, mouse-still, revering, hungry for more. And the spell did not break till he slumped down in his chair, exhausted, staring around with those pale blue sea eyes of the Breton, blinking at the tumultuously applauding audience.

What did he say? It was impossible to recapture the glamour of his words on the typewriter. In cold print the miracle was incapable of re-creation. The radiance did not linger. Perhaps music critics, not political observers, should have been sent to report the speeches of Briand. The contents escaped you as one misses the words of an opera. In vain do I rake my memory in an effort to recall a single one of his utterances. I remember one emotional exclamation: *"Arrière les mitrailleuses! Arrière les canons!"* and some wisecracks at the afternoon teas for journalists. The quintessence of the famous speech in Locarno remains vivid only because the satirical Léon Daudet never tires of quoting the words he spoke there: "The Germans are men. . . . They are not fools, the Germans. . . . They reason in Berlin. . . ."

That was the year 1928. That was the blossomtime of fate. The League of Nations was holding its ninth assembly. Foch had just informed the world that the German Reich had completely disarmed. Germany had a Social Democratic government. Its chancellor, Herman Mueller, who had come to Geneva, complained that whereas his country had destroyed its weapons of war, the other European states, far from following suit, as they had promised, were increasing their armaments and still pointed to Germany as the chief obstacle to world peace.

In reply to this eminently just observation, I heard the "violoncellist" go into action. He played the tune of—Poincaré. The other states could disarm only, said Briand, to the limit of their security. The disarmament of the Reich was not a sufficient guarantee. For two hours the *andante cantabile* filled the concert hall and the artist received an ovation. At the end, Tardieu, the man of the steel cartel, paid his compliments to Briand by saying that his policy had not differed materially from that the successive French governments had pursued since the war. All had been imbued with a sincere desire for peace. All!

Why should those governments have wanted anything else but peace, since France had nothing more to gain from war? The merit of Briand, if merit it is, consists in having colored with a veneer of humanitarianism the pacifism of the satisfied nations. Bismarck's pacifism!

In 1929, Briand was awarded the Nobel prize for peace along with Sir Austen Chamberlain, and fed us *petits fours* and champagne to celebrate the event. By that time there was no more talk of universal reconciliation. When the regeneration of Europe might have begun, the sinister spirit of conquest continued to prevail.

There was a caricature in a satirical boulevard sheet at the time, showing two Laplanders standing on a field of snow, muffled up in their furs. "We never seem to get that peace prize," said the one. "That's because we never make war," replied the other.

It has been said that without the occupation of the Ruhr by France, there never would have been a Nazi victory in Germany. I cannot share that view. For, although there is no question that the entire German people smarted under the outrage of their Rhenish fellow citizens being garrisoned by Senegalese troops, and that a French government really desirous of bringing about a reconciliation between the two peoples would not have been guilty of such a provocation, the decisive hour came much later. The Ruhr was still to be followed by Locarno, and Locarno once more revived the hope of German democracy to an unprecedented pitch.

I still see the scene at the Gare du Nord when Chancellor Bruening arrived in Paris. For the first time, a German statesman was back in the French capital after the humiliation of Versailles. The station was black with people, all eager to catch a glimpse of the German delegation. As Herr Bruening and his colleagues made their way from the platform to the waiting room, they passed a group of railway employees. Suddenly there was a cry, "*Vive l'Allemagne!*" and again, "*Vive la paix! Vive la fraternité humaine!*" The shout was taken up by thousands and thousands until the immense vault of the railway station reverberated with the roar.

That demonstration, absolutely spontaneous, by the workers of Paris, augured well for the Chancellor's visit. For days men spoke of nothing else but the reception accorded the representatives of the foe of yesterday. The German Chancellor, completely taken by surprise, had gravely returned the salute. It had been a moment of high emotion. I saw Bruening's eyes fill with tears. Everyone who witnessed the scene had to swallow hard.

But what was the object of Herr Bruening's visit to Paris? Before the imminence of a general catastrophe in the Reich, a financial and economic disaster of the first magnitude, the Chancellor of one of the great European states had come as a humble suppliant to plead the cause of the Reich with Monsieur Pierre Laval. "It was an act of desperation, foolish perhaps, and totally unexpected, but nevertheless an act of courage and greatness," as Jean Richard Bloch said at the time in *Europe*. The people felt similarly, and the instinct of the masses is seldom wrong.

France alone at that moment could have saved what remained of democracy and republicanism in the Weimar Republic.

Herr Bruening and his collaborators spent the night in conference. They had brought with them irrefutable evidence in figures and facts that Germany was on the verge of the abyss.

At seven in the morning—it was a Sunday—Bruening went to the Church of Notre Dame de la Victoire. He prayed for an hour and heard Mass. At ten o'clock he was received by M. Laval. The German Chancellor expressed his views, and pleaded with the French Foreign Minister for two hours. When he noticed that he could not soften the heart of the Frenchman, he fell on his knees. He spoke of the misery in his country, the sense of frustration of the German youth, the dull hopelessness of the situation if France would not lift some of the burdens imposed at Versailles. He warned of an economic debacle which might, through its repercussions, drag other countries, France herself, into a chaotic whirlpool. He named "the sinister forces" that were waiting to take over the reins in Germany if he (Bruening) should fail.

Laval shook his head. He would not even place Bruening's request for a loan, or a moratorium, before his colleagues in the cabinet. He refused to hold out the least strand of hope. He led the German Chancellor to the door with a polite expression of adieu.

It was a sunny day in Paris when Pierre Laval signed the death warrant of the German Republic.

Such incidents, which were scarcely noticed in the world at large, had their significance none the less as signposts pointing to the future. They led to the suspicion that while the statesmen were ostensibly as deeply concerned with peace as ever, a vast plot of international ramifications was being woven behind the scenes to bring to nought the ideal of a warless world.

While the eyes of the world were riveted on Geneva, where the interminable debate went on and on, few were aware that, from 1925 onward, representatives of French and German heavy industry were meeting regularly, now in Paris, then in Berlin. Both the German and French metal industry were incurring serious losses as a result of the suspension of armament contracts, and were desperately seeking ways and means to set business in motion again. This could not be done without intimate collaboration. In May, 1925, Arnold Rechberg, public-relations counsel of the Hugenberg and Thyssen trusts, came to Paris to propose the equipment by France of a German army of 800,000 which was to march into Russia and destroy the Bolshevik regime. Marshal Foch and President Poincaré received the German emissary in the company of Messrs. Robert Pinaud and Charles Laurent, directors of the Comité des Forges, the French steel cartel. They approved the plan which had been worked out by General von Hoffmann. After days of negotiations, François Coty announced triumphantly in his newspaper *Figaro* that Poincaré had approved a scheme which would have established a Franco-German condominium over the vast Russian market. He did not add, however, that this would have obviated the necessity of continuing the talk of general disarmament in Geneva. Foch approved in turn, and Tardieu sent Paul Reynaud to Berlin to arrange the final details. The plan was wrecked, said Herr Rechberg later,[1] by Lloyd George, who feared a still greater French influence in Europe. But contact between the French and German cannon makers had been established. It was never again broken. The French metal industry agreed to the rearmament of Germany as early as 1925, as being the only condition for the stimulation of the inner French market.

Strange personages were beginning to make their appearance in Geneva to assist the diplomats in clearing the last obstacle off the road towards universal peace and disarmament. Germany sent Constantin von Neurath, director of the Crédit Hongrois, a Hungarian banking institution controlled by Schneider & Cie., the French armament manufacturers. Carl von Schubert took charge of the permanent undersecretaryship for foreign affairs and the League

[1] *Edition spéciale, Documents politiques,* February, 1932; and Reichstag speech by Abel, January, 1932.

of Nations at the Wilhelmstrasse. He was a director of the Krupp metal trust. France, in turn, sent to Berlin as its ambassador François-Poncet, who had but recently been managing director of the Dillinger Huettenwerke, a German armament firm, but who was also a director of the Aciéries et Usines à Tubes de la Sarre, a French steel trust.[2] From 1928 onward, the Labor Bureau of the League was revealing the formation of strange new international business combinations. The Krupp Metal Works of Essen formed a subsidiary known as the Neunkirchen Eisenwerke and appointed French munitioneers and politicians to its board of directors: Georges Lenormand, administrator of the French Forges et Aciéries du Nord et de Lorraine, and Jean Bernard, vice-president of the Comité des Forges. Two German steel firms, the Halbergerhuette and the Dillinger Huettenwerke merged with a French company, the Aciéries de la Sarre. They appointed a board of directors consisting of six prominent French cannon merchants and six Germans.[2]

Paul Faure, deputy for the district of Le Creusot, revealed in the French parliament that Schneider-Cruesot, the mammoth French cannon trust, headed by the cousins De Wendel, one of whom was a member of the French Chamber and the other of the German Reichstag, was contributing funds to the infant Nazi party of Adolf Hitler, and that Skoda, the Czechoslovakian armament trust, which is largely controlled by Schneider-Cruesot, was supplying Germany with artillery, gunpowder and cartridges on credit.[3]

Why should Hitler have received French, Czechoslovakian and British money (for Sir Henry Deterding, chairman of Royal Dutch Shell, was also reported amongst the contributors to the Nazi party's funds)? The answer is simple. One needed but read the Führer's book, *Mein Kampf*. In that document, the upstart party leader, with scarcely ten thousand followers at the time he wrote the book, announced that his first task upon attaining power would be to rearm the Reich. Did not such a man deserve international sympathy and support? Armament factories all over the Continent were standing idle, dividends were sinking, stock quotations going lower and lower. And not a cloud on the horizon to give the deadly armament industry a little spurt, no danger anywhere to warrant the manufacture of a single gun! Would it not be a godsend if Hitler could come to power and make Germany dangerous once more?

[2] *Les Marchands de canons contre la nation, op. cit.*, p. 55.
[3] *Journal officiel* of February 12, 1932, pp. 575-576.

Wouldn't that be sufficient excuse to kill all this nonsense in Geneva about world peace and disarmament? Once Germany started to rearm, all could follow suit. For the primary condition of a general armament campaign is the rearmament of only one powerful state. With Germany on the way, "the tragic and ridiculous spectacle" (as François Delaisi called it once) of nations arming because they were afraid, and afraid because they were arming, could start all over again.

It did start all over again, and you felt sick at heart with the chicanery and the hypocritical palaver in Geneva about peace and democracy by men who represented the so-called great democracies, but who were scheming and conniving behind the scenes to sacrifice the German people to a barbaric militaristic authoritarianism because that was the condition *sine qua non* for setting the armament campaigns in their own countries in motion again. Before August, 1914, the most influential Parisian newspapers had been heavily subsidized by Germany to whip up the spirit of *revanche* in the French people, and so help the French governments pass ever heavier war budgets, and, in turn, give the Kaiser's cabinets the opportunity of obtaining more war credits from the German people. Now the chief task of international diplomacy was to kill the urge for peace and general disarmament in the peoples by introducing a new menace to peace in the center of Europe.

You saw the sordid mystification of Geneva, the murderous traffic to betray the hope of humanity, but who were you, a simple newspaperman, to denounce the contemptible trickery to set the peoples on the warpath again? Was it likely that anyone would believe that men like Austen Chamberlain, Baldwin, Briand, Stresemann, MacDonald, Simon and Paul-Boncour, who had the word "peace" forever on the tip of their tongues, were in reality playing with the life and death of Europe and the future of civilization? You managed to get some "revelations" printed in the periodicals and reviews of the Quakers and the Christian antimilitarists in Holland, Switzerland and France, but that was all that could be done about it. In the end you returned to France to seek forgetfulness in the company of the simple people you knew.

The consolation of being a resident of Paris—the greatest blessing, I think, that can befall any mortal—always remained. I am not a Frenchman, there is not a drop of French blood in my veins, but in Paris I felt at home more than in any other place on earth. Paris is the only city where a man can be happy without a pocketful

of money. It is a city to dream in, to wander in the rain, or sit and
watch the flow of life move by. I never felt an hour spent in Paris
wasted, even if I did not do anything. You could be silent in Paris
and let the cobblestones speak. Every paving block told its story.
From every sidewalk rose the voice of the past. . . .

I had made a habit of taking a daily walk, each day selecting
a new quarter of the city. Even after two years I was still making
discoveries. The official sights had little attraction, except Notre
Dame, where I dropped in occasionally to contemplate the restful
beauty of the rose windows. More frequently, I sat just across the
bridge facing the cathedral, in the churchyard of St. Julien-le-
Pauvre, where Dante slept when he had no money to pay for a lodging. Here I watched the tourists flock into a house across the street
where a chamber of tortures from the Middle Ages has been preserved. Or up to the Hill of Montmartre, on the terrace of the
Sacré Coeur, with its troubling spectacle of the whole teeming city,
and the citizens below in the street, taking off their hats to the
statue of the Chevalier de la Barre, the last man to be executed for
having refused to salute the Host as it was carried through the streets.
Every nook and corner was perfumed with reminiscences. Here
was the house of Marat, "the friend of the people," there the garret
where Victor Hugo hid before fleeing to Brussels, a few steps
farther the ruins of the palace in which Julian the Apostate burnt
his oil lamp over the Greek poets while the Gauls around him were
still barbarians. I would stray into the Père Lachaise cemetery to
look on the Wall of the Federated, where the Commune had made
its last glorious stand, and where now hung the commemorative
wreaths of poppies fastened there by the working-class organizations. Here was the house of Voltaire on the Quai, there the home
of the Admiral de Coligny, the most valiant of the Huguenots;
almost next door to each other, on the Rue Vaneau, the humble
dwellings that once housed Ernest Renan and Karl Marx. In this
narrow passage by the Bourse, Henri IV met his death at the hand of
an assassin, a stone's throw away the café where Jaurès was murdered
on the eve of the war. Here St. Roch's church, on whose worn-out
stairway the first shots were fired in the Revolution of 1830, and
in front of it the house where the Club of the Cordeliers met Danton
in the middle of the night. Or a visit to the *quais* and the bookshops
on the Rue des Saints-Pères to browse amongst the old volumes and
chat with the shopkeepers. I had friends everywhere, but they

were not the gentlemen at the ministries and embassies where my job brought me. They were the postman and the concierge, the waiter and the medical student, and the pastor of the little Huguenot chapel. They were men and women "who thought with their hearts and felt with their heads," essentially civilized and human. "Never," said Kurt Tucholsky, the German writer, one day, "have I met a single Frenchman who wanted to win the war all over again in conversation."

Life was never dull, even when there were no assignments in exciting places far away in Africa or Asia. Paris was a perpetual show that filled me with gladness from morn till night. I seldom missed a military parade and once a year, the anniversary of Napoleon's death, I went to the Hôtel des Invalides to see the dust and ashes of an empire whose glories had enthralled me in my youth. The fifth of May usually broke in a gray, melancholy way, with a blue haze hanging over the Seine, the pavements wet, and the pigeons of the Louvre flapping their wings forlornly in the weather-blackened niches of the statues. At dawn, an unknown hand would place the traditional wreath of flowers at the foot of the column on the Place Vendôme, on which stands the laurel-crowned statue of the Corsican Caesar. The violets would lay there fresh and fragrant in the soft rain of springtime, but across the river, beneath the gilded dome where he sleeps "in the midst of the French people whom he loved so well," the chapel of the Invalides would slowly fill for the annual requiem mass for the repose of the soul of the man who once threw Europe upside down.

They would come in one by one: Prince Murat . . . Count Bernadotte . . . the young Prince de la Moskowa, the descendant of Ney . . . the Duc de Talleyrand . . . Boni de Castellane . . . the family Jourdain . . . François Coty and the whole Corsican clan. . . . Widor would play the *Dies Irae* on the organ. From the ceiling at the back of the altar hung the massive draperies with white borders, and just above the perpetual light of the Sacrament, the huge silver-embroidered "N" on a field of black velvet. Priests would sprinkle the catafalque with holy water. "*Requiem aeternam dona eis, Domine!*"—Give him eternal peace, O Lord!

Then outside, on the square where he was wont to review the levies for the Grand Army, and where his statue still stands in one of the upper galleries, broodingly overlooking the rows of captured guns, a battalion of infantry, an artillery regiment and a detachment of dragoons would be drawn up. Those who had attended church would slowly file out to take their place behind the hedge of troops.

Standing in a corner of one of the upper galleries, the band of the Republican Guard would strike up Bonaparte's favorite song: *"Où peut-on être mieux qu'au sein de sa famille"*—Where Can One Better Be Than in the Bosom of One's Family. And then in the western door there would suddenly stand a detachment of soldiers holding the tattered battleflags of Austerlitz and Friedland, Moscow, Dresden, Leipzig and Waterloo. Once the music stilled, the eagle-tipped standards would begin to move slowly across the enclosed square.

Then, suddenly, without a word of command, in a single spontaneous gesture, inconceivable in Potsdam, five thousand bayonets and sabers would leap forth and from every mouth escape the sigh: *"Les Aigles!"*—The eagles!

I saw the great-grandson of Michel Ney bury his face in his hands. I looked at the officers: not an eye was dry. A young lieutenant by my side, in mystic exaltation, whispered: *"La Gloire!"*

The eagles passed, commands would ring out, and the band with cymbals and unmuffled drums would strike up the song at the sound of which the Emperor himself used to wag his head and stamp his feet:

> *Paraît que la cantinière*
> *A de tous les côtés*
> *Par devant, par derrière*
> *Un tas de grains de beauté.* . . .

The Quat-z-Arts ball was an annually recurrent affair which threw our whole *quartier* in an uproar. One year the students and their girl friends would appear in the streets impersonating the personages of Greek mythology in the garb of charming innocence affected by the immortal gods; the next year we looked upon a horde of wild Indians dragging captive squaws to the wigwams. The police were kept busy shooing wandering parties of Olympians and redskins from the more sedate residential quarters, for the prefecture had set a rule that the revelers must confine themselves to a certain area. On the other hand, the students had a tradition that a bath in the fountains of the Place de la Concorde was essential to a successful termination of the celebration. All night the riot squads would be busy removing unclad young humans from the intervening streets, usually by hailing taxicabs, shoving the offenders inside and directing the chauffeurs to drive them back to Montparnasse or the Boul' Mich. There was no roughness or violence. Everything went off in the best of humor. But one night the police were outmaneuvered. Towards three in the morning, the Grand Boulevards on the Right Bank were invaded by an army of nudes, who leap-frogged their way to the church of the Madeleine, and there, scaling the fence, disported themselves for an hour or so between the noble columns of that *ci-devant* Temple of Glory. When certain newspapers in the morning expressed the indignation of the bourgeoisie *bien-pensante*, whom they surely had not had time to consult, the Prefect of Police replied laconically that the spectacle had been so fascinating that he could not move from the spot, and plumb forgot to call out the riot squads.

Far more serious than these innocent games were the pranks of the royalist students, members of the Action Française. These gentlemen always gave a political tinge to their jokes, often with serious embarrassment to the authorities. Once they sent an epistle to each individual member of parliament, on an official-looking paper, which bore the inscription: "Bureau of the National Representation of the Republic of Terrania." The letter began by lauding the recipient's well-known sympathy for all oppressed peoples, his love of liberty, his broad universalistic outlook, and his many efforts in the cause of human brotherhood. It then set forth the woes of the Terranian people, ground to pieces under the cruel tyrant's heel, robbed of its liberties, its press muzzled, its cultural activities suspended by an arrogant conquerer, its noblest citizens rotting in the dungeons of the oppressor. France had always been champion of the small peoples; would not France again let her voice be heard in behalf of the Terranian Republic? Would not Monsieur the Deputy, recipient of the letter, lend the people of Terrania his moral support?

Sixty-three deputies replied to this hoax with a declaration, more or less eloquent, assuring the President of the Terranian Republic and the noble sister nation of Terrania of their solidarity and moral support. Thirteen promised to take the matter up with the French Foreign Ministry. Then the royalists exposed the hoax in their newspaper and Paris rocked with laughter. A sheet with photographs of the deputies who had run into the trap, with their replies, was sold on the boulevards, and for weeks the impromptu *conférenciers* in the cabarets of Montmartre analyzed, with bitter sarcasm, the contents of the letters in response to the appeal from Terrania.

Then there was the farce played on the government by Léon Daudet, the royalist leader. Not even the rich imagination of Dumas could have improved on this rollicking adventure. M. Daudet, one of the ablest journalists of the day, a man now well in his sixties, has all his life been one of the most determined opponents of the republican regime. No matter what political views a Frenchman holds, he reads Daudet, not only for the excellence of his language —he is a master of style—but because of his merciless lampooning of the chief personages on the political scene. He is a die-hard reactionary, of course, but he commands a vocabulary that holds the reader spellbound. One moment he is in Rabelaisian good humor, only to switch into mordant invective the next. He is the last exponent of the art of vituperation in journalism, but withal, a man of great culture, and not only a novelist of note, but a trail blazer in medical research. His public lectures, delivered with Gallic verve and frankness, are marvels of lucidity and attended by thousands. He is unquestionably one of the glories of the spiritual life of France. It almost goes without saying that Daudet is frequently at loggerheads with the laws on libel and defamation. As a rule, the government does not prosecute him, although for years he has been a pitiless debunker of the men who stand at the helm. The very prospect of seeing him in the courtroom fills the politicians with dread. M. Daudet is but all too eager to explain himself—and he can. Yet once when he had libeled a certain taxi driver, a man who was involved in the unsolved drama of Daudet's son, Philippe, a boy who was found murdered in a taxicab, the father was sentenced to six months' imprisonment.

But Daudet refused to surrender to the police and barricaded himself in the office of his newspaper *Action Française*, which faced the St. Lazare railway station. Squads of *camelots du roi*, young royalists, assumed the guard of their chief, and battalions of policemen were posted in the neighborhood to keep traffic moving. The intersection of the Rue St. Lazare and the Rue de Rome is one of the busiest in Paris. Tens of thousands of people milled about to see the siege in the heart of the city, in the hope of catching a glimpse of the royalist editor whose appearances on the balcony were greeted with wild ovations. Daudet's newspaper, containing a daily blast of defiance at the Republic, was selling by the hundreds of thousands all over the country. It was clear that the government could not tolerate the situation. It had to make a show of authority. This it did one morning by massing two regiments of the Republican Guard in the square before the Gare St. Lazare, in addition to hundreds of policemen, mobile guards, and all the available sections of the fire department, which is a branch of the military service in France.

My reporter's card enabled me to pass the cordon of troops which had been thrown around the neighborhood. Everybody expected a hot time and blood to flow. Instead of taking the building by storm, the Prefect of Police, M. Jean Chiappe, dispatched a policeman with a white flag to bring a message to M. Daudet. The message asked the royalist editor to appear on the balcony and to hear the Prefect's appeal. A hundred thousand people in the square waited breathlessly for the answer.

After a few moments the emissary returned with the white flag, the doors on the balcony opened, and M. Daudet made his appearance. The Prefect at once took a few steps forward, and saluted the royalist chief with a broad flourish of his hat. He remained uncovered during the entire parley. M. Daudet bowed in recognition, and the speeches commenced, M. Chiappe first. He made a discreet reference to the death of the editor's son, and asked M. Daudet to prevent the shedding of more innocent blood. Daudet was visibly moved by this appeal, and wiped away a tear. He consented to constitute himself a prisoner on the condition that his *camelots* be accorded full honors of war and be allowed to retreat. To this the Prefect consented. The *camelots* marched off in military formation and then Daudet came down to the door, again greeted by M. Chiappe. The two men stepped into a waiting limousine and drove away as the troops presented arms.

Six weeks later M. Daudet was out of jail and safely in Brussels. He has told the story himself, how one day, at noon, the director of the Santé prison entered his cell and asked him to pack up. "You are to be released at once by order of the Minister of the Interior," said the warden. When the puzzled M. Daudet leisurely began gathering up his belongings, the official pressed him to speed.

"You must be out of here in ten minutes. His Excellency the

Minister insists that you hurry, for he does not desire that the news of your release give rise to demonstrations on the part of your followers!"

All the formalities which ordinarily go with the release of a prisoner—the so-called *levée d'écrou*—were dispensed with in the rush, so that within a quarter of an hour M. Daudet found himself standing on the pavement outside. He walked a few steps along the Boulevard Arago and hailed a taxicab. To his amazement, he noticed that the chauffeur was a *camelot du roi*, a member of the monarchist organization of which M. Daudet is himself the chief. He jumped in and drove away. A few hours later Paris was rocking with laughter. Extras announced that Léon Daudet had escaped from prison. The whole detective corps was mobilized to scour the city for the fugitive editor; the police boarded all outgoing trains, boats and airplanes in every port, at every frontier.

How the *camelots* had managed to release their chief has never been cleared up. Government commissions to investigate the affair kept their conclusions a secret. It is certain that one of the *camelots* sat at the switchboard of the Ministry of the Interior during the noon hour when most of the employees had gone out for lunch. This man imitated the voice of the Minister of the Interior so perfectly that even the director of the Santé prison was deceived by it. Before releasing M. Daudet, this official took the precaution of calling back the Ministry of the Interior to verify the order. For answer the voice of the supposed Minister replied: "What? Daudet is not gone yet? *Nom de Dieu*, Monsieur, do you wish to embarrass the government? Please dispense with all the formalities and do as you are told. Your position is at stake, Monsieur, as well as the prestige of the Republic."

M. Daudet lived in Belgium for a year, but at no time revealed by what means and where he had crossed the borders. He was finally amnestied on the motion of M. Herriot, the man to whom Daudet refers habitually in his articles as "potbellied Eddy, the good-natured impostor with the pipe."

The kaleidoscope of ebullient Parisian life of which I was a silent spectator was frequently interrupted by trips abroad, but I lingered no longer in foreign countries than was strictly necessary: Paris had become my home, and every hour away from it I felt at a loss. In the city itself there was never any lack of material to write about. Definite assignments by the New York *Evening World* became more and·more rare. You merely let yourself drift along, and the story came your way, sometimes in the most unexpected places.

There was but one visitor in the reference room of the Musée de la Guerre that sultry afternoon in the late summer of 1930. He was a man well past middle age, with a grizzled moustache and a remarkably broad forehead. He was dressed in a tightly buttoned frock coat, and sported a pair of horn-rimmed glasses. When I entered the room he scarcely looked up from the table at which he was sitting, nervously turning the pages of a large illustrated volume, and merely mumbled something incomprehensible in answer to my word of greeting. An attendant, a man with a cork leg, who bore the ribbons of a World War veteran on his breast, stamped in and out of the room, lugging in piles of books that he placed at the visitor's elbow, bowing each time he deposited a load. The attendant's obsequiousness, coupled with the fact that the visitor had been permitted to keep his umbrella with him in the library, something which is contrary to the rules in vogue in all institutions classed as "historic monuments" in France, made it clear that the gentleman was a person of distinction, some higher functionary, perhaps, or a politician. Moreover, he looked the part every inch, from the rosette of the Legion of Honor in the lapel of his coat to his striped trousers and flowing black tie.

I had come to Vincennes to consult the original version of the Sykes-Picot Treaty, that half-forgotten diplomatic instrument, under the terms of which France and Britain, secretly eliminating their imperial Russian ally from a share in the loot, divided Arabia into spheres of influence long before they had expelled the Turk. This and other documents relating to the diplomatic history of the war are preserved in the castle of Vincennes, an early medieval structure dating from the time of Philippe le Bel. It stands just outside the walls of Paris. The castle still forms a part of the metropolitan defense system. I noticed that afternoon, when crossing the bridge, that it was garrisoned by a regiment of Tonkinese machine gunners. The donjon, which forms the chief edifice in a large complex of buildings inside the walls, is a broad stunted tower. A number of illustrious names scratched on the walls of chambers and crypt bear testimony to the extensive use of the donjon as a prison, first under the monarchy, which peopled the place with recalcitrant feudal lords, later by Napoleon III, who locked the friends of Victor Hugo in the caves, and still later by the Third Republic, which kept a batch of Communards there before shipping them off to Guiana. Besides the donjon, there is a fine Gothic chapel, a hospital, several munition depots, and a powder magazine, all within the fortified enclosure. From the windows of the library of the château proper, one can see the execution field. In the background, under a row of elm trees, stands the *poteau*, the sinister traitors' stake to which Mata Hari was tied when she faced the firing squad. Bolo Pasha, Duval, and scores of other spies in the days of war hysteria, were also executed there.

I had scarcely settled down to read and scribble a few notes, when the sky suddenly darkened, and I heard the rumble of an approaching thunderstorm. It soon became necessary to switch on the lights in the room. From where I sat I could see the lightning throw bolts of steel-blue around the delicate spire of the chapel. The wind began to howl through the chimney, and the first large drops of rain splashed hesitatingly on the windowpanes. The electric lights dipped warningly several times, and then went out altogether. The rain was now coming down in sheets, and I rose to walk over to the window as reading had become impossible. The elderly gentleman soon followed me.

Just as he reached the window, a crepitating crash of thunder shook the walls of the castle, and we saw the lightning strike a mason's scaffold around the donjon tower across the square. With a deafening rattle, the boards and boxes of tools clattered to the flagstones below. The wind ripped apart what remained of the scaffold and flung it to the ground. Before our eyes the square was turned into a seething pool of water.

"*C'est formidable,*" I said to the gentleman by my side. "I have never seen a rain like this in my life."

"*Oui, c'est une bonne petite pluie,*" he replied, nodding his head, "but I have seen worse; I once saw a road, which it had taken fifty thousand men half a year to build, washed out in a quarter of an hour—completely obliterated—like that!" He held up the flat palm of his hand by way of illustration. "Nothing remained of it. That was in Morocco. Yes, I have seen many of these sudden summer squalls. Once in Jerusalem, too, about forty years ago, I saw the streets turned into raging torrents in less time than that square was covered. I was marooned in my hotel. For several days I could not go out. The hotel was like an island in the midst of a lake."

"I thought it never rained in Jerusalem," I said.

"No rain in Jerusalem? *Mais si*, there is a heavy rainfall in Jerusalem," he answered. "Unfortunately it comes all at once, in the spring. The rest of the year the land is parched. This is what makes colonization work so difficult over there. It is the same in southern Morocco."

"I have brought you some light, *monsieur le maréchal*," interrupted the attendant as he walked into the room carrying two large brass candlesticks.

Monsieur le maréchal, I said mentally, not a little taken aback and looking in amazement from the attendant to the frock-coated gentleman by my side. I have been talking to a Marshal of France? Heavens above! But who was he? It wasn't Foch, Joffre, or Pétain. Who could he be? That hair combed in pompadour style, that upturned moustache, where, who? Ah, I had it: the old gentleman had spoken of Morocco; he could therefore be no one else but Lyautey, the builder of the Moroccan empire, one of the great colonizers of our time. Lyautey Africanus, the newspapers called him occasionally, bestowing upon him the title the old Romans gave to their conquering consuls: Scipio Africanus, Drusus Germanicus. . . .

Quickly I apologized for not having recognized His Excellency.

The storm was growing to tornado proportions, and since the Marshal showed no inclination of trusting his eyesight to the uncertain flicker of candles, we remained standing by the window and talked of the political situation in Morocco, and of the colonization work both there and in Tripoli and Palestine. M. Lyautey thought the Jewish reclamation scheme in the Holy Land an amazing performance and well worth watching. "Strange," he said, "how that old civilization of the Jews seems to be coming to life again. . . . There has been nothing in Palestine since the days of Christ. . . . What the Crusaders built, the Arabs and Turks destroyed. . . . Yes the Turks especially," he went on. "Once they poured westward and came near overrunning Europe, then they started to play checkers in Granada and Cairo and Baghdad and Jerusalem, and they forgot about the world. . . . They didn't deserve anything else but to be booted back into the hills of Anatolia. . . . *Et pourtant*, the Turk, too, driven back to his native habitat, seems to be getting a grip on himself once more. . . . *C'est un grand homme*, Kemal

Pasha. . . . He has put the Turks to work. . . . It's amazing when you come to think of it, all these nations coming back to life in Asia Minor! That whole area in the Hither East is in process of reconstruction: the Turks in Ankara, we in Syria, the Egyptians, the Jews in Palestine. . . . The Turks have even cast out the Arabic script and replaced it with an alphabet of their own, and the Jews, I am told, are speaking Hebrew once more. . . . Those are signs of life. . . . A language that was consigned to the petrification of liturgy coming back to life. . . . I wonder if Signor Mussolini will try to revive Latin. . . . That would be *épatant*. He should, to keep Rome abreast of Jerusalem. The Jews have taken up where they were interrupted by Titus in the beginning of the Christian era. . . . An amazing phenomenon!"

He was speaking calmly, but in crisp, unfinished sentences in the manner frequently affected by many military men. I noticed that the corner of his mouth was twitching nervously, and that he would suddenly draw up his left shoulder in a quick spasmodic gesture. Both these afflictions were remnants, no doubt, of an attack of infantile paralysis which also caused the Marshal's spine to grow crooked, so that he was obliged to wear a steel corset all his life. We stood in silence for a few moments. But the Marshal's reference to the days of Christ had given me an idea. I hesitated a moment, debating in my mind whether to put the question, and then I suddenly blurted it out:

"*Monsieur le maréchal*," I said, "you were the proconsul of the French Republic in Morocco as Pontius Pilate was the proconsul of Rome in Judea. How would Your Excellency, if I may ask, have dealt with a man like Jesus?"

"Ah," he chuckled, "that's an interesting question! I have thought of it myself sometimes. There is indeed a certain analogy in our positions, and I can tell you at once that Pilate, to my way of thinking, acted correctly as Roman proconsul, when he apprehended the Galilean. His task was to maintain the Pax Romana. What else could he do but put Jesus out of the way, the man who threatened law and order? It has always seemed strange to me that Pilate waited three full years before he had Him arrested. There must have been something wrong with the proconsul's intelligence service, or else the Gospels must have greatly exaggerated the stir Jesus created in the country. . . . Jesus had gone up and down the country talking and preaching and agitating. . . . Any man who can gather a crowd in the East should be watched—that has always been my view. During my term as *résident-général* in Morocco I was always kept informed of what those itinerant mullahs and ulemas and holy men were telling the people. Most of the time they were harmless individuals, perfectly innocuous, some of them are mere doddering idiots. . . . But look you, there is a little mullah born every minute. One of them may have the fire of a Mohammed and become the prophet of an idea. Such a one was Jesus. Unquestionably, a Roman governor in Judea could not tolerate a man who told the people things like this: 'Ye know that in this world the princes and mighty ones have authority, but in the Kingdom which I bring it shall not be so.' That's dangerous speech. . . . That's inflammatory, especially in the inflammatory East. . . . A fellow who talks like that should be watched carefully!"

"But Jesus also urged," I ventured to interrupt, "that the people give unto Caesar what was Caesar's."

"Did He?" snorted the Marshal. "Did He now, *parbleu*? Are you sure of that? I tell you I do not interpret that text as do the theologians. Jesus asked to be shown a coin, and, pointing to the imperial effigy, he said, 'Whose likeness is that?' 'That's Caesar's likeness,' they told Him. 'Well then, give it to him! Let Caesar have his coin. And be done with it!' *A mon avis*, Jesus replied contemptuously to that question as if he wanted to say, 'Leave me alone with your bosh about Caesar.' No, you may be sure of it: in that Kingdom of which Jesus dreamed and spoke there was no room for Caesar, or for Pilate, or for the princes and mighty ones. The whole Roman Empire was anathema to Him. What did the first Christians say when the Empire collapsed? 'She is fallen!' they shouted. 'She is fallen, the great whore, Babylon!' That's what they called Rome, those Galileans and their spiritual descendants. To them Rome was *la grande putain* with whom the kings of the earth had fornicated and who had fed on the blood of the saints. . . . The Christians rejoiced. They were happy about it. . . . They saw the reality of a destruction of which Jesus had only dreamed. . . . For He was first and foremost a nationalist Jew, this Jesus, a nationalist Jew with a religious idea, the archetype of a revolutionary, far more dangerous than a mere agitator of sedition. If Jesus' ideas had been translated into reality, not only in Judea, but in the world at large, there would be an entirely different story to tell, I dare say," chuckled the Marshal. "I do not think *nous autres Français*, we would be in Morocco

now, or the British in India. That is, if Jesus had realized His dreams.
. . . Fortunately Saint Paul came along later and effectively destroyed the revolutionary ferment in Christianity. Saint Paul made
Christianity respectable and acceptable to decent people instead of
a call to slaves and rabble. . . . But Jesus, ah, He, I believe, He was
just removed in time. . . .

"Imagine the situation in Judea in Pilate's days. It had been a bad
province for Rome ever since the conquest by Pompey. Little Judea
gave Rome more trouble than Gaul. The empire had to keep its
best legions in garrison there, legions that were sorely needed elsewhere: Batavi, Nervi, and Celts. The Jews were a restless crowd.
They had never, you might say, never, you hear, disarmed morally.
They had flown into the face of Assyria and Babylon and Egypt,
pitched themselves insanely against those mighty empires. They
had watched these colossi topple into the abyss of history . . . They
were waiting now for a chance to throw off the Roman yoke. They
were fanatical patriots. We sometimes talk of the Jews as a people
without a country, a people of Nomadic wanderers, but we forget
that the Jews defended their land with a heroism and desperation
seldom witnessed anywhere else. They never resigned themselves as
the Greeks did, for instance, to the loss of their national independence. Why, the very presence of Pilate in their holy city was a provocation to them. They had made him keep the emblems and banners
of the empire outside the city. Think of it, keeping the sacred
eagles of Rome from a conquered city! They would have thrown
themselves against Pilate's legions with their bare hands, had the
governor dared to set up an altar to Caesar in the temple courts, or
in the gardens around the Jahvistic sanctuary. . . . They were always on the verge of revolt. . . .

"Passover was the critical time of the year. That was the feast
when the Jews commemorated their liberation from the slavery in
Egypt. The city was filled with pilgrims, shepherds, peasants, fishermen, all of them burning with a mortal hatred for the Roman overlord and imbued with an expectation of a Messianic deliverer to restore their national freedom and independence. They awaited some
descendant of the House of David who would shatter the bonds of
foreign tutelage and crush the foes of Israel. Do you think Pilate
did not know all this? Believe me, he did. He had come specially to
the Holy City from some resort on the Mediterranean to be on
hand if trouble should start. . . . He knew what was up. . . . The

taverns in Jerusalem were filled with crowds of men who would have needed but one signal to storm the Antonia Citadel and massacre the Roman garrison. . . . Jewish women were out in the streets, shopping for the holy days. . . . Black-eyed damsels, powdered and perfumed, who swayed their hips sensuously under their thin linen garments as they walked through the bazaar. Can you see them? *Ah, mon Dieu,* what a show! *Quel cadre!* Can you imagine what would have happened if one of the these Germanic legionaries idling there in the sunshine near David's Tower, had suddenly made a suggestive gesture to one of these daughters of Zion in sight of those fierce Galilean fishermen? Can you? I can! There would have been a general assault! That is the way revolts start. An incident, *une bagatelle,* was needed in Jerusalem, a spark to set off a powder magazine. Believe me, Pontius Pilate was in an unenviable position. The peace of Judea—what do I say?—the peace of the world was at the mercy of an incident. Jerusalem was a seething cauldron. Judas Maccabaeus was dead, but his spirit lived on in a hundred thousand determined men. The mountains of Moab swarmed with bands of patriotic exiles. Ordinarily, these men roamed about in the desert regions, out of reach of the Roman patrols. But on the high holy day they filtered into the national capital to mix with the festive crowds, as the outlaws do to this very day in Morocco, when they come to the fairs of Marrakech and Fez and Meknes. These partisans met in the back rooms of caravanserais. They drank. They sang songs. Fists were clenched as the red wine mounted to their heads. They stamped their staffs on the floor. They were ready. They were willing to go out and fight. Now or never! Deliver the blow that would shake the imperial authority. But a few years ago we saw how such things are done, when the chiefs of the Djebel Druses sneaked into the city of Damascus to meet with the leaders of all the subversive anti-French secret societies in the metropolis. In one day we had a first-class revolt on our hands which cost us tens of thousands of men. Fortunately, a certain group of Syrian patriots co-operated with us by warning the authorities of the storm that was brewing, else we would have been taken entirely unaware and the disaster would have been incalculable.

"Such a group was the aristocratic sacerdotal party in Jerusalem. They wanted peace and quiet. They had a more realistic view of the position of their country than the overexcited revolutionary enthusiasts of the open spaces. They knew that the Roman imperium would not tolerate chaos because it could not afford a continual center of disturbance on the main highway between Persia and Egypt, and that, in the event of a major disturbance, Rome was determined to wipe out the Jewish state, be done with the Jewish people once and for all. I doubt not," went on the Marshal, "that Pontius Pilate was awaiting an opportunity to strike that blow for the peace of the world which history reserved for Titus Vespasianus. Here and there in the Gospel narrative, a sentence or two shows us what was really going on in that period of tension between the Jewish nation and the Roman imperium. The priests, it is reported, argued that it were better that one man should die than that the whole nation perish. Those priests knew what was in the air. They realized that Pilate would show no mercy if a revolt broke out. The memory of the Babylonian exile was very vivid. The members of the sacerdotal party saw the danger of a repetition—and worse.

"If it was they who quietly informed Pilate of the arrival in Jerusalem of the party of Galilean fishermen with that fanatic visionary at their head, they performed an act of the highest patriotism. Jesus had come to Jerusalem to make trouble. His own words can be cited in support of that. He had permitted His followers to stage a sumptuous reception in which He rode into the city seated on an ass, an honor that was reserved for the ancient kings of Israel. There was no mistaking His intention. He was confident that the trick could be turned. He believed God was on His side. They always do, these would-be deliverers. A few days later, when He paid for His foolhardiness on the cross, He reproached God for abandoning Him in the supreme hour. . . .

"Ah, no question, Jesus was a dangerous character. He had picked His friends amongst the plebeians. . . . He was always in the company of publicans, slaves and loose women; in short, He recruited his followers, like Spartacus in Rome, amongst an element that has been most prone to revolt at all times of history. When Pilate's spies brought him news of the presence of the itinerant exhorter, who talked of founding a new kingdom, the governor had no other course but to arrest Jesus. *Raisons d'état* demanded that short shrift be made with an agitator of that sort. 'Are you a king?' asked Pilate when he questioned Jesus. And what was the answer? Did he deny it? No, the Galilean carpenter replied in the affirmative. *C'était un peu ridicule tout de même*, but it was sufficient. Pilate sent Him away to be crucified. What else could he do?"

"But the Gospels say that the Jews demanded his crucifixion," I ventured.

"The Gospels? *Ah, mon cher monsieur*, did you ever consider who wrote those books? Were they not composed by missionaries, *c'est-à-dire* by propagandists, who sought to win the sympathy of the Roman populace for their creed of a man-god? Would it have been politic to put the blame for the death of a god on the shoulders of the prospective converts' compatriot? Was it not infinitely more expedient to fix the guilt on the Jews, who had always been enemies of Rome?"

"Then Your Excellency is of the opinion that Pilate was justified in putting Jesus to death?" I asked.

"Positively," came back Marshal Lyautey.

"Your Excellency would have acted in the same way under the circumstances?"

"*Parbleu*, no! I would not have waited till He had infected the crowds in the capital with his seditious poison. I would have had Him put before the firing squad in his home province, up north in Galilee."[4]

The most distressful aspects of war are not the great calamities which occur within sight of all the world: battles wherein thousands of lives are blotted out in a few hours' time, or the laying waste of homes, forcing terror-stricken and suddenly impoverished inhabitants to flee pell-mell and take the road of exile; but rather, the secret sorrows which gnaw at the hearts of men for years after, because of the futile, the senseless, and the unnecessary waste of beloved lives. Of one such an unexpected phase of war's inhuman cruelty I did not learn till many years after the cessation of hostilities, and then only by accident. At the Sorbonne, where I followed a course in Biblical exegesis, I made the acquaintance of several young Huguenots, pastors and theological students, who had made the resolve, on religious grounds, to refuse military service, in spite of the fact that conscientious objection is punishable in France, even in peacetime, with solitary confinement in one of those medieval dungeons that still serve as prisons in the twentieth century. In the course of the winter of 1926-27, I attended the trials of these men

[4] My interview with Marshal Lyautey was first published in *The Virginia Quarterly Review*, fall issue, 1931.

before the military court in the gloomy Prison du Cherche-Midi, where, it will be recalled, Alfred Dreyfus was incarcerated before his transfer to Devil's Island.

Situated on the Boulevard Raspail, which is one of the chief arteries of traffic on the Left Bank, the Cherche-Midi jail has retained so much of the medieval atmosphere that it was like stepping into another world when you entered it. I have always had a sinister dread of prisons. I could not pass by the Federal Penitentiary in Atlanta, when I lived in that city, the Loublianka in Moscow, or the Regina Coeli in Rome, without experiencing a feeling of almost physical nausea. The accumulation of suffering inside those places, where human beings are locked up in cages of cement and steel, seemed to be a living thing which penetrated the thick, soundproof walls. But the spectacle of those Huguenots walking around in a circle for their daily "recreation," just as Vincent van Gogh has pictured it in one of his immortal paintings, filled me with a loathing for modern society. At the same time, the fundamental helplessness of the state, which combats every revolt of the human spirit with violence, did not escape me either. In spite of their chains, I saw that those pale-faced young Huguenots were stronger than all the armed forces of France and that, intrinsically, the military machine was impotent against the spirit.

My regular visits to the Cherche-Midi made me aware of something else going on in that living tomb. I had noticed that nearly every afternoon small groups of elderly peasants and *petits bourgeois* would gather in front of the guarded gates to wait for the hour of two. Many times I had wondered what they were doing there, but one day, overcoming my reluctance to speak to perfect strangers, I learned from one man standing in the line-up before the prison gate that under pressure of several pacifist organizations, and one association of disabled veterans, the government had ordered the reconsideration by civil courts of scores of sentences pronounced during the war by courts-martial at the front. The peasants I saw in front of the Cherche-Midi were the parents and relatives of soldiers who had been shot for having been cowards in the face of the enemy. They had come in the hope of hearing their dead children and brothers vindicated in the eyes of the law.

In the matter of those revisionary trials in 1926 and the following years, it was difficult to understand the acquiescence of the general staff in permitting hundreds of these cases to come to public notice.

Men had been executed at the front, merely "to set an example." For it soon became clear, as those revisions proceeded, that most of the executed men had not been done away with because they had actually failed in their duty. In many cases the death sentence had been imposed merely "because expiatory victims were needed to hide the terrible blunders of the generals in charge of operations." Of course, the respectable press in Paris never breathed a whisper of these amazing revelations which were being made almost daily in the courtrooms of the Cherche-Midi. Foreign correspondents kept a discreet silence. It does not pay to incur the displeasure of the military clique in France. There may be disagreeable consequences later on. I cabled a synopsis of three of the trials to a syndicate which served thirty-odd American newspapers. But not a single paper published the reports. The evidence "seemed incredible" to my employers.

To this day, the general public in France remains unaware of the fact that thousands of Frenchmen were shot down by their comrades during the war, without a single serious charge being leveled against them. Many were executed on being designated by lot, or by pure chance.

Take, for example, the case of one Lucien Bersot, a middle-aged peasant who served in the 60th Regiment of Infantry. His retrial was one of those held in the Cherche-Midi. The periodical *Crapouillot* was the only publication in Paris that gave a résumé of the court proceedings. It was established that one day, in the winter of 1915-16, Bersot had asked his corporal for a pair of cloth trousers because it was extremely cold, and whereas all his comrades were warmly dressed, he alone in the company wore a tattered pair of cotton slacks. The corporal took Bersot behind a field hospital, and, picking up a pair of trousers which had just been pulled off a dead man, told him to put on the garment. Bersot took the trousers and held them up for inspection. Clots of blood dropped from the legs.

"That poilu must have lost his guts entirely," remarked Bersot, referring to the garment's former owner. "No, I don't want it, I don't want that stinking thing."

An officer, Lieutenant André, happened to pass by at that moment. "What's going on here?" inquired the superior.

"This man asked for a pair of trousers," replied the corporal. "I gave him a pair and he refuses to put them on!"

"Refuses?" scowled the officer. "Refuses an order? Quick, my man, put on that pair of pants, *quick*, do you hear?"

"*Mais, mon lieutenant*, the thing is soaking wet with blood."

"Put on those trousers, as I tell you!"

"You put them on yourself and see how you like it," laughed Bersot. "A French citizen does not need to walk around in a dead man's shit!"

"Eight days' arrest," barked Lieutenant André, "for refusal to obey!"

"*Ça va!*" Bersot shrugged his shoulders, "but I keep my old slacks."

The Colonel of the 60th Regiment saw the report a few days later. "That's mutiny," he declared. "Those fellows are getting out of hand. Call a court-martial at once. I will set an example of discipline!"

All this was put in evidence at the retrial in the Cherche-Midi. The company, witnesses recalled, was thrown into consternation by the Colonel's decision. Two soldiers, Dumoulin and Cottet, went to see Lieutenant André to ask him to modify his charge. M. Perruche de Velna, who had been recorder at Bersot's court-martial at the front, continued the story at the retrial. "It was the twelfth of January, 1916. We were near the château of Mardançons on the left bank of the Aisne. Colonel Auroux summoned me to headquarters and said: 'Sergeant, I asked you to come because I am faced with an open rebellion. I must set some examples. I must kill one or two of these fellows. Of course, I expect to observe the rules, that's understood. You are recorder of the permanent court-martial of the division, you are a magistrate in civil life. Well, you know what I want. I need a formula. Find it!'

"The Colonel handed me Bersot's file," went on M. de Velna. "There was nothing in it but a sheet of paper: Lieutenant André's report of the incident behind the field hospital. At the end of this report André had written that Bersot's comrades had asked him for leniency.

"'You see,' exclaimed the Colonel, 'just as I told you: open rebellion by the men, refusal to obey on the part of Bersot.'

"I drew the Colonel's attention very respectfully to the fact that if Bersot's comrades had made a mistake (for it is against military regulations to make a collective complaint), this certainly did not amount to rebellion. Insofar as Bersot was concerned, it was impossible to charge him with disobedience. Before a charge of refusal to obey can be laid against a man, a service order must be issued. I told the Colonel that he was going too far when he demanded a death sentence for a man's refusal to put on a pair of dirty trousers.

" 'All right,' answered the Colonel, 'let the others be charged with an infraction of the regulations, but Bersot shall be charged with refusal to carry out orders in the presence of the enemy. Draw up an order of accusation in that sense. After all, it is I who command here! Moreover,' he added, 'I am going to preside over the court myself.'

"At these words," continued the recorder, "I could not conceal my amazement.

"Surely, you are not thinking of anything as drastic as that? You are the prosecutor in this case: you cannot at the same time sit in judgment. Neither in civil law nor in military law can one and the same person be judge and accuser!"

" 'I am going to preside,' were the Colonel's only words."

The session of the court-martial was held a few minutes later in a dugout. The three judges were Colonel Auroux, his private secretary, the regimental sergeant major, and one of the other officers. Of the two soldiers who had spoken up for Bersot, one was acquitted, the other sentenced to hard labor for life.

Bersot was sentenced to death for disobedience in the name of the sovereign people of France.

At dawn the next morning the poor man was taken from his cell by the padre. He wept quietly and mumbled, "But this is not possible, I must be dreaming. For a pair of dirty pants, *non, c'est pas possible. . . .* This must be a joke. . . . A thing like that is impossible in France."

"The impossible sometimes happens in military matters," added M. de Velna in his testimony. "The justice of the military tribunal is not like ours."

Bersot was taken a few hundred yards up the road and led into a farm courtyard. The Colonel had arrived before. He was freshly shaven and dressed in his best uniform. Bersot's eyes were bandaged and his hands tied behind his back. When the Colonel gave the order to the firing squad to take aim, the condemned man screamed: "Marie Louise! Marie Louise!"

"That was his only child," M. de Velna explained.

The Special Court of Retrial in the Cherche-Midi in pronouncing sentence in this case declared: "Whereas on the one hand, Colonel

Auroux had signed the order of inculpation and yet presided at the session of the court-martial, and whereas, on the other hand, the order given to Bersot was not a service order for the accomplishment of a military duty, the sentence of the court-martial is hereby annulled."

Madame Bersot, who had been present at the trial of revision, and who had addressed a letter to the public press telling of the years she had been the object of disdain in the Breton village where she resided as "the widow of a traitor," decided to press charges against Colonel Auroux. However, the Minister of War, André Maginot, the builder of the Maginot Line, had the charges quashed. Further, he decorated Colonel Auroux with the cravat of a commander of the Legion of Honor.

A few days after this pathetic incident came to light, *Crapouillot* reported how, at another retrial, held in Metz, an ex-officer had calmly declared in court that General Reveilhac, on March 7, 1915, had ordered his artillery to take under fire a trench full of French soldiers, merely because their company had been thrown back the previous day, when they launched an attack on the German position at Souay. When the artillery commander refused to carry out this murderous instruction, without a signed order from Reveilhac, the General compromised. He demanded the names of any four corporals and any eighteen men belonging to the company, and ordered them sent out into no man's land to cut the barbed wire in plain daylight. The General obviously expected a protest on the part of the soldiers designated, and a refusal to carry out the insane order. But there was no refusal. The men went out, and were, of course, immediately taken under fire by a dozen German machine guns. They threw themselves into the shell holes and did not move until nightfall, when they cut the wires and returned to the trenches. The next day all were up for court-martial, on the charge of having displayed cowardice in the presence of the enemy. The four corporals were executed. Two of them were only wounded by the first salvo of the execution squad. The officer commanding the squad had just given these two wounded men the *coup de grâce* with his service revolver when Reveilhac's order arrived, calling off the execution.

The revisional court rehabilitated the men. A monument was elevated to their memory at Sartilly, in the Department of the Manche, but M. Raymond Poincaré, the President of France, who for the seven years of his tenure of office unveiled a monument to the dead every Sunday, did not unveil this one. Poincaré made General Reveil-hac, who was the owner of a château and of a rich winegrowing estate in the South, a grand officer of the Legion of Honor.

Then there was the *affaire* of Flirey, which came up for revision on July 24, 1929, before the special court. It was but one of the endless number of retrials going on all over France. In this case, a company of infantry, belonging to the 45th Brigade, appeared to have grumbled against an order to attack, after digging trenches during forty-eight hours in a torrential rain. All the surviving witnesses were unanimous in declaring that there was not a dry cartridge in the company. "Every man," said one witness, "was a ball of mud with a rifle sticking out." The artillery had not cut the barbed wire, so that it was obvious that the attacking column would be compelled to flatten out immediately after going over the top. Three hundred and fifty corpses still lay in the trench to remind the men what had happened three days earlier when their company had tried to attack from the same spot. However, the grumbling of the men had nothing to do with the order to make a new attempt. The order seemed unfair to the troops because it was not their turn to attack. Companies attacked in rotation. They were of the fifth company; the eighth was due to go into fire. The officers sought to calm the men by saying that the engagement was of no significance and that they would be relieved the following morning.

"It isn't fair, it isn't our turn," said the men of the fifth company when the zero hour arrived. However, they started up the storm ladders when the order to go forward was given. A blast of machine-gun fire cut from across no man's land at the sight of the first French steel helmets above the parapets. The French attack was held in check.

In reporting the maneuver, the Colonel informed the divisional commander that the fifth company had refused to follow its officers. The divisional commander's first reaction was to order the entire company executed by machine guns. Upon the supplication of colleagues, the general, a certain Delatoile, consented to execute only a certain number of men "to set an example." A discussion followed between the commanders as to how many. Delatoile first asked for "seventy-five heads." His colleagues cut him down to twenty.

Finally, after an hour of haggling, he declared himself content with six victims.

Lots were drawn for the six men who had to face a divisional court-martial. The first man to be questioned was Corporal Morange. He admitted frankly that he had not climbed over the top because it wasn't his company's turn. The second man, Coulon, affirmed that he had climbed into no man's land, but noticing the hail of bullets, and the fact that he was not being followed, he had slid back into the trench. The session was therewith suspended. The majority of the court was for acquittal.

During the few minutes of intermission, the defending advocate, a Lieutenant Minot, counseled the four other accused to repeat what Coulon had said. But those peasants refused to lie. "We have sworn to tell the whole truth," they informed their defender, "and we will." Upon a resumption of the session they assured the court they had always done their duty, but that this time they could not obey because it was not the company's turn.

The session was declared closed without a decision having been reached. The next day at dawn, however, the padre was sent to inform the six that they were going to be executed. "But this is a crime!" exclaimed Lieutenant Minot, the counsel for the defense. "The court-martial has not even pronounced a sentence!"

What had happened? In the night the divisional commander had had an interview with Joffre. Joffre, as usual, had recommended the utmost severity. The old generalissimo, whom the newspapers called "grandpa," was a firm believer in the system of "decimation" as a purely disciplinary measure to keep an army well in hand. This view was shared by the Italian Commander in Chief Cadorna: "If there is grumbling amongst the troops, have every tenth man step out of the ranks and put him before a firing squad."

The six soldiers were led to the execution field. The death squad was picked from a regiment of young recruits who had just arrived at the front. "When the news of the decision that they must die reached the six men, they were first struck speechless with emotion, but soon they were calling the names of their wives, their mothers, their children," stated *Crapouillot*, the only newspaper which published in detail the evidence submitted at the retrials.

One of the condemned men, Morange, died with the photograph of his wife and children in his hands. Another, Prevost, called out to the boys who leveled their rifles at his breast: "Now you are going to see how a French soldier dies," and he tore the bandage off his eyes. At the trial of revision, the court, after hearing all the evidence, declared that all of the six executed men were brave and disciplined soldiers, "the very glory of the regiment." The poilus of Flirey were rehabilitated. They, too, have a monument now.

For weeks, for months, for years, in every departmental courthouse, these investigations into the validity of the wartime courts-martial continued, always ending with the same sad result: innocent men had been assassinated on the slightest whim of superior officers who, in the majority of cases, were not front-line soldiers themselves.

The accumulating evidence became so fantastic that at last the press took notice of the trials, and the liberal newspaper *Oeuvre* exclaimed: "But where are the men whom Justice never disturbs, but whose remorse, nevertheless, should not let them sleep in peace?"

I will cite one more case, as reported by *Crapouillot* in its issue of August, 1934.

"On June 1, 1916, the 347th Infantry Regiment was 'in rest' behind the lines, in the region of Verdun. On the 3rd, the regiment marched into the line in the Thiaumont sector. A certain Lieutenant Herduin, a former colonial officer, bearer of the highest distinctions for bravery, the Military Medal and the War Cross, commanded the 17th company of the 5th battalion.

"On the 7th of June, the enemy started a bombardment which went on uninterruptedly for twenty-four hours. At eight o'clock on the morning of the 10th, a German attack was launched with extreme violence, two Bavarian divisions and one division of the Prussian Guard leading off. Colonel Lamirault was killed, Major Deverre taken prisoner. Only remnants of the 17th and the 19th companies hung on grimly to the French line.

"After a new barrage fire, Lieutenants Herduin and Milan and three hundred and fifty men, the sole survivors of two battalions still fought on. . . .

"At noon, however, the French artillery took its own lines under fire and sent a shower of high explosive into what remained of the 5th battalion. Signals were sent up, the range was corrected, but the situation had become critical, the communication with the rear had been cut, confusion reigned supreme.

"At 3 o'clock, Herduin tried to obtain reinforcements and addressed himself to the officer commanding the unit on his left: the

293rd Infantry Regiment. 'Take back the terrain lost by your division,' was the reply he received.

"At ten o'clock in the evening munitions ran out. The two surviving officers held a rapid council of war. What remained to be done? Surrender with the forty-two survivors or try to fall back? They agreed on the second alternative. But can retreat be interpreted as an abandonment of a post in the face of the enemy? The military law is precise on this point: whoever abandons his post without having carried out orders . . .

"Still no order had been given to resist until death. If all those who retreated in the Great War were to be guilty of abandonment of post, there would not remain many without sin in the French or in the German armies.

"The survivors marched back to Verdun and presented themselves to the commander of the Anthouar armory. Herduin wrote to his wife: 'Our division is finished, mowed down. . . . The regiment is annihilated. . . . I lived through five horrible days. . . . I looked death into the eyes every minute. I will tell you the details later. . . . I am the only officer left in my company. I am now in the rear of the line. Five days without food or drink, wallowing in mud under shrapnel. What a miracle that I am still alive!'

"On the evening of the 10th, Herduin learned that what was left of the 6th battalion had been reformed in the forest of Fleury. Followed by the handful of men, whom they had snatched from death, the two officers started out in the middle of the night to rejoin the sister battalion. The survivors were happy. They found many of their comrades whom they believed dead.

"But the faces of the poilus they met were somber and anxious. A brigade order had arrived that morning at the headquarters of the 6th battalion. Captain Delaruelle, its commander, carried it in his pocket. This officer, gulping down his emotion, finally gathered courage to tell two of his comrades what was in store for them.

"Captain Delaruelle had an order to have Lieutenants Herduin and Milan shot immediately!

"Herduin laughed: there must be an error. He was sure of his rights. He demanded to see the general commanding the brigade.

"Delaruelle granted the request at once. The orderly of a certain Lieutenant de Saint-Romain, a personal friend of Herduin, was sent off with a letter written by Herduin in which he asked for an interview.

"The brigade commander did not even open the letter and wrote on the envelope: "No idle talk. Immediate execution!"

"The two officers were lost. Herduin wrote a last letter to his wife. It was amongst the evidence submitted to the revisional court:

My ADORED LITTLE WIFE,

We have suffered a defeat, as I told you. My whole battalion has been wiped out by the Boches except myself and a few men. I am now reproached for having escaped. The brigade commander calls me a coward, as if with forty men I could have held out where a thousand would have been necessary. Well, I must accept my fate. I have nothing to be ashamed of. My comrades know I am not a coward. Before dying I am thinking of you, my dear Fernande, and of our little Luke. Insist that you get my pension. You have a right to it. My conscience is clear. I myself will command the soldiers of the firing squad to fire. They are weeping. I kiss you for the last time and I tell you: cry as loud as you can against military justice after my death. Those higher up always look for victims to get out of a scrape themselves. I kiss you once again and my beloved son, who will not have to blush for his father. I have done my full duty. De Saint-Romain is with me in my last moments. I have spoken with the Abbé Heintz before dying. One last kiss, my angel. I send you a kiss from Eternity. My hand is steady. My conscience is clear. I will be buried in the forest of Fleury to the north of Verdun. De Saint-Romain will give you all the details.

"At three o'clock the two lieutenants were led to the place of execution. The soldiers of the squad were pale as death. The regimental doctor refused to be present at the execution. He had locked himself up in his dugout. The condemned marched with a firm step. Until the very end they maintained their innocence. Captain Delaruelle read the fatal order with trembling voice.

"When nobody wanted to command the firing squad, Herduin threw down his helmet and took off his tunic. He bared his chest and detached a gold chain. 'This is for my son, later,' he said, and handed it to De Saint-Romain.

"Then addressing the men, he called out: 'My friends, we are charged with not having done our duty. It seems we did not hold out long enough. But I assure you we did our full duty. We did not deserve death. This will later be acknowledged. And now, you too, do your duty. Don't make us suffer. Aim straight at the heart. To my wife and my boy, good-by. Fire!'

"At the moment when the *coup de grâce* was administered, the order arrived that the execution was not to be carried out."

The Assize Court of Paris threw a full light on the Fleury affair. The widow of Herduin had lodged a charge of murder against the Brigadier General. *La Presse* published an article in defense of the commander, and Madame Herduin sued that newspaper for defamation. She won the case, but she had disquieted the government. The Minister of Justice, M. Louis Barthou, offered her one hundred thousand francs in a letter wherein he admitted that Herduin had been executed "by virtue of an erroneous application of the regulations." Herduin was finally "rehabilitated" and his "memory cleared of all dishonor" by the court of Colmar in 1926.

And so on and on and on. . . . Volumes could be filled with the agonizing evidence submitted before the courts of revision.

I have seen them buried one by one: Mangin, whom the people called "the Butcher of Verdun," Foch, Fayolle, Sarrail, Lyautey, Joffre, Franchet d'Esperey. They were followed to their graves by the kings of Europe, the cardinals of the Church, the diplomatic corps, the judiciary and the other old generals tottering on their feet.

One marshal remains: Pétain. I went to Verdun one day, the year before Hitler came to power. It was the anniversary of the Armistice, *le jour des morts*. Thousands of men, women, and children in mourning took the twenty-five special trains at the Gare de l'Est that morning to go and pray on the graves for the peace of the souls of their beloved.

On the blood-soaked hills near Douaumont, where the ossuary now stands, and where, up till 1932, each day ten cartloads of skulls and bones were collected, a German pilgrimage of several hundreds of men and women walked about. They were Lutherans, for they sang one of the old hymns of the Reformation. In the distance we could see the foreign visitors go down on their knees and raise their hands to heaven, while the words of their solemn oath drifted over to us, rumbling like the breakers on the shore: *"Nie wieder Krieg! Nie wieder Krieg!* Never Again War!" And then the other thousands of French women and children also fell to their knees and sobbed.

A few moments later I saw Marshal Pétain come along at the head of an official party, a little procession of gorgeous uniforms, frock coats, gold braid and dazzling decorations. He stopped by the side of a woman whose hands tightly grasped a wooden cross. She lifted her tortured face to him. The Marshal read the inscription on the cross.

"Was he your husband?" he inquired kindly of the woman.

"He was my only son, Monsieur."

"Ah, what a pity! I am deeply sorry for you. But never forget, your son was a hero. . . . He died for France. . . . He was one of the 'artisans of our victory.' If there is peace today, we owe it to them. It is men like your son who gave France back its smile and Alsace-Lorraine."

"You can have Alsace-Lorraine, Monsieur," said the woman, "but give me back my child!"

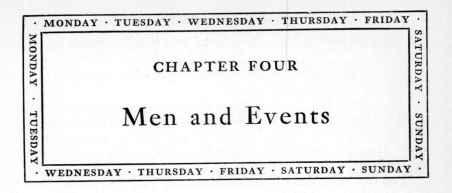
No RESTRICTIONS had been placed on my movements; I had virtually the entire Continent for my parish. Upon leaving for Europe, Mr. Ralph Pulitzer had given me letters of introduction to *The World*'s correspondents in Paris, Rome, London and Moscow, asking them to place the facilities of the bureaus under their direction at my disposal whenever I should make an appearance in their cities. I was not to send spot news, except on occasions when I would be definitely assigned to "cover" events, as happened later in the case of the Druse revolt, the Arabic uprising in Palestine in 1929, the British elections a year later, and other incidents. My real job was to complement the factual dispatches sent by the regular correspondents with a marginal story of background, milieu and, above all, "the human interest" element. In addition, I wrote my daily column "World's Window" for the editorial page of *The Evening World*, and a score of other American newspapers such as the Albany *Knickerbocker Press*, *The Atlanta Constitution*, the Boston *Globe*, *The Syracuse Herald*, *The Pittsburgh Sun*. . . .

That column was chiefly composed of what European journalists call *Kaffee-Klatsch*; I followed no definite line of thought, not even liberal. A scrap of conversation with a prime minister or a peasant, the election of a gypsy king, a sunset over the Zuider Zee, the execution of a bandit on the guillotine, a service in Rome's St. Peter's, anecdotes about the great, the famous, the renowned and the notorious—such were its usual contents.

Since I could not afford to be excluded from a single European country with so general an assignment, it was to my interest to remain on the good side of all the nascent censorships in Europe. Hence, many things I investigated or saw remained unreported.

For example, in 1928, when I accompanied Henri Barbusse on a trip of investigation in the Balkans, where he had gone to study the methods of the reactionary governments of Rumania and Bulgaria in suppressing popular movements—twelve thousand peasants and workers had been slain in Bulgaria alone that year—I could not send out a word. The police dogged our every footstep. After spending a day wandering around in the subterranean caves of the Doftana prison of Bucharest, watching people loaded down with chains, many of them reduced to hysterically idiotic skeletons, there was nothing that could be sent out but a yarn about the daring fashions worn by the women in the night clubs on the Calea Victoriei. That was the stuff expected of me. Nothing more, no delving into social conditions, no dishing up of unappetizing details about terrorism. The managing editor, Mr. John H. Tennant, warned me more than once that I had not been sent over on a crusading mission. He added, moreover, that there was no confirmation from any reliable source on that horrible business in Bulgaria. The local agency correspondents had not sent a word. So I, too, remained silent. It was the only policy. Correspondents like George Seldes, Samuel Spivak, David Darrah, Gedye, and myself discovered only too soon that if we did speak out, we did not last very long, either in the countries in which we were stationed or in our jobs. For when a correspondent is expelled from one country after the other, suspicion soon ripens that there is something wrong, not with the place he is forced to leave, but with himself. Gradually, as I grew somewhat more experienced, I found that I could "go the limit" in detailing my personal experience, so long as I placed the emphasis on myself. This fashion of reporting reached a downright ludicrous culmination with some newspapers which encouraged their correspondents to discourse at unlimited length on the style of hats or ties they wore, what their wives said when they returned from an assignment, or how much pocket money they were allowed by their generous employers. That was one way of diverting popular attention from the system that produces human misery as naturally as rotten cheese breeds maggots.

When I could not cry out in print about the events I saw, my blood boiled, and sometimes I would pitch in physically. I could never follow the sage advice of that veteran journalist, Arno Dosch-Fleurot, *The World*'s chief correspondent in France, who was somewhat of a mentor to me in my early days in Paris. He advised me to be simply "pro-story," and not bother about the rest. However, Fleurot did not follow that precious advice himself. He would grow livid with rage in the presence of the slightest injustice. I always forgot that my role was confined to that of a neutral observer and objective chronicler. I must say that it led me into an awful lot of trouble. In Jassy, coming from an interview with Professor George Cuza, I ran into a mob of students beating up a Jew, and succeeded in diverting their attention from their victim until the police intervened and escorted me to the station for my own safety's sake. In Russia, I ran around to the commissars' offices for a month, trying to get the man who had been my guide on a previous sight-seeing trip released from prison, until the GPU, in exasperation, finally took me to the border.

After fifteen years of this, I found myself a roving correspondent with hardly a country left to rove in. I was even expelled from France for a short time, until Léon Blum came to power and called me back. My first years were filled with going to and fro on the earth, wherever Mr. Tennant's fancy or that of subsequent employers directed me: to Beyrouth to see a casino opened by Pearl White in the deserted harem of a fugitive pasha; to Warsaw to dodge machine-gun bullets during Josef Pilsudki's "Putsch"; the antireligious activity in the Soviet Union; the white-slave traffic in Barcelona and Marseilles; mysterious apparitions in a rural community in Brittany; miracle-working rabbis in the snowy depths of Carpatho-Russia; the romance of Carol and Magda Lupescu; the signing of the Lateran Treaty; the inflation in Germany; the pilgrimages to Lourdes; the inauguration of the Dnieperstroy hydroelectric station; the finding of Roland's bones in Roncesvalles; a search for the ten lost tribes in the Arabian desert; the Anglo-Persian oil dispute; a visit to Oberammergau and to Therese Neumann, the girl on whose body appeared the divine stigmata on Good Friday; a revolt amongst the pearl divers of Hadhramaut on the South coast of Arabia; the co-operatives in Denmark; the appearance of a false Messiah in Hungary; the depredations of the *comitadjis* in Macedonia; the clandestine narcotic centers in Smyrna; the opening of Tutankhamen's tomb in the Valley of the Kings; the inauguration of the Vatican mint; Trotsky's arrival in France from Prinkipo; the mysterious death clouds in the Meuse valley near Liège; the filling-up of the Zuider Zee in Holland; the revolt of the Asturian miners; the bombardment of Damascus by Sarrail—all was grist for the mill and called for almost continuous travel by air, sea and overland by train and on foot.

There was scarcely a month that I could sit quietly at home and catch my breath. Barely had I returned from Ireland when I would receive a cable instructing me to proceed to Rumania or Russia. My luggage always stood packed, ready to move at a moment's notice, and I spent more nights in the carriages of the *grands expresses européens* and in distant cities than in the Rue St. André-des-Arts. The whole of Europe became a blur of station waiting rooms and hotel lobbies, and more than once I was unable to satisfy the curiosity of inquiring friends as to the picturesqueness or the strange sights of faraway cities I had visited. Circumstances often compelled me to rush about without looking or observing carefully what went on around me. For example, I have but a hazy recollection of Ankara and Smyrna, although I was in both places more than once. Only those impressions garnered in conversation with people remained. The words men spoke did not fade.

On looking back, it is curious to observe how my first interview with Herr Hitler back in 1928 was considered so unimportant that most newspaper members of the syndicate "buried it inside." Some prominent Jews in America to whose attention it was called dismissed it as a crude joke, and *Die Welt*, a Jewish newspaper in Vienna, denounced me as "a fantastic sensationalist." Nobody took Hitler seriously ten years ago. I did not myself. The man I saw in the Brown House in Munich impressed me so little that I came away from the interview mentally classifying *der Führer* as a crackbrained maniac with an *idée fixe*. Moeller van den Bruck, a Hollander in Hitler's entourage in those formative years of the Nazi movement, who wrote the final draft of *Mein Kampf* for him together with Gregor Strasser, and Horst Wessel, the composer of the song which became the marching tune of the victorious brownshirts, both of whom I knew in the *Nachtlokalen* of Berlin's Alexanderplatz, had given me a few hints on the great leader's private life. The company he kept was revealing: Roehm, who openly claimed "the German citizen's inalienable right to be a homosexual," and Goering, who was the much admired *pièce de résistance* in a crowd that staged the weirdest orgies at the house of Hanussen, the millionaire soothsayer. (Goering ordered Hanussen's assassination a week after coming to power.) These men were little calculated to inspire one with respect for the Fuehrer. It is not true, as Hitler's most intimate associates now proclaim, that they early recognized his almost divine qualities. Otto Strasser, who knew him better than anyone else, spoke to me with snarling contempt of *der Adolf* and of his frequent weeping jags. Goebbels, then only the upstart party's press chief, more than once had his tongue in his cheek when explaining some particularly incoherent passage in one of the Fuehrer's wild tirades. But he was unquestionably a spellbinder on the platform. Goering only succeeded in stirring up the crowd's amusement with his paunch and his lewd jokes; Goebbels was hated as a shifty and unreliable customer in the party itself. Hitler was the most useful as a propagandist because of his almost demoniacal vehemence, a quality the Germans mistake for sincerity. When he spoke, everything else was forgotten, even the unutterable contempt he expressed for the masses in his book. They hung on his lips, or rather, they seemed hypnotized by the dramatic act he put on, for even when he talked the rankest nonsense, you could hear a pin drop.

I recall one incident in 1932 which revealed not only the hold he had on the people, but also the manner in which it had been established. I had been assigned to follow the Fuehrer's propaganda campaign in the Rhineland, and followed him around from day to day, along with fifty or sixty domestic and foreign newspapermen, often trailing in the wake of the official motor caravan. One morning we left Elberfeld-Barmen shortly after lunch, Hitler's car leading off, with Bonn as our goal. We arrived there about six-thirty in the evening. The Fuehrer and his party went to the hotel for dinner. After taking some refreshment I drifted over to the hall where he was to make an address that evening. It was packed.

It was with difficulty that a Herculean usher elbowed himself up to the front to give me a seat at the press table. A band on the platform was playing *"Der Gute Kamerad," "Heil dir im Siegerkranz,"* and other patriotic songs. After about three quarters of an hour, a bald-headed Nazi mounted the rostrum and, after beckoning for silence, announced that the Fuehrer was being held up by a thunderstorm which had broken over the Rhine. He asked the crowd to be patient for a little while longer, and the band, amid general enthusiasm, struck up *"Die Wacht am Rhein."* When another half hour had passed and the Fuehrer had not put in an appearance, the same Nazi returned to the speaker's tribune and shouted that although the storm was redoubling in violence, Hitler had just telephoned from a village up the Rhine valley that he would be there in less than half an hour. "*Er kommt*," bellowed the announcer. "*Durch den Sturm*"—through the storm. Never will he disappoint us!"

Again the band struck up "The Good Comrade," and the crowd rose to its feet. When it had finally been worked up to a feverish pitch of expectancy, the Fuehrer, who had been sitting across the street all the time with his friends, walked in, dressed in his brown raincoat. He was splashed with water and mud from head to foot. The crowd was delirious and *sieg-heil*ed the unsmiling Fuehrer for five minutes. A middle-aged man, sitting in the front row near the press table, wiped the tears from his eyes and remarked to me, "*Alles tut er für das Deutsche Volk!*"—He does everything for the German people!

Yes, there lay the secret: not in Hitler, but in the German people. That people sordidly humiliated, without hope, reduced to starvation and poverty, with a youth feeling the frustration and futility of its existence, was ready for anything, any device, no matter how foolish or desperate, to throw off the chains of slavery imposed at Versailles. The German people had lost confidence in the parliamentary game and the methods employed by the diplomats to relieve the burden of Versailles when Hitler came along and behaved, as someone aptly said, "as a man with a cork leg throwing an epileptic fit on a tin roof."

The thing seemed incredible, without watching him perform; and I could easily understand why people, living thousands of miles from the spot, were inclined to dismiss the upstart party leader as a scatter-brained demagogue, a man who would never be taken seriously by a people as soberly analytical as the Germans.

In the course of that conversation in the Munich Brown House back in 1928, the Fuehrer revealed his intention of rearming the Reich, destroying the Soviet Union "to the applause of the whole civilized world," and reducing the Jews to the status of untouchables. "I promise," he said, bringing his fist down on the table, "that I will make life impossible for the Jews in Germany, and that I will not rest till I have destroyed the influence of the Jews in the whole of Europe—and in the world. Yes, I swear that the day will come when you in America will see the Jewish plutocrats stand with outstretched hands at the doors of the Christian churches begging for alms. They have been Germany's misfortune. They will pay dearly for their crimes!"

A little more interest was accorded the declaration of General Erich Ludendorff, who had just started to resurrect the pagan gods in 1928.

"*Sehen Sie*," said the Kaiser's quartermaster general, who graciously received me at his villa near Munich and who spoke to me, much to my inner amusement, as one Aryan to another, "the Jews are not our enemies because of their race, but because one of their subtlest rabbis, that man called Saint Paul, distilled the poison of the Christ myth out of the life story of Jesus of Nazareth. The Jews are the enemies of the Nordic race because they produced Christianity, which has been the poison that has destroyed the vitality of the Aryan peoples. Think of our Teutonic ancestors—the whole world was afraid of them! Rome launched its finest legions against the Rhine and Danube, but could never conquer the Germans. In the Hercynian Forest they hurled back the legions of Varus, who were the best-trained troops of the age and the conquerors of the Gauls, the Scyths, the Visigoths and the whole East. Against our defenses, the best Roman strategists could not prevail. One after the other, they went down to defeat. Unable to conquer the Germanic tribes by force of arms, Rome had recourse to a vile stratagem: it sent its missionaries up north. Trustful and kind as they were, our simple good-natured ancestors did not molest the tonsured strangers, such as Willibrord and Boniface. They received them with that hospitality for which the German race is famous, but which at the same time is one of its worst national faults. Incidentally, I would remind you," he went on, "that the Jews, Masons and Catholics used the same scurrilous tactics in defeating us in 1918, by having Marxist propagandists sap the German people's will to victory with pacifist propaganda, which is at bottom the same thing as Christianity.

"At any rate, what did the missionaries do?" resumed General Ludendorff. "They had a clearing made in the forest. They did not cut down the trees themselves. O, no, they did not soil their own delicate hands with hard labor. The kindhearted Germans did the work for them, and thus contributed to their own undoing. In the clearings the priests erected their altars. They donned their gorgeous vestments of gold and brocade and swung their golden censers. Then they genuflected and moved about with solemn gestures from the one side to the other, and intoned their strange Latin chants.

"You can imagine the amazement of those simple tribesmen," said the General. "The pomp and circumstance of the Latin service, it was like a vision from another world! They stared open-mouthed at the hocus-pocus. They were fascinated. They came under a magic spell. They were hypnotized, *bezaubert*, bamboozled, humbugged! The poison dripped into their pure souls by small drops, and has remained there ever since. The poison of a religion which taught men to turn the left cheek after the right had been struck.

"Of course, Jesus had nothing to do with this, you understand that," went on the General. "He was an Aryan himself, the son of a Batavian legionnaire named Pandor and of a certain Mary, probably an Arabic girl of easy morals who lived in a Syrian garrison town (*Dirne* was the word the General used). All this has been scientifically established. The real poisoner, as I said before, was Paul of Tarsus, the Apostle Paul if you wish, an epileptic fanatic, a man with a diseased body, a hunchback, probably a homosexual, with the fiendish mind of the pervert. His emissaries penetrated into Germany by a ruse, and began to talk to the Teutons of loving one's enemies, and of forgiveness and brotherliness. Sentimental and fundamentally good, our ancestors imbibed the alien doctrines. Germany was conquered and became the playball of Europe. They still sneer at us *dumme Deutsche*—stupid Germans—in the chancelleries of Europe. And we deserve it: for we Germans, sincere and frank as we are, *we* are the only ones who took Christianity seriously. We did not see that the evangelization of the Teutonic world was a trick to rob us of our birthright, of our place in the sun. We became the door mat of history. Every scheming bandit wiped his feet on us. Not until we get rid of the Christian mentality will we regain our independence of spirit. That a people of so fertile an imagination as the Germans, a tribe of such creative intellectual powers, should have accepted a Jewish religion that the Jews themselves rejected—that is the greatest imposture of history! Obviously, the whole maneuver," wound up the General, reverting to military terms, "was a snare, a pitfall, a *ruse de guerre*! And it worked—for fifteen centuries!"

As the prophet of Wotan and Thor, Ludendorff never succeeded in commanding a large following. He had more success with his theories of the totalitarian war, which the Nazi State adopted in their entirety. Fundamentally, there is not much difference: with the state imposing its criterion of what is good and bad on the citizen, and the cold scientific cultivation of hatred and lies for the one single purpose of destruction, Germany is much farther on the road to dechristianization than the Soviet Union, even if the churches in the Reich remain open and the incense still rises from the altars. In the place of God has come the would-be almighty state which, insatiable as the Moloch of old, demands man's entire devotion, mentally and physically. Whatever is of service to the state, be it mass murder or the worst of crimes, that alone is good and worthy of emulation and respect. Thus man, whose soul is considered more precious than the whole world by Christianity, is reduced to the value of an article, a machine, a cog in the machine. He becomes a mere automaton in the service of Mars and Moloch, the idols of old.

A Moment's Hope

From the window of *The World* bureau we could hear the procession come up the avenue: a human tidal wave roaring like a cataract. Like dead leaves racing before a storm, pedestrians were scampering in all directions, dodging into doorways, vanishing into the earth down the entrances of the underground railway. In a flash the terrace of the Café de la Paix was deserted and the long-aproned waiters were removing the blue-glass Seltzer siphons which, since the coming of asphalt, have replaced the traditional cobblestones of Paris as munition in street battles. Taxis ceased their hooting. The buses stopped running. Life was at a standstill.

Fifty abreast, arm in arm, led by the representatives of the people in their tricolored sashes, the Faubourg St. Antoine was invading the Place de l'Opéra, the central square of Paris. From the distance came the strains of the "Internationale," swelling in volume like the tones of a mighty organ, but the front ranks of the demonstrators were singing the "Carmagnole" of the sans-culottes: *"Ça ira, ça ira, ça ira, tous les bourgeois on les aura . . . !"*

A short trumpet blast, and from the side streets came the clatter of horses' hoofs. The brass helmets of the Republican Guard wheeled into view, and at a dozen points along the procession, long sabers gleamed in the afternoon sunshine. The government was breaking up a demonstration called to aid Sacco and Vanzetti.

This is one of the finest traits in the French character: when an injustice has been perpetrated anywhere on earth, be it in India or Portugal, in America or the depths of Indo-China, the Parisian "descends into the street," as he calls it, to demand that the wrong be righted. He does not need to be urged. He chokes with indignation and anger.

"For two anarchists so much fuss?" the reactionary *Liberté*, in a blood-red headline, had asked at noon, when it was clear that the temper of the popular *faubourgs* was rising. "They are men," came the answer of Armand Pelletier, a leather worker, when he appeared in court the next day on a charge of having smashed *Liberté*'s plate-glass windows.

For weeks there was a police guard in front of the American newspaper bureaus; the American embassy was surrounded by a battalion of the footguard to keep Myron T. Herrick from hearing the angry denunciations of American class justice by a million Parisian proletarians. Traffic was diverted and people frisked for concealed weapons and bombs. Every night the Bastille quarter, Montrouge, Villejuif, Saint-Denis, and the Faubourg du Temple rocked with mass demonstrations. Troops at Vincennes and the Invalides were confined to barracks, ready to march into the seething metropolis. Armored cars, the bullet-spraying nozzles of the machine guns uncovered, stood waiting in the suburbs. Old-timers predicted that the days of the *affaire* Dreyfus would come back.

Dreyfus! But he was alive! If anyone, *he* would understand the plight of the two Italian libertarians in Boston prison. Had he not, an innocent man, spent five years of his life on the burning rock of Devil's Island? We urged Joseph Caillaux, the financial expert and one of *The World*'s collaborators at the time, to appeal to the generosity of the American people and its President. Others telegraphed spontaneously: members of the Academy, ex-cabinet ministers, prelates, judges, intellectuals, newspaper editors, Professor Basch, Romain Rolland, Victor Margueritte, the Comtesse de Noailles, Barbusse, the League of the Rights of Man. . . . But no answer came from America. After keeping the two anarchists in torturing suspense for seven years, the Bostonian judge was ready to carry out his threat "to get those Reds."

Dreyfus appeared our last hope. If anyone could soften the hearts of men, it was *he*, with his moral authority as the living symbol of injured innocence. My colleagues on *The World* staff, Arno Dosch-Fleurot and Alfred Murray, suggested that I make the attempt to have Dreyfus speak out. There was not much time to lose: the execution was set for two days hence. But I found the home of the ex-artillery officer on the Avenue Friedland closed for the season. He had moved to his seaside villa near Deauville. Out to Deauville I raced in a taxi. . . .

I was received by someone who was either the Captain's valet or his secretary. When this man had heard my request, he refused to let me see Dreyfus. Monsieur could not interfere in such matters. Monsieur Dreyfus had retired from public life. An intervention on his part might be misconstrued.

"Misconstrued how, pray?"

"Let us not waste words," said the secretary, "Captain Dreyfus can have nothing to do with this affair. You must go. He is taking an afternoon nap in the next room. Our voices may disturb him."

"The lives of two men are at stake!"

"Too bad," came the answer. "Perhaps they are guilty."

"Perhaps," said I, "but was that not also the case with Monsieur Dreyfus? There was good reason to doubt then. There is reason to doubt here. We believe that Sacco and Vanzetti, as anarchists, are being made the scapegoats by a reactionary element in America, just as Captain Dreyfus, the Jew, was made a scapegoat by the Jesuits on the French general staff."

The door of the antechamber opened. Dreyfus! I looked upon the figure of the grizzled, nearsighted man over whose guilt or innocence men had battled each other in the streets, for whose sake France had skirted the brink of civil war and revolution. . . .

"Please leave this house at once!" commanded Captain Dreyfus angrily.

"As you wish, Monsieur! You know what I have come for."

"Not another word, please. Go!"

"Is that your last word, Captain Dreyfus?"

He did not answer.

On the day set for the execution, Paris offered the strangest spectacle I have ever witnessed: the boulevards were deserted, all vehicular traffic had been suspended, not a wheel turned in the factories. The silence was so intense that it was frightening. Yet no call had gone out from the labor syndicates or from the leftist parties for a protest strike or a final demonstration. The Parisian worker remained home that day, spontaneously and naturally, as if a great national emergency had suddenly arisen and everybody had to be on the alert. Paris was like a body from which the spirit had fled. To have seen mobs battling the police, or throwing up barricades, would have been more comprehensible and perhaps more comforting. It was as if the vast city held its breath in suspense. In its bewilderment the government rushed the army in, and the troops took up their positions in the deserted squares and along the inanimate broad thoroughfares, stacking their rifles and uncovering their machine guns, ready for action. That was shortly before noon. Not a sound was heard in the otherwise turbulent streets but the rattle of arms and the impatient pawing of the Guard's horses. In the crowded working-class districts, people closed their shutters in a gesture of colossal contempt for the martial display. The army stood facing a tomb. Nothing like it had happened since the year 1871, when the German army staged its insolent march of triumph down the deserted Champs-Élysées and, in consternation over the menacing silence and the barred windows, turned back before it had advanced a dozen blocks.

With nightfall the tension increased. Not a man or woman in the Faubourg du Temple went to bed. The guard in front of public buildings was increased. You saw nobody, but you felt as if a million eyes were watching your every move. Suddenly, about midnight, the electric service failed, and Paris was thrown into Stygian darkness. In the same moment thousands of shutters were flung open, and flaming torches appeared in the windows and on the roofs, as at a nocturnal funeral of some medieval prince.

The next morning everything reverted to normal. At dawn the troops marched off, and the Socialist newspapers came out with black borders and a manifesto saying: "Two more martyrs have been added to the long list of precursors of human freedom. They will be revenged by the workers of the world, not by the shedding of more innocent blood but by the building of a society in which no such injustice will be conceivable." These were the words of Léon Blum.

I spoke of the Dreyfus incident to Clemenceau, who once fought like a tiger for the innocent artillery captain. The ex-Premier remarked, "I could have told you that beforehand. Even at his own trials Dreyfus was impossible. He was the most arrogant militarist of the lot—*le plus cocardier de tous ces messieurs*. Dreyfus never concealed his contempt for the journalistic canaille represented by Zola and myself."

Clemenceau Sees a Ghost[1]

Clemenceau was undoubtedly one of the most interesting and representative personalities of the political history of France after 1870. His life had been a succession of tumults and thunderstorms. Like a weather-beaten mariner he had outfaced a hundred tempests, but his spirit remained fresh and inquisitive till the end. He had tasted the bitterness of the national defeat of 1870, earlier he had seen his father dragged away by the gendarmes of Napoleon the Little. Thereafter the wave of life had carried him to the highest crest of human endeavor, but when I met him in the summer of 1929, at the age of eighty-seven, he had been hurled down into the depths of forgetfulness. He was a bitter old man, who knew that he no longer had the strength to give blow for blow. His old enemy Briand, whom he had almost brought before the firing squad during the war, with the aid of the clericals frustrated the Tiger's last hope of terminating his career as President of the Republic. At the very moment when Clemenceau was putting on his frock coat and top hat to proceed to Versailles, where the National Assembly was in session to elect a new chief of state, word came that, with his persuasive power, Briand had switched the vote to Paul Deschanel.

Clemenceau had a feeling for truth, but he masked his sensitiveness by an ironic, blunt skepticism, an acid Voltairian satire. Perhaps he was not a great statesman, but he was a great agitator. When the French army, with admirable courage, had fought Von Kluck to a halt in 1914, the great task of the French government was to keep alive in the French people the faith in a final victory. That was Clemenceau's immense achievement. Clemenceau was the hero of the nationalist faith, a firm belief in the nation and the state. His life proves that this old intellectualistic nationalism was not a saving power, although it explains his deep sympathy for all the nascent nationalisms, all the Irredentisms, all the long lost national causes at the Peace Conference. He was praised for his attitude, and damned for it. One day when he had recovered from a serious illness and summoned the press to deny the rumors of his having sent for a confessor, someone, a Danish newspaperman, chided him for the bad treaty he had made: "It was the best I could do," said the Tiger quietly, "seated as I was between Jesus Christ and Napoleon Bonaparte."

[1] My interview with Clemenceau was originally published in the Herzl memorial issue of *The New Palestine*, New York, July, 1929.

Not Versailles, but his vindication of Dreyfus and Zola is his monument. There he fought without a truce. Like a torrent he raged through the trials, unmasking the lies of the general staff. He knew the enemy who had unleashed the Jew-baiting furor in western Europe. It was the old specter of intolerance. Behind the phantom stood the army with all its power and the Jesuit order. With the help of a few friends—Zola, Scheurer-Kestner, Jaurès—he wrestled with it in torment and agony, for he knew that France might go down in the struggle.

It was in May, 1929, that Meyer W. Weisgal, editor of *The New Palestine* in New York, asked me by cable to request Clemenceau, Anatole de Monzie and Painlevé for their reminiscences of Dr. Theodor Herzl, the founder of political Zionism. Clemenceau had known Herzl when he was correspondent of the *Neue Freie Presse* in Paris, at the time of the *affaire* Dreyfus. The American Zionists were about to commemorate the twenty-fifth anniversary of Herzl's death and intended to publish a memorial book in his honor. Mr. Weisgal wanted an article by Clemenceau or an interview on the subject of Herzl. Interviewing Clemenceau was easier said than done. Ever since the Peace Conference the Tiger entertained an unconcealed distrust for newspaper people. Moreover, he was old and ailing. In vain many journalists had attempted making the Tiger talk on questions of the day. He had "finished talking," he said. He wanted to be left alone with his books. He was in the midst of a treatise on Demosthenes and hoped to finish another volume before death should overtake him.

I wrote him a letter in which I reminded him of the little book of Jewish stories, *At the Foot of Sinai*, he had composed in his youth. I informed him that the work of reconstructing the Jewish Land in Palestine, in which he had shown a genuine interest at the Peace Conference, was progressing favorably, and finally broached the question of the interview. I handed the letter to the concierge of his apartment on the Rue Franklin and walked back to the office. When I reached the *World* bureau I was informed that M. Clemenceau's secretary had telephoned and that I was expected the same evening.

"*Ecoutez,*" growled the Tiger when I entered his room, "*j'ai une mémoire de tonnerre de Dieu.* I remember Dr. Herzl perfectly well, but what in the name of thunder is the matter with you journalists nowadays? In my time we wrote our own opinions, instead of taking dictation from others."

"*Monsieur le president*," I replied, "little has been written on Herzl. I have come to seek the testimony of one of his most illustrious contemporaries."

"No need of flattery, young man! *C'est bien superflu ici*," he retorted. "I knew Dr. Herzl slightly. Alphonse Daudet told me about him first, and about a book Herzl was going to write. Herzl was essentially a man of action, and a great man. When I say a great man, I judge greatness not by what a man has said or written. I want to know what he has done. Your own thoughts may astonish you any time. But what are the actions that follow? The world is full of verbal disguise. We have far too many literary masks in our time. There is far too much noise for the virtue of simplicity. Herzl looked life in the face. And he went his way, caring little for acclaim and popular approval. In certain things he was a little naïve. But are not all great men naïve, more or less?"

The Tiger dropped off into reverie. His head sank on his breast. For a moment I studied those massive and extraordinary, almost Mongolian features—the quick, brilliant brown eyes under the overhanging eyebrows, and the grooved pallor of the skin. With quick, nervous gestures he pulled at his mustache, jerked his old service cap askance, and sighed deeply.

"Did you know," he spoke up with a start, "that Herzl believed himself immortal? He once told me about it, on a night when we walked home after a session in the Chamber. It was at the time of the *affaire*."

Another silence. Then an almost imperceptible smile passed over the impassive features and he chuckled: "Myself, I haven't Dr. Herzl's certitude! Still, I suppose he was right. He has indeed survived!"

Another halt, while Clemenceau stroked his mustache meditatively. "In the memory of his people, *monsieur le president*?"

"Bah, *non*! Of course not. The Jewish people are no more grateful than the others. I say he has survived because I still see him occasionally. He comes to visit me here. If you were here at midnight or at two o'clock in the morning you could see him also."

"I am quite prepared, Monsieur le President. . . ."

"No, better have your sleep, young man. Young people need sleep. Old men do not. At any rate, they don't sleep."

Again his head dropped, imposing silence. Was this old realist, this "extinguisher of the heavenly lights," falling into the fallacies of spiritualism or necromancy in his old age? Was he going to tell me about lone seances with rapping ghosts and shuffling phantoms?

"Nothing foolish like that," he blurted out, as if he had read my thoughts. "The past is a refuge for old men like me. At nights, when this boiling caldron that is Paris simmers down at last, they come back here to visit me, those men of the past. They commune with me and spend an hour or so. After that they go off again, on their business, out there in the ether.

"Socrates, Galileo, Hugo, Goethe, Zola, George Washington, they all drop in from time to time. And many others. . . . Pope Leo XIII, for instance. . . . Pompous and ridiculous fellows some of them, who made a dreadful fracas when they were alive. They have quieted down a good deal since they died," he went on with a dry chuckle. "They are well behaved now when they visit me. They walk with muffled step. They are *en pantoufles*, you might say. Better behaved than some mortals." He was talking in quick, short sentences, rapping them out, snorting and puffing the while.

"Herzl, too, comes. He does not speak. He sits in that armchair over there, and his presence fills the room. He does not cry out his anguish over his people; he does not sing psalms of hope for his fatherland over there in Asia under the English. He only thinks, and his thoughts flit through the atmosphere and enter into my own mind. And I, too, think of the past. Herzl's image shakes me from my torpor as he shook the guilty and criminal nations who, in the course of history, have been responsible for the scandal of Israel.

"I am not going to analyze Herzl's philosophy. You younger men have that task. Only, when you write about him and dissect him, don't bury the *élan* of his thought, or entomb the fire of his vision and his enthusiasm into a mummified pile of words. If you do, you have missed your calling.

"A fire cannot be hidden," went on the Tiger. "There was a breath of eternity in that man Herzl. He had seen the burning bush, *le buisson ardent de Moïse*. He was a man of genius, not to be confounded with a man of talent. There are plenty of men of talent in the world. Men of genius are rare.

"How to draw the distinction between the two? Ah, that is the question! It must be sensed. Men of genius are recognized by their gigantic proportions, often enclosed in a framework of an ordinary existence. Their evolution is accomplished according to an unseizable process. Their way of acting, of understanding, of discovering the real substance of things and beings is manifested in an altogether personal and original manner. They are beyond ordinary logic: they surpass the level of their contemporaries and are therefore often misunderstood, or rather, not understood at all.

"Such a man was Herzl. Amid all the defection of character which marked his day, the weakness of thought, the furor of clashing interests, he dared to give himself. What audacity! What courage! What ardor of life! He was like a projector throwing light on the road ahead, a road to be traced by those who came after him. His 'emotivation' gave impulse to events that followed.

"He knew disillusionment. He was under crossfire, you might say. His own knew him not, or did not rally to him with spontaneous impulse, at any rate. He died without having seen his vision take shape. But he had given Israel a new sense of his destiny, which had become lost in the Dispersion. That cannot be denied. He forced it on Jewry!"

M. Clemenceau stopped talking. Piles of manuscripts on his desk and the general knowledge in Paris that he was working under pressure, a race with death, perhaps, to fling what he called "a last thunderbolt," made me realize the indelicacy of trespassing any longer on his time. I rose to leave.

"He was a fighter," added Clemenceau, himself a fighter for fifty years. "But for what did he fight? Tell me that!"

"For the recognition of Israel's claims."

"Nothing of the sort," snapped the Tiger. "He fought Israel."

"Fought Israel, *monsieur le président*?"

"Yes. Do you know Delacroix' painting at St. Sulpice?"

"Of Jacob battling the Angel?"

"Precisely!" he nodded. "It's a terrific combat that the artist presents there. A battle of Titans. . . . And still you gain the impression that they are not fighting. Jacob seems more concerned with holding the Angel near him on earth than resisting him. And the Angel is fully capable of overpowering Jacob but does not do it. If you look long at the painting you sense there is infinite love between those two, in spite of the struggle.

"And after the battle, what then?" asked M. Clemenceau sharply. "What happens? Tell me!"

"After the battle Jacob is no longer Jacob. He is Israel. He rises blessed from the celestial contact. Isn't that what the Bible says?"

"That's it, young man, *c'est cela!* Think of that when you write of

Herzl and Israel. No longer Jacob, but Israel, and Israel blessed by the contact. I feel," he said, as he led me to the door, "that Herzl brought the Jewish question a step nearer solution. His striving has resulted in an official recognition of the Jewish problem as a national and an international question, and not a mere matter of the integration of individual Jews in their non-Jewish environment. The recognition by the world of the Jewish people's national existence, of which modern Palestine is the practical evidence, is an important acquisition for all of us, for it implies a recognition of the right of every tribe and nationality to express itself freely in its own way, and that is the most essential condition of a truly human civilization."

Thus spoke one of the last of the humanists amongst Europe's statesmen. Whatever their faults, and I realize that the neohumanists failed to give man a program commensurate with the grandeur of humanity, a practical plan of action, a direct impulse and, most of all, a sure faith in itself, they nevertheless clung to an appreciation of man and his qualities, and sought to infuse life with an ideal of humaneness and humanity. That phase is ended. The new leaders cannot see humanity beyond the individual and the nation as instruments to attain that goal. They put up ever new barriers, new hurdles, new impediments, and in our time are driving the herdlike masses under their control along parallel roads, back into the night of medieval darkness.

Duce, Duce, Duce!

In the preface to his biography by Margherita Sarfatti, the Duce says that he detests those who make him the subject of their panegyrics. I must say that I never met anyone so eager to help me compose one. After a thundering denunciation of William Bolitho's articles on the birth of Fascism which had appeared in the morning *World*, and an even wilder outburst against Giovanni Giglio, the paper's correspondent stationed across the Swiss border in Lugano, Mussolini mellowed the moment I told him that my instructions were (I showed him the cablegram) to write a series of human-interest articles about him, his family background, and his hobbies.

Two minutes after he had bellowed: "No, I am damned if I give any more interviews! The interview is dead and it's the bad journalist who killed it," he was arranging for me to have a photographer occupy a balcony opposite the Palazzo Chigi on a day when he would make a speech to the Black Shirts. That was a rare privilege, for all the apartments in the neighborhood had been evacuated as a precaution against would-be assassins.

I had set out for Rome in trepidation. The Italian ambassador in Paris had informed me that anyone representing *The World* papers was bound to have a rough reception in the Eternal City. The Duce, he said, was fully informed on the nature of Bolitho's and Giglio's work. There could be no question of an interview with the Chief of the Italian Government. I was to put that hope out of my head definitely. However, he could not keep me from visiting Rome, and exacted a promise that upon arrival, I should report to Augusto Turati, the secretary of the Fascist party.

Although I fully intended to carry out the ambassador's suggestion, it proved unnecessary. For when the train on which I travelled passed Città Vecchia, the last stop before Rome, two Black Shirts entered the compartment and asked me if my name was Signor van Paassen. When I replied in the affirmative they bowed, and settled down in the corridor outside. When we pulled into the station it was they who picked up my luggage and carried it to a limousine standing before the exit. The chauffeur bowed and I bowed, but to myself I said: This looks bad . . . *Timeo Danaos . . . atque Dagos et limusina ferentes .* . . If only these fine fellows do not take out of my hide what is really intended for Messrs. Bolitho and Giglio!

I protested a little before entering the automobile, but a crowd was collecting and my bags were already inside, so that I followed automatically as it were, half dazed, puzzled, and not a little worried. I must confess that I expected to be driven straight off to the Fascist headquarters for a little question period at least, but to my amazement found myself a few minutes later being ushered into what turned out to be the bridal suite of the Albergo Ambasciatore, one of the smartest hotels in Rome.

"We have been expecting you, Signor," said the smiling manager, who showed me to my room. "On this table you will find all the books published on the subject of Fascism, including the speeches of the Chief of our Government, in both the French and the English languages. Here is a pass made out in your name for every theater in the city. You will notice that you are free to take as many friends on this *laisser-passer* as you desire. You are the guest of the Italian government, Signor. May I send you up some refreshments? A little fruit, perhaps? Some wine? This house prides itself on the reputation of its cellars. We have some dry Gragnono, *épatant*, allow me!"

I allowed him. For two weeks, from Rome to Palermo and from Messina to Gorizia, I allowed everything. My only regret was that I could not find a moment to tear myself away from the corps of gold-braided officials, state danseuses and pirouetting flunkeys who, it seemed, were detailed to smother me in kindness. I wanted to sit with more congenial company in one of those cool *trattorie* of the old Borgo, where the hack drivers, the costermongers and the other descendants of the conquerors of the world foregather around plain wooden tables and a bottle of Lachryma Christi.

But I could not see the Duce. Turati remained obdurate in spite of my daily repeated pleas, supported by urgent cables from my managing editor, that my only object in coming to Italy was to see the great man face to face. After ten days I had begun to despair and was ready to give up when, upon returning to the hotel one evening, after a day spent in visiting the catacombs, I found a letter from the press division of the Foreign Office, saying I had an audience with Mussolini on the following morning at the Palazzo Chigi.

The nomenclator left me standing in the door of the Premier's cabinet, and when the man at the desk by the window at the other end of the room, which seemed a quarter of a mile distant, gave no sign for me to approach, I began the long walk over the polished floor without being summoned. I stopped before the desk. Mussolini was scowling. I had no time to say good morning. Without looking up, he flew into a rage and pointing to a file of clippings: "*Ça, mais ça passe les bornes!*" The Duce was talking in French. "This really is the limit! Why does your paper have its Italian correspondent stationed in Lugano, in Switzerland? To collect the pearls of wisdom that fall from the lying mouths of a bunch of discredited fugitive politicians? Is that it? Why do you not come to Rome when you want to find out about Italy?" He bent over the clippings. "It is a lie," he shouted, "a contemptible lie, do you hear me? Benedetto Croce's library was not destroyed by the Black Shirts. Signora Matteotti is not in jail, more lies! Lies, lies, nothing but lies! Your whole paper is full of lies!" He had risen and stormed up and down the room, gesticulating, pounding the table. I noticed that he had short, stocky, peasant legs.

"But I have just come to Rome, Excellency," I said, when he sat down at last to catch his breath. "I have never written a word of what I have not seen with my own eyes or verified."

"Perhaps not yet, no, but what will you write when you are back in Paris? No, I am damned! I will not give you an interview. This is the end. The interview is dead, the bad journalist has killed it! Where do you go from here?"

"To Palestine, Signor Mussolini!"

"To Palestine? Ah, that is interesting." He brightened up at once. "When you go there you must call on my friend Ben Avi, the journalist! Do you know what he said to me, this Signor Ben Avi, sitting there right in that chair where you are sitting now? He said, 'Over there you have the Arch of Titus, with its inscription *Judea Capta*, the symbol of the destruction of the Hebrew state. I want to tear it down,' he told me, 'tear it down and rebuild it in Jerusalem, but then change the inscription to *Judea Liberata*!' What do you you think of that?"

"Fine idea," I said. "But what did you reply, Signor Mussolini?"

"I said, 'Signor Ben Avi, you tell the Jews of Jerusalem to try and get it!' Ha, ha, ha, how was that? Wasn't that a good one? Let them come and get it. Let the Jews try that!"

The Duce burst into a fit of laughter. But the ice was broken. I showed him the managing editor's telegrams. He nodded his head. I explained to him that there was a morning and an evening *World*, that I had nothing to do with the first and never wrote political articles for the second. The chin came up. He smiled broadly. A minute later he was telling me that his hobby was playing the violin. "Yes, music gives me mental quiet, you see. . . . I need music as a flower needs water. When I am tired I play."

"Your Excellency is like Frederick the Great in that," I said. "Is there a photograph in existence of Your Excellency in the act of playing?"

"I do not think so, but we will have one made right now." He rang a bell. He ordered his fiddle and a photographer brought in, and posed.

"Yes, and my other hobby is reading," he said. "I promise myself to read one canto of Dante every night, but I have never yet—never do you hear—been able to stop with one canto."

A few days later I received a photograph of the Duce in the act of playing the violin, with his eyes closed. Not a single postal box in Rome was large enough to contain the picture. The Duce had also given me a note of introduction to his brother, the publisher of the family newspaper in Milano. Arnaldo was a dutiful brother and knew what was expected of him; he gave me all the details of Benito's youth and career on a trip we took together to see the hydroelectric installation in the Apennines. I did not lack material.

The legend-building around Mussolini was in full swing even then. Arnaldo had casually referred me to Benito's dentist. This gentleman, who had a telephone call from the palace, understood what was wanted and promptly imparted the information that Mussolini was the only man he had ever treated who did not wince when the drill whirled into his molars. He even disdained the use of a local anesthetic when a tooth had to come out. I told this once to Pietro Nenni who for years was Mussolini's collaborator on the Socialist press. Nenni observed dryly: "He must have improved a lot since I knew him, for when he had to take injections of 606, he used to fill the office with lamentations of self-pity, and one of us always had to accompany him to the physician's office to hold his hand."

Time does wonders, indeed. For instance, that wound which was said to have been caused by a bullet passing right through Mussolini's nose—it had been but recently fired by a demented Irish woman. When I sat looking into the great man's face, not the slightest trace of a scar remained.

In the years that followed, when the nature of Fascism was better understood, I heard the Duce hold forth several times in a less naïve strain than on that first occasion, the last time to a group of French journalists, but it was always on the same theme: the might, the grandeur, the destiny and the military prowess of Italy. If he said anything of a more intimate nature, he always blue-penciled the words from the typescript which was to be submitted to him before publication. To neglect handing in an interview for his approval was followed by complete repudiation. Once I ventured, quite innocently, to ask him what I most wanted to know, namely, what had become of his earlier Socialist faith, and if he would still, as he had done once in a letter to Lenin, call Marx "our common, immortal teacher."

"Most certainly," replied Benito Mussolini. "I am still at heart an internationalist, but I consider that Marx's dream cannot be realized for thousands of years. Humanity must first pass through the stage of individual nationalisms." When I received the manuscript back, both the question and the answer had been deleted.

Mussolini, who lacks good manners, overreached himself in the beginning, like every parvenu. While I was in Rome the first time, back in 1926, he had a bust made of Caesar, but substituted his own physiognomy for that of the divine Julius. Next he posed for a photograph in which he appeared dressed in an imitation of Napoleon's old uniform, with the left hand in his breast pocket, a characteristic attitude of the Corsican. Five million postcard reproductions were made of this pose, but the picture did not make a good impression in Italy. He had to start all over again. He therefore learned to drive an automobile. Rural prefects were notified to keep the roads clear of all traffic, and stories began to circulate about the Duce's breakneck speed. By accident the secret slipped out that a double did the fast driving for him. Then he began to play with a lion like another fearless Androclus and had himself photographed in the act. Nobody who saw the pictures suspected that the animal's teeth had been extracted and that it was fed on macaroni and beef extract.

Two inches were added to the Duce's height by means of padded soles and high heels. One day he dressed as a leader of the Cossacks, the next as a Turkish grand vizir. He masqueraded in the getup of a drum major, a peasant and a Mameluke till he discovered that a foot-high white plume on top of a headgear that is a cross between a boyar's headdress and the Mad-Mullah's turban is most expressive of his unique grandeur. And wherever he went "the concessioned ovationists" came along to supply the applause, for when the claque stayed home there was disaster, as happened that September day in 1929, when I heard the Duce question the assembled employees at the Fiat Works in Milan in the stereotyped manner: "Who gave Italy back her self-respect? Who gave *dopolavoros*? Who defies the whole world?" When the workers maintained an obstinate silence, the Duce threw his precious Crimean headgear with the Byzantine feather on the floor and stamped off in a huff.

My instructions for the first trip to Italy were to delve into the Duce's private past. His role in world affairs was a matter of public record; it was no business of mine. But I could not help finding that in that realm, too, everything was based on bluff and intimidation.

The eight million bayonets that he began to mention more and more frequently as the source of Italy's military prowess are carried by the same men who allowed two hundred thousand Austrians to chase them all over the place after Caporetto, and by Black Shirt legions who repeated the performance of their elders at Guadalajara when facing poorly armed working-class battalions. Ludendorff, who was a fool when it came to religious matters, but who understood the military business as few others, wrote in the last issue of his *Zur heiligen Quelle der Deutsche Kraft* that a military alliance with Italy would be a millstone around Germany's neck in the event of war. And Ludendorff spoke the mind of the German general staff. Kemal Pasha, in 1935, when I was sent to ask him his opinion of the concentration of war material on the isle of Rhodes, in close proximity to the Turkish province of Adana, replied: "I will scratch out the eyes of any bandit who even dares to look at Adana, and I won't need any allies either to chop off his claws." But the best indication of what esteem is accorded the Italian armed forces in European military circles came in Paris in 1937. I had been invited to attend a luncheon at the opening of the Italian pavilion at the Exposition of that year, and sat at the table with a number of correspondents, French and Italian military attachés, and people from the Foreign Office. One young Italian officer, sporting the uniform of a *Bersaglieri* lieutenant and three rows of medals and tokens, began talking of the Ethiopian campaign and Spain. "Our Duce," he said, "ordered us to take Ethiopia and we took it in the face of fifty-one nations determined to destroy us. He told us to take the Iron Ring around Bilbao: the next morning it was ours. We have eight million bayonets—nothing can stop us. Let us be frank about it: if the Duce ordered his army to march into France tomorrow, what really could stop us?" he asked in a tone of victory. For a moment there was an embarrassed silence. Everybody knew that French wine is too heavy for Italians and that the lieutenant had imbibed rather freely. "Yes, who can stop us?" he demanded once more. "Monsieur seems to forget the French customs service," came back a French correspondent suddenly.

It is still admitted, even in Socialist circles, that the antimilitarist Mussolini, the agitator who counseled tearing up the railway tracks to prevent troop trains from leaving for the war in Tripoli, at least bravely accepted the consequences of his betrayal by enlisting as a private soldier and marching courageously to the front. But that, too, is a myth. There is no question, of course, that Mussolini enlisted, but he did not take part in a single battle. There are plenty of men alive today who served in the *Bersaglieri* regiment to which Private Mussolini belonged. I found half a dozen of these fellow soldiers of the Duce on my wanderings through Italy. Everyone shrugged his shoulders when the conversation turned to the subject of the Duce's war record. It appears that the man who had been rattling the saber,

from the moment he no longer ran the risk of being called personally, always managed to find a pretext to absent himself from the
front when an offensive was in preparation. The contempt with
which the turncoat was treated by his comrades provided him with
an opportunity of playing the misunderstood martyr's role in the
army which, in turn, gave him the facility to demand quick transfers
whenever danger drew near, generally on the pretense that the
soldiers were plotting to do away with him in the midst of an attack.
He was shrewd enough not to ask for an officer's commission, or to
be attached to the staff. He wanted the glory of having been a
front-line soldier without taking any of the risks. His wounds were
caused by the premature explosion of an Italian shell, not by Austrian shrapnel. The demagogue who talks incessantly of baths of
steel and baptisms of fire and of the regenerating effect of bloodletting
on the peoples, was not for a minute under shellfire himself. Of
course, in his autobiography, he talks about his habit of catching
hand grenades hurled across by the Austrians, and pitching them
back again, as though they were playing a baseball game on the
Isonzo. But if that is true, it may be said with safety that Benito
Mussolini is the only one of the twenty-odd million combatants in the
last war who has accomplished the feat.

Every act of Mussolini has been the cool scheming of an oppor-
tunist. Cold calculation blazes the way for projects which look fan-
tastically daring. He is a totalitarian egoist who identifies the universe
with himself. In this respect he differs fundamentally from Adolf
Hitler, who is utterly sincere in the belief that what he is doing is
right. Mussolini is not concerned with questions of good and evil,
morality and immorality, loyalty and betrayal. The same man who
sneers at the plutodemocracies is the one who has impoverished the
Italian people to a point where the social condition of the masses is as
pitiful as that of the French peasants on the eve of 1789. He knows
neither compassion nor mercy; pride rules his will. His record is an
unbroken series of betrayals—betrayal of the Socialists, of the agra-
rians, of the bourgeoisie, of the anticlericals and the end is not yet in
sight, as Hitler will discover in the hour of decision. The son of
poverty-stricken proletarian parents, he sold himself to the financial
interests, and with cynical design utilized his reputation as a champion of the humble to bind them hand and foot to the service of a
leviathan state which he heads. Priding himself on his kinship with
the humanists of the Renaissance, he produced a cultural stagnation

without precedence in the life of one of the most gifted peoples of Europe, in addition to militarizing every phase of life and bringing about a bankrupt national economy. He has accepted without scruple whatever serves him in the aggrandizement of his personal power. With callous ruthlessness he crushes what stands in his way. His fellow Fascists are sacrificed without a moment's hesitation whenever their popularity endangers the uniqueness of his position. He pursues his enemies with bestial ferocity, as the cases of Matteotti and the Rosselli brothers clearly show.

At the age of eighteen, before fleeing abroad to escape military service, young Benito was caught in the act of setting fire to a church in Bologna. At the trial, which followed, the charge was changed to one of having administered a beating to an aged cleric, a man of seventy-nine, who had accidentally come upon the incendiary as he was lighting a heap of rubbish behind a wooden altar. For these blows, the only ones he struck in his life, Mussolini was sent to jail for six months. The magistrate, in sentencing the youthful "direct actionist," expressed the hope that half a year of solitary confinement would cause the prisoner to reflect on "the folly of a single individual going to war against society."

Since that term of imprisonment the father of Fascism has suffered from acute claustrophobia. Till this day Mussolini cannot bear being alone in a locked room. Hence the enormous chamber in the Palazzo Chigi and the still larger hall wherein he does his work in the Palazzo Venezia. But the six months in jail do not seem to have cured him of his militant anticlericalism, for his first act upon liberation was to spit upon the cassock of a priest whom he met by chance on his way to the railway station. This brought only a fine, but it also opened the way for a series of paid lectures before a number of freethinkers' clubs in North Italy. Benito's subject was "The Crime of the Popes." He advertised this as "an inexhaustible subject." He was also engaged to write a *feuilleton* for several rural publications, and chose as the title for this opus, which ran interminably in half a dozen country weeklies, *The Cardinal's Mistress*. A pale, expurgated edition of this novel appeared in America in later years.

Mussolini was still considered a firebrand anticlerical and a convinced republican at the time of the famous March on Rome. This did not prevent King Victor Emmanuel from calling him to the premiership. Monsignor von Gerlach told me in a confidential mood that the night following the Duce's arrival in Rome the Holy Father

slept in peace for the first time in many months. Whatever else
may be said of the members of the Curia, nobody will deny them an
extraordinarily keen insight into human character. They recognized
Benito at first sight, and made a far better evaluation of him than
Badoglio, who called him "a dirt-mouthed labor agitator" and who
volunteered to smash the Fascist movement in one hour, and chase
the Duce and his cohorts "out of history" with a whiff of grapeshot.
Indeed, not many months after the March on Rome, the priest-baiting
Benito, who had composed a pamphlet at the age of twenty-seven
"proving" the nonexistence of God, had his union with Donna
Rachele regularized and his children baptized by the clergy, ordered
the crucifix back in every schoolroom of the Italian kingdom, had
himself photographed in the act of praying at the Tomb of the
Unknown Soldier, was kissing the relics of dead saints like any other
Sicilian peasant, and was currently referred to in the sermons of the
Roman clergy as a man of God.

Altogether a most wonderful conversion!

Léon Blum's Failure

Is it not a remarkable fact that so many of the leaders and thinkers
of Socialism in France have been drawn from the upper strata of
society? The church, the nobility, the arts, science, literature and
the magistracy—all have furnished their contingents. Almost without
exception, the tacticians of the ideal were men who abandoned
brilliant careers to throw in their lot with the proletariat and who
therewith voluntarily took on the yoke of poverty and obloquy.
What was the impulse that urged men like Gracchus Babeuf, the
Comte de Saint-Simon, a priest like Lamennais, or rich men's sons
like Blanqui, Jaurès and Léon Blum to turn their backs on their own
class? The materialist explanation of history does not apply in their
case, for it cannot be said that they sacrificed well-being, leisure and
friendships in obedience to material instincts. Their sentiments were
independent of their personal economic circumstances. When these
men embraced an ideal which was to serve as an instrument for the
creation of a new reality, they had their eye on something that was
in flagrant contradiction to their own environment. What motivated
them in taking a step which would be deemed folly in a world where
everything is done for the sake of gain?

Was it not their compassion, their deep love of humanity, the same
spirit that moved the Prophets of old?

How could they live in peace when they saw the morass of destitution, ignorance and inanition into which the majority of their
fellows were sinking? They suffered, and, at the risk of ridicule,
disdain, persecution and even martyrdom, they set about to alleviate
the burdens of the humblest. They gave up personal security and
took the cross upon their shoulders. For besides the instinct of self-
preservation, there is something in the human heart that lifts man
above the struggle for existence. This higher something is what
makes man speak words and perform acts quite contrary to his own
social and material interests. No doubt there are many whose attention is so exclusively focused on material things that they qualify
as good and just everything that is to their own benefit and advantage.
But there are others, men who measure their words and deeds by a
higher standard. Indeed, all the truly great in history were led by
considerations of an idealistic character, not by a hope of material
remuneration. At all times in history vast multitudes, not merely
exceptional individuals, have arisen to accept martyrdom for a great
cause with joy and enthusiasm.

The weight of material considerations is great—who shall deny it?—
but in decisive moments the spirit comes to the fore as the real
creator of history, the *Creator Spiritus*.

Only Marxistic one-sidedness, which has no eye for anything but
the material, has interpreted history as a series of class-war incidents,
and this in spite of the fact that everything worth-while in the labor
movement is the result of the unselfish sacrifice of individuals who
have gained nothing for themselves but hardship.

Léon Blum was one of that phalanx of men and women who, starting with the Saint-Simonists, the Fourierists, and the followers of
Proudhon, Buchez, Leroux, Montalembert and Lamennais, were
guided not by dogmas but by a certain socialistic mood or disposition. They did not believe in Hobbes' theory of *homo homini lupus*.
To the contrary, they were persuaded that a harmony exists between
individual and general interests, and that upon being given his freedom, the best in man will come to full fruition. It cannot be said that
Léon Blum is a Marxist, any more than that Jean Jaurès was one. For
neither believed in the domination of one class, but in the total
liberation of the human personality by the elimination of all classes.
It would be quite feasible to demonstrate in the light of orthodox
Marxist criteria that Léon Blum is not a Socialist at all. Men like
Blum and Jaurès before him drifted along on a current of opinions,

convictions and conceptions, which moved in the general direction of Socialism. They were in opposition to the dominant ideas of the ruling classes. Where the entrenched bourgeoisie always appealed to self-interest, they spoke of a community sentiment. Without stressing the class struggle, and therewith setting up another, a counter-egoism, these men wanted to break the barriers by which the social order was hemmed in. They were swept along by ideas and projects which aimed at widening the basis of social relationships.

Their failing was that they generalized. Their vision was an immense and splendid hope. In a broad but vague and indefinite way, they saw how the world could be arranged, if the majority of mankind should will it. But they did not show the way to a realization of the ideal. Like the greatest of the humanists, they projected the realization of their dreams into the distant future. Utopia was a mythical island in the midst of a mysterious ocean. The ideal remained too much a pure question of the intellect: a thought, a piece of the spirit. It was in a realm of almost celestial removedness that they placed that good and pure and salutary form of society for which mankind is groping. They fled beyond reality.

It is true that the ideal is the ultimate in beauty and joy our imagination can produce. The ideal can never in its entirety be translated into reality. It always eludes our grasp, always recedes into the future. And yet it must never be lost sight of. There may be a temporary compromise with the reality, but never at the cost of the ideal. The striving for it must never cease. Everything must be done to bring the ideal nearer.

I have often heard Léon Blum declare that his conception of Socialism was not a rigid system, a sort of marvelously articulated and regulated machine. He understood Socialism as being a high ideal of perfection proposed to individuals and peoples which sought an answer not only to immediate aspirations of demands of society, but to the most profound and permanent aspirations of the spirit and of the human heart. Contact with life and the problems of daily urgency led him to formulate a doctrine, if such it may be called, of revolutionary evolution. Out of the idealist conception of history of the French Utopians on the one hand, and Marxian absolute determinism on the other, he had distilled a synthesis marvelously adapted to the aspirations and the spirituality, always somewhat messianic, of the people of France. But the theory did not withstand the impact of the reality when the opportunity came to make the dream come true.

Léon Blum came to Socialism late in life. Nothing in his youth and early manhood seemed to predestine him for the role he was called to fill in later life. He came from that milieu of detached esthetes and literary snobs whose pontiff was Marcel Proust. But the *affaire* Dreyfus shook him awake, as it did his classmates, Romain Rolland and Paul Painlevé. The revelation came to him one night, as he was walking through the slums of the Faubourg St. Martin (still a pesthole today) and saw the sordid misery in which the mass of the people lived. How is it, he asked himself, that these men and women accept this state of degradation, these inhuman conditions? How is it that they have not revolted before this? And with a shock he discovered that the answer was that the proletariat had come to accept the situation as something inevitable, as a natural inescapable fate. In that hour he vowed: "Come what may, I will not rest until the flame of freedom has been lit in the hearts of the people of France."

A brilliant polemicist of unquestioned intellectual integrity who explained and commentated as perhaps no other in contemporary France, Léon Blum was not a leader. For a few months the masses of France were in a mood where they would have followed him blindly. Their confidence in him was entire, pathetically entire. Yet, anyone who closely watched Léon Blum's behavior at large mass meetings and political demonstrations must have been struck by a certain malaise which came over him in the presence of the people. In public Blum was shy almost to the point of femininity. To face one of those enormous multitudes in the Place de la République or in the Vélodrome d'Hiver was visibly an ordeal for him. When a half-million clenched fists were raised to him in the anti-Fascist salute, he became as flustered and as panicky as girlish André Gide. He could never bring himself to the point of answering that salute by raising his own fist. Blum seemed congenitally incapable of making a show of force, even by implication. He felt at ease in the study, in the editorial office, in the conference room, in that intimate circle which gathered at his apartment on the Quai de Bourbon when Madame Blum was still alive. There he rivaled in charm and wit his bosom friends: Tristan Bernard, the famous humorist, André Spire, the poet, Bracke, the veteran Socialist. . . .

But Léon Blum lacked what the French proletarians call *le sens de la soupe*. There was a spiritual barrier between this refined aristo-cratic-mannered bourgeois and the masses. He was with them, but they felt that this genteel-nurtured patrician, with his passion for precision in definitions, was not one of them. He was a stranger who had come over from the other camp. They admired the generosity of his heart, for his deep love of humanity was undoubtedly genuine. I have never met a man who was at the same time so deeply sensitive to the sorrows of others, and so completely devoid of personal ambition. Of the people and their cause he spoke with almost evangelic tenderness, and even when his voice grew harsh, as a prophet's must at times, it was still the harshness of love. But he was not, to put it bluntly, representative of the masses. He was a theoretical organizer, not a builder. Someone has said that Socialists of his kind are perfectly at ease in monarchical countries where the political institutions are not openly, or at least, not so brutally called into question. They need the fraternal shoulders of their fellows to lean upon.

Faced with the responsibilities of power, Léon Blum began to tremble and was full of hesitations. Instead of leaving the dead to bury their dead, he set himself up as a physician of the sick capitalist order. When the reaction was on the run, he sent out messengers to overtake the fugitive with reassurances of his good intentions. The fire he had himself helped to kindle burned so high for a moment that it threw a ray of hope into the darkest recesses of the slave camps across the Rhine and the Alps. His irresolution doused that light. In a time when the capitalist system had demonstrated its inability to provide the material needs of man, in a time when Socialism should have gone sailing before the wind, Léon Blum put the Socialist movement in France on the defensive. He did not doubt the people—he was afraid of life. The reality was stark and forbidding: his Socialist confreres in the cabinet had merely exchanged the ideal for a pair of striped trousers and the title of *Monsieur le ministre*. The plutocratic reaction said: "You are not a Frenchman of the French, Monsieur Blum." Capital ushered in a sit-down strike by exporting its gold hoardings abroad to sabotage "the Blum experiment" while the upper crust of the army took up a position of cold and watchful waiting.

There was a story current at the time of the Popular Front's advent to power concerning a group of Jewish captains of finance and industry calling on Léon Blum to persuade him not to accept the premiership. The representatives of official Judaism, whose sole concern is to be left alone in the enjoyment of their wealth and

privileged position, sought to convince their fellow Jew that an
eventual failure of his experiment would react unfavorably on their
coreligionists in France. Blum is said to have replied that all his life
he had hoped to bring a little more light, a little more happiness,
and a little more leisure to the masses and now, when the opportunity
presented itself, he was not going to fail them. Yet in every public
speech, he spoke almost apologetically of his race, as if the masses
care one rap for race. If Blum's father had been an Algerian Arab
they would have followed him. They were waiting for him to lead.
He was swept into office on an immense wave of enthusiasm. For
weeks the country was in a state of exaltation. It looked as if Blum
could have done whatever he wanted. He chose to wait for the historic opportunity.

"Do you not think my heart bleeds as much as yours when I see
what is going on in Spain?" he asked one day. "But every time we
make a move to help Madrid, we receive a warning from Downing
Street that if we become involved in a war with Germany and Italy
we must not count on England's support!"

He hesitated because, knowing the weaknesses of the French
working class, and seeing the attitude taken by the international
bourgeoisie on the Spanish question, he foresaw a struggle more
painful, more ghastly than that which raged in the Pyrenean peninsula. He wanted to prevent still more suffering. He was afraid to
face defeat. "We must make a stand for democracy pure and simple,"
he added, as if the democracy we have is democracy, and as if the
democracy which is democracy can be acquired without accepting
battle.

The Good Comrade

Almost immediately after being sent abroad, I made the acquaintance of that dangerous area of doubtful imperialistic compromises
known as the Near East, where the flame of war may burn low at
times, but where it has never yet been extinguished. Nothing is settled in Arabia. All the existing arrangements are temporary, for all
the frontiers are artificial. They were drawn up without consulting
the peoples and without paying the slightest attention to the natural
boundaries of race and religion. Ibn-Saud is kept in check, as he
was during the Great War, with a monthly stipend of five thousand
pounds sterling, the Imam of Hadhramaut with a share in the profits
of the pearl fisheries on the southern coast, Persia with a revenue

from the Anglo-Iranian oil fields. Military force, or the threat of its employment, insures a precarious peace in the rest of the Arabic world. "But every minute," said the Mufti of Beyrouth to me, "every minute a little mullah is born between Baghdad and Mecca. Some day in the fullness of time, there will be one, please Allah, with the imagination of a Mohammed. Then the Christian nations will have reason to tremble."

A tremor ran through Europe's chancelleries in 1925, only five years after Feisal, Britain's ally in the war against the Turks, had been chased from his throne in Damascus by the French. The Druses, one of the most intransigent of the Arab tribes, rose in revolt that year. Was this "the next wave" Lawrence had foreseen, the rising of the last inevitable and irresistible crest which is to overrun the peninsula and finally break the hold of the detested foreigner? Or was it but another intermittent skirmish, another instance of an Arabic tribe being made the playball in the gigantic duel of empires that Britain and France have never ceased to wage for the mastery of the Near East? Was it only Britain's subtle way of taking revenge for the ousting of her protégé, Feisal?

The Druses were armed with British rifles and British machine guns. Their women were loaded down with necklaces and bracelets made of golden sovereigns. What of it? Pure coincidence, the English in Baghdad and Jerusalem explained. Those guns and those trinkets were just remnants of the stocks Allenby's quartermasters carelessly left behind in the caverns of the desert rocks eight years before. France did not take the matter so lightly. She dispatched an army of a hundred thousand men to reinforce the eighty thousand Senegalese already on the spot. *Entente cordiale* or not, Paris was not going to allow the projected pipe line from the Mosul oil fields to run exclusively through British-controlled territory and have but one terminus in the British port of Haifa. France insisted on her share and a branch of the oil line.

When I arrived in July, Damascus seemed to be firmly held. Troops patrolled the city; the bazaar in the Meidan quarter swarmed with steel-helmeted Senegalese, Circassian and Armenian levies in French uniforms. The Foreign Legion had its camp around the Azem Palace. The Damascenes were known to be sympathetic to the Druses and were said to be awaiting an attack on the city by the hillmen, before joining in a general uprising which was to be spread to all the Syrian cities. Two frontal attacks were made, but the

Druses were easily stopped in the foothills of the Anti-Lebanon. Damascus failed to rise and General Sarrail could report that he had the situation well in hand.

Suddenly—it was the first of October—word came that the Druses had marched around the city and cut the railway to Beyrouth at Zebdani. At the same time, the green flag went up on the minarets in the Meidan quarter and fighting broke out in the suburbs. Thousands of Druses had filtered into the city and with the help of native Damascene had destroyed some French patrols. For a week the battle raged. No sooner was one section of the city subdued, but the revolt flared up in another quarter. Each night the Druse tribesmen were reinforced by bands of new arrivals. The battalions of the Foreign Legion had been sent out to restore communications with Beyrouth and the coast. Foreigners in Damascus were growing a little nervous. But there was still no genuine cause for anxiety. The fighting was sporadic and more in the nature of desultory rioting.

Then General Sarrail lost his head. He ordered the city bombarded. For three days, seventy-two hours long, he poured shrapnel and high explosive into the crowded *souks*, and then rushed the Legion back into the bazaar. An hour before the cannonade started, an officer of the intelligence service, Captain Baron de Chaunessay, who was, curiously enough, my own landlord over in Paris, came to tell me that I, as well as every foreigner, had to leave. I therefore did not see the massacre that followed. But I learned the gruesome details in a most unexpected manner four years later when I was back in Damascus. It was the most amazing story that ever came my way.

"Have you ever been inside a harem?" asked my friend Dr. Dantziger over the telephone in Jerusalem one morning in September 1929.

"I have been in some in south Morocco," I replied, "but they had unfortunately been deserted by the brown ladies, and wrecked by the white gentlemen of the Foreign Legion."

"You will see a real harem in full working order if you come along with me," replied the Doctor. "I have an emergency call from a sheik in the Djebel-Druse country. His favorite wife is sick. I suspect it is a case of acute appendicitis. I am starting in half an hour for Damascus."

We were in the midst of the so-called Judeo-Arabic riots in

Palestine, but the prospect of seeing Damascus again promised a happy release from the daily story of woe and anxiety in the Holy Land. Two hours after the Doctor's telephone call we were racing through Galilee in a sweltering heat, with Nazareth on our left, in full view of the glittering snow fields on the top of Hermon. Skirting the Sea of Chinnereth, and following a camel trail which ran parallel with the Jordan up to the waters of Meram, we struck out into the plain of Hauran, and then in a beeline over the scene of Colonel Lawrence's most famous train-wrecking exploits, straight for Damascus. We reached the outer gardens of the city when the sun was sinking so rapidly that we missed that spectacle of ineffable white splendor, which once, it is said, so impressed Mohammed that he could not conceive Paradise to be more alluring.

In Damascus we were met at the Hotel Unger by an emissary of the sheik whose wife was sick. This man had been sent to guide us into the country of the Djebel-Druse, which remained as jumpy and unsafe as I had left it in 1925. Our dragoman, who was armed *de pied en cap* with daggers and pistols that he prudently carried under his robes, told us that France still had seventy or eighty thousand men in the country.

It must have been two in the morning when we finally reached the sheik's mansion, a two-story stucco dwelling which stood in a walled-in court with a half dozen of the usual mud huts for servants and retainers in the rear. The proprietor, who spoke German (many Arabs in Syria do), welcomed us by the light of a pitch torch held aloft by a black slave. Dr. Dantziger introduced me as a medical colleague, and we were at once led into the sick room.

The ailing person, a chubby young girl of about sixteen or seventeen years, lay in a corner on a pile of sheepskins and rugs. She was attended by two white nuns from a neighboring French mission, who were no doubt responsible for the votive lamp in front of a highly colored plaster statue of the Virgin. The patient had a high temperature and was very uncomfortable, but when the Doctor began to examine her and ordered the woolen bandages removed from her abdomen, she began to weep violently. She protested that she would not submit to the touch of a strange man, and I had to go downstairs to fetch her husband to calm her fears.

The operation was a difficult one. Not only did it take an inordinately long time to heat and sterilize the water basins, but the Doctor got himself into a mild argument with the nuns, when he, rather contemptuously, I fear, removed the holy medals and scapularies which the sisters had inserted between every layer of the swaddling clothes.

We built a sort of table by piling up rugs and goatskins in the middle of the room. The patient was carefully placed on top and, by the light of a dozen torches, Dr. Dantziger did his job, while I held the ether cone and watched the patient's breathing and heart action.

We finished at dawn, and all I had seen of the harem was a mob of dirty women in ill-fitting cotton dresses who cackled and laughed and wept alternately as they boiled the water on an open brazier of charcoal and carried it upstairs. Whenever they caught sight of us, they hastily covered their tattooed faces and stared like frightened animals. In startling contrast to the squalid clothing of the harem ladies were their heavy necklaces made up of golden British sovereigns. The marvel was that the sheik had called in a foreign medical man at all, but then, as he explained over the morning coffee, he had heard of Dr. Dantziger's renown, and knowing him to be a German (the Germans have left an excellent reputation in Syria from Turkish days), he had preferred to confide his favorite wife to the care of an *Allaman* rather than take a chance with a local Arabic practitioner.

Noticing that the rugs upon which we were seated in the reception room downstairs were swarming with vermin, we decided to forego the sheik's polite conversation and the balance of the ceremonial three cups of coffee. We told him we were exceedingly tired, which was no lie, and that if he permitted, we would like to set out for Damascus at once to have a bath and a rest at the hotel before returning to Jerusalem. He spluttered a little, insisting that we spend at least the day with him, but the legions of lice, which had by now invaded our clothing, gave us the moral strength to overcome his objections. The Doctor received his fee in yellow coin of the British realm, and we drove off.

We did not reach the great city till late in the afternoon. After a thorough cleansing and a decent meal, the Doctor and I decided to enjoy the evening breeze in one of the large beer gardens in the Grande Place. Comfortably installed, we watched the moon come up from Baghdad and ride like a panther through the palm leaves and listened to the water playing in the fountain. We talked of this and that but mostly of Palestine, the good Doctor's home and his passion. Dr. Dantziger was a native of Hamburg in Germany. He had served in the imperial army as chief surgeon to the 1st Division of the Prussian Guard. At Langemarck and on the Somme he had watched the Guard go into action and he had seen the pitiful fragments of humanity carried from the battlefields to the operating table. An ardent Zionist from his student days, the Doctor had been the first surgeon of European reputation to settle in Palestine after the country was opened up to Jewish immigration in 1920.

As we dallied over our beer, really too tired to start back for the hotel, I noticed two officers in the uniform of the French Foreign Legion stroll into the garden and take a seat at the next table. We scarcely paid any attention to them until we heard one of the officers speak to his companion in German.

Dr. Dantziger put down his stein with a start and looked in the direction of the officers.

"Did you hear that?" he said to me. "They are speaking in German!"

To find a couple of Germans in the Foreign Legion was really nothing exceptional. In the years of the Weimar Republic no less than sixty per cent of the personnel of that eternally warring brigade were German boys. Even so, it was a strange experience to hear two men, who looked for all the world like Frenchmen, converse in the language of Hindenburg. The sound of German voices had the effect of reviving the Doctor completely from his drowsiness. Memories of Hamburg and East Frisia must have been stirring in his mind, and he was not content until I had invited the *zwei Landsleute* to join us at our table. The two men accepted with good grace and we soon had a set of four foaming Dortmunders in front of us.

They were from Stettin, both of them underlieutenants in the Foreign Legion with two years' service in Morocco against the Riff Kabyles to their credit, and three years' service in Syria, where they had come at the time of the Druse revolt. One had the *Croix de guerre* with several gold palms, and the other the Legion of Honor, gained "*au péril de la vie*," he said laughingly. I remember their names distinctly, but for reasons that will become apparent I cannot mention them.

Quite naturally, the conversation drifted to Germany, to the penurious circumstances of their relatives, the inflation, the chancellorship of Hermann Mueller, President von Hindenburg, and the rising Nazi movement. The hours slipped by unnoticed as the Syrian waiter saw to it that our glasses remained filled. Slowly we drifted into a *gemütliche Stimmung*, as they say in Vienna.

By three in the morning I had learned more about the methods of pacification employed by the French in the Syrian hinterland than in my three months of wandering to and fro over the length and breadth of the country at the time of the Druse rebellion when the censors worked overtime.

We never asked our two companions why they had enlisted in the Foreign Legion. Legionnaires do not like to expatiate on that subject. These men generally have some ulterior motive that has nothing to do with a sentimental thirst for adventure and romance, as readers of a certain type of story are led to imagine. In a fighting unit whose unofficial motto is *Marche ou crève*, which means "March or croak," a unit singled out for the most ungenerous task of crushing the resistance of native nationalist and patriotic movements, the glamour has worn off long ago. On the whole, a legionnaire's life is a monotonous existence in which a few days' leave of absence causes the solitude of camp life to bear down doubly heavy. But the Doctor did casually ask one of the legionnaires where he had served in the Great War.

"Right here in Arabia," came the answer. "We were both in the same regiment and went through the whole Turkish campaign from the attack on the Suez Canal in 1915 by Jemal Pasha, till the final bloody episode in Damascus in 1918."

"You were then probably amongst the adversaries of the famous Colonel Lawrence?" I interrupted.

"Yes, of course, we were, but we saw no British soldiers in all these years, except at the end in Damascus, when Allenby's advance guard made a juncture there with the irregular Arab forces under Feisal who had moved up north following the Hedjaz Railway. For nearly two years" went on the legionnaire, "the Turks kept the Arab tribes at bay. The Bedouin would make a raid on one of our positions, overwhelm it, load themselves with booty and go home again. There may have been some of their chiefs who were imbued with the idea of founding a great free Arabian Empire, but the mass of the tribesmen were out to loot and nothing more. In fact, if Jemal Pasha had been able to hold out the prospect of more loot than the British, they would just as lief have fought on our side. But neither Turkey nor Germany had the gold that England shipped in by whole caravans to keep the sheiks on her side.

"When retreat became inevitable, we Germans formed the rear-guard of the Turkish Fourth Army," he continued. "No regular battles were fought. The tribesmen would merely dash up and attack a column of stragglers. Their snipers would pick off as many as they could, but when we made a stand to fight, they would vanish. Our heaviest losses were not inflicted by the tribesmen: the British were the worst: towards the end they bombed us from the air—nasty business in open country. Lawrence speaks of this in his book *Revolt in the Desert*. He pays us the compliment of saying that our conduct was admirable."

The German was silent for a minute and then blurted out fiercely: "If our conduct was so admirable, why did the British allow us to be massacred by the Arabs, after we had thrown up the sponge, and we had been disarmed in Damascus? There was not the slightest excuse for that blood bath. When a soldier surrenders he is out of the war. His life is sacred. There were five thousand of us who surrendered to the British in Damascus. We felt that we could not hope to continue our retreat in the direction of Constantinople with a British army on our heels and Arab tribesmen on our flanks. The Syrian Desert lay ahead of us. We had left seven thousand men in the sands of Arabia. A third of the survivors were wounded or ill. We were all suffering from dysentery or scurvy. We were in rags and hungry. We had no artillery to protect our march and the Turkish air force was outnumbered twenty to one by the British.

"We surrendered here in Damascus and by all the rules of war, we should have been safe. Yet one night the prison camp to which we were assigned was invaded by a mob of Arabs. We were unarmed and there was no escape. They pounced upon us howling like devils, brandishing their swords. It was hell let loose! We retreated into a corner of the camp and tried to make a stand. Our front ranks had armed themselves with sticks and tent poles, but there was no use. The Arabs fired their revolvers point-blank at the stomachs of our men. They were crazed with the lust of blood. They hacked and slashed and slit throats and other things until five thousand men were slaughtered like pigs. No more than a dozen escaped that massacre, which was revenge for their inability to conquer us in open battle. . . .

"Yes, we made our escape, Erich and I. We hid in the city, in Damascus, in the home of a German citizen who had us transported to Beyrouth a month later. Some weeks thereafter we were able to obtain passage on a Greek steamer. We were interned at the Piraeus. We were finally shipped back to Germany in May, 1919.

"Things were bad at home," he continued again after a pause. "The Allied blockade had starved the Reich into submission. Troops were still returning from the Russian front. There was a strong revolutionary movement. We were drafted for the Iron Division which had just come home from Finland. That division was to restore order in the Reich. Rather than fight against our own German brothers, my friend and I decided to leave. We went to the Rhineland, which was then under French occupation, but finding no work, we enlisted in the Foreign Legion in order to get something to eat.

"We were shipped to Marseilles and from there to Sidi-bel-Abbès, the legion's depot in North Africa. After the campaign against Abd el-Krim, we were transferred to Syria to help crush the Druses. And so, you see," he smiled, "we were back where we had started, after five years."

A silence intervened. The dew in the gardens had scented the air with a sweet smell of peppermint. We were the only guests left in the beer garden where the day staff had already arrived to clean up. We started back for our hotel, for the Doctor and I intended to be off early for Jerusalem. The legionnaires walked up with us to our caravanserai. We passed the crumbled piles of stone that had once been mosques and the ruined triumphal arches of the caliphs which had tumbled down under the weight of Sarrail's heavy artillery.

"That was part of our revenge," said the legionnaire, pointing to the smashed masonry and the heaps of debris in the shadows of which the beggars and human flotsam of Damascus were sleeping peacefully. "There was really no necessity for this havoc. Damascus had not joined the Druse revolt. Sarrail merely suspected that some of the rebellious sheiks were hiding in the bazaar. He subjected the whole city to a cannonade and would not have left one stone if he had not been called off by telegraph from Paris.

"But not before the infantry had moved in," he added. "The Senegalese went into that bazaar there with the bayonet. They did excellent work, those black boys. *Ausgezeichnet!* They slaughtered these Arab swine till they were wading in their blood. The women and children were driven into the mosques and the buildings set on fire. It was a thoroughgoing cleanup. We of the Foreign Legion had been assigned the outer suburbs. We entered them at dawn,

before they had risen from their sleep. They squealed like rats when
our men spiked them. There was no resistance. They had no time
to flee. We took the houses one by one, finished the inhabitants,
and set the buildings on fire.

"I led the way myself," the legionnaire said grimly. "I listened to
no pleas for mercy. Had they listened to our comrades in 1918?
Die Schweinehunde! 'Here,' I said (he continued his story with
clenched teeth), '*here*, take this! That's for Friedrich Saltzer, my best
friend. . . . And this is for Paul Froehlich, and this for Gustav
Hackert. . . .' I slashed and I ripped and I disemboweled the women
till my arm grew tired and the sweat blinded my eyes. We kept it
up till noon when my men were ready to drop with exhaustion.

"After Damascus came the pacification of the interior. We started
with the Iraq border and the Ruellah tribes, those double-crossing
bastards who tortured our prisoners by making them swallow their
own sexual organs and then threw them into manure pits. . . .
We let them have their own medicine, and plenty of it. Our legionnaires did not need any urging.

"They slew five thousand of our good German comrades back
in 1918. Well, we have taken a triple revenge so far, and we are not
through yet, are we, Erich?" He turned to his companion. "*Pour un
œil les deux yeux et pour une dent toute la gueule!*" he said in
French. "That's our motto. We have not forgotten our German
brothers!"

Ten Days in Dachau

In spite of the German people's poverty and the general sense of
frustration and humiliation, Berlin was the most interesting city in
Europe in the years immediately preceding Hitler. It was a good deal
like Paris under the first year of the Popular Front: popular universities and theaters had made their appearance, houses of culture and
youth hostels opened up all over the country, the spirit of experi-
mentation and research in literature, art, science and architecture was
evident everywhere. Cultural and technical exchange with the Soviet
Union was ripening into a fruitful collaboration and was one of the
most hopeful aspects of the time. Russia and Germany complemented each other in a remarkable way. The Reich had the industries to modernize life in the Soviet Union and to place Socialism
in that country on a firm foundation. A close commercial co-operation between the two states could have helped Germany to over-

come the colossal handicap of the burdens imposed upon her at Versailles. It is amazing, in retrospect, how little advantage was taken of that opportunity which might have served to keep Adolf Hitler from marching to power on the empty stomachs of the German people. But even more amazing was the equanimity with which the advent of Hitlerite Fascism was accepted by the leadership of the powerfully organized bodies of the working class.

I was in Berlin in February 1933, when Von Papen was negotiating with Hitler, Goebbels, Roehm and Goering concerning the possibility of including a few Nazi ministers in his cabinet. The crisis lasted a full ten days. Couriers were running up and down between the Kaiserhof Hotel, where the Nazi chiefs were in residence, and the Foreign Office in the Wilhelmstrasse. Everybody in Berlin knew what was up: Von Papen, frightened by General von Schleicher's threat to expose the enormous corruption in connection with the *Ost-Hilfe*, a federal relief scheme for agriculture in East Prussia under which Von Papen's cronies, the land *Junkers* had been the sole beneficiaries, was trying to form a cabinet without Schleicher. Nobody expected that Von Papen would have turned to the Nazis, or that he would be successful in drafting Adolf Hitler for the vice-chancellorship. From Josef Goebbels, Berlin *Gauleiter* of the Nazi party, and chief of the press bureau, whom we buttonholed as he came out of the conference room of the Kaiserhof Hotel, we learned that the Nazis were holding out for the chief positions in the cabinet, and especially wanted the chancellorship for the Fuehrer.

Schleicher was looking on quietly. He felt that his turn would soon come. He had behind him the Reichswehr command and the great moral authority of President von Hindenburg. Anyway, so he thought. Much later it became known that Meissner, the President's private secretary, with the aid of Oskar von Hindenburg, the President's son, a *Junker* who had shared deeply in the *Ost-Hilfe* graft, kept the doddering old Field Marshal in complete ignorance of the true state of affairs. They told him that Schleicher was dickering with the Communists, which was true insofar as the General had consulted with Ernst Torgler, one of the Communist chiefs, on the possibility of forming a cabinet of national concentration, with the support of the entire Left and perhaps the Catholic Center.

In the course of the crisis Hitler called one hundred thousand of his followers to Berlin. The generals were quite willing to drive the brownshirts from the parks and suburbs of Berlin, and finish once and for all with the man whom the President had called an "upstart Bohemian corporal." Had Schleicher and they been able to get Hindenburg's ear that moment, it is not unlikely that Adolf Hitler would have given the world another exhibition of his fleet-footedness. His car stood ready night and day to carry him to safety if things should go wrong. It was from Ernst Roehm himself that we learned of *der Adolf's* hysterical pessimistic fits in the Kaiserhof, and of Goering's constant back-slapping encouragement. With the connivance of Major Oskar von Hindenburg and Meissner (both were properly rewarded by Hitler when he came into his kingdom), the President was kept incommunicado for days on end.

In the meantime the workers in the populous Wedding and Berlin-Ost suburbs had on their own initiative begun to chase the storm troopers down the streets. The people's instinct did not deceive them: the moment had arrived to fight and fight hard. The workers clamored for action. But in the upper circles of the Marxists reigned an unimaginable confusion. I recall a meeting in the Karl Liebknecht House where Thaelmann, Pieck, Torgler, Willy Muenzenberg, Katz—the whole Reichstag representation of the Communists—and the leaders of the trade-unions deliberated all night, with newspaper correspondents from all over the world camped in the hall outside. Left-wing Socialists, Brandlerists and Trotskyists came in to plead for direct action, urging the proclamation of a general strike, the immediate mobilization of a united Red fighting front, the creation of a workers' militia, demonstrations, barricades, anything! Nothing was done except that two streamers hung out of the window, one with the words: "Berlin remains Red!" and the other: "The third international will liberate the human race!"

The telegrams from Moscow had urged caution. "Let Hitler come. We will follow Hitler!" said Herr Thaelmann, repeating Stalin's diagnosis of the situation.

Seeing the organized workers of Berlin thus paralyzed at the psychological moment, and taking Goering's firing of the Reichstag as a signal that the Nazi repressional machine had gone into action, blasting the last hope of an insurrectionary move, I felt that there was just a chance of resistance crystallizing in the south and the east, notably in Saxony and in Bavaria, where the Spartacus movement had one of its strongholds in the Bavarian Soviet Republic. I went to Munich, little suspecting the experience that was in store for me in that familiar and pleasant city.

A few days after my arrival, I was visited by a German colleague, a subeditor of the *Welt am Abend* in Berlin. He had been my cicerone in the left-wing circles in the capital. He was terribly agitated and asked me to hide him in my room at least for a night. The secret police were on his trail, after shutting up the paper in Berlin and raiding his apartment. He wanted to attempt the crossing of the Swiss frontier, but had no passport, and suggested that I lend him mine. I objected that his features resembled mine so little that the fraud would be easily discovered at the border, when the officials compared my photo with his face, in which case we would both be in trouble. But he pleaded insistently, arguing that he was certain to lose his life if he remained in Germany—which was indeed a foregone conclusion, for he had been a bitter enemy of the Nazis. And then, what did I stand to lose, he said, if the impersonation were discovered? I could easily ward off suspicion by saying that the passport had been stolen.

I finally assented. It was decided that he would take one of the Swiss sight-seeing buses that ran through the Black Forest to Basel. Border formalities were said to be not so strict there as on the trains running into Switzerland, Czechoslovakia, Belgium, Holland and France. The Reich was facilitating short visits by tourists from these countries in order to catch foreign *valuta*, and even permitted the busloads of sight-seers from Switzerland to come in for a few hours without passports at all. There was one chance in a hundred that my friend would get through undetected. He remained with me till the following afternoon.

In the morning we both sat in the bathroom with the door locked, I singing a song and he still as a mouse, while the maid arranged the bed and busied herself with a vacuum cleaner. When she left at last, I went out to buy a passage for Basel. The police stamped a *laissez-passer* on my passport. I gave my friend the document, urging him to mail it back at the earliest possible opportunity, and took him to the bus.

When I had not heard from him two days later, I took the precaution, as we had agreed, to notify the authorities of the loss of my passport. That turned out to be a serious error. For the passport did arrive with the morning mail the next day, and was received by a desk clerk to whom I had spoken of the missing document. Three hours later I was trying to explain to the police what could not be explained: the stamp of the German and Swiss border police on my passport testifying that I had crossed into Switzerland, and the absence of another stamp proving that I had returned the same day.

The police fetched me from a beer hall where I was eating lunch, and took me at once to the Brown House. I had nobody to blame but myself, for it was I who had drawn attention to the loss of the passport. I conjectured that the desk clerk at the hotel, who had handed me my mail that morning, also notified the police that the passport had been returned.

I dare say that the brownshirts had a pretty clear idea of what had happened. But they could not charge me with anything definite: after all, the passport was in my possession. The *Scharführer* asked to see it. I gave it to him.

"Hm," he said, "three Soviet visas!"

"There are many visas on that passport: Russia, Jugoslavia, Palestine . . ."

"*Ja*, I see that," he answered in a drawling voice, "but why three visits to Russia in so short a time?" He was checking up the dates.

"I was sent to Russia on three occasions. Am I not free to go where I like?" I asked.

"Are you a Jew?" he asked in return.

"No," I said. "I am one hundred per cent Aryan, so Deutsch *wie, ja, wie, Herr Hitler selbst.*"

He looked at me with his fishy-pale Baltic eyes and said not a word, but in the next second he glanced at the leader of the policemen who had taken me from the *Bierstube*. Without the slightest warning this man struck me across the face with his clenched fist. I staggered and dropped on one knee but quickly recovered my senses and, without thinking, returned the blow. The Nazi would have gone down had he not grabbed hold of the table before which the *Scharführer* was sitting. It was the worst thing I could have done, for in the next instant blows were raining down from all sides and everything turned black.

When I regained consciousness, my clothes were soaking wet. Apparently they had tried to revive me by dousing me with a pail of water. I was sitting in a cell lighted by a lone electric bulb. My head was aching and I could not get my jaws shut. Several teeth were missing. In my mouth was the salty taste of blood. I was horribly thirsty. The torture of thirst became so great that my head was clearing fast. When my strength had returned sufficiently, I stumbled over to the toilet and drank the flushing water. As I bent forward, while sitting on my knees, there was a laugh behind me. A man had pushed open the spyhole in the door and was looking in. It was the Nazi who had struck the first blow.

"Dirty swine!" he said.

I did not know whether it was night or day, for there was no window and my watch was gone. The electric light burned eerily. I could hear footsteps outside my door and loud voices. They passed, and the stillness returned. I lay a long time on the iron bunk staring at the light, and was on the point of losing consciousness again when I heard a moaning sound. I listened, and when it grew louder and more poignant, I burst into an uncontrollable fit of weeping.

There was a short interrogation upstairs in the morning. The same *Scharführer* questioned me again. He wanted to know who the man was that had visited me in the hotel. I refused to answer, saying that I would like to communicate with my consul first.

"He was a Jew!" insisted the *Scharführer*, without paying heed to my request.

"Perhaps," I said.

"*Ein Kommunist!*" he snapped.

"Don't know," I said.

"You will remember everything before I am through with you!" he announced. "Take him back," he ordered the brownshirts.

"I want to say," I managed to blurt out before I was pushed out of the office, "that the consul will be notified by my friends at the hotel." This was a guess on my part, but it had its effect. The *Scharführer* looked up sharply. Subsequently I knew that I had guessed correctly.

That afternoon I was taken out in a police truck to a camp, along with seventeen other men. I learned later from fellow prisoners that I was in Dachau. There at last I had a chance to wash and I was given my first meal in fifty hours: coffee made of acorns and a slice of bread.

In Dachau we were housed in wooden huts. There was no other human habitation in sight on the other side of the triple fence of barbed wire. In the distance we could see the snowy tops of the Bavarian Alps. My eleven companions in the small barrack were all Germans, except one young fellow, who was an Italian libertarian. He had been employed as a chimney sweep in Munich, and had been taken from his job to the Brown House. Every day he was escorted to the *Kommandantur* of the camp and returned in an unconscious state. He nourished a hope that he would be returned to Italy, although there, too, prison awaited him. "At least," he would say, "I will see the sun of San Daniele once more." But he never did. At one of the interviews with the camp commander, his torturers, in order to extract names and addresses of comrades, applied wooden clamps to his testicles, an instrument which the Inquisition bequeathed to Benito Mussolini, and the Duce to the Fuehrer. Eugenio Narduzzi died in the camp hospital on March 23, 1933. The notice on the bulletin board said the cause of his death was appendicitis.

We were awakened at five in the morning and, after interminable setting-up exercises and a cup of coffee with a slice of bread, we were set to work erecting more huts and digging sanitary trenches. Every day new prisoners arrived from Munich, but we had little chance of talking, except in the evenings in the barracks. In the daytime a storm trooper kept careful watch, so conversation was impossible. But at nights we did talk freely. The men in my hut were *Gewerkschaften* officials, nearly all Social Democrats, and two had been connected with Catholic labor unions. One had been a Socialist member of a rural community council somewhere in Bavaria.

Jewish prisoners were housed in a separate hut. During the drill exercises they formed a squad apart. They were forced to bend their knees, or stand on one foot till they collapsed, whereupon they were revived with a pail of water, or left to contract pneumonia in the mud. At the roll call at dawn they had to answer to their names: "Present. I am animal number so much from the Egyptian wilderness!"

The commander of the camp, a fellow who bore an extraordinary resemblance to the pugilist Max Schmeling, took a delight in having the exhausted Jews march around the assembly ground after the day's work. Before the parade, Storm Troopers cut every button from the Jews' trousers so that they had to hold on to these garments if they were not to slip down to their heels. Yet at a signal of the commander, the Nazi who conducted the drill would shout: "*Die Hände hoch!*" and the marchers' trousers would drop to the ground. If they started to stumble over the disarranged clothing or stooped to pick it up, the cowhide whips of the inspectors who stood along the route of march lashed over their backs.

For a breach of discipline in their barracks—I think one man's bed had been made up in a nonregulation manner—the Jews were punished collectively one day by having to stand close together on the drill ground in the pouring rain from dawn till sunset. In the evening, after supper, they were commanded to sing the second stanza of the Horst Wessel hymn: *Wenn's Judenblut vom Messer spritzt geht's nochmal so gut!* and thereafter the German national anthem. When only one man's voice was too weakly heard to suit the commander, he ordered a beating for the entire company. Not one Jew had the strength to walk back to the barracks.

I was not maltreated at the camp. On the eleventh day after my arrest, I was driven back to Munich and put on a train to Switzerland, two Nazis accompanying me to the border. Journalistic colleagues, I learned later, who had noticed my absence and made inquiries, had succeeded in speeding my release. At the frontier I was given back my baggage, papers, watch and money, and signed a paper that I had no complaints to make.

Dr. Josef Goebbels, who banned the newspapers for which I was writing, motivated his decision in the following notice, published in *Der Angriff*. "The correspondent Pierre van Paassen, a Dutch Jew of Lithuanian extraction, whose real name is Pinchas Paskowitz, is an ex-rabbi, who engaged in atrocity-mongering while on Reich territory."

The Munich episode had a curious aftermath in Paris, a few weeks later, when I was asked to say a few words in the Salle Wagram in the course of a mass meeting of protest against the Hitler terror. When I expressed a fear that the outbreak of Nazi barbarism might evoke a nationalistic countercurrent of hatred and military chauvinism in France and other countries, I was rudely interrupted by someone who shouted in bad French: "This is no time for pacifist weaknesses! Let Germany be smashed!"

The heckler was the German journalist who had escaped from the house of bondage across the Rhine with the aid of my passport! He had regained his fighting spirit. He subsequently returned to the Reich to engage in underground work, and disappeared in March, 1934, exactly one year after his flight.

CHAPTER FIVE

The Street of Our Lady

I

WHEN WE MOVED from Paris to the village of Bourg-en-Forêt in 1929, we soon discovered that we had done more than change our residence. It was like another world. As a fog sometimes lingers over a swamp long after the sun is up, so the past still seemed to linger in Bourg-en-Forêt. True, the elementary gods had not failed to work their havoc; most of the houses were decrepit; their roofs sagged and the doors hung crooked; the rains of centuries had completely obliterated the features of the sculptured saints in the portal of the church, but life had remained untouched by the tumult with which the modern metropolis seeks to hide its secret anguish. Those peasants amongst whom we lived for almost ten years were poor in worldly goods; they had no automobiles or radios, but neither did they envy those who had them. Thoughts of tomorrow did not torture them. They did not lament when death came, nor were they afraid of life. And yet they had a remarkably clear conception of the problems of our time and did not hesitate to take definite stands when occasion demanded it. Their rule was to cultivate their own gardens. I think that the serenity of their existence, which often evoked the envy of strangers who watched them, resided in the fact that they insisted on being men before social beings. They were individualists. They were content to be human. Thus they had retained something of that fundamental dignity which is the sole condition of human happiness because it is both our physiological norm and the law of nature.

In Bourg life moved with a slower, perhaps a more graceful,

rhythm than in Paris. The parish priest, who became our friend, had not visited the capital in a quarter century, although the distance was but an hour by rail and on a clear day you could, by climbing the perilous stairway of a ruined mill, see the Eiffel Tower trace its lacy silhouette against the southern sky.

About eight or nine in the evening the peasants harnessed their heavy dray horses to the carts, hung a lantern on the whippletree, and settled down to sleep on a sack of straw in the front seat of their covered wagons. They let the horses find their own way to the night market in Paris. They were back before the larks winged their way to heaven and we heard the rumble of their empty carts on the dirt road as they passed our house. These men never saw Paris in the daytime. Indeed, to most families in the village a trip to the capital was still an event of importance for which provisions had to be prepared on the previous day—bread and sausage and chicken—as if no restaurants existed in the capital! Stiff Sunday clothes were worn on such occasions. Umbrellas, the device by which a French peasant thinks he raises himself to the rank of a bourgeois, never used in the village itself, not even in the heaviest downpour, were taken from the cupboards and carried for decorative purposes. Relatives went along as far as the station to see the voyagers off and stood waiting in the same place a few hours later to welcome them back home again. One morning one of my neighbors, "Papa" Vessières, a man well over seventy, who was the father of a professor at the Sorbonne, one of the greatest living authorities on tropical diseases, finding himself alone in the train compartment with me, whispered in evident distress, "Monsieur Pierre, when we come to the Gare du Nord, would you mind if I take your arm? I am afraid something might happen to me. *Les bicyclettes, vous savez, et puis les taxis. Ah, mon Dieu, mon Dieu, quelle horreur!*"

Our house stood on the Rue Notre-Dame de Bonne-Nouvelle. It was hidden from the road by a hedge of intertwining willows and by an eight-foot wall. In the rear it overlooked a rolling expanse of meadows and farmland bounded on the distant horizon by the somber mass of the forest of Montmorency. From the upstairs windows and from the garden which sloped down to a small stream, we watched the color of the valley change from the dull ocher of winter to an immense beggar's blanket with all the varieties of green in square patches. Ribbons of red, where the poppies grew, marked off the borders of the wheat fields. In midsummer the entire plain was overspread by a light sheen of azure caused by the millions of bluebottles and cornflowers pushing up in the pale oats and the ripening grain. A few weeks later, on the edge of the forest far away, appeared the first sprinkle of heather purple.

You could pick out the river by letting your eyes follow a line of stately poplars, which our Abbé called the most feminine of trees. The stream gleamed like a strip of blue mirror in the evening when the sun went down. On still evenings, too, you could sometimes see the miracle of the corn suddenly beginning to sway as if an invisible hand had brushed over it. The quiver communicated itself from field to field as often happens when a sudden squall darkens a portion of the ocean's surface on a seemingly windless day. . . . To the west were farmhouses, their gray roofs visible above clusters of oak and chestnut. Not a sound penetrated into our solitude except the whistle of the train which we saw crawling along the bottom of the valley, puffing out its smoke clouds as seriocomically as a man forcing his pipe to draw.

France is full of such valleys. They are of an incredible fertility, the richest land in Europe. Where else can you raise crops of sugar beets twenty years in succession without noticing a trace of soil exhaustion? Foreigners often marvel at the savor of the fruit and vegetables in France, and imagine that the mystery resides in the art of cooking. Preparation has no doubt something to do with it, but the generous soil holds the quintessence of the secret. Upon being imported to America to preside over some of those sterilized laboratories, known as cuisines in our grand hotels, the French masters of the culinary art seem to lose the knack of imparting the savor of a meal eaten in a French peasant's cottage. Go along the Rue de Sèvres in Paris on a summer day, or through the Faubourg St. Martin and see what the French workers have on their plates as they eat their noonday meal in the open. Yes, and inhale the odors of the little restaurants on the Buttes Chaumont. . . .

In my more philosophic moods I have sometimes wondered if we must not see in France's valleys of abundance a source of the enduring enmity of the Germans? Could it not be, I thought, that the knowledge, or the surmise, that to the west of them, where the rivers widen and the earth is watered more copiously, soil more nourishing and a scene more colorful than the dreary monotony of their own pine forests and arid swamps could be found, so roused their Teutonic imagination and cupidity that they came again and again in the course of history, breaking down the barriers the Caesars had originally erected, smashing their way with unbridled fury towards the fat and pleasant habitations of the Celts?

If this be contrary to the doctrine of economic determinism, so much the worse for that doctrine!

After the roar of cities and years of imprisonment between their tower-high stone walls, we rediscovered the land and stilled the nostalgia which gnaws silently at the heart of every city dweller. In our home the quiet of morning was disturbed only by the occasional rattle of a passing cart or the distant clangor of the blacksmith's hammer on the anvil. The bells in the stunted, moss-grown tower tolled out the hours of day a little sadly. But most of the time we were up at daylight and out in the fields. A peach tree in bloom, a cluster of wild strawberry shrubs, a mole heap with its labyrinth of galleries accidentally disturbed by the plow, the nests that the swallows built under our eaves—these were the marvels before which we halted in admiration. We learned again to wonder and to admire the virtues which have almost been banished by the frenzied agitation of modern life. For when a man is alone with nature he is astonished, he admires alone and at leisure. What do we know in our hectic cities of the sweetness and consolation of a flower, which is nevertheless as vast as space! There were moments when we felt prodigiously rich in the divine distraction of soil and sky and in the mere contemplation of the changing weather.

"Do you know," once asked Henri Bataille, "what is needed to shelter all the love under heaven, the greatest sorrow and the most pressing cares of earth? A solitary tree, on one of whose low-hanging branches sits a magpie blinking at the passing clouds!"

Before the open windows on those long summer evenings we watched the lamps being lit in the mansions of the Lord. It was at times as if we caught a breath of eternity: the riddle of human existence, the sense, the purpose and the mystery of life presented itself ineluctably to my spirit. From the Abbé de la Roudaire, our friend, whose hobby was astronomy, and who often brought his instruments to make his calculations by our window, I learned that it takes the light from one of those stars fifty million years to reach us, and that our life on the earth, which is but "an insignificant fragment of a grain of sand in millions of oceans of sand," is a pure accident.

Intuition violently contradicted the priest's calm rationalism. Like

Tagore, I never felt myself a stranger on this earth, but rather that we are here for a definite purpose and that it is our task to discover that purpose and to explain and arrange the world in accordance with it. I cannot tolerate the idea of a planless universe, or that the weary road of mankind is frustration and the end of the journey universal death. I believe that human instinct, the instinct of immortality included, never deceives.

How far removed we seemed in our rural retreat from the pandemonium of Paris and the heartbreaking struggle of the millions for bread and happiness! When you thought of it, which was frequently, it poisoned your life and made you ashamed of your privileged position and your own enjoyment of peace. No matter how I tried, I have never been able to conquer that anguish. It was a sorrow implanted in me from birth. It turned moments that should have been the happiest into bitterness and gall. I felt guilty of egoism, of desertion, of seeking an escape from the reality of life. What good is it, asked Renan once, when *I* live passably well but *humanity* suffers? And yet I wanted to go on dreaming forever in the charmed stillness of our valley where everything was sweetness and voluptuousness. . . .

2

From the railway station to the house was a good half hour's walk. Usually it took an hour or more, for you stopped here and there to pass the time of day with acquaintances. A delightful stroll: past the dilapidated *mairie*, the weather-beaten church and the Café du Commerce, in front of which the elders sat under the trees playing their interminable games of checkers and commenting on the political news from Paris. In winter they sat indoors and we generally took one of the fiacres, wherein your feet froze and your ears were deafened by the rattle of the windows. When spring came and the freshly painted chairs and tables were put out in front of the café again, you noticed how the old men had grown a little older, their hair a little whiter, and how their hands trembled a little more as they moved the pieces on the board.

Our way home led past the only public monument in Bourg. It showed a helmeted angel with a sword by her side, carrying a dead soldier in her arms. The monument had been erected to the memory of those from the village who had fallen in the Great War. On the commemorative plaque they were called *les enfants de Bourg-en-Forêt morts pour la Patrie*. Once a year, on All Souls' Day, a wreath was placed there by the Mayor, and Monsieur l'Abbé de la Roudaire made a little speech, followed by the pharmacist, who spoke on behalf of the Freemasons, the freethinkers and the left republicans about France the "Christ-Nation," the brotherhood of man and universal peace. It was a simple ceremony, but very touching, especially when the school children sang the hymn *Vers l'avenir*, accompanied by the quavering temple voice of the Abbé and the uncertain basso of the pharmacist, each with his own thoughts, no doubt, as to what that future should hold.

With our neighbors, who were farmers, we talked of the problems of agriculture, of the poultry yard and the seasons. Many nights I sat in the stable with Gaston Grèvecoeur and Raoul Mottet, playing a game of cards by the light of an oil lamp, while waiting for the birth of a calf. Mottet was a small farmer who was generally suspected of making his living by poaching in the forest, although he was sworn in as a rural constable with a special charge to watch for poachers. Grèvecoeur had served with a regiment of Zouaves in Africa and at Verdun in the Great War. He hailed from Carpentras, which is near enough to Marseilles to have endowed him with the Provençal's renowned cock-a-hoopness. To hear him talk you would suppose he had been on a most intimate footing with Joffre at the Marne. He spoke of Pétain as of a twin brother who had made his way in the world, and had we taken him seriously we might have asked him for details about the game of billiards which he was supposed to have played with members of the general staff. The years he had spent in Africa and the colonies served him as a perpetual source for bragging. He never tired of repeating that he had been a model soldier, for no other reason but to earn a sergeant's stripes which furnished him with the money to see the girls of Casablanca and Saïgon from time to time. "They all liked me," he said, "and the proof of it is that I used to sleep with the drum major's wife." Of life in the trenches he never spoke. His twenty months' captivity in Germany, where he had been sent to work on a farm in Bavaria, had made him thoughtful. "Monsieur Pierre," he would say after a spell of deep cogitation, "we should never forget that amongst the Germans there are people like ourselves." This glimmer of a broader humanity was invariably followed with the remark that it would be well to keep an eye on the Boche nevertheless. "And on our own Boches as well," Raoul would chime in.

Once a year, on the night of the fourteenth of July, Bastille Day, we had *une soirée artistique* in the festively decorated Salle des Fêtes. After speeches by the notables in which the ideals of liberty, equality and brotherhood were exalted with a flow of rhetoric from the works of Rousseau, Hugo and Jaurès, local minstrels, dressed in their Sunday best, gave us some of the latest chansons and wisecracks from the cabarets of Montmartre. Red wine flowed in torrents in the taprooms on the street and, judging by the ludicrous antics of the performers on the stage, the "Republic, One and Indivisible" was no less generously toasted behind the scenes. The evening not infrequently ended in a lively political debate. On the last occasion I attended, my neighbor Grèvecoeur, who for some unfathomable reason held the English in abomination, denounced the new *entente cordiale* between France and England (then maturing in the chancelleries) by singing with scandalously eloquent gestures the medieval sailors' ditty:

> *Buvons un coup, là, là!*
> *Buvons-en deux.*
> *A la santé des amoureux*
> *A la santé du Roi de France.*
> *Et—merde—sur l'Angleterre!*
> *Qui nous a déclaré la guerre.*

Upon hearing this, *monsieur le sous-prefet* hurriedly left the hall, but the citizens applauded and stamped their feet, calling for more and then joined in the chorus, which is far worse.

3

Everybody met at the weekly market and you could learn all the scandal and gossip of the neighborhood. There were always a few idlers on hand, who, in exchange for a glass of wine at the zinc-covered counter in one of the taverns on the square, volunteered to give away men's innermost secrets: which of the merchants and farmers most assiduously frequented the state brothel; what was going on at the château on those winter evenings when long lines of limousines from Paris were halted in the park; what was the real situation between the curé of a neighboring hamlet and the widow of a rich grocer whom he visited—most of it lies, of course, but it was good to hear them talk.

For a political debate the Café of the Golden Lion was the place. There Monsieur Tisserand had his permanent seat. "Un annarsheest" the villagers called him. If you wanted to hear him at his best you had to wait for the afternoon when the pharmacist and the rest of the Radicals dropped in. Monsieur Tisserand was the administrator of the public library from which he "*systématiquement*," as he was wont to say, kept away "the poison of clericalism and religion," something that was his right and even his duty, I dare say, under a republican regime which, as Viviani once exclaimed, has extinguished the heavenly lights. The clergy did not like Monsieur Tisserand, although no two men greeted each other with a greater flourish of hats and deep bows than he and the Abbé de la Roudaire when they met on the streets. From time to time these two citizens exchanged lengthy letters on a burning question of the day, and watched from behind the curtains in their respective parlors, as the mail carrier deposited the epistles in each other's letter boxes, for they lived vis-à-vis. I do not know who started that correspondence, but I suspect it was Monsieur Tisserand. He literally boiled over with indignation or enthusiasm, depending on the occasion, to inform his clerical neighbor of his views on a political event of importance. In those letters he let off steam. They ran into dozens of pages and were read in public in the café by Monsieur Antoine Tisserand himself: those of the Abbé in a voice that betrayed pitiful condescension, the copies of his own in the tone of majestic finality. He quoted voluminously from Voltaire and the philosophers of the Encyclopédie, but his hero was a certain Pierre Leroux, a Utopian freethinker of the seventies. In those missives to the Abbé, the librarian never failed to include citations from Lamennais, Alfred Loisy and other priests who had left the church. To these pinpricks the Abbé replied invariably with the assurance that he never ceased praying for the salvation of M. Tisserand's soul, as well as for the souls of those departed apostates, a remark that made the recipient of the letter as furious as a riled rooster.

Monsieur Tisserand was a Communist. As a boy he had carried water to the defenders of the Commune on the barricades in Belleville. He remembered those stormy days with pleasure and never tired of harking back to them. "They had no mercy, the Versaillais! The men of my precinct fought them for three days! If a worker had soiled clothes, or if he smelled of powder, or even if his hands were merely calloused, bang against the wall with him and twelve bullets smack into his skin! *Ils n'avaient pas de pitié, les Versaillais.* They were worse than the soldiers of Bismarck. My mother hid me in the sewer when they came to search our house. They beat her to death with the butts of their rifles when they could not find me. Ah, the clerical dogs, the black crows!"

When he grew calmer he returned to his other pet topic: America. He had never visited the country and I do not think he had the slightest inclination to undertake the journey. But what he had read of life in the United States fascinated, more often exasperated, but always puzzled him.

"They say," he would begin after the waiter had brought him the ritual glass of coffee, and he had taken the first sip, "that Jefferson was animated by what I would call fundamentally anticapitalist sentiments and Jackson even more, but how would you explain the fact that nothing has come of it? Why is there no Socialism in America? Can it be explained? Nobody has ever given me a satisfactory answer!"

"There is in the first place," I would tell him, "the influence of puritanical sectarianism in the United States. The spirit of that form of Protestantism which is entirely capitalistic has held, and still holds, an enormous section of the working class captive, as well as the petty bourgeoisie and the farmers. . . ."

"That is all very well," Monsieur Tisserand would interrupt, "but that is merely stating the fact—that is not explaining the absence of Socialism. The growth of the Socialist movement here in Europe has been extremely slow and painful. We know that. We also know the reason: capitalism itself developed but slowly and by easy stages in Europe. In America, on the other hand, capitalism developed in a tempo almost inconceivable here in France. Enormous fortunes were created. Wealth took on extraordinary proportions. And, from what I can gather, Proudhon's famous phrase about property being theft has been amply verified over there. Whether it was land speculation, or the building of railways, or the manufacture of steel, whether it was Astor or Field, Carnegie or Gould, it was the same endless chain of fraud, violence and gangsterism. *A mon avis*, there is but one description for that piling up of wealth: crime. Crime, I call it, because it came about without the slightest respect for the legal or moral rights of others. I have read a book by a certain Monsieur Gustave Myers on the history of those great American fortunes. What is the story? Men were robbed till they were bankrupt. . . . Millions of dollars for graft . . . whole railways stolen . . . judges and juries bought . . . foreign capitalists robbed. . . . *Mon Dieu,* it is awful! The history of the United States is frightening in its harrowing monotony. I think if I had to live in a country like that, I would go insane. And how did the working class take all this? That is the question. That the workers did not understand at once that it was principally their class which was being robbed, *that* I can understand. They were probably never told. We all know that they are bound to discover the fact some day and demand their just due. But how is it that there was not at least a vast movement of protest before this, a mass indignation against that monstrous injustice? Can you explain that? If you tell me that, I will at last know why there is no Socialism in America!"

"Dozens of economists have occupied themselves with that question," I would begin.

"I know, I know: Bernstein, Weber, Kummer," he would interrupt me with a gesture of impatience. "But they have not arrived at a satisfactory conclusion, any more than anyone else. They cannot explain it. Have you ever read the Declaration of Independence? *Eh bien,* what about that? When there is an accumulation of wealth as inordinate as in America, there must have been ruthless exploitation on the part of one class. That's clear, is it not? The social contrasts must have been enormous. We know that there were violent combats between capital and labor. Why did no militant Socialist movement emerge from these initial struggles? Why did not the workers at least invoke the Declaration of Independence?"

"But Monsieur Tisserand, you know as well as I do that that document was not written for the working class. The Declaration is the self-assertion on the part of a nascent American plutocracy and landed aristocracy against British imperialism, a cutting loose from British tutelage. The only battle American capitalism has had to fight against the feudal system or a remnant of it was the War of Independence against England. After that it had a free field of unlimited expansion before it. It did not pass through the struggle Europe had to wage against the feudal mode of production and the political restrictions of the old regime. That is the explanation of one of the world's greatest commentators of the evolution of Socialism. I mean W. Ravesteyn of Holland. American capitalism was free when it was born. For the proletariat this has been of fatal significance. For, whereas in Europe the struggle against feudalism brought the workers together with the bourgeoisie in a united front, in America the bourgeoisie was almighty without the help of the workers. The working class was never made the strong political element that the bourgeoisie in Europe made it, at its own great risk, in order to conquer feudalism, because feudalism never existed in America."

"That does not explain anything yet," Monsieur Tisserand would shake his head.

"*Eh bien*, will you allow me to finish?"

"Not today, *mon cher ami*, not today. My head is buzzing with what you have just told me. I must verify all that tomorrow in the original sources. Tell me now, *plutôt*, if you will, whether it is true, as I have heard it said, that Americans drink ice water in winter time."

"That's perfectly true. They do. And they eat ice cream with a cup of coffee!"

"How about cancer? Do not the doctors warn them?"

"The doctors drink ice water themselves!"

"But that is fantastic—Monsieur Beausart, did you hear that?" He was turning to one of his cronies sitting at the next table immersed in a game of chess.

"*Non, je vous demande pardon, Monsieur Tisserand*," replied the neighbor adjusting his pince-nez. "I did not hear."

"Well," resumed Tisserand triumphantly, "it is absolutely true what I once told you: *les Américains boivent de l'eau glacée en hiver!*"

"In winter time they drink ice water? *Parbleu*, but that is ridiculous, that is contrary to nature!"

"*Messieurs*," another chess player interrupted gravely, "you do not astonish me in the least. I have with my own eyes seen an American put lumps of ice in a glass of wine. *Oui, messieurs*, I have seen that. May I never move from this spot if it isn't true. It happened last year on the eleventh of November in the Café des Acacias on the Place Pigalle in Paris. The *maître d'hôtel* had the goodness to draw my attention to the incident. I need not say, *messieurs*, that I was scandalized!"

"No doubt you were," assented Monsieur Tisserand. "Such blasphemy!"

I knew Mme. Tisserand, the librarian's wife, but only for a short time. She was a woman of great charm and although no longer young, she belonged to that feminine category that Guy de Maupassant called "still appetizing." There were stories circulating about her past, but I did not pay any attention to that gossip. For when I knew her she was one of the Abbé's most devoted parishioners and far from approving her husband's militant republicanism.

Hers was the first funeral I was asked to attend in Bourg. I feared some embarrassing moments the morning of the ceremony, for she had insisted, in her lifetime, that she be buried with the full rites of the church. This meant that Monsieur Tisserand, her husband, would have to meet the Abbé de la Roudaire face to face. There were not a few who predicted a violent clash between the two old antagonists and many attended the service out of pure curiosity. However, there was no untoward incident. Everything passed off decently. After mass, the Abbé came into the librarian's house and sat down with the mourners. Monsieur Tisserand said to him, "Every morning I brought her coffee in bed. She deserved it. She was a good woman and beautiful in her youth. She gave me everything, Monsieur l'Abbé, everything, for she loved me!" After these words he grew pensive. The priest bowed his head and shook hands with him very decorously.

4

I was kept informed of the deaths in the community by Camille Villetorte, the gravedigger, whose place of work I passed every time I had to go to Paris.

"Today it's Monsieur Thurandot's turn," Camille greeted me when I hailed him one morning from the road.

"I don't know your Monsieur Thurandot," I said, stopping by the fence.

"Sure, Monsieur knows him, the cross-eyed little grocer with the long nose from the Rue de la Buanderie? Monsieur remembers?"

"He of the two beautiful daughters?"

"Precisely, the father of Lucienne and Suzanne." This with a wink.

"That reminds me: I don't see her around any more, the little Suzanne. She used to come by some evenings with a young man."

"Ah, no wonder, Monsieur, no wonder. She is in Paris. Monsieur had not heard of it? But yes, she is in the great city."

Camille dropped his spade on the bottom of the grave he was squaring off and clambered to the surface. He walked to the foot of a weeping willow, pulled a bottle of *pinard* from his haversack which lay there in the shade and took a swig.

"The whole commune is talking of that affair," he went on, sucking his moustaches. "I am surprised that Monsieur has not heard . . . It appears she is making little steps to and fro in the neighborhood of the Porte St. Denis. . . . Monsieur the collector of the direct imposts was telling me, *voilà*, two or three months ago. It appears he had to be in Paris one day, Monsieur the collector, ha, ha, and *tiens*! whom does he see there, but the *petite* Suzanne of the grocer. Wasn't that a coincidence? He's a man of fine instincts, this Monsieur the tax collector. He knows what's good. . . . I wonder if she'll be at the funeral *tout à l'heure*, the little Suzanne. . . . A fine shape she has, that girl, and of such a father! To be sure, one can never tell."

Camille dropped back into the hole, but presently threw two skulls and some human bones to the surface.

"What's this?" I asked in surprise. "What are you doing now?"

"They are a little crowded down here, Monsieur. I am throwing them out for the time being, till after the funeral. Then they go back. This is the head of *le père* Cochard, a rich farmer. Monsieur did not know him. He died before Monsieur's time. A scoundrel and a villain if ever there was one. He left not a sou to charity."

"What I don't understand," I said, "is how these skulls get out of coffins. How long ago was he buried, this Monsieur Cochard?"

"That must be going on to forty years, Monsieur, since we put *le père* Cochard away. My father dug his grave. . . . It's a moist patch down here. The pine boards don't hold, Monsieur. They rot away in no time. And then, the worms in France always had good teeth. . . ."

"Well, Monsieur Camille, I must be on my way!"

"To Paris, Monsieur Pierre?"

"To Paris!"

"Politics, Monsieur?"

"Not politics exactly. I must go to the Foreign Office!"

"Who's there now at the Quai d'Orsay, Laval or Tardieu?"

"Monsieur Laval is now the Foreign Minister."

"Ah, *le salaud!* It's that rascal and his gang who will bring misery upon us yet, mark my words! Ah, *les salauds!*" The gravedigger shook his head. "A dirty job *la politique*, Monsieur Pierre, a very foul business!"

5

We were not the only foreigners living in Bourg. About a quarter of a mile out of the village, on the road towards Clamercy, was a farm occupied by a Russian *émigré*. Unlike the other peasant cottages, his house did not border the roadway but stood a good distance inland and was almost completely hidden from view in summertime by clusters of shrubbery and the foliage of a small woods of willow trees. You reached the place by a sunken dirt road which followed the bends of a shallow creek formed by the seepage from the adjoining pastures. In the fall the road turned into a sea of mire and remained that way: virtually impassable till the warm weather of the following year. Yet, a small amount of money, a few loads of pebbles and sand and a little grading, altogether a few days' work, would have easily repaired the damage. But of this the proprietor would not hear. The *cantonnier* had spoken to him on the subject of the road more than once. He had dismissed the official every time with the remark that it was his own private property and that he could do with it as he liked; moreover, he wanted the road that way because it reminded him of Russia.

The farmer's name was Platon Klioutchevsky. A heavy-set individual with a small reddish beard and blue eyes, he must have been in his early fifties. He was something like our local man of mystery. There was a light in the window of his house at all times of the night, for he always neglected to close the shutters. Peasants driving by in their carts to or from the market in Paris said that some nights they had heard the Russian sing at the top of his voice. Often, too, they had been on the point of driving up the dirt road to investigate what was going on at the lonely farm house where they could see the vehemently gesticulating silhouette of the man moving against the light of the lamp or hear the crash of furniture, the screams of a woman and the raucous cursing voice of Klioutchevsky. What was going on at the house? Why were they always quarreling?

Madame Klioutchevsky was much younger than her husband. She was a woman of simple grace, not unattractive: tall, Titian-haired with soft jade-colored eyes and a skin as white as alabaster. She was obviously of genteel birth, for she spoke French in that melodious drawl affected by the former Russian upper classes. She carried herself with the dignity of a born aristocrat and although her clothes were old she always made a presentable appearance. When she came into the village to do her shopping, the women stood still to see her go by and then whispered: Was she Klioutchevsky's wife or was she his mistress? Why did she stay with such a brutal man?

"He beats her," said the men, "so she must be his legal wife. All Russians beat their wives. . . ."

Still others held that Klioutchevsky had been a general in the Russian army—every second Russian in France is either a general or a prince. But that surmise was based on nothing more authentic than that M. Klioutchevsky was invariably dressed in an old blouse with a broad leather belt around the waist and that he wore a pair of mud-splashed riding boots. There was nothing military in his bearing. He had a rather slouchy walk and always kept his hands in his trouser pockets. It is true that he kept a saber in his house. This I knew from Louise, our *femme de ménage*, who had served the Klioutchevsky family before she came to us.

"A funny kind of a farmer, that Monsieur Klioutchevsky," Louise would say. "For one thing, he never gets up till eleven in the morning, and then only to sit drinking one cup of cocoa after the other and smoking cigarettes till the room is white with smoke. If it were not for his wife the horses would never get fed. He'd let them starve!"

"When does he work?"

"*Eh bien*, he must work at nights—he does not stir out of the house till three or four in the afternoon when he is not drunk. When he is drunk he remains indoors altogether."

Drink, that was the trouble with M. Klioutchevsky. But for his drinking there was a primary cause. When he staggered around the village from one taproom to the other, or sat all by himself in a corner of the Lion d'Or with a somber stare on his face, contemplating the glass in front of him, the other customers shook their heads. "*C'est la douleur des hommes russes*," they would say.

"He's a White and as such I can have no sympathy with him," said Monsieur Tisserand, "but he is human just the same. . . . How would we feel far away from France in some strange country without hope of ever returning? The thought is enough to drive a man to drink and to insanity. But such is life. Those Russians we have here in France are paying for the sins of their fathers. There is retributive justice in this world after all. With a few noble exceptions, men like Tolstoy and the like, their class lived a life of leisure and affluence on the back of the long-suffering moujik, the same good-natured fellow as our own *Jacques Bonhomme* whom our nobles exploited like cattle. Until the *Jacquerie* revolts came and the manor houses went up in flame and the heads of the squires were carried around on pikes. That is the way it went in Russia. The jug goes down the well until it breaks."

I never had any personal dealings with M. Klioutchevsky except one day when he came to the house, in the fall of the year 1931. He had learned, he said, that I had been on a visit to his native country and would be glad if I could tell him some of my impressions.

I asked him inside and gave him a brief description of what I had seen: the mournful aspect of Leningrad and the general down-at-the heels appearance of the population. On the other hand, there had been an enormous amount of building and construction in cities like Moscow, Kiev and Rostov-on-the-Don, and feverish activity on the collective farms.

I told him of the huge crowds of kulaks I had seen sleeping in the streets of Leningrad near the Finland station. They were mostly Ukrainians who were on their way to the forests of Karelia. They were being removed to break up the sullen hostility against Stalin's agrarian reforms. But I also told him of the enormous amount of study and reading that was going on, the splendid theatrical experiments, and the spirit of daring and innovation in science and architecture. "Step by step," I said, "painfully at times, no doubt, the peoples of Russia are being imbued with a new vision. The difference between Russia and the rest of Europe is that whereas in countries like Germany and Italy culture is on the decline, and the standard of living going down, in Russia it is going up, imperceptibly almost, but going up just the same."

"Do you know any Russian?" he asked.

"I speak a little Ruthenian," I said, "and those with whom I came in contact understood me quite well."

"You were treated well, I mean not officially, but in chance meetings with people who did not know you were a foreign journalist?"

"Exceptionally well," I said. "I think the Russians are the most brotherly people on earth."

"And the army?"

"What I saw of the army gave me an impression of power and efficiency . . . But I do not like armies, the Red army no more than any other. The only good thing that can be said about Soviet militarism is that the leaders do not glory in their country's military prowess, but that they look upon armaments and all the rest of the killing game as an unavoidable evil. They would much sooner devote the wealth that is being produced to the improvement of the people's condition. But the others do not allow them. They must arm because they are menaced from all sides."

He sat silent for a while, rubbing his hand over his mouth and beard, looking out of the window.

All at once he said, "I feel like asking you to give me a blow on the head!" He rose from his chair. "*Je vous en prie, je vous en prie, flanquez-moi une gifle au moins.*"

"Why should I strike you, M. Klioutchevsky? This is a most extraordinary request: a man comes to my house . . ."

"Ah, you don't know," he replied, and buried his face in his hands. "Don't you see," he said, turning up his tear-stained face, "that's where I belong, over there. . . . The revolution was right. . . . There was hunger and there had to be a change. . . . Why did not I see it earlier? How can I get back now? I would do anything: sweep floors, the dirtiest work if only I could see Russia again, hear my own people talk. . . . I detest them, you understand. I have an unutterable contempt for everything Russian, but I am dying without Russia. . . . Do you think they will give me a visa, these others?"

"The Bolsheviks, you mean? Why not? Many are going back. I understand there is a standing invitation to the exiles to return." And I told him of the case of Prince Mirsky, who had given up his position as professor of Slavonic languages in the University of

London to return to Moscow where he had become the literary critic on one of the great dailies.

But Klioutchevsky did not return to Russia, although he entered into negotiations with the Soviet embassy in Paris for a return visa, and he did sell his farm on the strength of the good news he heard there.

It was the money he received for his property that brought about the tragedy. Unknown to his wife he had hidden the bank notes in the bottom of the stove. One day while he was away in Paris to make arrangements for their departure, the woman lit the fire and the money vanished.

Klioutchevsky came home around seven in the evening. From a distance he saw the smoke rising from the chimney. Those who met him on the road said that his face was terrible to behold, the face of a maniac. He bellowed like an ox in the abattoir as he raced along the road.

What happened when he reached the house the gendarmes learned from Madame Klioutchevsky just before she died the following day. Finding that his money had been burned, he had tied his wife's hands to the kitchen table and chopped them off with an ax.

6

In Bourg-en-Forêt the market was a weekly joy from which we returned light of heart and loaded with parcels. Its approach never failed to give me a holiday feeling. On Thursday, the school holiday in France, the atmosphere in the "grand" square was reminiscent of a kermis in Flanders than which, I think, there is nothing more joyous on earth. In the narrow alleys between the booths and stalls a dense crowd of peasants, rich and poor, from the surrounding district milled about with their wives and children. Their carts and horses cluttered up the side streets. You saw the notables, the school-teachers, the notaries, the mayors and officials from all the hamlets and villages in the neighborhood. The clergy were also present. Those priests, generally the sons of peasants themselves, examined the cattle with the eyes of connoisseurs, and their counsel was frequently sought when it came to making a purchase after hours of haggling. *Les paysannes* made you taste their butter from the point of a knife. When you bought a supply of potatoes for the winter you concluded the bargain by drinking a glass of white wine with the salesman in one of the taverns. Merchants and hucksters shouted their wares. "Ah, this good linen, ah, the delicious nougat from Montélimar!" Quacks sold remedies against all conceivable ills. According to the learned diagnosis of one rural Aesculapius, most of our maladies are due to the presence of worms in the human organism. There are worms, he would say, which eat away at your brain, causing premature senility; other worms gnaw away at a person's heart when a love affair does not run smoothly. This doctor, who wore a silk hat and a shining frock coat, had a sheet of linen spread out against the back of the stall on which was painted a worm of boa-constrictor dimensions gorging himself with a chunk of a blood-red human heart. It was a most convincing picture. He called the peasants over to his booth: "*Messieurs-dames, approchez-vous, approchez-vous,* health is within your grasp!" If they protested that they enjoyed perfect health, he made the peasants spit on their caps and then held a magnifying glass above the saliva which at once became alive with maggots. "And what do you think of your health, now, Monsieur? You are chock-full of worms!" The peasants looked aghast. It was nothing short of magic!

It takes a French peasant a long time to make up his mind before making a purchase. That is why the merchants poured forth an endless stream of sales talk which they shrewdly mixed with the bait of indiscreet references to prominent personalities of the neighborhood: "Now this pair of bed sheets—have a feel of the material, dear madam—one pair for the master and his goodwife, one pair for the children and one for the maid. . . . At the château the maids do not get sheets on the bed. *C'est pas nécessaire, d'ailleurs* . . . they crawl into the seigneur's bed. . . . The six sheets for two hundred francs. . . . Now is the best time to buy. . . . In a week the government is going to raise prices. The price of bread is going up, the price of bed sheets is going up. . . . *Monsieur le ministre* has discovered a new danseuse. . . . She's as poor as a church mouse, but from what I hear she has compensating qualities, *o là, là!* What that demoiselle needs is a trousseau. . . . You are going to pay for it, if you don't buy now. . . . *Vive la République!* . . . For good measure I throw in this fine rope to tie up the dog. . . . Where will you get such a bargain?"

One of the most popular personages in the market place was a troubadour who operated a wheezy harmonica. He was an ex-soldier, *une gueule cassée* whose face had been twisted into a horrible smirk by a piece of shrapnel. One eye was fully an inch lower than the other. This gave you the impression that he looked at you from a house with two storeys. He sang through his nose in the Parisian slang to which the peasants listened with a religious solemnity. His chants were mostly laments on the fate of dimple-cheeked milkmaids in the dens of evil in Montmartre. Sometimes, I thought, he exaggerated. Often, too, he repeated himself, which was understandable in the course of human events. But his moral code was beyond reproach: like Calvin Coolidge's preacher, he was against sin. . . .

Two or three bookstalls before which the intellectuals and the clergy met were a perpetual delight. They had a fresh stock of secondhand literature each week. One of the book merchants had the most vivid blue eyes of any man I ever saw. Next to the pharmacist, I was his best customer. He sold me some French pamphlets which had been printed in Holland in the sixteenth and seventeenth centuries. Their contents would have sent their authors before the execution squad in half a dozen European and American countries today.

And then there were the soothsayers and the dispensers of contraceptive medicine. They had to hide their illicit trade behind some innocuous false front. Madame Gabrielle, for instance, had her son, the pimply-faced Marcel, stand outside her little booth to urge you to have your photo taken, seated in a tin airplane. But once inside, she laid the cards for you and hinted in a mysterious whisper that she knew an address or two in the neighborhood where one could be *tranquil* in an *intérieur exotique* with a rural daughter of Venus who was said to be an expert in *caresses délicieuses* and all the games of love. If the farmers could get rid of their wives and children, leave them somewhere in a waffle booth or haggling with a Jew about the price of a mechanical eggbeater or a goatskin, they sneaked away to Madame Gabrielle. That woman was rich. She came to the market in her own automobile.

From one of the streets leading to the market square, the Rue Danès de Montardart, named after a long-since-departed citizen who had left his money to the poor, ran a narrow alley known as the Passage of the Sirens. In this alley were two "houses of illusion," easily recognizable by the red lanterns and the large numbers on their doors. The inmates of these temples, dedicated to a mercenary Aphrodite, leaned their bosoms on the open windows or strolled out amidst the crowds at the fair, triumphantly leading a customer off now and then to their haunts. They were no longer young, these ladies, and no longer fresh—Montmartre had left its traces—but they could do wonders with cosmetics. The farmers stared at them openmouthed and followed at a distance, swallowing hard, their eyes glistening.

We ended our day at the market by having a late lunch in the restaurant-kitchen of Mother Lunette which was located in one of the side streets off the square. Her house leaned against the church so that when the hours struck in the clock tower you could feel the walls of the dining room tremble. "Mama" Lunette, queen of French cooks, personally supervised the service in her establishment. The shoulder of mutton with string beans, the *ragoût de veau*, the *sole meunière* with wine sauce, or the omelet with mushrooms which she prepared in a corner of the room under the big chimney, came to the table so perfect, so well cooked, so appetizingly dished up that it made your mouth water. And with it a crackling loaf of bread, not wrapped in cellophane, thank heaven! and a choice of Burgundy, Haut Sauterne and Beaujolais. All of it for ten francs—thirty cents in our money.

"I do not expect to taste better in Paradise," the Abbé de la Roudaire used to sigh as he took his napkin from under his chin.

7

The Abbé Arsène de la Roudaire, parish priest of Bourg-en-Forêt, was in his seventy-eighth year when I first knew him. In spite of his age, he was subject to none of the infirmities of the old and could boast that he was still in possession of all his teeth. An ecclesiastic of the old stamp, a type rapidly dying out, he had nothing in common with the priests of the new generation in France "except the name and the costume." His piety was sober and reasonable, without sudden exaltations or mysticism; his religion a set of rules and dogmas which he defended as a general defends a strategic post entrusted to his care. Questions of criticism and research did not interest him; their meaning escaped him entirely, although he had started out in life by publishing a short treatise on astronomy. "If I had continued on that road," he said to me one day in speaking of his earlier studies, "I would have lost my faith." He had preferred to keep the faith intact and leave troublesome questions to others. Like everyone else the Abbé worked in his garden in the morning, took a nap in the afternoon and taught catechism to the children when school was dimissed. Just before supper he could be seen strolling on the main street, reading his breviary. "That is when he does his spying," said the anticlericals. It was quite true that the Abbé had his eyes wide open and that he knew everything going on in the village, but there was not a grain of malignity in his make-up. He was the most tolerant and the most polite man I ever knew.

To the Abbé came parents to inquire about suitable husbands and wives for their children. With him they discussed the amount of the dowry, the foreclosing of a mortgage, and the intricacies of the income-tax formula. I have known him to spend whole evenings going over the books of a shopkeeper who was menaced with bankruptcy.

One day I persuaded the Abbé to accompany me on a visit to the capital, but he felt ill at ease in the city and on the street he stopped frequently to mop his forehead with his red handkerchief. Together we walked down the Rue de Rennes on the Left Bank towards the close of the afternoon of an early summer day. I noticed the Abbé staring in amazement at the painted faces of the ladies who were walking up toward the Boulevard du Montparnasse to keep their vigil in the cafés on the hill at the cocktail hour. But he did not make any comment. Not till the following Sunday, in the course of his sermon, did he make a few remarks on the fashions of Paris, and then they were scorching. The Abbé had expressed a desire to see the Chamber of Deputies in session. When he entered the Palais Bourbon he shook hands with the ushers, remarking, when I pointed out to him who these men were, that they appeared to him more distinguished than many a parliamentarian. After he had blown his nose, he asked me to point out to him where the Communist representation sat. When one of their spokesmen mounted the rostrum—I think it was André Marty, the leader of the Black Sea mutiny in 1919—the Abbé half rose from his seat and bowed to the speaker. "I do this," he said, "because I see in him a representative of the sovereign people of France."

The Abbé had been to Rome in his younger days, but he was most reluctant to speak of his impressions of the Eternal City. I have noticed the same reticence on the subject of Rome in many other French clerics with whom I came in contact. In contrast to certain American priests of my acquaintance, whose voices drop to an awesome whisper whenever they mention the Holy Father, those men spoke of the Pope and the cardinals as ordinary human beings. Several were frankly suspicious of the *Italianità* of the present Vatican regime and its subservience to the policies of Duce Mussolini. Gallicanism is not entirely dead in France, and the saying of Piux XI that the French clergy are the most intractable on earth is quite understandable. But they are also the best instructed and the most exemplary clergy on earth. Amongst the French people you do not find that amused skepticism on the moral life of the clergy which you cannot miss noticing in Italy and the Mediterranean islands.

The Abbé's sojourn in Rome had coincided with the occupation of the city by Garibaldi's troops and the phenomenal proclamation by Pio Nono of the dogma of papal infallibility. He maintained a significant silence on both events. The only worldly subject on which he felt strongly and on which, on occasions, he would deliver himself with feeling, was the decline of France's influence in Near and Middle Eastern countries. A disaster, he called this, attributable solely to the Third Republic's anticlerical policy. By disbanding the monastic orders and closing their schools, the regime, he maintained, had prevented the emergence of a new generation of Catholic missionaries. This constituted not only a serious infringement on the principle of freedom of religious worship, but had been fraught with incalculable damage to the prestige of France abroad. The republican patriots, he used to say, and by this he meant the anticlerical Radicals, with all their ostentatious and wordy display of devotion to the fatherland, had not been able to inspire young Frenchmen to set out for such countries as Egypt, Syria, Turkey and Palestine, and by taking the places of aging missionaries, hold aloft the torch of French culture. This alone shows, said Monsieur l'Abbé, that the republican ideal lacks the quality of fire. Our youth is bereft of true heroism, because it is afraid of suffering.

Our parish priest knew too little about other sects to express an opinion. He looked upon the Huguenots as most Frenchmen do, that is to say he regarded them as strangers and aliens. No doubt the exclusiveness of the French Protestants is largely responsible for this sentiment. In France the Huguenots, although of the purest Gallic stock, are to this day a people apart, a nation within the nation as it were. Their gloomy history seems to have deprived them of the racial verve and a healthy *joie de vivre*. It may also be that Calvin's dour doctrine of predestination is at the bottom of it.

"I have never been in one of their temples," said the Abbé, "but I frequently listened to their congregational singing when I passed by and it always made a better man of me."

They were happy hours I spent in the old man's company. No matter what time of day I called, he would always ring for his old *servante* Marie, and ask her to bring a tumbler of red wine. Melting on the bottom of the glass lay two lumps of sugar, like two fine red crystals.

"Piping hot you must drink it," he would urge, "for the weather is damp and I do not want to have it said in your old age that you picked up rheumatism in Bourg-en-Forêt."

But one afternoon Marie was out when I ran into the presbytery for shelter from a pouring rainstorm. The Abbé was standing by the window, meditating upon the vocabulary of birds and the relative poverty of human speech. "Do you know," he asked, "that sparrows have three distinct cries of alarm, one to express hunger, one to warn of coming bad weather as today, and quite a different cry when their young are in danger of a prowling cat?

"But *mon Dieu*, you are soaking wet," he suddenly interrupted himself. "*Tenez*, help me light this candlestick! We will go down into the cellar and find a bottle of Vouvray."

We stumbled down the stone stairway together, the Abbé holding up his cassock. A rat scurried across his feet. I made a pass to kick the beast. "That is one of the baker's boarders," he said. "That fellow is on a foraging trip. He will soon discover that he was better off across the street. Don't hurry him and he will stay away for good."

"Can it be," he asked, when we had arrived at the bottom of the stairs, "that I saw you yesterday afternoon crossing the square in the company of a stranger?"

"Yes, Monsieur l'Abbé, I was showing a friend the sights of our town."

"A friend from Holland?"

"A friend from America, a tourist, who has traveled all over the world."

"*Tenez, un Américain* in Bourg. Have we been discovered at last? And what did he think of our village, *votre Américain?*"

"He thought that the light of the sinking sun on the moss of the old church tower was the most beautiful sight he had seen in all the world."

"It must be a sad thing," chuckled the Abbé, "to have to travel all over the world to make that discovery!"

He was now wiping the dust off the bottle of wine and holding it up to the candle. "This is a little too young," he muttered, and then turning to me: "But you have not told me where you have been of late."

"I was over in Germany, Monsieur l'Abbé."

"Ah, Germany, *comment vont-ils, les Allemands?* What are they doing?"

"They are up to their old tricks. They have donned the uniform again. They are marching again and will soon be ready to come over once more."

"Do you really think so?"

"Yes, they are in an ugly mood."

"Well, they have good reason to be," he said. "They were sorely humiliated."

"Humiliated? Didn't they start the war?" I taunted. "I think Clemenceau was quite right when he said that there are fifty million Germans too many in Europe. Foch should have finished the war in Berlin!"

"*Mon ami, mon ami*, what makes you speak so cruelly?" returned the Abbé. "Think of the additional suffering that would have entailed! Why can you only think of force to oppose force? Should our statesmen not have tried to be reasonable with the Germans long ago, stop humiliating them, I mean? Fundamentally, I found them always a good and noble people."

"You are too kind, Monsieur l'Abbé," I said. "You already seem to have forgotten how they behaved. You have an excuse for everybody. You would have a good word even for a damned soul like Judas!"

"A damned soul? Judas?" The Abbé suddenly placed his hands on my arm. "Why do you say that, my son?"

I turned around. The flame of the candle lit up his fine face. He brushed a strand of silver hair from his forehead. I knew that he was deeply perturbed.

"You should not say that, my son," he said, and I noticed that his voice trembled with emotion. "Let us not be hasty in our judgments. You must not say of any man that he is a lost soul. We are not the judge of that. For you may depend on it," he went on earnestly, "that if Judas in that last terrible moment when he hanged himself and just before he lost consciousness entirely, if in that moment, I say, he sighed his regret and his repentance, I assure you, my son, that that sigh was heard in heaven and that the first drop of Jesus' blood was shed for Judas Iscariot."

8

Then there was the hunchback of the Rue du Vieil-Abreuvoir and the tragic manner of his death which filled us all with shame and remorse. They called him Ugolin in the village, but I never learned his family name. He had been an outcast from youth; he had never known his father and of his mother it was said that she had been a drunkard and a loose woman who abandoned her children to the gutter. But that had been long before we came to Bourg. When I knew Ugolin he was approaching manhood: a monstrous creature with a closely cropped head, a heavy, clean-shaven face of unhealthy pallor and a protruding underlip. His arms swung loosely by his side as if he had lost control over them and the tips of his twitching fingers reached down almost as far as his knees. When he walked he threw his feet out sideways in a slow rotating motion, reminding you of the measured step of an ambling horse. There was something so repulsive about this dwarf that instinctively you felt like turning your face away when you encountered him so as not to humiliate him with your stare. But his eyes were wondrously beautiful. As if to compensate for all his other deformities, nature had given Ugolin the kindest eyes of anyone I ever saw. They were of a deep luminous black, extremely intelligent, and filled with an inexpressible sadness, like the eyes of a dog who seems to suffer because he cannot speak to you. When you had once looked into

Ugolin's eyes you forgot all about the man's ugliness. They made you feel as though you were speaking to another person.

Even so, many people shunned him, some going to the extent of walking around a block so as to escape meeting him face to face, for although the sight of a hunchback is said to be a good omen, there is a serious condition attached to that augury. Unless you can manage to see three of them in the course of a day's travel there are bound to be unpleasant consequences following the meeting of but one. There was no hope of fulfilling this condition in Bourg, for there were no other hunchbacks in the village or its vicinity. Ugolin was the only one.

He loitered in the streets late and early. When you had to catch the early train for Paris at six-thirty in the morning, Ugolin was at the station. If you returned late at night and took a fiacre home, you could be certain to recognize his misshapen head under the bluish light of some gas lamp somewhere along the deserted streets. Still, he had a home. For a few sous a week he was allowed to sleep in the garret of a house on the Rue du Vieil-Abreuvoir. It was a dilapidated structure, half ruined, dirty, and smelling of bad plumbing. Downstairs was a saloon of evil repute. On the floors above lived a great number of families in incredible promiscuity. It was a veritable pesthole. Ugolin, covered only with a few rags, lay on a straw sack under the leaking tiles of the roof. But he had to be up and away before daylight and did not venture back to his couch before nightfall. For there was always someone amongst the housewives in that slum who was pregnant and, as everybody knows, the mere sight of a hunchback by a prospective mother may cause the child to be born with the face of an animal. Ugolin never went home before midnight.

Those inhabitants of the street who sat in the doorway till all hours of the night chased him away more roughly than the merchants on the main street. Nobody could bear the sight of him. If he strayed into the neighborhood of the Place Adolphe Thiers, where the young toughs hung around in the evening to play catch, shake the dicebox, or merely to ogle the passing girls, some evil yokel was sure to pounce on him and give him a drubbing on his crooked spine. "Move on, you devil's spawn!" the boys would call after him. "*Engeance du diable! Enfant de grue!* Whore's child!"

Then Ugolin would shuffle away or he would take up his stand to watch the games they were playing from the safe distance of a side street, until there would be an angry rap on some glass again and an agitated hand would wave at him to move on, out of the street, out of sight!

I first met him one evening when I returned with the last train and alighted at the station in a driving rainstorm, lugging a heavy parcel. He stepped forward from some dark corner outside the station and volunteered to help me with my load.

"I am taking a cab," I said, dismissing him.

"But you have to climb seventeen steps on a rocky stairway at your house. . . . You had better take me. . . . Your parcel is heavy. . . . I can ride back with the cab driver . . . *et puis, patron*," he whispered, "I have not eaten in such a long time."

"Come," I said, "but sit inside, for it's raining hard and you have no raincoat."

We rode along in silence, the rain tracing small rivulets on the carriage windows. As we passed the church the hunchback crossed himself.

"Today is the feast of Our Lady of Consolation," he said.

"What about it?" I shrugged my shoulders. "It's a day like any other."

"This night," he said, "Our Lady goes around with the Jesus child in her arms to listen and to peek through the keyholes to see if there are mothers in tears and no wounded hearts. . . ."

I did not reply but looked at him. A ray of light from one of the lanterns near the driver's seat fell on his eyes. I saw that they had lost their sad expression. "Wounded hearts," he had said. Where had he heard this? And his own heart? How was it that this outcast, this pariah of the streets, could say such a thing? How was it that he had not turned bitter and cynical?

"Monsieur has a fine gramophone," he said suddenly, interrupting my thoughts. "Monsieur was playing this tune last night": he hummed Mendelssohn's "On Wings of Song." "Monsieur plays that tune very often. . . . *C'est beau, je l'aime aussi, moi!*"

"How do you know this?"

"I sometimes listen from the road."

"But last night—it must have been three o'clock in the morning! It was cold then. What were you doing out at that hour?"

"I could not sleep, Monsieur. I walked around."

"Too cold to sleep?"

"Too cold, yes," he nodded his big head.

I lit the oil lamp in the kitchen and made him sit down, put bread and milk in front of him and went upstairs. When I came back half an hour later, he had not touched the food.

"What are you waiting for?"

"I was waiting for Monsieur," he replied humbly.

"But I am not hungry. You eat, Ugolin. Here, begin with a glass of milk. I'll warm it up for you again. Don't be bashful."

I noticed that his hands trembled as he reached for the bread. Big tears were rolling down his cheeks. His lips moved and he crossed himself again as I busied myself about the kitchen, poking up the fire, piling some logs near the chimney. When he had eaten I sat down with him and smoked my pipe.

"Were you born in Bourg, Ugolin?"

"I was born in the house where I now live, on the Rue du Vieil-Abreuvoir," he said, "but not in the attic, on the first floor. I have never been outside Bourg in all my life except one Easter Monday five years ago. A farmer hired me to hold a pig he was taking home. I rode out in his cart. It was many kilometers past Clamercy. He gave me *vingt sous*, but he had promised me five francs. My rent is five francs a week. Fortunately, the next day someone gave me a tip and that made up for the loss. I always manage to pay my rent. They would not want me to stay where I am if I did not pay on time. They'd beat me and drive me out. But I have always paid on time, for I have always had something to work at and then—I have my sister. . . ."

He checked himself sharply. He seemed embarrassed. The words had slipped out before he was aware of what he was saying.

"Your sister? I did not know you had a sister, Ugolin!"

"Yes, I have a sister, Solange. . . . She is three years older than I. She knew my father. . . ."

He hesitated again and I noticed a great sadness creeping back into his eyes.

"Does she live here in Bourg?"

"She lives on the Rue Danès de Montardart, Monsieur!" He looked at me half fearfully, half defiantly.

"On that street? Is she—?"

"Yes, she is, she is a *pensionnaire* in one of those houses."

And then came the whole story of his life. The mother had died in delirium tremens, leaving the two waifs to the tender mercies of the neighbors. But the little girl had watched over her sickly rachitic brother. Somehow the two had grown up in that slum. At the age of thirteen Solange had been engaged on a farm in the neighborhood and paid for her brother's education and lodging. Three years later she had suddenly returned to Bourg.

"She was very agitated, Monsieur, the day she came back," went on the hunchback, "and no wonder. The gendarmes were after her. They came and searched our garret. That farmer, her former employer, had accused her of theft.

"*Elle était innocente*, Monsieur," said Ugolin fiercely, as he clenched his fist on the table.

"The farmer wanted to take advantage of her, Monsieur. That was the secret, for she was very beautiful. She resisted. But he had his revenge. Solange was sent to jail, Monsieur. Two years they kept her in Fresnes prison. . . ."

"Had you a lawyer, Ugolin?"

"Monsieur, she was a minor at the time. Minors do not come up for trial. They are dealt with at the discretion of the magistrate. Nobody spoke for her, except I, I wanted to speak, but the magistrate told me to get out of the room. . . .

" '*Elle est innocente*,' I cried, 'do not send an innocent person away to prison!' "

" 'She's too fresh and you are too fresh, Satan's imp,' the magistrate replied. 'If you do not get out, I will have you locked up, too, for a couple of years.' "

"I wished he had done it," said Ugolin. "I might have died. That would have been better. . . .

"When Solange came back from Fresnes," he continued after a pause, "she tried to obtain a position. Nobody wanted her. I was very ill at the time, Monsieur. I had caught a disease in the spine. I was not always this way." He placed his hand on his back. "My back grew crooked while Solange was in jail. I needed medicine and food. . . ."

He was silent for awhile. "She brought me the food and the medicine and a doctor came and I was taken to the hospital. I did not discover till I was discharged that she had entered that house on the Rue Danès to pay for all those expenses."

After that first night Ugolin came often to my home. I gave him a little work to do in the garden, but he was awkward and clumsy, always falling and hurting himself. He was coughing badly, too. We often sat chatting together or listening to the gramophone. But the dogs were his special friends. They would sit with him and watch his eyes as he told them stories as if they were little children who understood his strange tales. They whined when he left in the evening. Towards the end his walk was growing slower and more painful to behold. He complained of tiredness at times. He spent the day in the garden and instinctively had found himself a spot where he was out of sight, near the little brook at the bottom of the hill. One evening as he was about to leave, he said to me with a smile, "If there were a streetcar in Bourg, Monsieur, I would take the streetcar now."

"You could stay here tonight, Ugolin. We can fix you up something."

"*Non, Monsieur, merci.* It is good of you, but I have my own home. I have my dignity."

I never saw him alive again and only learned the following evening what had happened to him. I had dropped into the Golden Lion café where Monsieur Tisserand told me the appalling news.

It appears Ugolin on his way home had run into a crowd of people on the Rue du Vieil-Abreuvoir: men, women, boys and girls, all in a hilarious mood. Some of the men were drunk—I cannot otherwise explain the scandalous thing that occurred thereafter. Someone had jostled Ugolin. He had fallen and could not rise again. The crowd had formed a ring and danced around the man crawling there on his hands and knees. They had stepped on his fingers and bruised them and kicked him each time he was about to struggle to his feet. Then someone had finally raised him, but only to inflict new tortures. He was staggering so strangely that the crowd probably thought him drunk. To keep him on his feet the men had tied him up to a lantern post. And again they had danced around him, shouting their vilest epithets: "Devil's brood! Devil's brood!" and singing a song: "The lovers of my sister pay a franc apiece!" Utterly helpless, he had all his clothes torn off until he stood there naked with that crowd of yelling and screaming and laughing men and women around him.

"It was the priest who delivered him at last," said Monsieur Tisserand.

"The Abbé?"

"Yes, Monsieur de la Roudaire. He cut him loose and carried him away."

"Carried him away, Monsieur Tisserand? The Abbé, a man of eighty?"

"Yes, Ugolin was unconscious. The priest carried him away to his own house. That's where he slept. This morning, while the priest was at Mass, the hunchback got up and walked to the river. He drowned himself. The body has just been found. I saw the stretcher pass by an hour ago."

"Horrible," I said.

"Horrible, indeed," assented M. Tisserand, "but that is not yet the end."

"What else is there?"

"The girl, his sister, shot herself this afternoon."

"Dead, too?"

"Dead! The magistrates are at the brothel this minute, inquiring. Ah, *les sauvages*, the eternal barbarians that we are! For we are all guilty, Monsieur Pierre. It's not a question of where the gendarmes were last night when that mob of rowdies made sport of poor Ugolin. All of us, collectively, we are guilty and collectively we should be punished!"

I went to see the Abbé that evening. Monsieur de la Roudaire was in his study. His face was drawn and pale. I wanted to ask him, but being a Protestant, I scarcely dared, if the two suicides would at least have a decent Christian burial.

"I came to offer a small donation," I said. "I owed Ugolin a week's wages."

"That will be for a Mass of requiem," said the Abbé.

"Are they to be buried from the church?"

"Yes, for those children are not suicides. They have been murdered by society, Monsieur, by a society without mercy."

I never saw such a crowd at the church as on the day of the funeral. Even Monsieur Tisserand was there, and the mayor, and the pharmacist. Half the shops were closed in Bourg that morning. In the middle of the aisle, near the altar rail, stood the two coffins surrounded by tall silver candelabra. A heavy black cloth united them. The organ moaned the Miserere.

After the absolution the Abbé mounted the pulpit and stood there for a moment in his lace chasuble with its black stole, looking intently at the congregation and slowly turning his head from left to right as if he wanted to recognize every man and woman present.

Then he said: "Christians!" and the word had the effect of a whiplash. And again: "Christians! When the Lord of life and death shall ask me on the Day of Judgment, 'Pasteur de la Roudaire, where are thy sheep?' I will not answer Him. And when the Lord shall ask me for the second time: 'Pasteur de la Roudaire, where are thy sheep?' I will yet not answer Him. But when the Lord shall ask me the third time: 'Pasteur . . . de . . . la . . . Rou . . . daire, where . . . are . . . thy . . . sheep?' I shall hang my head in shame and I will answer: They were not sheep, Lord—they were a pack of wolves!"

9

On quiet Sundays in the month of August when the rye was ripe, the sky blue and the heather in purple, we frequently took a stroll through the cool forest to look at the farms in the small hamlets beyond, where we had some friends. I do not know how the birds knew that it was Sunday, but there was no doubt that they were aware of it, for they sang and chirped more joyously than on an ordinary workday. We would start out at break of day in order not to miss the miracle of the rising mist when the whole world would be sprinkled with diamonds for a few moments before the sun dried up the dew. The milkish vapors of the dawn would first lift from the ground and from around the basements of the houses we passed. Little by little the doorsteps and the lower lintels of the windows would become visible, then the upper sills and the rain pipes running along the eaves, until at last there was but a small plumelike tuft of white clinging to the chimney. When this suddenly evaporated, it was as if someone with invisible hands had slowly pulled their sleeping clothes from the cottages and in a final gesture had lifted their nightcaps. . . .

Almost imperceptible movements of the curtains in the windows made us aware that we were being watched and that some curious housewife was gathering her family around her, all of them peeping and squinting and peering through slits and cracks and openings, until I would deliberately break the good-natured spying by waving my hand in greeting. Then the curtains would be moved aside and the windows pushed open and a voice would call out: *"Bonjour, monsieur, madame! Vous êtes bien matinales, vous autres! Vous n'entrez pas prendre un verre de café avec nous?"*

But a little farther up the road breakfast would be over and every-

thing astir in the farmyard: the chickens were being fed; the cows
had gathered near the meadow gate behind the barn and were filling
the air with the clangor of their bells, impatiently waiting to be
milked; a woman was running out with a chamber pot in her hands
in the direction of the distant privy; children were going off to early
Mass; a boy was pumping up water, someone else forking manure
from a cart that had arrived from Paris the day before; banana
peels, cabbage leaves, rotten fish, lamp glasses, bundles of straw, dead
cats. . . . And the smell! you had to hold your nose as you passed.

And then to stop for an hour's talk about the beet crop and the
children and the rise in the cost of living with Armand and Marie;
or looking over his cherry orchard with old Louis Benoît, the
cripple; and hearing for the one-hundredth time the story of how he
came by that dragging leg of his; how he was halfway up the ladder
to the granary and a bolt of lightning struck him and killed his best
cow at the same time, and how he lay there unconscious by the side
of the dead beast all night until the postman passed by in the morning
and saw him there, ah, *mon Dieu, mon Dieu, quelle misère*, and how
he had been stuttering ever since, which was worse than the paralyzed
leg. And so on to the next farm to exchange a word with Aphasie,
the spinster, who lived alone.

And had Monsieur and Madame heard the news of the death of
François' wife? She had died the day before. Yes, in childbirth, as
was to be expected. What was he to do now, the poor man, four
cows and a calf, and his good wife gone! A disaster! Fate was hard
on the poor. . . .

"And five children, is it not, Mademoiselle Aphasie?"

"Seven, Madame, seven children, not counting the one that's cost
the mother her life. But the children, that's nothing. They grow up
anyway. Four big cows to take care of and the land. How will he do
that? He's too poor to take a maid. Must get himself an orphan girl
to help out, four cows to take care of!"

"And the calf, Mademoiselle Aphasie, don't forget the calf!"

"Monsieur and Madame ought to come to the rosary. It's tomorrow evening. The funeral is on Tuesday. It's heartbreaking! It spoils
my Sunday!"

And so to the tavern in Clamercy for a little refreshment, that is,
if it was quiet in the hamlet. Not on days when there was an election
or when the boys from the neighborhood were in town to draw
lots at the *mairie* for conscription in the army, two events which

always take place on Sundays. For then there would be a racket fit to raise the dead and drinking and a braying of the "Marseillaise" and other songs in the streets and dancing to the tune of a harmonica —and sometimes fights.

One experience of that had been enough. It had occurred right near the church, in front of the notary's house. We had come from the tavern run by a man named Chanelle, where everybody was excited and shouting about the election. "Monsieur," that is to say, the biggest landowner in the neighborhood, the squire, was running against a candidate of the Left.

"That's the reaction trying to get into the saddle," said a farm lad called Jean Binet, who had just returned from his service in the army.

"*Mais non, mais non,* he is not so bad 'Monsieur.' He stands for progress!" answered Chanelle, who rented his tavern from the squire and therefore spoke in his own interest.

"He's up to his ears in curés, that fellow!" shot back Binet.

"Don't speak disrespectfully of 'Monsieur,' " warned the host.

"Whom are you defending? I piss on your 'Monsieur,' that's what I do!"

"You keep your mouth shut about your betters and get a decent job, *fainéant!*"

"*Fainéant,* ne'er-do-well, me? I tell you something, Chanelle, I won't keep my mouth shut. I don't have to keep my mouth shut. There will come a time when we'll carry your 'Monsieur's' head on a pike, *nom de Dieu,* when the manor is going to burn and we'll be stripping the clothes off his fine daughters before . . ."

"You utter menaces of death, Binet," said the innkeeper. "I have witnesses. I will call the gendarmes."

"You call the gendarmes and I'll slit your throat, *vache!*"

"Shut up, Communist! You're drunk!"

"If I am drunk, it's your stinking rotgut that made me drunk. You dope the wine, anyway. Everybody knows that."

The gendarmes came on the scene without being called. They dragged Binet out of the tavern and up the street, handcuffed and swearing, with a crowd of peasants following in the rear. Suddenly in front of the notary's house, one of the peasant lads ran forward and stabbed one of the gendarmes in the back with a knife. The man did not die of the wound, but at the fall assizes Binet and the would-be assassin were both sentenced to penal servitude in Guiana.

The threats of death Binet had proffered against "Monsieur" had weighed heavily against him.

They still talked of the incident in Clamercy. We had been witnesses. In the eyes of the peasants that made us almost participants in the stabbing affair. We had never gone back to Chanelle's tavern, but whenever we were in the hamlet we dropped in at a humbler place, *chez le père* Guilbeaux, a Radical, a Jacobin, like the majority of the farmers in our part of France. All our neighbors were anti-curé and antichâteau. But they were not revolutionary; they were rather afraid of Communism because of the legend, steadfastly propagated by the reaction in the rural regions of France, that Communists and Socialists are against private property.

Guilbeaux was a man approaching his seventies, but still a robust customer with long mustaches worn in the style of Vercingetorix, blue eyes and a firm handshake. His *estaminet* was the center of Radicalism in Clamercy and he himself incorporated the opposition to the château, as the manor of the squire was ostentatiously called.

"It's not that individual in the château," Guilbeaux would say. "He's a good-natured fellow, *un brave homme*. . . . It's his class, his friends, his ideas. . . . They are our natural enemies, much more than the Germans. . . . That boy Binet, whom you knew, should not have spoken the way he did. He was excited. It was election day and the judge who sentenced him might have kept that in mind. *D'ailleurs*, we will get him amnestied when the government changes. For we are bound to get our own men in next time. Even so, we can never relax our vigilance. We put the reaction in its place once, at the time of the Revolution, but we have to watch them all the time. The seigneurs and the priests have not abdicated yet. . . . They think their day is coming. They laugh at the Republic, they hate her—*la Gueuse*, the slut, they call her. . . . Down in their hearts they detest democracy. And it's quite natural when you come to think of it. But they need not try and rock us to sleep with honeyed words. We know them for what they are. Let the cards be on the table, I say. We are not going to harm them if they keep in their places. . . . The people never start a scrap. . . . It's always the other side. That's why we must be on our guard and they better be on their guard, too, for I assure you, Monsieur, if ever they dare touch our liberties, I may be an old man, Monsieur, but if they touch our freedom, I take my rifle down from the chimney and I shoot 'em down like dogs!"

10

There are men who have the power to change themselves into animals. To do this they rub themselves with a salve that the Devil gives them on condition that they run around the countryside for a spell to frighten good Christians. Most times they adopt the shape of a wolf, less frequently that of a pig, but they are frightful to behold in either case. They breathe fire and are eager to draw human blood. They cannot be caught, but nevertheless must be hunted and attacked, for they cannot be "delivered" until their own blood has flown. We had a werewolf scare in Bourg in the winter of 1930, and not a soul amongst the more simple people ventured out on the roads after dark. The rumor began to circulate simultaneously with the disappearance of a farmer, a man by the name of Richard who lived alone in a hut by the forest and who had a bad reputation as a sorcerer. Years before, the villagers said, when he had asked for woman's milk and when he had been given an extract of oats, he had used this concoction to throw a spell on the corn, and that year the grain had dried up at the roots. Children were warned not to look him in the face when they met him, for it was certain he had the evil eye.

Richard prepared love philters. I saw one of these in the possession of a girl who worked for us. She had paid a month's wages for the brew. She gave the contents to drink to the young man with whom she walked out on Sundays and, I must admit, he duly married her, which was what she wanted. Upon the death of Richard there was found in his cabin a whole collection of the paraphernalia of sorcery, such as bottles of various herbs, magic stones, amulets with druidic inscriptions, the head of a calf, a pair of leather gloves (the Devil always wears leather gloves in the old stories), dried salamanders, an assortment of powders, and several small waxen manikins. These little statues were labeled with the names of different persons in the neighborhood, long ago deceased.

There was a strong suspicion, amounting to certainty amongst the peasants, that Richard had caused the death of the persons whose names were on the manikins by inserting pins in those parts of the effigies which corresponded with the location of vital organs in the originals. There was, for instance, one statue marked with the name of a prominent landowner. A pin traversed its throat from end to end. That landowner had died of cancer. Other manikins had pins stuck in their stomachs, in their backs, or in their heads. The implication was that Richard had been paid by the relatives of the dead to bring on or hasten their demise. Camille Villetorte, the gravedigger, told me one morning that the judiciary was going to start an investigation. But nothing came of that: the clergy bought up Richard's collection and had it destroyed by the beadle. "They always do that," said the villagers. I could not get a word out of the Abbé de la Roudaire on the subject. Yet that he attached some importance to the practice of magic and sorcery was obvious from the interest he took whenever a manifestation of it came to the surface. I do not say that he shared the trivial superstitions of the peasants. On the contrary, he was concerned with eradicating these remnants of the pagan past against which the church has fought for eighteen hundred years, sometimes with weapons other than persuasion, but never altogether successfully. What can the Church do against the secret veneration of certain wells and sources or the practice of burning incense at midnight under hoary oaks in the forest? I can show you a dozen such sacred trees within a radius of an hour from Paris where lovesick maidens go to pray at the forbidding hour. The only thing the Church can do is sanctify the practice by its approval and so lift the stigma of pagan practices in a Christian country in the twentieth century. This it has done: most of the druidical oaks are today hung with pictures of the Virgin and the wells are officially baptized with the names of Christian saints. Today the peasants see the face of Mary in an ear of corn where not long ago it was the Magna Mater, the generous mother of the gods.

Soon after Richard vanished from his cabin, the rumor spread that a werewolf had been seen one evening near the cemetery. Two nights later a pair of lovers had been surprised by the giant beast and chased back into the village. We heard their frightened screams as they ran past our house in the pitch-dark. The monster was said to be hiding amongst the tombstones. A battue was hastily organized with lanterns, cudgels and some firearms. But the chase ended in the tavern with everybody telling what he knew about werewolves. At an early hour the next morning, when passing the cemetery after the fruitless hunt, I myself felt the shivers run down my spine. Richard returned to his cottage toward spring and nothing more was heard of those manifestations.

Still it was not the end of my troubles with psychic forces, if such they were. Sitting alone in my room at nights, I had more than once heard a slight tapping sound on the walls. I had dismissed the matter from my mind and for years I scarcely paid any attention. We had two German police dogs. The bolts and locks on the doors were in good order so that there was not the slightest danger of unwelcome guests intruding without some more racket than a few taps now and then. Moreover, I did not believe in supernatural manifestations. We had a ghost tradition in the family on my mother's side, but that ghost had been left behind in Holland years ago, attached to its traditional haunts. A ghost does not cross the ocean, apparently, and the stories I had heard about it had almost faded from my memory.

One winter evening I felt the room growing chilly, and thinking that the coal in the furnace was burning low, I went downstairs to the cellar to throw a few shovelfuls on the fire. It must have been about eleven o'clock. Returning to my room, while ascending the stairway, I felt something brush past me and looking around I saw a large black dog running down. I must say that I was more surprised than alarmed. I turned on my heel and, switching on all the lights in the house, looked for the animal in every room. I could not find it. Then I unbolted the front door and called in the police dogs. They showed not the slightest sign of agitation, although their sense of smell was so acute that when I had stroked a dog somewhere on one of my trips, whether in Moscow or in Damascus or no matter how far away and how long ago, they wagged their tails in recognition as they sniffed my clothes upon my return home. This time they remained unmoved. The black dog I had seen had apparently not left a scent behind. I went back to my room, but found the door standing open, although I was certain that I had closed it before going down to the cellar.

The following night, again at the very same hour, I heard a noise on the stairs, a noise as if a dog were running down swiftly. The sound came from the second stairway on which no carpet lay. I flung the door of my room open and switched on the light in the hallway. I saw the same black dog running down the stairs. I began to tremble. I investigated again and called in the dogs once more. No trace of the intruder. . . .

I did not speak to any members of the household about the incident, not wishing to disturb anyone's peace of mind. Yet the manifestation repeated itself as regularly as clockwork on several ensuing evenings. Then they stopped abruptly. A short time thereafter I had to go to Rumania on a newspaper assignment—it was the time when Carol returned to seize the throne—and remained away five weeks. When I returned I was told that the maid was quitting our service because she would not remain in a haunted house. She had even then started to sleep out.

I questioned the girl. She said she had been awakened several times at night by a big black dog which pushed open the door of her room and walked about.

"You have been dreaming," I said; "there is no black dog in this house. I don't know of one in the whole village." But the girl would not stay with us.

The business was growing serious. The villagers would stop me and ask questions. I told my neighbor Grèvecoeur about it and he offered to come and sleep in the maid's room to clear up the mystery. He arrived one evening at half-past ten with his son, a boy of nineteen. They had armed themselves with heavy sticks and Grèvecoeur *père* had brought his army revolver. We sat in my room with the door wide open and all the lights in the house on full blast. And sure enough, at the stroke of eleven we heard the patter of a dog's feet coming down from the second storey. We ran into the hallway, all three of us, but saw nothing at first, until young Grèvecoeur called out, "There it is!" A big black dog stood at the foot of the stairs in the vestibule downstairs. The dog looked up at us. My neighbor whistled and the animal wagged its tail. We started down the stairs, keeping our eyes on the apparition. We had not gone three steps when the outline of the dog grew fainter and fainter and presently vanished altogether. Then we searched high and low once more, but no trace of a dog. For the rest of that night the Grèvecoeurs stayed at the house and we all slept peacefully.

There were two years to run on the lease and being poor I could not afford to sacrifice so much rent by moving out. Moreover, I had decided to see the thing through: so long as the canine phantom did not bite or bark, its presence for a brief moment each night was bearable. It was not pleasant and it was slowly wearing our nerves thin, but we had to put up with it. There was no other way out. We tried to joke about it, spoke about "Fido, the phantom poodle," and shrugged our shoulders when anybody inquired about the phenomenon. At the same time, nobody slept a wink before eleven in our house.

One evening I decided—I do not know why the idea had never occurred to me before—to bring our two police dogs into my room and have them present before the apparition should make itself heard and not afterwards. This led to a horrible scene. The dogs pricked up their ears at the first noise on the floor above and leaped for the door. The sound of pattering feet was coming downstairs as usual, but I saw nothing. What my dogs saw I do not know, but their hair stood on edge and they retreated growling back into my room, baring their fangs and snarling. Presently they howled as if they were in excruciating pain and were snapping and biting in all directions, as if they were fighting some fierce enemy. I had never seen them in such mortal panic. I could not come to their aid, for I saw nothing to strike with the cudgel I held in my hand. The battle with the invisible foe lasted less than two minutes. Then one of my dogs yelled as if he were in the death throes, fell on the floor and died.

I was like a man stricken with the palsy. I was still trembling from head to foot when the knocker banged on the front door and I opened it. It was my good neighbor, Monsieur Grèvecoeur. He made me drink some water and the first words I said when I recovered my wits were, "Tomorrow I move out of this place. I am damned if I stay another day!" I told him what had happened. Grèvecoeur examined the dead dog and his cowering brother who sat softly whining in a corner, still shaking like a reed.

"I am notifying the mayor tomorrow," I said.

"What for?" asked Monsieur Grèvecoeur.

"I want an official declaration that this house is haunted. He can send the gendarmes to investigate."

"The man to send for is the Abbé de la Roudaire," answered my neighbor. "The gendarmes cannot help here. You need the priest for this. He will rid you of the phantom if anyone can. The priests have a secret formula which they use to banish *les revenants*."

I looked up the Abbé next morning. He had already heard of the mysterious goings-on at our house. Instead of taking the matter lightly or laughing it off, Monsieur de la Roudaire was very serious. He promised to be with us that same night.

Grèvecoeur also came with his son. The Abbé was in the house promptly at ten o'clock. We took up our vigil again in my room and drank a glass of warm wine, for the night was cold and snow was falling. We had left the door open, so that we had a view of the stairs to the second storey.

At last the pendulum struck the hour of eleven. Silently we waited for the last stroke. As the sound died away, the patter of a dog's feet was heard upstairs. I began to shake. I do not wish to boast but I have never feared any physical foe. I do not remember having trembled in no man's land. Yet that night I was weak with fear. My nerves had been worn raw. As soon as the Abbé, who had been sitting nearest the door, heard the noise, he rose quietly and walked a few steps towards the entrance. I took up my stand by his side. The pattering footsteps stopped on the stairway. A big black dog stood on the stairs staring straight at the priest. The animal was wagging its tail. The Abbé did not say a word, but his eyes were fixed straight on the apparition. He took a step forward and the dog emitted a low growl. Then its outline became hazy and presently it vanished. The Abbé walked back into my room.

"Now we can drink in peace," he said.

"And sleep?" I asked.

"Sleep, too," he said. "This is over."

We telephoned to the café of the Golden Lion for a hack. When we heard the rattle of the carriage outside, the Abbé wrapped himself up in his cape and I showed him out. As I placed my hand on the bolt he paused and took me aside.

"You have a young girl in this house, fourteen, fifteen?" he asked.

"Yes, Monsieur l'Abbé, we have a girl who runs errands. She is fifteen, I think. She was recommended to us by her mother, a widow —you know her, Madame Germaine. Why do you ask?"

"Pay her a month's wages and let her go!" said the Abbé.

"You do not mean this girl has anything to do with the apparition?"

"I certainly do," he smiled. "Such instances of *Poltergeist* frequently center around a girl in puberty. But it is the first time I have seen it take the shape of a dog. *D'ailleurs*, there is nothing to worry about now. You should have called me before."

"*Mais*, Monsieur l'Abbé!"

"We will talk of this business again someday!"

But he never did.

CHAPTER SIX

Notes from an African Diary

IN AFRICA I learned why those Scythian tribesmen, whose habits are recorded by Julian, reserved their sharpest arrows to shoot at the sun. To Julian, who was a sun worshiper, that was sacrilege. Had I possessed a long-range gun on the journey to Lake Chad in the late summer of 1934, I would willingly have sent a charge into "that tranquil eye which knoweth not envy." In Africa I hated the sun with an impotent fury, the fury that made Giovanni Papini, before his conversion, speak of "the copper brute with the fiery face covered with black pimples." On the spur of the moment, Youssef ibn Avrahim and I invented epithets even more expressive of our helpless rage. "There are two things which detract from the dignity of our humanity," said a young clergyman, as he hunched beside me one day behind the firing line in France: "What we are doing now, and stuffing our mouths." Had I been through Africa then, I would have said that the sun also humiliates by making us aware of our human pettiness, "the wormwood and the gall" of Wesley's hymns. Throughout the waterless desolation of the Sahara the sun changed to a cruel stranger who sprang upon us at dawn and who shot death rays at us the whole day, piercing our bones and racking our frame till eventide.

Having been granted permission to accompany, at my "personal risk and expense," a scientific expedition which was headed for Lake Chad under the leadership of Professor Charles Perrault, greatest living authority on the native dialects of central Africa, I joined the caravan in Rabat, Morocco, on the ninth of September. Not being a scientist, I had nothing to do with the work of the expedition itself. The contact with the leaders had been made for me by the Evangelical Missionary Board to whom I submitted, on the termination of the journey, a modest report on the intense campaign of proselytization carried on amongst certain native tribes in the part of Africa I traversed, by the emissaries of the Islamic missionary bodies of Cairo, Fez and Mecca.

As is usual with modern expeditions of a scientific nature, the organization of this venture into the heart of Africa took a considerable time. For years I heard rumors and gossip about the expedition being about to start, but lack of funds repeatedly interfered with its departure. With the exception of the Soviet authorities who give most generous support to dozens of scientific expeditions every year, most European governments do not seem to be in a position these days, when the wealth of the nations is poured into armaments, to give much practical support to undertakings of this kind. In the end the cost of our trip to Lake Chad was entirely financed by prominent French industrial firms who furnished the motorcars, the mechanics, the instruments, the tools, the tents and the electrical appliances. I believe this was done primarily to advertise the value and the enduring quality of their manufactured articles which were to undergo a rigorous test on that journey. There were no less than forty white men participating: geological, geodetic and linguistic experts, medical men, representatives of several commercial colonization societies, as well as observers from the Ministries of Agriculture, Colonies, Public Works and War. With the native staff of chauffeurs, cooks and roustabouts, we made a column of a little more than a hundred souls and twenty-five lorries. While Dr. Perrault and his associates, as soon as Morocco lay behind, recorded native dialects and filmed native customs, dances, weddings and religious festivals wherever we halted, the chief object of the expedition was a study of the causes and of the possible consequences of one of the weirdest natural phenomena of our time.

It is not, perhaps, generally known in the Western world that the level of that immense inland sea, Lake Chad, which is the heart and nerve center of the Africa of the future, has been falling lower and lower in the last ten or twelve years. What this means can perhaps best be realized by referring to the formation of the Dust Bowl in the northwestern states of America. A disaster of breath-taking magnitude is in the making in the heart of the most fertile agricultural region of Africa, affecting an area almost the size of European Russia, menacing the physical existence of millions of people and animals, and threatening to deprive the human race of one of its greatest potential granaries. Broad and majestic rivers, comparable in sweep and volume of water to the Danube, the Mississippi and the Amazon, are mysteriously disappearing into the earth without leaving a single trace. Where there were formerly cataracts, rapids, waterfalls, and millions of cubic feet of water rolling toward the distant lake every hour, there remain today but murky rivulets of a dirty and sluggish yellow liquid. In the surrounding country, for thousands of square miles, the soil is dying. The spectacle grips your heart with an awesome, doomsday gloom. I can only explain the dread which that scene inspires by the fact that it must stir up memories in the subconscious mind of similar great natural disasters, floods, famines and droughts, in our own distant European past. And the worst of it all is that apparently nothing can be done about it. Whole tribes have moved away from their ancestral land which is visibly turning into a wilderness, animal life is almost extinct, the lake itself has become devoid of life and has begun to send up miasmic vapors. It is not a question of evaporation or of a disturbance of the moisture equilibrium in the atmosphere, as is the case of the Muscovite plains, where sandstorms from the Gobi Desert have lately come as far west as the Ukraine and Moscow, a situation the Soviets are effectually remedying by the creation of huge reservoirs and artificial lakes in the Volga and Don basins. In Africa the problem is of a far more baffling nature and appears insoluble. The most logical theory advanced so far is that several of the rivers flowing into Lake Chad, such as the Shari, the Aukadebbe, and others, have in some way or another established subterranean contact on the one side with the tributaries of the colossal Niger which flows in an opposite direction towards the Atlantic Ocean, and on the other with one or more of the numerous streams that go to feed the White Nile which flows in a general northerly direction through the Sudan and Egypt into the Mediterranean. Somewhere in the depths of the earth, it is suspected, these rivers are drawing off the water that formerly poured into the lake. Whether it was a seismic disturbance that tore a crack in the earth's crust and established a connection between Chad's supply carriers and the other rivers coursing in different directions cannot be said with certainty. What is certain is that the greatest natural enemy of mankind, the desert, will have conquered another vast stretch of the globe's surface in another quarter of a century, and that the chances of humanity's survival will therewith become slimmer. Thus, it is now surmised, the Sahara itself came into being. The innumerable habitations of the peoples who once lived on that now godforsaken plateau were buried under impenetrable layers of sand.

After Marrakech, our expedition's general course led south to Beni-Abbés and Lake Gurara, then eighteen days southwest through the desolate Tuareg country where no human or animal life can exist. We then came at last into green land, in the neighborhood of the strange cities of Tintellust and Agades, and then to the French military settlement of Baron on the great lake's shore. Beyond this point I did not accompany the expedition, as my purse did not permit further expenditure. From Baron I went east on one of the trucks of a German trade caravan, following the Wadi Batha river to El Fasher in the Anglo-Egyptian Sudan, and from there to Khartoum and out by motor launch down the Nile through the Valley of the Kings.

My first act upon arrival in Rabat was to engage Youssef ibn Avrahim Ishmal Abdul Saliman to drive the motorcar which had been placed at my disposal. Youssef remained with me to the end of the trail, and with the exception of the homeward journey in Egypt, when he fell ill with malaria, never failed me for a moment. Sick as he was, I managed to get him aboard the *Marietta Pasha* of the Messageries Maritimes steamship line at Port Said and brought him safely to Marseilles, where we embraced and parted. A Herculean young Arab of no more than twenty with a dash of Negro blood in his veins, the smile of a young god, and muscles that were coils of steel under a skin of olive-hued silk, he presented himself in my room at the hotel ten minutes after I had registered. Without a word he set to work unpacking my portmanteau. When I asked if he belonged to the house, he shook his head and said: "I belong to Monsieur. . . . I can cook, I can sew, I can drive a car, I can shoot straight and I will teach Monsieur Arabic, Berber, anything. . . ." That settled it. While we talked over *les conditions*, Youssef voluntarily reduced the wage I offered on the understanding that I should recommend him, on the satisfactory completion of his services, for a passport valid for ten years and for all countries.

"That will enable me to go to France upon our return," he said.

"What do you want to do there?"

"I would like to be a policeman. Do you think I will get the job?"

"What? Policeman? Why not? A most legitimate ambition! There is no limit to what a young man like you may aspire to under democracy."

Before going out together to report at the expedition's headquarters, Youssef informed me that he had some previous experience as a dragoman. The year before he had been engaged by a titled Englishwoman on a motortrip through Morocco and Algiers. From the pocket of his burnous he produced a greasy letter of introduction signed by his former employer. It was she who had taught him, he said, the half-dozen sentences in English, all of them of a phenomenal indecency, that he proceeded to recite for my benefit. Although I hardly felt shocked (the first words a man learns of a foreign language are generally of that type), I advised him never to use these words in introducing himself to English-speaking tourists, as such expressions were liable to get him in trouble. This first astonished him and then made him burst out laughing. The boy imagined he had been conveying the choicest compliments.

From the expedition's headquarters where I received the news of my promotion to assistant historian, we went to have my rifle permit verified and to lay in a stock of provisions. With the Jews in the bazaar Youssef spoke Spaniole, with the Berbers a mixture of French and Tuareg, at the native police on traffic duty he spat out a string of obscenities that would have made a Parisian taxidriver's hair stand on edge. But his Semitic blood made him an excellent bargainer. Going over our stocks the next morning, I noticed one more rifle than we should have had.

"Where did you get this?"

"From the son of a mule with the long nose of whom we bought the sugar."

"When?"

"Last night."

"How much?"

"He did not dicker."

"He did not dicker? How's that?"

"He was asleep!"

The expedition's main stores were picked up in Ben Nour, a considerable market place situated halfway between Rabat and Marrakech. It was there that Youssef and I went to the bazaar to buy cartridges and salt, the two chief mediums of exchange in the Chad country to which we were proceeding.

The merchant to whom we applied was lying on a carpet in the rear of his shop. Before him on a small table stood a silver narghile. His eyes were closed as he dreamily sucked the water-cooled tobacco. When he heard our voices he jumped to his feet, bowed, wished us the peace of Allah and motioned us to sit down on the carpet. He then filled the bowl of the narghile with fresh tobacco and ceremoniously handed us each a long tube with amber mouth-piece, whereupon he blew the charcoal into flame. Nothing was said of the errand on which we had come. When we had taken about a dozen puffs, he clapped his hands and a tall Senegalese, his naked torso gleaming with coconut oil, appeared bearing an immense brass tray. On the tray were three tiny porcelain cups filled with coffee. We drank in silence, two, three cups, noisily smacking our lips, as custom demands, while the merchant bowed acknowledg-ment of the clucking praise bestowed on his poisonous brew. Then we had another smoke.

Finally he asked my interpreter where I hailed from. Youssef did not know himself, but he had his answer ready:

"His Highness comes from Spain!" was the reply.

"Is it well with those of Spain? Have they peace?" asked our host.

"It is not well with the people of Spain," I answered. "They have no peace." For it was shortly after the troubles in Catalonia.

Upon hearing this the merchant burst into a violent speech. Yous-sef, too, began to gesticulate and in a minute both men blazed with anger. They forgot all about me. I wondered what was up.

"Just a minute, Youssef," I said. "Tell him that I am not a Spaniard, but that I merely happen to have traveled through that country."

"It is well," nodded the merchant after these words had been translated. "It is well. How many were killed in Spain?"

"Hundreds upon hundreds," I said.

"That is well. Praise be to Allah! That is good news indeed. . . . You are welcome to Ben Nour, thrice welcome." He made a deep salaam.

We talked for a while of the European situation and the prospect of a new war.

"It will be a great calamity," I ventured, "if ever it comes, this new war."

"No calamity at all," answered the merchant complacently. "Allah is just. The pestilential dogs will destroy each other. It is good news." He rubbed his hands in high glee at the thought of a European conflict.

Then we got down to the business of the sugar, which was black with flies, and then the salt and the cartridges. The transaction itself did not take us ten minutes.

In the afternoon we started at the tail end of the motor caravan for Marrakech, along a road which for miles ran parallel with the sea. On our right stretched the endless expanse of blue-gray water with a thin veil of mist hanging over it, on the other side the green panorama of the prairie; here and there a small domed building without any other habitation near by; the tomb of some Marabout, a holy man. We could only proceed at a snail's pace, for the road was crowded: indefatigable little donkeys carrying heavy loads of merchandise with the merchant perched on the beast's last extremity and the merchant's wife and daughters walking behind, burdened under baskets; trucks with sacks of wheat, gasoline cans, boxes of sugar; long strings of dromedaries moving with slow measured step, transporting dates, olives, wool and hides to the ports. In the opposite direction caravans passed with products of European origin: cotton and cloth, silk, paper, tea, matches and candles. . . .

One young camel in a caravan, moving in the same direction as we, took fright at the sound of our motor. He stretched his neck— a sign of distress, broke from the ranks and bolted. The camel drivers yelled and hurled imprecations at us, waved their hands and started in pursuit of the panic-stricken animal. But one old man with a short-clipped bristling beard, who headed the caravan seated on a white horse, raised his hand to stop our car, and having fired a volley of oaths at us, concluded by spitting voluminously on our windshield.

"What does the old boy say, Youssef?"

"He says, 'May Allah heat the fire seven times hotter when we two arrive in hell!'"

"Got your fire extinguisher, Youssef?"

"Yes, sir!"

"Let's take a chance!"

We may have driven some twenty miles and were approaching one of the cement bridges that Marshal Lyautey has built over the many streams and brooks which water the Moroccan lowlands when Youssef suddenly called out in alarm: "Cover your eyes, cover your eyes, for God's sake, cover your eyes!"

"Why?"

"Women," he shouted, "unveiled women. You must not see them. It is dangerous!"

"Dangerous? Where are they?" I asked, thoroughly aroused.

"There, there by the roadside," answered Youssef, pointing with both hands and letting go the wheel.

It was too late. In one glance I had seen what there was to be seen. The women of one of the villages were out doing the family washing in the little stream.

When the girls wash clothes, they take a bath at the same time, killing two birds with one stone. Their wardrobe is restricted to one gown and they wash this gown by placing it on a flat stone by the water's edge and stamping on it. There must have been twenty of them treading away rhythmically like a row of chorus girls. Youssef wanted to race over the bridge and flee that spectacle of charming innocence as swiftly as his namesake once hurried from Madame Potiphar's presence. But I stayed him.

"Wait!" I commanded.

"But it's dangerous," he said.

"Why?"

"Because their husbands will resent it! They will kill us!"

"Where are the husbands?"

"At the market," said Youssef.

"How far is the market?"

"A mile or so."

"Well, how will they ever find out? Wait until I get a good look."

"I implore you, let us drive on," wailed Youssef. "Cover your eyes. You don't know how dangerous it is!"

"Youssef," I said, "if those ladies are not to be seen, let them go up the creek out of the sight of the highway. Do you know what I think? I think they like the idea of being looked at. It seems to me they are waving at us."

"They are signaling us to go away!" explained Youssef.

"Are you sure? And what are the others doing all stretched out there in the shrubbery back of the water's edge?"

"They are waiting for their clothes to dry!"

"And those boys playing with them?"

"Those are their little brothers to keep them company!"

"I see. Little brothers."

I noticed that Youssef wasn't shutting or covering his eyes as some of the girls climbed up along a winding path to the main road.

They were Cleughs, a mixed Arabo-Negroid tribe. Their features were not beautiful, rather coarse: flat noses and high cheekbones, but there was a pleasant swing to their carriage. The wet gowns they wore were of a uniform blue calico, fastened together at the shoulder with a big safety pin and gathered at the waist with a cord—not very intricate.

As the girls came level with us on the road, they brazenly removed their veils and shouted something at us, laughing uproariously as they went along.

"What do they say?" I asked Youssef.

"They said we'll have to marry them all now, having seen them in undress!"

"Is that the custom here, Youssef?"

"Yes sir, an old custom!"

"If that is so, Youssef, let us get going. This is indeed a dangerous spot."

The peaks of the Atlas were visible in the distance: a curved stripe of silver traced the limit of the snow fields, as ethereal as a Japanese print. Without any warning of twilight, the mountains faded out and the world was plunged in darkness and we flashed on the headlights. Then we roared through the night over a road where Roman legions had marched, where Greeks and Phoenicians had come in search of new markets, and where Ali, lord of all the world, had led the green-bannered hosts of the Prophet. Pedestrians and horsemen passed us, an endless procession of camels, silently padding their way towards the coast—fantastic, eerie, in the gloom. . . .

And so into Marrakech, through narrow streets, in which white-robed silhouettes flattened themselves against the walls to afford us passageway. The din and clatter of the Arabic workaday world had ceased. From the windows of my hotel I could still see some shadows gliding about in roof gardens. Youssef rigged up the portable radio and before going to sleep we listened for a while to a transmission of a tom-tom from Berlin: *"Die Fahnen hoch, die Reihen fest geschlossen!"*

Marrakech

The cement in the red-towered walls which surround the city of Marrakech was mixed with the blood of enemies of the faith. The bodies of a hundred thousand captives were thrown into the imperial limekilns and baked into the bricks for the fortifications.

Into the foundations of every one of the dozen city gates went a load of freshly severed heads on the principle that there is nothing like a pile of skulls to prevent a building from cracking.

On the night of the new moon, they say, you can hear the sighs of all those immured, entombed and decapitated infidels as they suffer the pains of the damned in the nethermost pits of hell for having rejected Mohammed. I did not hear their groans myself, although I was there at the appointed hour. But then my ears, I am afraid, have never become quite attuned to the supernatural. Youssef heard them and he trembled like a leaf. I dragged him away from the place before he started to see things in addition to hearing what he described as "bad voices." For his eyes had already begun to assume that peculiar, faraway, glassy stare of the Moslems when they are in the contemplative mood. In such moments they see exactly what they want to see. . . .

Youssef, who tells me that his father is a *mullah* in Fez, is so deeply versed in Koranic lore that he is able to furnish a most minute description of heaven and hell. When he is on that subject he betrays so exact a knowledge of the inner workings of the administration of both places that I really suspect him of either having been there or of possessing blueprints showing the layout. It's uncanny. It fills me with a sort of fearful respect for him. Even so, his habit of scratching the inside of his ear with the aid of a match got us into serious trouble this morning. We were in a famous mosque, and I was inspecting the matchless mosaic of the walls when Youssef suddenly emitted a bloodcurdling yell. The sulphur had caught fire in his ear. He pulled it out, of course, and threw it on the floor, where it burned a hole in a prayer rug. While Youssef fled, head over heels, in the direction of a fountain in the patio where the believers wash their feet in a basin before entering the mosque, and plunged his head into the healing stream, all the imams, mullahs, scribes and Pharisees who hang around a Moslem temple pounced on me and stood there spluttering and frothing in throaty Arabic, shaking their fists.

I prepared myself for the worst. In a flash of the imagination, I saw my skull going to reinforce the foundations of some Mohammedan pothouse, when Youssef fortunately returned and started to explain. The incident ended with my making a donation of ten francs to the Mohammedan Missionary Society. This was gratefully accepted. Nothing was said of the carpet which must have been worth a hundred thousand francs if I know anything about carpets.

In the meantime the suffering Youssef is being treated with ointment of which a druggist in Paris made me a present before departing, saying that it was good for snakebites.

It certainly is good for earache!

Sultan aften Sultan from the tenth century onward has endowed Marrakech with palaces, mosques, gardens and citadels, even as every French king seems to have considered it his duty to build at least one palace in or near Paris to perpetuate his name and glory.

The greatest palace is that called El Bedi, which means the Marvelous. It was built by a sultan known as Ed-Dhahebi, the Golden One. He had been a slave in his youth and was the son of a Jewish woman and a Negro father. Short-legged, with an enormous head and bulging eyes, he must have been a frightful caricature of a man. But he rose rapidly and finally became grand vizier. Once in the higher spheres of politics he gathered a clique around him and began to intrigue against the reigning family. He arrested the sultan and had his twenty sons boiled in oil before their father's eyes. Then he had the old man put in a vat with seventy-seven starved rats— the holy number!

Subsequently this ex-slave conquered Senegal all the way to Timbuktu, where he burnt the famous library. Thereafter he crossed the Sahara—four and a half months on the march—and at the head of an army invaded the Sudan. He shipped the captives back to Marrakech and made good use of their skulls. With the gold he looted on the way—it took five hundred caravans to transport the booty—he built that palace called El Bedi, which is a city within a city. The ceilings are of cedar covered with beaten gold encrusted with jewels. Gateways are of marble with golden thresholds. Some of the gold has been stripped off. Subsequent sultans did that.

That monstrous dwarf had a hundred thousand slaves and a bodyguard of ten thousand men. He surpassed Solomon in the splendor of his harem. Historians assert that he had one army roaming his domains for no other purpose but to pick up beautiful girls and ship them to Marrakech. The plague got him in the end, him and all his slaves, bodyguard, and women.

The ulema who showed us around El Bedi, and who told us that story of the imperial dwarf, recommended the reading of Moroccan history. It is, he said, the most bloody collection of chronicles in the world. The ingenuity with which the sultans thought up means of torture for their predecessors is something that freezes the imagination. One of them had the prince he replaced on the throne cut into small slices. The process lasted seven days before death released the victim. Another was put naked in a glass cage filled with red termites. His wives and concubines were forced to come and watch the delectable spectacle of the man being devoured by the voracious insects. The ladies clapped their hands in delight, the historians say, when they saw him who had been their spouse battle the trillions of ants for hours. Finally when his strength gave out and the ants swarmed over him and crept into every opening of his body, they danced for joy. The successor to the throne smiled contentedly and ate a choice meal, sitting quite close to the crystal cage so as not to miss a single detail. Put in at the rising moon, the victim was a skeleton before dawn. Another was flayed alive, then smeared with honey, whereupon a score of beehives were carried in and the bees let loose to finish him.

Delicacy prohibits me from mentioning the really appetizing stories: suffice it to say that Nero was a pitiful upstart and that Torquemada did not know his business. These Moroccan sultans were past masters in the art of torture. Their imagination worked overtime when they were on that subject. But the prize must go to Al-Mansur, that potbellied dwarf from whose harem were carried every morning the fragments of the bodies of the women he had "loved" in the night.

Death in the Forenoon

Youssef and I attended a native funeral in Marrakech. When the procession got under way at ten in the morning, the men who were to be buried were not yet dead. They died two hours later, precisely at the stroke of noon. They were in their graves in a twinkling. Trumpeters were blowing a funeral dirge in the street when we emerged from the hotel. A full regiment of infantry marched by: Senegalese, stocky black fellows wearing trench helmets, their bayonets gleaming in the sunlight. They were followed by a group of military policemen in khaki. Between these policemen walked four young Arabs, heavy chains around their hands and feet. Behind came a military band of blacks playing Chopin's *Marche funèbre* and then a troop of spahis, red-robed cavalry, wearing turbans and mounted on white horses.

Bystanders informed us that there was to be an execution. Executions have become rather rare since the French control Morocco. Formerly the sultans held executions every day and arrayed the severed heads of the slain on pikes above the city's gates where the crows picked them clean as billiard balls before sunset. The pikes are still there.

Hordes of lemonade vendors and ice-cream and candy peddlers, surrounded and followed by an enormous host of children, marched out to the place of judgment in the wake of the military procession. With them came a swarm of old wives and young ones, shamelessly lifting their veils to catch sight of the criminals. The women were eating pistachios, peanuts and dates and spitting the stones in the direction of any white man they happened to see. I esimated the number of that chattering and hilarious mob which poured out of the city gate at thirty thousand. School must have been closed for the occasion.

Curiosity got the better of me and I decided to go along. We followed the procession through the main streets and part of the business quarter. No doubt the object of taking a route through the most densely populated part of town was to impress the people with the severity of the punishment meted out to men who murder a French officer. Whether the population was impressed or not I do not know. I venture to say, however, that if they were impressed, they were not inspired with the terror of it. Nobody seemed put out about it. The spectacle resembled a holiday picnic. The four condemned men themselves chatted amiably with the policemen. One of them grinned repeatedly and nudged his companion in order to draw attention to the spectators crowded on the roofs of the shops and residences we passed.

The place of execution was a green meadow sloping upward towards a hill. The condemned men were marched up to a trench about twelve feet long at the foot of the hill and made to stand there while the troops formed a square to keep back the surging multitude.

Then the hands of the condemned were united and their long cloaks of wool taken off. These were rolled neatly into a package and placed at their feet. The men took up a position about three feet

apart. A French officer advanced and started to read the sentence
first in French, then in Arabic. While he was reading the murmur
in the crowd grew to a tempest. I became nervous lest the mob
storm the lines and effect a liberation, but Youssef reassured me:
those behind were merely protesting because they could not see well
enough, or not at all, as the closely serried ranks of the soldiers
shut out the view.

The officer read on. I took my watch in my hand. I could see
him turning the pages, saw how much there remained to be read and
mentally calculated the minutes, the seconds of life remaining to
those four young boys. But the condemned men were utterly calm;
at least they appeared so outwardly. When the officer finished reading, the four men raised their right hands, pointing with their index
fingers to the sky. That is the way an Arab who expects death
awaits his last moment.

"Do you know what they think now?" Youssef whispered. "They
say to themselves: 'What is written is written. *Mektoub!*' If their
fate is not decided up there in heaven they are not going to die in
spite of the rifles that will be trained on them in a minute."

The crowd suddenly became mouse-still. Not a whisper came
from the four about to die. They may have prayed. But they did
not ask Allah to save them. An Arab never asks a favor of God.
Prayer is a recital of praise. There is no use in asking Allah to change
his will. Like Calvin's God, he has decided every man's lot from all
eternity and He never changes his decisions.

When the execution squad of twelve men advanced from the
ranks, the silence grew even more tense. My heart was in my throat
and my tongue was so dry that I could not swallow. I could have
screamed but my knees were trembling and I suddenly felt weak and
exhausted. The four condemned men turned around, facing the
trench, their grave, and waited. The platoon of sharpshooters took a
few more steps forward, raised their rifles and took aim. The young
man who had grinned so amiably in the streets turned his head to
see how near the soldiers were. Before he could quite turn, the salvo
rang out and I saw him leap forward in a strange contorted jump,
his head jerking backwards. The four bodies flopped into the
trench.

I stood petrified, sick with horror at what I saw next. The officer
who had read the sentence calmly walked to the edge of the grave

and, carefully taking aim, fired his revolver once, twice, thrice, four times into the ditch. The coup de grâce!

At the same moment the trumpets sounded the retreat. Commands rang out: "*A gauche par quatre! Avancez!*" The bodies were to lay uncovered in the trench till evening so that the populace could file past and look at the dead men. A few sentinels remained behind by the open grave. Youssef and I walked behind the troops. The band struck up a gay tune:

Si la femme du matelot
Pouvait monter sur le bateau
Le métier de marin
S'rait gentil tout plein

In the Mellah

Once a month, when the dirt and offal in the bazaar—that is to say, the business quarter—begin to look like a mountain landscape and the weary wayfarer thinks how useful an alpenstock would come in for travel in and over those malodorous hills, the Moslems of the town foregather, pick it all up, and amidst much Oriental hilarity (which is ten times as noisy as any other kind of a racket), dump it into the Jewish quarter.

That's an old custom with these people, something like getting a haircut, a regularly recurrent joy. They make certain to do the job on a Friday evening when the Sabbath begins and when they know that the Jews won't lift a finger for twenty-four hours. The Jews, who have a long memory, remember how the Pharaohs made them bring straw for the bricks for their pyramids. They clear away the piles of putrefaction on Sunday with philosophic equanimity.

"But why don't you complain?" I asked an old Hebrew as he was digging out the entrance of his home in the ghetto, much as a Canadian pioneer might shovel a path to the door of his shanty on the morning after a winter night's blizzard.

The old man shrugged his shoulders and raised his eyebrows in a characteristic Semitic way. "Did it help Moses when he complained?" he asked.

"Mordecai got results," I reminded him.

"Mordecai had Esther," he replied. "Our Esthers are *meshuga.*" He tapped his forehead. "They only think of fine clothes and jewels and of painting their faces!"

I thought of the Jewish girls I had seen in the ghetto: a pretty seedy lot they had seemed to me and I said, "But I haven't seen many very fine clothes."

"Did I say they have fine clothes and jewels?" the old man countered with another question. "They think of fine clothes. That's far worse. That's covetousness."

He went on with his job after telling me that it takes the Jews four or five days a month to clear away the dirt, and I walked into the ghetto to find the Talmud torah, the religious school.

A rabbi once said: "In Israel there are three kinds of people: Israelites, Jews and Moroccan Jews." The Moroccan Jews are the most backward Jews on earth. In every way they stand below the Arabs. Of course, there is a reason for this. No people or tribe on earth is naturally backward. To the confusion of the colonial empires, the Soviets are proving this with their nationalistic policy in Asia. When you find a backward people, you are certain to discover an historical circumstance which has interfered with their cultural development. In the case of the Moroccan Jews, who are descendants of those exiles who were expelled from Spain, centuries of brutal treatment on the part of a series of sultans whose religious fanaticism had made them singularly cruel is responsible. If Moroccan history drips with blood, a good deal of it is Jewish blood. It is a miracle that any Jews survive at all, for what all the warring, murdering factions had in common was their hatred of the Jew.

Here they are in the *mellah*, as the ghetto is called. You enter a courtyard through a door in the wall and there, grouped around a sort of patio, are a number of rooms occupied by innumerable families who, in unimaginable confusion, mix their vermin, their diseases, their children and their animals. From the door to the deepest darkest hole, a mass of human beings swarms and crawls and yells and sleeps and eats and does everything without the slightest regard for sanitation, decency or hygiene. The odor was atrocious. Everything seemed to be rotting, the air was heavy with a mixed smell of excrement, chickens, blood and putrefied vegetables.

But the most sorrowful spectacle was the Talmud torah, the school. Here the boys, unwashed and covered with dirt, sat in the semiobscurity of a shed on the stone floor. The teachers were not a whit cleaner. They were filthy brutal-faced fellows who walloped right and left with their sticks and stinging whips of oxhide.

As I walked out of the school where the boys were bellowing in chorus certain phrases from the Hebrew Bible—the girls get no schooling at all—I saw an old Jew who must have been seventy or eighty turning a wheel that put a pair of bellows in motion in a blacksmith's shop. The old man was naked to the waist and totally blind. I watched him for a while. When he did not produce enough flame to suit the Arabic blacksmith, one of the younger helpmates took a rod and struck the old man across his back.

A Day in Court

When a man is accused of a crime or misdemeanor and he enters the courtroom where his case is to be tried, he kneels down in the doorway and murmurs piously: "There is no justice in man. May Allah render justice here!" He stays on his knees, arguing with his fellow accused and the native lawyers, all on their knees, till his case is called.

The first question of the pasha on the bench is this: "How could you do that of which you stand accused?" He pronounces these words in a mechanical, offhand manner, as if to say: "It is hot in this courtroom: I wish I had a glass of cold lemonade!" The answer of the accused is also spoken automatically: "That of which I stand accused was Allah's will. Nothing happens in this world without Allah!" I think that is a good answer, for it should put an end to all argument, if the court is a consistent predestinationist.

There is often, alas! a wide divergence between the theories and the practices of religion, not only in Morocco. Though Allah may be responsible for the acts of his creatures in the final Islamic analysis, you cannot take Allah's fingerprints and lock him up in a subterranean dungeon, as is the custom here with a man found guilty.

All these attempts to throw the blame on Allah are mere empty formalities, just as are the shouts of the court attendants in the corridor who attempt to enjoin a little silence among the mass of arguing, quarreling, gesticulating disputants and litigants: "The Angel Gabriel is writing down your words, O believers! Put a guard on your tongues!" I must frankly say that, although I have considerable respect for angels, I do not envy Gabriel his job in the least. If this court business goes on much longer, with a thousand men all talking at the same time, I know Gabriel will be glad to end it all by that great trumpet blast on the last day, which I now realize will be something in the nature of a grand sigh of relief.

However, here we are. A black-eyed beauty comes up before
the court, lifts her veil and looks intently at the pasha. This gentleman, in his white burnous, looks her over from head to foot, allows
his eyes to linger on the golden bracelets around her wrists and
mutters, "How could you do that of which, etc.?" And the lady
replies that it's all Allah's fault. It seems from the evidence that she
has pulled her husband's beard, and has given him a stiff hiding to
boot. The husband, a little, fat, squint-eyed runt, makes the accusation. He carefully unfolds his handkerchief and produces two or
three hairs which, he declares, have been torn out of his chin and
hands them over to the scribe who sits next to the pasha.

Exhibit No. 1.

The scribe holds the hairs up to the light and nods his head. Then
he throws them on the floor. Next the plaintiff starts to undress,
showing the court and the crowd of lawyers standing around the
black-and-blue marks on his body where he says the lady scratched
and pummeled him. But as he does this, he bares his stomach which
is of so peculiar a shape, something like a puffed-up sausage balloon,
that everybody begins to laugh. The judge and the scribe almost fall
off their chairs with laughter. But the plaintiff cries out in a high-
pitched voice: "Why do you laugh, you fools? It's Allah's will!"
He means, of course, that misshapen abdomen of his.

Exhibit No. 2.

A lawyer advances and bows to the court and to the lady who
stands there with a look of indescribable disgust on her face.

"She," says the lawyer, pointing at the woman, whom he apparently represents, "she is a gazelle, she is an antelope, smooth and
lithe. She is as beautiful as a palm grove after rain. She is as lovely
as a fountain of crystal. Vivid are the colors. Wondrously has Allah
—praise to his goodness!—endowed her for the comfort of her lord."
Youssef ibn Avrahim who stands beside me is translating.

"*Attends un peu*, Josephe," I say. "I am going to write that speech
down. It's worth the trouble."

As I begin to scratch in my notebook, the pasha stops the proceedings and invites me in French to come up to take a seat by his side
on the bench. I accept, but not before Youssef whispers to me,
"Say you're unworthy, say you're unworthy!" I say it: "Grand
pasha, I do not deserve this great honor!" He answers with a royal
gesture of his fine long hands.

Then the lawyer goes on: "She," he says, "she is a precious jewel, glittering in splendor. She is patient and compassionate. She is a delight of paradise. She is charitable and modest. Her neck is a tower of ivory. Her lips as sweet as dew on the mountains. Her breasts . . ." He stops to clear his throat and consult his brief. I was secretly hoping that we were about to see Exhibit No. 3, *au naturel*, but I am disappointed. The lawyer points to the lady's husband and continues in a sarcastic, bitter tone, whereas a moment ago it was mellow as honey. "He," he says, "he is a brute. He exasperates his wives with his nagging. He has the means to possess but seven wives and he has thirteen." This is a great scandal apparently, for the judge clicks his tongue, followed by the scribe and then everybody in court: tsk-tsk, tsk-tsk!

Still another lawyer comes up to the rostrum and this man pours forth a stream of language such as I have never heard before in my life. He is as mad as a fighting cock. He yells at the judge, at the scribe, at me, at the accused woman, a harsh, never-ending stream of Arabic words, full of raucous consonants and harsh aspirations. He never stops for breath and, as he raves and splutters and waves his arms like a man fighting a swarm of hornets, he comes closer and closer to the judge, on the theory, I presume, that the nearer he comes the greater weight his argument carries. Finally the scribe has to ask him to step back a little as he is "causing it to rain on the court documents."

The trial ends by the judge pronouncing the divorce, whereupon the lady leaves the room, accompanied by her lawyer, to hear the proposals of marriage of a flock of new candidates who have waited impatiently outside for the verdict.

"She is good-looking," says the judge to me. "But she has a bad name. This is the third time. *Mon Dieu!* Her teeth are as sharp as a tiger's. I knew her as a boy!"

Beau Sabreurs

Twenty French soldiers and a top sergeant were sent out the day we arrived in Marrakech to investigate a complaint of the charcoal burners' guild. Members of this organization had been prevented from doing their work by irregular bands of Berber tribesmen in the forests which cover the foothills of the Atlas. The Berbers had warned the woodsmen not to come back on pain of death.

Of the patrol of twenty-one French soldiers five came back stark blind; the other sixteen had died from their horrible wounds on the way back to the military post of Djebel Laboun. We heard the story from the commander of the blockhouse who dined with the members of our expedition in the Cercle Militaire of Marrakech. The French casualty list for the summer of 1934, he admitted, ran into several thousands. "And yet," remarked the commandant, "this is a peaceful season!"

Every year it is announced in Paris that Morocco is pacified at last, and every year thousands of French soldiers die to give the lie to this official affirmation. With the coming of fall and the rainy season the so-called dissident tribes withdraw from the foothills towards their mountain strongholds in the Atlas and Anti-Atlas ranges where they hibernate. With the first signs of spring they are back in the valleys and the murderous raids resume.

"Qu'est ce que vous voulez?" said one of the officers of the Djebel Laboun post. "They are magnificent fellows, these Berbers. They do not know the word surrender. One of them will engage a whole patrol. They never run away. I admire them and love them, but I kill them on sight!"

The Berbers are not Mohammedans. They do not even speak Arabic, nor is their language of Semitic or Hamitic origin. They are fair and most of them have blue eyes. They are thought to be descendants of the Visigoths who conquered the south of Europe and therefore kinsmen of the Basques and of the old Vikings. I cannot say that they are exactly a recommendation for the race, for whereas the Visigoths of Spain became Christians in time and even invented the Inquisition, the Berbers of Morocco have not shown any aptitude for religion. With Islam they are on speaking terms, one might say, but with Christianity they will have no truck or trade. This strange antipathy against our gentle creed is well-nigh general all over Africa. For every heathen convert brought into the Christian fold, the Mohammedan missionaries enlist from ten to twelve neophytes.

We saw a good deal of the Berber settlements and, through Youssef, I spoke with a few of their chiefs. But you can search those villages as long as you like, you will never find a man with grey hairs. No tribesman survives the age of forty. War claims them all before they reach middle age. War is a natural state of affairs with these people. The Berbers do not need Franz von Papen to tell them that it is a shame for a warrior to die in bed. Not they!

To most clans, war is a source of profit and that is its only purpose. Besides fighting the French, the Berbers battle a good deal among themselves. Rifles come into play for the most insignificant reasons: a sheep, a well, a woman, a rifle, a handful of cartridges, anything might start off a tribal war. The prize is the opponent's possessions, including his children.

Eternally at war, and hostile as they are to new ideas, the Berbers would have exterminated themselves completely in the course of a century, were it not that by common consent they suspend hostilities from time to time to give the children a chance to grow up. Every clan sends a delegation to some holy man residing in the wilderness to whom the dispute of the moment is submitted for arbitration. This individual, after learning the details of the quarrel, advises an armistice and recites the fatiha, a Koranic benediction, whereupon he is paid and everybody goes home to raise a little corn and breed rapidly and indiscriminately until a new crop of humans is big enough to start fighting. I am speaking of a tribe of savages on the Dark Continent, of course!

"This summer," said the commander of the Djebel Laboun post, "the Berbers sneaked into a camp of three thousand soldiers, after first slitting the throats of the sentinels and crawling through the barbed-wire entanglements. They wriggled into the tents and cut the straps by which each French soldier attaches himself to his rifle during sleep. Our men who woke up were killed before they could make an outcry. Several had their throats bitten through. The Berbers got away with several hundred rifles. It was the most daring and amazing exploit we ever witnessed in these parts. When the alarm was finally raised and the searchlights played on the surrounding fields not a soul was in sight!"

The expedition halted for a day in the Scoura Pass of the Atlas Mountains. This is the approach to a position against which France, with her best troops, has been bumping her head every summer for ten years straight. The result? In the valley are a score of cemeteries whose little wooden crosses show that France lost as many as seven hundred men in one day. No statistics are available to show the total number of casualties in this region. Nobody knows how many men have died in the "pacification" of Morocco. The officials in the big somber building on the Rue Dominique in Paris, where the archives are kept, remain silent when you come to ask questions. The fighting in Morocco is mainly done by the Foreign Legion and by the Battalions d'Afrique, the dreaded "Bat d'Af," composed of men who are being punished for some crime committed while serving in regular units in France.

An incident that a soldier of the Foreign Legion told us will serve to indicate how things stood in 1934. A tribe of Riff Kabyles had flung down the gauntlet in the hated usurper's face by attacking a mountain post and killing half the garrison that summer. A detachment of the Foreign Legion to which our informant belonged had been sent to reinforce the regiments of the line.

"The first two or three days after we arrived everything was quiet," said our acquaintance. "Not a soul stirred in the mountain passes. Then one night during the second watch a shot rang out. Every one of the six sentries was found with his head severed. Their rifles were missing.

"The sentries were doubled the next night, but nothing happened. Five or six days passed and things seemed to have quieted down for good. Then one night the alarm was given again and of the twelve sentries only one man escaped with his life. But again all rifles were missing.

"Then our commandant had a bright idea. He ordered us all out in the daytime and we were set to work digging postholes in wide circles around the camp. In every one of these postholes a stake was placed rather loosely. Under the stake, in the bottom of the posthole, a hand grenade was hidden. The least jiggling with the stake and the grenade was bound to go off and the meddler blown sky-high. That's the way our commandant figured it out, and we too. We were on the alert the following night, but we heard nothing. Yet the next morning all the stakes were gone and with the stakes the grenades, two hundred of them. We got the grenades back two nights later, but then they came crashing and hurtling through the air. Now from this side, then from the other, killing eleven men and wounding a good many more.

"When daylight came we discovered that our own projectiles and our machine-gun fire in the night had been a pure waste. The Kabyles had crawled right up under our parapets and had tossed their bombs over lightly, while we had been replying by blazing away into the distance and by tossing our own hand grenades as far away as possible. The Kabyles' bombing had been much more effective, for they had but a comparatively limited space in which to center their attack. They couldn't miss.

"Reinforcements asked for by wireless were soon on the way, but the Kabyles ambushed the newcomers and only half of them reached the post. This gave them an additional fifty rifles. A third detachment of reinforcements came through, to within sight of the post, a month later. We had followed their advance day by day through information supplied by the radio messages from the posts they passed on their way up. So we knew when they would be near. . . . And to be sure, one day we could hear their voices in the stillness of the mountain pass.

"Then something happened that I will never forget," the legionnaire went on. "We saw the Kabyles riding by in the distance and we heard their raucous war cry: '*Arah-Sidi! Arah-Sidi! Allah il Allah!*' It was clear that they were about to throw themselves on the completely exhausted column of infantry coming to our aid. These men had several days' forced marching behind, over a terrain that trembled in the heat. If they could set up their machine guns they could perhaps beat off the stamping cavalcade. If not—" My informant threw up his hands in a hopeless gesture. "A terrible excitement reigned in the fort," he continued. "We realized that we were about to witness the destruction of the troops that had come to our aid.

"Our commander did not hesitate long. He ordered every man out, bayonets fixed and the light machine guns in front. We raced down in the slopes of the mountains. We could hear the yelling of the Moorish riders in the distance and the rattle of firing. Would we be in time? Could we avoid a new disaster? Every man ran for all he was worth! We got farther and farther away from the camp.

"Then suddenly shots rang out behind us. Another group of Kabyles had attacked the post and was already inside. The little hospital, the only wooden shack in the place, was going up in flames. A thick pillar of smoke was rising from the camp. In a flash it dawned upon every one of us that the Kabyles had outwitted us again. The attack on the reinforcement column had been a mere feint. They had waited till the troop of reinforcements was in sight of us, so that we would be drawn out and run to the aid of our threatened comrades.

"When the group of Kabyles which had attacked the reinforcements saw the column of smoke arise above the hills, they left off at once and galloped back.

"We too marched back, back to the fort, only to find the whole works in ruins, the wounded massacred or burned to death and even the doctor with his head cut off and horribly mutilated in the usual manner. The heavy machine guns were missing. The guns in the small-caliber battery were spiked. All the reserve rifles were gone. We had to wait another month before a supply column with new ammunition struggled its way up to us."

In Timhadit, in the passes of the Atlas, where General Weygand's son commanded the garrison, we learned that every pound of coffee, every box of cartridges, every rifle, everything in the form of rations or supplies destined for the troops had to be escorted and watched over every step of the way from the port of landing to the front in the Atlas mountains, a distance of fourteen hundred miles. More men were killed every month merely in bringing up supplies in Morocco than in five years of fighting in the Khyber Pass in India. Advance posts, we were told, were destroyed and their occupants massacred with the regularity of clockwork. And no matter how pitiless the reprisals, the Berbers were not daunted in the least and started all over again the next day.

Except for the machine guns and other latter-day appurtenances of war, such as the searchlights which send nervously shifting beams into the night, lighting up patches of the cedar forest to daylight clarity, the situation in Timhadit, which is one of the army's advance posts, does not differ a great deal from the perilous position in which the legions of Rome found themselves when King Jugurtha, who was a Kabyle, laid his ambuscades. Nobody ventures a step beyond the thick barbed-wire entanglements after dark. To do so is to risk a surprise. Like tigers watching their prey, the Berbers lie in the undergrowth, crawling up noiselessly to within earshot of the camp, and wait for any reckless man who should dare to leave after dark for a rendezvous with a native girl.

For that is one of their favorite tricks. They use women to lure the legionnaires out of their entrenched camps. This is not very difficult since the monotony of life in these tiny forts is enough to drive young men crazy with the blues. "Bring us ten rifles and you can have your pick from a score of beautiful children," has been a standing offer to the legionnaires since the days of Abd el-Krim, who inaugurated that system of enticing men to desert.

Timhadit is on a hill. A few tents, one shack with corrugated iron roof, heaps of rocks that serve as a parapet and thick layers of barbed wire all around. That's the whole camp. One narrow goat path leads to the summit of the hill. The nearest post is sixty miles away. Farther south there are no more posts. Farther south the Berbers are the masters. There are several parallel lines of such posts, all a considerable distance apart. Once a month a column comes through with victuals and munitions to relieve and to evacuate the sick and wounded. In the rainy season the relieving column may be weeks late.

Timhadit has a few pieces of mountain artillery and a set of machine guns. Six machine gunners were killed by Berber snipers in the month of August. For the moment there is no danger, as an extraordinary situation prevails around the fort. A great tribe of Kabyles is camped at the foot of the hill. They have erected a small city of tents. Their flocks of goats and sheep are peacefully grazing all around. Their women sit under the ramparts watching the strange soldiers. The Kabyles pretend that they are at war with the Berbers and have come to place themselves under protection of the fort.

That sounds all right. But it may be a *ruse de guerre*, a trick to lure the garrison from its stronghold. The forest may be hiding masses of Berbers ready for the attack and the massacre. Reconnoitering airplanes from Marrakech have flown over the forests. They have seen nothing suspicious. Patrols are now out on the extraordinarily dangerous mission of scouring the woods for miles around. They leave the camp early in the morning and must be back by sundown. When it gets dark and they are not in, the officers look worried and the searchlight swings in all directions. Are they still alive? Have they run into an ambush? The wireless crackles overhead. Other forts are asking whether the patrols are in. Finally there is a sigh of relief, a trumpet sounds in the distance, the men are on their way. . . .

Thus does France carry her share of "the white man's burden" in the outposts of the Sherifian Empire. But for how long? During the Great War, Marshal Lyautey, then *résident-général*, succeeded in keeping the peace from Timbuktu to the Mediterranean shores with but a handful of men. Virtually the entire Army of Morocco, native troops and Foreign Legion, were transferred to the Western front, where they were used in the defense of Verdun by Mangin.

Till this day it is considered nothing less than a miracle that Morocco did not rise in revolt when the army of occupation was absent. Had Abd el-Krim or some other native chieftains seized the opportunity they missed a few years later, there might be a different story to tell about French suzerainty in north Africa. It took half a million Frenchmen and Spaniards, one hundred and eighty generals and two Marshals of France, Pétain and Lyautey, to bring Abd el-Krim to his knees. Had he raised the green banner seven years earlier, he could have taken Fez and Marrakech and all the cities with comparative ease and dethroned the puppet sultan. Not only Abd el-Krim, but Germany also missed a chance to deliver a hard blow to France. This is realized in Berlin now. And that is why the Nazis, on coming to power, have made Morocco and Algiers the object of their most intensive propaganda. As early as the fall of 1934, the Moroccan cities were inundated by a flood of tracts and pamphlets in the Arabic language but printed in Germany, calling on the inhabitants to prepare for a struggle of liberation and not to let the historic opportunity pass when France shall again become involved in a European war. The occupation of Spanish Morocco by General Franco, Hitler's ally, has moreover, given Germany a foothold in the African continent from whence arms and supplies can easily be passed into the hands of the restless Arab tribes. In fact there is good reason to believe that if war breaks out between France and Germany, and under present conditions, the armies will most likely be deadlocked from the beginning on the Maginot Line and the German Rhineland fortifications. Morocco will be one of the chief theaters of war. Under the cover of the Spanish Civil War, Germany has prepared a new and deadly threat to France, and Nazi propaganda has found its most fertile soil amongst the Moroccan tribesmen and urban dwellers.

A Free Haircut

"Allah alone can make the grass grow, but only Achmed the barber knows how it is done." That's an old Arabic proverb. It may well be true. At all events, the barber in the native quarter of Marrakech, to whose tender mercies I submitted my cranium for curiosity's sake, knew a great deal, but he did not know how to cut hair. In the first place he started out by quarreling over the price with my interpreter, beginning by asking fifty francs and ending up with accepting a hundred sous—five francs. That was four times the regular tariff.

He ripped out the hair by bunches, talking the while with the eloquence of a Demosthenes. Did I not know what kind of a man my interpreter was? No? Well, he the barber, knew! (He had never clapped eyes on Youssef till that moment!) My interpreter was a robber, a low-down pickpocket, of a caste and a tribe altogether beneath contempt. How I could show myself in public with such a Satan's child was something he, the barber, could not understand! I was dishonoring myself, dishonoring the great, great white race, for which he had all the respect in the world, and it was more than likely that I would come to a bad end in the good Ibn Avrahim's company.

"Cut my hair," I interrupted, "and don't talk so much!"

He was cutting my hair, he said. It was good hair, better hair than these despicable Moroccans had on their heads. It was an honor to cut hair like mine. Where did people grow such fine hair?

"In Patagonia," I said. "But cut it—don't pull it out!"

He acted as if he hadn't heard me. He had once cut the hair of a French officer, a major. That gentleman had given him a tip of ten duros.

"Ten duros is a lot of money," I said. "I am not a major. I am only a corporal!"

It might have been five duros or three, he could not recall the exact amount. He had so many customers. They were all fine generous gentlemen. They all gave large tips.

"You will get no tip at all from me if you keep on this way!" I said. "You are tearing my hair out by the roots!"

"It's Allah's will," he said unctuously.

"Leave Allah out of this!" I ordered. "You are to cut my hair, not Allah!"

"Allah is merciful," quoth the barber.

"That may be so, but you certainly are merciless!" I said. "I have a good mind to report you to the police for taking money under false pretenses."

"There is a man in Marrakech who was blind," said the barber, "and who now has new eyes!"

"Liar!" put in Youssef, my interpreter, who was sitting on a stool in the corner of the shop waiting for me.

"Be still, Youssef!" I said. "Don't make trouble for us!"

The barber rambled on for another minute or so, and even dragged another customer into the conversation. This man, a tall Arab, had a harelip. Apropos of this man the barber said suddenly to me: "Do you know how the hares got that split lip of theirs?"

"No," I said, "I don't know."

"Well," he answered, "one day the moon sent an insect down to earth to tell the people: 'As I die and live again, so you will die and live again.' The insect was overtaken on the road by a hare who learned of the message and said: 'I can run faster than you can. Let me carry the message.' This was agreed. But the hare forgot the exact words of the message and he told the people: 'As I live says the moon, you shall all die!' The moon heard of this and when the hare came back, the moon took a piece of wood and whacked the hare over the snout. That's where the split lip comes in!"

"He's a liar and a blasphemer," Youssef suddenly called out.

"Youssef," I said, "I implore you to keep quiet!"

"Pig!" called out the barber.

That's a fighting word in Islam, and Youssef is a fighter. Without another word he hurled the stool he had been sitting on at the barber's head. It missed, but it struck an array of bottles of Eau de Cologne on a shelf. Youssef leaped forward like a tiger. He floored the barber with one blow, but the underdog set up such a howl that neighbors came running in. Everybody piled on. The barbershop was wrecked in a minute. Then the police appeared on the scene.

They arrested the barber and looked for Youssef. He had disappeared.

"You come to the pasha's court tomorrow," I was told, "to testify against this man." They pointed to the barber.

"But I don't want to testify against him!" I protested.

"He hasn't finished cutting your hair, has he?"

"No," I said, feeling my head. "I should say not!"

They all bowed and left. They always bow in Morocco, rain or shine. Youssef paid me a flying visit in the evening and told me that he'd wait outside the city for me till we moved out.

Where Dead Men Pay the Bill

Djema-el-Fna! Gathering Place of the Dead! That was the lugubrious name of the place we struck after Laboun and where the military escort which had accompanied the expedition through the danger zone turned back. The name is misleading: Djema-el-Fna is not a cemetery. It is a super-hotsy-totsy, an intertribal tom-tom fest and a carnival rolled in one, where "the quick and the dead" rub elbows. Here they shimmy and cancan till they drop with the foam on their mouths. Here the Arab sugar papas from Marrakech and Fez come to eat hashish till they see the hundred thousand houris of paradise sway into view on laughing camels with golden teeth.

The midway doesn't open until the moon is up and the mountain breezes begin to stir the palm trees. The first item on the program is a parade of the mannequins from every tribe in Africa in a hoofing act that would make Salome gasp. Such an act hasn't been seen in the vale of tears since the olive-hued damsels of old Babylon made their bangles jingle in the torchlit temples of Ishtar. It is a stomach dance, which means that the breasts and the haunches go into action. It begins with an extremely slow rhythm. The danseuses scarcely move: slowly the tempo increases, until in the end, panting and their torsos twisting and heaving in a tumultuous movement, the girls go into a self-intoxicated trance and finally look like a mob of devil-possessed furies.

The story goes that they gave this show for a Roman consul two thousand years ago and that he let his chance for the throne of the world go hang to watch it again. They put it on when Ali, Mohammed's grandson was in the neighborhood, and he swore by the Prophet's beard that he thought he had entered the golden gate.

"Tell me," I said to Youssef ibn Avrahim, as I gaped with my mouth open like any other yokel, at the scene where swarthy Cleugh girls, by the light of a hundred pitch torches, executed that breathless ring-around-a-rosy to the tom-toming of fifty grinning eunuchs, "tell me, Youssef, why do you call this Djema-en-Fna?"

"Because," replied the omniscient Youssef, "when a rich man is dead and his relatives fear that he may not be received at once in paradise, on account of his sins, they carry him up here, so that he may at least see the spectacle which is supposed to be next best to heaven—and may be better!"

"Dead men watch this show?"

"Oh, yes, there are several here tonight. They watch the show from under those palm trees over there!"

Sure enough, there they were seated on huge white camels, their bodies wrapped tightly in bandages, held up in a sitting position by leather straps fastened to high-backed saddles and surrounded by their wives and concubines who clapped their hands and beat little tinkling tambourines to the tune of the general racket. There were four of these dead men. I walked up to them to convince myself and saw the corpses lolling impotently to and fro as the cud-chewing camels, on which they were seated, shifted their weight from one foot to the other. Only their glassy, unseeing eyes had been left uncovered by the bandages. One servant stood tugging at his dead master's feet, rocking the corpse to the wild jangled tune of the screeching native string instruments.

By the side of another dead rider stood some women calling endearing names up at him. "Can you see, Achmed dear? See, Achmed, how that little dancing girl twists her body. It's all for you, my beloved lord: your duros make her daring and happy!" Youssef translated for me.

"What does she mean by 'your duros'?" I asked him.

"The dead man's money. He has paid the dancers and the musicians," replied Youssef.

That was the first time in my life I had a dead man pay for my entertainment!

Hashish and kiff, two narcotics greatly favored among the Arabs in Africa, were graciously distributed among those attending this nocturnal picnic, while the servants of the dead kaids poured sirupy lemonade in brass cups to anyone who made a bow of respect in the direction of the stiff white-robed corpses.

"Must have been rich men," I said to Youssef.

"Don't know them," he replied, "but I will ask." He whispered to one of the servants and presently returned.

"What does he say?"

"He says his master owned so many palm trees that he could make a river of oil run all the way from Marrakech to Fez."

A snake charmer came forward, bowed to the mourners, and started to do his stuff. He was a tall, skinny man, naked to the waist, with a matted beard and an evil countenance which was rendered almost demoniacal in the reflection of the ruddy glare of the lights all over the lot. He blew on a flute and made the snakes stand up on their tails in front of him. Then he let one of the reptiles grab hold of his tongue and two others sink their fangs into his breasts. He then began to hop and swirl around like a dervish, the snakes hanging on to him, swinging like a rotating green hoopskirt, and he, howling and screaming till I thought his lungs would burst. The spectators clapped their hands in delight, and everybody looked in the direction of the dead men to see, I suppose, if they, too, were enjoying the show. . . .

Boys in white robes, their heads and their waists girdled with orange-colored sashes, now held the center stage. They were all of uniform build, their faces were painted like women's and they danced like girls doing the cancan. The pantomime of obscenity made the corpulent merchants from the city lick their fiery lips in lecherous anticipation.

Divide and Rule

Before plunging into the wastelands of the Saraha, the expedition halted in one more small town, Tiznit. Inoculated though I was, I did not venture into the market place where there was a good chance of rubbing shoulders with men and women suffering from bubonic plague. Tiznit is on the confines of the so-called "dissident zone," land which has not been definitely conquered. The unconquered land extends two thousand miles southward to the borders of Sierra Leone. That land is French territory on the map only.

The market in Tiznit closes sharply at four in the afternoon, and every merchant seems in a precipitate hurry to leave town. This is because they are members of tribes who have not made their submission. They will not stop overnight in a settlement where the French flag flies. The French authorities do not treat them as enemies for that reason. It is impossible to tell by a man's exterior whether he belongs to a friendly tribe or not. It's their own bad conscience, I think, that makes the traders leave so hurriedly with nightfall.

They come to deal in sugar, the main staple commodity in the market and the principal food of both prince and beggar. Warriors and peasants carry nothing in their haversacks but a few lumps of sugar and some green tea.

But, it is not only sugar they trade in. If sugar was their stock in trade they would not need to run away so hurriedly. They trade in slaves. Caravans of little black boys are brought up from Senegal and sold on the outskirts of Tiznit. That is the unofficial market. These boys are trained for work and sold again when they are grown up, at a much higher price, of course. The two white inhabitants in Tiznit estimated the slave trade at from five to ten thousand a year.

In the town of Tiznit every merchant looks respectability personified. They suck their narghiles in the native cafés, play checkers, look at the dancing girls, and transact business in an undertone. Once outside the town the same merchant with the quiet manners changes into a warrior. Slaves, who have been looking after his horses under some palm trees, relieve him of his merchant's cloak and there is revealed an Arab warrior with a set of pistols in his belt. The slaves themselves suddenly bristle with long-barreled rifles and together they gallop back into the desert.

The slave trade is proscribed, only the slaves do not seem to know about it. Thousands of them are imported every year from Senegal which is also French territory, of course, but when one speaks of French territory in this connection, it must be considered that it concerns areas of the size of Germany, France and Italy combined, with probably one military post on the edge of it. There is practically no control.

Even in Tiznit itself, where there is a French commandant, things are not much better. The *grand seigneur* of the town is Si-Ayar, a magnificent Arab sheik of great wealth. He makes no bones about the fact that his wealth is derived from the traffic in human beings. The French officers are frequent dinner guests in his palace.

That palace is built over a stream and contains a harem of seventy-five women. The inmates of that harem change every two or three years. When Si-Ayar gets tired of a girl he makes a present of her to a friend or a sheik who happens to pass through the city on business and to whom he wants to be friendly. If a houri has displeased him he hands her over to a beggar covered with syphilitic sores. The disease flourishes here.

In addition, Si-Ayar has five hundred slaves in the palace. Many more are outside cultivating his lands and palm groves. They are not called slaves, of course. They are his servants. He has a radio set, several gramophones, six limousines, a minister of justice, a grand vizier or major-domo, a sort of comptroller of the household and a gallows. From Mauritania he imports ostriches, bald antelopes and royal eagles. He lives at peace with the French on condition they don't bother him, which they don't. It would be a bad day if the French and Si-Ayar had a falling out. For there are thousands of men (nobody knows exactly how far south the Sheik's influence extends) who would ride hard to his assistance—and willingly.

The French told me Si-Ayar's domains probably extend as far as Mauritania. That's a great kingdom—bigger than the whole of France. He is precisely informed as to political conditions in France. He owns two large buildings in Paris, and from time to time he sends a shipment of gold north by private car and across the Mediterranean to France. Si-Ayar is saving up for a rainy day, precisely as the late King of Jugoslavia, who had been putting his fortune in French banks for many years, always fearing that something would happen some day. It did in his case.

Si-Ayar has a mighty neighbor, another prince, who also draws his wealth from the slave trade. They are constantly at loggerheads and fights are not infrequent. They have their men raid each other's borders, whisk away whole caravans, damage crops, or rustle flocks of young camels. The French play the role of arbiters between these two *grand seigneurs* who own allegiance to the Sultan of Morocco, but who think their liege lord ought to be glad to get a few sacks of gold a year and not ask any questions.

"How do you expect to get these men completely under French control?" I asked the military commander here.

"Sometimes we flirt with them," he replied. "Sometimes we frown, sometimes we show our teeth. But since we have not the men and the equipment to carry out punitive expeditions on a large scale, we have the one punish the other at times, and so we have them both under control."

"But," said I, "suppose they tire of that little game some day and combine against you, what will happen?"

"We would be wiped out," came the reply without hesitation. "However, there is no danger that they will. When they get tired, both Si-Ayar and his mighty neighbor will move over to the Riviera. They each have a villa at Cannes and will live happily ever after on the gold they have shipped out."

"Then all that intertribal fighting here?" I began.

"All boloney," he replied. "We know what they are up to. But the tribesmen don't!"

The Holy Fire

In Uzdja, a city inhabited by Cleughs and Tuaregs, an oasis in the bad lands, we ran into what may be described as a Moslem revival service. Hundreds of tribesmen accompanied by their wives and children had squatted in a semicircle and were gazing with speechless awe at a wooden platform erected against the wall of a red-brick mosque, whereon a marabout was staring straight into the flame of a bundle of candles. Although he looked like the devil with his vermin-swarming beard and four or five snakes wriggling in and out of the opening of his filthy cloak, we were told that this man could read the future from the secret names of Allah.

"What is he up to?" I asked the omniscient Youssef ibn Avrahim when we had edged up as closely as we could to the elevation on which the prophet was performing. "Is he *maboul?*"

"*Maboul?* Crazy? He? No, he is holy and holy and holy. He is so holy he does not want to look at anything on earth any more. He has seen God," Youssef whispered.

"Could we speak with him, do you think?"

"We cannot speak to him now. He suffers terrible pain in his eyes. No man can see God without suffering. . . ."

"Let him stop looking into the fire."

"He cannot stop. When the pain becomes too great he will eat fire. We will all eat fire. All these people will eat fire!"

"What do you mean: we will all eat fire? I won't, I can assure you!"

"Yes, you will," retorted the imperturbable Youssef. "You will eat fire, too, if God commands."

"If God commands, that's a different matter. I'll take a chance on that!"

We waited a full hour before the marabout climbed down from the platform escorted by a group of men who were his immediate disciples. They crossed the square to a small whitewashed building— the tomb of one of his predecessors—and began building a fire around a knotty eucalyptus tree standing before the entrance of the tomb. The crowd helped to make a real bonfire by piling up twigs and faggots and potfuls of camel dung. Soon the flames shot up five, six feet high. But the tree did not burn. . . .

"Miracle! Miracle! Miracle! The tree isn't burning!" Everybody began to shout, to holler, to scream, to dance and beat their bare breasts. Some men ripped off their turbans and began slashing themselves across the scalp with daggers and knives till the blood trickled into their flaming eyes. Others stuck arrows into their shoulders, jabbing and stabbing themselves, filling the air with the smell of blood, ordure and sweat. The mob was working itself into mass delirium. Even Youssef became excited. Since the other members of our expedition had gone back to camp, and I feared that the revival meeting was not a safe place for a lone white man, I tried to get away, too, but had to give up the attempt. There was no way of getting out of that sweating, howling, groaning, bleeding multitude.

Branches of trees, logs, planks were heaped onto the fire. The flames shot up above the domed roof of the whitewashed tomb. The wood crackled and the crowd yelled itself hoarse. Suddenly the marabout snatched a burning twig out of the pyre and stuck it into his mouth. A hush fell over the crowd. Thousands of eyes lit up by fanaticism were devouring the holy man's every gesture. He chewed the red-hot embers as if he were munching a piece of marzipan. And then, to cap the show, he walked straight into the roaring fire. Now let me say this that fire was not merely a heap of glowing ashes. It flamed. It blazed. It crackled. It threw off a blistering heat. I felt its glow, and I was not hypnotized.

Walking in the midst of those flames did not seem to hurt the marabout any more than that fire into which Shadrach, Meshach and Abednego walked in Daniel's time. I stood aghast. I was rubbing my eyes and pinching myself. Had the prophet smeared his limbs with some kind of protective salve of a type used by some heretics in the days of the Inquisition when their legs were plunged into iron boots filled with boiling oil? I could see that he was stepping a little gingerly. But his bare feet were treading on blazing chunks of wood. His cloak did not burn, or even catch fire, or even get singed. . . .

All at once he turned about, and facing the congregation he began to shout like a lunatic. His cry was like the death rattle of that boy I once saw hanging on the barbed wire in France. I could see the snakes crawling up about his head, as he gesticulated and bellowed like an ox in delirium tremens.

"What does he say, Youssef? Does it hurt?"

"He calls upon everybody to step into the fire and be cleansed of sin and disease!"

Nobody seemed inclined to accept the invitation. Instead, some peasants pitched in a paralytic child. The youngster cried out in anguish as its clothes caught fire and its head was enveloped in flames. A deaf-and-dumb yokel was pushed in next. He roared like a steer who sees the deathtrap in the abattoir. A woman followed. She fainted the moment her feet touched the crackling branches. The next man became a living torch as the flames leaped to his burnous. But the marabout walked about untouched, and still screamed at the top of his voice: "Burn here, Believers, and you will not burn in hell!"

That roasting party kept up the whole night!

All the members of our expedition returned about midnight to see how things were getting along. Hundreds of pitch torches had been lit in the square by the mosque where the woodpile was now a smoldering, smoking heap. When our eyes grew somewhat accustomed to the smudge, we noticed that, under direction of that tireless marabout, the crowd was being put through a sort of breathing exercise. The Moslems breathed in unison, first slowly, then quicker and quicker like a locomotive gathering speed. When the ultimate speed had been reached, the marabout gave a sign and the process started all over again. Between gasps the men pushed out a guttural cry: "Allah!" The object of it all, as we later learned from a Catholic missionary, a White Father whom we encountered near Azouah, is to release the soul from the body. In such exercises the flesh is conquered, said the priest, and the spirit dominates. The body becomes insensible to pain. It is the same state of insensibility to environment which the Sufi acquires by intense meditation. "Those breathing exercises you witnessed in Oudjda are a remnant of medieval practices. They were always held before a campaign of conquest. This was the way the fighting men of Islam warmed themselves up for battle. After that they felt no pain or hardship. Even death became easy. Such orgies last from five to six days. It is fortunate," added the missionary, "that the Moslem refrains from drinking alcoholic beverages. For if that evil were prevalent in addition to this, no white man would be safe in Morocco."

Alcohol! As I thought back to that mob of ferocious fanatics in Oudjda it struck me that Mohammed did not know what he was doing when he reserved the use of wine for paradise. By that decree, the Prophet cramped his style, so to speak, and seriously limited the possibilities of Islam. After such exercises as we had seen, a dip into the fountain of Bacchus—and the Saracens would not have been brought to a halt by Charles Martel at Tours. With a little more gusto these swarms of lunatics, after conquering Spain, would have overrun France and Belgium and Germany as well, which would have been no great trick at that, since the Prussians had not yet learned to goose-step and were still tending their swine. A Moslem Europe! Napoleon a sheik! Karl Marx an ulema! Mussolini Khalif-ul Islam and the Pope a local preacher somewhere up in Iceland!

Perhaps not a bad arrangement!

The Black Watch

The guard turned out for our welcome in Agades, a city of mud hovels, built around an oasis in the heart of the desert. Talk about your Black Watch! The fifty men who made up this *corps d'élite* were the color of an ebony pianoforte and just about as shiny. Their uniform was a string of glass beads, two strings for the noncommissioned officers, and a loin cloth. The top sergeant had a *Croix de guerre* pinned on him. But they presented arms to the chief of our expedition with the perfection of the cadets of Saint-Cyr. The population received us with a beating of drums. They drummed all night and led us out next morning still playing the tom-toms. We had a dinner of antelope steak and tasted some native mead, which turned out to be as potent as Georgia "corn." In the evening a troupe of debutantes, drawn from the upper crust of society, entertained us with a dance which was filmed. No censors on earth would release that film for public showing. It was destined for the edification of the delegates to an anthropological congress to be held the year thereafter in Nice. After the dance a native medicine man called up the ghosts of his ancestors for us.

We owed that evening of pleasure to Koliko'mbo, which means literally "the Great One," the chief, the king, the emperor, the president or whatever you like. I addressed him as Majesty, at any rate, and he did not take it amiss. Koliko'mbo knew a few phrases of French. They were made up of words which are not to be found in any dictionary. They, too, would not pass the censor. I do not know who had been the teachers of His Majesty, but I suspect the Foreign Legion. Yet, it was amazing what a wide diversity of sentiments can be expressed with an extremely limited vocabulary. Koliko'mbo, like my own Youssef in speaking English, had not the slightest notion how scandalous his language was and probably thought he was discoursing in the best parliamentarian French.

That mead the natives of equatorial Africa brew out of grain is the identical stuff our forefathers in the Hercynian forest were so fond of. Ludendorff had endowed the ancestor of the storm troopers with an aureole of virtue, but Tacitus, who saw them on the spot, contradicts the General. They were lolling drunkards, wife beaters, lazybones and rowdies. I do not know whether it was that mead, but there was an awful lot of rough-and-tumble going on in Agades after the drinks were served. For instance, those debutantes who danced so entrancingly were not members of the tribe at all. They were slave girls, brought home by Koliko'mbo from his raids in the neighborhood. "They are all mine, these," he boasted. "Maybe I give you one?" he added questioningly, in a sudden burst of generosity.

"Not now, Majesty," I said. "Not now, but gladly on my way back!"

"But we don't come back this way," piped up Youssef ibn Avrahim, whom I did not know was so near.

"Youssef," I admonished, "you as a Moslem should not drink so much of that beer."

"You captured all these girls?" I asked Koliko'mbo.

"You think that's all I have?" he came back. "I have a lot more."

"But the French?" I asked.

For answer the great man winked, which made me conclude that the French do the same.

"Do these ladies not run away?" I asked.

"They don't get a chance," he came back emphatically, pointing to the whip of cowhide that hung by his side. "Moreover," he went on reassuringly, "I treat them well. I give them dazo and arachis oil and sesame and manioc and bananas. I also have some absinthe! Would you care for a spot?"

Finding the steak somewhat musty, I contented myself with a bowl of rice and melted camel butter. Ordinarily you dip your fingers into the bowl and make little balls out of the rice as in Arabia, but Koliko'mbo's dancing girls were graciously distributed amongst the guests to do the *honneurs*. The ladies fed us like babes in arms.

Youssef was sitting behind me. "This one," he tapped her familiarly on the shoulder, "is the best-looking one of the lot," he whispered. "You can have her for the asking."

"I don't want her," I said.

"If you don't want her, maybe you could ask for me?" he insisted.

For answer I ceded him my place in the noisily smacking circle and watched him devour rice balls at the hands of the damsel till he became ill.

Just before dawn a sorcerer was summoned to the long house where the revelry was in progress and commanded to call up the shades of Koliko'mbo's fathers from the nether world. The magician, a lean specimen, had been sitting outside chewing off the bones that had been left over from our repast. He donned a gruesome mask of carved wood which slipped over his head. On top of that went a bonnet, the shape of a Chinese pagoda roof, adorned with feathers, and around his loins a sort of hoop skirt of grass. The boys began to play the tom-tom, the girls clapped their hands, and while everybody joined in singing a wailing lament in which the words *Ayaya yer, Ayaya yer* recurred with tiresome monotony, the sorcerer began to dance. Pretty soon he had worked himself into a sweat and I could hear his breath come in asthmatic gasps. Faster and faster he whirled. All eyes were glued on this jumping, sliding, hiccoughing monstrosity. I expected him to collapse any moment, for the perspiration literally streamed down his torso and legs and each time he made a quick about-face, he sent a shower of sweat drops over the assembled guests. But the magician did not go under. Koliko'mbo passed out first. I noticed that as the dance reached its climax the chief's eyes had become dilated with terror. He was shaking like a reed. Suddenly, pointing with trembling hand, he emitted a scream that went to the marrow of our bones. Then he swooned. Everybody shrieked and the girls fled. They had all seen the ghost. As we left, both the magician and Koliko'mbo lay unconscious on the floor.

That night Youssef went A.W.O.L.

Prayer Code

When the moon came up in Azouah, it crept in and out of the moving clouds like a panther stalking its prey. Its shifty light peopled the night with mysterious shapes and phantoms. The searchlight beam on the first car of our procession (we traveled by night after leaving Morocco) lit up a wall of blue faïence rising perpendicularly from the salt plain. From the top of that wall gargoyles and dragons seemed to be looking down upon our caravan. We had passed through a hailstorm that evening. Our teeth chattered with the cold. Both Youssef and I sat with a blanket over our shoulders. Far away to the east, maybe fifteen miles distant, other travelers could be seen moving against the moon. From the flat hollow in which we traveled, their camels' legs assumed fantastic proportions against the lunar horizon. It was like trick photography on a quivering silver screen. We dropped still farther into a volcanic gully and the cinematographic vision vanished, but the play of shadows above our heads was accentuated. "On such nights," stated Youssef, who had his rifle gripped between his knees, "on such nights the *boudas* prowl about: *boudas* are men who change to hyenas at dusk only to resume human shape at dawn again. Bullets don't hurt a *bouda.*"

With the coming of day which broke like a thunderbolt of fierce, implacable light, we halted in the shadow of the blue wall. It was an outcropping of black schist veined with streaks of gneiss. In less than an hour the heat became terrific. The water in the radiators evaporated so rapidly that we had to replace it with an alcoholic preparation. But on top of the wall the sun's rays were a shimmering inferno. As we spread out the cars to camp, we saw a troop of white camels descending into the valley. The beasts were mounted by Tuaregs, the men who wear veils and who were at one time the shock troops of Islam. In front rode two young French officers. They also had kept their woollen cloaks tightly wrapped around their faces. There was a great deal of handshaking all around, and we sat down to a breakfast of coffee and bread. Youssef was pressed into service as headwaiter. The meharists of the camel corps had their own meal a short distance from us. They ate dried meat with water.

We learned from the officers, two young Parisian boys who were more interested in the latest news from the boulevards than in telling us details of their work in the desert, that their patrol was on the lookout for tribesmen out of Tripoli. The Azouah section of the Sahara in which we were traveling formed a part of a huge chunk of territory but recently ceded to Italy. The desert population was shifting: they wanted to get out of the way of the Fascists who would come to take over this district of seventy-five thousand square miles. Mixed with these subjects of France, who did not desire to change their allegiance, was a considerable number of Tripolitan Arabs who seized the opportunity of escaping from the clutches of Signor Balbo in the Libyan protectorate. If caught while trying to escape into French territory, the chiefs of the nomads were taken up in Italian airplanes and hurled to death on the rocks.

That was the punishment for insubordination inaugurated by Rodolfo Graziani, and it still prevailed in the Italian part of Africa.

The result was that the nomads from Italian territory, rather than being driven back into Tripoli, took a chance on fighting the French patrols.

"We seldom catch sight of these infiltering nomads," said the commander of the French patrol. "And even if we did, what can we do with them? They carry no identification papers. They do not know where the frontiers start. I do not know myself and I have my staff maps. However, they generally give themselves away by starting to shoot or ambushing a patrol. We are carrying five dead men with us now for burial at Fort Flatters. They were killed in an ambush three days ago. The corpses are putrid, but our Tuaregs insist on carrying their comrades back for burial. They won't leave them to the hyenas."

"Who were the attackers?" I asked.

The commander shrugged his shoulders.

"Did you inflict any losses on them?"

"I could not tell. They decamped as soon as they got the herd of young camels which we were bringing up to Flatters."

"So you really do not know whether they were Tunisians, Saharans or Tripolitans?"

"Not the faintest idea!" he said with a shrug of the shoulders. "There are no friendly tribes hereabouts. It would take a million men to pacify this desert. We have a few thousand. They fire at us on general principles, just to hear their rifles go off, I suppose. Your expedition might run into the crowd that attacked us. They cannot be very far," he added. "But you will meet another of our patrols first. We split into two parties after the ambush. One squad remains on duty while we go to the fort. You'll hear the others this evening. We are going to signal to them."

We were breaking up to resume our journey towards nightfall when the signaling took place. Slowly one of the Tuaregs rode up the path to the top of that granite hill. On the promontory and standing in his stirrups he called the evening prayer. His voice rushed down to us in the hollow as clearly as if he had stood next to us:

"O thou, enwrapped in thy mantle. Arise, magnify Him! By the sun when it retreateth! Praise Him! By the shadows as they lengthen! Turn ye to Allah! Allah is merciful, compassionate! His goodness endureth. . . ."

The meharists were kneeling on their prayer rugs. The camels stood with lifted necks patiently blinking their long-lashed eyes. The French commander of the camel troops puffed nervously at his cigaret. The stillness was immense.

We were waiting for the answer. After a few minutes it came, a faint piping voice, as that of an infant's wail: "O thou, enwrapped in thy mantle. . . ."

"Everything is fine," said the commander with a sigh, after the distant prayer ceased.

"How can you tell? It seemed to me the other man recited exactly the same prayer."

"We can tell by the tone in which he pitched his chant," replied the officer. "That is our code here!"

"White Man, My Brother!"

Before leaving the expedition I stayed at Fort Baron for three weeks. I wanted to send off a batch of articles and to rest a little after the exhausting push through the Sahara. During that time the expedition split into small groups, each with his own task to perform. We two, Youssef and I, made several excursions in the neighborhood, generally accompanying Professor Perrault and his assistants who wrote down whatever sagas and legends they could hear from the tribal medicine men and chiefs, while recording for phonographic reproduction the war and love songs of the different clans. I had the satisfaction of being useful, at least once on that long journey, when it was learned that one tribe, the Bobo Ouleh, who live about a hundred miles west of Fort Lamy had a script which they preserved with religious veneration on one of their long houses. We heard about its existence from one of the French officers at Fort Lamy. But it took a lot of cajoling and flattery before the headman consented to let us have a look at it, and then not until they had spent two whole days and a night in deliberation.

The magic document turned out to be nothing more than a crumpled scrap of paper and contained but a few lines written in ink, half in French and half in Flemish. By diligent questioning, Dr. Perrault extracted from the tribesmen the information that the paper had been left there by a white man who had lived in their midst, or rather with their fathers. When he left, the whole tribe—

men, women and children—had accompanied him safely to the next tribe, carrying him across the ravines and rivers on the way. When they saw the stranger finally disappear in the distance, they told us, they had all wept. They were still inconsolable over his absence. "But some day," the tribesmen said, "the holy one will come back and the good days will return." He had been their father. He had cured the sick and had carried the little children in his arms. He had sung songs for them in the evening and told them strange stories of the good god.

"And what did he look like?" the Doctor asked.

"He was white, all white; his clothes were white; his face, his hands, all white."

"A White Father, obviously," remarked Dr. Perrault. "A missionary, who must have passed by here on his way to Nigeria or the Congo."

Finally we were handed the script. It read: "White Man, my Brother, whoever you are, be kind and gentle in your dealings with the people of the Bobo Ouleh. They are a good people, trustworthy and loyal. There is no guile in them. I have lived with them for a year and have learned to love them. Remember: whatever you do to one of the least of these it shall be done to Our Father in heaven." Then there followed the sign of the cross and an illegible scrawl.

"He hasn't signed his name," spoke up Dr. Perrault. "What a pity!"

"That name is known in heaven," I said, for I felt that we had crossed the path of a saint.

Amongst the Bobo Ouleh the relations between the sexes seemed somewhat reversed. It was the boys who wore the skirts and the married women who presided at the collective tasks of the community. The husbands attended to the affairs of the household, which was not as onerous a task as would appear on first sight, for there were no dishes to wash. A myriad of curs took care of that. The principal industry, as far as I could see, among the youth at least, consisted of hairdressing. This ancient profession was not carried on in shops. It was done in the open. Perfectly oblivious of their idyllic nudity, the young women of the tribe spent the lifelong day sitting in the shade of their parents' huts or under the trees dressing each other's hair, surrounded by a swarm of gaping skirt-wearing yokels who watched the performance with unbounded fascination. The trick is to clip, snip, smoothen and plaster with oil the kinky curls till (the delicate operation lasted for hours) they resemble in outline the shape of some animal, in the manner of a landscape gardener trimming a fancy hedge. According to Youssef, who did nothing else for ten days but watch the female beauticians, the height of achievement was considered the form of a giraffe, but when they were through it was always and again the same old disappointing shape of a chicken that emerged.

If ever a giraffe-shaped coiffure is produced, Youssef had learned, the bearer is forthwith escorted by the whole guild to the local chief, who promptly adds the beauty with the ineffable coiffure to his harem. Few attain to this high state of perfection, but they never weary of trying. Ordinary mortals, the equivalent amongst the Bobo Ouleh of greengrocers, lawyers, streetcar conductors and news-papermen, must be satisfied with sweethearts with chicken-shaped coiffures.

There was of course, more to all these hirsute manipulations than struck the eye. In fact, the hairdressing business was mere camouflage, It was the Bobo Ouleh's substitute for cocktail hour at the Ritz, only it took longer before coming to a head.

Yet all the gossip and giggling and sighing and sly holding of hands came to an abrupt stop the moment a white man put in an appearance. The smiles froze on the girls' faces. The general attitude of the boys grew stiff, formal, suspicious, hostile. The fun was over: the white man was there. Amongst all these innocent people in Africa we white men have the devil's own reputation. On the hunt, in their struggle against wild beasts, snakes and pestilence, and on the warpath against other tribes, they are without fear. But when they see a white man they tremble. I strolled around the village of the Bobo Ouleh one morning. At one point I saw something dis-appear behind a silo and when I followed, I found a woman no longer young, standing with her face against the wall, howling in fear. I walked away as quickly as I could to calm her apprehensions. It was a most mortifying experience, too, to see the black urchins in all those Chad villages open their eyes wide with dread at my approach, run as fast as their little legs could carry them, as if the big bad wolf were on their heels, and scamper into the huts. From the inside of the hovels you could hear them weep as if their hearts would break.

Who and what has frightened all these people so dreadfully? Are we then fiends that even little children are afraid of us? Entire regions in Africa, the size of European kingdoms, are deserted. The inhabitants have moved away to escape the sight of the white man. They give up their villages, rivers, lakes and hunting grounds and prefer to hide in the jungle and feed on roots and snakes so long as they do not have to come in contact with the representatives of what is known as Western civilization.

Oh, yes, we bring them blessings galore if one goes by exhibits in museums and by statistics in colonial ministries. But almost everywhere in colonial Africa the natives see their land expropriated by the whites. Amongst the Bolo Ouleh their collective property, which is called "the soil without a master," has been concessioned by the French governmental authorities to colonization trusts under leases running for ninety-nine years, that is to say forever. Without a cent of compensation to the native owners, these trusts extract all the natural riches from immense regions and have the military forces of France at their beck and call to crush resistance, and even press the natives into service for the exploitation and despoliation of their own soil and wealth.

From the Chad region batches of young men are shipped away every spring into Nigeria and equatorial Africa to work rubber plantations, a distance fully equal to that from New York to Salt Lake City. They never return. Their parents and relatives never hear of them again. If they refuse to leave they are beaten with whips of hippopotamus leather. If they hide, the village elders are imprisoned; frequently the women and children are maltreated before their eyes to make them give up their resistance. Passive resistance on the part of a tribe or a clan is followed with collective punishment: destruction of their villages of straw and mud and relentless man hunts in the forests where the populations go into hiding. What life is like for the native laborers in the concessions may be gathered from the report of M. Albert Londres[1] on the construction of the railway which is to run from Chad to the coast of Equatorial Africa, that is to say to the Atlantic Ocean. Of the thirty thousand contract laborers employed in 1928, but seven thousand were alive a year later. Of the twenty-seven thousand driven to work the next year, eighteen thousand perished before nine months were over. It will take at least ten more years to com-

[1] Albert Londres, *Schwarz und Weiss: Die Wahrheit über Afrika*, Agis-Verlag, Wien-Berlin, 1929, p. 216 *et seq.*; see also André Gide, *Le Voyage au Congo* and *Le Retour*, Librairie Gallimard, Paris, 1927.

plete that line, after which it is to have branches running off into the Congo.

Besides sleeping sickness which claims tens of thousands of lives annually, the natives are subject to a disease which the doctors dismiss as "machinitis," but which is in reality nostalgia. After a week a Negro starts daydreaming. In two weeks he is finished. The blacks cannot bear to be away from home. They cannot stand the rhythm, the pace of steady labor. They lose flesh, they lose their strength and their inborn *joie de vivre*. They wither like flowers. For a time they work like automatons until they collapse and are left to die.

Work? That was not work! That was bestialization. Everything in Africa is done with the aid of the whip. Freeborn human beings are beaten and lashed to tasks that should be left to machinery or elephants. If they revolt against the inhuman treatment and want to return to their peaceful peasant existence, they are driven back at the point of the bayonet!

I watched lumbering operations for a few days in Ubangi, south of the lake's shore. Eight thousand black men were employed there. As in wartime, there was a daily list of casualties: on Monday ten killed, Tuesday nine, Wednesday fifteen—and so on. The wounded and maimed were not even mentioned. Who cares? Tomorrow another gang arrives. Ten villages had just been raided. The young men have been rounded up. They will take the place of the human cattle that become unusable today.

Forty men were poised over a gigantic log which had to be lifted to a flatcar on the forest rail. Another hundred men stood looking on, the reserve. The whips of the European slave drivers cracked. "*Allez!*" Lift! The forty blacks strained on the log, their muscles bulged, their eyes protruded from their sockets. "*Allez, Allez!*" Down came the whips on the naked flesh, lacerating it, tearing the skin off, making the blood run down the men's legs. The log did not budge. "*Allez!*" Ten more. Make room for ten. "*Quick!*" The whips zoomed through the air again. One black, who stumbled, received such a beating that he could not rise. A guard jumped on his face with two heavy-shod feet and crunched his heel in the fallen man's mouth. The man did not let out a whimper. The others looked on, silent, sullen, the sweat of fear pouring down their limbs. Again the whips crashed down. The four guards worked themselves into a hysteria beating the blacks, running along the lines, kicking, battering, lashing. At last the log moved. But one fellow's arm was caught under it. He howled, not in pain, but for what he knew was coming. Two guards jumped on him, stamping on his abdomen, his chest, kicking him in the face, until he groaned and lapsed into unconsciousness.

Forced labor, known as the contract system, is one of the most ferocious institutions of our time. Those black men, faraway from their native lands, work under penal sanctions—that is to say, if they break their contract, they become liable to imprisonment. If they try to flee and are caught, they suffer the most cruel bodily punishment.

The late Sir Arthur Conan Doyle made the world stand aghast at his revelations on the treatment to which natives in the Belgian Congo were subjected. But the world's indignation soon subsided. Today the terrorization of the native is universal from South Africa to the Sudan and from Rio del Oro to Ethiopia. And, whereas in Europe as well as in America, public opinion, Christian traditions, and democratic freedom as well as the working-class organizations rise against the brutality of the exploiters of the colored peoples, in Fascist states that check is altogether lacking and the native races in their colonies are delivered up like so much merchandise into the hands of the exploitation companies.

The colonial record of Italy in Libya is perhaps the most distressing episode in the history of African colonization. There, according to the official statistics published by the League of Nations, the Turks left a population of two millions, six hundred thousand, when they ceded the territory to Italy. After fifteen years of Italian administration two million natives had perished or had emigrated, one million and a half of these under the reign of the famous Graziani. I have seen refugees from Italian rule in Tripoli trudging through the desert of Sinai. They had walked across Libya and Egypt and were making their way wearily and hungrily to the Holy Land, not unlike the ancient Hebrews three thousand years before. Viceroy Graziani, it may be said in passing, had not entirely forgotten his former subjects in Libya when he was conquering southern Ethiopia. For the benefit of his Eritrean infantry, who did all the fighting and whose casualties were never listed by Rome, he imported hundreds of young Libyan boys and girls to serve as prostitutes.

Modern psychoanalysis has made us understand something of the dangerous consequences of the instinct of domination. The European in tropical countries easily degenerates. There is no question but that amongst the thousands of young Europeans who go out every year to serve as administrators, agronomes, organizers and factors, a small minority of idealists can be found to be of genuine help to the native population. But few can resist the ennervating and demoralizing influence of the environment in which they move. Few can resist the terrible temptation of the quasi-unlimited power the white man exercises. Moreover, instead of improving, the moral and intellectual standards of men who go out to the colonies are constantly sinking because an ever greater number is required. Such critical observers of the African colonial system as André Gide, H. Roland Holst, Albert Londres and Andrée Viollis established the fact that a high percentage of the guards on the plantations have lost their mental equilibrium. Under the influence of solitude, boredom, alcohol, and abnormal social and sexual conditions, they become psychopathic. It is the same with the troops. All these people have the power to wreak vengeance for their disturbed mental condition on poor defenseless creatures. The details are too ghastly to mention. The victims dare not complain. The dominant race, the colonial armies and the exploiting companies are one: they work hand in hand. There is no escape. No escape except in a gigantic St. Bartholomew's, a slaughter of all the whites, good and bad.

That the fear of such an eventuality haunts the colonizers is evident from the constant nervousness in official quarters and from the ruthless ferocity with which every attempt on the part of the natives to improve their lot is suppressed in blood. Every administrator I met felt himself the object of silent hatred, a hatred which does not relent. The white man has destroyed not only the native's but his own peace of mind. Both are pursued by fear. The characters of both are destroyed, for the native is fast losing his joy of life. Our expedition went out to record dances and songs because the natives are dancing and singing less and less. Native art is disappearing. Wood sculpture, for which the Bobo Ouleh were once famous, and which is of an almost classic Chinese perfection and serenity, had grown so rare that it was with difficulty that we could acquire a few specimens. Everywhere the mores become more bestial and the oppression more cruel. Greed is turning a continent into a world of blood and tears.

CHAPTER SEVEN

Ethiopian Interlude

WHEN IT BECAME KNOWN in October, 1934, that Mussolini was assembling large quantities of war material on the island of Rhodes, a rumor gained currency almost simultaneously in European diplomatic circles that Italy was about to lay claim to that part of Turkish territory which had been promised to her by the Allies in 1916 as an inducement to enter the Great War on their side. At first, it did not seem far-fetched to suppose that Mussolini, who had for years been feeding the Fascist regime with speeches about baths of steel, would at last start to live dangerously and collect that belated debt once he considered the Italian army sufficiently strong to deal with Kemal Pasha. In 1934, Russia, then Turkey's only friend, was passing through the upheaval attendant upon Stalin's forced collectivization of the peasantry; Soviet industry was known to be suffering from wholesale wrecking campaigns, while Japan was constructing a significant number of airdromes on the Siberian border in her recently acquired Manchurian domains. It appeared extremely doubtful that Russia could have given Turkey any effective aid in the event of an Italian attack. Mussolini's opportunity for keeping the exaltation in his country at the required fever point by making a quick raid on Adana appeared, superficially speaking, quite favorable.

However, the Duce's real objective could not remain hidden for long. When the Italian governors of Somaliland and Eritrea in East Africa did their best to pick a quarrel with Haile Selassie, Emperor of Ethiopia, the mystery concerning the war preparations in Rhodes vanished. But what was curious about the rumor of the planned attack on Turkey was the fact that it had first been launched in circles close to the French Foreign Ministry, where M. Pierre Laval was presiding at the time. For this raised the question as to what motive the Prime Minister of France could have had in helping Mussolini in masking his real intentions. France and Italy were not on the best of terms at the time, at least so the world believed. To the left-wing parties in France, Mussolini, the ex-Socialist, who had crushed Italian democracy, was the villain par excellence. Joseph Paul-Boncour had called him the Caesar of the Carnival. Briand had persistently refused to meet him. Barthou had met his death in Marseilles at the side of Alexander of Jugoslavia, France's stanchest ally and Italy's most determined opponent. Why should the successor of these foreign ministers, M. Pierre Laval, go out of his way to render a service to the man in Rome, a man who made his Black-Shirt claque shout every time he made a speech that such French territories as Tunis, Nice and Savoy would soon belong to them? Was Laval under personal obligations to the Duce? Had these two former revolutionaries—for Laval was the ex-Communist who invented the class-war slogan of "Class against Class"—arrived at a secret understanding? What was the meaning behind this collaboration of the two statesmen whose countries were apparently drifting apart more rapidly than ever before?

Laval's attitude grew still more puzzling when he paid a visit to Rome in the beginning of 1935. By this time nobody was any longer in the dark as to who was to be the intended victim of Mussolini's war preparations. Laval, as Prime Minister and Foreign Minister of France, signed an accord with the Duce under the terms of which the French Government gave Italy: 1. twenty-five per cent of the shares in the Franco-Ethiopian railway; 2. a stretch of territory in the south of Libya in the Lake Chad region; 3. the promise of a larger measure of cultural autonomy for the quarter-million Italian nationals in Tunis, and, what was doubly significant, 4. control over one of the tiny Seven Brothers islands in the straits of Bab el Mandeb, that narrow passage leading from the Red Sea into the Indian Ocean, which is the strategic counterpart of the Suez Canal.

Why had Laval made these considerable concessions to Mussolini without apparently receiving anything in return?

Not till the Ethiopian war broke out eight months later did the full significance of that important diplomatic transaction between Laval and Mussolini become clear. For then it was seen that under the terms of the Rome protocol of February 6, 1935, Laval had given Mussolini what amounted to a free hand in his attack on the Ethiopian Empire. But French public opinion never suspected the accord's sinister implications until Pierre Laval launched into a definite policy of procrastination by withholding from Britain France's co-operation in making the League's sanctions against Italy really effective. To the amazement of the people of France, it will be recalled, Laval refused point-blank to place the French war harbors of Toulon and Bastia on Corsica at the disposal of the British navy when Britain requested their use as bases for an eventual anti-Italian blockade. And this in spite of the fact that the French people had given unmistakable indications that they wanted to go the limit in making Mussolini desist from the rape he contemplated in east Africa. While the Left clamored to bring "the bloody tyrant" to his knees, Prime Minister Laval followed a policy diametrically opposed to popular sentiment. Later, after Laval's defeat by the Popular Front, there were several demands to bring the ex-Premier before the High Court of Justice on a charge of high treason, but by that time the fate of Ethiopia had been settled and the agitation against Laval petered out in partisan newspaper attacks.

It can now be revealed that Pierre Laval was animated by more than a personal friendship for Mussolini when he facilitated the Duce's seizure of the Ethiopian Empire. Laval smoothed Italy's path to imperial power in return for a service of inestimable value the Duce rendered to France in the summer of 1934. In the month of July of that year, it will be recalled, when the German dictatorship was purging the Nazi party of oppositional elements, the Fuehrer suddenly flew to Italy, met Mussolini on a flying field near Venice, and after two hours' conversation raced back to Berlin. I have since learned from a responsible French statesman that Hitler, on that occasion, had gone to solicit Mussolini's aid in a venture which, if carried out, might well have thrown the world out of balance. The Fuehrer proposed nothing less than a secret mobilization of Germany's air fleet and a nocturnal attack on Paris, Lyons, the Longwy-Briey steel-manufacturing district, the Schneider-Creusot armament mills, and France's chief centers of communication. The blow was to come from the blue as it were, without ultimatum or declaration of war, and without even a preceding "incident" to disturb normal relations between the two countries. Paris was to be covered with a blanket of poison gas in the night. A fleet of two thousand bombers was to rain a great shower of their heaviest torpedoes and incendiary bombs on the capital's three million inhabitants. The members of the general staff and the personnel of the administrative services and the ministries, taken totally by surprise and before effective means of defense and protection could be devised, were to be exterminated in a few hours. That, thought the ex-paper hanger, would have meant the elimination of France from the European concert for a long time to come. General Kurt von Schleicher got wind of the fantastic project, so my informer told me, and was assassinated by Goering's police. Roehm, another opponent of the diabolic scheme, met a similar fate.

The purge had eliminated the opposition to the plan in the higher circles of the Nazi party when Hitler flew to Venice. Mussolini, after hearing his German colleague detail the fine points of his plan, which had originated in Goering's fertile imagination, indignantly refused to be a partner in the undertaking and dismissed Hitler with the prediction that such an attack would be followed by a world rising in arms against Germany and revolutionary outbreaks at home. In a huff, Hitler flew back home. Mussolini, after seeing the Fuehrer off, remarked to the correspondent of the Vienna *Reichpost* that he had just been talking to *"ein schwätzeriger Mönch"* (a gossiping old monk), but telephoned his friend Franklin-Bouillon, leader of a right-wing group in the French parliament, who happened to be staying at the Lido at the moment. An hour later French troops were pouring into the Maginot Line and all the resources of French aviation had received order "to stand to." We in Paris imagined that these extraordinary military measures, as far as we knew, were merely a precaution on the part of the French government against the possibility of the effervescence over the blood purge in the Reich spreading to the confines of French territory.

In spite of the fact that my employers urged me repeatedly, from the month of May onward, "to be on hand for the first battle in Ethiopia," if and when war should break out between Mussolini and the Negus, I delayed my departure till July. I had a feeling, or rather a secret hope, that Mussolini could not pull that tour de force without meeting with serious difficulties at home. I still feel that he would not have succeeded had the workers of the world, Russia's included, instead of docilely following their governments, proclaimed and enforced an embargo on the shipment of war goods to Italy.

I knew from the start that the British government had no intention of doing anything that might have brought about the collapse of the Fascist regime. Mussolini's elimination and the replacement of his

dictatorship—or of Hitler's dictatorship in Germany, for that matter
—by a democratic parliamentary regime or by a Socialist form of
government were then, and till this day remain, eventualities
tories in England and rightists in France would give almost anything to prevent. To be sure, they did not like the idea of Mussolini
making ready to cut himself a share in the imperialist loot on the
shores of the Red Sea where England had hitherto held a virtual
monopoly. However, that was preferable to forcing the Duce to his
knees, something that would almost certainly have dragged Hitler
down in its wake and might have culminated in the red flag going up
over the Quirinal and the Wilhelmstrasse. Moreover, if the two
dictators, or but one of them, should fall, what would become of
the new wave of prosperity Stanley Baldwin's rearmament campaign had ushered in? In a democratic parliament the Italian people,
groaning under the weight of the Duce's war burdens, would surely
have insisted on ending the masquerade of a poverty-stricken agricultural country playing the role of a first-class power. Then the
League would have been seized with a new passion for disarmament,
and all the work of recent years, reducing the Geneva institution to
impotence and making the general rearmament campaign possible,
would have been in vain.

No, Mussolini had nothing to fear on the part of England. Sir
Samuel Hoare proved that conclusively in December, 1935, when he
advised the Negus to give up the struggle just when the Ethiopian
warriors had fought De Bono to a standstill and Italy was for a
moment faced with the prospect of a repetition of the disastrous
defeat of 1896.

But there seemed just a possibility of the Italian people putting
a spoke in the wheel. Before flying to Addis Ababa and while the
war fever was already mounting in Italy, I began traveling up and
down the peninsula cautiously pulsing the public sentiment in
regard to the forthcoming military campaign. After hearing the
Duce promise me solemnly, in the course of an interview, that there
would be no war, that war was the thing farthest from his mind,
that Italy needed peace more than anything else and all the rest of it,
I visited popular milieus such as *dopolavoros* and intellectual and
business circles, and could not discover the slightest enthusiasm for
the campaign against Ethiopia.

As soon as I set foot in Italy I fell under the gloomy spell which
has settled over that country of warm colors since the Black Shirts

swarmed over the landscape like a flock of crows. The port of Trieste was deserted, Brindisi a dilapidated conglomeration of slums. In Naples the Café Esposito was turning off its lights before eleven. I noticed hundreds of abandoned villas around the Lido di Roma and a mournful silence in the taverns and *trattorie* of Milan. The price of bread was rather more than a lira a pound while the average daily wage fluctuated between twelve and fifteen lire. Coffee was about twenty lire a pound; milk sold for a lira. The cost of living was staggering. The walls of Rome, that capital of melancholy since Mussolini came to the Palazzo Chigi, were covered with notices of all kinds of new taxes and, as it happened in June, 1935, with a poster containing a new Caesarian decree forbidding "the detestable custom of poking fun at mothers-in-law" as "tending to diminish respect for the family."

I witnessed mass demonstrations before the rural prefectures in Sicily by the hungry *cafoni* and sulphur-mine workers. They walked around with their trouser pockets turned inside out in token of their total destitution. I saw the women of Mantua's proletariat prostrate themselves on the railway tracks, as Mussolini had advised them years before at the time of the war with Tripoli, to prevent the departure of their sons for the mobilization centers. I was present when the embarkation quays of Naples were brutally cleared by the Fascist police because the populace showed signs of sympathy with a northern regiment whose members shouted: "Down with the Black Shirts! Down with the war!" Crossing the border, I interviewed some of the hundreds of deserters from northern garrisons who had escaped into Jugoslavia and Austria. Everywhere gloom and a spirit of hopelessness reigned. But always and again when returning to Rome I heard the paid chorus of "concessioned ovationists" roar their bellicose approval of the man who is "always right." The few military men with whom I came in contact shrugged their shoulders with a fatalistic gesture when questioned on the prospects of the war in Ethiopia. Everybody knew the story about Marshal Badoglio having voiced a strong protest against the Duce's African plans. Victor Emmanuel was said to have the familiar feeling of his throne tottering under his feet, and the Pope, it was rumored, was plagued by nocturnal visions of the Roman proletariat singing the "Internationale" under the dome of St. Peter's in celebration of the tyrant's fall. In short, the situation seemed laden with immediate trouble.

"If Britain gives him one push," declared a professor of economics in one important Italian city, who received me as stealthily as Nicodemus, "one push, by closing the Suez Canal, for instance, we Italians will give him the second push and eventually we will administer the *coup de grâce*. Everything is ready." That was in June, 1935, on a day when the wineshops in the old Borzo buzzed with the news that thirty-five Fascist legionnaires had been tortured to death in the dungeons of the Regina Coeli for having distributed anti-Fascist literature. Farinacci, the podesta of Cremona, the powerful leader of the extreme right wing of Fascism, was literally crazed with fear in the presence of secret demonstrations which he interpreted as the beginning of an open revolt. Against the slogans "Death to Mussolini," which were chalked up on the walls at night all over Italy, the old Fascist standbys—the whipping post, castor oil, and the little wooden clamp that is used to squeeze men's testicles— were once more brought into play. That was the atmosphere in which the Duce opened the Ethiopian campaign.

From my employers came insistent cables to cut short my travel in Italy and proceed to Addis Ababa. A Belgian aviator, Auguste 't Serstevens, an acquaintance from the days when I had espoused the cause of Flemish nationalism, invited me to accompany him in a machine which he was to deliver for his firm to the Negus by mid-July. 'T Serstevens was planning to stay in Ethiopia and enter the service of Haile Selassie. On the ninth we took off from Brussels, spent a day in Geneva, and then roared off to Athens. In Egypt we followed the course of the Nile as far as Assuan, then veered west through the Sudan, and after a total of six days' travel reached the flying field of Addis Ababa.

The full three months that were to elapse before De Bono crossed the Eritrean border to attack the undefended town of Adowa, in the first week of October, gave me an opportunity of seeing something of life in the last independent African state before it was swallowed up by the Roman imperium. Having watched Italy's preparations—the concentration of war material at the ports, the departure of troopships, and the drumming up of the martial spirit by press and pulpit, I could not share the general optimism I found prevailing in leading Ethiopian circles. They thought that the most the Duce would seek to obtain would be a slice of Ogaden province

in the south, the right of way for a railway across the Danakil desert
in order to link Eritrea with Italian Somaliland, and a larger share
in the exploitation of the inner Ethiopian market. The mobilization
of Italian troops on Ethiopia's borders was dismissed as a mere
gesture on the Duce's part to exercise pressure on the European
chancelleries not to forget him in eventual negotiations for a division of the east-African market. Prominent Ethiopians, time and
again, expressed their absolute confidence that Britain would not
abandon the Christian Emperor and that the League of Nations
would see to it that justice was done.

Haile Selassie himself, who summoned me to the palace shortly
after my arrival, seemed to be the only person to have a realistic
view of the situation. At a second audience, he frankly said that
he was worried about the secret negotiations between M. Pierre
Laval and Signor Mussolini in the month of February, 1935. Why,
he asked me, was it impossible for him, the Negus, to buy munitions
in the European market? Why had Laval ceded twenty-five per cent
of the shares in the Franco-Ethiopian railway to the Duce? Bending slightly forward in his chair, the Emperor asked me whether it
was generally known in Europe that France had promised to provide landing facilities for an Italian army in Somaliland in the event
that the invasion from the north into Tigré miscarried. Pensively,
Haile Selassie recalled the plan for a division of his empire into
spheres of influence by Britain, France and Italy which he had frustrated a few years earlier by bringing it to the attention of the
League. As I listened to the Emperor, it seemed to me that the
project of a joint protectorate over Ethiopia by the three great
powers appeared preferable to the Emperor in July, 1935, to the
idea of facing Mussolini alone. From the Duce he expected no mercy.
But he was not bitter: his declarations of policy at the innumerable
press conferences which were to follow never descended to the
level of vulgar expressions of hatred for the Italian people. The
Negus perfectly understood the game the diplomats were playing
with his country. He still had faith in England and in the League of
Nations, arguing that if Mussolini were permitted to attack Ethiopia
with impunity a precedent would be set up which would destroy
the moral basis of international relationships and pave the way for
a series of bloody wars. As he spoke in a listless voice and sighed
deeply after every sentence, I read the doom of Ethiopia in his
big melancholy eyes. "Divine justice," he said to me on the day

when Aksum was captured, "divine justice will settle its accounts to the last penny some day!"

I returned from my first audience with Haile Selassie convinced that the Emperor had abandoned hope and that he believed no arguments in the world would cause Mussolini to desist from his design of seizing the lion's share of the empire. The Abuna, head of the Coptic Church, thought differently. This ecclesiastic, His Holiness Mathias, a lusty, robust fellow with a graying beard and a hearty laugh, who seemed mentally to be living in the Middle Ages, entertained the naïve notion that world Protestantism would not permit the conquest of Ethiopia by a Catholic power. He was thinking, he informed me, of preparing a manifesto to the Archbishop of Canterbury and the Free Churches of Britain, America and the Scandinavian countries, calling upon them to stand by the Coptic Church, one of the oldest branches of the Church Universal, in its hour of danger. In the Abuna's imagination Europe was already divided into two hostile camps with the Protestants—Germans, Englishmen, Dutchmen and Scandinavians—standing shoulder to shoulder for the defense of the religious liberty of the Ethiopian people. He saw an alignment pro or contra Ethiopia cutting squarely across the international scene, obliterating for the moment, or putting into the shade, all existing national-political issues. He spoke of the deeds of Gustavus Adolphus, the Prince of Orange, of Luther, Wycliffe, Knox and the Huguenots, as if we were living in the heroic times of the Reformation and not in the pale era of the Oxford movement.

On one point the Abuna did not think far amiss: he suspected that Mussolini had concluded some sort of an agreement with the Vatican whereby the Roman Church, in consideration for its support of Italy's raid on Ethiopia, was to be given a free hand in the territory to be conquered. A dispatch setting forth in brief the Abuna's declaration on this point, sent to the American and Canadian newspapers I represented, raised a storm of indignant protest from the Roman clergy, and for the second time in three months I found myself denounced as a prejudiced bigot and an enemy of Christianity. On the previous occasion the wrath of the *monsignori* had been kindled by my observation that the papal nuncios in Paris and other European capitals seemed to be showing more zeal for Mussolini's cause in east Africa than the ambassadors of the Italian state.

In spite of these protestations, it is to be noted that within six months after Graziani's triumphant entry into Addis Ababa, shiploads of Sicilian and Maltese monks were on their way to Ethiopia to "evangelize" the Coptic Christians of Tigré and the Amharic plateau. The new "Italia in Africa" was divided into five ecclesiastical provinces with a papal prefect at their head, and the Pope even went so far as to recall the French Catholic missions who had worked in Ethiopia for three-quarters of a century. Thus the Vatican's complete subservience to the policy of Fascist imperialism was completely demonstrated. In 1937, moreover, the Abuna of the Coptic Church was arrested, shipped to Italy and incarcerated in the prison of Venice.

It did not take me long to discover that Haile Selassie, in the event of an armed clash with Italy, could not count on the undivided support of the peoples and tribes under his suzerainty. His reforms had not made him popular. Even the Abuna, although superficially correct, had his doubts as to the wisdom of the Emperor's social program. When I arrived in the country in July, these two men, the two mightiest in the Empire, were in the midst of an acrimonious debate on what disposal was to be made of the vast domains of the Coptic Church. Haile Selassie wanted to expropriate the immense properties of the monastic orders and hand them over for settlement and exploitation to the slaves whom he was setting free at the rate of sixty thousand a year. The Coptic clergy, on the whole a lazy and ignorant lot, but who made up no less than one tenth of the total population in the central Amharic provinces, objected as vehemently to the distribution of the land as the monastic orders in France on the eve of the Revolution. Some of the rich Ethiopian abbots with whom I talked made no bones about it: they would resist the land decrees of the King of Kings with every means at their disposal. By mutual consent, the Negus and the clergy decided to shelve the projects of land reform till the Italian crisis should have blown over.

Opposition to the Emperor was not confined to the Coptic hierarchy. Several of the rases, or provincial governors, were openly flirting with the Italian consuls in their capitals, and we know from De Bono's book of reminiscences that at least half of these kings were bought by Italian money. In vain did Haile Selassie summon some of his vassals to Addis Ababa. To be sure, they did send part of their military forces, for they dared not rise in open rebellion against their liege lord (it was just possible, after all, that the Negus would be upheld by the League), but personally, they respectfully declined his pressing invitations to attend the war councils in the capital. It must be admitted that their caution was more than justified. Haile Selassie was not a ruler famed for the gentleness of his manners.

Tens of thousands of followers of Lidyi Yassu, the Emperor who had been deposed by Haile Selassie and the Abuna, were thirsting for revenge and for an opportunity to put the imperial prisoner back on the throne. Lidyi Yassu, the rightful successor of Menelik the Great, whose grandson he was, had flirted with the Mohammedan religion without ever formally embracing it. When still Ras Tafari, governor of the important city of Harar, Haile Selassie had led the revolt against Lidyi Yassu with the aid of His Holiness the Abuna Mathias, and at the time I arrived in Addis Ababa still kept him a prisoner in the cone of an extinct volcano in the neighborhood of Aouash on the rim of the Danakil desert. There, under heavy guard, Lidyi Yassu remained till the end of the war, when the Italians set him free and allowed him to take up residence in Djibouti. Several of the grandees, who had been Lidyi Yassu's closest friends and advisers during the few years he occupied the throne, had been arrested by Haile Selassie and executed in the most fiendish manner imaginable. After having had their bodies wrapped tightly in bandages, which first had been soaked in melted wax, the men had been tied to the stake and the strips of cloth set on fire. This form of punishment was not of Haile Selassie's personal invention and that is the best that can be said for the Emperor in the circumstances. However, he had personally watched the agonizing suffering of his victims in the market square of Harar. Many of the relatives of the executed were waiting for a chance to pay the Negus in kind. The entire Mohammedan population of southern Ethiopia, several million souls, was hostile to the rule of the man who had supplanted the one ruler who had shown an inclination to become a Moslem.

I saw some instances of Haile Selassie's repression with my own eyes. In Harar, one of the doctors of the leprosarium of the French Catholic mission, where I was a guest for several days (owing to the lack of proper hotels), showed me a sample of the Emperor's ferocity one day while we took a stroll about town. In a round straw hut, guarded by a soldier of the Imperial Guard, sat a creature with an iron collar around his neck. At our approach, this man crawled towards the opening and stared at us with the uncomprehending eyes of an idiot. The short chain with which his collar was fastened to a stake in the center of the hut's floor forced him to move about like a beast: on his hands and knees. He was totally naked and covered from head to foot with filth, for he was wallowing in his own excrements.

"This man," said the missionary, "is Ras Hailu, former King of Gojjam, one of the richest princes of the realm. He was educated in Paris, and Haile Selassie appointed him his ambassador to France. Two years ago he was recalled, ostensibly for a conference. No sooner had he arrived in Addis Ababa than Haile Selassie had him thrown into prison. It is said," continued the missionary, "that he had incurred the displeasure of the Emperor by receiving the Soviet trade commissioner in Paris and proposing a commercial agreement between Ethiopia and Russia. The Emperor, who has several White-Russian émigrés amongst his personal friends, saw a plot and lured his ambassador back to Addis. This is the outcome," said the missionary, pointing to the pitiful creature groveling at our feet.

"But that is not all," he continued, "when this man's brother, a powerful ras in Tigré, came to intercede with the Emperor for his brother and threatened to take up arms, Haile Selassie had him executed by the saw; he had him placed between two boards of oak, the planks were tightly roped together, and he was sawn in twain."

As we stood there looking at the hut, a woman, whose noble rank was indicated by the pink color of her gown, came to the door of the hut, and placed a small basket of peas on the ground for that man who had lost all semblance of a human being.

My arrival in Ethiopia coincided with the last phase of the disturbance over the collection of a tax that Haile Selassie had imposed on his subjects to defray the expense of building his new palace. It took eighteen military expeditions by the Imperial Guard in the course of 1934 and 1935 to collect that tax of one thaler per head for the entire population. If a district was tardy in paying its tribute, the Emperor simply dispatched a battalion of his guard. The commander of the guard would inquire as to the number of inhabitants in a given village, and having learned this, would demand the payment of an amount of thalers equal to the number of souls in the village within twenty-four hours. No excuses were accepted, not even a plea by the elders and the clergy that the village did not possess the required amount of silver—something which is quite understandable in a country where the chief medium of exchange is not money but salt. The troops hemmed in the village, trained their machine guns on the huts, from which rose the wail of the women and children, and, after expiration of the ultimatum, sent their bullets crashing through the thin mud walls until not a soul remained alive.

Thus ruled the Christian Emperor of Ethiopia, but so ruled also Charlemagne, the butcher of the Saxons, who was crowned by Pope Leo III. It is perhaps unjust to compare conditions in pre-Fascist Ethiopia with the age of feudalism in Europe. One must go back further into history to gain an approximately fair perspective: the Stone Age perhaps, or the patriarchal era in Canaan previous to the Israelite conquest.

Although I felt little sympathy for Haile Selassie's personal plight, there was no question in my mind as to the justice of Ethiopia's cause. Mussolini had no business there for the same reason that the other great imperialisms have no right to lord it over the native races of Asia and Africa. The motive of the white man's civilizing mission has always been a pretext for ruthless exploitation unworthy of a truly human society. Though Ethiopian civilization had remained intact since times immemorial, it had also drawn into its own shell. It had crystallized, retrograded more than it had advanced, bringing to mind the course of Egyptian and Greek civilization, but it was still valuable. To awaken it out of its dormant state was an ineluctable necessity. But that should have been the work of the Ethiopian peoples themselves. It must be admitted that Haile Selassie was vaguely aware of the necessity of steering a new course. It is to his credit that he chafed under the knowledge that his country was a startling anachronism in the modern world. But the inconsistent part of the scheme of things in Ethiopia was that Haile Selassie was an imperialist conquerer himself. He was the ruler of the dominant race of the Amharics, which had subjected twenty-seven other nations and tribes in the course of history. He ruled these others with an iron hand. Only the backward conditions of the country in general prevented him from exploiting the tribes in a manner as profitable as the European imperialisms manage to. He ruled by force and intimidation and by the right of the strongest and was therefore bitterly hated by most of his subjects. Several important tribes, such as the Gallas, refused to come to his aid even when the Italian army was smashing its way forward through Dessye.

From the moment I landed in his capital the Emperor showed me extraordinary kindness. The evening of my arrival a messenger from the court came to the hotel to bid me welcome in His Majesty's name and to fix the date for my first audience. The first reception was a stiff and formal affair, with the Emperor strictly observing the court etiquette of not saying a word in a foreign language, although he speaks French tolerably well and of course understands it perfectly. He spoke in Gué on that occasion, an ancient Semitic idiom which is now only used by the high clergy and the court. His words were translated into French by the *dedjaz* Lorenço, the master of ceremonies, a young man with a European education.

I found Haile Selassie much darker of skin than I had imagined. Most men and women of the Amharic tribe are of considerably lighter hue than the Negus; the majority of them have the deep olive-colored skin of the Jews of Yemen, but as a rule they are much taller than the Yemenites. Haile Selassie had his chair placed against the wall between two windows, an arrangement that enabled him to scan the visitors' features at leisure, while from their side the callers had the sun beating into their eyes. We sat there on the first occasion, Tambouras Bey and I, on the edge of our chairs, in rented frock coats, each taking our turn in making a pretty speech in French, while the Negus, much to our embarrassment, remained as silent as a clam. He had been studying us, the *dedjaz* said, after we had walked out backwards. But we had made an impression on His Majesty and we were bound to be summoned again.

That prediction came true. On the next occasion, a few days later, the Emperor unbent considerably. He talked freely in French of his apprehensions of a betrayal by the European powers, and wondered if any foreign volunteers would rally to his banner. Leading the way into the hall, he showed me his collection of photographs of the European kings and princes who had been present at his coronation, and seemed highly pleased when I said of a lithograph showing the boy Jesus disputing with the doctors in the Temple, which hung between the silver-framed photos of the Duke of York and the Italian Crown Prince, that we had one exactly like it in my parents' home. At one point in the conversation which was resumed in his private cabinet, he burst into laughter. That was when I remarked to Ras Mala Guetta, the aged War Minister, who kept harping on the Emperor's descent from the Patriarch Abraham and was saying that a prince of so illustrious a line would not be lightly treated by the European governments, that I would not put much stock in that, seeing that the prestige of Abraham's fatherhood had not served the Jewish people to any advantage. When the Emperor thereupon asked me about the Abuna's idea of calling on the heads of the Protestant churches, I said that I had no hope at all of any good resulting from such a step. The Protestant churches, I said, had no more a policy of their own than the Vatican. Both conformed to the exigencies of the national states in which they found themselves. I respectfully submitted that an immediate liberation of all slaves in Ethiopia would at that time be a gesture far more calculated to impress the world than an appeal to Christendom in the name of Abraham or Solomon. In the bottom of my heart I knew, however, that all this was mere talk. Mussolini was going to resort to violence and the only thing that could stop him was concerted action in making the embargo on war material destined for Italy a concrete reality.

"The only thing that can save the Ethiopian Empire," I said rather bluntly, "is an international strike by the stevedores and the transport workers."

"But His Majesty, as the Emperor of Ethiopia, can scarcely be expected to make an appeal to the workers of the world," interjected Lorenço.

"Why not? The workers have a sense of justice!"

"The working-class organizations," said the Emperor quietly, and his remark showed that he was a keen observer of world affairs, "have no more independent policy than the churches you mentioned."

In those first three months, I tried to learn something of the traditions of the lordly race of the Amharics on the subject of their racial and national origin. But I found the greatest scholars of the realm hopelessly vague in their explanations. That the Amharic language is a pure Semitic tongue was obvious: the first word I heard in Addis—the cry of a water seller in the street: *"Maim, maim!"*—made me think I was back in some neo-Hebraic colony in Palestine. The Emperor's name, Haile Selassie, which means Glory of the Trinity, and the name of the capital which the natives pronounce Addis

Aviv—Flower of Spring—are quite recognizably Hebraic. In fact, half the place names in the Amharic provinces of Ethiopia were taken from the Bible. That there had been contact with Jerusalem in the days of Solomon seemed well established. The deliciously lascivious miniatures in the great cathedral of St. George in Addis Ababa, showing scenes in the Hebrew king's bedchamber in the Holy City, were adduced as proof of the Ethiopian royal family's descent from David's son and Balkis, Queen of Sheba. One of the manuscript writers in the chief Coptic monastery in Addis Ababa went so far as to suggest that the Song of Songs, which he had no doubt had been composed by Solomon, was obviously referring to the Ethiopian queen when the writer called his beloved "black but comely." I thought this at least as acceptable a theory as that of the fundamentalist exegetes who see in that passionate Oriental ode a monologue of Christ addressed to his mystic bride, the Church.

However, this has nothing to do with the racial origins of the Semitic Amharics. How had they come to settle in the heart of Africa and impose themselves on the Negro aborigines? Who were they? Had they wandered through Arabia in the opposite direction from their Hebraic kinsmen bound for the Holy Land, and crossed to the African mainland from Yemen or the Hejaz coast? After consulting with the keepers of the holy books, which are all written in Gué, a tongue as Semitic as the common language of the people (although it is still used only in the liturgy of the Coptic Church), and having obtained no satisfactory answer, I felt emboldened to make a guess myself. Can it not be, I wondered, that the Amharics are the descendants of those Hebrews who refused to accompany their kinsmen on the great tribal exodus from Egypt? It is known that all of the children of Israel did not follow Moses and Aaron into the desert of Sinai any more than all the Jews left Babylon when Cyrus gave the exiled people permission to return to Palestine. Egyptian Pharaohs, following the Nile to its sources, did conquer east Africa as far south as the present colony of Rhodesia and the island of Madagascar. Armies marched back and forth over that route which is today covered by the Cape-to-Cairo airway. Why could not the Pharaohs have set aside a territory in the heart of Africa, on the Amharic plateau to be exact, for a tribe of their subjects, to form a sort of bulwark of their empire on its southern extremities? The Romans followed such a policy: the modern Rumanian nation descends from a batch of Trajan's legionnaires who were planted on the Danube to form a bastion on the northern boundaries of the imperium against the Scyths, Gepidae and Visigoths. Why could not the Pharaohs have followed a similar policy in protecting their domains against incursions by raiding tribes? As time went on, Egypt was drawn into the interminable struggle with the Chaldean and Babylonian empires for the trade routes to Persia and the Mediterranean coast, causing her attention to be centered wholly on her Sinaitic borders. Her armies were recalled from central Africa, but the Semitic Amharics were left behind to hold the empire's outposts at the sources of the Nile. For long centuries the contest for world power between Egypt and Assyria continued with alternate defeats and successes, and the Amharics became isolated in the fastnesses of the primeval forest, isolated and forgotten by their overlords, who were too busy elsewhere.

A theory!

But a theory that is supported, I think, by the ruins of that gigantic temple to Jehovah, which can be seen near Elephantine in Lower Egypt, near the modern city of Aswan.

The Christianization of Ethiopia, we know, followed in the third century of the Common Era, although the Abuna maintained solemnly that there is no doubt of the historic authenticity of the New Testament story of Saint Philip, who, en route to Gaza, baptized a Moorish nobleman whom he found reading the book of Isaiah. This princely man, whose name has been forgotten, is deemed by the Coptic clergy to have introduced the Christian faith into Ethiopia.

At the Abuna's palace where there was good cheer, I took a liking to the bread which comes in the form of a huge brown pancake. It tasted like the *galettes du roi* we eat in France around the Feast of Epiphany. A slave seated at your feet tore off chunks and handed them to you. But I could not stomach the meat, which was so rare that it seemed scarcely to have touched the grill. After the meal, there was Turkish coffee and the traditional glass of *tatja*, an extract of honey which, besides making one drunk in record time, also acts as a narcotic. On the Abuna it had the effect of loosening his tongue and his laughing muscles. When we came to the *tatja* all the native guests would throw off their *shammas* and sit on the floor, their torsos naked.

The Abuna, who had been educated in Egypt, and old Ras Mala Guetta, the War Minister, who made theology his hobby, would commence a discussion on the doctrines of the church. Themselves Copts, that is to say Monophysites, they ridiculed the Catholic dogma on the subject of the two persons of Christ. They grew terribly excited when I, for the sake of enlivening the discussion, quoted from the Fathers to combat their ideas, which were the old Nestorian heresy all over again. How I should have loved our old dominies in Holland to have heard me hold forth!

Ras Mala Guetta had been to Paris in his youth and remembered the Latin Quarter and its cafés, sighing deeply each time he thought of them. But for decency's sake, in order not to scandalize His Holiness, I imagine, he put in a hasty question as to whether such and such a place in Paris still existed, and then quickly returned to theological subjects. Did the Holy Spirit proceed from the Father and from the Son, as the Western Christians maintained, or only from the Father? The very question had the effect of a bombshell on the Abuna. "Your Excellency, Your Excellency," the prelate would admonish the ebony-hued Mala Guetta, "please set a guard on your tongue! Your Excellency makes me feel that the apostolate of our Coptic Church has been totally in vain. Who doubts such things now? Of course, the Holy Spirit proceeds from the Father alone! A little child knows that!" After he said this, the Abuna laughed till the tears came to his eyes.

Ras Mala Guetta, ashamed of his ignorance, would swallow a whole tumbler of *tatja*, and we all followed suit so that harmony was soon restored.

Those people were very much in earnest about such abstract and metaphysical questions, which Europe, too, had tried to settle, although not by laughing them off, but by bloodshed and war. Hardly were matters dismissed by the Abuna's authority but they would start all over again and go on disputing for hours, most vehemently at times, although there was nobody to contradict them seriously in their cherished beliefs. I think that their anger was most aroused by the thought that after all these centuries the Bishop of Rome, the title they used in speaking of the Pope, was going to impose his views. For the Abuna blandly interpreted the coming war with Italy as a resumption of the long battle between Rome and the Eastern schismatics. He did not blame Rome for using Mussolini's sword to put an end to the old controversy, for he saw nothing incongruous in that fact. The Ethiopian emperors had employed similar methods in converting different black tribes to their own particular brand of Christianity.

The eyes of Ras Mala Guetta, the old warrior, would light up at the thought of going to fight the battle of faith with the Italian Black Shirts. The old man was positive of victory. He had been at Adowa forty years earlier. When I gently remonstrated with him by citing Italy's enormous superiority in engines of war, he shouted that this would not prevent him from giving the Italians an awful drubbing.

"Why," he exclaimed, "at Adowa we beat them down with sticks!" Later I saw that Ethiopian Minister of War actually distributing leather shields, swords, old flintlocks, and even bows and arrows from the stores of Menelik the Great to his men departing for the front. But I was also with him in the mountain passes of Tigré a few months later when they carried the body of his youngest and last son back into camp, the victim of Italian poison gas.

The Ras had his servants take me back to the hotel after those nocturnal sessions, one to light my steps on the uneven path, several to beat off the hyenas that swarmed into the capital at nights with their eerie howling during the long rainy period. You could have imagined yourself back in the Middle Ages. Here and there you would see a couple of Ethiopian *prominenti* wrapped in their long black cloaks, wearing those broad-brimmed hats which in shape more resemble the headgear affected by the burghers of Rembrandt's days than the latter-day hats of cowboys and Mexican peons. Barefooted slaves walking backwards preceded their masters with a miserable oil lantern and halted respectfully whenever their lords stood still to emphasize some point in their conversation.

Unlike the much older towns of Harar, Dessye, Makalle and Gondar, Addis had little of the picturesque. It was an immense sprawling village set in a forest of eucalyptus trees. But the environs were of great natural beauty. In fact, the whole Amharic plateau, over which I flew in all directions, reminded me, with its wooded, sloping hills and innumerable streams and brooks, of the Ile de France. I have often wondered how the impression gained currency abroad that Mussolini with his costly Ethiopian campaign was merely adding one more desert to his already extensive collection.

Ethiopia is a land of incredible fertility and has a good climate.

It fully deserves the name it had in antiquity of being the garden of Africa and can easily take care of a population of fifty millions: in other words, there is room in that country for all the Italian Fascists in the world. Mussolini's difficulties consist in exploiting this vast empire. That takes capital. That there was so much ignorance on the subject of Ethiopia's natural resources must be chiefly attributed, I think, to its geographical position, separated as it is from the Red Sea and the Indian Ocean by the most inhospitable wilderness on earth, the Danakil desert. This desert, a godforsaken, barren inferno where the temperature is downright murderous, much hotter in fact than the atmosphere in the Plain of the Cities, the legendary site of Sodom and Gomorrah, south of the Dead Sea in Palestine, which I had always imagined the worst place on earth, has served throughout the ages as a natural barrier to keep explorers and settlers out of Ethiopia. It extends eastward from French Somaliland to within eighty miles of Addis Ababa, but then changes rapidly into volcanic tableland and gradually into pleasant meadows and rich forests.

If the Fascist Empire of Rome survives the next world cataclysm, which is a most likely eventuality, for the Duce, that master of opportunism, is bound to range himself on the winning side (that is to say, with England) long before the final battle, the Ethiopian Empire will become one of the most prosperous colonies on earth, for its resources are inexhaustible.

Before that distant day, however, Italy must do a lot of work. Disease, for one thing, must be wiped out. It is estimated that there are a quarter-million lepers in Ethiopia. In Addis Ababa there were fifteen thousand at the outbreak of the war. They moved about freely in the streets and were not subject to any segregational measures, although those in the last stages of the malady were in the habit of congregating in the neighborhood of the cathedral of St. George, where they sat in hundreds, sunning themselves and dying against the wall which encloses the great courtyard of the church. It was virtually impossible to walk through that district, first because in the rainy season you sank up to your knees in the red mud, and secondly because the nauseating odor emanating from a myriad of open sores made the atmosphere positively unbearable.

I recall the first morning I strayed into those streets of horror. My old friend Tambouras Bey, editor of a French newspaper in Athens, *Le Messager d'Athènes*, had taken up residence in Addis a year before the outbreak of the war because, as he said, he had smelled a rat. He was with me that morning and led me up to a group of men sitting against the wall of a monastery. It was one of those clear sunny hours between downpours, for the rainy season was on. "Look at those men," said Tambouras. "Take a few small coins out of your pocket and hold them up to them. But do not hand over the coins until they walk up to you," he warned.

I did as I was told and to my amazement I saw those men, who appeared to be sitting on what looked like sacks of cement, struggle to their feet, and carry the sacks in front of their legs with both hands. Only then did I notice that the things on which they had been sitting were attached to their bodies: their testicles. Elephantiasis! I could scarcely believe my eyes.

Nothing was being done to eradicate this disease, or the leprosy, or the syphilis which was endemic in Addis Ababa. Here and there throughout the land was a small missionary post with an infirmary or small clinic, but the members of the medical profession in Addis Ababa itself catered to the needs of Europeans exclusively. There was not a medical school in the whole empire. The native medicos operated chiefly with herbs and roots. Even when the war had started, a gunshot wound was often treated by stuffing it with tree leaves or grass. Out in the big open spaces disease was much rarer. The Gallas, for instance, a magnificent tribe of broad-shouldered black men, were absolutely free of syphilis. It was in the cities where the natives were in contact with the white man that this evil flourished.

When viewing all that misery in the slums of Addis Ababa, I used to say that it would be a godsend if some European power stepped in and helped the Emperor clean up. I could not then imagine in how dreadful a manner the Italians would acquit themselves of the civilizing task for which Mussolini declared himself a candidate in his flamboyant speeches. For the Italians are today indeed cleaning up Ethiopia's diseases, but they are doing it by sterilizing both men and women. Every minor ailment that comes to the attention of the Italian military doctors is an occasion for the application of sterilization. The point is that now that Ethiopia has been conquered, there are too many Ethiopians, healthy as well as sick.

The first question every correspondent asked of us who had preceded them by a few months in Ethiopia concerned the slave trade.

At the press conferences in the Ministry of the Interior they were told that it had been abolished long ago by the Negus Theodore II and that Haile Selassie had devoted his entire reign to wiping out its last remaining traces. This was somewhat of an exaggeration. There were still a million slaves in Ethiopia in 1935, and the trade flourished not only in the provinces of the interior but in the larger cities and even in the capital. The Emperor himself was unquestionably antislavery, although the Abuna looked upon it as a divine institution. The great obstacle to its abolition resided in the Emperor's precarious authority. Fifty miles outside the capital his antislavery decrees had made not the slightest impression. The governors of provinces like Gojjam, Tigré, Sidamo and Ogaden were in reality independent rulers and a law unto themselves. Official slave markets, it is true, had been abolished all over the realm. But girl slaves were offered to Tambouras Bey and myself not only in Harar but also in Addis Ababa itself. The offer, it is true, was on both occasions made by Moslem dealers. One evening the Greek consul told us that he had been offered six slaves that day in the market of Addis in exchange for two Russian wolfhounds he had imported from England. The offer had been made by the district governor of Dessye. The usual price for a man in full strength was one hundred thalers, fifty thalers for a *koudjo baria*—literally, a beautiful one.

One day in the early hours of the morning, when returning from a visit to the home of the Belgian consul in the company of some newspapermen, we saw a group of several hundred boys and girls being escorted through one of the main thoroughfares of Addis Ababa by men armed with rifles. We stood still to watch the strange nocturnal procession, wondering what was up and who the prisoners could be, for that they were prisoners seemed clear from the manner in which the armed guards shouted at them and prodded them with their rifles. It also seemed (but this was not easily verified because of the darkness) that they were bound together with ropes fastened around their necks. A flock of mules bearing sacks of provisions brought up the rear. Upon making inquiry of some European businessmen of our acquaintance, residents of Addis, who happened to be passing by, we learned that the boys and girls were slaves, probably Oumallas, a tribe of Negroes inhabiting the south of Ethiopia, who were being marched off in the general direction of the Somali coast to be shipped off to the slave markets of Arabia. Somebody reminded us that the report, submitted to the League of Nations' antislavery commission by Lady John Simon but a few months earlier, stated that in 1934 the slave trade between Africa and Arabia still ran into the hundreds of thousands and that most of the slaves came from Ethiopia. The captured slaves, generally young people such as we saw that night, after being caught in raids on their villages, were taken to some little-frequented spot of the Somali coast, in the neighborhood of Djibouti, and there kept until an Arab ship, eluding the vigilance of the British naval patrols in the Red Sea, would hastily embark for one of the ports in southern or eastern Arabia.

After we had seen that midnight caravan we returned to the hotel where a discussion arose amongst some of the newspapermen as to whether there had been any girls in the mournful procession. We decided to hire a car in the morning, try to catch up with the caravan and see them in the daytime. This was done. After a morning's search we came on the pitiful crowd camped, but some of them still bound together, in a narrow valley called Soloulda. They were all stark naked. In return for some baksheesh paid to the slave drivers we were allowed to come closer and inspect the human merchandise. Only then did the full horror of the spectacle dawn upon us, for then we saw that most of the black boys had been recently emasculated. Many of them were sick unto death, the wounds having begun to fester or blood poison having set in. All of the lads were weak from loss of blood. They lay around on the ground silently or groaning with pain. Through Boul-Boul, my interpreter, we learned that there were several deaths each day and that the slave drivers considered themselves lucky if they reached the point of embarkation by forced night marches with forty per cent of the boys in a condition to move at all. The marching was done at night because officially the slave trade was forbidden. These slaves were still hundreds of miles from their goal. They were to walk north, skirting the Danakil desert, eluding the French frontier posts in Somaliland, and so reach the coast.

While Boul-Boul was talking to the chief, I noticed a boy who was lying with his head against the trunk of a tree. He may have been fifteen years old and was evidently in great distress; his legs were spread out wide; he rubbed his swollen abdomen incessantly, whining pitifully. I took a step nearer and called over Tambouras Bey to take a look. Aghast, Tambouras stepped back. "That boy has not merely been castrated!" he exclaimed.

"Sure, sure, *saballa, saballa*," explained the slave driver whom Boul-Boul had called over. "We make these little eunuchs with one clear sweep of the sword. We cut off everything. That is the way the Arabs want them."

"But how about the others, these who have not been cut?" I asked. "What are they used for, just ordinary slaves?"

Boul-Boul and the slave driver went into a long discussion with a lot of gesticulations at the end of which both laughed obscenely. No, they were not going to be slaves. They were to be prostitutes. *Lustknaben* the Germans call them.

It is from sexual intercourse with these boys that Mohammed commanded the Believers to abstain during the holy month of Ramadan.

Greeks, Armenians, and a few Russians and Turks made up the European element in Addis Ababa. They were the shop- and café-keepers who catered to the aristocratic section of the native population and to the foreigners. The common people went to the native market for their purchases, or to the department store of Mohammed Ali, a gentleman from India, who has a similar establishment in Aden, across the Red Sea. Mohammed had his own staff of clerks, all Moslems from India. The clerks were the first to flee the country when the war broke out, but the proprietor remained until Signor Graziani expelled him on the suspicion of being the author of an anonymous letter to the London *Times*, wherein was told the story of the massacres that the new Italian Viceroy ordered when he took over from Marshal Badoglio. The Greeks and the other European inhabitants, unless they freely consented to become Italian citizens, were also packed off on the train to Djibouti. This will not be surprising to anyone who knows something of the bitter feelings between Italians and Greeks wherever they come together in the Near East. The Greeks are excellent businessmen and would occupy a dominant position in the commerce of the Near Eastern countries, but for the Italians whose enterprises, if not subsidized by the Italian state, at least are heavily protected by the political organizations of the Fascio, which squeeze out the Hellenes wherever they can.

I witnessed a sample of the almost unendurable tension between Greeks and Italians in Egypt two months after the outbreak of the

Ethiopian war. The Italian Fascii of Cairo and Alexandria, fifty thousand men strong in each city, were openly defying Great Britain to close the Suez Canal. But the Greeks were arming. "If England gives the signal," they said, "we will see to it that not an Italian remains alive this side of Sicily." No signal came from England or from anybody else and as the hopelessness of the Abyssinian cause became more and more apparent, the Greeks in Egypt calmed down and those in Ethiopia quietly left to seek their fortunes elsewhere.

As the fateful month of October drew near, several of the foreign merchants departed. Their closed shops on the main street of Addis gave the city a mournful appearance. But the environs of the Guebi, or political center, where the old palace of Menelik is located, fairly seethed with activity when the rainy season drew to a close in September. Large contingents of warriors were daily arriving from the interior. Some coal-black detachments, who had journeyed all the way from the Anglo-Egyptian Sudan on silver-caparisoned mules, joined the fighting forces of Ethiopia in a pure spirit of Pan-African solidarity—and the prospect of loot. The native tribes arrived under the supervision of provincial and village rases and *dedjahs*. You saw a mass of barefooted men, in close formation, enter the city on the trot. They were all dressed in white, except the chiefs, who rode on horses and mules in the middle of the horde. The chiefs, men of unusually distinguished bearing, flashing eyes and square-cut beards like Assyrian bowmen, wore black capes which they wrapped around their shoulders in a striking, majestic manner. But even the greatest ras went barefooted. They came to the Emperor to offer their services, like feudal lords in Europe's Middle Ages, and they camped in and around the Guebi until Haile Selassie deigned to take notice of them, which was a complicated and rather ludicrous ceremony.

For several days, the Emperor, who drove by in a limousine at least twice a day, acted as if he did not notice the warriors who swarmed in thousands around the Guebi, where all the ministeries and the imperial council chamber were located. It was then arranged that he should meet one of the chiefs accidentally, although both knew where and how the meeting was to take place. The chief would fall on his face and kiss the Emperor's garment and weepingly assure his lord and master that he had come to the defense of the Empire. At first Haile Selassie would pretend that he did not know the stranger and brusquely order him begone. Then the ras would set up a bloodcurdling yell denoting, so I was told, injured pride. This promptly brought his waiting assistants to his side, whereupon the lot of them groveled in the dust and wept in chorus. This had the effect at last of touching the Emperor's heart. He would take a closer look at the stranger, who was no stranger at all, and, with an exclamation of feigned surprise, at last recognize his dear old trusted lieutenant and press him to his bosom. Seeing the King of Kings in fraternal embrace with their immediate chief and both of them weeping scalding tears, the thousands of warriors who had been aware of the simulation right along, but were waiting for the culmination of the melodrama, would leap to their feet and with a wild shout of joy and brandishing their weapons, rifles, lances and cutlasses, race forward to the Emperor to fall at his feet and pay him their fealty.

Then there was rejoicing and the city rang with the ululating war cries and the braying notes of the military trumpets carved from the tusks of elephants. The refreshment parlors were invaded and the jugs of hydromel and *tatja* opened, and everyone was gloriously drunk in no time. For that honey brew of the Ethiopians is, as I have hinted before, a potent mixture, something that was immediately noticed by that connoisseur, Signor Graziani, who forbade its use to his blackshirted *arditi*. On these joyous days Addis Ababa was in a turmoil, and it was not always safe for a stranger to be abroad. Haile Selassie's troops carried their armament wherever they went, even into the shrines dedicated to Venus, which in that particular city, curious to say, were marked not with a colored lantern and a big number as is the case in Paris and other civilized places but, for some unfathomable reason, with a red-cross flag flapping in the open doorway. This was not a wartime regulation, some *ruse de guerre*, I hasten to add. That flag has been the symbol of the daughters of Rahab in Ethiopia since time immemorial. The prevalence of the red-cross emblem led to some curious misunderstandings, one of them being that nearly every arriving correspondent, after a hasty glance around the capital, sent a cable to his home office announcing Ethiopia's preparedness in the matter of hospitals. I was the first to run into the trap.

The *maisons d'illusions* operating under the sign of the red cross were the *bordels honnêtes*, those frankly and honestly dedicated to the sensuous Lubentina, but there were also scores of speakeasies. In fact, it was so difficult to distinguish between an ordinary taproom and a brothel I would not know whether it would be correct to say that every saloon was a lupanar or that every lupanar was a saloon. The Abuna told me that no decent Ethiopian would want to be seen in those ill-famed houses of either sort. But this did not prevent him from owning half a dozen of them himself. All the others, I discovered, paid a license tax into the imperial exchequer as is the case in France. They did a roaring business night and day.

After paying tribute to the voluptuous goddess, the troops were generally in, what our provost marshal in the base camp of Etaples used to call, a window-smashing mood. For lack of windows they seized upon anyone with a pith helmet and a white face, on the chance, no doubt, that the possessor might be an Italian. Walking back from the imperial palace to my hotel one evening, I ran into a crowd of these high-spirited celebrants, who began stoning me and then drew their knives. I do not know if they mistook me for Il Duce or one of his bright young heroes and I never inquired. I ran back to the palace as fast as I could and got a squad of the Imperial Guard to see me home—at ten piasters a head. When I told the Minister of War of this mishap a few days later, malicious old Mala Guetta laughed heartily: "What were you afraid of?" he asked.

"You told me yourself that your soldiers feed on raw meat," I said.

This, in fact, they did, and I am told that it is this habit which preserves them, in spite of their bare feet in the rainy season, from many of the ills to which we Europeans were heir in a time when you could count on seeing the streets of Addis Ababa turn into a swirling river at least once a day.

The weather was beastly from July to September. No amount of blankets could keep your teeth from chattering at night. The hotels were unheated, and the dampness entered by a legion of cracks, for the buildings were ramshackle. Four newspapermen died of pneumonia in that period, one, a particular friend of mine, a Spaniard from the monarchist journal *ABC*, who bore such a striking resemblance to King Alfonso that he had frequently been mistaken for the ex-monarch in places where the journalist himself explained, one would not expect a king to be a habitué. The only remedy against the bone-chilling damp was provided by the local Greeks who kept vodka, slivovitz and schnapps on tap, all known in Ethiopia by the common denominator of *araki*. I am glad to say that the

Greeks got rid of their entire stock of that vitriol to the newspaper- and lens-men before the evil days came that drove them out of business.

For want of something else to do, I braved the downpour to attend the services at St. George's on Sundays and holy days. These feasts came with astonishing frequency. The Ethiopians did honor their saints, and I had nothing against that, but the services were decidedly too long. Had it not been for the crutches which were handed out at the door of the cathedral to whoever could pay a few piasters, I would have fainted with exhaustion, for the place was devoid of chairs and benches, and the atmosphere humid to the point of suffocation. The Emperor's crutches were gold-plated, the rases' silver-plated and so on down the grade: brass, iron and tin, until the Ethiopian *Lumpenproletariat*, the beggars and the foreign newspapermen who had to content themselves with plain wooden supports devoid of all adornment.

The service resembled that of a Roman Catholic Mass, except that after the blessing of the chalice, the priests stepped aside from the high altar and made place for a group of young acolytes who executed a religious dance before the communion rail. This, of course, is nothing unusual in Africa, where nearly all tribes express their religious, as well as all other emotional reactions, by the dance. Even the converts of the Roman missions in certain parts of Africa are taught religious dances. But they do not perform before the altar, of course.

The Emperor Haile Selassie's interpretation of the ceremony was curious. When he questioned me one day on my impression of the services in the cathedral, I mentioned that as a Protestant I had little sympathy with any creed using a ritual language that the common people do not understand, but that I found the dancing to the tom-tom, although vastly entertaining, a strange custom in a Christian place of worship.

"Strange?" asked the Negus Negusti. "Did you not know that our father David danced before the Ark?"

There was no preaching, just an endless ceremonial, with antiphonal choirs and genuflecting priests in green and silver vestments and the chanting of the Gospel in Gué. On the high altar, above the monstrance, stood the Ark, a cedar chest covered with gold and topped with two golden angels or cherubim whose wings touched. Of this mysterious box the clergy stoutly maintained that it was the identical Ark of the Covenant which the ancient Hebrews carried on their wanderings through the desert into the Promised Land. Its transfer from Solomon's temple in Jerusalem to the Coptic cathedral in Addis Ababa was said to have been the work of the first Menelik, the legendary son of Solomon and Balkis. The Abuna used to announce from time to time in those days preceding the war that if the Italians should dare to invade Ethiopia, he would personally escort the Ark into the forefront of the battle as Joshua ben Nun had done of yore. Its presence there, the prelate felt, would strike terror into the hearts of the Black Shirts. Nothing came of that interesting project, a circumstance much to be regretted, for it might have injected into the campaign that element of surprise which had once played havoc with the walls of Jericho, and, earlier yet, produced the debacle, as we know, of Pharaoh's host in the Red Sea. The only surprise in the war came from the other side, when Badoglio employed poison gas. The "savages" of Ethiopia did not know all the resources of "modern civilization."

After his defeat at Dessye, the Emperor hastily removed the Ark from the cathedral and concealed it in the hills, where it is awaiting his own return or that of his successors.

Having made early application to travel north in the event of war, I had bought myself a mule for three hundred francs and tried to accustom myself to this mode of locomotion by riding out into the country and exploring the neighborhood. I was accompanied on these trips by my Galla boy, Boul-Boul, who spoke French. Our first trip, some thirty miles into the interior west of Addis Ababa, brought us to the powder factory, the main supply depot of the Ethiopian army. The arsenal was administered by a White Russian officer, Colonel Piotr Theodosiev, a gallant gentleman who had fought with Denikine under the walls of Petrograd against Leon Trotsky. He enjoyed the full confidence of the Emperor and had the reputation of being a strict disciplinarian, something that was fully attested by the twenty-one human bodies dangling from the trees in front of his office. The dead men, Colonel Theodosiev explained, had been employees of the powder mill who had been caught in the act of supplying some friends and relatives with cartridges. With characteristic Russian thoroughness, he had punished these "wreckers" by stringing them up and leaving their bodies as a horrible example to other would-be *saboteurs*. But only a Russian could have stood for the putrid odor emanating from those decomposing bodies. The vultures perched on the dead men's shoulders were having a foretaste of the full repast that was in store for them up north a few months later.

On the way back to Addis, after one of these exploration trips, we picked up a lad whom we found lying by the side of the mule track and who implored us to take him along. He was about seventeen or eighteen years old and had his right arm severed at the elbow and his right leg cut off at the knee. These horrible wounds were not the result of an accident, but punishment for theft: the boy had stolen a lamb. We placed him on my mule and brought him to the capital where nobody wanted to have anything to do with him. In the end we left him in care of the lepers and the monks near the cathedral—for a consideration, of course. I did not see him again till the last day of August when I caught sight of him among a batch of criminals who were being led to the execution field to face the firing squad. Supporting himself on the shoulders of a couple of fellow condemned, he was hopping blithely to his death.

The executions in Addis Ababa were carried out in a courtyard near the model prison. The building of this jail was one of the reforms instituted by the Emperor Haile Selassie. I heard that he was very proud of it. The amazing part about it was that only men condemned to death were housed in it. Minor criminals were not incarcerated at all. They were given a beating with an oxhide whip in public and sent on their way with the admonition to sin no more. It was somewhat difficult to discover what constituted a minor breach of law and what was a major crime. Wife beaters were punished with the lash, thieves had to pay with the loss of a limb or two, lying and perjury were visited by branding the offenders on the forehead. But debtors were chained up to their creditors and kept attached till they had paid the last cent. How a debtor could go about earning the money that would ensure his release I never discovered. He remained chained to his creditor, day and night inseparable, so long as his debt remained unpaid. You frequently met a pair of individuals, their hands attached with an iron chain, in the streets of the Ethiopian cities. More often yet one ran into sessions of a court of justice. There was no special hall or tribunal in Ethiopia for the settlement of legal disputes. Any elderly citizen coming along could be instantly pressed into service as judge and arbiter in a quarrel. The elderly one accepted with alacrity, first because it was a mark of honor to be singled out by his fellows for the judicial position and secondly because there was a fee attached to the job.

A few boxes were piled up and the law was hoisted on his throne and a boy was placed behind him to chase off the flies with an umbrella of straw. Then the litigants advanced with bows and obeisances and the arguments began amidst the deathly silence of the otherwise tumultuous Ethiopian street crowd.

"It is so still," Boul-Boul whispered on one occasion, "that you can hear the witnesses lie." The pleaders would withdraw about fifty paces from the throne of justice and suddenly rush forward with outstretched arms, shout out their case with many gesticulations, and withdraw again to a safe distance. This game went on for hours amidst the rapt attention of the bystanders. To anyone not understanding the language, the strain was considerable, but it was not hard to see who was the winner in the case under consideration, for upon pronouncement of the judgment one of the parties would rush forward, kiss the hem of the judge's gown and walk off with him arm in arm to the nearest taproom.

Fantastic as a court trial might be, more animation was provided by a funeral. The burial ground in Addis Ababa was located in the consoling nearness of the cathedral of St. George, adjoining the sheep market and the street of the butchers' guild, where the slaughtering was done in the red mud, under the gaze and sometimes with the assistance of the idling lepers from the neighborhood. The funeral processions had to pass through this street of blood and bleating, but interfered little with the activity of the butchers. Preceded by a priest, who read aloud from a holy book and a boy who sounded a bell, the mourners walked backwards in front of the corpse, screaming and bellowing out their sorrow. At the open grave, as the uncoffined corpse was unceremoniously dumped into the hole, the mourners broke into a frenzied dancing. This was not part of a prescribed ceremonial, but a spontaneous manifestation of grief. The vociferous expression of sorrow passed as quickly as it started, for no sooner was the last clod of earth stamped into place than the tears stopped flowing and the procession moved off with that mark of congenial hilarity characteristic of a wedding feast.

At the monastery of St. Abo on Mount Zekouala, some twenty-five miles outside the capital, I visited the miraculous chapel whither the Emperor retired more and more frequently to pray as the Italian menace loomed nearer. The monks received me with a simple ceremony at the entrance of their retreat, offering bread and salt before crossing their threshold. During the meals I was given the seat of honor on the right hand of the Abbot, with Boul-Boul sitting behind me on the floor to help in the conversation. Having been told that the chief occupation of the inmates was the copying of holy books, I expressed a desire to see the library and was duly allowed to inspect the fine collection of original manuscripts. Some of the documents dated back, so the Abbot informed me, to the third and fourth century. They were priceless in value but no doubt the greatest treasure in the library was that crumpled and half-deteriorated scrap of parchment which the Abbot carefully unwrapped from a layer of silk. It carried about ten lines of a marvelously flowering Arabic script, probably of Persian origin, obviously the work of an artist. The Abbot explained to me, and I let Boul-Boul repeat his words three times, that it was a letter written by the Prophet Mohammed, wherein that notoriously illiterate Bedouin certified the immaculate conception of the Virgin Mary!

The Negus used to go out to St. Abo's shortly after sundown, riding on a white mule, the traditional conveyance of the Israelite kings and priests. On those trips he was accompanied by hundreds of torchbearers. These attendants waited outside the chapel all night while Haile Selassie lay on his knees, a pathetic and helpless figure, illuminated by a solitary oil lamp. Only in circumstances of extreme national peril were the doors of the chapel opened and the sovereign alone was permitted inside. Menelik the Great had prayed there forty years earlier on the occasion of the first Italian invasion and, before him, the mad emperor John, he, who when all had deserted him, withdrew within the fortress of Magdala and defended the walls alone against the British troops of General Napier.

It was in the neighborhood of Mount Zekouala that Menelik was said to have buried a war chest of three hundred million thalers. The hoard was supposed to be hidden in a cavern at the foot of an extinguished volcano of which the opening had been sealed by an avalanche of rocks let loose from the top of the cone. Only the royal family knew its exact location, for the workmen employed in the excavation of the vault and the transfer of the treasure had been massacred on the principle that dead men tell no tales. It was generally expected that Haile Selassie would open the cache if and when the need for money to buy munitions should make itself felt. I accompanied my friend Tambouras Bey and some other Greek gentlemen on a fortnight's expedition, undertaken in the greatest secrecy, in search of Menelik's pile of gold. Our search was conducted by a German expatriate who had devoted long years of study to the problem. But we never used the dynamite we had brought along. The imperial safe remained a secret in the solitary mountains.

But we did stumble on another curiosity: the local *dedjaz* or chief of the village at the foot of the St. Abo mountain was the proud possessor of an electric chair. This deadly instrument, quite harmless in that rural Ethiopian environment, was one of the famous trio imported by the Emperor Menelik from America. Another specimen stands in the old Guebi in Addis Ababa and a third lies somewhere in the desert near Aouash, where it is said to be venerated with superstitious awe by the Danakil tribesmen. Menelik ordered three metal chairs from America when he heard that his own method of executing criminals (he had them ripped apart by letting two saplings to which their legs were attached suddenly spring back into opposite directions) was decried as un-Christian by his missionary friends. It was found impossible to make the chairs do the work for which they were intended without an electric current and as this was not available in Menelik's days, the great Negus used one of them as a throne; the second he gave away, and the third never reached him, for the vehicle in which it was conveyed across the Danakil desert was wrecked two hundred miles from home.

When I arrived in Addis, the Negus Haile Selassie had abandoned the old Guebi as a residence. He had built the new palace in preparation for his coronation. It was really a large-sized country house, furnished in modern style. In the reception hall among innumerable elephant tusks, lion skins and other trophies of the hunt stood the Emperor's precious collection of China—huge dragon-painted pots— and clusters of swords and sharp-tipped metal spears and a few cases filled with neatly bound annual trade reports in German and Italian. The imperial bedrooms were modest, a crucifix and religious pictures being the only ornaments.

It was the building of this palace which had led to the military raids in 1934. For, although he was reputed an extremely wealthy man, the Emperor forced his people to pay a tax for the construction of his new home. In July, 1935 when I came to Addis the tax troubles were not at an end. Detachments of the Imperial Guard would swoop down on the market place to ask the peasants to show the small slip of red paper which had been handed out as a receipt for the payment of the tax, and woe to the man who could not produce the scrap of paper! The soldiers would belabor him and his wife and children with the butt ends of their rifles and drag them off to that famous model prison where life was hard and death a release.

Around the old Guebi, a bizarre-looking collection of palaces, brightly painted kiosks and barbaric churches, a miniature Kremlin, where the Negus held his state councils, nothing had been changed since the days of Menelik. The compound was surrounded by three brick walls. The narrow passageways leading up to the imperial headquarters were lined on both sides with cages containing lions. It was said to be the intention of the Ethiopians to let these beasts loose on the Italians should they ever venture near the capital city. They were indeed set free in April, 1936, but instead of attacking Badoglio's men they were intelligent enough to disappear into the forest.

The value of Addis Ababa as an observation point in the war was practically zero. Haile Selassie's intelligence service furnished the correspondents with a daily bulletin on preparations for the defense of the empire and a crop of rumors. One day it was said that Japan was landing an expeditionary corps in Yemen, and the next that Kemal Pasha had dispatched some of his ablest strategists to aid the Emperor in drawing up a plan of campaign. The only definite information we had were the broadcasts from Rome—of all places. These indicated that as soon as the rainy season was over, De Bono would take the offensive.

Since all requests for permission to go to the front were refused, I decided to go outside the country, speculating on the possibility of re-entering Ethiopia from the west by way of the Sudan or Kenya. Hence I had to travel by railway to Djibouti, the port city of French Somaliland and there catch a steamer for Suez. Arrived in Djibouti and awaiting a steamer in that city of scorching sun and fleas, I found the unexpected opportunity presented itself of going to Yemen across the Red Sea on a Greek trawler. In Yemen I convinced myself that the stories of a concentration of Japanese troops and war material were without the slightest foundation. From Yemen I traveled back to Aden on a British coast-guard cutter which was on the lookout for a convoy of slaves from Assab. After a week's wait in Aden I obtained permission to cross to Massaua in Eritrea on one of the British-owned tankers which supplied the Italian expeditionary army with drinking water.

I visited Italian headquarters in Massaua but when I had given my name and been made to wait two hours, I was promptly escorted back to the harbor by order, I was told, of Count Galeazzo Ciano, who handled the publicity on the Italian side. The Count did not like the dispatches I had sent from Italy in the month of June. However, upon finding that the tanker on which I had come from Aden after discharging its load of water had lifted anchor, I was locked up for safekeeping by the Fascist police till the next British tanker should call.

My prison was a shed of corrugated iron. From ten o'clock onward when the sun stood directly overhead, the place was the nearest thing I can imagine to a frying pan. There were some sixty or seventy Italian soldiers in that prison awaiting shipment back to the motherland. They were charged with antimilitarist propaganda and other crimes and were going to be tried en masse. I was not permitted to communicate with them, a Black Shirt having been detailed to keep me confined to a corner of the shed. This fellow, a good-natured boy from Verona, passed the time with me playing cards and teaching me a game called *jocare digiti*, which consists in sticking up a number of fingers with lightninglike rapidity and having the opposing party call out the number of fingers not raised. We had a pleasant enough time of it. But the food they gave me was atrocious. I have never since been able to overcome the disgust I conceived for macaroni and spaghetti. Fortunately the duress ended after four days and I returned to Aden, whence I crossed back over the Red Sea to Djibouti in French Somaliland. In this city I learned from Tambouras Bey, who had come from Addis by rail, that the Negus desired to see me, so together we returned to Ethiopia, but this time we traveled on a free ticket.

The Emperor asked me to draw up that manifesto of which the Abuna had spoken: "an appeal to the conscience of the Christian world." I delivered the document the following day and read it to the Emperor in French, in the presence of Tambouras Bey, the Greek consul general and the *dedjaz* Lorenço, the chief of the press service. In the evening it was put on the air and dispatched to the capitals of Europe. It was published in about fifty American, Canadian, and European cities.

I pleaded with the Emperor to be allowed to go to the front with Ras Mala Guetta, the War Minister, but he said he could not guarantee my personal safety and refused point-blank. I decided thereupon to start off on my own, after coming to an understanding with Mala Guetta that I would place myself under his protection if and when I would reach the front. And so I was off again for the second time across the Danakil desert for Djibouti, where I boarded a French ship bound for Egypt, this time in the company of the famous and mysterious oil man, Mr. F. C. Rickett.

Not until November did I find a journalist in Egypt ready to share the hazard of flying south via Khartoum and Tanganyika to the shores of Lake Tana in central Ethiopia, against which point, I figured, the Italians would make their first drive. While in Egypt, Tambouras Bey, who had remained behind in Addis, kept in touch with me by means of a private sender installed in the garret of an international travel bureau in Addis.

In the meantime, De Bono had crossed the Mareb River and had captured Aksum, the holy city of Tigré, and Adowa, the town where General Baratieri at the head of an invading force had been crushed by Menelik in March, 1896. With the capture of Adowa, Mussolini at last had his revenge for the humiliating Italian defeat of forty years before and many observers believed that he would now offer Haile Selassie a compromise. The Emperor himself was quite willing to enter into negotiations, but on the suggestion of the British consul general in Addis Ababa, who held out hopes of a rapid intervention by the League of Nations, the poor man was led to declare that there could be no question of peace until the Fascist legions had evacuated Aksum. This demand, of which the least that can be said was that it sounded ridiculous, did not even evoke a response in Rome. Mussolini knew by then that the early calculations of his espionage service, which had placed the number of mobilizable Ethiopians at half a million, were grossly exaggerated. Haile Selassie decreed a general mobilization after eight months of hesitation and when the Italians had already advanced thirty miles into his territory. Only then did he find out that he did not have the means to transfer the bulk of his troops to the front.

What did he have? He did not dispose of any credits to acquire the necessary war material abroad. He had approximately two hundred pieces of artillery and a dozen combat planes and no poison gas. His army lacked trained officers. There was not a single general in Addis capable of drawing up a doctrine of strategy and tactics, or even to prepare a plan of campaign to oppose a redoubtable invader, who was "powerfully armed, carefully prepared and fanatically determined to conquer."

Even so, after De Bono's first rapid advance as far as Makalle, the Ethiopian tribesmen fought the Italian juggernaut to a standstill. That was in December. Up till that time the Fascists had not met with any serious resistance. As they moved away from their bases, their lines of communications were attacked by bands of Ethiopians who filtered through the mountain passes, unobserved by the aviation, to wreck bridges, burn stores and wipe out convoys proceeding along the newly constructed military roads. De Bono was pushing ahead regardless of consequences. His ambition was to come to grips with and annihilate the main Ethiopian force which was moving northward at the rate of about fifteen miles a day from Dessye. His right flank, however, wavered in December and was pressed back on Makalle. For a few days the whole Italian expeditionary force was in danger of encirclement and De Bono escaped Baratieri's fate of 1896 only by a hair's breadth. By a prodigious effort he saved himself in the battle of Dembenguina on December 15. But the shave had been so close that Mussolini hastily recalled the man whose only recommendation for the position of commander in chief had been his record as Fascist police prefect of Milan in 1922, and other distinguished services rendered to the Duce in the burning of Socialist newspaper offices and forcing castor oil down the throats of handcuffed labor leaders.

There is no question but that Mussolini himself was thoroughly upset by De Bono's blunders. He saw the specter of defeat staring him in the face in December. It was at his request that the Pope conveyed a desire for a compromise peace to Sir Samuel Hoare and Pierre Laval. The Foreign Ministers of England and France acted on the suggestion with a promptitude fully warranted by the dangerous position in which their friend, the Roman dictator, had maneuvered himself. Yet to the outside world the Duce did not betray his disquietude by as much as a whimper. He kept a stiff upper lip.

The battle of Dembenguina had shown that the Negus was going to give battle in the European style—that is to say, by opposing large masses of troops to the Italian expeditionary corps. Badoglio, who succeeded as commander in chief, liked nothing better, for with his immense superiority of equipment, he could now turn the war into what amounted to an easy and ceaseless massacre.

From Egypt I flew in a Fokker monoplane, piloted by Baron von Epp, the representative of a Berlin newspaper, first to Khartoum and then to Gallabat in the Sudan, crossing into Ethiopia at Metemma and landing at Gondar on January 2. But in Gondar we were still one hundred and fifty miles from the nearest fighting. A reconnoitering flight, undertaken on January 4, showed that no landing facilities were available nearer the line. We decided therefore that one of us should make the rest of the journey to the Tigré province on mule, and establish a courier service back to Gondar, and that the other man should take the dispatches out once every ten days by plane to the Sudan, where at the same time the machine could be refueled and overhauled.

Because I was not able to pilot the plane, it fell to my lot to try and reach the fighting zone. And so, my belt loaded down with thalers and with two pack mules laden with a month's provisions, a small cooking outfit, blankets, rubber sheets and my old homeopathic medicine chest, I started out on the tenth of January for the Tembien district with five boys and a guide who knew exactly twenty words of French. I had no weapons whatever, for the British border police in Metemma had confiscated our revolvers on the ground that an embargo had been placed on the importation of arms into Ethiopia. Not until I had been on my way a few days did the full hazard of the undertaking dawn upon me. We walked in single file, the guide leading off, and I bringing up the rear. All day the boys chattered like monkeys and I could tell by their glances that I was the frequent subject of their conversation. The first night I was restless. I remembered the warning of the officials in Addis Ababa that not even the Emperor could guarantee my personal security outside the capital, and I also recalled that in order to bring a scientific mission from the Kenya border safely to Addis

Ababa the year before, Haile Selassie had deemed it necessary to send a protective escort of two thousand men. I had six men whose language I did not understand and who might be taking me a stretch up the trail to get rid of me. I could not even have defended myself in the event of an attack by my escort.

The five boys were Amharics, but the guide was a Galla, a quiet coal-black man of about forty, of vigorous built and fully six and a half feet in height. I was aware that he had noticed my nervousness and this only served to increase my apprehensions. I was constantly debating in my mind whether or not to turn back and give up the venture. My worries became an obsession until one evening—it was the sixth day out—when we had been drenched to the skin by a sudden downpour at twilight, the boys first began to mutter and then shout their discontent. Mentally I was debating whether I should not announce a raise in wages and give the signal to start back for Gondar. We had made camp under a giant birch by the side of the Menna River about fifty miles due west of the town of Sokota. Tawfik, the guide, and I were strolling up and down, while the lads were cooking rice and dried meat, he chewing tobacco and I smoking my pipe, when all at once he said to me in his broken French: "You, *patron*, a man—me, Tawfik, a Galla man— No fear. . . ." I looked into his eyes and took his hand. "Tawfik, *frère*," I said, "that's fine of you!" The tears came into his eyes but the dread apprehensiveness left me completely. We did not separate for two months, Tawfik and I, and we became dear friends. Before leaving Ethiopia I bequeathed to him by deed, which was witnessed by the archpriest of Gondar, the two mules and all the travel equipment.

The hike across Ethiopian territory revealed to me the richness of the country Mussolini was acquiring. That was no desert by any means: fruitful black soil of the kind you see in the Ukraine, meadows of astounding green filled with large herds of splendid cattle, an abundance of streams. In the villages I was received with the greatest of kindness. Women and children brought us milk and honey at every halt and would not hear of receiving payment. In fact, it was considered an insult to offer money at all. Although the children stared at the strange white man with a certain shy curiosity, I managed to disarm them completely with a tune on the old mouth organ that had done glorious duty in a much more painful situation—amongst a mob of hostile Arabs in Janin, Palestine, six years before. The elders treated me with a quiet dignity, bowing from a distance and then halting to await a beckoning motion from Tawfik to advance. What astonished me was the fact that so few men in Gojjam province had left for the front. Life went on as if no danger threatened. The explanation was that the ruler of that part of Ethiopia did not join Haile Selassie until Gojjam itself was invaded, which did not occur till April.

Not until we could discern the peaks of Abbi Addi to the east, on January the twenty-second, did we run into hordes of warriors making their way forward to the firing line. On the following day a squadron of Savoia-Marchettis roared overhead, and we learned from the peasants that a great battle had been fought in which the Italians were completely defeated. This was, of course, an exaggerated version of the engagement of the latter part of December. What had happened was that after a few critical hours in which the Ethiopians launched a mass attack, De Bono had extricated himself from an enveloping movement by uniting his right wing with his center. Ras Kassa, one of the Ethiopian commanders, thereupon united his forces with those of War Minister, Mala Guetta, on January twenty-fourth, and together these two chiefs with about eighty thousand men were attacking the Italian line when I arrived in the zone of operations. We made contact with Mala Guetta's headquarters at Kobbo on January the twenty-fifth.

One did not have to be a military expert to realize that the Ethiopians were literally destroying themselves in hurling mass formations into the fire of machine guns and artillery. Had they confined themselves to guerrilla tactics, harassing the enemy and attacking his lines of communications, they would have held up the enemy's advance, not indefinitely to be sure, but long enough to prolong the war another year. For with the beginning of a new rainy season toward the end of May, 1936, Badoglio would have been immobilized for months. The Emperor was extremely ill-advised by his foreign military advisers when he ordered his commanders, Seyoum, Kassa and Mala Guetta, to fight in a manner to which the warriors were not accustomed and for which they showed neither aptitude nor understanding. With his mass attacks, Haile Selassie was playing right into Badoglio's hands. For with his enormous superiority in technical equipment and especially his bombing squads, the Italian generalissimo demoralized the Ethiopian defense in less than two months' time. From February onward he used, moreover, poison gas, which turned the Ethiopian forces into a panic-stricken multitude streaming south to Dessye.

On the thirtieth of January, the town of Kobbo, where I stayed because Ras Seyoum had established his headquarters there, was subjected to an aerial bombardment. Three times the Savoias wheeled overhead dropping their torpedoes and machine-gunning the terror-stricken inhabitants. The first bomb struck in the middle of the market square, killing about sixty people. But the majority of the projectiles came down on the dense masses of warriors who were trotting up to the line. The enemy flew at an altitude of five hundred feet and emptied his racks without being in the least disquieted. Here and there a musket was fired at him, that was all. When they had flown off, I re-entered the town. . . .

Chunks of human flesh were quivering on the branches of the trees. . . . A half dozen houses were burning. . . . Mules and horses were pawing in their own entrails. . . . The whitewashed church was bespattered with blood and brains. . . . Men were running about howling with insanity, their eyes protruding from their sockets. . . . One woman was sitting against a wall trying to push her bleeding intestines back into her abdomen. . . . A man lay near by, digging his teeth and his fingers into the ground. . . . A child sat on a doorstep whimperingly holding up the bleeding stumps of its arms to a dead woman whose face was missing. . . .

That night while my boys and I helped drag the bodies out of the ruins and placed them in a row by the side of the church, where the moonlight looked down into their open eyes, Count Ciano, I learned later, was handing out medals to the flyers of the Disparata squadron in the salon of the military club of Asmara. It was one of the bombs Mussolini's son hurled that day on an Ethiopian cavalry squad that was later described in the boy's book as having had the effect of "a sudden blossoming of red roses."

The Ethiopians fought three battles in all and then gave up the struggle. But the armies of Kassa and Seyoum lost two thirds of their men in the engagements of February and March. By the tenth of the latter month, the Ethiopian force was a disorganized mob of half-insane creatures. Badoglio no longer met with any serious opposition, except in the center where the Negus sought to group the remnants of his armies, reinforced with the famous Imperial Guard. At Dessye Haile Selassie made a last stand to bar the road to Addis Ababa.

Badoglio pushed him up against Lake Ascianghi, where the Guard was massacred on April 4.

The only actual battle I witnessed was that of Chiré on February 25 and 26, in the presence of Ras Seyoum. This commander used sixteen pieces of artillery with which he attempted to hold up the enemy advance long enough to enable his infantry, if such may be called a vast mass of untrained and badly armed men who did not have fifty rounds of ammunition per head, to carry out a flank attack. Seyoum had distributed about twenty thousand of his warriors in a row of enormous caves overlooking the valley of Dedjan. They were to pour down into the hollow when Badoglio's Eritrean Askaris should venture to push forward.

The Ethiopian chief danced about in joyous anticipation of the moment when his troops should pounce on the enemy and exterminate him. But he had not counted on Italian aviation. Badoglio's scouts had observed the whole maneuver. Twenty batteries of quick-firing guns of the seventy-five type had wheeled out to bash in Seyoum's left. When this wing was in full route, the guns advanced to a point opposite the row of caverns where the Ethiopian infantry was massed, and for six hours poured a murderous fire into the densely packed twenty thousand men. It was pure slaughter, for when the Ethiopian infantry finally poured out of its holes, thirty Savoias bombed them and raked them with machine-gun fire. Less than a thousand men survived Seyoum's maneuver.

Badoglio's overwhelming victory necessitated a precipitate flight on my own part in a southerly direction as far as Korissa, where Rases Mala Guetta and Imru were trying to form a new army with the reinforcements the Emperor was sending up in an almost uninterrupted stream.

We moved at the rate of three or four miles an hour, for the road ahead was filled as far as the eye could reach with transports of wounded men. They hung in clusters on the exhausted pack mules or were carried on the shoulders of their comrades. Their gaping wounds had been dressed with tatters of clothing. Literally thousands perished on the way to the rear. Their bodies lay under every tree. There was no time to bury anyone. Nobody bothered to chase the swarms of vultures and ravens which trailed in a lazy aerial procession behind Africa's last army. In the night the jackals devoured what the vultures left. As a man died the ropes with which he was tied to the mule were hastily undone, and his body was carried to the side of the road. The air was putrid with the smell of blood. Twice on the way to Korissa, an Italian aerial patrol passed over that disheveled mob at a low altitude and pumped machine-gun bullets into them. The mules would throw up their heads when the zoom of the motors became audible far off and stampede with their loads of wounded men. The animals that broke away were left to their fate. At the sound of the airplanes, we moved off the trail as best and as quickly as we could, and, throwing the mules' guide ropes around a tree, hung on for dear life. There is only one consolation about a death-spraying pursuit plane: it passes by in a flash. The Ethiopians moving south scattered in all directions when an aerial patrol hove in sight, but the inexperienced troops marching up to the front kept their formation and even fired their muskets at the winged marauders. They were cut down in swathes.

We found Korissa in an incredible state of confusion. The Italians had bombed it into ruins, and the victims of those raids lay in piles along the main streets. At every step I was surrounded by women and children who knelt and stretched out their hands imploringly for help. They took me for a foreign medical man or missionary. That they did not kill me—a white brother of the poison-spreading Italians—showed the innate goodness of these people. Had I been an Ethiopian, I think I would have smashed in the head of the first white man to have come within my reach.

The whole of Korissa was filled with creatures moaning and screaming in pain and anguish. They crawled around in the streets on their hands and knees. Hundreds had gone insane. Mothers carried blood-dripping fragments around of what once had been laughing children. The warriors squatted around in little groups. But no fires had been lit. Food was extremely scarce. Our own stocks were down to one last sack of millet. It was necessary to guard our mules day and night to protect them against foraging parties of soldiers who were prowling about and slaughtering whatever animals came within their grasp. Some of the troops busied themselves with burning the corpses. Since no combustible was available that might have consumed them quickly, a thick pestilential cloud hung over the town. Demoralization was absolute. The Ethiopians had not a grain of fighting spirit left.

Old Ras Mala Guetta was found at the *dedjaz'* house, which had escaped destruction, although a torpedo had struck the stables in the rear. The old warrior was sitting on the floor, as was his habit, holding in his lap the head of his youngest son, who had been badly gassed. The War Minister looked up dully when I entered, but without a trace of hostility. His sorrow was too great for words, for he had just learned that his other three boys had fallen at Chiré. Had I been able, I would have fled that moment to escape the silent reproach I thought I detected in the old man's weary face. As a white man, I was filled with shame and for the first time I understood what Julian meant that day when, seeing the Christian mob attack with axes and then befoul the priceless statues of Praxiteles in the streets of Antioch, he remarked to a companion: "Does it not fill you with loathing to know yourself of the same blood as these barbarians?"

It was from Ras Seyoum, who joined Mala Guetta at Korissa, that I heard the story of the destruction of the Italian column which had started out from Moussa Ali, the nearest point to the port of Assab, on the tenth of October of the preceding year. It will be recalled that Ethiopia was invaded from three points: De Bono led off for Adowa; Graziani entered the south from Italian Somaliland; a third corps was to march around French Somaliland through the Danakil desert, to cut the Franco-Ethiopian railway at Addi-Galla. The Italian communiqués never mentioned anything of this expedition beyond the fact that it had started out. In the glorious accounts of the Ethiopian campaign which have been produced by the score in Italy since the conquest, one searches in vain for information on the outcome of that march of the two thousand Askaris through the blistering inferno of the Danakil.

There is good reason for the official silence: for the whole column was annihilated. These men set out with fifty trucks and twenty small-caliber tanks. They had six hundred kilometers to go to the first water holes at Hala. Small groups of Danakils, a wicked tribe of black men who dyed their hair a henna-red, and who were armed only with spears and hatchets, retreated before them, but led them nearly a hundred kilometers out of their course, by acting as if they would give battle and then fleeing as fast as they could whenever the Italians were about to come to grips with them. These Danakils did not have the benefit of the advice of European military experts. as did the Emperor and the Rases Seyoum, Kassa, and Imru and the other Ethiopian commanders. They fought in the style in which their ancestors had fought since time immemorial. And they were successful! Had Haile Selassie pinned his defense on guerrilla tactics of this sort, Badoglio would have had a much harder time in reaching Addis Ababa.

When the column arrived at Hala, the Italians found the water holes poisoned. Had they been reasonable then, they would have returned immediately to their base. Instead, they set out in pursuit of the Danakils, with the intention of pushing on to Addi-Galla, eight hundred kilometers beyond. But the Danakils remained invisible for days and then suddenly attacked from the rear. At last the Askaris had a chance to empty their machine guns, but their march was held up by assaults that grew ever more frequent, and water became scarce in the Italian column. Yet they pushed forward in the terrific heat over ridge after ridge of sun-burned flint. For fear of nocturnal attacks they made camp at sunset by ranging their vehicles in a circle. The Danakils crept up in the few hours of darkness and cut down the sentinels with their razor-sharp crooked cutlasses, which were shaped like sickles. (In Aouash a Danakil tribesman gave us a sample of expertness. He hurled his knife as an Australian bushman throws his boomerang and cut off the head of a dog at a distance of thirty feet.) The Italian sentries dropped without muttering a sound, their heads rolling away from their bodies.

The Italians were six hundred kilometers from their base when a cloudburst immobilized their advance for three days. Then they resumed their march but with the knowledge that they were doomed men. For on all sides they were hemmed in by masses of tribesmen, who kept out of range, but followed the slow progress of the column. One morning at dawn as they were breaking camp the Danakils closed in on them in a sudden mass attack. The tanks had gotten a start on the rest of the column. Like an army of ants the savage tribesmen clambered on the lumbering machines and, heedless of the bullets and the falling bodies of their own comrades, poured crocks with some highly inflammable liquid over the outside of the tanks and into the firing holes. In a few minutes the attack was over, but the tank crews had been roasted alive. The sustained fire of the rear guard drove the tribesmen away. Yet the damage suffered was fatal to the success of the expedition. The Italians kept open ground to prevent surprise attacks. Ahead lay the narrow ravines of Haddelleh, wedged between volcanic cones of loose lava blocks. To venture into those narrow passages would have meant the end of the remaining tanks and motor trucks. To turn back now was an impossible feat. The water supply was so low that the trucks could not have made the two hundred kilometers to the poisoned wells of Hala. It was decided therefore to put all the available water into the radiators of the four swiftest motor trucks and send these back to the base for supplies and reinforcements. The rest of the column would strike camp and fortify itself behind a circle of trucks and rock and await the arrival of help.

For a white man to uncover in the Red Sea area is fatal. In the Danakil desert, where the heat cuts like a razor, to remove one's headgear produces almost instant unconsciousness. The sunstroke hits the vertebrae of the neck and paralyzes the brain, or else it enters through the eyes and strikes you blind. Without water the fourteen or fifteen hundred remaining Italians were given over to the tortures of hell. They were doomed to an enervating inactivity, for the Danakils did not show themselves for five days, leaving the sun to do its murderous work.

Then a flock of scout planes hove in sight and the pilots signaled to the beleaguered expedition. The next day they were back to drop food supplies, munitions and containers of water. But the Danakils were on the watch. Fearful that their prey which they had lured to the jaws of death might yet escape, they crawled up to within close proximity of the camp and then launched an attack under cover of darkness.

The last defenders were being slaughtered when the Marchettis returned and peppered the Danakils with shot, but it was too late. A few crazed men wandered about in the desert and these were cut down one by one by the tribesmen.

To prove their victory, the Danakils employed the method of the young warrior David of the Old Testament: they carried baskets full of putrefied severed foreskins across the Golima River on the western border of the desert and presented these trophies to Ras Seyoum, who had his headquarters then at Kobbo.

Upon learning of the swift advance of Marshal Badoglio's motorized columns, I rode back from Korissa to Gondar, arriving in the latter city on March twenty-eighth. The population had been warned by leaflets dropped from airplanes that a column of two hundred Italian motor trucks was coming down from Daka. From every window floated a white rag in token of submission. Baron von Epp and I took off in our monoplane on the thirtieth. The Italians entered Gondar two days later. In Khartoum we learned of the desperate efforts of the Negus to halt Badoglio's advance at Dessye, a belated maneuver which failed because of the same error committed since the beginning.

Only after the Italians had installed themselves in Addis Ababa, and the foreign military advisers had departed, did the Ethiopians, left to their own resources, resort to the tactics which would have brought them a larger measure of success had they employed them during the campaign. They slipped away from the cities and began to blow up newly constructed roads, attack convoys, destroy bridges, harass isolated blockhouses and military posts. And although they had no unity of command and no definite plan, they so effectively embarrassed the usurper of their country that in February, 1938, when Mussolini's press proclaimed the complete subjugation of Ethiopia, the London *Times*' correspondent in French Somaliland could report that the Italian garrisons of Magdala and Makalle had been wiped out, that the Franco-Ethiopian railway was choked with goods at Dire Dawa because the tracks had been blown up near the Aouash valley, that a serious food shortage made itself felt in Addis Ababa and that the Ethiopians were killing off the livestock and burying their grain in order to deplete the Italian food supply.

In fact, as late as November, 1938, the Italian conquest had made so little headway that an army of Ethiopians was reported on good authority to have fought its way to within less than fifty miles of the capital. Italy, at that time, had 500,000 men in Ethiopia, that is to say, 300,000 more than the force with which Badoglio had smashed his way to Addis Ababa. The pacification of Ethiopia by Italy was as far from being an accomplished fact as the total subjugation of Morocco by the French.

· MONDAY · TUESDAY · WEDNESDAY · THURSDAY · FRIDAY ·

MONDAY · TUESDAY

SATURDAY · SUNDAY

CHAPTER EIGHT

After Seven Centuries

· WEDNESDAY · THURSDAY · FRIDAY · SATURDAY · SUNDAY ·

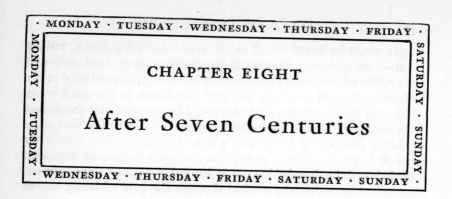

IT WAS THE HOUR when the waters are asleep. A strip of yellow gold on the edge of the world marked the spot where the sun had fallen off. The flowers had lost their courage with the coming of autumn and the meadows now lay a tarnished green in the fading light of day. The smell of oak and of fallen leaves hung in the air, mingled with the pungent odor of burning peat. Like a wisp of incense a haze had come up from the darkened stream. In tufts of whitish wool it clung to the naked branches of the willow trees. A flock of crows, tracing a wide curve against the fading blue, flapped their way, eerily cawing, from the Forest of the Eight Beatitudes towards their nocturnal home in the stunted village tower. With a nervous flutter of wings they nestled in the sloping louvers of the sound holes. From the chimneys of the straw-thatched huts the smoke rose in thin candle-straight pillars. Hushed in the evening stillness, a wind-mill traced the sign of the cross over the clustered dwellings at its feet. The silence which follows the "Ave Maria" in the Flemish land brooded over the hamlet of Paeszdaele.

Shadow pockets were deepening from grey to mauve under the eaves of the seigneurial mansion when a man, dressed in the somber robe of a penitential friar, bareheaded, with unshod feet and leaning on a heavy cudgel, was seen to make his way slowly between the two rows of poplars which led to the drawbridge of the manor. He paused by the moat, placed his mendicant's bag and his staff on the ground, and, cooping his hands in the form of a trumpet, called out in a voice that reverberated against the battlements: *"Deus le veult! Deus le veult!* God wills it!"

That call shattered the peace of descending night. The metallic grating of unbarring and heavy wooden doors swinging on rusty

347

hinges could be heard on all sides. Yellow-haired peasants, pulling
on their sheepskins, tramped out on the frostbitten road, followed
by a horde of half-naked children who stared openmouthedly at the
unfamiliar sight of a flaming torch moving about on the castle walls.
While the figures of helmeted men could be seen busying themselves
in lowering the bridge, the priestly stranger was wielding his cudgel
against a snarling pack of curs which were attempting to rip his
cassock to shreds. With a sound like the swift crackle of flintlocks,
the chains of the drawbridge suddenly rattled through their hawsers.
A moment later the friar walked through the gate of honor where
he was saluted by the armed men of the watch.

An ancient chronicle, written in medieval Latin, and preserved
to this day in the library of St. Jerome's of Bruges, affirms that the
monk, one Jean d'Hennemont, surnamed the Ass of Balaam, was the
bearer of letters-patent from our holy father, the Pope Innocent,
and from Baldwin, the Count of Flanders, calling upon his faithful
liege, the lord of Paeszdaele, to lend his assistance in clearing a path
to the Sepulcher of Jesus Christ, held by the infidel Saracen.

Before greeting his host the papal messenger was asked to sit by
the log fire in the low-ceilinged refectory, and there, the chronicle
relates, partook of "some light refreshment" consisting of "a few
egg cakes, a portion of eels stewed in vinegar, a slice of ham on
baked sausage, a leg of hare cooked in black sauce, a portion of
calf's kidneys, pig knuckles, *le cul d'un poulet*, a fried woodcock
or two, and a pudding," the whole washed down, no doubt, by an
equally "light" assortment of Burgundy wines, "famed for their
power of reviving drooping spirits." Then Jean d'Hennemont
picked up his pilgrim's staff and his sack and stumbled up the stairway to convey the Pope's and the Count's desires to Peter Paesz,
lord of the manor. The time was anno Domini 1198.

Peter Paesz was then in his fifty-ninth year, a man of middle
height, with a deep scar across his forehead. A crude drawing of
him by an unknown artist still exists in the priory of St. Michael's of
Zoutezeele. It depicts him as a man of considerable weight, with
a double chin and lively eyes, and holding a beaker in his right
hand. The chronicle holds that he was a knight of great valor, but
pious withal, who married three wives in rapid succession and
died in the sure hope of the resurrection. He had two sons, Hadriaen
and Hugues, the latter a canon of the chapter of Ypres. Hugues must
have been somewhat of a scholar, for he advanced the theory, since

grown into popular dogma, that the angels of heaven changed their speech from Hebrew to Flemish after the crucifixion of Our Lord.

The monk's recital of Christendom's woes brought tears to the eyes of the chatelain. Jerusalem, the capital of the Latin Kingdom, suffered under the domination of the Sultan whose horses were trampling the sepulcher of the world's Saviour. The Eastern Emperor, Isaac Angelus, with treasonable design, had allied himself with Saladin, whose aim was "to purge the air of the air breathed by the demons of the Cross." The castles and fortresses erected by earlier Crusaders in Syria and Asia Minor were falling one by one before the savage onslaught of the unbelievers while heaps of bleached bones along the road to the East testified to the sad defeat of the Christian arms. So grievous and desperate indeed was the extent of the disaster that the Pope had caused the words—"from the furor of the heathen, good Lord, deliver us"—to be inserted in the Latin litany. Jean d'Hennemont's appeal, which ended with the divine message he had sounded before the gates of Paeszdaele, left the good seigneur trembling with indignation and sorrow. But it was a promise of forgiveness of sins and eternal salvation, as well as d'Hennemont's alluring description of the beauty of Greek women which decided him to ride forth with his bondsmen and serfs, under the Count of Flanders, to fight for the liberation of the holy places.

The peasants were called in and the glad news of mankind's "new path to heaven" communicated to them. Upon learning that their servitude would end in that hour when they should depart with their master for the Orient, their joy, says the old chronicle, knew no bounds. They danced around the lord of the manor while the women, falling on their knees, kissed the garments of him who had been the harbinger of such good tidings. The bagpipes were brought in, more torches were lit, and fat lumps of meat brought up from the kitchen. Soon the tables were covered with earthen tankards. Tin jugs were filled to the brim, and salvers laden with sides of pork were taken down from the inside of the broad chimney. The pots were set a-boiling until a thick steam of fat enveloped the Virgin Mother whose marble statue, in prayerful attitude, stood still and forgotten upon the mantel shelf. Casks of beer were rolled into the refectory, the *dudelsacks* started their absonant caterwauling as peasants and seigneur stamped about on the wooden floor bellowing in raucous chorus: *"Deus le veult! Deus le veult!"*

Towards dawn, when the last girl had been kissed and the seigneur of Paeszdaele had been lifted to his couch, the drunken peasants, as the chronicle relates, were pelting Balaam's Ass with chewed-off ribs of beef and smearing his cassock with liver paste and mustard. . . .

In the spring of the year 1199, Peter rode off with his small lifeguard of halberdiers and archers to join similar groups of Crusaders at Liége, whence the pilgrimage to Palestine got under way by summer. Led by Guy de Lusignan, they stormed the walls of Byzantium, planted their standards on the dome of Constantine, locked the reigning prince in a cloister, and proclaimed their own leader—Baldwin—Emperor of Constantinople. Before proceeding southward to Jerusalem they looted the city of Edessa and put the Moslem and Jewish inhabitants to the sword. At one time, it appears, they considered continuing their victorious march to India and Cathay. They spent months in festive deliberation on that project until an epistle from the Pope, reminding them of "their holy task," caused them to "turn their faces regretfully" towards Jerusalem. But Peter rode back home. The King of France, Philip Augustus, who participated in the Crusade, had secretly returned to Paris, feigning illness, but in reality to seize the Flemish land which was denuded of its defenders.

Two hundred and fifty years later, a descendant of the squire of Paeszdaele, Simon, who had killed the canon of St. Gilles at Ypres in a brawl over cards "in a pothouse by the eastern gate," set out to do penance on the tomb of Our Lord in Jerusalem. He reached Constantinople about Easter, 1453, but was slain in the basilica of Aya Sophia when Mohammed the Great invaded the imperial city, and, wading up to the altar through the blood of the fallen, spat upon the image of the crucified Galilean.

Since that day no member of our family had attempted to reach the Holy City, until in 1925 the New York *Evening World* sent me to "cover" the Druse revolt in Syria.

Seven centuries had elapsed since Peter set forth from our ancestral home.

I

In a blistering heat on the rocky goat paths between Jaffa and Jerusalem, struggling with his obstinate pack mules, beset by a cloud of venomous mosquitoes, his caravan trailed from afar by a pack of jackals, in hourly dread lest his military escort prove inadequate to ward off an attack by bands of robbers whose scouts he could see prowling on the horizon, the Vicomte de Chateaubriand looked upon the dreadful solitude of the Judean hills and noted the following in his diary: "This desert is mute with terror since the Voice of God has reverberated through the waste places. . . . These valleys have been turned into an arid, barren plain. . . . Here the wilderness has conquered. . . . Never will this land lift its voice again!"

On my first visit to Palestine in 1926 I raced over the splendid asphalt road which links the Mediterranean with Jerusalem, and covered in less than two hours what took Chateaubriand nearly a week of travel. That road was built by Jewish pioneers. It is part of a system of modern highways that cover the Holy Land like a net—all of it the work of the last fifteen years! In the country where Mark Twain saw nothing but sackcloth and ashes, and where in 1907 the Prime Minister of Holland, Dr. Abraham Kuyper wept over the poverty and the godforsaken loneliness of the landscape, there stands today a living monument to the revival of Judaism— a land of pleasant gardens interspersed with cities teeming with every branch of modern human endeavor.

The transformation of Palestine is one of the wonders of our age. The all-engulfing desert has been pushed back: the wastelands have been reclaimed, and the sick soil has been nourished back to health. It is a miracle of creative love. For with that rare selfless devotion to which man has risen in great moments of history, bands of Jewish boys and girls from the squalid ghettos of eastern Europe have redeemed for the coming generations of their people what had been lost for centuries. Theirs was essentially a religious zeal. For whatever task renders a man capable of sacrifice, veneration and a pure heart, that is his religion. No immediate prospect of well-being spurred the efforts of the *Chalutzim* (pioneers). There was nothing to relieve the monotony of the unfamiliar work, no pay day in the offing, no restful comfort at the conclusion of the day's hard toil. They had nothing but the bare earth beneath them and a pitiless sun above their heads. Yet with their bare hands they set about digging up the stones which encumbered the soil. On their frail shoulders they lugged the building materials for the foundations of a new civilization. Because the machinery which could have speeded the sanitation work was lacking, they succumbed by the score in the malarial pestholes of the plain of Esdraelon. The flower of European Jewish youth, the intellectuals, the teachers, the idealists who were destined to be the leaders in Israel's renascent national life perished by the hundreds in making the country habitable. But in response to their call the land did lift its voice again. . . .

When I landed, dynamos were zooming their deep basso on the spot where Jonah took ship in Jaffa. An entire city, Tel Aviv, spotless and white, had sprouted from the barren sand dunes to the north. In the seaboard region I walked through an endless array of orange groves whose perfume in springtime mingled with that of the rose fields of Sharon. On every side was heard the clatter of hammers and the grating sound of saws ripping through the board. Factories, buildings, schools and homes were rising from the ground. Everywhere the plow was turning up the fields of festering weeds which had for centuries poisoned the Arab goatherds and sent them to a premature grave. Swamps were being drained. Olive-skinned Jewish boys were dragging baskets of earth up the mountain slopes and restoring the vine terraces and the hanging gardens of Solomon. Motor trucks with building material roared through evangelic Bethany of Martha and Mary. A hydraulic pump plunked out its rhythmic singsong at that ford on the Yarmuk River where, the legend says, the majestic figure of Abraham entered history. There were wheat fields on Armageddon, a dairy farm in the bogs below Gilboa where disaster overtook Saul and Jonathan, prospectors at work in the blood-drenched land of the Philistines, surveyors setting up their instruments in Ramoth Gilead, telephone wires being strung out to Jericho, a hydroelectric station rearing its steel towers where the Baptist met Jesus. There was talk of a real-estate boom in Sodom. Costly machinery was being installed on the shores of the Dead Sea to extract the sixteen-billion-dollar chemical treasure in the accursed lake.

That was the Palestine I saw. . . .

Travel in the Holy Land does not mean the same thing to everybody. In our time, when man has lost so much of what once gave his life direction and filled it with meaning and content, when he has allowed the struggle of life to replace the spiritual traditions that once enveloped him with their beneficent warmth with a set of exterior occupations, so that he has become as restless as a hunted animal, seeking happiness everywhere, yet finding it nowhere, the prey of violently changing moods, sudden unreasoning fears and of a desperate loneliness in a universe he no longer understands, in such times it is difficult, if not impossible, to feel that there is a tie which binds all of us Westerners to that little notch of land on the eastern shore of the Mediterranean.

Yet, it was in this insignificant country, from the heart of an insignificant tribe of nomads, that there sprang the impulse which gave humanity a new hope and a new vision, annihilating the ancients' gruesome wheel of fate and put in its place the conception of the oneness, the holiness and the absoluteness of God, which is the final condition of the oneness of man and the vital source of history wherein grows the root of freedom and humanity.

It was not Palestine's natural beauty which attracted me: the amazing white light of the sun, the magic nights when the stars swayed to and fro like lightships dancing on the swell of a darkened sea and heaven seemed so near that you felt like reaching out and touching it with your fingers. It was the mystery of it all—the mystery of Israel, the mystery of that people whose history is a series of *gesta Dei per Hebraeos*: ". . . a people," as Denis de Rougemont said, "like no other in that it has sacrificed philosophy, fine arts, science, industry, all culture, in fact, for the accomplishments of one thing, a spiritual vocation!"

Also present in Palestine were those intangibles which enkindle the "spiritual sensibility" of a Protestant even more than his familiarity with the place names, the legends and the mythology of the Old Testament, which Ramuz called the real antiquity of the peoples of Protestant Europe; I mean the Calvinist tradition of my fathers who considered themselves the spiritual kinsmen of Israel, in that their church, like the people of the Jews, was a Congregation of the Living God, concerned only with the highest good, a search for the supreme sense of life, "predestined to persecution and revilement because of its testimony of the coming Kingdom in an unbelieving and unregenerate world."

If Palestine is the Jews' national home, it is my spiritual home. I could well understand Allenby's gesture in 1917 when he and his officers walked bareheaded through the gates of Jerusalem. . . .

The Alps are undoubtedly more impressive than Hermon and the Lebanon. The Jordan cannot be compared with the majesty of the Danube, the Mississippi, or the Rhine. By the side of Baalbek and the Acropolis, the Holy Land's ruins are lowly heaps of dust. I met tourists, among them Jews, to whom a visit to Palestine seemed a waste of time and money. They found that there was little to please the eye. And yet ——

"Rome," said Kuyper, one of the last great Calvinists, "in all its glory cannot compare to the world-historical significance of Jerusalem. Babylon may have searched the heavens, Athens given man his highest literary and esthetic values—Jerusalem was and remains the city of cities, the Holy City, the heart and soul of humanity. Deeper than any other motif, that of religion has been woven into the texture of mankind's evolution."

That motif came from Jerusalem!

2

I went the rounds of the holy places like any other pilgrim. Their gaudiness dismayed me. The commercialization of sacred shrines of dubious authenticity made me think of Luther's denunciation of Johann Tetzel. A Franciscan monk led me, half-a-dollar taper in hand, up a stairway in the basilica of the Tomb and said we stood on Calvary. I saw a goat nibbling grass next to the chapel erected on the spot where once, my guide explained, stood the veritable cross. An Abyssinian priest, surprised in his morning ablutions on the roof, grinned in a friendly fashion and dressed hastily to collect a few coppers.

Through the thorns and weeds of Gethsemane's garden, I waded to a cave said to be "the real grave" prepared by Joseph of Arimathea. I put my hand, for half a shilling, on an imprint in a wall on the Via Dolorosa where Christ supported himself on the way to Golgotha. I saw Greek and Latin monks chase each other around with brooms in the holiest shrine of Christendom. I sat with a local English official who explained his presence in the basilica as the end of a search for the coolest place in town; I attended a Mass celebrated by the Latin Patriarch and heard the Greek clergy, before the Patriarch had intoned the "*Ite, missa est,*" start a racket with bells and gongs because the Latin service had that day impinged for half a minute on the time allotted the Eastern rite. I stuck it out to the bitter end and viewed the basin "made in Germany," in which Jesus was said to have washed the feet of his disciples at the Last Supper; I beheld the saddle—yes, the saddle—on which He rode into Jerusalem on Palm Sunday, and I came away with the coin (sold to me by a sly Arab for ten piasters) lest by the woman in the parable. When I scraped the dirt off it later, I saw the rubicund effigy of King Carlos of Portugal and the date 1898!

That was the Old City, the Jerusalem of the past, of moldering ruins and sacred sites, of fakirs and beggars, pilgrims and tourists, crumbling synagogues and silent monasteries, of the Wailing Wall and the multitudinous bazaars. There, in a perpetual twilight, in the "stables of Solomon," brown men and black men, men with green turbans and dirty headcloths, men with red fezzes and men with fuzzy bonnets of rabbitskin—all push and stumble their way forward over the slippery cobblestones in a labyrinthine maze of alleys, rubbing elbows with English soldiers in tropical uniform, Greek priests with parasols and cylindrical hats, Protestant pastors with Roman collars, Dominican monks with Bombay hats, veiled women in soiled clothes that drag in the filth, half-naked camel drivers, Bedouin peasants, Chasidic rabbis, Mohammedan ulemas, blind mendicants rattling tin cups, ice-cream vendors rattling brass cups, lemonade merchants jingling silver bells, hashish peddlers, Levantine guides, Russian nuns, Syrian money-changers, Ethiopian manuscript writers, Turkish dragomans, Arabian sheiks, Greek tourist agents, Armenian prelates and Egyptians porters.

Every second hole in the wall is a refreshment parlor with a gramaphone going full blast. From an early hour the bazaar roars with the shouting and bellowing of merchants, hucksters and beggars. Each guild or confraternity has its own distinctive call. A camel driver's demand for passage is an unearthly screeching yell, a blind man announces his approach with the monotonous singsong call of the hoot owl, while the porters, bent low under staggering loads, emit growls like wild beasts if they do not simply rely on bumping their way through. Every transaction before the vegetable stalls makes you think of preliminary sparring in a prize fight. Instead of the American rule that the customer is always right, the bazaar's fundamental principle seems to require a demonstration of blazing enmity towards a prospective client. During the first dickerings in a business transaction the parties involved eye each other through narrow slits of suspicion. Soon their voices rise to a crescendo, hands begin to fly out, and the faces of the customers and salesmen become red and swollen with the heat of an argument carried on in hoarse guttural expletives. The antagonists look each other straight in the eye, fists are clenched, the veins in their necks protrude, their bodies grow taut with the pent-up tension of boiling kettles. You pause in expectation of the first blow. They are almost spitting into each other's faces. Then with a roar both burst into laughter. Half a minute later the debate resumes.

Of cleanliness there is not a trace: the blood of slaughtered animals gushes into the streets; a million flies zoom over the heaps of refuse and offal into which little brown children dig for overripe figs or cucumbers. Here is a donkey taking advantage of a traffic jam to relieve itself. The urine spatters over a row of crackling flat loaves of bread that a baker's assistant has spread out on the edge of the roadway to cool off. The baker, viewing the scene from his cellar through an opening just level with the street, emits a stream of vile names addressed at the mother of the donkey's owner. This gentle-man, until then calmly sucking a pomegranate, suddenly purses his lips, spits out the pips, and hits the baker smack in the eye. A gale of laughter greets this performance. Business is suspended. There are explanations to passers-by who have missed the show. A police-man elbows his way through the crowd and traffic begins to move again. Life goes on: "Moslem, Believers, beloved of Allah, take a look at these gifts from God. They can be had for the asking. Brighten the eyes of your spouses. Take a pound of grapes from my stores!"

Under the high vault of the Jaffa Gate, a coal-black storyteller hunches down, puts his begging bowl in front of him on the flag-stones and waits for some customers to collect. Presently a group of strolling Bedouins, on a visit to Jerusalem, clink their coins in the box and squat down in a semicircle around the Nubian. He begins talking to them in a whisper so that they have to bend their heads forward to catch his words. The listeners' mouths are agape. He is making curves with his hands, casts his eyes to heaven, licks his lips with an enormous blood-red tongue and places his long fingertips on his breasts. The audience grins obscenely and huddles closer in order to miss not a word of the delectable yarn. That story will be retold tonight in the villages of the plain. Now the minstrel's features betray a growing anxiety. Terror leaps into his eyes. He cowers and trem-bles and his listeners bite their fingernails in bated suspense. Some-thing gruesome must be happening to the houri he has just described so alluringly. The climax is coming. The Bedouins, their faces contorted with apprehension and fear, lean over to within a few inches of the Nubian's face. At this moment, letting his eyes wander over the environment, he catches sight of me watching the scene a few paces away. He gives me a colossal wink and holds out the collection box with a smile which reveals a row of marvelous teeth. A policeman ambles up and, swinging his club in a casual metropolitan manner, shoos audience and storyteller out of the way of pedestrian traffic. . . .

On a quiet side street men and women are squatting in a circle to watch a cockfight. They laugh like happy children as one rooster picks out his opponent's left eye. The spectacle is interrupted by the arrival of an individual who is rolling over the ground. A boy calls out that we are in the presence of a holy man. He expects to roll all the way to Mecca. The holy roller bellows at the top of his voice that Allah is God and Mohammed God's prophet. He has accumulated so much dirt on his garment that he looks like an animated bale of dung. His wife brings up the rear guard, clinking the collection box and toting a sleeping baby on her back. The child is almost hidden under a quivering mass of verdigris—flies!

A sheik stands before a public letter writer's booth and watches intently while the scribe traces the flowering Arabic script from right to left across a piece of cheap paper. The cackle of quarreling women before a silversmith's shop across the street disturbs this primitive idyl. The hags take down their veils and reveal their tattooed and toothless faces. A crowd of yokels gathers and egg the women on to fight; the silversmith cautiously puts up the shutters of his shop. When the females tear each other's clothes, and one of them bleeds from a scratch over her cheek, the sheik interrupts his dictation and stops the fight by walking over and kicking both women to the ground.

Just before sunset, when the muezzins sing out their ululating call to prayer, the bazaar suddenly grows silent as a tomb. In less than an hour all activity ceases, the shops are made invisible by the rows of shutters, and the only sound in the night is the echo of the slow step of the military watchmen in the vaulted passages. But before dawn the pious Jews are up. Long-caftaned shapes on slippered feet can be seen flitting ghostlike through the semiobscurity. The muffled sound of fists pounding on doors and shuttered windows can be heard: the call to prayer in the synagogue or before the Wailing Wall: *"Steht auf fuer Shacharis!"*

3

The new Jerusalem lies outside the walls. Spread out over a dozen hills, it has grown far beyond the limits of the city of both the Solomonian or the Herodian epoch. Brand-new suburbs encompass it. These are inhabited by the Jewish intelligentsia, the modern businessmen and officialdom. Jaffa Road, with its European cafés, restaurants, movies, concert halls, bookshops, banking houses, art exhibits and shops, is the central artery where a cosmopolitan night life is developing. In daytime this district is teeming with activity. There the Occident is pushing the East out of the way. With the exception of Moscow, there was perhaps not a single spot in all of Europe where so much building was going on in 1926 as in Jerusalem and in the booming coast cities of Tel Aviv and Haifa on the Mediterranean shore. A distinctive Hebraic style of architecture had not yet made its appearance. The influence of Le Corbusier and Berlage was predominant in the suburbs, while in the more elaborate edifices variations of all the European and Near Eastern architectural styles could be detected. If this was to be regretted, one had to take into consideration that the new Palestine was still in the embryonic stage. There were more pressing problems than esthetics. Beautification was bound to follow as soon as life could be organized on a permanent basis, and the emerging Hebraic civilization put its stamp on every manifestation of life.

Building, making room, redeeming the soil, creating possibilities for the steady flow of newcomers, setting up new industries—these were the major objectives when first I visited the land in 1926. It was an amazing spectacle: tens of thousands of Jews building roads, mixing concrete, plowing the fields, milking cows, laying bricks, digging wells, driving trucks, raising chickens and livestock, wielding hammer and saw and spade and ax in a manner and with a determination of which the Western world had perhaps not thought them capable. A Turkish officer whom I encountered one day in Cook's office in Jerusalem and who had resided in the Holy Land before Allenby's conquest, in speaking of the changing scene, remarked that after an absence of only nine years he could not believe his own eyes. "It is like a dream," he told me. "I would not have thought it possible."

Every steamer was bringing new immigrants. The population of the city of Tel Aviv had jumped to eighty thousand. One of the most brilliant theatrical companies in the world, the Habima, had transferred its home from Moscow to Tel Aviv. Houses could not be built fast enough to accommodate the new arrivals. Foreign money was being invested. Banks opened their doors. New agricultural settlements were started every month. Book-publishing houses began to make their appearance. The country had half a dozen excellent newspapers. The number of schools had almost doubled every year since the beginning of the Zionist era.

The Jews were building hospitals and clinics. They were laying out new roads, exploring the waste places in the infernal heat south of the Dead Sea, harnessing the River Jordan with an ingenious hydroelectric system. The plain of Sharon was slowly being filled with orange groves and the immense valley of the Emek, which a few years before had been a deathtrap for the Arab tribes, was beginning to be filled with prosperous agricultural colonies. Forests were planted to stop soil erosion. Plans were being laid to make Haifa the largest port in the eastern Mediterranean. Work had been started on the pipe line from Mosul. . . .

The wandering Jew seemed to have reached the end of his age-long journey. He was building himself a home. The Judean night was filled with the song of liberation. Lovers whispered in the language of Amos on the darkened shore of the Old World Sea.

Then came disaster!

4

The general atmosphere here in Jerusalem is reminiscent of 1914 behind the lines in the cities of France and Belgium, I cabled to *The Evening World* a few days after my return to Jerusalem, three years later, in August, 1929. The school buildings are crowded with refugees from the danger areas and the hospitals filled with wounded. Small parties of prisoners are dribbling in under heavy escort. Fast observation planes and slow-moving bombers of the Royal Air Force are circling over the city, drowning out the incredible cacophony of the bazaar. Infantry detachments are constantly patrolling the streets or marching out to relieve military outposts in the country districts. Sentinels with bayonets are guarding the approaches to the holy places: the Wailing Wall, the mosque of Omar and the Sepulcher basilica. English officers posted on David's Tower turn their telescopes on the crowd streaming in and out of Jaffa Gate. The walls are plastered with proclamations as in the northern towns of France during an enemy drive. In the evening the Angelus rings in the curfew. After this hour the city is as dead and deserted as a graveyard. But from the roof of the Hotel Allenby we can see the flames of burning villages in the night.

Upon receipt of Mr. Vincent Sheean's dispatch from Jerusalem, wherein a minor disturbance at the Wailing Wall was attributed to the provocative attitude of young "Jewish Fascists," the publisher of my paper, no doubt perturbed by the storm of indignation the story produced in American Jewish circles, instructed me to proceed post-haste from Paris to Palestine and investigate. The New York Jewish community, which had for years been thoroughly informed on day-by-day events in the Holy Land by a corps of resident correspondents representing the three great Yiddish dailies, unanimously rejected Mr. Sheean's interpretation that a parade by a troop of Jewish boy scouts in the vicinity of the Wailing Wall had been responsible for the outbreak of the disturbances. That incident, these journals argued (and they were subsequently proved correct), had been a mere subterfuge on which the Arabs had seized to bring their long-smoldering revolt to a head. In fact, no person even superficially acquainted with Jewish aims in the Holy Land and with the eminently humane record the Jews had established in their dealings with the Arabs, could possibly believe that the Palestinian Jews in one moment deliberately destroyed what they had striven for long years to establish: a close collaboration with the Arab population as the sole basis for a successful restoration of the Jewish land.

Those who remembered what had happened eight years earlier realized at once that the party of Arab landlords, headed by the Mufti of Jerusalem who had been sentenced to ten years of hard labor in 1921 for incitement to riot and soon thereafter amnestied by a Jewish High Commissioner, had returned to the attack. The flag-waving incident at the Wall had been as good a device as any to throw sand in the eyes of public opinion. Clever propagandists could easily—and did—magnify this intrinsically insignificant demonstration on the part of children into a challenge of Jewish chauvinists. The Mufti had carefully prepared the stage for what was to follow: early in the upheaval of 1929 foreign public opinion was provided with a false premise on which to judge later developments.

The riots of 1921 had given a first intimation that certain influential Palestinian Arabs were not in agreement with King Feisal of Iraq, who, as chief spokesman of the Arabic peoples at the Peace Conference in Paris, had expressed his entire satisfaction with the international plan to set aside Palestine as a National Home for the Jewish people. Feisal, who was unquestionably the ablest of the Arab chiefs, had welcomed the Jew back to the Near East, convinced that his return would prove a real blessing to the Arabs. Scarcely had Feisal spoken when the Palestinian Arabs rioted. However, that was nine years ago, in 1929. Time, the great healer, had produced a general prosperity in the country, and the oppositional elements to Jewish colonization were thought to have dwindled to an insignificant proportion. The Arab masses were thought to be reconciled to the Jew who had actually proved their benefactor. However, the year 1929 was to demonstrate that this sanguine expectation was ill-founded. The Arab landlord class reasserted its stranglehold on the Arab masses and launched them in a bloody assault against the Jewish community. In the late summer of that year, while delegates to the Zionist World Congress in Zurich were singing for joy when an influential section of non-Zionist Jewry decided to join in the building of the National Home, the Mufti of Jerusalem tried to drown the hopeful beginnings of the great Jewish experiment in a sea of blood.

Why were these bloody outbreaks against the Jews in Palestine occurring at almost regular intervals? Who was the Mufti? Why did England permit this upstart madman, who was a government officeholder, to wreck a scheme that England had promised to bring to a successful issue? Were the Zionists trying to force something down the Arab's throat? Was the Jew pushing the Arab off the land? And if so, was the British overlord permitting that injustice to be perpetrated on the original inhabitants of the country, the people whose civic and religious rights he was pledged to protect under the very terms of the Balfour Declaration? What role was England playing in Palestine? And finally, was British power, which holds millions in India within bounds of law and order, insufficient to cope with a few thousand rioting Arabs in Palestine?

I had been sent to investigate these questions in 1929. I admit that I was sympathetic to the aims of the Jewish national movement of which the rebuilding of Palestine is the central motif. The idea of Palestine's redemption seemed a fascinating adventure to me. To behold the land of Jesus rise again from the dust was something to which I looked forward with anticipation. In order to wrest this land from the hands of the Moslem, all Christendom had once faced East. Of course, I was not looking forward to a new Crusade. I entertained no feeling of antipathy towards the Arabs. On the contrary, I commiserated deeply with their hard lot under Turkish domination and under a rapacious landlord class of feudal nobles. But I agreed with Lord Cecil, Smuts, and Lloyd George that Palestine's liberation from the Turkish yoke was one of the few really worth-while things born out of the Great War. As the son of a Bible people, I looked forward with lively anticipation towards the fulfillment of the age-old dream of the Jewish people. But I was unwilling that the Hebraic Renaissance should come about at the expense of the Palestinian Arabs. If Jewish nationalism should have attempted to grow strong by discriminating against the Arabs, I would have been willing to champion the cause of the Arabs.

It will perhaps be argued that the objectivity of my approach to the Palestinian problem was vitiated by a pre-existent sympathy with the aims of the Jewish national movement. The Arab leaders took this view at once when they became aware of the nature of my published observations in the American press. The Mufti of Jerusalem led off with a vehement denunciation in the Arabic newspapers of Palestine, Syria and Egypt. I was called "a hireling of the Jews who had been sent to concoct anti-Arabic propaganda." The press campaign for my expulsion from the Holy Land was too clearly an attempt to divert public attention from the implications of the murderous assault upon peaceful Jewish settlements to have merited a refutation. Not my journalistic activity in the Holy Land, but, rather, the Mufti's personal share of responsibility in the massacre was one of the things that required investigation. I would therefore not have paid the slightest notice to that personage's verbal fulminations, considering that I had merely done my duty in pointing to him as the evil puppeteer in the bloody disturbance, if it were not that I began to receive telephone calls and anonymous letters threatening me with violence and even death. They were not idle threats, either. On two occasions I was fired on by Arab snipers. I owed my life to the presence of mind of my friend, Captain Marek Schwartz, and his chauffeur, Menachem Katan, who had managed to circumvent one ambush which had been prepared in the neighborhood of Lifta and another one near Bethlehem. On both occasions we had come safely through the shower of bullets that beat down on our car. But when I reported the second attack to the commander of the British police post in Hebron, this gentleman, a certain Captain Saunders, remarked: "I should think that half the fun of being a journalist is to go about unarmed and still come through these scrapes unscathed. Moreover," he added, "why do these things happen to you? I have received no complaints from your colleagues of the press in Jerusalem."

Upon my return to Jerusalem that day something flew past my head as I was about to enter the hotel. I saw a dagger quivering in the doorpost. Had it not been that some boys of the *Haganah*, the Jewish Self-Defense Corps, voluntarily constituted themselves into a bodyguard, the intimation of the Palestine government (in the latter part of September) that my further presence in Palestine was undesirable would, I feel, have been quite unnecessary.

I believe my offense was that I took nothing for granted. I did not depend on press handouts from either the Jewish or the Arabic propaganda bureaus. I questioned everybody, from the Mufti down to the most destitute Arabic peasants in the country and the murderous hooligans in the jails of Hebron and Jerusalem who had been caught, their blood-dripping knives in hand. Only when I refused to accept the explanations of a "spontaneous" uprising against the Jews, with which the Mufti and his agents and spokesmen sought to impress foreign correspondents, in several instances quite successfully, did the Mufti denounce me as a hireling of the Jews and did I become *persona non grata* at Government House. The coincidence was significant!

5

Ai Hameen el Husseini, "Grand" Mufti of Jerusalem proved to be an amiable young man with a silken red beard, a disarming smile and big blue saucer-eyes. *Ein gemütlicher* Viennese one might have said, had he been dressed in a frock coat with striped trousers. Only he was not attired in the European style. He wore a gown of dark red silk and on his head a white cloth wrapped around a green fez, in token of an accomplished pilgrimage to Mecca. His strikingly Nordic features clothed in that Oriental costume made him look like a European dressed up for a masquerade ball. I had waited for ten minutes in an antechamber where a mixed crowd of ulemas, eunuchs, beggars and bodyguards was posted to impress the stranger with the importance of the man who was about to receive me in audience. Before being ushered into a high-ceilinged chamber overlooking the gardens of the mosque of Omar, I had also been prompted to address the "Grand" Mufti with the title of Eminence. The advice came from Jamal el Husseini, the "Grand" Mufti's cousin and chief secretary. Once in the great man's presence, I was informed by Jamal that His Eminence was a direct lineal descendant of Mohammed's only daughter, Fatima, and a prospective candidate for the office of Khalif-ul-Islam. When I opened my eyes rather incredulously at this startling announcement, the secretary went on to say that it was generally recognized in the Mohammedan world that since the apostasy of Kemal Pasha and his deposition of the Turkish Sultan, the office of supreme spiritual head of Islam should be laid in religion's second holy city: Jerusalem. And who could be more suitable for the position than —? He bowed in the direction of his smiling cousin. I also bowed. I could see Ai Hameen liked the idea tremendously.

"But," I asked naïvely, "isn't His Majesty Ibn Saud of the Wahabites also a candidate?"

The King of the Hejaz was too much of a sectarian. He was not a man of the world but a regional puritan reformer, a man who did not have a sufficiently catholic view of Islam. Moreover, Ibn Saud was already Sherif of Mecca.

"But that is neither here nor there," the Mufti interrupted in a pompous Levantine French. He wanted to know where I was staying. He hoped that I had found comfortable quarters, for my stay in the Holy Land, he thought, was going to be a long one. We were in for quite a spell of restlessness—in fact, the disturbances, he brusquely announced, would not terminate till both the Jews and the English had evacuated Palestine. When I said that I was stopping at the Hotel Allenby, the two cousins threw up their hands in consternation: "What, in a Jewish hotel? In that breeding nest of anti-

Arabic intrigue?" I told him that all the correspondents I knew were staying there and that we had had the Acting High Commissioner for dinner on the previous evening.

"Incredible!" came the reply.

"What seems more incredible to me," I said, "is that Your Eminence should think that the English are ever going to go home or that the Zionists will give up their plan for redeeming the land of Israel."

"There will be no peace in this country until they go," declared the Mufti. "In the English we recognize our real enemies. It is the British government and not the Jews who have foisted the scandalous Balfour Declaration on us. It is Ramsay MacDonald who has misrepresented the situation in this Holy Land in his book *Palestine*. We have clearly shown the world our attitude in this issue and we are determined to fight it out to the end," he added. "The British will have to put a soldier with a bayonet in front of every Jewish home if they want peace without a wholesale exodus of the Jews. Our people are at the end of their patience. They cannot bear the sight of the Jews any longer."

"The outbreaks are to be taken then as an organized attempt on the part of the Arabs, under the leadership of Your Eminence, to thwart the establishment of a Jewish National Home in Palestine?" I asked.

Hameen was on the point of replying to this question, when Jamal stayed him. The two cousins exchanged a few remarks in Arabic. At the end of their consultation Jamal informed me that His Eminence was going to furnish me with a written declaration at the close of the audience. I was now asked to honor him by accepting a cup of coffee.

The "Grand" Mufti was toying with a gold box of cigarettes. He eyed me from the side, but when I turned my head and looked him in the face he smiled—the same candid baby smile he had worn when I entered. He asked me to step over to the open window to take a look at the garden while a black servant in a white gown arranged the trays on the low table of carved ivory. . . .

The whole marvelous scene lay at my feet. In the clear light the immense garden seemed almost unreal, a frame on which God had embroidered the world. Ulemas were strolling around in the poplar lanes with their disciples or reposed in little groups in the shade of the palms. Believers were washing their hands and feet at the fountains. The sun had imposed a golden luster on the ocher façades of the kiosks. Above the treetops, against the incense blue of the Judean hills, I could see the gleaming porcelain dome of the great Byzantine mosque with its challenging inscription: "Remember, Moslems, God has no son!"

"That is the sanctuary," said the "Grand" Mufti at my elbow, "the Jews want to tear down. Here they plan to rebuild the Temple of Solomon."

"Do they?" I asked in surprise. "I have never heard of that."

"Oh, but that is common knowledge," His Eminence nodded, and stepping over to a small Louis XVI *secrétaire*, he drew out a sheet of paper and read: " 'Lord Melchett declared that he will consecrate the remainder of his life to rebuild the Jewish Temple.' And here is something else," added the "Grand" Mufti: "Professor Einstein believes that Palestine without the Temple is to the Jews like a body without a head.' Do you see the real aims of the Jews? They want to destroy this mosque."

"I do not think so," I retorted. "That is really not the inference I would draw from those remarks. Lord Melchett and Professor Einstein's reference to a temple are most probably to be taken in an allegorical sense. They hope that the new social order that the Jews plan to institute here will be a temple of humanity, a model of justice in human relationships. I cannot see a man like Dr. Einstein advocating a restoration of the ancient sacrificial ceremonies with oxen and bullocks slaughtered, and all the rest of the primitive symbolism. The Jews have outgrown that bloody business centuries ago."

"Have they?" exclaimed His Eminence in turn. "Then read this." He handed me another clipping, this time an excerpt from an article by Professor Joseph Klausner. The words to which he drew my attention were the following: "We (the Jews) are not different in that respect. When you puncture a Jew's skin, blood issues. . . ."

"You see," exclaimed the "Grand" Mufti triumphantly, "it is blood they want. The Jews are always thirsting for blood. Their whole history is soaked in blood."

I looked at the man in astonishment. Was he serious or did he think I was a fool? The Jews thirsting for blood! It was he, the Mufti, who had just been wallowing in Jewish blood. That was a little too much. I almost lost my composure. Jamal noticed my indignation. "Lest an erroneous interpretation be placed on His

Eminence's words, we would prefer you to be guided only by what is in the written declaration we will give you upon leaving," he said.

"What His Eminence says here is not for publication then?"

"It is merely supplementary. His fundamental thoughts are outlined in the document you will receive."

His fundamental thoughts: All the trouble started at Zurich, where the Jews held a conference in August. There the rich Jews of America promised to support the rebuilding of the Jewish National Home. This announcement had made the Jews in Palestine so arrogant that they thought they could start expelling the Arabs. The government of Palestine has formally acknowledged that the Arabs were provoked and that their cause was just.

"Please tell me," resumed the "Grand" Mufti, when we had taken our seats again and he had lit a fresh cigaret, "what is the general impression in the world on the present deplorable situation in Palestine? What is your personal view? You have been in Palestine before; I understand you live in Paris. Surely, you have formed an opinion? Who is held responsible for these horrible outbreaks? The French people do understand, I trust!"

"It is my personal opinion," I said, "that these riots were an attempt to strike terror in the hearts of the Zionists at a moment when they had secured the co-operation of an influential section of Jewry to speed up Palestine's industrial and agricultural development. This bloodshed was intended to paralyze the process of building a Jewish National Home. Am I right?"

The Mufti did not reply. "*Continuez, je vous prie,*" he said.

"As to the responsibility," I continued, "for what Your Eminence calls 'these horrible outbreaks,' public opinion in France and in America, I am sorry to say, points directly to yourself. And not only in those distant countries; the most influential newspaper in Egypt, *La Bourse Egyptienne*, in one of its latest issues to arrive here in Jerusalem, declares that 'the murder of the Palestine Jews is an echo of the Mufti's inflammatory exhortations in the mosque.' "

At these words the grandson of the Prophet jumped up from the divan, threw his cigaret away, and quickly walked towards me, his eyes blazing with anger. Jamal casually uncovered his belt so that two silver-handled daggers came into view. The Mufti was striding up and down the room with quick nervous steps. His fury made him gnash his teeth.

"Your Eminence asked me a question," I said. "I answered truthfully. Why grow angry? I came here to find out to what extent the foreign public opinion is in error."

His Eminence calmed down at once. He lit a new cigaret. "Look at these hands," he said dramatically, stretching out his rose-perfumed palms, "There is no blood on these hands. I declare before God that I have no share in the shedding of Jewish blood. Moreover," he went on, "it is not true that foreign public opinion favors the Jews. We have distinct evidence to the contrary. We have telegrams from Moscow upholding our stand. Only this morning we had a wire from Henri Barbusse, president of the Antiimperialist League in Paris, assuring us of the sympathy of the members of his organization in our struggle against the Balfour Declaration and Jewish usurpation. Why," he went on, "the whole Moslem world is solidly behind the Arab people of Palestine. Mass demonstrations of protest are held every day in the large Egyptian cities. I have a telegraphic offer from His Majesty, King Ibn Saud of the Hejaz, to send an army of a hundred thousand men across Trans-Jordan to chase the Jews out of Palestine.

"However, we do not need the King's aid," the Mufti went on. "We will win by means of an economic boycott. The Jewish industries in Palestine cannot exist without the market of the surrounding Arabic countries. We have proclaimed a world boycott against Jewish goods. That boycott is growing tighter every day. We will not rest till the Jewish industries are broken and the English, in pity, take their Jewish protégés away on their battleships.

"It is a horrible shame to put the responsibility of these riots at the feet of the Arabs. It is a crime. A dastardly ignominy. The Arab is a kind and loyal creature. The Jews, fortunately, cannot easily forget what Colonel Lawrence has said of the Arabs. We are not murderers or fiends, I would have you understand. Why do you say Arabs are responsible for this slaughter?"

"Did those Jewish women and children and old men in Hebron and Lifta and Safed commit suicide?" I asked.

"No," snapped the Mufti, "we were provoked. We were challenged in our holiest possessions. The Hebron Arabs learned that the Jews had decided to drive them out, to push them into the sea. The Jews are stealing our land. They want everything we have." The Mufti broke down and buried his head in his hands. "My country is being ruined by the Jews," he turned up a dramatically tearful face. "My country, Palestine, just when we had shaken off the Turkish yoke and turned up the road of freedom!"

"The Turkish yoke?" I asked. "Did Your Eminence not serve as a volunteer in the Turkish army?"

At this question the Mufti looked straight at his cousin, said something in Arabic, and left the room.

"Could I see the telegram from Barbusse and from King Ibn Saud?" I asked Jamal.

"Copies will be attached to the document you will find at your hotel later in the day." he replied.

"One more question please," I said, turning to Jamal: "On that fateful Friday in August, when the rioting broke out in Jerusalem after the morning service in the mosque, where was His Eminence?"

"He was in Amman [capital of Trans-Jordan]. Why do you ask?"

"The Egyptian press avers that His Eminence applied for a visa to go to Syria to escape a possible accusation that his sermon that morning had incited the Moslems to draw the sword, but that he was refused by the French authorities."

"His Eminence was in Amman, I tell you. Why do you pay attention to the gossip column in an Egyptian newspaper? I thought you had come to find out the truth."

"Quite," I said, "that is what I have come for; but it is true, is it not, that a large number of out-of-town Moslems attended the service in the mosque that morning?"

"There were some, no doubt!"

"Peasants from the Mufti's family estates?"

"I cannot tell. Why do you ask?"

"I ask because the sentence of seven years at hard labor which the government of Palestine imposed upon His Eminence in 1920 was to punish him for a previous seditious sermon in which he called upon village leaders to bring their men into Jerusalem to exterminate the Jews."

"His Eminence never was in prison!"

"I know that: he fled to Damascus. It was Sir Herbert Samuel who amnestied him two years later."

"You ought to be careful," warned Jamal, as I went out, "that you do not get poisoned in that Jewish hotel."

"Or shot from ambush on the road to Bethlehem?" I retorted.

6

Falsified photographs showing the Omar mosque of Jerusalem in ruins, with an inscription that the edifice had been bombed by the Zionists, were handed out to the Arabs of Hebron as they were leaving their place of worship on Friday evening, August the twenty-third. A Jew passing by on his way to the synagogue was stabbed to death. When he learned of the murder, Rabbi Slonim, a man born and bred in the city and a friend of the Arab notables, notified the British police commander that the Arabs seemed to be strangely excited. He was told to mind his own business. An hour later the synagogue was attacked by a mob, and the Jews at prayer were slaughtered. On the Saturday morning following, the Yeshiva or theological seminary, which stands away from the center of the town on the road to Jerusalem, was put to the sack, and the students were slain. A delegation of Jewish citizens thereupon set out to visit the police station, but was met by the lynchers. The Jews returned and took refuge in the house of Rabbi Slonim where they remained until evening, when the mob appeared before the door. Unable to batter it down, the Arabs climbed up the trees at the rear of the house and, dropping onto the balcony, entered through the windows on the first floor.

Mounted police—Arab troopers in the service of the government—had appeared outside by this time, and some of the Jews ran down the stairs of Slonim's house and out into the roadway. They implored the policemen to dismount and protect their friends and relatives inside the house and clung around the necks of the horses. From the upper windows came the terrifying screams of the old people, but the police galloped off, leaving the boys in the road to be cut down by Arabs arriving from all sides for the orgy of blood.

What occurred in the upper chambers of Slonim's house could be seen when we found the twelve-foot-high ceiling splashed with blood. The rooms looked like a slaughterhouse. When I visited the place in the company of Captain Marek Schwartz, a former Austrian artillery officer, Mr. Abraham Goldberg of New York, and Mr. Ernst Davies, correspondent of the old *Berliner Tageblatt*, the blood stood in a huge pool on the slightly sagging stone floor of the house. Clocks, crockery, tables and windows had been smashed to smithereens. Of the unlooted articles, not a single item had been left intact except a large black-and-white photograph of Dr. Theodore Herzl, the founder of political Zionism. Around the picture's frame the murderers had draped the blood-drenched underwear of a woman.

We stood silently contemplating the scene of slaughter when the door was flung open by a British soldier with fixed bayonet. In strolled Mr. Keith-Roach, governor of the Jaffa district, followed by a colonel of the Green Howards battalion of the King's African Rifles. They took a hasty glance around that awful room, and Mr. Roach remarked to his companion, "Shall we have lunch now or drive to Jerusalem first?"

In Jerusalem the Government published a refutation of the rumors that the dead Jews of Hebron had been tortured before they had their throats slit. This made me rush back to that city accompanied by two medical men, Dr. Dantziger and Dr. Ticho. I intended to gather up the severed sexual organs and the cut-off women's breasts we had seen lying scattered over the floor and in the beds. But when we came to Hebron a telephone call from Jerusalem had ordered our access barred to the Slonim house. A heavy guard had been placed before the door. Only then did I recall that I had inadvertently told a fellow newspaperman in Jerusalem about our gruesome discoveries.

On the same day of the Hebron massacre, the Arabs had rioted in Jerusalem, crying: "Death to the Jews! The government is with us!" The fact that the attacks on Jewish communities in different parts of the country had occurred simultaneously was interpreted by the Mufti's newspaper *Falastine* as irrefutable evidence of the spontaneity of the outburst of Arab indignation. The Acting High Commissioner, Mr. H. C. Luke, had informed newspapermen that the government had been completely taken unawares. Yet a full ten days earlier it was he who had ordered the various hospitals, and especially the Rothschild clinic of which Dr. Dantziger was chief surgeon, to have a large number of beds in readiness in view of the government's expectation of a riotous outbreak.

The same scenes which occurred in Hebron had taken place in the Holy City. Upon the conclusion of the morning service in the mosque, where an unusually large crowd had been in attendance so that the congregation had overflown into the gardens, the Arabs, who had ordered their women to stay indoors that day, streamed into the city and began to attack any and every Jew they encountered. There were no street battles. There was never any question as to whether the first slain were Jews or Arabs. For the Jewish merchants in the Old City were indeed completely taken unawares. As always, the Jews were unarmed. Groups of them ran in the direction of Government House, pursued by Arabs brandishing their long knives and clubs. Mr. Luke and Mr. Keith-Roach saw the crowd running up and in all haste ordered the mounted police to close all the approaches to the building. The Jews were trapped. In order to return home, they had to break through the lines of the rioters. Many of them perished in the very shadow of the union jack.

For an hour or so it seemed as if the Arabs were going to attack the seat of government. Large numbers of rioters were assembling near the building. From their excited behavior, it could be deducted that a serious move was under consideration. Spies brought word that the crowd was still divided as to whether to march down the Jewish quarter first to put man, woman and child to the sword, or attack Government House. The majority finally seemed to favor the last course. When Mr. Luke learned of this, he realized that there was not a minute to lose: he ordered that arms be distributed to the Jews. The nearest British troops were somewhere on the high seas between Malta and the port of Haifa.

An hour later Jews manned the guard at Government House and Mr. Luke was safe. Order returned to the city. As had been the case in Hebron, after the damage was done, a few shots fired into the air dispersed the bloodthirsty mob.

Until the first contingent of military reinforcements arrived a few days later, the knowledge that Jews had been armed by the government maintained law and order. With the exception of attacks on outlying Jewish settlements in the country, the whole of Palestine remained quiet.

The Jews alone had saved British prestige in the Holy Land and in the entire Near East. But they did not take advantage of an opportunity afforded by circumstances to show the world the service they had rendered to the British cause. They should have occupied the post office and a few central buildings in the city (there was no one to stay them), hoisted the Zionist flag next to the union jack, and announced that they were holding Jerusalem till the arrival of the destroyers carrying the British troops from Malta.

The Jews in the agricultural colonies stuck to their plows. There was no panic or wild *sauve-qui-peut* for the comparative safety of the large cities. Everybody remained at his post. Rishon-le-Zion, the central winegrowing colony, harvested the largest crop in history. When two thousand Bedouin tribesmen massed on the outskirts of the city under the leadership of Sheik Abu Kishek, who had been the leader of the attack on the colony of Petach Tikvah in 1921, a handful of Jewish boys showed themselves with arms and the would-be assailants withdrew. Mayor Dizengov of Tel Aviv did not learn of the incident till evening and then only by chance. The leader of the *Haganah* informed him that he had not thought it necessary to alarm the citizenry. Business had continued quite normally throughout the day.

7

"After eight years of comparative tranquillity the Palestine government had come to believe that the Arabs had finally acquiesced in the establishment of the Jewish National Home. The dreadful events took the government completely by surprise. It is evident now that the Arabs have not changed their oppositional attitude one particle. They will go on resisting." Thus spoke Mr. H. C. Luke, Acting High Commissioner of Palestine when I sat with him in his office. "The reports from Zurich," he went on, "where Zionists and non-Zionists reached an accord on the measures to be taken to accelerate the building of Palestine, made the Arabs realize that in the future they will no longer deal with a minority of the Jewish people but with the entire, united Jewish world. The Arabs fear that more of their best land will be bought up by the Jews and they themselves gradually confined to the mountainous regions. It is quite clear," said Mr. Luke, "that if the troops were withdrawn the outbreaks will immediately be repeated and on a much larger scale. The government fears that in such an event the Moslem unrest would not be confined to Palestine alone, but that the whole Near East would go up in flames."

Mr. Luke had welcomed me with extraordinary warmth. "As a correspondent of the most influential liberal journal in America," he said, "you are the man I want to see. Moreover, I understand from Mr. Edwin Samuel [to whom I had applied for the interview with the acting chief of the government] that you are a British subject, a Canadian. Thus, you are one of our own. That is fine. The Palestine Administration and the British government are extremely susceptible to American public opinion and you can render us valuable services. I am glad you came to me. I am sure you must be tired of being bombarded with all sorts of silly propaganda, both from the Jewish and the Arabic side.

"You see," he resumed in that intimate now-I-am-going-to-let-you-in-on-the-secret tone of voice that politicians all over the world adopt when they want a favor from a newspaperman, "you see, we British are really in a difficult position. We are trying to strike a balance—steer a neutral course, you might say—between the two sections of the population. We are charged with unfairness by both Jews and Arabs, something that is of course the best possible proof of our impartiality. We are caught between Scylla and Charybdis. We are damned if we do and damned if we don't. What impressions have you gained in Palestine yourself?" he inquired kindly, leaning forward with arched eyebrows.

"A difficult task, no doubt," I admitted. "Britain is charged by the League of Nations to make it possible for the Jews to build their National Home. Some Arabs object and have recourse to violence. That is the way it looks on the surface. But what is harder to understand is that these Arabs believe the government to be on their side, for that was the general battle cry of the rioters in the recent attacks. I do not presume to suggest that the government gave the Arabs carte blanche to try and drive the Jews out, but were the Arab leaders not justified in believing that the Administration itself is, let us say, not wholly in sympathy with the idea of establishing the Jewish National Home here in this corner of the Near East?"

"I do not know what makes you say that," retorted the High Commissioner.

"If the Administration is itself in full sympathy with the realization of the Jewish plan of building a homeland, why does it permit a constant agitation on the part of a few Arabs against the project? The Mufti of Jerusalem openly declares that he cannot guarantee peace in Palestine so long as Britain adheres to the Balfour Declaration. He says that the British authority will have to place a soldier in front of every Jewish home in Palestine and, further, that he is determined to crush Jewish endeavor by a pan-Islamic boycott; in other words, he advocates violence and sabotage of an enterprise which Britain is sponsoring and expected to protect."

"To whom did he say this?"

"To me," I replied.

"Yes, he is alleged to have made a similar declaration to the correspondent of the London *Express*, but when he was questioned by the government, he made a wholesale denial. What can you do with a man like that?"

"Does the Mufti receive a stipend from the government?"

"Yes, as the spiritual head of the Moslem community of Jerusalem."

"That is to say, from money paid in taxes by the Jews?"

"Oh, the Arabs also pay taxes, I assure you!"

"How much would you say?"

"Something like fifteen per cent."

"But the Arabs own ninety-five per cent of the arable land, that is to say, a few Arab families do, amongst them the family of the Husseinis to which the Mufti belongs?"

"Ninety-five per cent, yes, something like that! By the way, you are not a Jew?" asked the High Commissioner.

"No, sir!"

"Then why should you take, eh, such interest in the Jewish side of the question?"

"My dear High Commissioner I am merely trying to understand what is going on in this country. I see menaced by collapse a project which was considered by British statesmen one of the few valuable acquisitions of the Great War. I am trying to discover what is at the bottom of it. I cannot take the Mufti seriously when he says that all Moslem Palestine is with him in his opposition to the Jewish National Home, for this is simply not true. As to the Pan-Islamic character of the Mufti's agitation, that is downright ridiculous. You, Mr. High Commissioner, intimated that the government has reasons to fear a general conflagration in the Mohammedan East in sympathy with the Mufti's ideas. Yet the Mohammedan peoples did not lift a finger when Britain in 1914 went to war with the Turkish Sultan, and he was a great deal more than a Mufti—he was the spiritual head of all Islam."

"If you will inquire in Egypt and Saudi Arabia, I think you will find a widespread sympathy with the Palestinian Arabs," said Mr. Luke.

"I will make an inquiry there," I said. "In the meantime I would very much like you, Mr. Luke, to tell me how I am to explain in my dispatches certain incidents that occurred here recently."

"For instance, what?"

"For instance, the case of Mr. Brozen. Here was an old man with forty years' residence in the Holy Land. He owns a little canning factory near Motza. The other day a band of Arabs from the nearby village of Lifta attacked his house while he was absent. They were bad Arabs, just cutthroats and highway robbers, even in Turkish days. They killed his wife and two daughters. Then they moved onto the factory. Brozen saw them coming, locked the door, and pointed a rifle between the bars of a window. At this the Arabs contented themselves with smashing the machinery in the out-lying buildings and withdrew. But we," I said, speaking as a British subject, "we had Mr. Brozen arrested and I saw him a week ago as he was being brought to Jerusalem in chains, an old man of sixty-five—an enterprising citizen in chains, Mr. Luke, led by British soldiers!"

"Ah, yes, he was arrested on a charge of concealing weapons!"

"Was he? That makes it ten times worse," said I. "The American public will not easily understand that sort of an interpretation of the right of self-defense."

"Oh, that matter is easily settled. I will sign an order for Mr. Brozen's immediate release. Does that satisfy you?"

"I thank you, but I am not satisfied. There is another case. Fifty Jews took refuge in the flour mills of Haifa to defend themselves the other day when attacked by a crowd of two thousand Arabs. Those Jews are in jail today, and the Arabs went free."

"All right, the evidence has been sifted in their case; they, too, will be released tomorrow, I can assure you. We are not unreasonable. Naturally mistakes do occur in a time of stress such as this. What else is there?" He rose to signify that the audience was at an end.

"You speak of accidents," I said. "Will you kindly explain why the Jewish colonies were searched for concealed weapons just a few days before the outbreak of Arab violence?"

"I think you are wrong there," answered the Acting High Commissioner, his voice hardening perceptibly. "No such order was issued by the government."

"There wasn't?" I asked. "Perhaps you will let me tell you then what happened in the colony of Hulda."

"Yes, I would be glad to hear."

"In Hulda the Jews had thirty rifles. They were Lee Enfield rifles—the same type of rifles we used in the Great War. They had been placed there by the government after the rioting in 1921. These rifles were kept in a tin box called an armory. Every month an inspector from the military department in Jerusalem came to Hulda and to all the other colonies which had such an armory to look over the rifles. The inspector would go to the headman of the colony and ask him for the key of the armory. Together they would inspect the rifles, hold them up to the light to see that the barrels were clean, verify the locks, and then put them back in the box.

"In the month of June, 1929, the government's inspector came on his usual monthly visit to Hulda and told the headman of the colony: 'I have orders to take these rifles away.'

" 'Why,' asked the Jew. 'Did we ever misuse them?'

" 'No, I do not think you ever took them out of the box except on the occasions when I came here to inspect them,' replied the inspector, 'but it is a general rule. All these armories are to be called in.'

" 'But,' stammered the Jew, 'these guns are our only guarantee of security. The Arabs in the neighboring villages know of their presence. If they get to know that the guns are gone, we will be in danger. No! I will not give up these rifles without a written order from the chief of the military department in Jerusalem.'

"The inspector shrugged his shoulders. But on his next visit, sir, he had the written order from the government, signed by the chief inspector of His Majesty's military forces in Palestine.

" 'If you must take away what is our only protection,' said the Jew to the Englishman, 'please take them away in the night so that the Arabs out there in the surrounding villages will not know they have been removed. Does that sound fair to you?'

" 'Very fair!' said the inspector.

"The next day, Mr. Luke," I continued, "at high noon, an Arab patrol was sent with a truck to collect the rifles by the authority of the Palestine government. Nine days later the colony of Hulda was destroyed."

"I am amazed to hear this," said the High Commissioner. "Where did you learn all this?"

"In Hulda from the headman of the colony!"

"I promise you that I will investigate the matter at once. I am very sorry for the colony of Hulda. I was there once. It seemed a very happy little place."

"It is in ashes today, and the colonists have abandoned it after burying their dead."

"You will realize now how difficult it is for us," said Mr. Luke, as he led me to the door, "to maintain a balance between Jews and Arabs."

"But are we really supposed to maintain a neutral position?" I asked. "Whatever your personal opinion of the Jews may be, you cannot deny that the mandate imposes a duty on the British authority to facilitate the building of a Jewish National Home in Palestine. Not build the Jewish National Home—the Jews are doing that themselves—but protect them and aid them in their task. You cannot deny either that the Jews here in Palestine represent the progressive element, that they are in a sense the bearers of Western civilization. How can we strike a balance between civilization and barbarism? How is that done? Aren't we already out of balance the moment we compromise with barbarism?"

"It is undeniable, of course, that Jewish culture is superior to that of the Palestinian Arabs," said Mr. Luke. "But the law does not make a distinction between the races. By following any other procedure than that which it is following, the government would lay itself open to charges of injustice to the Arabs. We do not intend to do anything contrary to the mandate's terms or the spirit of the Balfour declaration. I deny specifically the charges emanating from the Zionist side that the government has systematically sabotaged Jewish endeavor. Immigration was curtailed, it is true, during the critical years of economic stagnation when the country could not absorb a large influx of newcomers. Our position is clear in this quarrel between Jews and Arabs: we must keep the peace. Don't you agree?"

"It does not look to me, sir," I said in leaving, "that this is fundamentally a quarrel between Jews and Arabs."

8

Between alarms and sporadic outbreaks of violence, which paralyzed certain sections of the country for hours, sometimes for days, I started to visit the Jewish colonies and settlements in the outlying districts in the company of Marek Schwartz. Marek had served in the Austrian army as a captain of artillery during the Great War. He had been detailed for service with the Turks in the campaign against the British under Fahkri Pasha, the butcher of the Armenians, and had taken part in the retreat from Medina. He had been left in charge of a sacrifice unit of artillery when Jemal Pasha, the Turkish commander in chief, had been forced to abandon the Holy City to General Allenby, with instructions to "blow Jerusalem to hell" the moment the British should enter. On the personal orders of Jamal Pasha, Schwartz had his batteries trained on the mosque of Omar, and ammunition lying ready for a forty-eight-hour intensive bombardment. When Jemal left for Megiddo to make his last stand before Damascus, Captain Schwartz, rather than destroy Jerusalem, quietly spiked his own guns and walked into the British lines. He had remained in Palestine after the war and had built up a prosperous business.

When we roared out of the Holy City in his swift roadster he would sometimes look down on the old city where Arabs were killing his Jewish compatriots and wonder if it would not have been better had he buried that hotbed of conspiracy under a mass of ruins, as Sarrail had done in Damascus at the time of the Druse revolt. . . .

We found work going on normally in the colonies. The Arabs had only attacked places where they knew that no or little resistance could be offered, for instance in Talpiot, a residential suburb of Jerusalem, where many of the professors of the Hebrew University lived. I stood in the deserted study of Professor Joseph Klausner, the author of a scholarly work on the Jewish background of Christ's ministry. The Arab hoodlums had pillaged the house, and all the neighboring houses. They had started a fire with the books. British soldiers with fixed bayonets walked between the blackened ruins.

Farther north we saw the synagogue of Safed in Galilee where the old Jews like those of Hebron, had been slaughtered while they were at prayer. But in the colonies of the Zionists with their population of young people, the Mufti's henchmen had not dared set foot. The little colony of Gedara had taught them that it was expensive business to attack the Zionists. Eighteen times in the course of one night they had hurled themselves against Gedara in a mass assault. When morning came two hundred Arabs dead lay before the stockade while just one Jew had been wounded. The day Schwartz and I visited the colony a British military patrol was examining the damage and looking for the rifles with which the Jews had defended themselves!

In the neighborhood of the Dead Sea, where the first plants for the extraction of potash were under construction, thousands of Arabs from Trans-Jordan hovered in the neighborhood, apparently waiting for an opportune moment to pounce on the works. At nights the workers went aboard the barges and rowed out to the middle of the lake. Only two or three watchmen remained behind. Had the Arabs ventured within the camp enclosure, they would have been blown sky-high, for every building was stocked with dynamite. Schwartz and I spent two nights sitting in a boat waiting for the attack that never came.

The friend, who was to have been our companion on these trips, Dr. Wolfgang von Weisl, the correspondent of the *Vossische Zeitung* of Berlin, had been stabbed in the back by an Arab in the streets of Jerusalem and lay dangerously ill in the Rothschild Hospital. One of our drivers had his arm ripped open by a bullet in an ambush on the Bethlehem road. For the rest, with the exception of a fusillade near Lifta, where our car was riddled with shots, we came through without mishap.

The Zionist colonization work in Palestine was distinguished from all other enterprises of a similar character in the world by the daring nature and the great freedom of its social and economic experiments. Man may make his choice of half a dozen different socialistic and co-operative formulas before entering an established colony or founding a new settlement. The simplicity of communal organization in some of the *kevutzoth*, like that of Tel Yosef, for instance, which is part of the vast socialistic agricultural canton of Ain Harod in the valley of Esdraelon, made me think of the primitive Christianity mentioned in the Acts of the Apostles and of that sect of the Essenes of which Philo wrote that its members eschewed all trade and commerce, refused to manufacture any article that could be made useful for purposes of war, and whose social life was based on human co-operation, mutual aid and confidence. In Tel Yosef the use of money was even unknown in the interior work of the colony. The village was organized like a religious community. Every collective undertaking by the colonists was determined by a general council of all the members who had an equal voice in the assembly. Men and women were subject to a self-imposed, freely established discipline, not the Potsdam or the Henry Ford kind.

A mile to the west of Tel Yosef was the purely Socialist colony of Kfar-Yezekiel, where everyone owned his implements but where the work in the field was carried out co-operatively. Beth Alpha, in the same general group of Ain Harod, was a collectivist village of still a different type.

The central village, Ain Harod, which gives its name to the canton, is the largest single socialistic agricultural experiment carried on in Palestine. In 1929 Ain Harod was already entirely self-sustaining and self-sufficient. It possessed a small canning plant, a shoe factory, a brick factory, a communal bakery and a clothing factory. The Habima, the national Hebrew theater, a group of the most talented artists in the world, formerly of Moscow and Paris, and now established in Tel Aviv, gave regular performances in the communal halls of those colonies in Esdraelon, where lecture courses on every conceivable subject in the world were currently given. But the diversity and variety in communal structure which were still increased by colonies operated on a capitalist basis and others run on purely orthodox religious lines constituted no obstacle to the single purpose and unity of the Zionist enterprise to reconstitute Jewish life on a national basis and give it a national scope.

Life in those colonies interested me more than Tel Aviv, Haifa and Jerusalem. The attraction resided in the fact that the all-Jewish city of Tel Aviv, clean and white as it was, was a purely bourgeois creation with many of capitalism's evils transplanted to the new land. In those rural communes, however, tens of thousands of men and women were making a new approach to life. In those *kevutzoth* (collective farms) there was no exploitation of one man by another. There was no private property. Man and woman were perfectly equal. Children were brought up and educated by the community. No manager or owner drove the pioneers to work. Labor had acquired an entirely new meaning. Nobody desired to accumulate riches for himself. The only pity of it was that those *kevutzoth* were but small islands of Socialism in a capitalist sea, advance posts of the new life in an alien world and as such they made me think of Vienna, at that time also a precarious advance post of Socialism.

It was on the whole amazing, too, how little the colonists talked or seemed to care about the disturbances. The excitement about the Arab attack was all in the coffeehouses and night clubs of Tel Aviv and New York. In the colonies the Arab attack was taken almost as a matter of course. Life went on. A comrade had fallen here, another one over there. Yes, it was a bitter struggle. But something fine and good was being built. Sacrifices were necessary, but the work could not be interrupted.

Tourists seldom visited those Socialist colonies, Christian pilgrimages to the Holy Land not at all. The pilgrims, of whom there are still thousands going to the Holy Land each year in spite of Russia's elimination from the pious traffic, spend a few days around the holy places: Nazareth, Bethany, Bethlehem, Emmaus. They never bother to look at one of the most modernistic colonization schemes in the world. And this is not merely indifference. Many of the leaders of pilgrimages, whether from France, Belgium, Ireland, Germany or Poland, I met on boats coming from or going to the Holy Land on my annual visits to Palestine were deeply indignant over the fact that Jews were fishing in the Lake of Tiberias, for instance, or that a dairy farm had been laid out or a hydroelectric station put up near some spot where Christ once lingered. Galilee, in their idea, should have remained as it was, undisturbed and poetic, as in the days when the Lord walked on earth. With their perverted sense of sacredness, which they always associated with the past, they considered the development work in Palestine nothing less than desecration. Strange as it may seem, this attitude need not cause any astonishment, for Christianity itself has to many Christians become something that is linked with and belongs exclusively to the past. As soon as something new or strange appears, they are filled with fear and trembling in its presence. The future frightens them and they clamp themselves anxiously to the past, because they know it or think they know it.

Jewish reticence on the socialistic and idealistic aspects of the new life in Palestine had another source: it was also fear. Fear that the world would find out that something really different than the

Bronx or Temple Emanu-El was being attempted in Palestine. The emancipated Jews of America—as the Jews of Germany before them—who considered themselves the elite of Judaism, that is to say those who had carved themselves a place in American life, occupying prominent positions, owning property and wealth, imagined that they collaborated in the defense and in the regeneration of Judaism by building hospitals and concert halls, endowing universities and by seeking to impress the non-Jewish world in general with the fact that but a slight confessional difference separates them from their non-Jewish fellow citizens. When other Jews thereupon went to Palestine or talked about the Jewish Land, *Eretz Israel,* and worked for the building in Palestine of a civilization that is distinctly Hebraic, with a different basis than ruthless competition and greed, this has a disturbing effect on the peace of mind of those whom Zangwill called the grand dukes of Judaism.

In reality these Jews, who pride themselves on their American, German, French or Brazilian patriotism, who are everywhere *plus royaliste que le roi,* are the worst enemies of an emerging civilization in the countries in which they dwell, no matter how often they call themselves, in distinction to the Zionists, "Jews who are Americans," or "Jews who are first Frenchmen and Jews afterwards." They withhold the distinctive contribution they as Jews could make toward the sum total of American or French civilization. They play down their Jewishness and do not seem to realize that the world must despise whatever does not esteem itself. Had the Jewish masses accepted *their* leadership, instead of developing what is richest and strongest in their native and inborn tendencies, we would have even more quaking, psychologically sick, and valet-minded Jews in our midst, the French poet, André Spire, once said.

When this type of Jewish bourgeois consents to visit Palestine—for in the end they all come (the work in Palestine having assumed proportions of which every Jew in the world may be proud), he prefers to sit in the boardwalk cafés of Tel Aviv and discuss the fall and rise of real estate, the performances of the Habima Theater and the latest developments of the Arab question. Their highest ambition is to be asked to a party of tennis on some Englishman's lawn. Of what goes on in the colonies they want to hear as little as possible. They don't want to know because someone is bound to ask some such question as to whether or not it isn't really all the same as Bolshevism over there in the colonies: women owned in common and children not even knowing their parents, and red flags flying from the granaries and factories.

Obviously the pioneers are not saints. Many have thrown the old ritualistic traditions of their people overboard, even as millions of workers in other countries who see in Christianity a power of the past, bound up with reaction and conservatism. And yet fundamentally there was, at least to my way of thinking, a deep ethico-religious basis in the striving of these *Chalutizim* for a share in all the intellectual and material products of culture, including manual labor. Theirs was not the religion of the "Lord, Lord" sayers, to be sure, but that of the doers of God's will.

However, in contrast to the most modern agricultural and industrial advance, there still remained a good many Jews of the old school in Palestine. Pious and *gesetzgetreu*, they lived lives of study and meditation over Torah and Talmud, in the never-wearying expectation of a personal Messiah.

As I alighted from my car one evening, shaking the dust off my feet in front of the Hotel Amdursky in Jerusalem after a sizzlingly hot trip from Galilee, the proprietor of the establishment, an old man with a beard like Aaron's, who was enjoying the cool of evening on the porch with some fellow patriarchs, walked up to me swiftly and, taking me aside with a great ado of mystery, whispered in my ear, "There are a couple of Jews waiting to see you."

"What? A couple of Jews in Jerusalem? Surely that is nothing to get excited about."

"Wait till you see this delegation and you will change your opinion!" he assured me.

"Where are they?"

"In the parlor on the first floor. They have been waiting since eleven o'clock this morning. They say they must see you on a most urgent matter." He chuckled and nodded his head meaningfully as he stumbled up the stairs in his embroidered slippers to announce my arrival. We followed the proprietor to the parlor, Marek Schwartz and I.

Two men rose from the red plush divan as we entered the room. They came forward, bowing several times in grave salutation: "*Shalom!* Peace upon you!" One was a youth with a coal-black beard and hollow cheeks. He had the largest pair of eyes I ever saw in a human being, except the Negus of Ethiopia—the kind of eyes

Max Band likes to paint: shimmering pools of jet with a flame in the pupils. I noticed that he kept his hands in the sleeves of his violet caftan like a Chinese mandarin.

His companion was an old man who leaned on a stick and whose beard almost came down to his waist. Both wore the fuzzy bonnets which the Chasidim have brought with them from Carpatho-Russia: those strange contraptions of yellow bushy fur which seemed the most incongruous headgear a man could possibly wear in the blistering heat of a Judean summer.

"Please be seated, Father," Marek Schwartz, who was to serve as interpreter, said in Hebrew.

The old man looked at him reproachfully. "We do not use the holy language in daily life," he said. "We are not Zionists!"

"That makes it easier, for then we'll all speak Yiddish," I interrupted.

"Kabbalists," whispered Marek.

"What can I do for you, sir?" I asked, when the old man refused a glass of tea, although he must have been starving. He signified his intention to remain standing during the interview.

"Are you Mr. van Paassen?" he began.

"That is my name."

"You are a friend of the Jewish people?"

"I don't like the expression, Master," I said. "Has anyone ever heard of a friend of the Bulgarian people or of a friend of Albania. There is too often an element of condescension in that term."

"You have spoken well," he answered. "But you are nevertheless a friend. Were you not instrumental in having some Jews set free from jail?"

"I may have had something to do with that."

"You are a friend of Israel then. We cannot repay you for your services."

"Oh, that is all right, Father. I have done nothing—I only wish I could . . ."

"The Eternal One, blessed be He, will himself reward you. It is said: the holy ones amongst the Gentiles . . ."

"Please, Master, do not include me in their company. I assure you I am not worthy."

"You are in a position to do something for Israel," he resumed after a pause.

"I would be most happy to do that," I said.

"It may be difficult for you, for I do not know your circumstances," he went on. "But we think you can be of immense service to us Jews here in Palestine and to all the world. You must leave the Holy Land at once!"

"Leave Palestine? At once?" I gasped in amazement. "How can I be of the slightest service to you if I leave this country. Do you mean that I should go to England or Geneva and relate the plight of the Jews?"

The old man made a gesture of annoyance. "God forbid!" he said, throwing up his hands. "That would be worse than remaining here."

"Then what is it?"

"You see, it is this way," he said, moving a little closer and talking with great earnestness. "We are Kabbalists. We have a holy book called Zoar, the book of light. Now there is a prophecy in that book which has bearing on this very time we are living. The prophecy says that there will come a day when three rabbis will be slain in a city of the south."

"Yes?"

"Three rabbis have just been slain in Hebron, and Hebron is a city of the south, is it not?"

He came still closer until our faces were but a few inches apart.

"Now, in the book of Zoar it is further said that seven times seven weeks after the slaying of these *Rabonim*, Messiah will come."

"Yes?"

"But in the interval the Jews must suffer and suffer as they have never suffered before. They must suffer till their cries of pain are heard in heaven, till the Eternal One, blessed be He, takes pity on them."

He paused a moment and looked at me appealingly. "Don't you see," he said, "what you are doing? If you seek to alleviate Jewish suffering, you may succeed. But if you succeed, you delay the coming of Messiah. You see? Won't you please go away, leave this country so that you will not be tempted to help the Jews. The best way to help the Jewish people is to let them suffer. You would not stand in the way of Messiah, would you?"

"God forbid!" I said in turn. "I promise you to leave in a few days!"

The young man kissed my hands in gratitude.

9

By a freak of circumstances I was the only correspondent whose reports and observations on the disturbances in Palestine were published in Jerusalem itself. They were relayed from New York to London, whence a syndicate distributed them to its member papers in Europe and Asia, of which *The Palestine Post* of Jerusalem was one. Every word I wrote therefore could be scrutinized daily by Arabs, Jews and British alike. This put me in a most embarrassing situation, for not a day passed without an attack being launched against me, either in the Arab press, or in a section of the Jewish press. The British authorities set a watch over me to check up on my every movement. This was not difficult since they controlled the telegraph service, and I was in the habit of cabling at the close of every dispatch what I intended to do the next day.

In various governmental communiqués an attempt was made to minimize the importance of my dispatches: the conversation with Mr. Luke had not been a formal interview, but a mere social chat. Moreover, I had placed the wrong emphasis on the words of the chief of the government. Of my visit to the Mufti's chambers it was said that I had expressed a fear of assassination at the hands of the Jews and I had asked the Mufti outright for a bodyguard to take me back to my hotel. On top of that the rumor was publicized that I was an inveterate French-Canadian nationalist who was out to damage Britain's reputation. All this left me quite unperturbed, although I was embarrassed with the importance people attached to my personal views. I began to shun public places, not out of a motive of fear, but because I noticed I became the object of everybody's attention the moment I was recognized. There were disagreeable incidents, too. One day a British tommy, stationed in front of the post office, with a blow of his rifle broke the arm of an Arab who rushed me with a long knife as I emerged from the building. I was glad to accept the gracious hospitality of Lia Rosen, Marek Schwartz's wife, who had given up her distinguished artistic career with the Reinhardt Ensemble in Berlin and Vienna to come to live in Palestine. At her home, overlooking the Mediterranean shore, I spent my remaining days in Palestine in the company of a small group of friends.

However, I still attended the journalistic conferences in Jerusalem where Gershon Agronsky came to express the official Zionist interpretation of events and someone else the Arab view. I began to notice that whenever I entered the conference room a significant silence rushed in. Some of my English colleagues walked out when I entered. One man accused me of having taken sides in the quarrel between Jews and Arabs and declared that I injured the cause of England. I argued that since I believed the Jews absolutely innocent there was no reason in the world why they should not be defended. Others took my side. John Gunther, who had come from Vienna for *The Chicago Daily News*, was the most sympathetic.

In the meantime, *Falastine*, the official organ of the Mufti's party, returned to the charge of Zionist gold having been more persuasive in my case than the righteousness of the Arab cause. Some of my fellow newspapermen began to hint that the allegation was probably not without foundation. It was the old question of *calumniez, calumniez toujours*—fling as much mud as possible, some of it is bound to stick. I received an unsigned typewritten note saying: "Jew-bastard clear out!"

More serious was the threat of a government's emissary who came to tell me that although no interview of mine with European statesmen had ever been repudiated, every word of mine would henceforth be refuted if I continued what he called "my hostility to Britain." In that moment I regretted that I was no longer a Dutch national. I literally boiled over. Another Dutchman, Dr. van Rees, did let loose a couple of months later, and then in a manner that made even the British Foreign Secretary squirm. In a full session of the Permanent Mandates' Commission of the League in Geneva he calmly reviewed Britain's "sinister role" in playing with the holiest ideals of a people. That was the very thing which had exasperated me. I could not bear that sanctimonious prattle about fair play and the impartiality of the law in the presence of bloodshed. Perhaps it was not becoming in me to have stated it as bluntly as I did, but that was perhaps "the dark and mysterious blood of Flanders" in me. I could not have kept silent even if I had tried. Like every son of Thyl Uilenspiegel's land, I carry on my heart the ashes of Klaes. They knocked on my breast when that dressed-up pantomime doll, known as the Mufti, justified the mass murder of those humble souls in Hebron. They knocked again when Harry C. Luke smirkingly talked of striking a balance between barbarism and civilization. And they fairly thundered when in the end an Anglican clergyman, of the Bishop of Jerusalem's staff, in a last attempt to convert me to "objectivity," came to tell me that all the suffering of the Jews was but a rightful punishment for the crucifixion of Jesus. . . .

10

In the second half of the sixteenth century the Spanish armies occupied Holland and Flanders and the glare of the Inquisition's autos-da-fé lit up the market squares of the cities great and small. After a long vigil in prayer, the silent man with the cruel eyes in the Escorial had decreed the extermination of the new religion in the Netherlands. In less than a decade there perished by his will in the torture chambers, on the gallows and on the pyres two hundred and fifty thousand men and women of the Dutch race. Nobles and burghers, old and young, rich and poor, all were dragged from their homes, frequently on secret denunciation, to face the Grand Inquisitor—the monk Titelman—and his helpers, who knew no mercy. From Amsterdam to Lille and from Maastricht to Ypres the bells were tolling for the dead each morning and a procession of priests, halberdiers and archers could be seen conducting the heretics to the place of execution. Before the victims were at the stake, their skin was cut off their feet so that they could not run away, and their tongues were pulled out or twisted into a knot so that they could not blaspheme God and his Son in the midst of the flames. Then the torch was applied to the faggots and the priests sang:

> Si de coelo descenderes
> O sancta Maria

When the first wisps of smoke rose from the stake, the tambours rolled their drums and from the towers came the deep clangor of the Borgstorm, the heavy bell which is usually rung when the country is in danger of invasion. Upon hearing its mournful sound the citizens would close their doors and windows to shut out the cries of pain and anguish of the men and women burning in the square and the sickening smell of cooking flesh that drifted through the streets with the acrid odor of smoldering wood.

And the Spanish King inherited the goods of the executed heretics.

One morning the gendarmes halted before the door of the cottage inhabited by Klaes, the charcoal burner, and Soetken, his wife, in the town of Damme in Flanders. They took him away. Klaes had inherited a thousand ducats through the death of his brother in Liége, but he had also laughed at the vendors of indulgences on the steps of Notre Dame.

Titelman had him tortured with the aid of candles that burnt the hair off his head and arms. But Klaes looking on his son Thyl and his wife Soetken, who were held to witness his sufferings, did not utter a sound. He spoke but once. That was when the tribunal sitting under the four sacred oak trees sentenced him to the flames: "May storm and drought," said he, "blast these trees from the free land of Flanders for having witnessed in their shade the condemnation of a free conscience!"

Klaes was burnt by slow fire in the market square of Damme on the first day of the month of Our Lady as the bells of Notre Dame tolled for the dead. Soetken could not see her husband twist his body in pain, for a white cloud of smoke enveloped the martyr. But she heard a great cry above the tolling of the bells and above the chant of the clerics when the flames suddenly leaped to his throat: "Soetken! Thyl!"

That was the end. The consumed wood crumbled into a heap of ashes at the foot of the stake, but the charred body of Klaes remained suspended by the neck.

In the night that followed Soetken took her son by the arm and led him through the silent streets to the Grande Place. Crows were sitting on the dead man's shoulders feeding on his burned flesh. Thyl wanted to chase the evil birds from his father's body, but the sergeant of the guard prevented him.

Then said Soetken to the guard: "Messire Sergeant, this is the orphaned son of him who hangs there and I am his widow. We would kiss his dear face and gather some ashes to preserve his memory. Give us permission, Messire, you who are not a foreign mercenary but a son of this land."

And the sergeant consented.

Then Soetken and Thyl walked over the burnt wood and came to the body and they touched the face of their husband and father.

But Soetken took from the region of the heart, where the flames had seared a deep hole in the body, some ashes. And she knelt down with the orphan and prayed for the peace of her man's soul.

When the first pale streaks of dawn came they still lingered, and the sergeant bade them begone in fear of a reprimand for having shown good will to the family of a heretic.

And coming home Soetken took a piece of red silk and a piece of black silk and she made a sachet of them. She sewed two strings to the ends and placed the ashes in the sachet and fastened it around Thyl's neck and she said: "My son these ashes are the heart of Flanders. The red is my man's blood and the black is our mourning. I place these ashes on your heart and on the heart of every son of these Netherlands in all eternity. And whenever or wherever in this world there is an injustice or a wrong committed these ashes will beat on your heart. And you will speak out without fear, even at the danger of death, for all those who are reviled and oppressed for their conscience' sake."

And Thyl said: "It will be so."

And the widow embraced the orphan and the sun rose.

II

One would have expected Cairo, capital city of the most progressive Arab state, to be the logical fountainhead of Pan-Arabism because it is unquestionably the spiritual center of Islam since Kemal Pasha's abolition of the khalifate. Its great school of Koranic learning, Al-Hazar University, in addition to training tens of thousands of muftis and ulemas, for the far-flung communities of the Mohammedan world, from India to Morocco, is also the supreme tribunal of Koranic law and philosophy with a decisive voice in all the doctrinal disputes that arise each year in countries as far apart as Java and Persia, Palestine and Indo-China. But Egypt had, on the whole, maintained a stolid indifference towards events in Palestine, and this in spite of the Jerusalem Mufti's personal attempts to enlist the support of the Mohammedan clergy and the Egyptian intellectuals in his anti-Jewish campaign. The Mufti had given me to understand that the Egyptian government was seriously perturbed, and the British High Commissioner in that country even more, about the agitation in Palestine. There had been mass demonstrations in Alexandria, Cairo and Port Said, he said, when the news reached there of "the slaughter of Arabs by Jews." He had himself inaugurated a campaign to raise money in Egypt "for the relief of the victims of Jewish terror."

This campaign, I learned upon arrival in Cairo, had taken the form of distributing tens of thousands of the well-known forged photographs showing the mosque of Omar in Jerusalem a pile of blackened ruins. The inscription on these pictures brazenly announced that the second holiest shrine in Islam had been bombed to pieces by the Jews. Pamphlets also had been scattered in the Egyptian bazaars setting forth in detail Professor Einstein's and Lord Melchett's plan to rebuild the Hebrew Temple on the site of the Moslem sanctuary now destroyed by Jewish vandals. But the acme of deceit was no doubt the publication of a photograph of the wrecked Jewish theological seminary in Hebron, showing the bodies of the slain students lying in the foreground and capped with a heading saying that this was what the Jews had done to an Arab home and its inhabitants in Jerusalem.

When I showed my own photographs of that scene to the editors of the different Arabic newspapers in Cairo, these gentlemen immediately took action to refute the Mufti's faked pictures and its intents and purposes. The Egyptian Gazette of Cairo, a newspaper subsidized by the British intelligence service, indignantly pounced on me and asked in an editorial if "this troublemaker who has just been shown the door in Palestine should be permitted to carry on his subversive activity from Egypt."

This led to an invitation from the editor of the most important newspaper in the French language in the Near East, La Bourse Egyptienne, to write a series of articles on what had happened in Palestine. It was also the beginning of my regular collaboration on that journal, for which I subsequently reported the campaign in Ethiopia. In the second place I was honored with a reception at the home of the Sheik-President of Al-Hazar University who had called in the ulemas and the teachers of that famous institution of Koranic learning to hear, as he said, a firsthand account of what had taken place in the Holy Land.

Giving an exposé of the Palestinian situation in the French language before a group of Arabic religious notables was one of the most difficult jobs I ever undertook. When I called in the evening at the Sheik's house in one of the fashionable suburbs of Cairo, in the company of an Arab interpreter, who was a journalist attached to the staff of a newspaper published by Dr. Moissieri in Cairo, the reception room was crowded with the most distinguished scholars and theologians in Islam. We sat in silence, our legs crossed Arab-fashion on low divans arranged in a square along the walls, which were, in that orthodox Moslem home, devoid of the least adornment. Servants passed cigarettes, and we had several cups of coffee in silence before our host came downstairs from his harem and introduced me to the other guests of the evening. The Sheik-President himself was a man of striking appearance, slender and tall, with a carefully groomed coal-black beard and features that seemed chiseled from yellow marble. He was dressed in a spotlessly white burnous with a hood laying in ample folds around his neck and shoulders. From time to time his pitch-black eyes narrowed to glimmering slits as he looked at me through the smoke of his perfumed cigarette. But his voice was a pleasant melodious basso which rose to a high-pitched Semitic vehemence when, in the course of the evening, he expressed his contempt for the Jerusalem Mufti's claims to being a descendant of Fatima, Mohammed's daughter.

What I said to that assembly is immaterial. The Sheik-President's views on some phases of the Palestinian situation are, however, of a certain value. For instance, when in the course of my causerie I referred to Ai Hameen Husseini as the " 'Grand' Mufti" of Jerusalem and as "His Eminence," all those who understood French burst into laughter. When the merriment had somewhat subsided and the President noticed my astonishment, he remarked kindly that there were no "grand" muftis or "eminences" in Islam.

"Before Allah all men are equal, and it does not behoove a religious teacher," said he, "to assume such redundant titles."

"But," I objected, "perhaps the illustrious descent of the dignitary in Jerusalem entitles him to more respect than is accorded an ordinary Koranic exhorter."

"What illustrious descent?" rapped out the Sheik-President in Arabic.

"I was told," I said "that the Mufti of Jerusalem is a direct lineal descendant of Fatima, granddaughter of the Prophet."

I got no further: the Sheik jumped to his feet, and flung his amber prayer beads on the rug at his feet. His face impassive the moment before, was now distorted with anger.

"Son of the Prophet, he, Ai Hameen Husseini of Jerusalem? A son of Satan, that is what I call him for making such a statement!" The man's eyes shot out sparks and, turning to the ulemas, he broke into a crackling gutteral speech, rasping out the sentences in rapid, grating sounds.

Suddenly he calmed down and addressing me, he said, "The Mufti of Jerusalem has no right to make such assertions. There are ten thousand descendants of Fatima in Arabia and their names are known, but they do not bear titles to distinguish them from ordinary Moslems. That would mean a sort of spiritual aristocracy. There is no room in Islam for such things. With regard to the suggestion of a restoration of the khalifate in Jerusalem," he continued, "what the Mufti's cousin told you is a vile abomination. I am shocked beyond words."

"But who and what is he then, this Mufti?" I asked.

"A mufti," came the reply, "is a teacher in Islam. The man of whom you speak is not really a mufti, for he has not finished a single course of studies here at the University. He owes his appointment to political influences and family connections. He is a younger son of a family which owns extensive estates both in Palestine and in Syria. He is a politician."

"Yes, that is obvious," I assented, and then cautiously I asked the question that I wanted answered more than anything else: "Would it be correct to say that in the political controversy in which the Mufti was engaged with the Jews, the religious chiefs of Al-Hazar University supported him and that he could count on the sympathies of the Egyptian people?"

A long whispered conversation with the ulemas followed this question. At the end the Sheik-President dictated the following statement to my interpreter: "When the Mufti of Jerusalem expounds a sura from the Koran to the Believers in Jerusalem and he does it in orthodox manner, all Islam is at heart with him. For the Koran is the truth, infallible and eternal. But when the same man seeks to create the impression that we in Egypt are interested in the petty political issues of his insignificant parish of Jerusalem, he is mistaken. We are not interested in his quarrel with the Jews. We know perfectly well that the Jews have no designs on the mosque, but that they have very different ambitions in Palestine. They want to reconstitute their national life. That is a legitimate aspiration. We, too, here in Egypt want to rebuild an Egyptian culture. We are Egyptians first. We have nothing in common with Pan-Arabism. Its aims are absolutely outside the sphere of our national interests. . . ."

12

Although the interviews with the chief of the Palestine Administration and with the Jerusalem Mufti go back to the year 1929, I have reproduced them here chiefly because of their intrinsic value as reflections of a fundamental attitude on the part of two out of three of the contending forces in a conflict that, instead of diminishing with the passage of time, has grown steadily more acute until, in less than a decade, the violence unleashed by the Mufti, who fled abroad in 1937 but who in the meantime had acquired the precious support of the world's two chief troublemakers, Hitler and Mussolini, had put the whole enterprise of Zion's redemption in jeopardy. My own concern with the building of the Jewish National Home in Palestine did not cease with my return to France in October, 1929. On the contrary, it deepened as I returned again and again to the Holy Land to see with my own eyes the progress of that most significant undertaking in a land which is sacred to all Christians and where Jews, even through blood and tears, were engaged in translating into reality the precepts of Christ by the practice of justice and compassion in their relationships with their fellows.

In 1929 I had come to feel—for I am more often led by the heart's inclinations than by reasons of cold logic—that there was more at issue in Palestine than the failure or success of a mere scheme for the resettlement and rehabilitation of a number of hard-pressed European Jews. I felt that here was something intimately linked with the fate and destiny of the entire Jewish people.

What grieved me most was not the Arabic opposition to the Zionist enterprise—I understood the Mufti's motives thoroughly—but the fact that the insinuations of the oily-tongued spokesman of the Arabic feudal order were being accepted at their face value by certain of my journalistic colleagues—men who subsequently cried out their indignation in books, not over the slaughter of Jewish scholars and little Jewish children, the wanton destruction of agricultural colonies, the uprooting of eucalyptus forests and the general terrorism of bands of savage hoodlums directed against an essentially peaceful community, but over the "injustice" of Zionism's indirect interference with the absolute hegemony of a small group of Arabic landlords who kept their mass of destitute peasants on a level comparable only with that of chattel slaves and just a little above that of the beasts of the field.

That the Zionists had made clinics available for the healing of the Arabs' diseases, that the Jewish laboratories had prepared serums for the improvement of the miserable breed of native cattle, that their agricultural experimental stations had heightened the quality of Arab wheat and barley and citrus fruit, that the Jews had supplanted the straggling goat paths of the past with a system of modern roads, that hydroelectric stations had been installed by Jewish capital and initiative for the comfort and betterment of all, that the swamps which annually claimed thousands of Arab lives had been cleaned up at an immense cost of money and of young Jewish lives, that innumerable wells had been dug by Jews in that land which had become parched and barren through centuries of Arab neglect and suicidal deforestation, that on top of that not a single Arab had been asked to contribute as much as one cent or make the least sacrifice for the work that had led in the first place to his own betterment—all that was considered a mere bagatelle which did not compare to the mental sufferings of the handful of feudal Arab nobles who had suddenly discovered that they wanted self-determination and democratic freedom for the Arabic people.

For having set in motion what I consider the greatest single instance of practical Christian endeavor in modern times, the Zionists were denounced as usurpers who schemed to drive the Arabs out of house and home. One man made it appear, on the erratic testimony of an excited Jewish girl, that the Zionists had secretly planned, or at least had consciously contributed to, what was unquestionably an Arab attack. Another sought to justify the fears expressed by Ai Hameen Hussein and his dagger-toting cousin concerning a Jewish attempt to establish a land monopoly, without mentioning the fact that these two members of one of the feudal families which own five sixths of the soil of Palestine were personally selling large tracts of land at the back door of the Jewish land purchasing agency when the disturbances were at their height. Still others argued and went on arguing for years, without ever producing or looking up an official document, that the establishment of the Jewish National

Home in Palestine constitutes a breach of promise made to the Arabs, in the course of the war by Britain, to the effect that the Holy Land was to be included in some sort of confederacy of independent Arab states in an eventual postwar settlement.

There were indeed different agreements drawn up in the course of the Great War among France, Britain and even Russia for the ultimate arrangement of affairs in the Near East, but Palestine was neither included in the scheme for an Arabic confederacy which never materialized nor was it ever officially mentioned as one in a set of independent Arab states that were to replace the Ottoman Empire after the war. And this in the first place because the Vatican would never have acquiesced in leaving the Christian holy places in charge of a purely Arabic state. Under the terms of the Sykes-Picot treaty of the autumn of 1915, which provisionally divided Arabia into spheres of French and British interest, or in the earlier arrangement of the spring of 1915 in which Russia was a partner, the Holy Land was in each case considered as something quite apart. The Arab princes, it should be noted, had not protested by as much as a word against the exclusion of Palestine from any of the schemes envisaged by the great powers for the settlement of Arabia's postwar status. King Feisal, the chief spokesman of the Arabs at the Peace Conference, welcomed the idea of a Jewish National Home in Palestine, and although the Mufti and his friends for years drew great comfort from the unpublished correspondence between General McMahon, the British chief of Staff in Egypt and the Sherif of Mecca on the subject of Arabic participation in the war on the side of the Allies, that bubble was finally pricked, too, by the General himself when he published a letter in the London *Times* in 1937 wherein he declared that he had never discussed the future status of Palestine with the Sherif.

The truth is that the Palestinian Arabs did not play the slightest role in Turkish days. They did not side with the Allies in the war, any more than Ibn Saud. Before the Zionist era, Palestine was a wilderness as Trans-Jordan is today. Only with the coming of the Jews did the Palestinian effendi class begin to realize that it would ultimately have to relinquish its stranglehold on the Arab peasants. Only then did the representatives of that class give to their anti-Zionist opposition the cachet of a nationalist movement. The Arab landlord class, which disposed of a clique of hangers-on, petty politicians, journalists and coffeehouse intrigants, early recognized the menace to their privileged position in that primitive feudal society if the Jewish enterprise were to develop unchecked. They saw that the transformation of the poverty-stricken share croppers and tenants into a prosperous industrial and agricultural community would inevitably lead to fraternization and amicable co-operation between the Jewish workers and those Arab peasant proletarians whom they had exploited so long for their own exclusive benefit. Such fraternization was to be prevented at all costs. Everything possible was to be done to prevent the Arab masses from discovering that they had a common basis of interest with the Jewish workers. But since nobody could deny that the Jewish influx was highly beneficial and profitable to the Arab fellah, the Arab urban worker, and the small Arab businessman, false issues had to be concocted in order to mislead the illiterate and credulous Arab population. In 1929 the Mufti raised the issue of religion: behind the peaceful behavior of the Jews loomed a sinister design to secure a numerical majority in the country. Once that was attained, the great mosque in Jerusalem was to be replaced with a Hebrew sanctuary. For months this myth was assiduously disseminated throughout Moslem religious circles all over the country until, with the incident of a small group of Jewish boy scouts in August, 1929, the attack was launched.

Seven years later, when not even the most backward Arab could have been aroused with an appeal to his religious fanaticism, not even with the aid of forged photographs showing the mosque lying in ruins, the Mufti raised the cry that the Jews were crowding the Arab off the land with the intention of pushing him into the sea. That for every Jew who had come to settle in Palestine, no less than five Arabs had entered, and that neighboring Trans-Jordan had virtually emptied so that the Emir Abdullah complained that he was fast becoming a king without subjects; that vast numbers of Arabs had been attracted to the Jewish-created prosperity in Palestine from Syria, Lebanon, Iraq, and from as far away as Italian Libya—these and whatever other benefits the Arabs got from this Jew-created prosperity were scornfully dismissed by the Mufti. The Jew was robbing the fellah of his land. Jewish prosperity had come about at the expense of the Arab peasant. There was not a moment to lose if the Jew was not to enslave the Arab people.

Again the country was plunged into terror and bloodshed, but the Arab landlords, the Mufti's family included, secretly kept on selling land to the Jews, so that if the indignation of the masses could have had any justification, it should have been directed against the very men who were setting them against the Jews. The Jews bought land, it is true, and there was nothing abnormal or illigitimate in that, but they took good care to compensate the poor Arab tenants they found on the estates they took over from the effendis by buying them land elsewhere, often better land, land they could henceforth own outright and not merely work for a grasping owner who collected four fifths of the profits as his share. The Arab Higher Committee, the Mufti's political creation, sent out its bands of terrorists to ravage the land. This campaign of organized violence and destruction, which started in 1936, and which went on almost uninterruptedly for two years, was declared to be a spontaneous emanation of an exasperated Arabic national sentiment. Murderers and bandits who threw bombs into Jewish hospitals and orphan asylums, who killed from ambush and tore up young orange plantations in the night, were elevated to the rank of national heroes. Commentators compared the wave of Arab terrorism in Palestine with the civil-disobedience movement in India, and the criminal Mufti of Jerusalem was put on a level with the holy personality of Gandhi, as if the Mahatma had not always insisted on nonviolence as an essential condition in passive resistance. A section of the British and of the American press began to speak of "an Arabic general strike conducted with an amazing display of discipline." Liberal journals of opinion hinted that no other result could have been expected from the Jewish policy of usurpation in the Holy Land, but it was left to the Communists to utter the weird absurdity that the wave of banditry was "a struggle on the part of the Arab people for full democratic freedom."

When in the course of history has a class of feudalist landlords fought for democracy?

Even so, in the confusion of false slogans and deliberate muddling of the situation, it generally escaped attention abroad that the Arab peasants never for a day interrupted their work on the land and that the so-called general strike was kept going in the cities only by means of a bloody terror and acts of violence, not only against Jews, but chiefly against Arabic citizens. The mass of the fellahin did not participate in the strike. They harvested and threshed, tended their truck gardens and watered the orange groves as if no Higher Arabic Committee existed. Ninety per cent of the Arabic civic and governmental employees refused to join the strike. They continued to draw their salaries from the exchequers, which were full to overflowing since the Jews had started to come into the land.

"Why," asked a correspondent for the *Neue Wege* of Zurich, a man who made an exhaustive inquiry amongst the Arab peasants of Tul Karm, a hotbed of Arab nationalism, "why do you not cease work and join the attack on the Jews?"

"Only the effendis can afford not to work," came the answer. "They live of the labor of others."

Every day the peasants brought their products to market in the cities. It was there that they were set upon, beaten, robbed and often killed by the Mufti's gangsters. This is the simple truth about that "phenomenal explosion of Arabic nationalist sentiment," which filled the British press with amazement. The Arabic village was subjected to a constant bombardment of anti-Jewish propaganda. The local muftis, following the lead of their spiritual leader in Jerusalem, Friday upon Friday delivered the most inflammatory harangues in the Mosques and still the fellah refused to budge. In the end paid terrorists and gangsters from neighboring countries had to be imported to keep up the fantastic fiction of an Arab revolt, and thirty-five hundred prominent Arabs emigrated from Palestine to escape the depredations of their own countrymen. Mussolini took a hand in the matter. Large quantities of German manufactured arms and ammunition found their way into Palestine. Bands in the pay of the Duce and the Fuehrer filtered in. Again the Jewish national enterprise came to a standstill. Violence interrupted the work of creative peace.

Humbly and patiently the Jewish pioneers have set about to make the Land of Israel, the hope and prayer of their people for two thousand years, a habitable place not only for the weary wanderers still in Europe, but first of all for the destitute and disease-ridden masses of Arabs. They had not come with weapons of war, building forts and strongholds as a conqueror who protects his gains in a captured province. Spontaneously the Jewish people had rejected the counsel of those who urged, for the sake of national prestige, the bloody panoplies of imperialism. Instead of arsenals and military bastions, the first foundation on Zion's hill had been a school of learning, a tribute to the universality of the spirit, the Hebrew University. Israel had returned to the land of his fathers by virtue of a decree of the civilized world, which in a moment of high idealism had conceived the will to set right an ancient wrong.

Not to trample underfoot, therefore, to crush or to break the bruised reed had those pioneers come, but to fight the battle of the Lord which is to open the eyes of the blind, to bring out those that sit in the darkness of the prison house and to intone a new psalm of peace and human brotherhood. Not domination, not outward success, not even possession was the *Chalutzims'* goal. Zionism's object was to bring to a close Israel's two thousand years of exile, to terminate the scandal of history, to end our own Christian shame of a people of human brothers being hounded and hunted from pillar to post.

Not all the Jewish people were expected to come to Palestine. The geographical limits of the country would not have permitted the settlement of so great a number. Only a kernel of the Jewish people, withdrawn from the galuth, was to there build a civilization marked by the ethos of the Hebraic spirit and make a contribution to the sum total of human civilization in accordance with the national character and the national genius of the Jewish people. This, it was expected, would also fill with new meaning and a new dignity the life of the Jews who remained behind in the Diaspora. The deeper significance of Zionism was therefore that the thing called Judaism should not disappear from the earth, but that Israel in a personal-national sense would become again one of the collaborators in the building of humanity's fatherland—the Kingdom of God, "the world to come," a world wherein not one man shall plow and another reap, not one man build and another inhabit and not one man cause hurt or damage to another man.

In that place where he had entered history at the hand of his God, Israel had come to take up the threads of the past and "renew the mystery of his national existence through a rebirth of the moral ideals of Judaism." So much sweat, said the Hebrew poet Bialik to me, so much blood, so much love is being poured into the soil of *Eretz Israel* that sooner or later the womb of the earth will grow pregnant and a Prophet will issue again! Israel, the timeless witness of the unity of God and, therefore, of the oneness of humanity, had returned to Jerusalem to rekindle those lamps which had been a beacon to mankind on the long and weary climb to the human ideal. His Messianic urge, the undying hope of a better world wherein God is to be the principle of life and justice, the cardinal principle in man's relationships with his brother, which is the tie, the fabric **of** the tie that has more than any racial bond kept the Jews together through the storms and flames of history, had led the Jewish people back to the land of its youth. Again the Law was to go forth from Zion and the word of God from Jerusalem, yet not in the form of a ritual or a liturgy, but as a new Commonwealth of Labor, based on justice, as an inspiration and a hope to all mankind.

The fundamental directive of the Jewish approach to the Arab problem resided in that precept of Hillel, who said: "Love thy neighbor as thyself," and "Do not unto others what thou wouldst not have others do unto thee." Since in that precept lies the whole sense of Judaism, any departure from it in political or international relationships would have caused the Jewish spirit to suffer damage. And, inasmuch as the whole sense and purpose of Palestine's redemption was and is to create a home, a territory where the Hebraic spirit may be itself again, unfold and blossom in full amplitude, any attempt to make the scheme for the redemption of the Jewish land conform to the usual methods of chauvinist nationalism would have been a vitiation of the aims of Zionism. The Jews are not saints—we have no right to expect that of any people—but it cannot be denied that what was known as Jewish nationalism had been service not oppression, love not hatred, "a humanized nationalism which finds its justification only in the human conscience and in the divine laws which are the same for all peoples."

And what had been the world's answer?

Blood and terror! Lies and sneers and calumny! The liberals were turning over their specious shibboleths about the rule of the majority. The British talked of striking a balance between two groups of "natives" and of protecting Arab rights. In a land where some of the finest movements of Socialism had been started, the Communists supported the henchmen of the reaction and stabbed the Jewish working community in the back. Others pretended to be concerned over the safety of the dust-covered holy places which nobody menaced. The Christian Church as a body stood aside. In the presence of Albert Schweitzer, the great savant who had given up his scholarly work in Europe's universities to devote himself, in a spirit of expiation for the white man's sins, to his black brethren, and who had gone to work as a medical missionary amongst them, the Protestant community was full of praise and admiration, but on the work of the Zionists who had freed the Arabs of trachoma—that terrible scourge of the Near Eastern peoples, it turned its back.

13

Someone asked Lloyd George at the Peace Conference why he had been so persistent an advocate of the conquest of Palestine by British arms? "Because," replied the Welshman, "it was not only the surest way to break the backbone of the Ottoman Empire, but the promise of a National Home for the Jewish people in the Holy Land gave the war a certain halo of righteousness in the eyes of my Methodist constituents."

In spite of this implied avowal of the profound interest in the restoration of Zion on the part of the Free Protestant Churches in England, it would be puerile to see therein a determining factor in Britain's assumption of the mandate over Palestine. England is in Palestine neither to bring fulfillment of the age-old aspirations of the Jewish people nor to speed the second coming of Christ, an eventuality for which, in Christian fundamentalist milieus, a return of the Jews to those sacred landmarks is deemed to be pre-essential. Imperialism is moved by more realistic considerations. Great Britain is in Palestine for weighty reasons of empire. The Holy Land's occupation by the British armies was the culmination of a struggle for supremacy between rival imperialisms in the Near and Middle East. Jemal Pasha's attack on the Suez Canal in 1915 at the head of a Germano-Turkish army and the Turkish commander's declaration that after the war he proposed to return to Constantinople via Alexandria made the objectives of the Central Powers in that part of the world perilously clear. The Germano-Turkish campaign on the borders of the Red Sea was not primarily a maneuver to lessen British power of resistance on the Western front: it was a threat to the most vulnerable link in Britain's imperial line of communications—Suez.

Britain parried that threat with a concentration in Egypt of Indian and Australian troops, who first repulsed the Turkish attack and then crossed to the Arabian peninsula where, two years later, after certain Arabic tribes had been persuaded by Colonel T. E. Lawrence, on the promise of boundless loot, to revolt against the Turk, the age-old Ottoman dominion over Arabia was broken by General Allenby. In this campaign Palestine fell into British hands in the latter part of 1917, shortly after Lord Balfour, the British Foreign Secretary, made public his famous note, known as the Balfour Declaration, wherein the British government declared itself favorably disposed towards the establishment of a National Home for the Jewish people in Palestine.

At the request of the Jewish people, represented by the Zionist Organization, Britain was charged by the League of Nations to assume the mandate over the Holy Land. At the Conference of San Remo in 1920, that mandate was ratified by all the League's members, fifty-three states in all, and subsequently under the terms of a separate diplomatic instrument by the United States of America. Before ratifying, the then Secretary of State, Mr. Bainbridge Colby, specifically asked Britain what her intentions were in the Holy Land, and the answer Lord Curzon gave was that England had but one objective—the facilitation of the building of a National Home for the Jewish people.

However, even before the ratification of the mandate, Britain had taken charge of Palestine and had placed the administration of the country in the hands of the Colonial Office, instead of the Foreign Office as France had done in the case of Syria. This move indicated that the manner and spirit of approach to the untried mandatory question would not differ essentially from that which governs a crown colony; that is to say, the development of Palestine was to be made subservient to British imperial considerations. Whether a Conservative, a Liberal or a Labor administration was subsequently in power in England, the British policy in regard to Palestine has fundamentally remained unchanged: the chief object was, and remains till this day, not to speed the building of a National Home for the Jewish people, but to integrate the country in the British system of imperial defense, and this because Palestine's geographical position makes it an indispensable link in the chain of British imperial defenses. For Palestine is nothing less than Britain's overland bridge to her Indian Empire.

Since the rise of the new Roman imperium as a challenger to British supremacy in the Mediterranean and the Red Sea, Palestine's value to the British Empire has increased in a measure that had not been foreseen. For Mussolini's conquest of Ethiopia has made of Eritrea a most formidable potential threat to British communications with India, the Far East and the antipodean dominions of Australia and New Zealand. Before Ethiopia passed into Italian hands the value of Eritrea as a military and naval base on the Red Sea was nullified by an Ethiopia that was friendly to Britain and that could, in the event of a war between Britain and Italy, be quickly militarized through Kenya and the Sudan, and thus become a threat in Mussolini's back.

Mussolini was therefore not wrong when he denounced the Ethiopian Empire as a menace to Italy's imperium, and his occupation of that land was a master stroke of imperialist maneuvering. Furthermore, the installation of Italian gun emplacements at Ceuta on the north African coast opposite Gibraltar has seriously diminished the value of that ancient rock as a key position of British imperial power. The occupation of the Canary Islands and of the Basque coast by General Franco, a mere mercenary in the Duce's service, leaves the possibility open for a speedy transformation of these strategic points into submarine and air bases. The militarization by the Duce of the island of Pantelleria, halfway between Messina and the north African coast, has made of the western Mediterranean an Italian sea. The constant reinforcement of the Libyan coast, where Italy now has two important submarine bases, has made Malta, for more than a century Britain's chief naval concentration point in the Mediterranean, on the admission of the British admiralty itself, untenable in the event of war. If to this is added a consideration of Egypt's progressive evolution towards complete independence, and that country's scarcely concealed pro-Italian attitude, it becomes clear that Palestine and Cyprus are Britain's only remaining bases for the naval, aerial and land defense of the Suez Canal.

In fact, since the Ethiopian debacle and the Spanish civil war, Palestine is the key to British world power. Haifa is not only the terminus of the pipe line from the Mosul oil fields, the most important fueling station for the navy, the air force and the modern mechanized armies, but at Haifa starts the route, aerial and terrestrial, to India. The radius of the Palestinian airdromes brings British aerial power within easy striking distance not only of the Soviet Union's oil fields in Southern Caucasia, but also of the Dardanelles, Russia's access to the Mediterranean, of the Persian Gulf, which is the road the products of the British-owned Iranian oil-fields must take and last, but not least, of the entire Arabian peninsula with its doubtful kings in Yemen and Mecca. In addition to being the strongest *point d'appui* of Britain's interempire lines of communication, Palestine is also England's great bastion in the Arabic world.

In this area, the very pivot of British world power, which is destined to become one of the most decisive factors in the coming struggle for power, the Jewish people are building their National Home. That National Home is today in its infancy with less than half a million Jewish population. Yet the increasing pressure of the Jewish masses in Central and eastern Europe makes extension of that National Home a crying necessity.

What is Britain going to do? Is she going to let the millions of Jews who can no longer remain in Europe come into Palestine? Or will she, taking the cue from the Arab nationalists, declare her mission of facilitating "the close settlement of the land by Jews" fulfilled, and stabilize the Jewish National Home at its present stage of development? If Palestine were a crown colony the latter course would no doubt be adopted without further ado. Being in reality only the guardian of the Holy Land, and exercising her mandate merely on behalf of the League of Nations, Britain is obliged and treaty-bound to give an accounting of her administration of Palestine before the bar of world opinion.

How is she to explain her failure to maintain order in Palestine? How is she—she who holds hundreds of millions in check in India—to make the world believe that she is powerless to prevent or put a stop to the depredations of a mere handful of terrorists in Palestine? How is she to justify her deviation from the solemn task entrusted to her care by the League of Nations and by the government of the United States of America? How can she explain her turning Palestine into a military and naval concentration point exclusively in the service of British imperial interests?

How? By submitting evidence, of course, that Jews and Arabs cannot get along together, that the obstacles placed in the way of the further development of the Jewish National Home by a growing Arabic nationalism are insuperable, that Arabic hostility to the Jews may in time become a movement of Pan-Arabic dimensions, affecting all the Near Eastern countries and thus endangering Britain's position, as the protector of the Jewish National Home, in the entire Arabic world. In short, Britain must show that her task in the Holy Land is an ungrateful and impossible one and that she must be released—not of Palestine, but of trying to maintain peace between Jews and Arabs in Palestine by giving in to Arab demands with respect to a curtailment of Jewish immigration and Jewish agricultural and industrial expansion in Palestine.

There have been investigations from time to time in the disturbed condition of Palestine, not by bodies of experts appointed by the League, but by British commissions of inquiry. Every one of these commissions has been unsparing in its criticism of both Jewish and Arabic conduct, but the role of the mandatory power itself was on each occasion left out of consideration. That aspect of the Palestine situation, England's own role and conduct, was definitely excluded by the British government from the terms of inquiry permitted to the investigating bodies. This manner of procedure left Britain in every instance in the role of the long-suffering, innocent, good-natured big brother of Jews and Arabs alike.

When a revolt was brewing in one of the Roman Empire's provinces, the first question the Senators asked was: *Cui prodest?* Who is counting on becoming the beneficiary of this disturbance? That is the question which should have been and which should be asked in connection with the periodic outbreaks of violence in Palestine. To whose interest is it that Jews and Arabs do not get along? Why does the Palestine Administration persistently discourage attempts on the part of the Jewish Labor Party and the leaders of Arab labor, who together represent the bulk of the country's population, to arrive at a peaceful mode of collaboration? Why does the English police threaten Arab workers with jail if they do not cease their contact with Jews and why are joint Jewish-Arab labor unions refused recognition by the Administration? Arab villagers, in the course of the riots in 1937, asked for a charter to start an organization to spread "a moderate attitude towards the Jews." They were refused. Why?

One of the latest (1937) English-manned commissions of inquiry has reached the conclusion that the mandate is unworkable. It so happens that this verdict is precisely that of the permanent staff in the Colonial Office and of the Palestine Administration. On the face of it, this verdict looks quite plausible. But—*cui prodest?* An investigation by non-British members of the League of Nations would have shown not that the mandate is unworkable, but that the representatives of the Colonial Office in the Near East have from the outset been of the opinion that the exclusion of Palestine from an eventual Arabic Confederacy was an error. Mr. St. John Philby, for many years the British agent at Jidda; Lord Lloyd, onetime High Commissioner in Egypt; General Bols, one of Allenby's lieutenants, and H. C. Luke, Chief Secretary of Palestine till 1931, and finally, Gertrude Bell—all have intimated at one time or another that in their opinion a Jewish Palestine would in the end be more of an embarrassment than a benefit to the British Empire. This point of view was that of the first officials in the Palestine Administration who entered the country in the wake of the Allenby army—men chiefly of military extraction who became the administrators of so delicate a task as supervising the building of the Jewish National Home in the midst of an Arabic world.

The history of the seventeen years of mandatory regime in Palestine reveals an unbroken succession of restrictive measures, acts of pettifogging chicanery, niggardliness and outright opposition on the part of the Administration to the Jewish National enterprise. When the Arab mob in 1929 shouted: "The government is with us," and threw themselves upon the Jewish colonies, which had first been disarmed by the Administration, they gave a true expression of the situation. I know this is a grave charge to make, but I convinced myself on the spot that the uprising of that year was deliberately fomented by the authorities, and that the terror and destruction were but a camouflaged attempt on their part, not only to discourage the Jewish spirit of initiative, but to show the world in an unmistakable manner that the establishment of a Jewish National Home in Palestine was a foolish Utopian dream which would ultimately go to pieces on the rock of Arab intransigence. The impression had to be created that while England had done all in its power to carry out its pledges to the Jewish people, it had found its plans thwarted and nullified by Arab opposition.

Every instance of friction between Jews and Arabs has from the beginning of the mandate been cited as evidence of Judeo-Arabic incompatibility. Every act of Arab hostility against the Jewish national enterprise was grist in the mill of that school of thought amongst British colonial experts which holds that the British Empire needs a strong Arabic imperialism as a factor in the maintenance of the Empire's equilibrium in the Eastern world. When H. C. Luke and others spoke of Pan-Arabism as a movement Britain had to reckon with, at a time when Pan-Arabism was nonexistent, they were thinking wishfully and trying to force the issue. By these very words, which were repeated over and over again to every commission of inquiry and to every investigating journalist, and which implied the necessity on Britain's part to proceed cautiously and slowly with the building of the Jewish National Home, these Englishmen were actually fostering Pan-Arabism in that they tried to lift it from a chimera in the imagination of a handful of European-educated Arabic bourgeois to a reality in Near Eastern affairs.

As time went on Palestine became in fact Britain's chief instrument for the cultivation of Pan-Arabism, for in Palestine the Zionist colonization work could be held up and cited as a growing obstacle to the ultimate realization of Pan-Arabism and be used as an alarm clock, as it were, to stir the Arabs from their political lethargy. And because that was their fundamental aim, the British colonial experts in the Near East and the spokesmen of the Colonial Office at Geneva could always be counted upon to pay verbal loyalty to England's task of facilitating the upbuilding of the Jewish National Home, because the more important the Jewish National Home appeared in the eyes of the world, the more was Arabic opposition to its edification prickled and the more likely was it to coalesce first in a local Palestinian Arab nationalism and later in a widespread movement of Pan-Arabic opposition all over the Near East. In other words, Zionist colonization in Palestine has been utilized by Britain to give the Arab peoples the one common collective task which does not imperil British hegemony in the Near East. Coolly and cynically those British agents in the Near East are playing with the holiest things the peoples under their control and influence possess. They believe neither in the Arabic ideal nor in the Jewish ideal. They are obsessed with the idea of the British imperium. They may well say with Lawrence, in whose footsteps they are following, that they are playing hide-and-seek with Jews and Arabs alike by exploiting their highest ideals as instruments in Britain's power politics.

By presenting those first outbreaks of terrorism and hooliganism, inspired by the Jerusalem Mufti, who was the Administration's paid servant, as manifestations of an awakening Arabic national consciousness, the British authorities in Palestine sought to impress world opinion with the immense difficulties confronting Britain in the discharge of her task of transforming Palestine into a National Home for the Jewish people. One energetic word would not only have put the politicians of the Mufti's clan in their place, but would have earned the Administration the gratitude of the bulk of the Arab people in Palestine who desired and still desire nothing better than to work in peace and harmony with the Jewish population. No action was taken until the Mufti had been able to build up an organization, largely by terrorism and intimidation of his fellow citizens, which looked indeed like an Arab nationalist movement. Then only a few of the ringleaders were arrested, and the Mufti fled to Syria to conduct the campaign from the safe distance of Beyrouth. But the repression of the terrorism was carried on in so haphazard and romantic a way by Britain that the Palestinian press could ask sarcastically if the dispatch of Scottish regiments to Palestine did not signify that the Administration intended to go sparingly with ammunition. Roving bands of gangsters, recruited by the Mufti in Syria, paid with Italian money and equipped with German Mausers and time bombs, roamed the country with impunity, shooting down Jewish laborers in the fields, burning crops, hurling bombs into market squares, synagogues, homes and shops—right under the nose of twenty thousand British troops who could not even keep the eighty miles of railway in Palestine clear for traffic.

The Arab attacks, it should be noted, increased in intensity at the moment the Jewish people's representatives at the Conference for Refugees in Evian-les-Bains asked Britain to translate her verbal assurances of sympathy for the victims of the Nazi terror into practical, definite, and concrete assistance by opening the doors of Palestine to Jewish immigration.

Immigration at a time when Palestine was seething with unrest! What were the Jews thinking of? Could they not see that England had her hands full in a dozen spots on the globe and that their precious National Home would have to wait?

The truth is that the Jewish National movement has served the purpose for which the British Empire entered into an alliance with it in 1917. In that year, Germany's unrestricted submarine campaign threatened to force England to her knees: France was slowly bleeding to death, the British armies in Flanders were hanging on by the skin of their teeth, and America was far from having thrown her full weight into the scales on the Allies' side. Then it was that the Balfour Declaration had been issued to win the moral and financial support of the Jewish people. It had brought about that desired result. It had, moreover, enabled Great Britain to establish a bulwark for her empire on the northeast side of the Suez Canal. That was the end of Zionism's usefulness insofar as the British imperium is concerned.

It is true that Britain has not said so in so many words. British opposition has remained verbally unexpressed, because Britain cannot openly and before the whole world disavow her solemn pledges to the Jewish people. Instead she used Arabic feudalist hostility to the Jewish National Home as an opportune pretext to limit Jewish enterprise and to stabilize the building of the National Home before the Jews shall have attained a majority in Palestine and therewith lay claim to a deciding voice in the direction of developments. To the British, sponsorship in the building of the Jewish National Home was and remains an embarrassing imperial commitment of which England would gladly have rid itself long ago if that had been possible. In the present state of international affairs, from British imperialism's point of view, the ideal situation in Palestine would be a country sparsely inhabited by a poor class of Arabs who could be employed as laborers in the exploitation of the asphalt, salt and potash deposits (indispensable in the production of armaments) in the Dead Sea area, the extension of the Haifa naval center, and the building of airdromes, munition depots, strategic railways and highways, amongst them the projected road from Gaza on the Mediterranean to Akaba on the Red Sea, an overland alternative of the water route in the event the Suez Canal is made unusable. The Jews want to build and develop; the British do not like to see the country, which they intend to be the military defense base of their Empire's key position, cluttered up entirely with collectivist agricultural colonies and peopled with a tribe to which war and the things of war are anathema.

Had it been possible, on the other hand, to utilize the Jewish national movement as an instrument for the maintenance and strengthening of the British hegemony in the Arabian peninsula, no doubt Britain's attitude towards the building of the Jewish National Home in Palestine would have been entirely different. Jewish immigration would then not have been curtailed and it is safe to say that if Zionism had consented to have an eventual Jewish commonwealth in the Near East function as a sort of bastion and spearhead for Britain in the Arabic world, there would not be half a million Jews today in Palestine, but millions of Jews and the nationalism of the Palestinian Arabs would scarcely carry that halo of injured righteousness with which it is generally presented today. England would have taken care of that.

It is in the intensely pacifist sentiment which animates the Jewish people and their unshakable determination that their collaboration with the Arab people must be founded on a basis of mutual trust and respect that we must see, I think, the crux of the entire Palestinian problem, the fundamental motive of Britain's antagonism to the building of the Jewish National Home.

Alluring though the prospect might have been of seeing the Land of Israel become one of the brightest gems in the British imperial diadem, the Jewish spirit could not accept the condition of playing the imperialist game of guile and oppression with England at the expense of the Arab people. The Jews felt by instinct—and their political conduct has clearly established the fact—that they have been guided by one fundamental sentiment, namely this: that it is not permissible to realize a sacred ideal by all the means at one's disposal, least of all by violence in the form of chauvinism and imperialism. For the Jew knows that whoever uses incompassionate and dishonest means also gambles away his sacred goal.

It is for this reason that British imperialism has not only never, in the course of the seventeen years of mandatory regime, striven for a Judeo-Arabic reconciliation, but that it has systematically sabotaged each and every successive effort in that direction. And this not by reason of some secret animosity towards the Jewish people, although the Tories could not but look with contempt on the forward-looking, not to say socialistic, experiments carried on by the Jews in the Holy Land, but because an eventual Judeo-Arabic rapprochement would be laden with an infinitely greater capacity for contravening British imperial interests in the Near East than a perpetual state of disturbance in Palestine. Under the circumstances, so long as Zionism is not willing to be the hand-maiden of British imperialism, a Judeo-Arabic understanding is definitely contrary to the interest of the British Empire. A collaboration between Jews and Arabs, predicated on a recognition of their common and mutual interests, would inevitably and quickly produce a movement of opposition to Britain's own designs in the Near East. And it could be a puissant movement, extending far beyond the confines of Palestine. For Jews and Arabs can work together. We know that the precious collaboration of these two Semitic groups under the caliphs of Baghdad and in Spain produced one of the parent streams of Western civilization.

In order to forestall the materialization of such a Judeo-Arabic alliance, Britain has for seventeen years pursued the old Roman policy of divide and rule.

But while this policy was for many years applied to Palestine in a sly and covert manner, the advent of Neville Chamberlain to the premiership of England has brought a decided change. From the moment Mr. Chamberlain occupied himself with Palestine, the

British attitude to the Jewish National Home has been openly hostile.

In his "realistic" striving for a *détente* in Europe, the British Prime Minister has preferred an understanding with the Fascist dictatorships of Italy and Germany to the formation of a united front of democratic states with which to counteract and eventually check the dynamic expansionism of Rome and Berlin. In that policy, the Jewish masses in Europe and in Palestine rightly see an adoption by Britain of Fascism's theoretical solution of Europe's problems.

Ethiopia and Spain have been sacrificed to the Fascists. Hitler's road to the East is made smooth by subtle diplomatic pressure on France which is offered security through a new Entente Cordiale with Britain in exchange for loosening her ties with Czechoslovakia and the Soviet Union. It is not the prospect of war which alarms the Jewish masses, but the Fascistization of all Europe. The Jews know by experience that they are the first and worst sufferers from Fascism. Seeing Britain, on the side of their worst enemies, calmly sacrificing what remains of the League and collective security and democracy in Europe in order to placate the Fascist dictatorships, the Jewish people, whose fate is bound up with democracy, are inevitably turning against a Britain that is lined up with her mortal enemies. On the other hand, lest the Jews, alarmed by the approaching thunderstorm, turn in desperation to the Arab masses for an alliance and seek to constitute with them a united front not only against British imperialism but against Arabic feudal Fascism as well, the rhythm of the disturbances in Palestine is accentuated so that the cleft between Jews and Arabs appears more and more unbridgeable. Without a word of warning, Britain cut down the proposal of a Jewish state in a partitioned Palestine, made by and adopted by Britain after the Peel Commission's investigation in 1937—a scheme under which the Jews were to control no more than four hundred square miles. Not only did this encourage the Arab nationalists to keep up the campaign of terrorism but it may well have provoked the Jews, in turn, to measures of violence. A full-fledged civil war in Palestine would give Britain the excuse to say that neither of the two parties is mature for self-government—and the Jewish National Home should be allowed to stagnate.

Thus the struggle for Jewish national emancipation enters into a new phase, both in Palestine and on the European and American fronts. Imperialism unchains the very forces which speed its own doom. Arab nationalism has been awakened. Palestine has definitely entered the phase of industrial capitalism. But not only Palestine, the whole Arabian peninsula has turned up the road of modern technique. And, although the influence of the Jewish workers on the Arab masses remains insignificant for the time being, the nationalistic agitation of the ruling class of effendis, which begins to take the form of a glorification of Hitler and which is now also motivated by the opposition to "Jewish Bolshevism and Communism," reveals itself more and more as an effort to put the reality of the class struggle in the shadow. The antisocial character of the effendis and landed families is obvious. Their aim is not an independent democratic republic, but independence on the model of Iraq, Trans-Jordan, and Syria, that is to say, an arrangement which leaves the foundation of the feudal state intact under the "protection" of a great power with its advisors and attachés.

In the course of time the Arab peasants and workers will come to see that not the Jewish workers, but British imperialism is their social enemy. They will realize that in the struggle which they must wage as an historic necessity their own landlord class is not a dependable ally, and that their salvation lies in a close collaboration with the Jewish workers and nowhere else. For this reason, it is manifest that Zionist policy should be directed towards transforming the Arab nationalist movement into an anti-imperialist and antifascist struggle through a productive movement for the building of Arabic independence. Rapprochement between the Jewish and Arabic masses is the condition for this, but also the detachment of all Jewish national endeavor from British imperialist considerations.

Of an abandonment or even a curtailment of the scope of the Jewish National Home, by a cessation or a limitation of Jewish immigration into Palestine, there must be and there can be no question. It is true that if obstruction be England's plan—and all signs point to such an eventuality—the Zionist movement and the Jewish people will probably have neither the strength nor the political influence to parry so cruel and so undeserved a blow. But others have. And others must act. For the Jewish problem, of which Palestine is the kernel, is no longer an academic question on which men can afford to debate and discourse at leisure. By their ostracism of the Jew, the Fascist states have made of the Jewish question an integral and inseparable part of the greater problem confronting civilization, and one that can no longer be solved by the establishment of partial or temporary havens of refuge.

We are living in a time when the eternal barbarian is camped before humanity's door. If he should be allowed to enter farther and install himself, society is heading, not towards a new medievalism, as the Russian philosopher Berdjaev seems to think (for the Middle Ages ushered in the free unfolding of the human personality), but towards a new barbarism and a slavery far blacker than the bondage of oldtime Egypt. In one country after another, life is being pressed into one single form; the nations are being turned into single-minded homogeneous units, the thoughts, feelings and desires of whose members are to be permeated with one exclusive national ideology. Here that objective is being attained by violence, elsewhere by mass suggestion in which press, pulpit, radio, and sport actively collaborate. In the states that have adopted a totalitarian regime this process of regimentation has assumed such fantastic proportions that there, as Paul Claudel once said, "The eyelids of man have been sewn together, as it were, and his ears stuffed with cement." His news is being chewed and masticated for him in wads by functionaries before being handed out. Everything possible is being done to prevent him from seeing and hearing humanity beyond the nation. "Everywhere," says H. Roland-Holst, "a suggested standard of values is being imposed on the people, in which the individual, the human personality, the family, and the conception of God as the sole principle of life are all ruthlessly sacrificed to the interests of the collectivity in the form of quasi-almighty superstates," which are as jealous of their prerogatives as the idols of old. The new leviathan state stifles every expression of independent judgment, replaces the criterion of conscience with a criterion of its own, and bases this on what is of service or disservice to the state, rejecting the rights of the individual and the demands of justice and morality. Man is being reduced to an article, to a soulless automaton, to a cog in the machine, generally a highly perfected war machine. His daily life is regulated by the police whistle and the revolver. He has lost the freedom of his hands, his intelligence and his conscience. His beliefs, aspirations, and hopes are to conform to the dictates of autocratic pontiffs who tolerate no more divergence than Torquemada and who do not even hesitate to invade his bedroom with an order to produce more slaves. In short, "Man is no more than a brick in the temples erected to the false gods, an inanimate object that can be disposed of at the will and to satisfy the whims of a few almighty individuals who stand at the top of the human structure. It is in this absolute destruction of the individual that the essence of barbarism resides."

Because the Jew represents the most striking element of dissimilarity in the democratic Christian society of the West of which the touchstone is diversity and respect for the diversity of the contributions to be made by various groups and nations to the sum total of civilization, he becomes the first victim of the process of leveling ushered in by the totalitarian state. This is no accident. Totalitarianism recognizes in the Jew, as the bearer of Judaism, that is to say the bearer of a philosophy of life which makes justice the cardinal principle in man's relationship with his fellow, a natural enemy, and rightly so. The Jew must therefore be eliminated, because there can be no room for Judaism in a society based on violence and brute force. He must go. He must be exterminated. For not before the Jew is crushed can the forces of darkness attain the other citadels of humanity—humanism, democracy and Christianity, the three daughters of Judaism.

And the Jew is going. He is being stamped upon, hounded and driven out of one country after the other. He is hunted as if he were a wild and ferocious beast, not for what he has done but for what he is, a Jew, the eternal contradictor of violence and bloodshed and slavery and barbarism. Germany has reduced the status of the Jews to that of the untouchables of India. Poland has declared that its three and a half million Jewish citizens are superfluous. In Rumania the Jew lives in a constant atmosphere of pogrom. Inexorably the tentacles of the Nazi octopus stretch out in easterly directions where the mass of the Jews of Europe live. When Vienna succumbed, fifty million semibarbarians in eastern Europe passed under the direct influence of a Pan-Hitlerite philosophy of the destiny of man which predicates that the Jew is anathema henceforth in that entire broad strip of territory which runs from the Baltic to the Aegean where in days of peace, such as we are having now, the Jews live under conditions that can scarcely be qualified as human, and, where in days of further tension and war—for that area, because of the Soviet Union's proximity, is destined to be the battleground in the next war—they must inevitably become the victim of all the exasperated nationalisms, all the economic rivalries and of the designs of Nazi imperialism.

And not only is the Jew eliminated because he represents an obstacle in the homogenization of the nations, but his prostrate body is the most accessible and convenient steppingstone to ulterior objectives of Fascist power politics. In Germany at a moment of historical transition when the choice lay between turning up the road towards a full-fledged democracy on the one hand, and falling back into pre-medieval barbarism on the other, the Jewish question served to divert the attention of the masses from the real issues at stake in society. In Poland, the deliberately pauperized Jewish masses serve as an instrument of bargaining in the hands of a Polish imperialism avid for colonies and markets: give Poland colonies and she can settle her superfluous Jewish population there. By suddenly accentuating the Jewish question, the Rumanian Iron Guard, at the behest of Germany, not only turned out a quasi-liberal government that held its hands somewhat protectingly above the head of the Jew, but it put into its place a government that wanted to break off the French alliance and orientate itself toward Berlin.

And now comes Italy. After years of protestations that anti-Semitism is a sentiment alien to Italian Fascism and that the forty-five thousand de-Judaized, assimilated and Italianized Jews of Venice and Rome are amongst the most loyal subjects of the state, Mussolini suddenly declares them enemies, a menace to his vast empire—and at the same time elevates Arabic to a compulsory subject in the high schools of his country and announces the foundation of an Arabic university in Ethiopia. The trick is obvious: the Duce, who would like to become the protector of Islam, like Wilhelm II before him, makes an appeal to the Arabic world over the head of Britain, and the Jew is again made the scapegoat, the victim, the instrument.

Overnight, without warning, in spite of centuries of common life with the Italian people, sharing its weal and woe, contributing without stint to its culture, fighting in its wars, aggrandizing its power and wealth, the Italian Jews are suddenly brought to the level of outcasts and undesirables. After that, can it be said that there is one place on earth where the Jew is safe? Do not the Jews, by their mere presence, constitute to any dictator or aspirant dictator, or to any group imbued with the totalitarian ideology, a temptation to be utilized as a steppingstone to power? All over Central and Eastern Europe the Jew is sinking into a state of destitution and misery hardly conceivable in the West. He is driven into the lowest strata of the *Lumpenproletariat* without hope of rising again so long—we may as well be frank about it—so long as there prevails in this world a social system which finds in anti-Semitism too facile an instrument for its own perpetuation and domination. Of course, as Christians we know that the day will come, the day of which Renan once spoke, the day when this cruel world, this world of blood and guile, "this bourgeois world, this world of pigmies will finally be swept into the discard by the heroic and idealistic forces of mankind," and every nation and tribe, Israel included, will be assured free and full unfoldment of national culture and of the human personality. That day will come, and the times through which we are passing are proof of its advent, for they are "the birthpangs" of a new era of regeneration and renaissance. But in the meantime there can be little doubt that at no other time in their long and melancholy history has the future loomed darker and more forbidding to the Jewish people than it does in our day. Blood and tears and still more blood and tears seem to be Israel's portion. André Gide once asked: "Is it not amazing that the Christian peoples alone should have been capable of creating the civilization that is furthest removed from the precepts of the Gospel, the most contrary to any form of Christian life?" To be sure, judging by what we Westerners, and not this or that tribe of Asiatic barbarians, have done to the Jew, often in the name of Christ himself, in the light of all the woe and cruelty and revilement heaped on his head by our hands, must we not confess that it is we who have been the barbarians, the unconverted pagans?

Must this—"the scandal of history"—continue forever? Is there then no balm in Gilead, and is there no physician?

Yes, there is. There is one last hope, one last solution: the *solutio Christi*.

If the Christian Church would yet, at this late hour, understand the signs of the times and realize that the attacks on the Jew, as they multiply in our day, are but a prelude to an assault on Christianity's own foundations, that in order to attain the last bulwarks of Christianity and humanism and democracy, the forces of darkness, the false gods of state and race, who have been set up in our time, must first crush the Jew, who has been the guardian of the spirit throughout the ages, if the realization would penetrate and deepen in Christian circles that the salvation of the Jewish people through the rebuilding of the Holy Land is a phase of the struggle for the establishment of the Kingdom of God on earth, I believe, there is still hope. And not only hope of saving the Jewish people from frightful disaster, but hope of saving society!

If the Christian Church, in a great and sacred gesture of audacity, should recapture something of its old prophetic spirit—the power of moral expression it lacks at present—it could still establish a new contact with life and take up the conduct of human society. For that Church, which is now almost entirely left aside by life, remains nevertheless, as James Darmesteter, the philosopher, said, "the only organized force of the West whose heartbeat could be made to be felt to the ends of the earth and whose word could still evoke a thrill of hope and of filial obedience amongst men."

It is more than a hundred years ago since Carlyle wrote in *Sartor Resartus* that the noblest enthusiasms of human nature—the religious principle and the idea of humanity—are wandering up and down the earth like a body without a soul, seeking their earthly organization here, there, and everywhere, indefatigably, indestructibly searching for a home, for incorporation, for incarnation.

If the Church is to fulfill its destiny and be that incarnation, the incorporation of mankind's hope and ideal for which the instincts and aspirations of man have groped and striven throughout the ages, it must make the cause of all the oppressed its own and let up being an apologist of a social system based on violence, class egoism and war. It must sever the attachments that bind it to Moloch and Mammon and stop striving for a "meaningless outer conformity" and instead, for the sake of peace on earth and the brotherhood of man, march forward in a community of spirit with all the forces of the future against the citadels of sin and darkness and poverty and misery and sorrow. The Church must become again, what its Master called it to be, a ferment in society, the salt of the earth, a conscious, rational, responsible, human force of action in the service of the coming day, the new man, and the society of the future. In other words, the Church must cut the Gospel loose from the ways and things of "this world" which it was commanded to overcome, and bring back from heaven, where a spirit of lassitude and compromise has relegated it, the immense and ultimate hope of mankind, which is the establishment of the Kingdom of God on this earth and in our time.

Such a Church, such a newborn Christianity would show the world and the Jews the face of the Master in the conduct of the disciples and redeem itself by seeing that the stain on Christ's name, the stain of the persecution of the blood kinsmen of Jesus, be removed at last. Such a Church, having returned to its task as builder of the City of God, would rejoice that in this age, when the idols of the past have returned, Israel, too, driven by a mysterious and divine urge, has set his hand to rekindle those lamps on Zion's hill which once illumined the universe of man.

Such a Church of Christ, having regained its independence and its courage, would dare to speak to England in Nathan's words: "Thou art the Man," and insist that Britain's pledge, freely given to the whole world, be kept, and that the doors of its national home be opened wide to the tired and weary People of the Book. For the Jew has a home and there is room in that home for millions of Israel's homeless. When statesmen and diplomats persuaded at last that no other solution for the plight of European Jewry can be envisaged but exodus from the lands of terror, in apparent bewilderment scan the horizon for a haven of refuge for the hard-pressed Jews and alternately suggest the swamps of Guiana, the frozen tundras of Alaska, the inhospitable shores of Ceylon or Madagascar as a possible asylum, and country after country debates in embarrassment what can be done about increasing immigrant quotas, why is Palestine overlooked, the Land of Israel, where, with a view to precisely such a calamity as has now overtaken European Jewry, the framework and the machinery for the reception and the integration of millions of Jews into the economic, social, cultural, and religious fabric has been set up and perfected by the Zionists? Palestine, it is said, cannot take care of all the refugees and prospective refugees. Perhaps it cannot. Yet, vast tracts of land are available for settlement and acute shortage of labor prevails. Eretz Israel is calling its wandering children home, and millions of Jews have a passionate longing to enter its gates. Let a beginning be made in taking the Jew there before it is too late and the barbarians carry out their threat to exterminate the remnant of Israel by the sword and the fire.

More cruel, more inhuman than persecution and ostracism and the imposition of ghettos and of the yellow badge of shame it would be to keep the door of their home shut in the face of the clamoring multitudes of Israel.

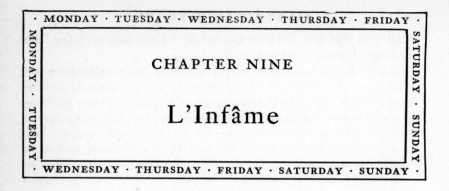

CHAPTER NINE

L'Infâme

I

In the course of the month of May, 1936, a number of reactionary journals in Paris suddenly started to print most alarming reports about conditions in republican Spain. Disorders, it was said, had broken out in Barcelona; there were strikes in the fruitgrowing districts of Andalusia; the peasants of Estremadura, exasperated with the long delays in agrarian reform, were said to be marching on Madrid; the Asturian miners, who had rioted but two years earlier, were once more in open revolt; churches had been set on fire, the homes of prominent citizens looted by wild-eyed mobs of revolutionaries; priests and nuns had been assaulted in the streets; banks had closed; business had virtually come to a standstill; in short, the whole of Spain, where but three months before the democratic and proletarian parties had won a signal victory at the polls and where now a government of the Frente Popular was in power, was described as being in a state of utter chaos and disintegration. The situation was pictured in such dismal colors that the French newspaper reader may well have believed the announcement that a wholesale exodus of the Spanish nobility and persons prominent in the business and financial world of the distressed peninsula would shortly be on its way to Paris. In fact, thousands of Spain's decent and law-abiding citizens, it was reported, had already sent their wives and children out of the country for safety's sake. Every available villa in the resort cities on the Côte d'Argent and on French and Italian Rivieras, such as Biarritz, Saint-Jean-de-Luz, Cannes, Rapallo, Mentone and

San Remo, was said either to be occupied by or reserved for "distinguished Spanish refugees."

Of course, those reports had to be taken with more than one grain of salt. The intent and purpose of the Spanish scare was a little too obvious. Its primary purpose was to influence the French electorate, which was itself about to be called to the polls a few weeks later. Since a similar combination of political groups as that which had triumphed in Spain was about to enter the electoral contest in France, the reactionary press was doing its utmost to frighten that not inconsiderable element on the periphery of the proletariat which fluctuates between Left and Right in French elections.

Nothing works as effectively on your petty bourgeois as a Bolshevik scare. Tell him his property will be taken away from him, and the average member of the lower middle class will at once forget that it is capitalism which actually does pauperize and proletarianize him. He will rally to the support of his own worst social enemies. Homes were being looted under the Frente Popular, nuns were being raped, banks were closing, farms were being expropriated, the whole Bolshevist prelude was being enacted in Spain. Was that what the French electors wanted in their own country? If they did, they simply had to cast their votes for the parties represented by the Messrs. Daladier, Blum, and Thorez of the Popular Front, and their wish would be promptly fulfilled. That was in substance the message the French reaction sought to convey to the French elector with those sensational stories about Spain.

The Spanish Republic was in reality about to enter on a very timid program of agrarian reform: the expropriation of some of the immense latifundia in the hands of the nobility and the Church. In this respect Spain was merely following the example, although in a far less thoroughgoing manner than the Frenchmen's own glorious ancestors in 1789, of every liberal-democratic state in Europe. She desired, instead of abolishing property, to create out of a multitude of near-serfs, share croppers and the poorest peasants a new class of peasant proprietors. Of course, the French elector was not informed of this by the reactionary journals. The old Bolshevik bogey was trotted out to obscure the issue. And, although the French middle classes paid no heed to that typical rightist propaganda, but gave the Popular Front of Léon Blum an overwhelming majority at the polls, immense damage had been done: a convenient weapon had been made available for the international Fascist conspirators who were about to plunge Spain into a sea of blood and tears. Thereafter every detractor of the Spanish people in its heroic struggle against the political and spiritual tyranny of Fascism pointed to the "unimpeachable authority" of the French press in claiming that Spain had been on the verge of Bolshevism and chaos when General Francisco Franco, in a spontaneous burst of indignation, rushed forth, as he announced in July, to restore "respect for the family and for the traditional morality of Spain."

After discounting the usual exaggeration that the French rightist press injects in any presentation of conditions in countries where the political and social institutions are not to its liking, it still seemed to me that there was sufficient warrant for a short trip of investigation on the other side of the Pyrenees. So, without waiting for instructions from the newspapers[1] I represented, I set out for Spain in the latter part of May.

It was not my first trip to the Iberian peninsula. I had been in Madrid for the North American Newspaper Alliance in 1931, shortly after the proclamation of the Republic, to interview Señor Manuel Azaña, the leader of the left-wing liberals. Once again, at the time of the cruel repression of the miners' revolt in Asturia by the reactionary government of Alejandro Lerroux, I had wandered up and down that sun-scorched country where, a dozen steps beyond the capital in the direction of Toledo, I felt as if I were back in the African desert. I am physically ill at ease in southern climes, but most of all in Spain. That yellow baked earth, the rocks and stones, always produced a feeling of nostalgia for the green pastures of Holland and Normandy. There is nothing sadder, more desolate on earth than that wind-swept plateau where the soil is the color of sulphur, and only a cluster of houses here and there swaying in the heat breaks the monotony and the immobility of the landscape. If it were not for the gardens of Galicia and the green strip along the Mediterranean coast, Spain could be taken for an outcropping of the Sahara in Europe. When crossing that land in a motorcar, or as was more often the case, in a slow-moving, wooden, third-class railway carriage as hot as an incubator, looking on those denuded and stark hills where God, according to an old legend, fashioned the sun and then dropped it on Toledo, I was filled with perpetual wonder that this was the country which at one time had been the heart and

[1] Federated Press of America; Canadian Central Press, and Seven Arts Feature Syndicate.

the nerve center of one of the mightiest empires mankind has ever known. What had come over the Spanish people that they had forfeited the mastery of the universe? On Charles V's dominions the sun had never set. My ancestors in Holland and Flanders had been subjects of Spanish lords. What had caused Alva and Sidonia, Cortés and Don John to be pushed from the pinnacle of history by an upstart republic in the tenebrous north, a handful of Calvinist burghers, and then elbowed out of the world's markets one after the other, until Spain, deprived of its colonies, had shrunk to the position of a third-rate power in Europe?

Were those ragged peasants in the Castilian plain with their somber faces and bony frames the people who had sent out conquistadors and armadas to capture the fabulous trade of America, the spices, the precious stones and the costly woods of India and Cathay? Spain had heaped treasure upon treasure, had circumnavigated the globe, planted the banner of Jesus and Mary in the farthermost corners of the earth; Spaniards had devirginized the pampas of the Argentine, the forests of Peru, hauled home the gold of Aztecs and Toltecs until the country was gorged to the bursting point with richness and splendor. What had become of all that wealth? What caused the strength to ebb from the hands of the conquerors of the Moor, the Turk and the Frenchman? Italy, Flanders, Portugal, the dominions beyond the sea—all had paid their annual tribute to Spain in gold and silver. Where was the glory gone? Where the empire?

The former mistress of the Seven Seas I saw now was a land of miserable peasants, illiterate, priest-ridden and ragged, mere peons exploited to the bone. Next to cathedrals and palaces of sheer beauty and breath-taking grandeur in Seville, Murcia, Granada and Valencia, cities which stand in an agricultural region of incredible fertility, where every tree bears from six hundred to a thousand oranges a year, a land of vineyards, luscious plantations, rich estates and olive groves, I was amazed to find filth, hunger, and vice in slums swarming with myriads of half-naked children. Who owned that rich land outside those wondrous cities which could have stilled the hunger and have been a source of well-being, if not of affluence, to the innumerable starvelings of the streets? A small number of absentee landlords, the grandees, the *señores*, who spent their winters in Biarritz and Paris. Who exploited those vast estates, the forests, and the farms? It was the Church which virtually controlled the Andalusian citrus crop, from planting to export, from banks to railways and steamship lines.

I had seen religious processions in 1931, one in Seville and one in Saragossa, still another in Cáceres, a small town where there were thirty-eight monasteries, the one standing next to the other in an endless row like the cathedrals in the Kremlin of Moscow, processions carrying a golden-diademed statue of the Virgin which was literally buried under jewels, diamonds, rubies, smaragds and other precious stones, including decorations and stars of the kind worn by victorious generals and diplomats on their gala uniforms. Priests in golden vestments walked under baldachins of purple and damask, swinging censers of silver and filigree, preceded by banners of silk and jewel-studded croziers, surrounded by lace-wearing acolytes, train bearers and boys in violet soutanes carrying glittering boxes containing relics, followed by a monstrance of a value of three million pesetas that burst upon the eye like a cluster of diamonds. And looking on, pouring from the putrid alleys of the Triana quarter in Seville, and saluting the Real Presence by dropping on their knees, I had seen the hollow-cheeked, ragged, barefooted Magdalenes, the disheveled women, the unkempt hungry children, the very flesh and blood of Jesus.

Tourist agencies did not lead their clientele to the Triana, to the so-called Chinese City in Barcelona, or to the even more evil slums of Madrid, Murcia and Granada. And why should they, when every city had a hundred *verdaderas maravillas*, real wonders of architecture and art and beauty? That cloak of jewels on the Our Lady of Valencia's statue, easily two million pesetas, *Señor*. The altar pieces in the cathedral of Burgos? Well, everything was solid gold, including the altar itself. At the same time it could be said without exaggeration by Señora Nelkin, shortly after the Republic supplanted the monarchy, that not half the children of Spain had ever eaten their fill once in their lives. On the Gran Via and the Calle de Alcalá in Madrid you saw more fashionable gowns in one hour than on Fifth Avenue during a whole year. Yet, one minute's walk away from those thoroughfares you landed in dark courts off the side streets which swarmed with barefooted urchins and hungry-eyed women. The only visitors there were the gentlemen of the white-slave traffic who came to select their merchandise for the thousands of brothels in the cities of Spain and South America. What the Republic took over from Alfonso was a land peopled with hundreds of thousands of monks, treasure-stuffed monasteries and churches, whole districts inhabited by idiots, and overcrowded jails—a land filled with typhus and malaria. A people that had written one of the most brilliant pages of history had sunk to a position of a backward Balkan country.

In 1934, at the suggestion of Don Miguel de Unamuno, whom I found back in Salamanca, where the Republic had appointed him Rector Magnificus of the University, I visited the Las Hordas district in the province of Estremadura, east of Toledo. There, within a stone's throw, so to speak, of the most fashionable capital in Europe, I found a peasant population that was on a social and cultural level with the Arab fellahin of Trans-Jordan. Every person you met on the road went barefooted. Men and women were dressed in rags, the children suffered from pellagra and rachitis. Bread was an unknown luxury in that part of Spain. Hunger was proportioned to age: the older ones had been hungry a long time, the younger ones less, but they felt the pangs the more, not having been inured to suffering. People slept on heaps of straw without cover, and this was not the case in one hut, but in all those cottages with their earthen floors which were devoid of the most elementary comforts and even bereft of furniture. Yet all about were forests of oak and birch and enormous areas of the most fertile soil. The peasants were not allowed to set foot on these rich estates. Armed guards were posted all along the roads and in the woods, ready to spring into action if the hungry and poverty-stricken masses should make an attempt to occupy the seigneurial farms. Even the gathering of chestnuts and acorns on the properties of the nobles and abbots was forbidden, as it had been since time immemorial. Caught in the act of snaring a rabbit or a squirrel or picking off a crow, the "poachers" were shot down without mercy. This had been the law of the land for ages. The Republic could not change that overnight. For the seigneurs still had too many friends in the Cortes of 1934, dominated as it was by Lerroux and Gil Robles.

There were no schools in Las Hordas, except a room adjoining the village churches where the children were taught prayers and catechism. Ninety per cent of the adults were illiterate. I heard there the story of two Socialist doctors, the only medical men in fifty years to have come to settle and practice in an area of more than a hundred square miles inhabited by a half-million people. These two medical practitioners had been driven out by the Civil Guards upon a denunciation by the clergy that they were advocating birth control. They probably were, considering the fact that in spite of the injunction to be fruitful and to multiply it was difficult to see how the people of Las Hordas could be driven still deeper into shame and human degradation by having still more children. These people literally possessed nothing except a profound respect for what General Franco was to call "the traditional morality." For, although the seigneurial estates which could have given them bread were not even exploited agriculturally, but merely kept as hunting domains, these starvelings would humbly apply for work to the major-domos, who had been left in charge. They were refused. Even the great hunting parties at which the peasants were engaged as beaters had been suspended in 1934. The seigneurs were in Paris, in Fontainebleau, where Victoria Ena had set up her court, or in Biarritz and Deauville following Alfonso around the cocktail bars. No work of any kind was to be provided so long as a "Red" government (the agrarian-Fascist government of Gil Robles) remained in power in Madrid. The peasants had sent delegations to the capital, delegations of barefooted men who had walked all the way because all the villagers put together had not the money to provide their spokesmen with a speedier conveyance. At the Ministry of Agriculture where they had gone to ask how matters stood, that is to say with the agricultural investigations then in progress, they were told time and again that the government was still examining the situation. For the time being they were to go home and insist on being set to work.

"Let those fine Socialist *compañeros* of yours in the city, whom you put in power, give you work," the major-domos would tell them.

King Alfonso had wandered into the Las Hordas district quite by accident the year before his abdication. Upon his return to Madrid he called in the newspaper editors and told them the unbelievable story of peasants in relatively close proximity to the Spanish capital "feeding on roots and herbs." He had seen it with his own eyes, he said. For days thereafter the Madrilenian papers and the European press had been filled with harrowing eyewitness accounts and breath-taking photographs. And the King has said that something was to be done for the people!

That was in 1930. But nothing had been done to improve the lot of the peasants in the meantime. I visited orange plantations in May, 1936, in Andalusia where pickers received four pesetas a day for sixteen hours of work. On one property a strike was in progress because a quarter peseta was being deducted from the daily wage for the water taken at mealtime from the owner's well. Yet in Seville, the directors of the citrus trust, of which the Church was the richest and the most influential member, cried out that "the Bolsheviks" were filling the heads of the people with outrageous ideas. The Civil Guard shot down the strikers as if they were cattle. In Seville the cards were on the table. "Blood is going to flow," people said.

Conditions in rural Spain closely resembled, I imagine, those prevailing in France on the eve of the Revolution of 1789. The Republic had done very little to change the desperate situation. The successive republican governments since 1931 had all been more or less reactionary and had been following the same agricultural policy as the monarchy: all had held out promises of amelioration but had failed to apply the only measure that could have brought alleviation: confiscation of the feudal estates and their division amongst the peasants.

Of course, since the Frente Popular had come to power, there had been a few excesses in isolated spots. What else could have been expected when a people shook off the yoke under which it has been burdened for ages? Here and there certain individuals had taken the opportunity to wreak vengeance on their oppressors, but collectively the parties of the Popular Front had maintained an amazing discipline in their hour of victory and had severely condemned the isolated outbreaks. To one who had seen something of conditions before February, 1936, it was a downright wonder that no more damage had been done.

On my round trip in May of that year, I investigated a few of these disturbances. In Robledillo for instance, the peasants, tired of waiting for the distribution of the land, had seized an estate belonging to a grandee. The grandee himself had not been near his place for seventeen years, but the major-domo and his assistants had put up a fight. When the peasants had begun cutting down the oak forest to build themselves a communal center and to replace their hovels with wooden houses, the major-domo, a certain Don Pablo Periquino, at the head of his fellow servants, had surprised them with a salvo of bullets. Seven peasants had been killed, ten wounded. They had withdrawn, taking the dead and wounded with them, but the next night the château had gone up in flames and the major-domo, the village priest and the other defenders of the estate had had their bowels opened with pitchforks.

Another spontaneous land occupation had occurred in the neighborhood of Navalmoral. But there the Civil Guards had interfered. The personnel of these troops had not been changed when the Frente Popular came into power. They were the same brutal repressionist machine the governments of Lerroux, Gil Robles and Primo de Rivera had used for years. Without waiting for instructions from Madrid they had massacred the peasants and set their huts on fire after locking the women and children inside. Then there had been revenge. Peasants from the neighborhood had come to the rescue. There had been a pitched battle, the guard driven off and the seigneurial mansion and the church set on fire.

In a little hamlet in the province of Cáceres there had been disturbance of a different nature. A young corporal, home from garrison duty in Valencia, had insisted that his marriage be performed by the civil authorities, as was permissible under the laws of the Republic. Under the governments preceding the Frente Popular the civil-marriage law had remained a dead letter in the rural regions. But this corporal—Damian López was his name—was a Popular Frontist. He had insisted that at his wedding there be no sacerdotal sanction. The mayor had tried to dissuade him. It would be the first civil marriage in the village. Damian should go to the priest who knew more about such things. Everybody, the best citizens, Damian's parents, his uncles and aunts—all had had their marriage solemnized in the house of God. But Damian would not listen. It was his right to have a civil marriage. He would abide by the laws of the country. He wanted to be the first to be married at the town hall.

On the day of the wedding, I learned, the village priest had appeared at the town hall, and made a scene. He had protested against the godless ceremony. He had called it a scandal and a sin. He had said that Guadalupe, Damian's fiancée, would be the same as a prostitute if she married without the rites of the Church. At this Damian had struck the priest, beaten him down, right in front of the mayor. And then Damian had been arrested and put in jail, but the villagers had set him free in the night that followed and they had burned the church and the vicar's house so that there could be no more church marriage either for Damian and Guadalupe or anyone else. But then the civil guards from Cáceres had been summoned and there had been a battle, many killed on both sides.

In May the populous quarters of the cities were seething with excitement. New contracts were under discussion, new wage scales were being drawn up. Every taproom was full of arguing and gesticulating men and women. Meetings were being held and sometimes parades organized and demonstrations, for the owners did not always submit to the new order of things with very good grace. They resisted. They closed their factories and plants, saying they would be ruined if they paid the higher wages demanded by the workers. It was the same petty chicanery, bickering, vexation and sabotage of the regime that attended the application of the labor legislation of the Roosevelt administration in America and the Popular Front in France. But nothing serious occurred: the workers used no violence or direct action; there was not a single sit-down strike in Spain. "If there have been some instances of violence," said the Governor of Toledo, Señor de Semprun Gurrea, a leading Catholic writer, who happened to be one of the first men I saw in Madrid, "they had their immediate antecedent, if not their entire justification in the senseless, egotistical and despotic antipopular policy of the preceding governments of the Right." In fact it seemed to me as soon as I had taken cognizance of the state of affairs that the Popular Front upon coming to power had been exceptionally lenient and magnanimous. Of a wholesale exodus or a wild stampede for the borders, as had been the case in Russia after the defeat of Denikine, there had been and there was no question in May. Business was operating normally. A few churches and cloisters had been burned, but no banks had been touched. The railways were running in the same old inefficient way. I found the Cortes discussing a program of land reform and the monarchist and agrarian opposition sending one deputy after the other to the rostrum to voice disagreement, sometimes in the most vehement terms. All this did not look like a Red dictatorship or like any dictatorship at all.

Nonetheless, trouble was brewing. But not on the Left. It was the Right that would not abide by the decision of the majority of the people. Four days after the elections rightist students in Madrid made an attempt on the life of a Socialist professor, Señor Jiménez de Asua, and accidentally killed a policeman who was accompanying the professor. (The latter had been warned of an impending attempt on his life.) A few days thereafter one of the judges who had imposed sentence on the murderous students was shot down in the streets. Then came the celebration of the fifth anniversary of the founding of the Republic when Fascists threw a bomb at the presidential tribune just at the moment when Señor Azaña, the President, had finished his speech. The deadly engine missed him by a couple of inches. In protest the workers of Madrid decreed a twenty-four-hour strike. They did not retaliate by attacking leaders of the Right. They simply demanded that the government immediately dissolve the Fascist leagues—a little matter that had been neglected up till that time.

We were to see the same thing in France a few weeks later, when Léon Blum, driving peacefully home from the Chamber, was suddenly set upon by a band of Fascist youths, and he and his wife were so unmercifully beaten and kicked that Blum's life was in danger for several days. Mme. Blum died of the consequences a year later. And what took place in France when the Popular Front came to power had its parallel in Spain when the Frente Popular formed the government in Spain. To embarrass the government, the reactionaries exported their capital abroad, paying as much as twenty per cent in commission for transfer. That was the first move in the bitter economic war which preceded the armed insurrection by Franco and the army.

The government of the Frente Popular, which had come to power in a legitimate constitutional manner, as the result of elections held under the auspices of the preceding reactionary government of Señor Gil Robles, represented the very opposite of a dictatorship. The masses put Manuel Azaña, the distinguished liberal, in power because he was opposed to any and every form of dictatorship, whether from the Left or from the Right. An attempt was to be made for the first time in history to govern Spain in a constitutional manner. That the experiment was launched with the support of the proletarian parties, even with that of the handful of Communists, is evidence of the genuine liberal-democratic character of the regime which the reaction sought to destroy.

Most of the men I met in the course of my tour in the months of May and June, while happy over the turn of events, entertained grave apprehensions for the future. The electoral victory of February was not to be taken as a final triumph of the progressive elements. Señor Giral, professor of pharmacy at the University of Madrid, one of the liberal party's chief lieutenants who preceded Largo Caballero in the premiership, said frankly that February had been but a preliminary skirmish and that the real struggle between democracy and the defenders of predatory interests was still to come. Don Miguel de Unamuno, whom I visited again, was in a gloomy mood. "Dire events are in the offing," said the Basque sage. "The atmosphere is charged as if a thunderstorm is approaching. . . . In fact, I do not think it can be long before the present tension snaps. . . . The old clique has not abdicated by any means. . . . It is foolish to think that the elections have made Spain safe for democracy. . . . The Republic has made the enormous mistake of leaving the old generals in charge of the army. For in Spain," he added, "the real menace is not Bolshevism, as the Right would now have the world believe. . . . Bolshevik theories never made the slightest impression on the Spanish masses. . . . There is no Communism here. I said that in Paris six years ago and I repeat it now. Our greatest danger is the military. We have more officers here in Spain right now than the German Empire had during the Great War. The Republic has not dared to send these fellows packing, for fear that their rancor would cause them to plot. History has shown that our militarists need not be dismissed from the army to become conspirators. . . . They form a pretorian elite which has strong links with the higher clergy and with the financiers. They are nearly all aristocrats. . . . They were plotting yesterday. They are plotting today. . . . I do not think they aim at a restoration of the monarchy, for it is they who betrayed the monarchy in its dying hours. They are playing for higher stakes. They want to rule without the monarchy. But such a pretorian republic would be infinitely worse than the regime of Don Alfonso or Primo de Rivera, for I doubt if it could maintain itself without foreign aid."

These words were spoken in May, 1936!

I went from town to town: Salamanca, Valladolid, Saragossa, Avila, Escorial, Madrid again, Toledo, Seville, and thence up the coast to Cartagena, Valencia and Barcelona, the same route I had taken two years previously. On the outside there was little changed. Life went on in the usual way: factories worked, the peasants were out in the fields, the *señoritas* strolled up and down the main streets accompanied by their duennas, people went in and out of the churches, the cabarets and night clubs were full to overflowing— everything was as it had been. No, not everything: for one thing there were more bookshops; the labor halls, the so-called People's Houses, were no longer located in dilapidated slum dwellings. Popular evening classes had been opened, concerts were given, the walls carried announcements of new hospitals and clinics having been made available to the public, the entrance fee to the bullfights had been reduced, and there was an enormous number of meetings being held. But to my amazement I saw young dandies, of the type Parisians call *fils de papa*, come into a popular meeting in Seville and throw a lot of stink bombs. I learned, after the whole audience had fled outside to escape the odor, that this was not an unusual occurrence. In fact, the windows of labor halls in that city and others were regularly smashed by the same hoodlum elements. Every day the papers reported cases of lone workers being waylaid on their way home at nights in dark corners of Madrid, Socialist and libertarian militants being assassinated—all the usual tactics of French Fascism with which I was too well acquainted. But here in Spain Fascism was supposed to have been conquered, whereas in France the Popular Front was still in formation. What kept the government from putting an end to these depredations?

"If we retaliate—and it would be the easiest thing in the world to ask the workers to take revenge," said Señor Azaña, the new President, in an interview, "we show ourselves the same uncivilized barbarians as the reactionaries."

"But the churches?" I objected. "Have they not been fired in retaliation?"

"We know perfectly well who the incendiaries of the churches are," he said. "In every instance where the perpetrators of these outrages have been caught in the act they turned out to be members of the Fascist *falange* or of the extreme Right. In several cases they were found with membership cards of labor organizations in their pockets—plain *agents provocateurs*. It has been clear to the government that the reaction finds the victory of the Popular Front too hard a pill to swallow. It is doing its utmost to create the impression abroad that unbridled license and terror have come to Spain with the triumph of the democratic parties."

That was indeed the argument Franco gave the world two months later when he betrayed the Republic: Spain had been plunged into chaos by the anarcho-Communist-Socialist coalition and he, Franco, had been chosen by God to be the country's savior. Three times, declared Queipo de Llano, the insurgent broadcasting general, in his first press interview after the rebellion broke out and he had seized control of Seville, three times Spain had saved European civilization in the past: once from the Moors, once from the Jews, and once from Protestantism (by Philip II's cruel extermination of the new religion in the southern Netherlands); this time Spain was going "to preserve Christian civilization in Europe by blotting out the menace of Marxism." The same efficacious methods which had been so successful in the Middle Ages were apparently to be employed again, for Generalissimo Franco complemented the statement of his lieutenant by declaring that even if he had to kill off one half of the population he would go through with his plan to restore "respect for religion and the traditional morality of Spain."

2

Having returned to France after my round trip in May and June, I rushed back to Spain when Franco's revolt, which at first had looked like an insignificant garrison brawl in the Moroccan protectorate, jumped the Straits of Gibraltar to the mainland. Right then the incident of the Italian airplanes made it clear that the Spanish Republic was not confronted with a mere military pronunciamento of the kind General Sanjurjo had attempted two years earlier, but that Europe was about to witness a brazen looting expedition on the part of Mussolini and Hitler in the Spanish peninsula.

On July 30, three Italian bombing planes, for want of fuel, had been forced to land in French Morocco. Two others crashed in the Oran region of Algeria and a sixth fell forty kilometers from Nemours, near the mouth of the Moulouya River. Every one of these planes had ten machine guns on board. After examining the wrecked planes and interrogating the surviving aviators, who had first pretended to be Spaniards, the French High Commissioner in Rabat informed his government in Paris that the six bombers had left the military airdrome of Milan on the morning of July 27. But, he added, the order to transport the six machines to Spanish Morocco, an order which had been found on the dead bodies of the aviators, had been issued by the Italian military authorities on July 15.

In other words, three days before Franco started his revolt, Italy had begun its war against the Spanish Republic!

When I arrived in the Catalonian capital on July 22, the decision had already been made: Fascism had been extirpated. One of the ablest military commanders of Spain, General Goded, who had scientifically prepared the crushing of Catalonia and had occupied all the strategic points in the capital and in the whole autonomous republic with forty thousand picked troops, had been defeated and made a prisoner. It seemed almost unbelievable. For Franco and his fellow conspirators had been well aware that the sharpest opposition to their *Putsch* would develop in cities like Barcelona and Saragossa where the workers were better organized than anywhere else. They had taken ample precautions to drown resistance in blood and the ablest staff officers were on the spot when the hour struck. In Saragossa the unarmed masses were overwhelmed and tens of thousands slain. But exactly in the sector where the Fascist chiefs had concentrated their most efficient troops they were defeated most decisively. On July 19, only three days before my arrival, Barcelona had been virtually under the heel of the Fascists. Further opposition had seemed futile. Goded dominated the city from a dozen points which seemed invulnerable because of the absence of arms amongst the people. Any attempt on the part of the people to dislodge the military from its strongholds was bound to turn into a wholesale slaughter.

Even so, remembering 1931 and 1934, when Barcelona had been given over to a pitiless White terror, the workers had rushed Goded's troops. Against his machine guns and artillery they advanced with miserable pistols, butcher knives, muzzle-loaders, old flintlocks and commandeered motor trucks. It was sheer insanity, but within a few hours, at the cost of about a thousand dead in the workers' ranks, feudal Fascism was swept away, and in a few weeks' time the whole of Catalonia was liberated.

And Catalonia was the crux of the situation. On Barcelona Franco had pinned his hopes. For in Catalonia resided twenty-four per cent of the total population of the Spanish peninsula; the province contained fifty per cent of the natural resources of Spain and was the center of seventy-five per cent of the Peninsula's light industry and commerce.

Whatever the Fascists did subsequently in Spain does not begin to compare with the heroism of the unarmed and military unorganized workers of Catalonia. There was nothing heroic about that massacre by the Moors of the thousands in Badajoz whose names were found on the list of subscribers to a local public library in which there may have been some books by Karl Marx and Piotr Kropotkin. Nothing heroic about the crushing of the Catholic

Basque Republic by powerful and perfectly equipped foreign armies. Judged by standards of military chivalry and fair play, such an episode as the siege and relief of the Alcázar fortress in Toledo, which was subsequently held up to the admiration of the world as a sample of deathless Fascist courage, was simply an instance of brute force smashing down helpless masses of people. But it does take courage to storm churches and monasteries when from every window and crack leap the little flames of death and you have nothing but your bare fists, or a club, or at best a twenty-two-caliber hunting rifle. To do that a man must have an ideal and be willing to lay down his life for it.

3

Alarms were still frequent in Barcelona in the latter part of July; most of the time they were false, but very often Fascist resistance flared up dangerously. I was walking on the Paseo the afternoon of July 23, when a stream of limousines, packed with men and women of the militia, raced by at breakneck speed and came to a stop a few hundred yards up the street. I increased my pace to see what was going on. While the *milicianos* were alighting from their cars and standing about scanning the street in both directions and looking up at the houses, apparently wondering whether they had come on but another useless errand, machine guns suddenly began to rattle from the roofs and windows of the apartment houses on both sides of the avenue. In a flash the *milicianos* disappeared and passers-by scurried for the nearest doorways, but not without leaving a few dead and wounded on the pavement.

Those firing the machine guns from the apartment houses then extended their range, and in a few minutes their fire dominated one of the main thoroughfares of Barcelona in both directions. Windows were smashed from the inside in other houses and the broken glass clattered into the deserted street. Everywhere the nozzles of machine guns and *mitraillettes* appeared in the windows, and the roofs were dotted with Fascist snipers.

I was caught in a most dangerous position. I stood in the hallway of the apartment house where I had taken refuge. A shower of glass crashed down on the sidewalk in front of me, evidence that

the building, or at least its upper stories, was occupied by the
Fascists. To remain might have meant a bullet from the first militiaman entering the building. To make a dash for it seemed even more
risky, for it meant running the gauntlet of half a dozen machine
guns and heaven knows how many snipers. Heavy trucks loaded
with men were roaring by outside and the firing turned into a sustained fusillade. Nobody came into the house where I stood, and
nobody left. Through the iron lattice of the door I could see a
man crawling from the middle of the street to the sidewalk. He was
keeping one hand on his stomach. Another lay flat on his back, his
eyes wide open, beating the pavement with the flat of his hand.
A truck racing by at express-train speed missed the wounded man's
head by an inch. . . .

I had stood there for twenty minutes, helpless, with the sweat
running down my face, when a body crashed down on the sidewalk
in front of the door. It struck the concrete walk headfirst and the
sight of the brains spattered over the *trottoir* almost turned my
stomach. In another minute a second body plopped down and a
third and a fourth. What was going on? Were the Fascists jumping
out of the windows?

A few minutes later the puzzle was solved: the militia had gone
across the roofs and had invaded the houses occupied by the
Fascists by way of garrets and the fire escapes. When the victors
came downstairs leading some of their prisoners and carrying the
captured machine guns, I merely had to show my pass signed by
García Oliver, the chief of one of the big labor unions, to be
allowed to proceed on my way.

4

Three months later when I visited Barcelona again, there remained not a trace of disorder. The old regime was making way for
a new order of things. Theaters had reopened. The transportation
system, including the taxicabs and the underground railway, was
functioning normally, and food was plentiful. But the false Montmartre atmosphere in the Paralelo neighborhood had completely
evaporated. You could walk through the quarter known as the
Chinese City without an army of pimps and harlots and dope

peddlers hanging on to your coattails. The brothels, night clubs, gambling casinos, peep shows, honky-tonks and obscene movies had been closed. That was the work of the working-class committees. On the other hand, the churches and convents which had escaped the fury of the masses in July had been turned into kindergartens, cultural centers, hospitals, lecture halls and popular universities. Scores of small bookshops had made their appearance. People apparently were turning to reading in a country where letters and learning were for ages, if not proscribed, then at least the privilege of a minority of *monsignori* and bourgeois lawyers. The famous monastery of Montserrat, located on the mountain overlooking the city, had been transformed into a sanatorium for tubercular children, but nobody could tell me where the monks had gone, nor did anyone seem to care a great deal.

By chance I met one of these Benedictine friars, a man who was an old acquaintance of mine, on the deck of the prison ship *Uruguay*, which was lying in the harbor of Barcelona. Several years before, in 1927, I believe, he and I had shared a cabin on a journey from Cyprus to Naples. He had been engaged in a new translation of the Bible and had been summoned to Rome to be present when the first book was offered to the Pope. When I suddenly stumbled on him there on the deck of the prison ship, we talked of that trip, of our arrival in Naples where the Fascist police, apparently tipped off about the presence of some Italian anti-Fascist on board, had subjected every debarking passenger to a grilling interrogation and then had gone so far as to order my cabin mate to shave off his black beard which he had grown in Palestine. Nothing less would do to convince the Black Shirts that the clean-shaven face on the passport was not that of the bearded priest in front of them.

"But I am in a far worse predicament now," said the friar laughingly. "This time I am going to be shot. Everybody on board here is going to be shot."

When I asked him why he had been arrested, he only shrugged his shoulders. Before leaving the prison ship, I learned from the commandant that my old fellow traveler had been captured in the Carmelite cloister which stands near the intersection of the Paseo and the Rambla in Barcelona. He had been dressed in the uniform of a Civil Guard when he surrendered and was under suspicion of having operated a machine gun along with some young seminarists. He was to be court-martialed and his fate was not uncertain.

From Santillan, the libertarian leader, who supervised the introduction of revolutionary tribunals in Catalonia, I managed to obtain
a pass, a few weeks later, to attend the monk's trial. But when he did
not even make an attempt to deny the charges of having taken part
in the Fascist-military conspiracy, and nobody had a good word
for him, I asked for the privilege of addressing the court. This was
granted at once. I began by telling the judges of our trip to Italy
and of the days and nights spent in discussion in our cabin and on
the decks of the *S.S. Lotus.* It was from the prisoner at the bar, I
said, that I heard the whole marvelous story of the age-old struggle
of the Benedictine monks of Montserrat for Catalonian cultural
autonomy. They had kept the flame of Catalan independence alive
in the darkest days of Primo de Rivera's governorship. They had run
a clandestine press right under the nose of the dictator and they had
fought the centralizing policy of the monarchy with every means at
their disposal.

The judge interrupted me to say that the monk was being tried
for high treason and carrying arms against the legally-constituted
authority. He deserved death by the firing squad. I asked the court
to show mercy and thus set an example to the barbarian Fascists, who
were shooting down their prisoners without so much as the semblance of a trial. I told of an incident I had witnessed at the front
in Sietamo where Durruti, one of the people's leaders, had intervened when the militia was about to execute a batch of Fascist
prisoners.

"He is a traitor!" said the president of the court with finality.

"He is a misguided patriot, *compañero,*" I said. "He is also an
eminent scholar." And then I tried to describe the system of scientific research of ancient manuscripts that was once carried on in
Montserrat monastery; how the prisoner himself was the inventor
of a chemical preparation which washed out the superimposed
scribblings of medieval copyists and laid bare the original Greek or
Latin texts.

All this had nothing to do with treason and rebellion, of course,
but I was playing to the gallery and the court listened attentively—
Catalans like the sound of the French language anyway, even when
it is pronounced with a Dutch accent. In the end I argued that the
execution of so renowned a scholar would impoverish European
culture. Would that serve the social revolution?

In the end I had the satisfaction of hearing my Benedictine friend sentenced to banishment for ten years and the loss of civil rights for fifteen years.

On the last occasion I heard from him he was preparing to resume his work in the famous Ecole des Chartes at the Sorbonne.

5

I spent the first weeks of the civil war behind the lines in Catalonia with a column of libertarian partisans. The Catalan labor unions had performed the miracle of beating down Goded and his army of forty thousand men in Barcelona proper. Whatever war equipment was available for the campaign to dislodge the Fascists from the provincial cities in Catalonia and Aragon had been collected from the abandoned stores of the defeated insurgents and from the monasteries and churches in the capital.

Even so, supplies for a campaign in the rural regions were ridiculously inadequate: no artillery, no machine guns, no trucks. When on my first contact with the militia on the outskirts of the town of Sietamo I saw the poverty of their equipment my heart sank in my shoes. How could these men in overalls and canvas slippers expect to halt the drive that would certainly be coming from the direction of Saragossa? Thoughts of Ethiopia flitted through my mind. Men were lying about in all attitudes alongside a rural road, sleeping, eating, discussing what was to be done. Hundreds of farmers from the surrounding districts had joined them. They wanted to enlist. But there were no rifles to hand out. Three planes zoomed overhead and dropped their bombs on the railroad tracks and on the orchards. A wheat field had caught fire. Fragments of high explosives clattered on the barn roofs. Machine-gun bullets pecked away at the plaster walls of the cottages. One group of *milicianos* sat about under an umbrella tree staring somberly at the evolutions of the metal birds in the sky. One pursuit plane veered around and almost touched the roofs of the houses and rattled its death spray. The machine flew so low I could see the observer swing his machine gun around.

"If he comes again," I said to a group of men who watched from the cover of a railroad culvert, "you can drop him with your rifles.

Surely, someone is bound to hit the gasoline tank, if you give him a salvo."

"Sure, we could," came the answer, "but we have no cartridges, *compañero!*"

No cartridges, no medical supplies, no blankets, exactly two hundred old shells for the antiquated cannons that had been found in the fortress of Montjuich. But those shells were now crashing into the tower of Sietamo. Men who had never fired a gun in their lives: schoolteachers, dock workers, typesetters, Ford employees—all had found the range after a dozen misses. You could see chunks of masonry crashing on the cathedral roof. Smoke puffs were issuing from the belfry.

"We must take Sietamo before the Fascists bring their artillery and tanks from Huesca," said Durruti, the leader of the column. "With the stores we capture in Sietamo we can advance."

Advance? One *miliciano* looked around the corner of the first house on the street leading into town. There was a sharp rap as of an anchor chain slipping a dozen notches through the hawser, and the *miliciano*'s brains splashed out against the whitewashed wall.

"We'll go over the roofs and through the cellars," said Durruti. "We must take that church over there by morning."

A violent explosion cut his words short. Everybody got up. The air was filled with an acrid smell. Cautiously some men crawled forward to investigate.

"A shell?" I asked.

"No, Jimines has wiped out that machine-gun crew," came the answer. "That was Jimines' brother who was just killed, the man who looked around the corner. Jimines threw a packet of dynamite. We have another machine gun now, brand-new."

"Now we can take a step further," announced Durruti.

An armored train came rumbling up the track. There was a red-black flag on the locomotive and the letters FAI, initials of the Anarchist Federation. The train stopped at the level crossing behind us. The engineer came over to talk with Durruti's general staff, which was composed of an English boatswain, named Middleton, who had deserted ship at Barcelona, a French journalist of the newspaper *Barrage*, and a Señor Panjanú, the only one of the forty-nine colonels in Barcelona who had not joined Goded's revolt.

Three men were carrying the body of Jimines away. They had wrapped his broken head in a newspaper. The door of the house on the corner opened and an old man stepped out driving five chickens before him. He greeted me with a flourish of his tattered hat.

"Why do you stay here?" I asked.

"Why shouldn't I?" he returned. "This is my house. Everything is in order, except that the Whites took my donkey yesterday. The chickens they missed."

He laughed and showed his toothless gums.

"How many were they?" I asked.

He shrugged his shoulders.

"They're in the church," he said, pointing in the direction of the city's center. "They have fortified it. Have you heard whether they are sending up any rifles from Barcelona?"

"Do you want to fight, too?" I asked in amazement.

"Why shouldn't I?" replied the old peasant. "My eyes are good!"

The armored train rolled on. It had twenty machine guns on board.

"Unless the Whites get a direct hit on that train with their guns, we will be in the railway station in an hour's time," remarked Durruti.

The body of a boy lay slumped against the side of a house. His left hand was stretched forward towards his rifle, which had fallen a few paces ahead of him. His mouth was stuffed with bread. Death had caught him in the act of eating. In his right hand he held the rest of the loaf. The bread was soaking up the blood that trickled in a thin stream from his side. . . .

A tank came lumbering towards us. It crunched over the barbed-wire entanglements fifty yards up the street. The *milicianos* grabbed their rifles and jumped to their feet. I was ordered into the rail guard's cabin. After ten minutes a *miliciano* told me to come out: "It's all right. That tank is one of ours," he said. "Some peasants captured it." Everybody crowded about the engine to look it over. The boy who had driven it over was being questioned by Durruti. He climbed on top and tumbled inside leaving the lid open. Presently he reappeared and began handing out sacks of hand grenades. Durruti smiled.

"We'll soon have as much ammunition as Franco," he said.

Death lurked around every corner. Every house had to be carried by storm. From every window snipers picked off *milicianos* and peasants. A man would suddenly grasp his head and sink to his knees. Another running across an open court would stumble as a little boy who stubs his toe, his rifle slipping from his hands and clattering on the cobblestones. Before his body struck the ground it was riddled with bullets.

I saw a Fascist lying in the rain conduit of an official building quietly emptying the drum of his *mitraillette* into the street below, until a *miliciano's* head appeared behind him through a garret window. The Fascist turned sharply and fired at the militiaman and brought him down. But in his fall, before plunging into the street below, the *miliciano* grabbed the Fascist and both rolled off the edge of the roof. Their bodies locked together came down with a smack in the street. A worker quietly picked up the *mitraillette*. A few minutes later it was spitting bullets in the direction of the central square.

Darkness came. Some houses were on fire. The reflection of the leaping flames on the flanks of the tower gave the scene a strange, unreal aspect. It made me think of a Fourteenth of July celebration in France with Bengal fire, before the days of floodlighting. But the square in the middle of which stood the church remained untaken. Only the captured tank had ventured into the bullet-swept area to reconnoiter. It had not returned. From all sides the *milicianos* were converging upon the medieval building with its massive walls and buttresses and counterforts. They fired blindly at the windows and porticos. Short tongues of flame would leap in answer from a sound hole in the tower and from between the pillars of a broad balcony that ran in front of the façade. That was the point where the Fascists had concentrated their machine guns, that balcony. The place could not be approached. Durruti said: "We will wait till dawn, but then we must go into the square. We will bring up a piece of artillery and blow away that balcony."

At daybreak he was told that not a single shell remained.

"Then we'll dislodge them with hand grenades!"

The hand grenades did not reach the balcony. Those who pitched them did it awkwardly. They were shot down the moment they ventured into the open. The square was littered with motionless little mounds. By the first streaks of dawn they looked like piles of clothing. Wounded men were calling from the square, cursing the delay. Others crawled back slowly, inch by inch, into the safety of the side streets. The Fascist machine guns barked in quick, nervous bursts. The *milicianos* stood silently flattened against the walls impotent, disgusted.

"To make a rush means to be cut down like ripe corn," said Colonel Panjanu.

Durruti looked at him sharply, questioningly.

"We are going to rush the square," replied Durruti, "and you will lead us."

But no mass attack was necessary. Two barefooted, ragged peasant boys quietly wrapped bundles of dynamite around their waists, inserted the caps in one of the sticks, and then, with a lighted cigarette in the one hand and the short fuse in the other, suddenly dashed across the square. One fell wounded by a burst of machine-gun fire, but he crawled on and reached the cathedral's porch. His companion had already applied his cigarette to the fuse. There was a moment of suspense and then the ear-tearing rip of an explosion . . . and another one. The boys had blown themselves up. The balcony with the machine guns crashed down in chunks to the flagstones.

A minute later the militia stormed across and a thick column of smoke poured from the tower. The Fascists in the bell chamber were roasting to death. Those inside the church surrendered.

The town of Sietamo[2] was taken. But one horrible surprise awaited the victors. In the dank cellars of the municipal building, where a detachment of Whites held out till the afternoon, were found the bodies of the hostages, the labor leaders and the liberals of the community. They lay in pools of fresh blood, but the clots of brains adhering to the mildewed walls showed that they had been shot at close range.

The inhabitants were circulating freely in the streets towards sunset when a batch of prisoners was being led away. They were all military men, several officers amongst them. On the west side of the church they were halted and placed against the wall. A crowd collected to see the execution. Just as the firing squad had taken up its position Durruti appeared on the scene.

"What are you doing?" he asked the *milicianos*. "Who gave orders for this? Are you going to shoot defenseless men?" There was an

[2] An error in the transmission of two separate dispatches on the capture of the small town of Sietamo situated on the outskirts of the provincial capital of Huesca made it appear as if I had reported the taking of the provincial capital itself, which is also named Huesca. In this city the loyalists secured but a precarious hold and were driven back after a few days' occupation of the outer districts.

angry murmur at these words and shouts of hate. "They executed our *compañeros* you say?" shouted Durruti, his face livid with anger. "Does that mean that we have to do the same? No!" he thundered. "Down with your rifles! These men are going to Barcelona for trial. They are human, even if they behaved like swine."

He did not finish. The *milicianos* burst out laughing. One of the Fascists had dropped on his knees and was making the sign of the cross with a lightninglike rapidity.

As the prisoners were being marched off, five airplanes came zooming down from the direction of Saragossa. The entire population of Sietamo ran out into the streets to see the machines. The balconies of the houses and the roofs were black with people. When they were overhead the machines let go their bombs. A series of terrific explosions followed.

I went to the quarter where the first torpedoes had fallen. Several houses had collapsed; *milicianos* were already digging out the wounded whose cries could be heard under the piles of pulverized masonry. A little girl was the first to be dragged out. A beam had crushed her chest. Then came the body of an old woman. Far away the detonations of other exploding torpedoes were heard.

"Were they Spanish planes, *compañero*?" a *miliciano* asked me.

"They were Junker planes, *compañero*, German planes!"

"Don't those German bastards have mothers and children?" he asked.

6

With the Fascist rebellion crushed in Catalonia and the Moors halted on the outskirts of Madrid, the republican authorities found time to examine and classify the enormous number of documents which had been found in the homes and clubs of fugitive nobles, ecclesiastics, military men and Fascist leaders as well as in the abandoned offices of the German Nazi sections that flourished all over Spain before July, 1936. These papers established definitely that Hitler and Mussolini had not rushed to the aid of Franco in a spontaneous and disinterested élan of brotherly feeling when he set about "to rid Spain of Marxism," but that the conspiracy had been hatching a long time. One of the first documents to come to light was a procès-verbal of a conference held in Rome in May, 1934, between Mussolini and the Spanish monarchist leader, Antonio Goicocea. At this conference the Duce had promised to furnish the rightist parties with two hundred thousand rifles and two thousand machine guns. Another document showed that General Sanjurjo, who was to have been the leader of the revolt, visited Berlin in May, 1936, and came away with a donation of two million pesetas for the work of stirring up trouble in the republic.

Even more remarkable were the instructions sent by the Nazi Bureau of Propaganda and Enlightenment in Berlin, under the direction of Dr. Goebbels, to Nazi clubs and consuls in Spain telling them to invent "Red" atrocity stories for publication in the German press. There were piles of documents, fifty thousand in all, showing beyond doubt that the German government had made up its mind to capture the trade and commerce of Spain and that the Spanish military party, the nobles, and the Fascists had been in complete accord with the Nazi plans.

During the Great War Alfonso XIII once made the remark: "Only I and the Spanish rabble are for France and the Allies: every one of my generals is a pro-German." The papers that the Frente Popular government brought to light showed that the generals were not only pro-German but that Sanjurjo, Mola, Franco, Goded and the whole upper military clique were in the pay of the Nazi Reich.

I was permitted to inspect documents which established that the German airplane factories of Junker, Dornier, Krupp and Messerschmidt, whose names were later to figure so often and in so tragic a manner in the dispatches about Guernica and Gijón and Bilbao, had been dickering with Sanjurjo and Juan March, Franco's banker, a full eighteen months before the rebellion "broke out." In the light of those documents, which the Spanish government had the good sense to publish, everything that happened subsequently became clear; for instance, where Franco obtained the equipment to arm several divisions of Moorish tribesmen. The material had been shipped to him when he was governor of the Canary Islands in March, April and May, 1935.

The German Nazi party, not trusting Franco's espionage service in republican Spain, had had a spy of its own in every government post office and in every ministerial department for months. The names were there and the sheets setting forth their instructions and the reports they made. Most illuminating, too, was the endless correspondence between Nazi group Fuehrers in Spain and their head office in Berlin on the subject of "new potatoes."[3] From this exchange of letters the authorities learned at last the secret of the vast amount of small arms—160,000 revolvers in Madrid alone—which had found their way into the possession of Fascist sympathizers on the eve of the rebellion in July. The Frente Popular discovered, too late, it is true, that Germany had had no less than six thousand agents, all trusted Nazis, on the ground in Spain to prepare the insurrection for Franco and with the complicity of thousands of rightist officials in the different branches of the government service.

Of course, the Nazi agents had flown the coop at the first sign of danger and were now concentrated in the areas under rebel control, but the Spaniards who had conspired with the enemy were being arrested wherever they could be located. They were brought before the Tribunals of Public Safety, which the government had reluctantly established under pressure of the working-class organizations. In some instances the workers' indignation got the better of them. Some of the traitors were hauled before the workers' revolutionary courts and executed without long palaver by lawyers and attorneys.

7

The last military engagement I witnessed was the siege of the Alcázar fortress in Toledo. In the light of what followed—the horror of hundreds of cities and villages destroyed by "the civilizing action" of German and Italian bombers, the incredible massacres on the road from Almería, the sadistic bacchanalia of the Basqueland and the Asturias, Guernica, Durango, the aerial bombardments of Barcelona and Valencia—Toledo may perhaps be considered mere child's play. Still there was something so contemptible about the siege of that walled-in complex of medieval buildings that it sticks in my memory as the place where I saw Fascist ignominy sink to its lowest depth.

Most of the loyalist defenders of the town withdrew in good order in the direction of Madrid when Franco's troops entered. Only the prisoners and the sick were killed by the five battalions of Moors who marched in the vanguard of the "Christian" army.

[3] O. K. Simon, *Hitler en Espagne*, Editions Noël, Paris, 1938, p. 209.

This bloody exploit took place while Franco and his aides repaired to the cathedral to attend a solemn service of thanksgiving for the capture of the city, which is the seat of the Primate of Spain. While the Generalissimo was on his knees, the Riff battalions entered the municipal hospital and spiked every patient with their bayonets.

At the same time the world rang with the praise of the Fascist defenders of the Alcázar who had held out for months in the caves and subterranean chambers of the fortress and who were now at last set free. The siege of the Alcázar became a universal symbol of Fascist courage and endurance. Goebbels, over in Germany, ordered restaurants and night clubs which bore the name of Alcázar to change their name to something else. The word Alcázar was too sacred henceforth for profane use.

To have been locked in that fortress with their women and children and to have held out for months against the daily assaults of the "Red rabble" was deemed a feat of unsurpassed heroism. It was an epic that would go down the ages when everything else about the civil war would be forgotten.

It might indeed go down the ages, but not as an epic of heroism, but as one of the most disgusting exhibitions of Fascist cowardice and cruelty. For there is only one thing wrong with that story of Fascist fortitude: the women and children locked up in the fortress were *not* the relatives of the defenders—*they were the wives and children of the besiegers!*

The garrison of the Alcázar was made up of army cadets and their instructors. As a rule, cadets studying at a military academy are not old enough to be married. Such was the case at the Alcázar. Of course, the lads and their officers, most of them scions of noble families, were in the general military plot to attack the Republic. On July 20, when all eyes were riveted on Morocco and Barcelona, the cadets of the Alcázar suddenly poured out of the gates of the fortress and began rounding up as many women and children as they could. This was not a very hard job: the Alcázar stands in the neighborhood of the most populous quarter of the city. It was shortly after noon of a warm day when most of the slum inhabitants in Toledo, as in all southern cities, sit in the doorways. The men had gone off to work. In less than an hour the Fascist nobles had dragged off a few hundred women and children and locked them up in the cellars of the castle. Then the gates of the fortress were bolted and the nationalist flag hoisted on the parapet of San Pedro's tower. When the alarm spread through the city and the workers streamed back from work, they were received with salvos of machine-gun fire if they ventured into the open spaces bordering on the castle.

What could the loyalists do after that? Bring up some guns from the arsenal or from Madrid, only two hours distant, and blow the fortress to smithereens? But that would have meant burying their own wives and children under the ruins. For weeks no decision was taken. Sentinels were posted in the streets abutting on the Alcázar, and snipers took up their position on the roofs of neighboring houses and monasteries. Shots rang out now and then in the invested quarter but for the rest the town was quiet. *Milicianos* going to the front in the Tagus valley, where Franco was advancing with rapid strides after the insane butchery of Badajoz, passed by within a few blocks of the Alcázar. There were no mass assaults, no bombardments, no regular siege. The *milicianos* were undecided. There were repeated orders from Madrid to take the stronghold at all costs and finish an episode that kept thousands of loyalist men and women from joining the republican forces up the line at Talavera and Valdeglesias where Franco's Moors and the professional killers of the Foreign Legion were battering the Republic's defenses with artillery, aerial torpedoes and tanks.

On September 12, the Fascists hoisted the white flag and sent out an officer to ask for a priest. One of the cadets was said to be dying and was crying for the last sacraments of the Church. A loyalist priest, Don Alvarez Ponchón, was summoned in all haste. He was blindfolded in the square. Led by the hand of the officer who had come to parley, he disappeared within the gate. In a flash the square filled with men and women. From the wall floated the white flag. The Fascist cadets walked up and down on the battlements, their rifles slung over their shoulders, or they leaned over the walls to look down on the crowd below.

"*Caballero*," a woman would call up, "please tell us are the children well? Have they enough to eat? Where do you keep them?"

Others shouted imprecations: "Wait, you bastards, till we get a hold of you! Gangsters you are! Cradle snatchers! Have you no decency? We'll tear you apart with our teeth when we get you!"

The noble cadets on the walls just laughed. "You will never get us. General Franco is on the way. It is you who will be ripped up. The Moors are in the lead! Don't forget the Moors, brothers and comrades! Just a few more days and we'll be playing football with your cut-off heads!"

Then the priest returned and the crowd surged around him. "Have you seen the children, Don Alvarez? How are they treated? Have they enough to eat? Did you see my wife, Father, you know her?"

But the priest shook his head. He had had his eyes bandaged all the time, he explained, except in the hospital by the bedside of the dying man.

"They're hungry inside," he remarked abruptly. "They have killed their last mule. There is no bread."

"But that is monstrous, Don Alvarez. Our children are starving!"

The square was filled with wails and sobs. A soft rain had begun to fall. The moment the firing had ceased the sparrows had returned to the wet chestnut trees and chirped their joy on being back home. Then a machine gun in one of the towers rattled warningly. The square was deserted in a minute.

A gang of miners from the Asturias paused en route to the front in Toledo on the last day of September. They tossed a few packages of dynamite over the walls. The Fascists replied by having the captive women and children walk along the battlements in full view of the attackers. The loyalist snipers immediately held their fire. The *dinamiteros* were told to move on.

There were days when not a shot was fired on either side, but parleys would be frequent. One afternoon the white flag went up and an officer came out with some companions to ask the loyalists to post a letter to his wife. The letter was accepted and posted without even being read.

"What do you fellows want? Why don't you release the women and children at least?" The *milicianos* crowded around the Fascist officers. A quarrel broke out: "Franco is a word-breaking son of a bitch. . . . He has no ideals, no honor. . . . Even if we gave him Toledo, he'd order us to be massacred. . . . You, too, you are not *caballeros*. . . . You hide behind the skirts of women and children. . . ."

"It is you who have neither honor nor ideals," answered the officers. "You are fighting for Moscow!"

"For Moscow?" a cry of derision greeted the remark. "We are for the Republic! But you *caballeros*, you are the lackeys of Hitler."

Another day the Fascists parleyed for medicine. They brought out a whole list of items they lacked in the hospital. Gauze, bandages, iodine, antitetanus serum and 606. The loyalists sent for the supplies to the municipal hospital and allowed their enemies to carry off the load.

Beginning in October, Franco began sending airplanes over the Alcázar to drop sacks of foodstuffs. The loyalist planes from the nearby Getafe airdrome let them accomplish their mission and allowed the machines to return unmolested. It was not till one of the sacks, which fell on the roof of the medical building inside the Alcazar, exploded, that the decision was taken to attempt the capture of the fortress by mass attacks and by blowing up the underground passages which ran from the castle to the monasteries in the neighborhood.

But first another parley was held. Don Alvarez Ponchón, the loyalist priest, was dispatched to plead with the Fascists once more to let the women and children go. "Let them give us back the children and we won't harm a hair on their heads," the *milicianos* told the priest as he set out for the Alcázar accompanied by a white-flag bearer. "But tell them also that if they don't surrender we will blow the whole place to hell."

The priest was back in half an hour. He shook his head. "There is no use talking. The women and children are massed in the tunnels. They will be the first to get killed if you start to use dynamite. The commander told me that if he and his men are to die, your wives and children will die first. The women and children are in a pitiful state," went on the priest. "I have seen them. . . . They have been warned that they must die if you men attack. . . . Several women have gone insane, three babies have been born down there in the cellars. There is no food or milk. . . . I am afraid you will never see your loved ones again. . . ."

This prediction of the priest came true, for when Franco entered Toledo, the surviving wives and children were taken from the Alcázar and handed over to the pleasure of the Riffs. There is a saying among the Spaniards that when the Riffs get tired of playing with a girl they kill her.

8

When the prediction was freely made abroad that in the event of a loyalist victory the Church in Spain would be reduced to the status of Orthodoxy in Russia and that the freedom of worship but so recently (1931) established by the republican regime would be abolished again, it was not easy to discover in the country itself what basis there was for these prognostications. The government of the Frente Popular promulgated but one decree touching religious matters in the course of the war: all buildings belonging to the religious orders were to be confiscated. But this did not mean the abolition of worship. In France a liberal government had taken precisely the same measure thirty years earlier and yet no Catholic had thereafter been prevented from worshiping. The church buildings and their contents had merely changed ownership. They had become national property.

A service was held every morning by loyalist priests in Toledo, and on the Guadarrama front in the early days of the war when I was there. Attendance, however, was not compulsory for the militia, as it had been for the regular army in the days of Alfonso. It must be said too, that very few *milicianos* took part in those religious exercises, but this is not something which can be attributed to any malevolence on the part of the Madrilenian authorities. That men decline to go to church shows that the Church has failed to win or that it has lost their confidence.[4] Services were also held in many private homes, with the knowledge of the republican authorities, in Madrid, Barcelona and Valencia, the cities where I spent most of my time. But the churches in those cities remained closed. In the Catalan villages no religious activity of any kind went on, as far as I could

[4] The distinguished Catholic monarchist writer, Georges Bernanos, whose son served in Franco's army and who himself spent the first eighteen months of the civil war on Majorca, declares that the anticlericalism of the Spanish people cannot be attributed to Communist or Protestant propaganda but that it has been latent for long. Nor, says he, have the Spanish people been influenced by a public, nonsectarian public-school system as the French have. He puts the blame for the intense anticlerical sentiments of the people squarely on the shoulders of the Spanish religious authorities and . . . on the Devil.

Georges Bernanos, *Les Cimitières sous la lune*, Plon, Paris, 1937, p. 214.

discover, not because the Government had decreed it so, but because of the intense anticlerical feelings of the peasantry.

I have never seen a country where the priesthood was held in so general and so thorough a detestation by the masses as in Catalonia. That hatred had more of a social and political motivization than an antireligious character. Yet, in spite of this popular hostility towards the Church, no break occurred in the relations between the Vatican and the government of Madrid. Neither at the commencement of hostilities nor thereafter was the papal ambassador recalled, nor did the Republic's diplomatic representative come home from the Eternal City. President Azaña declared as late as January, 1938, that in religious matters the government intended to abide strictly by the constitution. There is nothing in the Spanish constitution about the interdiction of any religious cult.

Although it is undeniable, of course, that the war in Spain had certain ecclesiastical and even religious implications, only a man of the type of Queipo de Llano, whom Europe heard over Radio Sevilla give expert hints to his Moorish mercenaries and the soldiers of the Foreign Legion on the most pleasant way to rape the woman adherents of the Frente Popular, dared to qualify it as a holy war. But neither the Vatican nor the Spanish or French episcopates ventured to go that far. For that would have meant excommunicating the majority of the Spanish people who were definitely attached to the cause of Madrid.

Since intellectuals and not militarists express a people's aspirations and ideals, and many of the leading Catholic intellectuals of Spain, the Basqueland, and France stood with the Madrilenian popular government, I took pains to consult them for my newspapers on their attitude to the religious issues involved.

There was, in the first place, Don José Bergamin, editor of one of the most important Catholic reviews in the world, *Luz y Raya*, published in Madrid. I had known of Señor Bergamin for years, because of the influence of his periodical in Catholic milieus in France. He was not a defrocked priest or a runaway Jesuit. Señor Bergamin was and remained to the end in full communion with his Church. He was, moreover, one of the most appreciated collaborators of *Esprit*, the important periodical in Paris to which Jacques Maritain, professor at the Catholic University in Paris and one of the foremost Catholic scholars of our times, is a frequent contributor. In his own magazine and in *Esprit*, Don José Bergamin had for years, and long before the

Franco rebellion broke out, by virtue of the Christian principles he professes, denounced and combated "the sacrilegious impiety" of official Catholicism in Spain,[5] where religion, "emptied of all spiritual content," served only, in Bergamin's own words, "as a cover for the profit system and the oppression of the people." He openly sided with the government when the civil war broke out and continued publication of his intensely Catholic periodical all during the war right in Madrid. At no time did either the Spanish hierarchy or the Vatican even threaten to place *Luz y Raya* on the Index Expurgatorious. The elite of the Spanish as well as the French Catholic clergy continued to read what Señor Bergamin had to say on the issues involved in the struggle.

I saw Señor Bergamin on the day when the rebels dropped a box containing the mutilated body of a loyalist aviator who had fallen into their hands on the Gran Via in Madrid. Hand-to-hand fighting was going on in the gardens of the Royal Palace; Franco's Moorish battalions had just entered University City. On the wavering front line before Talavera and Getafe whence I had just returned, the *milicianos* had assured me that Franco would be halted before Madrid. But I had seen their defenses smashed one by one on the Toledo highway and I told Señor Bergamin of the roads being crowded with fleeing militia units.

The quiet sun-browned and weather-beaten face of the Spanish mystic wrinkled into a smile.

"The workers are right," he said. "Franco cannot take Madrid. With all the technical resources of the country at his command, which he stole from the government, he is incapable of capturing the capital. For instead of sinking as a result of the exhausting and uneven struggle, the morale of the republicans is taking the form of exaltation. In the country the new order is installing itself and is beginning to bear fruit."

The new order? I thought of the reports appearing in the foreign press about "Red" atrocities, about the closing of the churches, the assassination of priests and nuns and all the rest of the Fascist propaganda, and I wondered how a devout Catholic like Señor Bergamin

[5] This attitude on the part of devout Catholics is not exceptional. When the late Cardinal Mercier, on the occasion of a visit to Madrid, was congratulated on having had an opportunity of seeing and admiring Spanish Catholicism at close quarters, the Primate of Belgium replied after a long silence, "Spain a Christian country? Do you really think so?" This is quoted by Bernanos, *op. cit.*, p. 222.

could speak hopefully of the new order and even more how he and his Catholic partisans tolerated an association with men who were currently described in the safe and sound press abroad as Muscovite atheists and enemies of religion.

"But we Catholics get along marvelously well with the anarchists and the Bolsheviks and the Socialists," he replied. "We are friends, we are allies, we are brothers."

"You are perhaps only tolerated?"

"No, we are respected and honored and even a little spoiled, I am afraid," he answered. "The first time I had to speak at a popular mass meeting after Franco's coup, I must admit, I was afraid of the reception a man like myself, who came as a Catholic, would receive. But I was greeted with an unexpected enthusiasm. It was overwhelming. My fears entirely vanished. . . ."

"To what do you attribute this sympathy with which you Catholics are treated by the masses of the Frente Popular? We hear that they are antireligious fanatics and despoilers of churches."

"Well, you see," answered Señor Bergamin, "the people regard the official church as a supporter and symbol of all who oppress them. Religion in Spain means money, power, domination, inhumanity, capitalism, Fascism. . . . The union between the Church and Fascism became patent to everybody in the present struggle, not merely by the action of this or that bishop in exposing the Blessed Sacrament for Franco's benefit and declaring that Christ and the right-wing parties represented one and the same cause, but by the stocking of monasteries and churches with war material and then turning them into Fascist strongholds. The people's reaction to this betrayal has been cruel, I know. But I am surprised that it has not been worse. Yet in spite of all that, the people do retain a respect for true religion, for spiritual things, for Christian love," he went on. "On the other hand, they feel, as if by instinct, the sacrilege of those prelates and priests and monks who betray Christ while pretending to serve him— covering themselves with his name and falsifying his teachings. Yet, when a Catholic says to the people: 'We think as you do,' confusion disappears and they are filled with joy. Therefore, the place of true Catholics is in the midst of the people."

"How many priests have taken the side of the Frente Popular?" I asked.

"Not many in Castile, Andalusia and Catalonia, but in the Basque-land, the clergy and the faithful, perhaps the truest Catholics of

Spain, are unanimously on the side of the Republic. Yet, priests who do not take sides and who restrict their activity to religious affairs, are not molested. It is quite true, on the other hand, that many priests and monks in Spain have exchanged the cassock for the Fascist uniform. Others are waiting and hiding, for there are thousands of clerics who have refused to sign the declaration of neutrality. They are waiting for Franco's victory and the return of their privileges. They are incorrigible!"

On my last day in Madrid I had an interview with a canon of Segovia, professor of philosophy at the University of Madrid, who was amongst the signatories of a manifesto calling the world's attention to the insurgents' bombardment of an open city. I asked him: "How is it that Your Reverence has not left Madrid? General Franco may be here any moment and he is not likely to be very merciful towards an ecclesiastic who has made common cause with the Frente Popular by protesting against his bombardment of this city."

"My place is here," said the prelate, "with the people, in defense of the cause of righteousness!"

"But General Franco and Queipo de Llano call this a holy war, a crusade in defense of religion."

"They have no right to say that. A Catholic has full liberty to place himself on whatever side he deems to be representative of the cause of justice. I consider that I am serving my Church best by supporting the legitimate government of Spain."

"But the Pope?"

"The Pope does not condone war. He has said that war is always terrible and inhuman, more so when it is a war between brothers. Not war, but love; not to destroy, but to preach and to guide and to teach and to draw men's souls to Christ—those are the words of the Pope. I stand with the government of the Frente Popular because I consider that the Church still has an apostolic task to perform in Spain. I do not think that the cause of Christ is served by blessing the arms with which Franco is shooting down the humblest and the poorest of the people."

Then there was François Mauriac, ultraconservative member of the Académie Française, author of a *Life of Jesus* which bears the imprimatur of the ecclesiastical authorities in France, a man so influential in European Catholic circles that it was upon his insistence that Cardinal Pacelli telegraphed, in the name of the Pope, to the Archbishop of Toledo charging that ecclesiastical dignitary to plead with Franco for the utmost moderation in his operations in the Vizcaya sector, where he was dealing with an exclusively Catholic population.

"The constant teaching of the Catholic Church has been," wrote M. Mauriac, "that we owe obedience to the established authorities. Nobody can deny that on the day when the Spanish generals revolted, a legitimate and legal government had been established in Madrid. Even if we would concede that in the circumstances the Basques should have understood that insurrection suddenly became the most sacred duty, no mistake was ever more excusable than theirs. You do not assassinate an old Christian people because it did not believe it necessary to revolt.

"The legal government of Madrid said to the Basques: 'You are free!' Why should they not have defended inch by inch that independence of which they had dreamed for centuries and which the rebels refused them and which they had legitimately acquired? If they refused to hand over the iron mines and the steel mills of their country to Germany, the French should at least be indulgent. Some day we in France will understand that that poor people of the Basqueland suffered and died for us. May God grant that on that day we will not have to bury our dead where they are now burying theirs. It is a crime to treat as criminals such heroes who died for a liberty which they had not taken, but which was granted them freely.

"The Basques were not the accomplices of Moscow, as General Franco charges. That is a lie! They had no part in anything that took place in Barcelona or Valencia. They fought at home in defense of their homes. When the history of this war is finally told, we will know how little support they had from Madrid (which did not have the means to help them, it is true), how they were abandoned to their fate without airplanes, without antiaircraft defenses. Hitler and Mussolini had an easy time of it at Bilbao. What the world does not know either is that the Basque priests, who were covered with calumny and dragged through the slime by Franco and his propaganda service abroad, had built up a trade-union movement which was fully the equal of that of the anarchists and the Socialists. A noble work crumpled to pieces in the Basqueland when Franco entered, a work which was the honor of the Catholic Church in Spain and the Catholic Church in general. Whatever their error might have been, those Basque priests deserved clemency on the part of those who refused to admire them. In the most tragic hours they remained with their decimated flocks. All they could do was to await the conquerors who came in the name of God.

"We, Catholics of France," M. Mauriac went on, "are trying to reassure ourselves. We know that the Church never abandons its children. We turn towards our common father, to him whom St. Catherine of Siena called Christ on earth, towards the 'Servant of the Servants of God.' We know that he has done much, that many lives have been saved through him. But what is that when you consider the wholesale and legal massacre of priests and faithful by the insurgents? General Franco is also one of the faithful. There is only one power on earth that can stop the hand ready to strike: the power of Him whose Kingdom is not of this world."

M. Mauriac was speaking before Franco overran the entire Basqueland. Guernica had been gruesome. What happened in Bilbao the Catholics of France learned from their own Catholic newspapers and periodicals: *La Croix, Sept, Esprit,* and *La Terre Nouvelle.* If that news had come from Moscow, it would have been charged to Bolshevik propaganda. It is true that the excellent weekly *Sept,* which was published by the Dominican Fathers in France, was suppressed by Cardinal Verdier of Paris after its spirited defense of the Basques. But *La Croix* and *Esprit* printed the endless lists of names of Catholic priests executed by orders of Franco and the circumstances attending their martyrdom.

Here are some examples: Don Alejandro Mendicute, aged forty-five, vicar of Hernani, famous orator and sociologist. He was arrested at his home by Juan José Pradera, the son of an aristocratic family of San Sebastián, who first insulted him in an unmentionable way and then locked him up in the prison of Ondarretta. Don Alejandro was executed by the firing squad at the entrance of the cemetery in the presence of his brother, the curate of the village of Hernani.

Don Martin Lecuona and Don Gervasio de Arbrizú, respectively twenty-nine and sixty-four years of age. Both were priests in the parish of Rentería. They were executed in the village of Hernani by the Phalangists who first forced them to pull off their cassocks. Their bodies were transported on a wheelbarrow to the cemetery. Don Martin was the first secretary of the Basque group for Social and Christian Endeavor (*Agrupación Vasca de Acción Social Cristiana*) and was the founder of the Christian Basque working-class youth.

Don Joaquin Ariú, Don José Marquiegui, and Don Leonardo de

Guridi. The first, archpriest of the important parish of Mondragon, the other two priests of the same parish. The archpriest was sixty-four years old. He had the finest reputation of any man in the diocese and kept himself wholly free from all political activity. The Abbé Marquiegui was a well-known Basque writer. All three were executed on the day on which it is customary in Spain to celebrate the feast of Christ the King.

One could continue almost indefinitely citing names of Basque priests executed by the Phalangists and Carlists. This is admitted by the Catholic press itself. I will give one more instance reported by *Esprit*. Don José Penagaricano and Don Celestino de Onaindia, aged sixty-three and thirty-six respectively, the first vicar of Marquina-Echeverria and the second vicar of Elgoibar. The first left his house because it was in the line of fire of Franco's advancing army and sought refuge with the Abbé Onaindia. Both were arrested in the church at the moment they were celebrating Mass. They were thrown in a cell with three other priests. The five clerics were shot together in the cemetery of Oyarzun. As he faced the firing squad with his four sacerdotal colleagues, the Abbé Onaindia was reciting a *Te Deum*, and the tears ran down his face, reported the priest of the Phalangists, who confessed him. His tears, added the confessor, were not an expression of sorrow: he but felt that he was about to enter heaven. The Abbé Penegaricano uncovered his head as he faced the execution squad, because the Ave Maria was tolling at the moment. The bodies of the five priests were dumped into a hole with those of seventy other persons who had been executed. Their families were not permitted to erect a monument on their tomb.

"Are these things related," asked Motley, in discussing the terror unleashed by Alva and the Inquisition in the Netherlands, "to excite superfluous horror? Are the sufferings of these obscure Christians beneath the dignity of history? Is it not better to deal with murder and oppression in the abstract, without entering into trivial details?" The answer is that these things are the history of the epoch, that these hideous details furnish a compendium to this age in which the last traditions of Christianity and of humanism were cast aside by a generation that had readopted the cult of violence from the somber past of mankind.

The murders related above were carried out before Franco entered the ancient capital of the Basqueland. After his arrival the persecutions grew worse. The priests were slaughtered wholesale. And if that was the fate of the priests one can imagine in what manner the laity was dealt with by the blood-crazed Moors from Africa. Yet the Catholic press of France certified: 1. that not a single Basque priest was an adherent of the Basque Nationalist Party, whereas many priests in other parts of Spain are members of Right-wing organizations; 2. that during the entire civil war the Basque clergy kept itself apart, confining its activity to ecclesiastical affairs, and were respected by everybody, even by the Marxists; 3. that not a single chaplain with the troops was armed, whereas it was a well-known fact that chaplains serving with the rebels carry revolvers and frequently do not even take them off when celebrating Mass; 4. that not a single Basque priest served as a combatant in the national army (they were with the troops as chaplains and confessors); 5. that Franco personally forbade the publication of the names of the priests who were executed by his troops; 6. and that no Masses of requiem were allowed to be said for the repose of their souls.

Nowhere did Fascist ruthlessness reach such a depth of ignominy as in the Catholic Basqueland. Not satisfied with shooting down men and women whom the Moors, Italians, and Carlists found peacefully laboring in the fields, or locking inhabitants in their homes and setting these on fire, they systematically destroyed evacuated villages. Bombs on the churches where large congregations were at worship. Bombs on the hospitals. Bombs on the schools. Hand grenades thrown into the maternity ward of San Sebastián's clinic, mixing in one bloody mass mothers, infants, and nursing sisters. . . .

On the afternoon of October 7, 1936, José Antonio de Aguirre was sworn in as President of the Republic of Euzkadi (Basqueland). In the basilica of Begoña, in the midst of an enormous crowd, at the foot of the statue of the Virgin of Viscaya, his eyes on the crucifix and his hand on the Bible, Aguirre pronounced these words: "I swear by the Sacred Host fidelity to the Catholic, Apostolic and Roman faith. I swear loyalty to my fatherland Euzkadi. . . . I swear this with all my soul before the Sacred Host!"

Yet it was Franco who fought for God and to restore respect for the traditional morality of Spain! Sixty-nine thousand of the most ardent Catholics in the world were slain in the one month of April, 1937, in Euzkadi. But Hitler got the mines!

Amongst the Basque refugees in St. Jean-Pied-de-Port, a representative of *Esprit* met the father of Pedro Elquizabal, a Basque nationalist who fought in the Loyola Battalion (mark the name! not the

Nikolai Lenin battalion, but the Ignatius-de-Loyola-founder-of-the
Jesuit-order-Battalion!). Young Pedro was captured along with
Kortabania, another nationalist, and Estabillo, a militant Socialist, in
the battle of Otchandiano. They were led out to be executed the
next morning—for Franco shot his prisoners of war on the charge of
having taken up arms against him. Elquizabal had written a touching
letter of farewell to his parents. In that letter the boy mentioned the
fact that during the last night they had talked with the Socialist
Estabillo of spiritual things. In the morning they asked to be confessed, but were refused. Yet a priest came into their cell, and "we
had the joy, dear father and mother, to see our friend Estabillo kiss
the crucifix!"

Exterminating Bolshevism!

"If the Frente Popular is victorious," said Señor de Semprun
Gurrea, perhaps the most authoritative of the Spanish Catholic intellectuals, "the Church will have absolute freedom. A great freedom,
a terrible freedom! May it please God that she is not tempted to
abuse that freedom! From the reawakening and the liberation of the
people, the Church has nothing to fear. On the contrary, she will be
freed herself, delivered from the chains which bind her now to big
business. She will find back her lost virtue, which is to love and to
serve and not to command!"

"But it will be entirely different with the Church in Spain if
Fascism triumphs definitely," wrote back an anonymous priest in
Esprit. "That the Church in that case will recover, exteriorly and
temporarily, much of her past influence is not doubtful. That there
will be grandiose processions again with participation of official
corporations, that religious monuments will be erected on the public
squares and that the Sacred Heart will be enthroned in the city
halls, all that is certain. But what good will it be if the old routine
returns and with it ignorance and a total absence of authentic
spiritual life? Will a victory which leaves behind it an imperishable
hatred not also produce an absolute divorce between religion and
the people? Would it not be better to start again from the truth—the
irreligiosity of the people—and without mystification or deceitful
appearances have recourse to the almighty means of prayer and
sacrifice to recover the souls of men? In living by the spirit and for
the spirit, would the Church not again, and more so than in the past,
be the light of the world and the salt of the earth?"

To this François Mauriac of the Académie Francaise added these words: "It must be admitted that there is one crime the most abject assassins of Barcelona did not commit: they did not compromise Christ. How many years, how many centuries will it take the Church in Spain before it washes off that terrible stain and before the sons of the women murdered in Guernica, Durango, Barcelona and in the whole of Spain will have learned not to confound the cause of their crucified God with that of General Franco."

But these were merely the view of exceptional personalities. The Vatican and the Catholic hierarchy took the side of Franco, Hitler and Mussolini against the Spanish democratic regime, invoking the pretext that Madrid was Bolshevistic and stood under the direct influence, if not under the control, of Moscow. The argument was false and was denounced as such by many prominent Catholic intellectuals both in Spain and abroad, but it served the dual purpose of strengthening the cause of Fascism in the world and of masking the Roman Church's persistent opposition to democracy, scientific progress, and the modern spirit in general.

From the days of the Restoration of 1815, when the Pope recovered his temporal power and his kingdom which Napoleon had confiscated, the Roman Church has never ceased to strive in countries like Spain and France and Italy to recapture the hegemony it lost with the French Revolution. In April, 1814, Rome re-established the Jesuit order in all its rights and with it, in Spain, the Inquisition. Everywhere else, it sought to reconstitute ecclesiastical property. It seized every opportunity to proclaim its hostility towards all liberal principles. It especially singled out countries like France whose political institutions guaranteed religious toleration and freedom, countries which, to use the words of a papal encyclical, "had dared to place on the same level with heretical sects, and even with perfidious Judaism, the Holy Spouse of Christ, the Church outside of which there is no salvation."

There was a good deal of surprise in democratic countries like America when the Vatican and the Catholic hierarchy openly took the side of absolute reaction as represented by a traitorous general in his attack on the legally constituted, democratically elected government of his country—a general, moreover, who had the active support of the most intransigent foe of democracy and of Christianity in the world: Hitler. But there need not have been any astonishment, for in rallying to the side of Franco the papacy remained perfectly true to form and principles. Since the year 1832, when Pope Gregory XVI issued the encyclical *Mirari vos*, the Roman Church has been in a constant state of war with a modern society founded on freedom of conscience and on freedom of the press, "which latter," the encyclical states, "can never be sufficiently execrated and cursed, and through which all the bad doctrines of the freedom of scientific research are propagated. Pius VII condemned the liberal-monarchist French constitution of France in 1814. Gregory XVI, using the same arguments, damned the constitution of Belgium in 1831 as not Catholic enough in that it did not constitute the clergy the supervisors of the civil and the intellectual life of the country. The papacy, which had not joined the Holy Alliance against Napoleon because that "Christian" pact was not exclusively Catholic, became everywhere, as soon as Bonaparte had been removed from the European scene, the champion of the old medieval order. In every country it made common cause with the bitterest enemies of liberalism.

As there are in our day many Catholics who are sincere liberals and who are filled with anguish before the spectacle of their Church officially concluding concordats with every reaction, whether in Austria, Italy, Germany or Spain, so, too, there were many clear-sighted men inside the Catholic Church in the last century who saw that the Kingdom of God had nothing to do with that blind passion with which the Vatican stood by every tyrannical potentate in his campaign against political freedom, religious tolerance and modern democracy. Voices went up in the Church itself: Lamennais, Montalembert, Lacordaire, Littré. . . . Rome squelched them. "The Pope," says Professor Guignebert,[6] "sent his encouragement and his marks of approbation to those in each country who taught and championed the dogma of divine sovereignty and to those statesmen who, under the inspiration of the Jesuits, sought to link the Church, in the home politics of the various countries, with doctrines of the most narrow absolutism and reaction. The Vatican has fought democracy from the very outset: it allied itself with the Carlists of Spain, with the monarchist reaction under the Comte de Chambord in France, with the Portuguese Miguelists. The Pope was the most determined foe of Italy's national unification. Everywhere the papacy

[6] Charles Guignebert, professor at the Sorbonne, *Le Christianisme mediéval et môderne*, Flammarion, Paris, 1927, p. 267.

declared legitimate the very servitude from which democracy had vowed to liberate mankind."

Not only did the Church of Rome acquire a reputation during the last century for being the sworn enemy of all the political interests of democracy, but it placed itself squarely across the path of science. "There is not a single great scientific doctrine," adds Guignebert, "no matter whence it came or in what direction it moved, that did not encounter the condemnation, or at least the opposition and the ill will of the ecclesiastical authorities. This is the reason that science and Catholicism are almost contradictory terms."

When Rome discovered in the course of time that it could not stem the mounting tide of popular freedom and scientific research, it sought to head off the trend towards democracy by permitting Catholics to participate in popular political movements, without, however, for a moment abandoning its old reactionary principles. Leo XIII, who is generally taken as the most social-minded of the Popes, consented that Catholics in France should at last rally to the republican regime, but then the damage had already been done: because of Rome's protracted opposition to the democratic republic, millions of middle-class people and virtually the entire proletariat had become estranged from the Church and, what is more serious, from Christianity. Finding the Church always in their path as a tremendous obstacle, always in opposition to the two great movements which have determined contemporary evolution—democracy and modern science—liberals and scientists left the Church alone and stopped arguing about the claims of Rome to have the last word and to impose its views.

When the hope of a restoration of the old feudal order, which was destroyed by the French Revolution, did not materialize in the course of the nineteenth century, but instead the labor movement gained steadily in strength and in the consciousness of its strength, the papacy changed its tactics but not its fundamental policy. It encouraged the formation of Catholic political parties in the democratic states whose constitutions it had formerly denounced. Such parties came into existence in Belgium, Holland, Germany, Austria, Switzerland and Italy. The chief task of these Catholic parties was to prevent political democracy from moving towards its logical consequence: social and industrial democracy. They set out to stultify the growth of the labor movement by withdrawing the Catholic masses from the influence of the general labor movement and to canalize the entire working-class movement into channels where it should offer no threat to the existing order.

There should have been no surprise, therefore, when the Vatican took the side of Franco in the civil war in Spain. Franco attacked the emerging democratic regime with the aid of the Fascists of Germany and Italy and with the intention of turning Spain into a totalitarian state with a totalitarian religion.[7] For today Rome considers the Fascist regime the nearest to its dogmas and interests. We have not merely the Reverend Father Coughlin praising Mussolini's Italy as "a Christian democracy," but *Civiltà Cattolica*, house organ of the Jesuits, says quite frankly: "The very Christian idea of class collaboration has been widely diffused and its translation into reality takes on the most diverse forms. But whereas everywhere else its realization is slow and indecisive, in Italy alone it advances energetically and with rapid strides towards its complete fruition. In Italy it has chosen the form of the corporate state, which is, without doubt, the most audacious experiment amongst those we know in the postwar years. It is to be noted that the condition of success of this regime is its double nature, for it includes simultaneously positive and negative elements. On the one hand, these move away from the liberal and Socialist ideas and, on the other hand, they approach the principles exposed in that magnificent document of the Roman Church (the encyclical *Rerum novarum* of Pope Leo XIII is meant), which should be called the charter of the Christian labor movement."[8]

There you have an authoritative declaration which holds that Fascism is the regime that corresponds most closely to the concepts of the Church of Rome. In other words, the regime which is based on the ruins of the working-class organizations it has destroyed, including the Catholic organizations in Italy, Austria, Germany and the Basqueland, the regime which has reduced the workers to the level of famished slaves, who have no more rights in this life but to work for the aggrandizement of the imperialist states of Mussolini and Hitler and to prepare themselves for slaughter on the battle-field—that regime has the approbation of, and receives its inspiration

[7] Bernanos relates that in the Balearic Islands the clergy, with the help of the insurgent military, forced backsliders into the confessionals on pain of death. *Op. cit.*, p. 141.

[8] Franz von Papen declared on January 14, 1934, in *Der Völkischer Beobachter*: "The Third Reich is the first power which not only recognizes, but which puts into practice the high principles of the papacy."

from, the Church which claims its authority directly from Christ the King!

General Franco's cynical boast that Spain, after liberating Europe from Protestantism, as its last great achievement of world-historical significance, was, under his leadership, about to resume its glorious destiny by proceeding with a restoration of "the traditional morality" of the country, not only cut me to the quick, but served as a singular clarification of the issues involved in the civil war. What Franco was doing in Spain, the Duke of Alva and the Cardinal de Granvelle had tried to do in the seventeenth century in Holland and Flanders, and Catherine de' Medici and the Duc de Guise in the savage night of St. Bartholomew's in France: Franco and his cohorts desired to slip the collar of servitude back on the necks of the Spanish people who had just thrown it off.

This was *l'infâme*! And again it was wearing the mask of pious hypocrisy and Christian morality under which every single inhabitant of the Netherlands was once condemned to death by the Inquisition for the sake of his soul's good. This was the oppression against which Calvin and William of Orange and the Beggars of Holland and Zeeland had revolted, and to escape which the Puritan Fathers had founded a new Republic in America: the imposition of a totalitarian creed in a totalitarian state, the substitution for God as the sole source of authority of the authority of the human institutions of State and Church. The struggle that Franco unleashed had nothing to do with Marx or Lenin. It was by virtue of our own Protestant logic and principles, which gave birth to modern democracy, and which demand a radical independence of conscience, that the Spanish people decided spontaneously on a defense to the death against the Fascist usurper. And it was those ideals which sustained them, although poorly armed, in the struggle against two of the mightiest military states on earth which were backed by an international campaign of slander and vilification.

I hope I will not be charged with being afflicted with what the Germans call a *Weltverbesserungswahn* or of being a perpetual *frondeur*. I am perfectly well aware of my humble station in life. I am a simple and not a very good journalist, and know from long years of experience that my voice does not carry very far. But I am also a Protestant Christian, and as such, I not only consider myself

a member, even the least one, of the Militia Christi, but I have the
right and even the duty to speak out whenever I see the pagan powers
of this world, even when they shield themselves behind the banner
of the Cross, seek to impose an authority which rests on a violence
that pretends to be authority. I did not see the Spanish war as a
struggle between the "ins" and the "outs." As such it would not
have deserved much attention. It was a clash between two fundamental ideologies: Caesar's and Christ's. I do not hesitate to say, as
do those Catholics De Semprun Gurrea, Maritain, Mounier, Bernanos and Bergamin, that the cause of the long-suffering and patient
Spanish people, so inhumanly exploited for ages by their worldly
and spiritual overlords and so hideously reviled in their fight for
freedom, did and does represent today the cause of Christ.

I am perfectly well aware that the masses in Spain did not
predicate their resistance to Franco and his international allies on an
expressed religious motivation, any more than modern Socialists,
in their striving for a better world, invoke the words from the
Lord's prayer: "Thy Kingdom Come." But when I see men demand
their independence and fight for it, affirming their right to their
personality and refusing to become mere articles, cattle or cannon
fodder in the service of a would-be almighty state, there I recognize
an affirmation of the sole authority of God in human affairs. For
every attempt to deliver the souls of men into the hands of human
authority appears to me not only as an infraction on the rights of
man, but as a usurpation of the rights of God. It is in the name of
God that Protestantism demands absolute freedom of conscience in
the presence of traditions and ordinances which are no doubt necessary in the maintenance of order in society but which nevertheless
remain at all times, as Calvin pointed out, "human, contingent and
revocable things."

9

Rumors that Franco, who gloried in the expulsion of the Jews by
Ferdinand and Isabella—an event that was accompanied by an inhumanity which after all these years still makes the heart stand still
with horror, was singling out the Protestants in Spain for special

torture and the most ignominious death came not as a surprise to me. But when my uncle, who was *Scriba* of the North Holland Synod of the Dutch Reformed Church, inquired by letter to verify the reports current in Huguenot circles in France and amongst Protestants in Holland about Franco's deliberate cruelty "to our people," I placed myself in communication with the leaders of the Evangelical church in Spain.

I found them rather conservative theologians and confirmed fundamentalists. They related to me the hopeful beginnings that had been made by the various Protestant missions in Spain since the Republic had been established in 1931 and freedom of worship had been decreed for all cults. Two years before Alfonso's abdication a humble woman of the people had actually been jailed by the Inquisition for affirming to some friends gathered around the village pump that Our Lord had had little brothers and sisters (as the New Testament definitely states), and those who wanted to worship outside the official temples had still been doing it in great secrecy and in dread of the *carabineros*. All that was changed by the Republic. The Protestant missions had gained a hundred and fifty thousand adherents in Spain in four years' time. Those godless workers in the slums of Barcelona, Madrid and other cities had sent sixty-seven thousand of their children to the Protestant day schools. No less than a million Bibles had been distributed by the British and Foreign Bible Society, of which three hundred thousand had been purchased. Yes, the Gospel had prospered wonderfully under the Republic, and our brethren of the evangelical branch of the Anglican Church, I was told, had taken a special interest in Spain. And even after the trouble broke out with Franco's revolt, the people had not burned or disturbed a single Protestant chapel. All had remained open and crowded, even on days of bombardment and terror.

As to the Protestants in territories occupied by the insurgents, there was news only from a few places. Communication between the capital and the cities and provinces in the hands of Franco was not only difficult, it was dangerous to boot. But at least the following incidents were known on the undisputable authority of refugee Protestants from Toledo. Upon the conquest of that city by Franco, the Moors and the soldiers of the Tercio had been let loose in the hospital where a Protestant pastor, Don Jaime Oredo, and his wife were confined to bed with illness. They were bayoneted along with the other two hundred and fifty patients in the institution.[9] Another pastor in Toledo, Don Miguel Almorán, was arrested in his house and kept a prisoner for a month, then led to the execution field in the company of all the Jews who could be rounded up in the city by the Fascists, and shot down by a Riff firing squad.

At Saragossa, Fascist troops pillaged the Protestant chapel, befouling the Bible and the pulpit with their own ordure and arrested the pastor, Don Benjamin Heras. He was led out in the square in front of the cathedral after a mass of people had been summoned into the streets to see the show. There the pastor and the local liberals and labor leaders, amongst whom was one deputy to the Cortes, had their hands and feet tied and were left in the middle of the street to face two oncoming forty-ton tanks.

At Granada, the two Protestant pastors, Don José García Fernández and Don Salvador Iniguez, were seized by rebel soldiers and shot. The wife of Dr. Fernández faced the firing squad with her husband and his colleague after she had been raped by a number of Moslem troopers of a spahi cavalry regiment.

In Santa María, Franco's troops, unable to find "the heretic" they sought all over town, seized the wife of the "local preacher," soaked her clothes in gasoline and set her on fire. She was horribly burned and thereafter, while screaming with pain, executed by a Moor who was allowed to chop her body to pieces with an ax.

In San Fernando, Pastor Miguel Blanco was executed in the presence of his mother. His death was decreed by the commanding Fascist officer to serve as an example to the other forty "evangelicals" in the town. The minister of Puerto Real, Don Francisco López, underwent the same treatment.

Nothing was known concerning the fate of the evangelical minister of Mijadas, Don Carlos Linan, nor of the Protestant Sunday-school teacher of Santa Amalia, Don Luis Cabrera. They were supposed to have been the victims of the general Fascist terror against Protestants.

In Ibahernando, in the province of Cáceres, the Protestants were

[9] Bernanos says the same thing happened on Majorca when the insurgents took over. Every patient in the hospitals was massacred. Priests, revolvers on their hips, standing by, splashing in the blood, confessed the victims and passed them over to the military. Bernanos, *op. cit.*, p. 139 *et seq.*

executed en masse: pastors, men, women and children, among them a nobleman by the name of Don Francisco Tirado. The same happened in Prajedon in the province of Logroño. The congregation there numbered thirty souls. Six only escaped death. In Badajoz, where three thousand persons were machine-gunned in the bull ring, the Protestant pastor and all his flock were dragged to the arena of death, because most of their names figured on the list of the subscribers to the local public library. In Santa Amalia, the Protestants were handed over to the Riff troops by the Fascist officers . . .

Are the sufferings of these obscure Christians recorded merely to excite additional horror, asked Motley in writing of the mass-executions of the Protestants of Holland by the armies of Philip II at the behest of the Spanish Inquisition. His own answer was, as we have seen, no: they are part and parcel of the record and of the spirit of the times. We may therefore well add in the case of those tens of thousands of humble souls in Spain that their sorrows and martyrdom are testimony to the failure and fall of Christianity in that after twenty centuries of teaching of brotherly love by words alone man has not yet learned mercy and compassion.

From the day General Franco attacked the democratic Republic, the Spanish hierarchy, as the business partner of the reaction in landed estates, banks, railway lines and urban real estate, charged itself with the word-breaking General's propaganda service abroad, utilizing the Catholic press and enlisting the services of innumerable pulpiteers throughout the world. That the Spanish hierarchy, with its Jesuitical and contra-Reformation traditions, should have taken the attitude it did was in itself not surprising; but that "the social-minded" Vatican should not have recognized in the Popular Front movements of Europe the labored breathing of the world's weary and heavy-laden, and in the striving of the democratic and proletarian masses in Spain and elsewhere for a classless society a fundamentally Christian impulse, shows that Rome has severed its last remaining link with Christianity. The class consciousness of the papacy drives it to league itself with every reaction, be it in Spain, Germany, Mexico, Holland or Austria. It has not uttered a word of protest against the mass murder of working-class leaders in Italy, Austria, Germany and Spain. Rome only protests when its organization is menaced, or its influence curtailed, or when the capitalist conception of property is challenged. The Papal Secretary of State, Cardinal Pacelli, did telegraph[10] an apostolic blessing to a man like Dollfuss on the day when his police were hounding and hanging the dispersed remnants of the Viennese Social Democrats; Mussolini's bloody work in Ethiopia was described as a holy task by the *Osservatore Romano*, while the episcopal conference of Fulda has lauded Hitler as a man of God. The day the Nazis marched into Austria and the last remaining bulwark of Christianity and humanism in eastern Europe went down before the jack-booted barbarians, Cardinal Innitzer declared the Fuehrer "a man visibly blessed by Providence." In Spain, those who used the utmost violence in trying to suppress an emerging social order which aims at lifting man to a higher dignity than that of beasts of burden in the service of grandees and abbots were placed on a level with saints and martyrs of the faith by the agencies of Rome.

This is what could be read under the heading "Mola, Promoted Ambassador to Christ the King," in the *Diario de Navarra* on June 15, 1937, by way of an obituary notice on General Mola who massacred the Basque Catholics and whose death was caused by an act of sabotage on the part of his own Phalangist allies: "One morning in June, on the eve of the feast of the Sacred Heart of Jesus to which he had consecrated his life and all his aspirations, he mounted to heaven, filled with blessedness, to celebrate a grandiose triumph at the court of the King of Kings. He was called to rule Spain from heaven in a cabinet in which figure such illustrious Spaniards, such glorious heroes, such sainted martyrs as Calvo Sotelo, Goded, Sanjurjo, and Fanjul. What a feast in heaven, my God! At the doors of glory to receive our general, the whole immense galaxy of the Martyrs of Spain and—at the head of the august procession—the Christ-King, who pressed him to His sacred bosom. In the midst of the music of Paradise, these words of gratitude were heard: 'Blessed are those who die for My sake!' The death of Mola is the seal of God's recognition of our imperial rebirth. Our chief, by the force of destiny, has entered those eternal regions to represent awakening Catholic Spain before the throne of the King of Kings, the throne of the Christ the King."

[10] *Reichpost* of Vienna and *Neue freie Presse* of February 14, 1933.

10

Mola in heaven, but on earth. . . . In the course of the month of April, 1935, two years before Franco hoisted the banner of revolt in Morocco, a series of conferences was held in the Ministry of Economic Affairs in Berlin and in the Adlon Hotel of the same city at which were present Dr. Alfred Merton, chairman of the board of directors of the Metalgesellschaft, the steel trust of Frankfort-on-the-Main; Dr. Edward Kloenne, of the German metallurgical consortium which bears his name; Dr. Ludwig von der Porten, head of the Rheinmetal trust of Düsseldorf; Dr. Hjalmar Schacht, Minister of Economic Affairs in Hitler's cabinet; Dr. Krupp von Bohlen of the Essen cannon trust; Dr. Friedrich Opel, president of the Opel Motor Works; representatives of Siemens & Halske, tank manufacturers; representatives of the Vulkan rifle factories and three directors of the Farben Aktien Gesellschaft, the mammoth German chemical trust; furthermore, Señor Gil Robles, leader of the clerical-Fascist agrarian party of Spain; Señor Juan March, Spanish banker and steamship-line operator; General Sanjurjo, leader of an abortive military *Putsch* against the Spanish republican regime, who lived in banishment in Portugal, and, finally, General Ingeniani, director of industrial mobilization in Italy; Signor Guido Mazolini, chief of the trade division of the Italian foreign office; Colonel Benni Stefano, of the Italian general staff, and Signor M. Giurati, director of the foreign affairs department of the Italian Fascist party.

These gentlemen were informed by Dr. Merton that with the approval of the Spanish Government, which was then headed by Señor Alejandro Lerroux, an international consortium was about to be formed for the exploitation of the mineral resources of the Iberian peninsula, including Portugal and the Spanish colonial domains in north Morocco. The Italians had been invited to this meeting on the personal suggestion of Hermann Goering, because the Reichswehr command, so it was stated at the meeting, was of the opinion that, in so vast an undertaking designed to acquire raw materials for the German war industry, friction in the international field was apt to develop and that it would therefore be more politic to be assured of Mussolini's support and co-operation from the beginning.

I have before me the minutes of one meeting held in the Ministry of Economic Affairs on April 21, and also some of the agreements drawn up in the course of that month back in 1935 between the various aforementioned corporations and the Spanish government. These papers are of indisputable authenticity and were supplied by an international banker in Paris who was indirectly represented at the conferences in Berlin.

On behalf of the Federation of Italian Industry, Colonel Benni Stefano announced that this organization offered to participate in the preliminary investigations by a contribution of twenty million lire per annum. These funds, he said, had been placed at the disposal of the Federation by the Italian insurance companies.

At subsequent meetings of the international industrialists in Berlin the discussion centered on the exploitation of the vast mineral resources of Spanish Morocco. The agreements for an intensive exploitation of all these properties, both on the Spanish mainland and in Africa, the division of exploitation cost and the shares Germany and Italy were to have from the output were finally signed with the owners in the course of the month of January, 1936.

However, in the month of February of that same year, the political parties banded together in the Spanish Frente Popular triumphed at the polls, in spite of the fact, it is to be noted, that Señor Gil Robles, one of the negotiators in Berlin, controlled the election machinery. One of the first reforms to be taken in hand by the new Spanish government was the nationalization of the mines. When the news of the Frente Popular's victory reached Berlin, plans for the execution of the contracts were dropped for the time being. Indalecio Prieto showed me one day at the Ministry of the Interior in Madrid the files of the correspondence exchanged between the government of Gil Robles and Lerroux on the one hand and the international trusts on the other. Not a single letter had been received after the Frente Popular came into power. The negotiators had known that there was no use in trying to enlist the new democratic government in Madrid in a scheme which aimed at the rearmament of the two most powerful Fascist states in Europe. The incoming government did not have the confidence of Hitler and Mussolini.

Even so, the need for raw materials was pressing. Germany's war stocks were of the scantiest. Rather than forego the unlimited supply that the mines of Iberia and the Riff offered, Hitler summoned

General Sanjurjo from Lisbon (where he was living in banishment) to Berlin in March, 1936, and the plot for a military insurrection against the Republic with the aid of the Fuehrer and Signor Mussolini was hatched. The presence of fifteen Communist deputies in the new Cortes of the Frente Popular (France was to send seventy-three Communists to parliament a few weeks later) was deemed a sufficient peg on which to hang a campaign of international propaganda to the effect that Moscow had designs on Spain—and the trick was turned. Within a week Spanish Fascists began terrorizing the population; their *agents provocateurs* who had slipped into the labor organizations began setting churches on fire; capitalists exported their valuta abroad to hamper the government in the execution of its financial policy, and kept up the sabotage of the constituted authority until Sanjurjo would be ready. Then the monarchist Sotelo was sacrificed, murdered by Phalangists in Civil Guard uniforms, and Franco in indignation moved to the attack in Morocco, Cabannelas in Burgos, Mola in Madrid and Goded in Barcelona. Hitler had justified his terror on the grounds of an impending Communist revolution in Germany; Franco, who succeeded as Generalissimo when Sanjurjo crashed on the way from Portugal to Seville to take command of the insurrection, justified his attack on the Spanish Republic with the same argument.

In December, 1936, Germany had the satisfaction of receiving the first shipments of iron ore from Spanish Morocco and a year later had not only the mines of the Asturias under her control, but had ordered Franco, in exchange for artillery tanks, Junker planes and ammunition, to have one million tons of ore, antimony, tin, copper and lignite in German ports by the end of 1939.

II

It is not unlikely that if the French government had carried out its first impulse in July, 1936, of sending to Morocco the forty-odd bombing planes which were standing ready for delivery (on an order dating back eighteen months) in the various French aviation factories, Franco's rebellion would have been nipped in the bud. The Generalissimo's equipment at that time was far from impressive. The insurrection had miscarried in such important cities as

Madrid, Barcelona, Alicante, Valencia, Cartagena, Murcia, in the entire Basque country and in the Asturias. His military force was restricted to the Tercio (Foreign Legion) and the Moorish regiments in Africa. The bulk of these troops, moreover, were stationed in Morocco. He had no navy to transport them to the peninsula. Only Seville and Saragossa of the great Spanish cities had been brought over to his side, and in the latter city, the stronghold of libertarian Communism where Franco had concentrated his most dependable regiments, the struggle went on right through the month of August and did not terminate until a wholesale massacre eliminated the left-wing elements. France could have squelched Franco's threat to a friendly sister republic in a week's time had she followed the advice of Edouard Daladier, the War Minister, and Pierre Cot, the Minister of Aviation, both Radicals, in Léon Blum's cabinet. Blum was the one who hesitated the moment the French reactionary press began to protest against delivery of the long-ordered war equipment for which the Spanish government was calling. Heedless of the outcry raised by the French Fascists, M. Cot nevertheless ordered the bombing planes assembled at the airdrome of Villacoublay and notified the Spanish ambassador in Paris that the machines could fly off as soon as the Spanish aviators should arrive to take them to Madrid. The Spanish ambassador in Paris, who betrayed the Republic simultaneously with Franco, instead of telegraphing his government, informed the former Prefect of Police, Jean Chiappe, an extremely wealthy Corsican and a personal friend of ex-King Alfonso and of Benito Mussolini. M. Chiappe revealed M. Cot's decision to send the planes to *Gringoire*, a Fascist newspaper of which his (Chiappe's) son-in-law, Horace Carbuccia, another Corsican, is the publisher. In a few hours the entire rightist press in Paris took up the hue and cry about France going "to the aid of the Bolshevik nun rapers in Spain," and Léon Blum countermanded not only the order for the dispatch of the bombers, but in panic ordered the Spanish border closed.

Subsequently, after Franco had taken Toledo and subjected Madrid to its first bombardments, word was brought to Léon Blum that the working-class leaders in Madrid still entertained the hope that France would relent and revoke orders against the buying and shipment of munitions. Léon Blum replied: "My heart bleeds as much as any man's for the people of Spain, but every time we make a move to help the Spanish Republic, we are warned by Downing

Street that if we become involved in war with Italy and Germany over Spain, France cannot count on British support."

Even so, from a national point of view, an insurgent victory in Spain would be a serious blow to France. With Franco, a puppet of Hitler and Mussolini installed in Madrid, France would have a third frontier to defend in the event of war: to the Rhine and to the Alps would be added the Pyrenees. And yet, officially France did not lift a finger to frustrate the design which would ultimately result in her being hemmed in on three sides by the Fascist coalition. In vain did the Left Republicans plead for the opening of the frontier to war supplies, not merely in the interest of the Spanish Republic, but in the interest of France herself. In vain did the friends of France throughout the world point out the danger to her national existence involved in an eventual insurgent victory and call upon her to make a stand for democracy against the Fascist aggressors.

To every objective observer it seemed incomprehensible that France should adopt a policy of strict neutrality in a situation where her national security was jeopardized to a graver extent even than by Hitler's remilitarization of the Rhineland. What held her back from sending an army corps across the border and restoring order in a territory which her foes were about to turn into an armed camp, into a new base for attack against her southern provinces?

Mussolini would have thought twice to launch his Fascist legions against a French army and Hitler could not, because of his shortage of raw materials, have plunged into war. From whatever angle one looked at it the attitude of France seemed a puzzle. Why did not France prevent the Fascistization of the Spanish peninsula? Why did the French general staff not intervene when Mussolini installed himself on the Balearic Islands and built a submarine base on the Canaries, thus putting under the control of his guns the two sea routes along which France's colonial armies must be transported from Morocco, Algiers, Tunis, on the one hand, and from Equatorial Africa, on the other, in the event of a European conflict? Why did the mighty British Empire permit the erection of naval fortresses at Ceuta and Algeciras opposite Gibraltar, imperiling the freedom of her Mediterranean route to the Near East and India, and allow the Biscay coast—the ports of Bilbao, Santander and Gijón—from where the Germans waged their unrestricted submarine campaign against British shipping in the last war, to pass into the hands of the Italians and Germans and thus countenance the setting up of a threat to Britain's alternate route, around the Cape of Good Hope, to her Far Eastern possessions and the antipodean dominions? The liberals abroad saw the danger to the democracies of Britain and France: why did not England and France themselves realize the hazardous position into which the Fascist states maneuvered them?

With Belgium detached from the French alliance, with Hitler on the Rhine, Mussolini on the Alps and now Franco on the Pyrenees and the whole Iberian peninsula on the way to become a military camp for the Fascist allies, could the French government not see that France was being isolated from her allies of the Little Entente and from the Soviet Union and that her freedom of action in Europe, already seriously impaired by Hitler's occupation of the Rhineland, was further compromised by events in and around Spain?

"Are our reactionaries so blinded by their hatred for democracy that they do not see that the Fascist ring is closing tighter every day around France?" I heard a deputy ask in the Chamber of Deputies.

The government did not answer. But a Fascist paper in Paris gave the following reply the next day: "We can see plainly what is going on. France is being rendered impotent in the foreign field. Her friends in central and eastern Europe are turning away from her, realizing that we can do nothing to help them in the event of trouble. But it is not enmity against France that has driven Mussolini and Hitler to this course in Spain. It is our unholy alliance with the Bolsheviks of Russia which is at the bottom of the policy of the Fascist encirclement of France. The Fascist dictators are not thinking of attacking France. They are building up a defense against Bolshevism and rendering France harmless by isolation. Shutting France up in a ring of steel is the instrument Rome and Berlin have devised to prevent us from going to the aid of Russia. The aid given Franco by Germany and Italy is an integral part of Fascist defense against Russian intrigue. If the Fascist ring around France is closing, our national policy should be to break out of our isolation by coming to an understanding with the Fascist dictators. Such an understanding alone will guarantee peace in Europe, for it would call into existence a solid bloc of civilized countries against the Asiatic barbarians of the Kremlin. We should grasp the hand of friendship that Italy and Germany have extended to us before these same powers deem it necessary for their own self-preservation to attack us and destroy the Bolshevik vipers of our own Popular Front, who are conspiring with Stalin to plunge Europe into chaos."

That was the view of an outspoken Fascist newspaper. But as that paper spoke, so thought many on the Right in France. All the reactionary newspapers in Paris—and they form the great majority of the daily press—hailed every victory of Franco with shouts of joy. Fully one third of the French population, but the most influential third—the upper bourgeoisie, finance and business—pretended to see in the Moors, *requêtes*, and Carlists the champions of law and order, decency and religion. To the French bourgeoisie the loyalists were just scum and rabble, the ideological kinsmen of the French Popular Frontists, whom the reaction considered a far greater menace than Hitler, Mussolini and Franco combined.

I happened to be in the Chamber of Deputies in Paris when the question of allowing individual foreign volunteers to pass the border into Spain was being debated. Maurice Thorez, the secretary of the French Communist party, was addressing the Foreign Minister, Yvon Delbos, member of the Popular Front cabinet: "At least," he exclaimed, in winding up his appeal, "accord the proletarians of France the right to go and die for democracy under the walls of Madrid!"

To this a right-wing deputy, M. Tixier-Vignancour, retorted: "Yes, Monsieur the Minister, let them go. . . . Franco will never kill enough of that leftist canaille."

The upper strata of the bourgeoisies, Europe's economic royalists, who are at the same time the real internationalists, men without a fatherland and with no God but profits, had recognized the meaning of the events in Spain on first sight. They stood together, reached each other a helping hand across the borders and conspired to bring about the death of a Republic which wanted to institute a real democracy.

Hitler's declaration of war on Communism is a masterpiece of Machiavellian diplomacy. In raising the hue and cry against Moscow the Fuehrer has frightened the bourgeoisie of every country of which he desires the disintegration into looking toward himself as the champion of the established order and as the savior of Europe. With the aid of the Bolshevik bogey the class spirit swept aside the national spirit, so that General Franco, under the direction of Duce and Fuehrer, could launch his war against the Spanish Republic on the pretext of ridding the peninsula of a nonexistent Bolshevism to the applause of European conservatism, especially of the reaction in France and of British Toryism. In reality, the civil war in Spain strengthened Hitler so enormously that in the perspective of history that dolorous episode may well come to be known as the starting point of the Nazi mastery of Europe.

For as a direct result of his acquisition of a vast share in the mineral output of Spain and of Spanish Morocco, which is largely owned or controlled by British and French interests, Hitler was enabled to speed up Germany's rearmament sufficiently to venture on the annexation of Austria in March, 1938, and, almost simultaneously, to usher in a policy of pressure designed to dislocate the Czechoslovak state, the keystone of the French system of alliances, and the only formidable military barrier separating him from his ultimate objective—the Russian steppes and the port of Odessa.

By his intervention in Spain, Herr Hitler, moreover, rendered Britain the immense service of laying the ax to the French military hegemony in Europe (which had been a thorn in Britain's side ever since Versailles). By the creation of a third hostile frontier, he made the Quai d'Orsay so absolutely dependent on England that France lost her freedom of action entirely and was to all intents and purposes reduced to the status of a second-rate power, as much a vassal of Great Britain as Portugal or Greece.

British foreign policy, it is quite true, had paved the way for the destruction of France's military and political supremacy in continental Europe by urging Paris to countermand the plan of the French and Czechoslovakian general staffs in the spring of 1936 when Hitler was making preparations to remilitarize the Rhineland. Upon learning of Hitler's intention to occupy the Rhenish provinces, the military chiefs in Paris and Prague submitted to their respective governments a plan which provided for a French army to cross the Rhine, and a Czechoslovakian army to invade southern Germany, the two forces to effect a junction at Munich. Bavaria was then to be detached from the Nazi Reich and to be joined with Austria under the kingship of Otto of Hapsburg. Had this plan been carried into effect—and in March, 1936, three years after Hitler came to power, the Reichswehr did not command the artillery, the aviation, or the men to offer serious resistance—the Germanic world would have been split in twain as it was before Bismarck's unification in 1871 and a North and a South Germany would have confronted each other (the Hapsburg policy would logically have been directed against reunification) for half a century or more to the benefit of peace in Europe.

Britain persuaded the French government to shelve this plan in return for the promise of a renewal of the *Entente Cordiale* (Baldwin at the time stated that Britain's frontier henceforth was on the Rhine), and thus the Nazi regime was spared what would unquestionably have been a disaster of the first order, if not total disintegration and collapse.

While secret diplomacy thus pursued its own objective, the peoples of Europe were fed the myth of a coming alignment of Fascist versus democratic states. In the minds of the masters of the world's game there never was thought of such an alignment. That line-up was mere wishful dreaming on the part of Georges Dimitrov, the secretary of the Communist International, a last, desperate expedient of the Soviet-inspired collective-security school of thought under which one group of imperialisms—France, Britain, and their satellites—with the aid of Russia was to have made a firm stand and ultimately destroy the Italo-German combination in what would have amounted to a preventive war. For such a conflict might indeed have spared the Soviet Union the prospect of facing a much stronger Germany later on and alone.

The liberals in every interested country caught the vision at once and began urging their "democratic" governments to greater speed in arming against the Fascist menace. The Socialists, blinded by their hatred of Hitler and Mussolini, and, as has been the case with them whenever they were confronted with a major problem in international affairs, being unable to formulate a definite program to combat Fascism, easily fell into line. In the whole world all the ideologists of the "against war and Fascism" school accepted the idea of war as the sole means to fight Fascist encroachments, as if war whether "democratic" or "totalitarian," in the present state of perfection of the instruments of destruction, would not impose on every belligerent a Frankenstein which nobody could control and of which the inevitable consequence must be everywhere hatred, brutality, and contempt of men. War today will impartially distribute amongst victors and vanquished nothing but ruin, human degradation, and slavery. Even so, under the inspiration of the slogan "democracy versus Fascism," the Communist parties in France and Czechoslovakia went so far as to change their tactics from revolutionary antimilitarism to intense patriotic chauvinism. The entire Left joined in every country in building up the militarist spirit, which is the mother of Fascism and dictatorship, and thus strengthened, unwittingly perhaps, the very bourgeoisie which, in the Marxist plan of the ages, the proletariat is called upon to overcome and obliterate.

The theoretical alignment of democracy versus Fascism was predicated on the assumption that Britain and France are in reality democracies. That these two states are as imperialistic as Germany and Italy was overlooked. In their colonies—India, Morocco, Cochin-China—they have been pursuing a policy of ruthless exploitation of millions of human beings long before Mussolini and Hitler appeared on the horizon. The difference is merely that not possessing colonies, Italy and Germany are compelled to practice British and French colonial methods on their home population. Because of their colonial wealth, too, the contradictions in society have not been so rudely challenged in Britain and France as they have been in Italy and Germany; at home, therefore, London and Paris have been able to carry on with a semblance of democratic procedure.

A Fascist-democratic world struggle might still have become a reality if the Spanish and French popular fronts had been permitted to function consistently, that is if both in Spain and France the liberal forces had proceeded to strip the reactionaries of their power and influence. That is why Mussolini, the ex-Marxist, who understood what was at stake, was in so great a hurry to crush the emergent democracy in Spain, and why Britain played the sinister comedy of the nonintervention policy, which prolonged the civil war long enough to give the French bourgeoisie (which went on the run the moment Léon Blum assumed the premiership) time to catch its breath, regain courage, and bring about the disintegration of the Popular Front.

This task fell to the party headed by Edouard Daladier, the Radical Socialists, who had entered the Popular Front coalition with the Socialists and Communists for no other purpose than to stand guard over the bourgeoisie's interests against popular aspirations. One of the Popular Front's aims was the formation of a democratic bloc of nations in Europe under the leadership of France. By dexterous political maneuvering (the Radical Socialist majority in the Senate overthrew Léon Blum by refusing to accord him power to rule temporarily by decree), Daladier took over the direction of the government. Thereafter, international class considerations, always stronger than national interests with the upper classes, took precedence, and France, at an enormous cost to herself (it meant abdicating her position as a first-class power), began to play the imperialist game as an adjunct of Great Britain.

That game consisted in seeking to prevent at all costs (sacrificing the whole system of Versailles—collective security, the League of Nations, and the French system of alliances) an internecine, fruitless, suicidal imperialistic war between the four great European imperialisms of Britain, France, Germany, and Italy. For such a war, fought on ideological alignment of democracy versus Fascism, might conceivably have ended not only with the destruction of the bourgeois-Fascist regimes in Germany and Italy, but would also have meant strengthening the Soviet Union, and, what is more, it might have led to the emergence of a genuine social democracy in France and Czechoslovakia.

In order to spare the international bourgeoisie that immense and final calamity, it became necessary to prevent the French Popular Front not only from utilizing France's system of alliances for the waging of an ideological war but also to render impossible a continuation of France's policy of checking Germany's so-called "dynamic expansionism" by keeping the Reich encircled in a wall of steel. For both expedients meant disaster for Germany: either she would be defeated in a war for which she lacked the required equipment and foodstuffs, or, deprived of the opportunity to expand, she would have collapsed through inner contradictions.

The disintegration of the Nazi power, either through war or isolation—the possibility that all of Central Europe might turn up the road to genuine democracy and the resultant shock to the entire European economy—was the formidable danger presented by the French system of alliances controlled by a leftist Popular Front. That is why both had to go by the board.

On the other hand, against the evil of Germany's collapse stood the alternative of giving Adolf Hitler, under a Four-Power accord, carte blanche to break out of his dangerous isolation by clearing himself a road through Czechoslovakia to the oil and wheat fields of Rumania, thus putting him in possession of the wherewithal to risk a war of long duration with the Soviet Union. For it is Russia, which Herr Hitler, by a stroke of the pen, has relegated to Asia, that is to provide Germany with the markets and colonies she lacks at present. In this way Germany's pressure on the Western imperialisms, it is thought, will be lessened, and at the same time the intolerable burden of carrying the Reich's colossal war machine will be shifted, at least partially, from the shoulders of the German people to those of the prospective colonial tribes in the Muscovite plan.[11]

To prevent an interimperialist European war by coming to an understanding with Nazi ambition for expansion in eastern Europe has been the fundamental directive of England's foreign policy under Baldwin and Chamberlain. Having her eyes on the Far East, where Japan has arisen as the next historical challenger of British naval and colonial power, Britain desires above all else to have her hands free for the struggle she must wage in the Pacific. For, as England in the past has successively destroyed the naval power of Spain, Holland, Louis XIV, Napoleonic France, and Imperial Germany, she must sooner or later envisage checking Japan before her spheres of interest in China and her Indian, Malay, and Australian possessions are threatened by that new and determined rival.

England will fight, therefore, not for democracy and not in Europe if she can at all prevent it, but to safeguard her imperial interests where they are at stake and where her prestige with all the colonial peoples has been at issue for a decade—in the East.

When France permitted the remilitarization of the Rhineland without even a word of protest against what was equal to the establishment of an unsurmountable wall between herself and her east European allies, what had been darkly suspected since London and Paris abandoned the Spanish Republic to Hitler and Mussolini became clear: that powerful influences in Paris, Rome, London and Berlin were collaborating above the heads of the peoples and their parliaments to bring about quite a different solution of the European problem than checkmating Nazi expansionism, or, what would have amounted to the same thing: the destruction of the Nazi empire. It could therefore be predicted with reasonable certainty after the smoothly effected annexation of Austria that Czechoslovakia would be the next link in the chain encircling Germany to be sacrificed, and, thereafter, that Poland, Hungary, Rumania and Jugoslavia are to be similarly abandoned when Hitler judges the time opportune to take another step in easterly direction.

[11] Publisher's note: The foregoing was written several months before the Munich accord of Sept. 1938.

To some of us foreign correspondents, who were aware of the vast superiority of the French, Czechoslovak and Russian armed forces over the young, insufficiently equipped and underofficered Reichswehr and its inflated Italian ally, and who therefore never took the idea seriously that it was fear and trepidation which made Britain and France repeatedly back down before the Fascist aggressors, but who knew, to the contrary, that not a single one of Hitler's major moves had been undertaken without a consultation (and the approbation) of the inner circle of the British cabinet, the only puzzle, after the Fuehrer's victorious march into Vienna, was how the four great imperialist Powers would manage a justification of the dismemberment of Czechoslovakia in the eyes of the democratically-minded peoples and, at the same time, prevent the Soviet Union, whose territories would be directly menaced if and when the barrier of the Czech fortifications should be eliminated, from mobilizing and sending the Red Army crashing through Northern Rumania to the defense of Prague.

The colossal dupery of September, 1938, was the answer. Chamberlain, Hitler, Daladier and Mussolini, in complete and perfect accord, staged a drama which caused the entire world to hold its breath in dread suspense for ten days. Europe was made to appear as hovering on the very brink of the most ghastly cataclysm of history. France mobilized. A million men poured into the Maginot Line. The civil population was evacuated from Strasbourg and the rural regions of Alsace. London and Paris were blacked out and millions of gas masks were distributed while churches filled with awe-stricken crowds. Half a million Parisians fled to the comparative safety of southern cities. The British fleet took up its wartime stations at the Skagerrak. Stock exchanges suspended operations. The peasants abandoned their plows in the fields of Lorraine. The whole world stood still. Not a sound was heard save the crackle of the transatlantic radio broadcasts which grew more ominous as the hours ticked away. One hasty careless move by a diplomat, it seemed, or one random shot by an excited peasant-soldier on those borders now bristling with guns, and the Continent would be aflame and great cities leap into the air under an avalanche of aerial torpedoes. That is the way it looked.

Then the show was suddenly called off. Czechoslovakia surrendered. But not to Hitler. Against Hitler Prague could have defended itself successfully six months and more, long enough to have exhausted Germany's reserves of war material. President Beneš did not consent to hand over the Sudeten areas and the fort circles of Czechoslovakia until he had before him a secret ultimatum from Daladier and Chamberlain containing a veiled threat that France and Britain would take a serious view of it if Prague should dare to invoke the aid of Moscow.[12]

For Moscow did offer Prague not merely a few hundred bombing planes, but "the full support of the Red Army and all the resources of the Soviet Union's industry in an eventual conflict." The terms of Russia's offer of support, which were conveyed twice over by Foreign Commissar Maxim Litvinov to Georges Bonnet, were deliberately falsified by Bonnet.[13] Thus, not only an entirely false picture was created of the situation, but panic increased amongst the French people, who were led to interpret Bonnet's statements on Russia as if the Soviet Union intended to leave her allies completely in the lurch.

Fearful lest certain members of the British cabinet, seeing an opportunity to finish with Hitler in a short time and in a comparatively easy manner, would in the last moment urge Chamberlain to make a stand and bring Hitler to his knees or force him into war that would lead to his perdition, the same French minister, M. Bonnet, withheld from the British cabinet the full text of a technical report drawn up by General Gamelin, wherein the Commander in Chief of the French army, after citing the difficulties of invading the Reich in the presence of the newly constructed Siegfried Line on the right bank of the Rhine, nevertheless urged an immediate intervention in favor of Czechoslovakia and concluded with a confident prediction of the annihilation of the Reichswehr in less than a year's time.[14]

That Hitler's threats were pure bluff, even when bolstered up

---

[12] The knowledge that Dr. Beneš before going into exile had prepared a photostatic and certified copy of this ultimatum, which showed that not German might, but Anglo-French perfidy, had brought about the Republic's destruction, caused the German government to agitate for the former President's detention in Czechoslovakia and for his extradition to the Gestapo.

[13] Reported by Le Voltigeur, organ of the Christian (Catholic) liberals, one of the most responsible journals of Paris (issue of Oct. 19, 1938); by Le Peuple (of the same date); by Leonhard Ragaz in his magazine Neue Wege (issue of Nov., 1938) and by the diplomatic correspondents of several other important European newspapers. Le Temps remarked: "On a menti sciemment sur les conversations entre M. Litvinov et le Ministre français des Affaires Etrangères" (Oct. 5, 1938).

[14] A challenging statement made to this effect by Léon Jouhaux, secretary of the General Confederation of Labor, has not been refuted by the French government.

with Charles A. Lindbergh's declaration minimizing the efficiency of the Soviet Union's aerial equipment (Spain had shown the very opposite), everybody knows today. But best of all, this is known in Germany, where the Chief of Staff, General Beck, risked and actually ruined his career in warning the Fuehrer that the German army was far from ready to face even France and Czechoslovakia, let alone Britain's navy and the Soviet forces, and, where another Reichswehr Commander, General von Metzsch, added the more significant reminder that even if the army had been ready and stocks at full completion for a war of long duration, the Fuehrer was "not yet protected against commotions in the popular soul," too many millions of Germans being dreadfully afraid of war, "which might end with a worse debacle than that of 1918."[15]

Hitler could bluff his way through to the end because he had the personal assurance of Neville Chamberlain that he would not let it come to war. Hitler was not alone in bluffing therefore. The mobilization of the French army and of the British navy was also bluff. That mobilization was the trick to strike panic in the hearts of the peoples and make them subsequently grateful to the imperialist intrigants for having maintained peace even at the cost of Czechoslovakia's sacrifice.

Neville Chamberlain and Edouard Daladier were not for a moment afraid of an Anglo-French defeat. They were afraid of victory. They dreaded the consequences of an annihilation of the Nazi regime. They knew beforehand that they would not only have had the entire support of the French, British, Czechoslovak and Russian peoples in a war to defeat German Fascism, but that Poland, the Baltic States, the countries of the Little Entente and even Turkey would early have joined, and that without much prodding, in a war to defeat the voracious monster that threatens to swallow them all ultimately.

But an Anglo-French victory, as has been said, would also have meant a victory of the democratic principle not only in the allied countries but in Germany itself. Democracy, a revival of the League of Nations, collective security based on general disarmament, international collaboration and an era of creative peace in the world, that was the prospect involved in a defeat of Adolf Hitler. That was also a state of affairs the Tories of Britain and the reaction in France

[15] Geneviève Tabouis, *Chantage à la guerre*, Flammarion, Paris, 1938, page 168.

would not face. For that eventuality might well have spelt the doom of their own cast in several lands.

The idea which has gained such wide currency since the World War that the British Empire is a thing of the past, a giant staggering on his last legs, without the strength or the gumption to stand up to the dictators, never returning the blows raining down from right and left, first in Manchuria, then in the Ethiopian affair, even more in the Spanish imbroglio, and in the cases of Austria and Czechoslovakia, naturally served to dishearten all those well-intentioned souls who nourish the notion that the British Empire is "the greatest power for good in this world," but it accorded perfectly with the "realistic" policy pursued by Mr. Chamberlain. The idea of a weak and helpless Britain was the smoke screen under cover of which the small group of men at the head of the British imperium, the inner Tory council, carried out its designs to a successful issue. England was not "just muddling through." These men knew what they wanted. The series of seemingly humiliating incidents, culminating in the Munich accord, the abandonment of Czechoslovakia, and the liquidation of France's military supremacy in Europe, was a triumph of the British imperial cause. At Berchtesgaden and Godesberg, Chamberlain seemingly gave way before superior pressure; in fact, he achieved what he had constantly striven for—he turned Hitler eastward. In forcing France to leave her eastern allies in the lurch, the British Tories saved themselves the trouble of fighting a European war in the defense of interests which were none of theirs or which were at best only of secondary consideration.

While it is true that Chamberlain and Daladier delivered a staggering blow at Munich to the cause of democracy, it would nevertheless be wrong and inconsistent to accuse these statesmen of weakness, of truckling to the dictators, and of treachery. A man is not guilty of treason to what he detests when he tries to kill it. In the case of men to whom the slogans of democracy and international morality are but expedients to further their self-interests, mere oratorical phrases to be mouthed for opportunistic reasons, Munich did not constitute a betrayal. Munich was a mere expedient to protect what they considered their primary class and national interests.

If Paris was well worth one Mass to Henri IV, half a dozen Munichs are not too high a price to pay for the stability and safety of Britain's imperial interests. And other Munichs are bound to follow, for without them the first Munich would indeed become a useless sacrifice. In spite of Munich Britain is not yet in a position to deploy her strength exclusively in the settlement of problems confronting her in the Pacific. Neither is Adolf Hitler completely assured that he has been accepted on a basis of full equality with Britain, France and America. For the Munich accord and the acquisition of the Sudeten areas, although considerably extending Germany's freedom of action, did not yet place her in a position where she could refuse to pay for economic and financial concessions with political guarantees. For that she must still create herself a vast economic dominion over Eastern Europe where Britain and France still have too many commitments and interests.

In this and other respects England will be required to show her good will. It is not enough that the road to the East has been opened if Germany cannot advance. Hence Germany will demand a settlement of the civil war in Spain in a way that will enable her to continue drawing on the mineral resources of the peninsula. This may be done by a division of Spanish territory between loyalists and insurgents, leaving General Franco in possession of the mining areas he has conquered for Hitler. Or, if the loyalists object to splitting up the national territory, diplomatic and eventually even military pressure may be brought to bear by Britain and France on the Madrid government to force its surrender.

The Reich must furthermore have back some of its colonies. Not, to be sure, for the purpose of extracting food supplies or raw materials (Germany's former colonies do not possess either) but to utilize the commodities produced by Togoland and the Cameroons as objects for barter in the world market in exchange for food and steel. When this demand is made, Britain and France will no doubt, "in the interest of general peace," insist that Belgium, Portugal, and Holland share in the colonial sacrifices to be made to Germany. Then, finally or first (for the sequence of Germany's demands may be reversed at will, the Reich having captured the initiative in international affairs) Britain will have to consent to a revision of the Anglo-German pact of 1934, which limits the German naval power to one third of Britain's, because the Reich's present naval strength is not judged adequate in Berlin to protect the landing of armies in Finland and Esthonia for an attack on Leningrad and at the same time to convoy the steady flow of supplies from Spain and Morocco and elsewhere. Britain must, moreover, agree to an air pact limiting her aviation to not more than half of Germany's and therewith give practical evidence of her intention of benevolent neutrality in an eventual war between the Reich and the Soviet.

In return for all this, Germany and Italy may finally, but not before Britain has scrupulously conformed to all the Reich's demands and given Italy ample compensation at the expense of France most likely, consent to detach Japan from the Anti-Comintern pact, which will be a tremendous concession on Hitler's part considering the assistance Japan could render him in a war with Russia, and England will at last be free to devote her undivided attention to her rival in the Far East; the Russian and Chinese markets will be divided between the four European imperialisms, and prosperity and peace will be assured "in our time."

That, in broad outline, is the vast scheme maturing in the European chancelleries. It may work. So far it has worked. Franco's rebellion was the first act, the Austrian annexation the second, and the destruction of Czechoslovakia the third in the historic drama. Every hurdle has been cleared so far. But the sea is full of shoals and rocks. The conquest of Russia may not prove an easy matter. There may be a hitch there. On the other hand, the prospect of a victorious German army in Europe and an attempt by Hitler to make an advance, perhaps with the aid of Turkey now that Kemal Ataturk, the anti-German, is dead, towards the Suez Canal, Arabia, Baghdad, and Persia, into Britain's imperial sphere, may cause a sharp reversion of policy on London's part. The point is: will Hitler prove worthy of the confidence imposed in him at Munich? Will he content himself with Russia? Chamberlain has repeatedly expressed himself as convinced of Hitler's sincerity. So has Daladier. Co-operation seems therefore assured.

The danger of victory is past. Armies and navies can now be built up in a feverish tempo, in order that on the day when the spoils are to be divided not one of the four partners will be able to steal a march on the others. Italy, which received no compensation for her share in "maintaining the peace" of Europe at Munich, may have to exercise a little pressure on France to obtain a loan from France's suzerain in London for the exploitation of her Ethiopian Empire, or some other advantages in the Mediterranean and the Red Sea area before she considers herself entirely satisfied and takes up her role as a full and equal participant, and not merely as a vassal of Hitler, in "the redivision of the world's markets," of which the Duce in speaking to a group of correspondents in 1930 said that he thought it would occur about a decade or twelve years hence, that is to say around 1940-1942. But Italian pressure on France may also strengthen Daladier's or someone else's hands to set up the authoritarian-militarist regime Paris must have if France is to perform her share in the great *Kladderadatsch*. There are a hundred ways of giving a lift to a friendly enemy when Machiavelli is prince.

The only remaining obstacle to Hitler's attack on Russia is Poland. However, France's ties with Warsaw have been sufficiently weakened by the German guarantee to respect the Alsatian frontier for the Reich to venture (while war stocks are accumulating for the final episode) upon an intensive diplomatic and propagandistic drive to bring about the disintegration of the Polish state in the same manner Czechoslovakia was eliminated. Rumania, a possible ally of Poland, will in the meantime have to be weakened by an internal upheaval and Jugoslavia, another potential ally, if she should show signs of siding with Poland, held in check by an Italian threat on the Dalmatian coast. The Ukrainian minority in Poland has been selected by the Reich to play the same role as the Sudeten Germans did in Czechoslovakia. Germany will recognize their right to self-determination. Hitler is going to "liberate" the Ukraine. Bereft of all outside help, Poland will most probably, in order to escape complete annihilation, give in to German pressure and will lose Silesia in the bargain. On the other hand if Poland, in desperation, turns to the Soviet Union for assistance, Germany might have to use an alternate scheme to bring about Poland's neutrality by an arrangement under which Warsaw is given the Baltic States in exchange for the Ukraine. That done the Reich will support the clamor for reunification of the Polish Ukrainians with their forty million "oppressed" brethren in the Soviet Union and the casus belli with Russia will finally be there.

With the exception of a few minor adjustments, which the Reich confidently expects to effect without war, the stage seems to be pretty well set therefore for the realization of the final and fundamental raison d'être of the Nazi power: the dismemberment of the Soviet Union. Another year or two! . . .

"*On va remettre ça*," as the French say. The youth of this generation is going to be sacrificed, as the youth of the preceding generation, on the altars of Moloch. Unless . . .

There is one imponderable, which is still causing some anxiety in high places: it is what that German general called the possibility of "commotions in the popular soul." It is comparatively easy to start a war, it is much more difficult to foresee its end. Of that could testify the gentleman woodcutter in Doorn, the Romanoffs and the Habsburgs whose thrones were carried away by the torrent in the last upheaval. History is not a chain of events following each other in logical sequence. At every turn one finds mysterious and inexplicable incidents "not the result of hazard or of personal initiative" and which seem to be "injected by the creative force of spiritual currents." In a world situation which seems to lack all logic there are a great many unpredictables and unforeseeables. For one thing there is this: the muzzled and propaganda-drugged peoples may yet awaken from their stupor and ask the meaning of the huge armament campaigns and take their fate and the fate of their children out of the hands of the avowed and unavowed Fascists and put an end to the monstrous imperialist game of guile, greed and blood and make this beautiful and bountiful earth a garden for all God's children to walk in.

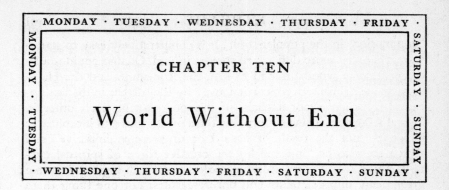

· MONDAY · TUESDAY · WEDNESDAY · THURSDAY · FRIDAY ·

MONDAY

· TUESDAY

SATURDAY

SUNDAY

· WEDNESDAY · THURSDAY · FRIDAY · SATURDAY · SUNDAY ·

CHAPTER TEN

World Without End

SLOWLY THE TRAIN STARTED, imperceptibly almost, without a shock. The tooth-paste girl in the advertising poster on the station wall began to move. Her blue eyes turned into misty blurbs, then receding, froze hard and rigid in the pasty paper mask. The train quivered over a fork in the rails, rattling the couplers. From behind a smoke-blackened steel girder a luminous purple sign, proclaiming the merits of yeast, suddenly rushed forward, its letters bulking large and menacingly like the onrushing subtitle in a horror movie. They retreated as rapidly as if sucked back into place. The scarlet cap of the stationmaster, its band of gold braid just level with my elbow, flitted by the compartment window. Porters were unloading heavy trunks from a baggage truck. The boxes struck the platform with the rattle of old tin. From the locomotive the first plumes of steam flew past my face. For a moment they wreathed themselves around the form of a young woman, who placed her grip on the platform and stretched out both hands towards a man. Laughingly she threw back her head. But the sound of her voice was lost. Dark silhouettes moved about in the reddish glow inside the waiting room. A life-insurance poster showing an angel shielding a woman in widow's weeds leaped forward in flaming colors. Then the picture of a rosy-cheeked old gentleman with a crock in his hand who promised that Schiedam gin brings health. The train was picking up speed. The acrid smell of wet coal crept into the compartment. As the carriage emerged from under the glasshooded vault of the station, a gust of wet wind breathed a film of white moisture on the pane. In a minute the milky sheen vanished as the temperatures equalized again. We clanged over a steel bridge. Below, the bottle-green Meuse gleamed with a pallid luster under the day's wan sunlight. Around the basalt pillars whirled innumerable little eddies and foam pockets, the color of spittle. With a metallic roar the train started up a viaduct. We ran along the rear of a row of tenements; a crazy quilt of rain-sodden wooden balconies with radio aerials, dovecotes, rickety fire escapes, bird cages, provision boxes, flowerpots and clotheslines with strings of cheap underwear hanging listlessly in the smudge-charged drizzle.

From one window a man, his face half lathered, peered at the passing coaches. In one squalid back yard I saw a woman place one hand on her back and look up wearily from her washtub. It was seven o'clock in the morning. The viaduct ran over a square filled with tarpaulin-covered market stalls before skirting the roof of a gray church. In the background was a blue patch of sky. The chimneys of invisible ocean liners, like huge cannon muzzles turned skyward, appeared above a row of trees. Beyond that, the steel fingers of hoisting cranes threw perplexing signals against the murky horizon. An early morning streetcar clanged under my feet. Umbrellas danced over the black mirror of the wet pavement. We crossed another bridge, a long one with pillars that boomed by one by one, reminiscent of soldiers calling out their names on parade. A tug, laboriously pulling a string of barges against the stream, sent up a dense column of black smoke. The compartment filled with the rancid odor of oily grease and tar mixed with coal gas. A long street, flanked by endless rows of red stone apartment blocks of a monstrous architectural monotony, wheeled by. Men and women could be seen walking swiftly, fearfully almost, as if in dread of being late for work. And then tenements again and billboards, smokestacks, aerials, arc lights, warehouses, coal yards, stables, oil tanks, rubbish heaps, abattoirs, unmade beds and pale faces above the flowerpots in the windows.

How good and how pleasant it is for brethren to dwell together in unity!

The train whistled its joy to be out of the city as it rounded a curve and ran into the open fields at last. Rotterdam lay behind. A windmill, turning slowly in the morning breeze on top of a dike, waved a dignified welcome. Through the open window now came a smell of clover, of fresh manure and ripening grain. The cows had turned their tails to the wind in the soaking meadows. A red-legged stork stood watching for frogs by the side of a ditch. Here and there the lonely shape of a church tower loomed dimly through the haze only to melt again in the fog like a phantom in the light of dawn. I lost count of the bridges we crossed. The train slowed down going through a station. On the platform stood a group of farmers. They were dressed in their short black jackets of the province of Zeeland, round silk caps on their heads and silver buckles on their low shoes. They carried small linen provision sacks. Their faces were grim and wrinkled. As we slid past I caught the gleam of steel in their gray-blue eyes. Through the girders of another bridge, above a forest of ships' masts and Renaissance roofs, I caught sight for a moment of the massive cathedral of Dort, a name once mentioned in the same breath with that of Rome as the citadel of Calvinism.

In that city I was baptized and this broad stream we now crossed was the Merwede, the river of my youth. Every detail of the dear and pleasant landscape suddenly assumed an uncanny familiarity, as if I had been away only a week. The windmills, the polders, the dykes, the villages, the trees—I knew them all. Every one of those rural roads I had trodden. Sliedrecht, Giessendam, Hardinxveld. . . . I let my mind race over the names of the communes. Softly I murmured a greeting to them. There were the castle of Schelluinen and the green drawbridge where we went fishing in the canal. There the tower of St. John's! In the distance the old bastion near the school. . . . Just as the train came to a stop with a creaking of brakes, a squall of rain lashed fiercely against the windowpanes. A voice on the platform called out: "Gorcum! Gorcum!"

I walked through the station waiting room into the square. The little park where geraniums bloomed every summer was gone. Motorbuses were parked on the spot. The trees leading to the Chancellery Gate had been cut down. Gorcum lay bare and stripped of foliage behind its triple ring of old-fashioned green earthworks, canals and moats. I walked across the wooden bridges through the gate. The main street I had thought so broad seemed to have narrowed down to a mere alley. The buildings looked like dolls' houses. I rounded a corner. There was the old church. A shiver passed down my spine as I glanced up at the small windows near the top from where I had caught my first glimpse of the world. Around the next corner, I knew, stood my father's house. How would it look? Who would be living in it? Would the new owners permit me to have a look at the garden? I stepped faster. My heart was beating violently. The house wasn't there. It had been gutted. I could look right through it. There was a back yard full of oil vats and gasoline cans. But no trees. Bicycles and motorcars and tools cluttered up the sidewalk in front. There was a sign above the open doors: INTERNATIONAL GARAGE.

When the heavy bell began to strike the hour of noon I was in the still street of the *Gymnasium*. The brown oaken door opened and some boys stepped out carrying books under their arms. They were laughing. One, who came running up behind, called out a phrase in Latin to his companions. An old man stumbled down the stairs of the building, leaning on a cane. "There's Jupiter," I said to myself, for so we once called the Rector. Instinctively I raised my hat. He threw me an uncomprehending suspicious glance and continued on his way without returning my salutation. I walked in the other direction towards Uncle Kees' house. I saw it from the distance. The door and the windows were boarded up. The paint was peeling off the eaves. Tufts of grass had sprouted between cracks in the stones near the ledge. To one of the shutters still clung a yellowed scrap of a notary's sale announcement. Children had drawn marks with chalk on the stoop and on the space between two windows someone had scrawled, in big white letters, that *Hendrik loves Anna*. I walked to the river edge and sat on one of the benches where an old man made room for me.

"It's a bleak day," he said. "But there are lines in the sky—it's going to clear up." A gentleman walked by, swinging a walking stick, apparently a citizen of standing.

"Who's that?" I asked the old man by my side.

"That's Mijnheer Verhey," he said.

"Klaas Verhey of the People's University?" I wanted to get up and shake his hand.

"What People's University?" asked the old man. "We have no people's university here. You must be mistaken. Mijnheer Verhey is an elder in the church. He's a rich man. He owns the brewery. His daughter is married to the Baron van Asperen."

I tried to swallow and found that my throat had suddenly gone dry. I looked up the river and saw the twin towers of Loevesteyn through the haze, the prison of Grotius. The blunt spires were tipped by a silver light. But the smoke of a river boat spread over the horizon and blurred my vision.

"You must be a stranger here?" asked the man by my side.

"I lived here once," I said, and told him my name.

He shook his head. "I don't remember that name," he said.

I got up and walked around the walls of the town and entered the cemetery. I found my brother's grave, next to my grandfather's. Weeds had grown over the tombstones. I shoved them aside with my umbrella, but they jumped back into place. The keeper was coming along one of the paths. He was carrying a rake on his shoulder. I recognized the man, but he merely nodded. I stopped him by telling him that I was looking for Uncle Kees' grave.

"You are standing right in front of it," he said.

"That slab there?"

"There's an inscription," I said. "Could I scrape off the moss?"

"His name isn't there, I can tell you that, if that's what you are looking for," replied the keeper. "He didn't want his name on it. No dates either."

"His name isn't there? That's strange. But what are these words then? I can see some letters here," I said, bending over the stone.

"Yes, some words, to be sure," the keeper assented. "It's a little song he wrote down in his testament to be put on his grave. I don't remember the words myself. But if you want to see, sure, you can scratch off the moss. I'll give you my rake. Here it is. Leave it at the gate house when you go out." The keeper shuffled off. I scraped the tombstone clean of the creeping vine and fungi and found these words:

> *Ik leef en weet niet hoe lang,*
> *Ik sterf en weet niet wanneer,*
> *Ik reis en weet niet waarheen,*
> *Vreemd dat ik zoo vroolijk ben.*

> *I live and know not how long,*
> *I die and know not when,*
> *I travel and know not whither,*
> *Strange that I am so cheerful.*

So those were the words he had wanted to be remembered by, that old mediaeval saying of which he used to tell me that it was one of Erasmus' favorite bywords. *I do not know where I go and do not know whence I came.* The words kept drumming in my head. But is that not the lot of all of us and of all mankind? We do not know how long we have been on this star or when we shall disappear. There had been an ice age once and there will be an ice age again. What profit is there then in all our striving? O, the cheerful pessimist that he was, Uncle Kees!

I strolled out of the gate and wandered back into the streets. The lights were being lit in the shop windows. People greeted each other with a flourish of hats. High-school girls walking arm in arm passed up and down the main street. Near the church some boys were playing football. I stood in front of the bakery across from the house where I had lived and saw the baker wrap up a loaf for a lady who was accompanied by two children. I recognized her. She had been in my dreams twenty years long. She stared at me with a haughty frown when she emerged from the shop and gathered her children close to her side as if she feared contamination.

At last I decided to enter the only local hotel. I had never been inside in my youth, for then it had not been a proper place for Christians, because of its barroom and the things that went on there occasionally. The waiter spoke French to me. When I looked up at him questioningly, he changed to German. I ordered in Dutch and he understood me. A group of young officers came in noisily, flinging the door wide open and clinking their spurs. They unclasped their sabers and deposited them in the umbrella stand. Then they walked up to the bar. They were speaking of women. One pulled a crumpled letter from his tunic. He proceeded to read it to his comrades in an undertone. What they heard made them laugh till the tears came to their eyes.

There was a rattle of wooden shoes outside. From my seat by the window I looked through the transparent curtain. Workers were passing on their way home. I pulled the curtain aside slightly to look at their faces. I did not recognize one of them. But a red-headed boy, sauntering by slowly, hands in his pockets, noticing me at the window, stuck out his tongue. Other men followed behind. A cart came rumbling by, pulled by three big dogs. On it sat a man, quite erect, with one hand at his side. In the other he held a whip. His long tousled hair was white. He brushed his hand through the ruffled locks. All at once I noticed that he had a cork leg and that it lay stiff in front of him. Nardus de Smet! I tapped on the window and caught his eye. I nodded my head. He stared back fiercely, pursing his lips in anger. With a gesture of contempt he whipped up his dogs. Nardus still believed in the class war apparently, and was showing it by not greeting any strange bourgeois.

The waiter brought the food, but I did not notice what I ate. The words on the tombstone kept rushing back: "I travel and know not whither, I die and do not know when." But I could not be cheerful as Uncle Kees had been. Gorcum was not the same. People had changed. They did not recognize me. I was a stranger in my own land.

Suddenly I felt very lonely. Cannot you, too, remember a day when snow fell and the change that came over yourself and the world, when the light grew dim and drab, the sky mournful and opaque, and the houses, the roofs, the fields, suddenly became other houses, other roofs, other fields, unfamiliar and strange? Or when a beloved face was covered for the last time and the universe seemed suddenly bereft of sense and pity and you felt as if you had been the plaything of a cruel illusion? Where shall man find the fortitude to sustain him in moments of doubt, when the light goes out, the inner voice is silent and refuses to be drawn into further dialogue?

I walked out of the restaurant. The streets had grown dark. Pairs of lovers, holding hands, strolled out through the town gates. A bus honked for passage. I looked into the lighted garage which stood on the spot where I was born. The carillon in St. John's tower began to play. I stood still to listen. It was a familiar old hymn: "There sounds a voice, there is a noise, of shouting in Jerusalem!" I waited for the end and leaned against the old stones to feel the tremor of the heavy bell when it should start to strike the hour, as we had done so often as boys. Then I had to smile as I thought of Goethe's word: "*Da steh ich nun, ich armer Tor! Und bin so klug, als wie zuvor!*" And then again those other words came back: "I live and know not how long, I travel and know not whither."

It was dark when I sat down on the steps in the deep porch of the tower. How many times in the course of the last twenty years, in moments of sorrow and loneliness of wandering in the world's crowded highways, had I not wished to be back where I now was at last. There were times when I had almost cursed the fates which had made of me a stranger in nearly every land under the sun, and when I would have given anything to feel again the consoling warmth of this environment. And now this refuge, too, was evading me. The clammy stones against which I leaned were almost symbolical of the feeling of frustration and estrangement that had come over me the moment I stepped off the train. Had I changed, or had the people of Gorcum changed? Where was my fatherland, my

last anchorage, in this whirlpool of contradictory forces and currents that we call contemporary society and in which I had been
swept along now by this, then by that, stream?

My mind flew back over the road trodden in the past decades:
the religious enthusiasm of college days and the raw reality of the
War which had shattered that naïve idealism; the voyages to the
ends of the earth in quest of news that seemed as futile and worthless now as extinguished ashes; the bloody experiences of Palestine
and Ethiopia and Spain. Where was the recompense, the consolation?
I lit my pipe and listened to the singing-tower above my head.
Slowly the Stygian darkness around me became peopled with faces.
There was a tumult of voices on the old porch. A weird and fantastic procession passed before my unseeing eyes. There they were
again, all those I had seen: the lone fighters for great causes, who
suffered opprobrium and forgetfulness in bare prison walls for
scattering the seed from which the humanity of tomorrow will
grow; the masses of silent men and women in the world's great cities
who toil and sweat and strive for light and happiness. But also their
eternal adversaries, the men on horseback, who ride in the day's
fierce limelight, the saber rattlers and poison-gas philosophers,
ermine-draped and glittering with jewels. I heard and saw them all
again, the comrades with whom I had marched to war, the workers
groping in the subterranean darkness of the mines, the pleasure-
hungry crowds in Montmartre, the prisoners in the Doftana and
Cherche-Midi, the *rentiers* in their self-sufficient little world around
the coffeehouse table in Bourg-en-Forêt, the friends found in the
world's highways and by-ways: restless Panaït, prophetic Ragaz
and De Ligt, loyal Youssef Avrahim. The anguish of the watchman
peering into the Judean night came back to mind, the senseless
cruelty of the black children of Ethiopia choking on mustard gas,
the deathless courage of the valiant men of Sietamo and Barcelona.
And in the background, licking the heavens with voracious tongue,
the flames of China and Spain. And the sea of fire crepitating audibly
as it came nearer and nearer, casting a blood-red glow before it as a
harbinger of evil days to come!

Poor man! Must it be again? Have the fires of humanity then
burned in vain? Have the teachings of Christianity and of humanism
been all for nought and the self-sacrifice and love poured out by the
saints and martyrs entirely futile that we have not yet learned
goodness and peace? Is humanity to make yet another attempt

to wipe out its name with its own blood? Is it not all an endless cycle, a horrible wheel of suffering to which we are chained forever?

The clock tower's boom shook me from my reverie. A dog ran by barking at the crescent moon which appeared like a silver horn on the summit of the old bastion. Then all grew peaceful again. The town was asleep. I was alone with my thoughts again. These people have changed, I mused, but I have changed too: the whole world has changed. Can I still look to the future with confidence and have the same moral certainty that there is a profound sense to the confusion and chaos around us; that, in spite of the storm and stress of contemporary history, humanity is nevertheless growing to a fuller and more beautiful life by the acquisition of new spiritual values which will ultimately place human relationships on a higher plane?

I felt like a man who stands by the ruins of his own house. There in the presence of the worthless remains he feels himself helpless and weary and he lacks the courage to build again, because he is afraid of life and dreads the future. He sees the old values, the sacrosanct institutions undermined or cast aside, religion, authority, freedom of conscience held in contempt. And his thoughts revert to his lost paradise which always lies in the past. His own heart fails him and his old herd instinct comes to the surface and he seeks consolation and forgetfulness in the company of other fearful and frustrated brothers, and they put their trust in the capacities of a strong man, a savior, a messiah. They accept his guidance and they abdicate their will and their conscience and their intelligence and their personality into his hands. That is what has happened in our time.

How can we have faith in a higher destiny of man when we see countries that were once the homes of great cultures revert to slavery? How can there be hope when books are burned, when the most diabolical instruments of death are pressed into the hands of little children, when doctrines of hate and frenzy are hammered into the heads of brutalized millions and multitudes prostrate themselves at the lifting of the policeman's stick before some obscene idol with the shout: "Thy will alone be done!"

The process of man's dehumanization attains the one land after the other. Christianity and the centuries of humanization reveal themselves as but the thinnest veneer imposed on paganism. They come off at the first rub bringing to the surface the old atavistic instincts from the human race's somber infancy. What land is immune today? Everywhere a single standard of values is being imposed on the peoples. Every statesman speaks in terms of brute strength. True, in one place men still protest passionately that they desire to maintain the old liberties, democracy and the economic status quo but at the same time we see them band themselves together to restrict freedom (with force if needs be), to frustrate the natural evolution of democracy and seek to patch up dilapidated systems of credit and exchange in order that material well-being be confined to their class alone. Over there they loudly condemn the other man's discrimination against the Jew but themselves hang out a sign that reads "Gentiles Only." All lament the growth of anti-God movements and while professing a religion of brotherly love engage in the blasphemy of keeping millions of brothers in subhuman living conditions while preparing to destroy their neighbor by poison gas, bombing plane and dreadnought.

"This is to me the agony of life," I heard Schermerhorn say one day in my youth, "that I am a member of a society, an integral part of a social order, in which the most flagrant injustice, the most inhuman exploitation, the most barbaric practises not only occur, but are accepted as normal." But life would be unbearable if I should think this "normality" the law of Nature or the will of God and life therefore a chaotic, purposeless tumult instead of an eternal orderly process.

No, what we see in this world today is not proof that evil is immune or that the triumph of inhumanity and injustice and lovelessness is final. Long ago it was said: what a man sows that also shall he reap. The apparent triumph of evil in a historical period such as ours is not a mere accidental, unrelated phenomenon. Precisely because there is violence and oppression and hatred, there is a divine order and not chaos. Effect follows cause with inexorable accuracy. God's mill, the divine law, operates with relentless precision. When the fundamental law of nature, which is coherence and respect and brotherhood, is trodden underfoot, no other result can be expected but confusion and hatred and war. The whirlwind follows the storm. In the reflection of the flames of China and Spain our whole social order stands revealed to its very foundations as being built on colossal greed, mammonism, heartless exploitation, disregard of elementary human rights and violence. A peace based on vengeance, as someone has said, could not produce anything but Hitlers and their ugly entourage.

Europe and the world will in all likelihood have to pass through the phase of Fascism. The old democratic, parliamentary institutions cannot be saved. They have had their time. A new type of man is emerging, the mass-man, "who can no longer be considered in the perspectives of his own individual inner existence." No doubt a terrible spiritual abasement stands before the door. But Fascism carries in its bosom the seed of its own disintegration. Out of man's dissatisfaction and longing new worlds are born. As in the time of the decline of the ancient world, when man was nothing more than a plaything in the hands of the deified autocrat and his destiny riveted to the terrible wheel of fate, the hope in a juster dispensation produced a profound religious inspiration and Christianity was born. In our time too, before long, the urge will become manifest to bring the rights of the human personality in harmony with the demands of the collectivity. For even if the oppressors and tyrants, be they quasi-almighty superstates or individuals, appear inviolate and intangible as they govern with death and destruction, there will come a time when the peoples are no longer afraid of death, or, as Paul Claudel said, when men will refuse to be treated as minors and semi-idiots, and will demand a return of the freedom of their hands, their intelligence and their conscience. The last word does not belong to the poison-gas philosophers and the sabre-rattlers. Not all are going to bend the knee to Baal. The struggle that is coming is a struggle for man. In that struggle Christianity will triumph, "for Christianity alone stands for man and the freedom of the human personality and social justice and the fraternization of the peoples and enlightenment of human existence." But that triumphant Christianity will not be the Christianity we know. The old Christianity, which identified itself with this world, will perish with that world. It has been weighed and found wanting. It will be a new Christianity that comes up from the depths of the catacombs of suffering and sorrow. Its apostles will be the martyrs and saints of a new religion that will solve the elementary problems of human existence, the conquest of economic slavery and poverty and peace. . . .

The voice of a rooster, crowing in a long elastic stretch, brought me back to the reality. I had not noticed the passage of the hours. But now I felt chilly and I rose. At the same time a figure detached itself from the shadows of the houses opposite. By the light of the street lamp on the corner, I saw the gleam of a policeman's helmet. The man came up to me. "A good thing you rose," he said not unkindly, "for it is quite cool. I was coming over in a minute to see if anything had gone wrong with you. Had you fallen asleep?"

"Yes, I think I did fall asleep."

"Well, it's almost time for everybody to get up. See," he said pointing east, "there is the first light. Where are you going?"

"To the river!"

"But halt," he stopped me suddenly, "your voice sounds familiar, your face, too. . . . Now, where have I seen you before?"

"Right here, Willem!"

"You are . . . ?"

"Yes, you have guessed right!"

"Have you come back for good?" he asked.

"No, I was just here for a few hours to see the old town once more. I am taking the first ferry across."

"Well, then you're going my way and I'll accompany you." And he added, "Do you remember the time when I ran after you and took you to the police station for throwing a snowball into the open window of the girls' school?"

"I do remember it very well, Van den Oever," I replied. "You frightened me terribly that time."

He laughed and took off his helmet. I saw that his close cropped hair was white. His lips had sunken and there were a myriad of wrinkles around his eyes.

"By the way," he asked hesitatingly after we had walked a stretch, "you are not in . . . in straitened circumstances that you were sleeping in that porch?"

"No, Willem, happily not. How is it with you?"

"I am retiring on pension next year."

We stood by the shore waiting for the ferry boat. The river was splashed with dancing patches of quicksilver. But the wooded bank opposite was still wrapped in the half shadows of twilight. Midstream a fishing raft, accompanied by a tug, drifted lazily with the current. The men were busy hauling in the catch of the night. Their voices traveled to us over the water and their words were as clear as if they had been spoken by our side. Leisurely picking its way around the raft, the paddle steamer was making for the shore. The gangplank was finally lowered on the wooden wharf and the echo carried the rumbling sound over the water. I shook hands with the old policeman.

"*Den zegen*, Pieter!" he said.

"To you, too, Willem, blessings without end!"

In a quarter hour I walked on Brabant soil. It seemed but yesterday that I passed by here with Uncle Kees on one of his painting trips, for this had always been our starting point. The elm-shaded road lay very still before me. I felt strangely cheerful. The silence came singing its way into my heart. After some refreshment in the old tavern by the side of the dike, I started in the direction of Almkerk. But now the curtain of night had parted. Starting from a small patch of pale gold, no larger than a man's hand, the clouds were tearing asunder to north and south and east and west. In a flash the heavens were all aglow. The whole world looked like an open book, full of precious miniatures. I reached the abandoned fort of Altena and stood still to look at the old fire pieces pointing over its earthen walls. Suddenly a swallow, frightened by my presence, flew from its nest in the mouth of one of the rusty cannons. The next instant a troop of towheaded boys tumbled down the green slope of the bastion, pummeling each other and filling the air with shouts. I climbed to the top of the fort. Beyond was a field ripe for the mower. A farmer stood among the stalks and raised his hand in greeting. From the south a warm breeze had come up. Under its touch the wheat rustled softly with the promise of coming days.

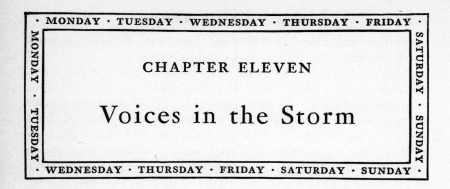

CHAPTER ELEVEN

Voices in the Storm

THEY CAME TO MY HOUSE or they came casually sauntering into the garden where I was tending the vines, villagers with whom I had scarcely exchanged a word in all the years that I had lived in their midst. From their shy and cautious behavior I knew at once that they had come to talk politics. For to talk politics—*parler politique*—is not an easy, natural thing with them. It may be that with the city man, but not with peasants. When peasants talk politics they always behave in a somewhat abnormal manner: they appear purposely distraught and casual as if they were afraid to compromise themselves. They beat around the bush, and hem and haw, before coming to the point and even then they act furtively as if they were taking some hazard, like trespassing on forbidden ground or setting out snares for rabbits on the seigneurial domains. And, to be sure, they are not altogether wrong, for politics has indeed its risks. You are apt to let yourself go when you talk politics. You may become heated, say something bold or audacious, say something you might come to regret later on. If you want to talk politics you had far better go to the tavern of an evening, where the doors can be kept closed and the shutters are bolted and where you are among neighbors, men you have known from childhood. That is much safer than standing there in the open for every passer-by to see and for him to draw his own conclusions. At the inn you feel protected, shielded against I don't know what danger. In the back room filled with tobacco smoke, and with the wine on the table, you have more courage, more hardihood, you can say what you like. You can speak "with logic," as they say, and not fear that anyone goes blabbing about it outside.

This time, too, they did not speak without a certain hesitation

505

when they came to me. Yet there was more urgency in their approach than usual. Something seemed to compel them. What overcame their reluctance, I suspect, was the hope that I might know something, that I might know of a way out, know the answer to the question that was uppermost in their minds: *Ce qui se passe maintenant, vous pensez que c'est bon pour le pays?* Do you think what is happening now, is good for the country? After all, I go to Paris very often, do I not? I may know somebody there in the big world; ministers, deputies, or professors, *tout ça.* I may have heard somebody of importance say something that's worth knowing. *Alors?* Will it be war? *Est-ce que c'est vrai qu'on va mourir pour la Pologne?* They are already a little reassured, seeing me at work so early. For that means I am not going to Paris today. I must feel rather at ease about the situation, about *les affaires,* by which they mean that mysterious and sinister realm from which are rising those storm clouds that have suddenly come to darken their lives with gloom and anguish. *Alors, ça ne va pas?* The Germans then are sure "to march"? *Ah, quels salauds tout de même!*

It was from the strange demeanor of Henri Loyau, the old *cantonnier,* that I had first become aware that there was something more seriously wrong in the village than the periodic disquietude to which the long war of nerves had almost habituated us. Often I had watched Loyau at work mending the road, spreading shovelfuls of gravel over the highway in deft, fanlike sweeps, and I had marveled at the energy and the strength of the gnarled and weather-beaten old man and the apparent delight he took in his work.

Now he was going about his task quite listlessly, without the slightest animation. He was not humming his monotonous ditty about going to pick apples in Neuilly as he lingered near my hedge that last Wednesday in August, 1939. It was, in fact, his silence that perturbed me and caused me to walk over in his direction. I noticed that the old man looked sick.

"*Alors!*" he called out abruptly, without the usual formalities about the weather and other preliminary verbal maneuvres. "*Alors!* it's for Poland this time, *hein?*"

"That's not what the posters say," I replied. "The government tells us that freedom is menaced and that we must defend it with all our might."

My answer made him think for a moment. Before he answered he spat out a stream of yellow juice.

"For freedom, *hé? Pour la liberté?*" he came back at last. "Ah," he added, "there is always some excuse. Isn't that what we were told last time? And what has it brought us, I ask you? Is there more freedom in France now than before the war? Are we better off now? Everybody knows that things have become far worse these last few years. Isn't it idiotic to try again a remedy that turned out to be poison?"

He fell silent and scraped the road in quick, angry blows, and again spat contemptuously. Suddenly he turned his furrowed and wrinkled face to me and he spoke in a hoarse whisper:

"Monsieur knows my son?"

I nodded.

"*Eh bien*, all my life I have worked to bring up that boy, to give him a better start in life than I had. I am not ashamed to tell you that I myself was brought up in a foundling's institute and that I was turned loose in the world at the age of thirteen, set to work in a cotton spinnery in St. Etienne. I married late, for I had not the income to keep a wife. But ever since the birth of that boy, who cost his mother her life, I have worked for him so that he would not know poverty. I have done it gladly, with a joyous heart, I mean. For he is a good boy, and he is now a teacher in Dijon...." Loyau was silent for a moment. He took up a rake, but dropped it back immediately. In a voice trembling with sadness he said: "He leaves tomorrow, monsieur. I haven't slept for a week. I have not eaten, I cannot swallow the smallest crust of bread. It sticks here. Here!" he pointed to his throat.

"Tomorrow," he muttered. "For Poland... or, as you say, for freedom! My boy, for Poland!" And then, with a vicious snarl that showed his yellow stumps of teeth: "*Ah, nom d'un nom de Dieu! Why do we have children? To see them slaughtered? What freedom is that? Quel horreur!*"

Slowly the village emptied of its men. The first day of mobilization the horses went. Even the old horse of the garbage cart was requisitioned. In the long tail-switching procession I recognized that old acquaintance by his soft, melancholy eyes. Fifteen years I had known him, and I had sometimes dreamed for him of a grassy meadow by the side of a still pond at the end of the trail. Now he ambled off to the battlefield with his tired and sagging knees.

Only women were about in the streets. They stood talking in little clusters at the garden gates. When I came near they looked askance and their conversation stopped. I felt like an outcast. The blood rushed to my cheeks. What had I done, what was my crime?

I went to read the posters put up at the *mairie*. They indicated the classes that were called to the colors, what articles and personal effects the mobilized men had to bring along to the depots, which butchers were to supply a neighboring military concentration point, which houses were to be requisitioned. I noticed that mine was one of them. There were also long printed explanations about the dangers of air raids. Incendiary bombs were declared not dangerous. Only, you were not to try and put them out by dousing them with water. Water would only cause them to burn the more fiercely. You were advised to have a pail of sand in readiness. When one of these bombs fell on your roof or in your back yard all you had to do was to sprinkle it gently with sand, and it would be extinguished in no time. Sprinkle it gently—*doucement* was the word—as if any human being can come within reach of one of those things which develops a heat of 2200 degrees and which burns through the average roof and three floors below in less time than it takes to say a paternoster.

The water in your faucet will be colored red, warned another poster. This is to indicate that the source has been subjected to bombardment by poison gas or disease germs. When high-explosive bombs are dropping, go at once to your cellar or to the neighbor's. Unless there is a direct hit on the house in which you have sought refuge there is not much danger. Not much, no! But if the high-explosive bombs are of the kind the Italians and Germans dropped one day on Barcelona by way of experiment, every living creature within a radius of five hundred yards will have his lungs burst by the concussion. And four-storied houses not directly hit, as I recall it, will crumple like children's toys, the walls bending inward and the ceilings crashing downward, all in the twinkling of an eye, long before any one can run out of the cellar—that is, if his lungs are not exploded beforehand.

I was summoned to the police post. The place swarmed with military men. Our own rural gendarmes looked worried and busy. They spoke in crisp and harsh tones, and somehow did not seem to recognize me. My fingerprints were taken. A lieutenant who sported a monocle wrote on my identity card that my movements were henceforth restricted to the village of Bourg. "*Mesure de guerre*," he said. "Have you any arms?" he asked.

"No," I said.

"No hunting rifle? No revolver?"

"No," I repeated.

"You mean, you live alone there near the forest and you have no defensive arms?"

"*Non, mon lieutenant!* Against whom should I defend myself?"

"*Eh bien, rôdeurs*, vagabonds, marauders...."

I shook my head.

"That's strange," he mused. "You know, I might send some one to search. It will go badly with you if any arms are found on the premises."

"But surely you have some *armes blanches*?" he questioned again.

"White arms? What do you mean? Bayonets?"

"No, I mean knives, cutlery, that sort of thing. Those too must be surrendered by aliens."

"I have a kitchen carving knife."

"Go and fetch it!"

Then the government passed a decree ordering the destruction of all domestic animals de luxe. A measure to safeguard the food supply it was called. I waited till the last hour of the last day on which notification of the possession of such animals had to be made. Then I sat with my old friend of twelve years, who had been like a child in our home and a brother to the children, and who had roamed over the world with us. He had to die. I knew there was a tin of *pâté de foie gras* in the provision box, and I knew he liked it.

"Please open that tin," I said to the maid, "and I'll give it to him."

"Monsieur is not thinking of feeding that dog *pâté de foie*?" she came back icily. And she added: "Not while our brave French soldiers are eating dry bread in the Maginot Line."

So the veterinary came, another military man. I held my hand over old Michel's trusting brown eyes and whispered in his ear the lie that all would be well, while the functionary administered the mortal injection....

I walked out and met the Abbé de la Roudaire and told him about Michel's death. "Monsieur," he said, "he will be waiting for you at the gate on that day. He won't go in till you have come."

"Monsieur," I replied, "heaven would be misery without him."

As I stood on the darkened railway platform that night, waiting for a train to take me to Paris, a sharp female voice cried out that it was *les metèques*, the aliens, the damned foreigners, who were responsible for all the woe. "It is they who have been laying down the law to us all these years, eating and drinking of the best France has to offer. Why shouldn't they be made to fight and....bleed?"

I returned at dawn, having managed to escape the police patrols in Paris, who would have had to run me in had they stopped me with only a *carte d'identité* for Bourg in my possession. I entered the garden gate just as the milkman was making his delivery.

"You are a Huguenot, are you not, monsieur?" the man asked.

When I replied in the affirmative, he went on: "Well, then, what do you people make of all this? Is this justice? Is this the work of a God of love, this gruesome slaughter of innocent men, women, and children we are about to see? What is the sense of this existence, to slave and slave, and then be butchered in the end? Is there a God?

"There is a God, Monsieur Beaumont," I said, "but I do not believe that God has anything to do with this war. This war, in my opinion, is entirely the work of man. I can only tell you what an Englishman once said when others, before you, blamed and even cursed God for the calamity of war. 'If men do not like war,' he said, 'let them not fight!'" The milkman went off shrugging his shoulders.

Before taking the train in the evening of the tenth day of the war I lingered for a while in the Café du Commerce, opposite the railway station. On a seat near by sat an elderly man in the uniform of a colonel of infantry. At his side was a boy of eighteen or nineteen, obviously his son. The boy had a haversack slung over his shoulder, and at his feet stood a small leather grip of the kind recruits and reservists take along when they leave for the army depots. The colonel and his son were holding hands. They did not speak a word. Both were perfectly oblivious of what went on around them. Every once in a while the older man leaned over and put his grizzled head on the lad's shoulder. At last the sound of the train's whistle could be heard in the distance, and the boy made as if to rise from his seat. But his father held him down.

A world of sadness came into the man's eyes. He aged as I watched. Then the tears started rolling down his cheeks. And the two walked silently, hand in hand, to the station.

On the platform stood a reservist, a man I knew well. He was a widower. He had brought his four small children. They stood there with him, three girls and a small boy, a mere infant. The reservist caught sight of the colonel.

"*Eh, mon colonel*," he exclaimed, "colonel, look—look at this, *mes quatres gosses*, my four kids. They have no mother. I am leaving. I have been called, Colonel! I am going! *Pour la Pologne!* For Poland!"

The man screamed the words. The colonel tried to hush him: "Be quiet, my friend. What is the good of shouting? *Voila*, there is the train!"

But the reservist continued to cry out at the top of his voice: "*Pour la Pologne! Ah, merde de la merde! Mes quatres gosses!... Pour la Pologne!...*"

My neighbor Jules Carnot was not taken. He is the handy man who lived up the street a little way from us. The medical board rejected him. He came to tell me about it.

"*Eh bien*," he said, "here I am. I am free. I am apparently the only man of military age to stay behind in Bourg."

"How is that, Jules?"

"It was like this," Jules explained. "They had us all lined up in the *mairie*, stripped naked, and looked us over. Grèvecoeur and Vingtier and the others, all had passed. *Bon pour le service*. Fit for every branch of the service. The boys were already putting on their clothes. Then my turn came. 'But you,' said the doctor, after he sounded my lungs, 'what are you doing here? You have consumption. You know you have consumption. You haven't got six months to live!'

"'Is that so? And they?' I asked the doctor, pointing at Grèvecoeur and the others. '*Et eux?* How long have they—can you tell me that?...'"

Four days later the postman rang. "A registered letter, Monsieur Pelletier?"

"No, monsieur, not a registered letter. Monsieur," he hesitated a little, "I have a card to deliver at the widow Garnier's across the way."

"A card? *The* card?"

"Yes, *the* card. Here it is...."

"I read: "The Government of the Republic regrets to announce that your son Garnier, Raoul, has fallen on the field of honor...."

"I am carrying this card in my sack these three days," said the postman. "I have not the courage to deliver it. Raoul was her only son, you know that. What am I to do? Look, monsieur," said the postman, "there she stands at the gate waiting for me to pass. She is expecting a letter from Raoul. What am I to do? Life will not be worth living for that woman if I deliver this card. Monsieur, will you go and talk to her, sort of prepare her? Will you, monsieur? I can't bring myself to hand her the card. Upon my soul I can't. Maybe you could speak to *monsieur l'Abbé* about this? I am not on speaking terms with the priest.... Will you?"

I promised, and I watched him pass the cottage across the way with a friendly wave at Mme. Garnier, who was still standing in the doorway.

On my way out of France I read the censored newspapers on the train and learned that the French people were determined to finish with Hitlerism once and for all. There was no weakness, it was said, no room for sloppy sentimentality; the French soldiers were resolute, of one mind. In the forceful official communiqués Daladier and Chamberlain were saying that France and Britain were going to fight to the limit of their material and human resources.

Human resources!

And then I thought of the villages of Bourg, of Vingtier and Grèvecoeur and Pelletier, and their wives and children, of the Maginot Line and the bone-crushing, fire-spewing tanks, of the bombing planes and of the glory of the mass attacks. And I prayed God to have pity on the hearts of men.

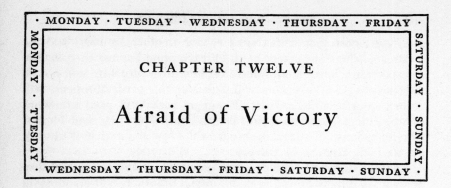

CHAPTER TWELVE

Afraid of Victory

How ANYONE COULD HAVE expected French diplomats who were members of Franco-German munition trusts; ministers of the Government who sent their wives and mistresses to Berlin, Munich, and Vienna to be entertained by the Nazi bonzes; financiers who were seen night after night in the salons of Mme. des Portes, the Marquise du Crussol and Mme. Georges Bonnet walking arm in arm with Abetz, with Sieburg, Arnheim, Funk, and the other emissaries of Goebbels and Ribbentrop; cardinals and bishops who returned from the periodic visits *ad limina* dazzled by, and firm protagonists of, Mussolini's corporate state; generals who, like De Castelnau and Weygand, were the moving spirits in the order of the Gagoulards, a secret terrorist and anti-Semitic organization which affected the hood and robe of the Ku Klux Klan; newspaper publishers, like the directors of *Le Temps* and *Le Figaro*, who were shown to be recipients of subsidies from Rome and Berlin; utility magnates like Pierre Laval, Flandin, and Colonel de La Rocque, who rejoiced over the surrender of fifty divisions at Munich; and, finally, statesmen who treated the parliamentary representatives as so many irresponsible schoolboys and who ruled by decree, the censor's gag, and the threat of the gardes mobiles' machine guns—how anyone could have expected all that corrupt and reactionary crowd of avowed and unavowed Fascists, which in the hour of France's crisis effectively held and operated the state's levers of control, to be capable of leading the French people to a victory of democracy over Fascism —that is beyond comprehension.

Yet a mere glance at the newspaper files covering the first six fateful months of the year 1940 will show that until the very end the belief or the hope was entertained by editorialists, commentators, and expert correspondents that somehow or other, by miracle even, in Weygand's "last quarter hour," France would contrive to snatch victory from the jaws of defeat and hurl the Germans back across the Rhine. Which of our metropolitan journals or national commentators had the courage or even the simple honesty to paint the situation in France in its true colors by making it known that under the administrations which had succeeded the Popular Front government France had ceased to be a democracy, and thus to warn the American people that with men of so pronounced an antidemocratic disposition at the helm as Laval, Bonnet, Flandin, Reynaud, Ponçet, Weygand, Ybernégaray, Déat, Leméry, Badouin, Pétain, Gamelin, Daladier, and Bérenger no democratic victory over German and Italian Fascism was to be looked for or was even intended? Every conceivable contributing factor to the defeat of the French Republic has been explored and explained in our press: the lack of equipment, the shortage of man power, the treasonable manipulations of the Communists, pacifist sentiment, moral degeneration, Britain's failure to send sufficient reinforcements, Leopold's betrayal, Russia's slap in the face to the Western democracies, the petrification of the French high command, which clung to the antiquated strategical theories of 1914 and which had been dismissing its critics of twenty years with the facile rejoinder: "I am Sir Oracle, and when I open my lips, let no dog bark." All these aspects of the internal situation and the international position of France have been analyzed until even congressmen and a presidential candidate oracled about the conduct of Léon Blum and the Popular Front being at base the cause of France's downfall.

One thing was not said, except in the leaflets and pamphlets of Leftist minorities: that the democracy of France lay gagged and bound long before the struggle started. Yes, the sinister truth is that the politicians who led the dance in 1940 themselves sacrificed the French people in a war which not only was lost before a single shot was fired, but a war, also, which they deliberately set out to lose.

Oh, I do not doubt that enemy agents were at work before and during the German drive and that a German spy or so with a radio transmission set hidden in a wooden leg was actually caught signaling to Goering's bombers, but the work of these petty agents did not weigh up against that of the brains of the Fifth Column, Hitler's real allies in France, who were at all times safely installed in the War Office, in the parliamentary bureaus, and even in the Hotel des Invalides, the seat of the high command. The party of treason in France was not a clandestine organization of alien or alien-inspired wreckers and *saboteurs*. It was made up of unfingerprinted, unmolested native-born Frenchmen, most respectable gentlemen all of them, and superpatriotic to boot: generals, big industrialists, veteran politicians, and newspaper proprietors, who had never so much as set foot in a pacifist meetinghouse or taken any more interest in alien isms than to damn and curse them.

The last thing on earth these people wanted was a democratic victory for France, something which by the nature of things would have entailed a victory for democratic principles in Germany also, and, conceivably, the institution of a new social order in postwar Europe, probably a federation of European states by the free consent of the peoples and a unified economy operating not for the exclusive benefit of one particular group, but a Continental economy to satisfy the needs and to assure the well-being of all classes and of all groups in every European nation.

That, to these men, was the dreadful specter which loomed behind a victory for democracy. They hated democracy like the very pestilence because the evolution of democratic institutions threatens the privileged status of their own class in society. What they wanted was Fascism, because Fascism protects the interests of their class and makes their inviolability the state's chief concern.

The story that Pétain, who was General Franco's teacher, and Laval, Mussolini's personal friend, turned to Fascism as a last desperate resort, so to speak, in that they adopted the drastic remedy of authoritarianism to counteract the chaos and confusion which were bound to follow in the wake of the army's disintegration—that story is not borne out by the historical facts of the last decade. Nor can Pétain's sudden decision to co-ordinate the French social order to the Nazi-Fascist norm be interpreted and accepted as a gesture to placate Fuehrer and Duce, or as a tacit appeal to the two dictators for leniency.

We have been told that the French people were in a stupor in those tragic hours when disaster overwhelmed their country. The French people, yes. But not Weygand, Laval and Pétain. These men were not groping their way. They moved with the somnambulistic sureness of an Adolf Hitler. They knew what they were doing. They and their class did in July, 1940, what they had plotted to do for a long time; they seized upon the German military victory as a supreme, godsent opportunity to slip the collar of servitude around the necks of the French people.

In June, 1940, it became clear what the chief organ of Fascism in the French capital, *Le Jour*, had meant in June, 1936, when it proclaimed in a six-column headline, on the day when the Popular Front assumed power: *"Plutôt Hitler que Blum! Rather Hitler than Blum!"*

While it is generally admitted that it was not the might of the German army alone but the subversive activity of a Fifth Column which served as the principal instrument in the defeat of France, the disastrous events of the months of May and June, 1940, are consequently taken as the result, the culmination of a long process of sabotage of France's defenses and undermining of the people's morale. It is argued that an entire nation does not grow listless and soft all at once, but that the preceding course of events, the social and economic conditions of the masses must be taken into account as having had a definite and determining influence on the spirit, the morale, and the capacity of the people to resist a hostile onslaught. Most of the analysts of the French debacle in our American press have ascribed the amazingly swift collapse of what Mussolini, as late as 1938, called "the best and finest army in Europe," to the social follies of the Popular Front governments, which, it is said, instituted a sort of New Deal: costly and far-reaching social legislation, shorter working hours, paid vacations; new educational facilities, theater and public-work projects and the like. The program of these governments, it is charged, was executed at the expense of national defense. It absorbed and drained the country's financial resources. Under the Popular Front governments, it is said, France gave herself up to luxuries beyond her means, indulged in an orgy of spending, and allowed her pivotal departments of government to fall into the hands of a Red radical bureaucracy whose members and fellow travelers, international or antinational in spirit, provoked dissension, laxity of discipline, and civil strife in the rear, thus weakening the national defense to the point of paralysis.

This explanation, which we have seen repeated with varying degrees of literary felicity and noble indignation, had the advantage of placing an opportune weapon in the hands of the opponents of the New Deal in America. Can you not see what happened to

France? Those French Reds and dreamers went on a spending spree, they frightened business with their extravagances; they shocked the sane and sound citizenry with their threats of revolution, they undermined confidence, and in the end plunged the country into a depression which deflected that national energy and those funds which should have gone into the fight against Germany. This is the interpretation we have most insistently been given. The moral is: beware of New Deals! But this argument, which was ostensibly aimed at the men of the Popular Front in France and which was intended to strike at the Roosevelt administration, is a poisoned dart, false and malicious from beginning to end!

The first effect of the coming to power of the Popular Front was an amazing upsurge in national sentiment. For the first time in the history of the Third Republic three great political parties had united to carry out a program of social reform which was to assure bread, liberty, and peace to every man and woman in France. As Prime Minister the coalition chose Edouard Daladier, the chief of the Radical-Socialist Party, which was the political organization of the middle-class liberals, and therefore neither socialistic nor radical in the sense generally attributed to these words in America. Daladier announced as his fundamental thesis of government that in order to be free France must needs be strong, that is to say, mistress of her own destiny and able to command respect for her voice in the international concert. He therefore set to work strengthening the army and organizing and reinforcing the production of war materials.

At the same time, the government ushered in the program of social reform which was to bring the French working class and the poor peasants somewhat nearer to the standard of living long since attained by the workers of America, Britain, Germany, and the Scandinavian countries. The horrible slums of the capital and the great industrial cities, foul breeding-nests of crime, of vice, and of generations of anemic and tubercular human beings, were to be cleared. Higher educational facilities were to be provided for the children of the proletarian masses and the rural inhabitants. The airless and sunless school buildings erected in the last four and five centuries were to be torn down and replaced with modern edifices. Clinical facilities were to be provided for the sick amongst the destitute. Maternity hospitals were planned and begun. The labor syndicates or trade unions were conceded the right of collective bargaining, and company unions were proscribed. The number of hours of work, which was still twelve and fourteen and even sixteen a day in the mines of the Pas de Calais and in the textile plants of the Roubaix and Lyons districts, was reduced to forty-five a week, giving the workers a free Saturday afternoon and a week's vacation with pay every year. In a few months' time hundreds of vocational schools were opened, and the country was dotted with youth hostels, to which tens of thousands of boys and girls from the crowded cities tramped or bicycled for week ends and holidays.

"Is this Socialism that you are introducing?" I asked the Vice-Premier, Léon Blum, one evening in his home on the Quai de Bourbon.

"No, it is not," said Blum. "We have no mandate to introduce Socialism. We are merely trying to extract from the capitalist system the fullest possible measure of well-being for the underprivileged. We are out first and foremost to raise the standard of life for all citizens. We desire to create such social conditions in France as will make every citizen proud of the fact that he is a Frenchman and therefore willing and eager to defend France if a threat to her national existence should ever arise."

"But suppose," I ventured, "the people who are sometimes called the ruling class, or the *bourgeoisie*, refuse to co-operate with you, and they withhold their capital or in other ways hinder the efforts of your government. What will you do then—employ force? Will you in that case institute a dictatorship of the proletariat as the Marxists did in Russia, that is, crush your opponents and liquidate them as a class?"

"Ours is not a workers' government," replied Blum, "but a government of national concentration. We are the government of all Frenchmen and of all classes in France, also of the *haute bourgeoisie*, the bankers, the trust magnates, the big industrialists, and the press. It is true that these are our opponents. But I do not think we are trespassing on their interests. Have they themselves not always insisted that France must be strong and free? How can France be strong and free if the majority of her citizens live in stinking holes, when her children perish from malnutrition and her adolescents grow up to despise and hate the land which is always praised as free and generous but which denies them an elementary measure of well-being? Our program is one of national regeneration, and in this we expect all classes to collaborate for the common weal. However, it is quite well possible, as you suggest, that the *bourgeoisie* will obstruct the government in its program of social amelioration and will place great obstacles in our way. If that happens," said Léon Blum, "I will go to the workers and I will tell them frankly: 'It cannot be done, my friends; you have enemies who deny you a place in the sun; it is up to you to decide what to do next.'"

And, to be sure, side by side with a splendid enthusiasm which swept France from one end to the other, the installation of the Popular Front produced a storm of opposition. The *grande presse* almost unanimously disapproved of the government's program and launched a campaign of criticism so violent and vituperative that one might have gained the impression, in reading it, that gangsters and highwaymen had managed to seize the reins of power in France. Even so, new schools went up in the sordid suburbs. Popular theaters arose as by magic in the tumultuous *faubourgs*. Garden cities were laid out and constructed. Hundreds of old buildings in the capital and in the other cities, which had stood dark and deserted at nights for many scores of years, now blazed with light in the evenings as the youth of France returned to school. Pregnant mothers obtained a few months' release from the deadening monotony of conveyor belt and whirling bobbins. The railways could scarcely accommodate the droves of vacationists who deserted the sweltering factories in summertime to seek refreshment and recreation in the forests and the mountains and at the seaside. The Parisian and Lyonese slum dweller was seeing and feeling the beauty and the loveliness of his own fatherland for the first time. He was learning what the trees have to say and what the sun and the wind write in the sky, and he heard the language of silence in the still flowers on the mountains and in the fields.

It was as if a new life had started. France without doubt was big, as the people say, with good hope, looking for a happy birth hour and blessed fruit. The long-expected light that will be born out of the hopes and aspirations of all peoples and all nations seemed to be drawing nearer. Men held their heads higher. They had new courage and a new pride. There was new vigor in their step. They had jobs. Gone were the horrible long queues of bedraggled and hungry mendicants in front of the soup kitchens and the Hôtels-Dieu. The government's work projects had absorbed unemployment. The French were working and eating, and it was not the bread of charity. At nights the boulevards swarmed with the strolling inhabitants of the *faubourgs*. Sometimes they came singing, arm in arm, tens of thousands of men and women. And the song they sang was not some *Carmagnole* or *Vive la dynamite*, but the *Marseillaise!*

If some of the chroniclers of medieval social conditions are right when they aver that manual labor was both an honor and a joy in those days of cathedral building, one might have believed a renascence of the Middle Ages to have returned. At least, that is the way I felt as I went the rounds night and day of the factories and workshops of Paris and its industrial vicinity. I had never witnessed such a general elation of spirit, such an outburst of *joie de vivre*. The boisterous celebrations at the time of the Armistice signing in 1918 were nothing in comparison with this, for the happy mood was sustained and the quiet joy was not marred by memories of blood and suffering. Everybody sang. On buses and trains, or when you looked in at the ateliers and *chantiers*, you were greeted with a cordiality, with a genuine brotherliness that made your heart swell with emotion. "*Hé, les copains, voici un frère d'Amérique qui vient nous voir!*" Not a word of hatred or rancor. The sordid past seemed already forgotten. The world of slums and saloons, of gutter poverty and ugliness, had taken on a rosier hue. It still existed but it was wrapped in the crepuscule of a sinking sun.

Will I be believed when I say that I saw workers who were anxious to work, who thought and spoke of nothing else but of work? I heard them go to their factories at Boulogne-Billancourt and Sartrouville, at Neuilly and St. Dénis, at six in the morning, singing, yes, singing in unison *La Jeune Garde*, the *Internationale*, and the song of the stationmaster's beautiful wife. "They went and they sang," wrote Victor Hugo of the workers of his day. And you had not believed the old master, for you had never heard them yourself. But now work was their joy, which they went out to meet as a sweetheart. "There was once," said Charles Peguy, "an unbelievable honor in work, the greatest of all honors, the most Christian. It is for that reason that I say that a freethinker in those days was more of a Christian than the pious of our time." That honor had been restored. When work is a joy it is like a healing herb. You sensed in those days that men had begun to look upon work no longer as an ineluctible evil, but with an intensity of feeling, with what the Italians called *pietà*, a religious devotion.

And the effect in practical reality? Statistics prove, although they are never mentioned by the detractors of the Popular Front, that under that regime the workers took such pride and care in their work that they pushed the desire to turn out a perfect article to the limit of the handcraftsmen of the Middle Ages. And statistics also prove—and these are totally ignored by the enemies of democracy —that the quantitative output of France's industry, including the war industry, never rose to such a height as it did under the Popular Front. Only when the war had started, and Reynaud speeded up industry under the menace of the German Stukas, did the production again reach the tempo of the Popular Front days.

Even so, all this time *la grande presse* kept up a frenzied tom-tom of slander, attack, and misrepresentation against the leaders of the Popular Front and their intentions. The capacity for evil of these men was made to appear of almost superhuman dimensions. Daladier, of course, had sold out to the Bolsheviks. That was a fundamental maxim which apparently required no demonstration. Of a bourgeois who deserts his class only the worst is to be believed. It was as clear as daylight to the tone-setting editorialists—who had lost most of their income through the cancellation of the item "for secret funds" in the new government's budget and who now appeared at the pay window of the big utilities as regularly as honey bees near a sugar factory—that the Popular Front, with Edouard Daladier at its head, intended to disarm France, demoralize her, and then hand the country and people over as a delectable morsel to Joseph Stalin and his barbarian Mongol legions. Daladier, it should not be overlooked, had once, back in 1934, dispersed an attempted Fascist *Putsch* with a few whiffs of grapeshot.

As to Léon Blum, the Vice-Premier's racial antecedents naturally indicated him as the easiest target of all to those chivalrous knights of the pen. What else, do you think, could that sly *youpin* be doing but carrying out the orders of the invisible and intangible but ubiquitous Jewish world syndicate? Was he not known as a charter member of the executive committee of the Elders of Zion, was he not also a Bulgarian by birth and, moreover, engaged, with Trotsky and Litvinov, in the international counterfeiting business? When the Popular Front came to power Blum had at once given vent to his base Semitic instincts by beginning the spoliation of France in the interests of the universal Jewish bankers' cartel. For assistants in this task he was importing the dregs from the Jewish ghettos across the Rhine and from eastern Europe, whom he was naturalizing as French citizens at the rate of seventy-five to one hundred thousand a year. With these human mongrels, whom Herr Hitler and the Endeks of Poland had manfully and wisely cast off, Blum was spending his days and nights in endless carousel in the châteaux he had bought up with money stolen from the exchequer. The Rightist papers gave descriptions of banquets and feasts, at which the Socialist leader was said to preside, that surpassed in lustful delirium the most fantastic saturnalia of the ancients. At those feasts the filched gold plate of the former kings of France reflected the glory of chandeliers presented to *monsieur le ministre* by a grateful House of Rothschild.

If anyone should think me guilty of exaggeration, let him turn up the files of the journal with the largest circulation in France, *Gringoire*, a paper owned by Jean Chiappe, the Prefect of Police whom the Popular Front dismissed. Let him read there the front-page articles on Léon Blum by "the master journalist" Henri Béraud. Blum, austere ascetic that he is, paid no attention to the filth, of course, and merely shrugged his shoulders—and a free press is one of the bulwarks of democracy too, isn't it?—but Roger Salengro, the Minister of the Interior, when his turn came to be "exposed" by the Messrs. Béraud and Carbuccia, could not bear the shame of it, and after the twentieth article in the series went and committed suicide on the grave of his wife in some town up north. Yes, let any doubting Thomas also read the outpourings of Jacques Doriot in *La Liberté* and of Pierre Dreux La Rochelle in *Emancipation Nationale*, and, if he is immune to nausea, glance through a book entitled *Bagatelles pour un massacre*, by Ferdinand Céline, which was scattered in millions of copies—and then let him tell me whether vituperation and calumny and insinuation have ever descended to more abysmal depths.

By trying to create the impression that the French nation had become decadent and corrupt and hence was no longer worthy of being considered the chief torchbearer of culture in the world, the reactionary press in Europe, with the Mussolinian house organ in the lead, had unwittingly indicated the source from which it expected the most determined and the most principled opposition to the fascistization of the Continent to emanate—the country, namely, whose working class had, historically, shown itself possessed of the surest revolutionary instinct. The victory of 1918, it was said, had not led to a spiritual revival in France, as had been the case in Italy and even in defeated Germany. The French people were dishonorably resting on the laurels won for them by British, American, and—chiefly, of course—Italian arms. They had lost the virility of their ancestors; Democratic corruption and love of luxury had made them grow soft and effeminate. The working class, lulled by the demagogic slogan of *l'Allemagne paiera*, had fallen into indolence, was given over to vice, alcohol, and degeneracy, while all moral restraint and religious authority had naturally broken down under regimes headed by Freemasons and Jews.

This campaign of calumny suddenly reached a crescendo when the pro-Fascist sections of the British press, followed by their American imitators, seized upon the wave of strikes in June, 1936, to treat the country of France as a boiling hotbed of anarchy in Europe, as a most dangerous hearth of violent revolutionism which, with Russia's collaboration, might soon set all the world aflame. Although Paris and the provincial cities had remained perfectly peaceful throughout the weeks of labor's demonstration, the most blood-curdling stories were sent out to England and America by certain correspondents: about tourists fearing for their lives, about scenes of horror, looting, lynching, rapine, bloodshed, and misery, all personally witnessed, it goes without saying, or based on the testimony of "usually reliable sources." The flood of misrepresentation rose so high that the French government, unable to bear the ignominy any longer, issued a communiqué saying that it could "not allow the publication of such flagrant lies without making a categorical protest." No "signs of either violence or horror," it said, had occurred in Paris. Nowhere in France had there been any rioting. What effect this protest had may be seen by consulting the editorial pages of certain American journals, the columns of the English Rothermere press, and the Hearst press in the United States. The France of the Popular Front remains to this day a horrible example of the confusion, of the class-war ferocity and the misery that any country must expect when it proceeds from mere theories to making democracy a reality.

It is quite true, on the other hand, that France lost the leadership of Europe at once after the Great War. But this can in no way be attributed to a decadence of the national spirit, or even less to a loss of historical perspective on the part of her working class. France's leadership was lost because her British allies, who feared the reactivization of the revolutionary instinct of the French workers, tied her hands from the day peace was signed at Versailles, and thus prevented her diplomacy from organizing Europe in the light of political common sense and historical experience. In fact, British imperialism decreed long before the end of the first world war that the hegemony in Europe should, in the event of victory, not go to a France where the strong sentiment for international brotherhood, especially among the workers, might some day upset Britain's balance-of-power policy by breaking up the armed camps and creating a European federation. In his famous memorandum of 1916, which Lloyd George praised as "the height of statesmanship," Sir William Robertson, chief of the British General Staff, wrote: "What Britain needs above all after the war, is a strong Germany." From the moment peace was signed in 1920 until the invasion of Poland in September, 1939, successive British governments have not veered one iota from that disastrous program.

Fear of France because of its working class, which had built barricades a dozen times "for the extension of democratic rights and the clarification of human thought"—there you have, I think, the fundamental explanation of the events which led to the debacle of 1940. That fear, which was deeply shared by the French propertied classes, produced a halfheartedness in the defense effort amounting to paralysis. Nay, worse, it caused the French *bourgeoisie* to deliver up the country to Hitler as the lesser of two evils, rather than face the prospect of victory and with it the likelihood of seeing a consistent democracy emerge after the struggle. And to go one step further: Hitler's attack in the spring of 1940 saved the French *bourgeoisie* from the humiliation of calling in the Fuehrer to restore what they would have called order, that is to say, their order, an eventuality at which the Rightist press had hinted more than once in the days of the Popular Front government. That this hint was not a mere bogy threat may be seen from the past: on two other occasions in the midst of a great national crisis did the French ruling classes prefer passing under foreign domination to facing a democratic transformation of the state, and actually called in an alien conqueror. Once after the defeat of Napoleon at Waterloo, when the Bourbons called in the Russian Czar and his Holy Alliance to prevent the people from setting up a democratic republic. And once again in 1871, when the Parisians were determined to continue the war against Prussia and proclaimed the Commune as the instrument to fight a revolutionary war, the *bourgeoisie*, headed by Adolphe Thiers, hastened to make common cause with the German General

Staff. Rather share power with a national enemy who recognizes the bourgeois order than allow history to take its normal course towards the institution of a genuine democracy—that has been the governing maxim of the French ruling classes for a century and more.

Even so, no matter how loudly the pack howled, the caravan continued on its way. The Popular Front held the reins and was regenerating France. A new life had begun. There was joy and hope and confidence in the future. The masses of the people, seeing their government genuinely concerned about their health and happiness and well-being, felt that they had something to live for—yes, something to defend and die for if necessary.

The France of the Popular Front would never have been the victim of Hitler's violence. For that France had recaptured the deathless spirit of the ragged and barefooted sans-culottes of 1789, who faced and overcame a reactionary Europe arrayed in arms against them. It was a united France that Germany would have had to face in 1937, not the totally demoralized and confused French people with which the politicians who succeeded the Popular Front pretended to hold back the Reich's mechanized legions in 1940.

For the France of the Popular Front, besides being innerly united, had strong allies. Not only was Czechoslovakia, powerfully equipped, still standing guard at Germany's back door, but the Soviet Union was bound to both Prague and Paris by a pact of mutual assistance. At that time Russia, which had good reason to believe her territory the first major objective of the Nazi expansionist program, would not have been averse, we know, to waging a preventive war on the side of France, Britain, and their allies against Germany. Russia's attitude caused the Communists in France, who had entered the Popular Front, but not the government, to appear in the unaccustomed role of fierce and even chauvinistic nationalists. It was they who in 1937, strange as it may seem in the light of later events, were the most vociferous supporters in the parliamentary committees and in their press of the national preparedness campaign. If their zeal was so great that it rendered their motives suspect, it unquestionably at the same time proved the serious intent of Moscow to check Hitler. It is true that nothing hampered Daladier and later Blum, when he became Premier, so much in their efforts to build up a strong national defense as the warlike clamor of the neophyte Red nationalists who received their instructions from the Comintern. For now the reaction could and did raise the cry that the preparedness campaign of the Popular Front was designed merely to have France pull the chestnuts out of the fire for or save the skins of the Bolsheviks of Moscow. Hitler, from his side, seeing the value of a possible break in the single-mindedness of the French people on the subject of national defense, vigorously supported the contentions of the Popular Front's opponents, by giving out the assurance that he entertained no hostile intentions against Paris, and even that he intended to respect that clause in the Versailles Treaty whereby Alsace-Lorraine had been ceded to France.

The men of the reaction in France, the same who were to institute a Fascist-authoritarian regime under Hitler's protection in the month of July, 1940—Maxime Weygand, Pierre Laval, Paul Baudouin, Henri Leméry, Philippe Pétain, Pierre Flandin, Jean Ybernégaray, Emile Mireaux—and who then proceeded to take a frightful revenge on the adherents of the erstwhile Popular Front, charging them with high treason and culpable neglect in the building of French national defenses—that is, fixing the blame for the military disaster of 1940 on the political parties in power in 1936— these same men were falling over themselves denouncing the Popular Front as a warmongering outfit, bent on pushing France into war on Russia's side and murdering the French youth for Stalin's sake, when the Popular Front insisted on building up the country's diplomatic and military defenses.

The same Pierre Laval who, when he was Prime Minister in 1936, prevented Britain from enforcing the League's sanctions against Italy by withholding the use of France's war harbors from the British fleet, and who, he surely, thus most effectively sabotaged France's national interests by preventing the elimination from the scene of history of his friend, the back-stabbing Mussolini—that man caused to be put to death hundreds of patriotic Frenchmen for the crime of having desired to help Britain bring Mussolini to a fall, for the crime of having wanted to support the anti-Nazi opposition in the Reich, for having wanted to prevent Spain from becoming a base of attack in the hands of Franco, Mussolini, and Hitler against Britain and France herself, and for the crime of having wanted to take a strong stand, together with no matter whom, with the Devil himself, against Adolf Hitler at a time when the German dictator could still have been stopped.

Of course, the crime of the Popular Front was not that it neglected the national defense. The crime for which Laval and Weygand, under the protection and with the approbation of Hitler, will exact—or will have exacted when these words appear in print—a bloody expiation from the adherents of the erstwhile Popular Front, is that these men, when they were in power, sought to enlarge the basis of the social order in France by inviting the lower middle classes, the workers, and the poorer peasants to a fuller measure of representation in the administrative departments of the state, to bring about a more equitable distribution of wealth, and "to liberalize the control of vast industries lodged in the hands of a relatively small group of individuals of great financial power." Their crime was the same crime for which Hitler murdered, tortured, incarcerated, and drove into exile hundreds of thousands of Germany's noblest sons: the crime of having believed in democracy.

It has been openly charged, and more often insinuated, that the Popular Front in the minds of its protagonists was intended to serve as a sort of opening wedge for—or, rather, as a prelude to—a Bolshevik revolution, with Léon Blum consciously or unconsciously playing the role, providentially attributed to him by the French section of the Comintern, of a second Kerensky. But that allegation will not stand up either, in the light of what actually occurred. No doubt the Communists did enter the Popular Front for reasons of their own—I make no pretense to knowing the fluctuations of Stalin's and Dimitrov's dark and mysterious counsels—but there is no question, I think, that their chief motive in supporting the governments of Daladier and Blum, two men to whom till that time they habitually referred, and with bitterest venom, as a Social-Fascist and a Social-Traitor respectively, was to strengthen Russia's international position.

It so happened that in the prevailing international conjuncture Russia's interests coincided precisely with those of France; that is to say, together with Czechoslovakia, France and Russia constituted, for their own and Europe's protection, an insuperable barrier to Hitler's projects of conquest. It will be recalled that the Fuehrer did not unleash his assault on civilization until the Franco-Russian pact of mutual assistance had been nullified, if not by formal

abrogation then at least by events—chiefly the surrender of Czechoslovakia—which rendered the pact inoperative. More than once both
Daladier and Blum sharply reminded the Communists that their
support was desired only in so far as it affected national regeneration through social reform and military preparedness, and that the
government would under no circumstances tolerate the furtherance
of revolutionary aims that they might secretly harbor.

"Might secretly harbor"—for in reality revolution was the farthest thing from the minds of Stalin and his followers. Stalin
favored the maintenance of the status quo in Europe. He was
anxiously guarding against the slightest change in the postwar order
of Europe either by revolution in any given country or by a shift
in the alliances. He did not want to embarrass France in the least,
and so had pledged to Pierre Laval on the occasion of that politician's visit to Moscow in 1935, when the Russian leader passed
the word through Laval to the Communists of France that henceforth they were to drop their opposition to the passage of military
budgets in the French parliament, withhold criticism of the French
colonial policy, in short, be zealous supporters of their governments so long as these pursued a policy of collaboration with the
Soviets in the international field. That meant also not to play
any revolutionary tricks. It goes without saying that the French
Communists strictly obeyed this ukase of their Russian chief. I
have never heard of a single instance where Communists, in no
matter what country they be, did not blindly follow Moscow's
instructions. But if they obeyed Stalin in this respect—that is to
say, if they refrained from any action that might in the least have
disturbed France's relationship with Russia or that might have weakened or changed France's position in Europe, through a revolution,
for instance, or through revolutionary propaganda—if that is true,
the Popular Front was in no way a revolutionary government, or
intending to become revolutionary. For the other parties in the
Popular Front, that is, those headed by Blum, Daladier, Paul-Boncour, and a few others, were in fact definitely antirevolutionary.

Whatever aversion one might feel to the Communist ideology,
steeped as it is in capitalist materialism, and especially since the
day when the Muscovite directorate ordered the party's adherents
in every land to become abettors, not to say allies, of the Nazi
marauders of humanity—an action which must stand utterly condemned, even as an opportunistic makeshift, as absolutely incom-

patible with and detrimental to the workers' interests, as well as at variance with the fundamentally humane and humanistic aspirations of Socialism—in spite of all that one must admit, if one looks at the matter without prejudice, that during the days of the Popular Front the Communist party in France conducted itself with exemplary correctness from a purely national and even from a nationalistic point of view. Chauvinist Bayonet Bills of the type of Weygand and Pétain surely should have had the least cause for complaint, unless it was a case of being jealous of the Communists for outhurrahing them in patriotic demonstration.

We have the word of Mr. Winston Churchill himself for it in his *Step by Step*, published in October, 1936, that in the days of the Popular Front "they [the Communists] not only vote all the credits for defense; they urge that even more intense efforts should be made. They do nothing to hamper the preparations of the French Army, and would tomorrow support and smooth out its mobilization in the face of a Nazi menace. Communist conscripts present themselves with the utmost punctuality at the depots, and in many cases prove model soldiers. Communist agitators use their influence against serious interruption in the production of munitions of all kinds in the factories. I am not at the moment commenting on these facts. I am merely stating them."

Day after day *L'Humanité*, the official organ of the Communist party in France, printed the words of the *Marseillaise* on the front page, so that the people, its readers, might learn the words of a national anthem which had virtually become the monopoly of the *haute bourgeoisie*. The same paper and the provincial journals of the party urged the masses to "go out and acclaim the army" on the Fourteenth of July, the national holiday, because it was now the people's army, "the mighty, unconquerable organization of defense of the people's bread and liberty," whereas in former years the annual military parades on the fashionable Champs Elysées had been staged as a glittering entertainment for the upper classes alone.

Under the Popular Front there was a spirit of fraternity and patriotic fervor on those days and on the days when the Popular Front staged its immense demonstrations at the foot of the statue of the Republic and around the two statues of Joan of Arc, "the symbol of the peasantry of France," who up to that time had basked, strange as it may seem in the light of the facts of her death, in the exclusive veneration of clerics and royalists—such an exalted feeling of national solidarity that the like of it had never been seen in human memory. Never had the reaction been able to produce such a sentiment of national feeling as the Popular Front engendered spontaneously.

And who, we may well ask, had more right and more reason to rejoice and to rededicate themselves to the principles of 1789— Freedom, Equality, and Brotherhood—on a day set aside to commemorate the fall of the Bastille, that somber symbol of feudalist reaction—who: Weygand and Pétain and the other plotters of democracy's strangulation, who were standing there gnashing their teeth in the official reviewing stands, or the others, the millions, the sons and daughters of the sans-culottes, the spiritual descendants of Danton, Desmoulins, and Lafayette? What would Europe have been without the French masses, who had intervened so often at the decisive historical moment to send humanity on new paths of triumph and hope?

In the interval between the electoral victory of the popular parties in February, 1936, and the formation of the new government in the month of July of the same year, the reactionary opposition made it abundantly clear that it would not abide by the decisions expressed at the polls by the overwhelming majority of the French people. Through the newspapers they controlled, big industry and the banks declared openly that they never had recognized, and never would recognize, labor's right to collective bargaining, that the program of social insurance, old-age pensions, paid vacations, and shorter working hours, which the new government was pledged to carry into effect, would cause the ruination of France, and hence that it was men's patriotic duty to resist and hamper the incoming administration with all their might.

This sort of intimidation, not to say provocation, had the effect of throwing the working-class organizations into confusion. The elections had brought an unqualified success to the progressive parties. After more than half a century of hope which had always and again been blasted, but which nevertheless had been kept alive, the forward-looking elements in the nation at last had the satisfaction of seeing a government of socialistic inclinations in formation. Were they now, on the threshold of success, again to be robbed of the fruit of their victory? Would the leaders of the Popular Front stand firm, and not be intimidated into seeking a compromise by those threats of noncollaboration and obstructionism on the part of the reaction? The fear of a retreat on the part of the leaders was spreading when the trade-unions, taking the bull by the horns and without consulting the wishes of their chiefs, ordered the occupation of the plants whose owners were amongst the most vociferous opponents of the Popular Front's social legislation. The workers felt that the government had to be shown that in coming to power it could count on the support of the masses, and that no retreat would be countenanced before the battle had even started.

Sit-down strikes broke out everywhere. Strange to say, the strike movement was encouraged by the reaction, by the simple device of adopting an intransigent attitude towards the coming government's social program, for the purpose of showing that the Popular Front's promises to the workers had been so extravagant as to cause the leaders to lose control over the masses. More than that, the reaction expected that the epidemic of strikes would effect a breach in the solid front presented by the parties that made up the Popular Front. For France is, after all, a country of small proprietors, and the respect for the right of property is ingrained in the vast majority of Frenchmen as one of the inalienable principles of a stable social order. The sit-down strikers were clearly flouting that right. The Rightest press took full advantage of this circumstance to foment confusion and strife between the trade unions and the middle-class members of the Popular Front.

The maneuver of throwing the Popular Front off its hinges almost succeeded before a ministry could be formed. The Right wing of the middle-class parties—Radical Socialists and Left Republicans—was on the point of quitting the coalition and forming an alliance with the landed proprietors on the Right when Daladier and Blum came into power and at once took measures to restore calm, by assuring the workers that the sit-down strikes had become wholly superfluous now that they had a government which would take care of their interests and would fulfill its obligations towards them. The workers were asked to clear the factories and conform to the law of the country, which they did at once and with good grace. It was universally admitted that during the occupations they had conducted themselves with excellent discipline, and had nowhere caused the slightest damage. Alcohol had been kept off the premises, women and girls had been sent home at night, and no violence had been reported from any part of France.

But the reaction was not done for. It renewed the attack by a wholesale export and freezing of capital. Like the moneyed classes in Spain when the Popular Front came into power in that country, rich Frenchmen streamed across the borders into Switzerland and Holland (alone in the community where I lived no less than sixty-two families moved to Switzerland and England in less than a month's time), and many more shipped their funds out of the country before the Popular Front government, which had no such intention, should proceed with a capital levy. The Rightist press, which was by far the most influential and widely read, kept up a ceaseless campaign of sowing panic and fear. That old stand-by, the Bolshevik bogy, was trotted out in all its frightening trappings of the assassin with the knife between his teeth, confiscation of property, the rape of nuns, the nationalization of women, and the massacre of the *bourgeoisie*.

At the same time—the Popular Front had not been quite a month in power—the Fascist International, using the discredited clerical-military clique headed by Sanjurgo, Franco, and Mola in Spain, launched a bloody attack on the newly born democracy in that country. For simple reasons of national interest and self-preservation, the clear duty of any French government would have been to supply the authorities in a friendly neighboring state with the means to defend themselves against a treasonable insurrection of that kind. And not only the means of self-defense: the threat of a victory for Franco, backed as he was by the two Fascist dictators in Rome and Berlin, warranted nothing less than the immediate dispatch of a French corps to the aid of the democratic government of Madrid.

Since those days it has become a reality, but even back in July, 1936, any schoolboy could see that if General Franco should be victorious he would remain the flunky of Hitler and Mussolini for the rest of his criminal career. This meant that France, in the event of a war with Germany and Italy, would have a third front, that of the Pyrenees, to watch and guard. And not only that, but the territory of Spain might conceivably become, in the event of a defeat of France, the overland route of attack against Gibraltar and British naval supremacy in the Mediterranean.

These things may have come to pass when these words are

printed. But they will not end General Franco's usefulness in the Fascist world cause. It is through that individual, who is going to lay claim to the former Spanish dominions in the New World, that Hitler and Mussolini will try to obtain a foothold in the Western hemisphere when the time comes for that "simple stride across the Atlantic" of which the Fuehrer has spoken. When that day comes it will also be seen that the volunteers of the International Brigade, who were held up to contempt and calumny by the black Franco front in the United States as Communist rabble and Jews, in reality fought America's battle.

The French high command, which stood under the direction of Maxime Weygand in 1936, with Philippe Pétain serving under him as vice-president of the Council of National Defense, recognized the danger of the Franco insurrection as clearly—and no doubt much more clearly, since they had access to secret information supplied by the intelligence service—as did the friends of France who urged intervention. One French army corps, it was agreed in French military circles, would have taken care of the entire Italian expeditionary force in Spain, while Hitler would have thought twice before launching into a war which would have seen Czechoslovakia and the Soviet Union on France's side. It will be recalled that the Fuehrer immediately withdrew the troops he had landed in Spanish Morocco when he saw the entire French nation aroused over this direct threat. Why did not Weygand, who posed as a super-patriot after the defeat of his country, counsel and insist with Daladier and Blum on a prompt intervention in Spain at a time when France might still have been saved, in that the Fascist march to world conquest could have been arrested at the start? Weygand and Pétain called the military situation "irreparable" when they took over from Gamelin and Reynaud in June, 1940. But the military situation was far from irreparable in July, 1936, when General Franco, as the instrument of Duce and Fuehrer, began to pave the way for the Fascistization of Europe. Where were Weygand and Pétain at that time, and Laval and Flandin, Leméry, Marquet, and Reynaud?

The answer is: the national leaders of 1940 were in the Franco front in 1936. They were in that front, which was the spearhead of a Fascist world movement directed principally against the French Republic and the British Empire. Considerations of class interest overshadowed the vital national interests of their own country with these men. Franco was their friend because Franco was bold enough to have come out in the open and to have unleashed a campaign of violence against the democratic government of his country. They admired him for it and did all in their power to facilitate his murdering march to Madrid and Barcelona.

By chance I attended a garden party and bazaar in August, 1936, in the interest of Spanish rebel relief on the estate of the Duchesse d'Uzès at Saint-Germain-en-Laye. There I saw *monsieur le général* Weygand, in the midst of a crowd of cooing princesses and baronesses, auction off ropes to hang, as was solemnly announced, not Hitler or Mussolini or Franco, the avowed enemies of France, but Léon Blum, Vincent Auriol, Léon Jouhaux, Largo Caballero, La Pasionaria, Negrín, Prieto, José Bergamin, Victor Margueritte, Romain Rolland, and other French and Spanish labor leaders and liberal intellectuals.

Although the leaders of the one-time Popular Front, who were brought to trial by Pétain's authoritarian regime on charges of having contributed, by their neglect of the national defense, to the military debacle of 1940, cannot be said to have been wholly without blame in the matter, the charges nevertheless remain grossly unjust. In fact, those charges constitute one of the most cynical and dastardly perversions of the truth recorded in the history of governmental provocation and treason.

For if Daladier and Blum, for their pusillanimous attitude on General Franco's revolt, merit censure because they allowed that agent of the Fascist axis an easy victory and in that way permitted an all-important breach in France's national security, who was it that prevented Daladier and Blum from doing otherwise?

France was not defeated on the plains of Flanders: the Battle of France was merely the inevitable culmination of a long process of undermining the morale of the French people and of breaking the spirit of resistance. What happened in July, 1940, was the inescapable result of a long-handed preparation to bring to a fall the last remaining Continental democracy. That process started with the secret understanding arrived at in February, 1935, in Rome between the two ex-Communists Pierre Laval and Benito Mussolini to destroy the League and the League's principle of collective security by rendering ineffective the policy of sanctions in the forthcoming Ethiopian conquest. That process was greatly accelerated by the actions of the Franco front, of which the very men who came to rule France as proconsuls of Hitler and Mussolini were the most vociferous animators in France. Who yelled "Treason!" and "Bolshevism!" when Blum and his associates in the Popular Front government debated the advisability of succoring the democratic government in Madrid with arms and equipment and making an attempt at least to prevent the Fascist dictators from gaining a first important advantage in their struggle against the allied democracies? It would have seemed logical to have seen charges of high treason lodged against Pétain and Weygand themselves, military men in charge of the military organization of the country, who must have seen through the plans of the enemy in Spain, who were, moreover, supposed to stand aloof from party considerations and look upon the interests of France from a national point of view only, but who nevertheless sabotaged the security of the Republic by aiding and abetting the enemy.

The enemy? Did men like Pétain and Weygand really look on Hitler and Mussolini as the supreme enemy? If they did, why was there never a word from them to encourage the French people in the struggle against Fascist expansionism? Why did not they, who were the masters of the army and therefore the supreme guardians of France's national territory, who were never refused a vote of supply for military equipment by any government, whether of the Popular Front or not—why did not they once raise their voices in warning or protest when the two dictators, through the intermediary of Francisco Franco and Leopold of Saxe-Coburg-Gotha, tightened the ring of death that encircled France, or when Alexander of Yugoslavia, France's most dependable ally, was assassinated by the Duce's henchmen; when the Rhineland was remilitarized by Hitler and therewith the Maginot Line's protective value nullified, or when Czechoslovakia's mighty army was sacrificed? Why? The answer to this question contains the key to the puzzle—if puzzle it is—of France's amazingly swift collapse in 1940.

On Hitler and Mussolini the Messrs. Weygand and Pétain at all times expressed themselves in terms of the highest admiration. What they liked especially about the methods of the Fascist dictators in Rome and Berlin was the way in which they had put labor in its proper place, that is to say, the way in which the growth of democratic institutions had been checked in Germany and Italy. Although M. Weygand's position as a military man required of him strict abstention from political activity, he was frequently seen occupying the seat of honor at Fascist meetings where Colonel de La Rocque, chief of the Croix de Feu, held forth, urging his bravi to wreck the labor temples and beat up the leaders of the working class.

With Charles Maurras, the royalist leader—who is said to have been Mussolini's mentor in Fascist doctrine, who in his newspaper *Action Française* promised time and again that some day he would execute the chiefs of the liberal and labor parties by drowning them like dogs in the Seine, and who actually had his gilded gangster youths, the *camelots du roi*, attack and almost kill Léon Blum on the Boulevard St. Germain in June, 1936—with that individual Pétain and Weygand were elected members of the Académie Française. Not because of the intrinsic literary or artistic merit of their published works, to be sure, but because the Academy had grown into a stronghold of antidemocratic reaction, and its members wanted to defy the government of the Popular Front by elevating that government's most outstanding foes to a position of eminence in French national life.

The issues involved in the Spanish revolt by far overshadowed all the other events on the political scene in France during the lifetime of the Popular Front administrations. On the Spanish question the Popular leadership allowed itself to be intimidated by the incessant clamor of the Franco front into withholding from a friendly sister republic the assistance that could have saved her. Blum and his associates bowed to the demands of the reaction, first by refraining from open military intervention, and later by enforcing a cessation of the clandestine aid which was rendered democratic Spain by private initiative. Blum closed the frontier and even denied volunteers "the right to die for democracy under the walls of Madrid."

Carlyle held that revolt may, under certain circumstances, become the citizen's most sacred duty. This assertion was invoked by the Franco front in favor of the Spanish rebels on the ground that they and their allies, Hitler and Mussolini, were combating the Bolshevization of the Iberian peninsula. Hitler's subsequent pact of collaboration with Moscow proves the falseness of this claim. However, it served its purpose well in drumming up support for General Franco in reactionary, conservative, and clerical circles all over Europe and America.

That Blum and his associates in the Popular Front government desisted from carrying out what was their manifest duty—namely, nipping the Franco-Hitler plot in the bud—showed the world that even if the parties united in the Popular Front had acquired political power by the ballot, effective control of the machinery of state remained a fiction. For one thing, they lacked freedom of action in the foreign field. On the Spanish question they were thrown off their course by a reactionary minority which, although defeated politically, nevertheless managed to keep the financial and economic reins in its hands. This minority was linked by ties of caste and class to the army command and virtually the entire officers' corps. It was determined, if possible without the aid of Hitler, to bring an end to the regime which marched under the slogans of Liberty, Equality, and Fraternity.

Behind the military hierarchy and the *haute bourgeoisie* stood another implacable enemy of the Third Republic, that most inveterate foe of democracy—the Roman Catholic Church. Completely ultramontanized in France, that is, made subject in every detail of action and of opinion to the dictates of the Italian Fascist Popes, that Church was thirsting for revenge over the alleged loss of prestige it had suffered in the matter of the separation of Church and State back in 1903. Unable to dominate after that event, the Church had declared itself deprived of its freedom and despoiled of its possessions, and had assumed a pose of injured martyrdom. But that martyrdom is in no way to be confused with the pious resignation that Rome so warmly recommends in its encyclicals to the poor and the underprivileged. On the contrary, the French section of the Roman international turned itself into an *ecclesia militans* to combat, mostly by intrigue, undercover work, and subversion, every democratic measure the Republic ventured to take, beginning with universal suffrage, of which the Roman pontiff, speaking to the members of a French pilgrimage, said that it was "one of the most horrible sores on the body of human society and ought justly to be called the universal lie."

Not only did the Catholic newspapers and the diocesan press in France consistently speak of democracy and of democratic institutions with supreme contempt, but in the history of the Third Republic there are a number of incidents which were of dangerous portent to those institutions. They are linked with the names of Galliffet, MacMahon, Boulanger, and Dreyfus, and are associated with violent antidemocratic movements. All of them, like the insurrectionary spirit that Rome inculcated in the unhappy French clergy and in its adherents over the separation law, were inspired by the military-clerical reaction.

René Viviani once said the same thing that Unamuno said with respect to Spain, namely, that the greatest danger to democracy in France did not come from the side of Germany, but that it lay in the presence of an officers' class steeped in clericalism and royalism. Clemenceau opposed with all the energy at his command the elevation of the victorious generals of the World War to the dignity of marshals of France. "It is dangerous," he said, "to add one grain to the prestige of these men who are *jusqu'au cou dans les Jésuites.*" Clemenceau was overruled in the case of Foch, Pétain, and the others, but he held out against the granting of a marshal's baton to the man whom he considered "the worst of the clique," Maxime Weygand. Events proved him correct in that evaluation. For it is to the evil represented by Weygand that the Third Republic finally succumbed and from which democracy in Europe received its death blow.

Having consistently denied the fundamental democratic principle of popular sovereignty, the Church could not but condemn in turn every modern liberty such as freedom and equality of religious denominations, freedom of conscience and of the press, civil marriage, the separation of Church and State and, above all, the nonsectarian public schools. There are encyclicals and other authoritative papal pronouncements specifically naming these "pestilential democratic abominations."

In France the Church, exercising an enormous pressure behind the scenes through its surreptitious alliance with the military hierarchy, the landowners, and the big industrialists, and by the sway it still held over the souls of women and the peasantry in backward sections, fought the principle of freedom of religion and of conscience as "a Protestant, Kantian, revolutionary, Communistic, Masonic abomination"; the public school, the most carefully nurtured institution of the Third Republic, it characterized as "social atheism" which with regard to the faith was to be considered "pure heresy," with regard to reason "mortal and insane error," and with regard to history "a monstrosity." The regular reports of the League for Human Rights, which were issued up to the time of the great debacle of 1940, showed that the rural *curés*, almost without exception, threatened parents with excommunication, with loss of income or position and respectability, and with hell-fire in the hereafter, of course, if they dared send their children to the public schools or if they took in public-school teachers as boarders.

One learned from these sermons and from a devoted perusal of the diocesan newspapers such as *La Semaine religieuse*, as well as from *La Croix*, *Le Messager du coeur de Jésus*, and *La Foi catholique*, that the Roman Church learns nothing, forgets nothing, and remains loyal to its ancient device of *semper eadem*. To this day, as in the "glorious" days of the Inquisition, it comes out with a demand for the death sentence of its opponents as soon as it regains the position of a state religion, as is the case in Italy and Spain. No sooner had Mussolini restored the crucifix in schoolrooms and courtrooms, a procedure Pétain or that man's successor in France is bound to follow, than the Italian clergy demanded the institution of a special ecclesiastical tribunal to judge . . . heretics. These, it was recommended by priests of Christ, were then to be handed over to the civil authority, which is to punish them by striking hard, not shrinking even to apply the death sentence: *"al potere civile che devrà copirlo, anche spingendosi all 'estrema pena."*

Anyone who is not altogether a stranger in the Jerusalem of papal affairs knows that, by virtue of a number of pronouncements by the various popes since the famous encyclical *Quanta cura* and the so-called *Syllabus errorum* of 1864, the Vatican is the uncompromising foe of liberalism, Socialism, democracy, Americanism—in short, of modernism in general. It was therefore to be expected that, as soon as the reaction against all these isms should begin to concretize, the Pope was most likely to sympathize with that reaction. In our day that reaction was crystallized in Fascism, which is the synthesis of all the forces of reaction, and the Vatican has indeed chosen to take its position on that side of the barricade to triumph, as it thinks, with the pagan dictators on the ruins of Christian civilization. It sees decay and error and pestilence in everything that has been gained since the Protestant Reformation and the French Revolution, including the Declaration of the Rights of Man, the Bill of Rights, equal suffrage, the nonsectarian school—in fact, all democratic institutions.

The Vatican's resumed intervention in world politics after long years of relative inactivity dates from the rise of Fascism. The present Pope and his immediate successor, Pius XI, have done their utmost to intensify the reaction against the democratic institutions of the Western world. Not only in France and in Spain, in Italy and in Germany, where the Vatican allied itself with the most ruthless extirpators of democracy—in the last-named country it dissolved its political institutions, sacrificing many of the noblest Catholics in order to placate Hitler and win his favor, and had the Bishops' Conference at Fulda in 1940 uphold the Nazi regime immediately after the crushing of the Scandinavian, Belgian, and French democracies—but also in Mexico and in the United States, where it recruits armies of squadristi and terrorists in the Christian Fronts, the state legislatures, and the police forces, the Church has its henchmen and propagandists in the pulpits muddying the waters by fastening the label of Communist or anarchist or atheist on every person in public life who does not believe that the last word on social reform has been said with the encylical *Quadragesimo anno.*

In France the priesthood contributed to the general debacle. They preached sedition. They incited the people to distrust and despise the principles on which the Republic was built. For years they implanted in the minds of the people of France the idea that some day they would expiate in a horrible bloodletting the sins of "the godless, atheistic 'lay' Republic." "O God," the diocesan journal *Croix du Nord* instructed the faithful to pray when the German armies were battering away at the Belgian defenses, "O God, Thou strikest us again for the sins of our dearly loved Fatherland, sins of our legislators who in criminal folly have denied Thy name, persecuted Thy church, despoiled Thy servants, educated children in atheism; sins of the voters who have elected representatives without religion and who have therewith become their accomplices. Make us understand, O God, the terrible consequences of having used the vote. . . ."

That prayer was passed by both the French and the German military censorship!

It was a divine chastisement for France that the Germans broke loose again in September, 1939, a collective punishment justly deserved, and predicted by the clergy over a number of years, especially the years following the separation of Church and State, which was, as the Cardinal Archbishop of Bordeaux said, "an insult to God, deserving of the severest penalties." To the Roman Church, the self-styled heir of the Galilean pacifist and the martyrs who refused to enter Caesar's service to kill, war has the triple character of just punishment, expiation, and providential preparation. "As soon as a people ceases to be virile and to love sacrifice [in other words, when it begins to adapt itself to the ways of democracy], or yet when it grows tyrannical, oppresses conscience and threatens the freedom of God's truth on earth [read: when it rejects the Roman pontiff's claims to universal sovereignty by divine right, when it laughs at his thunderbolts against the exigencies of science and criticism, and refuses to listen to the lullabies which are sung in the Vatican to rock human misery to sleep], God calls another nation to strike the corrupt, dangerous, and wayward people with a redoubtable execution of divine justice."

That is the way in which one of the most popular Catholic writers in France, Léon Gautier, foreshadowed the *Blitzkrieg*, placing Adolf Hitler in the role of the great avenger in the service of divine justice. There was nothing to do for the French people but patiently await the ordeal. War was coming and that war must be lost, in the previsions of the clergy, because the Third Republic, that execrated instrument of democracy, must at last be rendered impotent, and eliminated if possible. Hence the felicitations of Pius XII to Philippe Pétain, whom he called "the most representative of the noblest traditions of his race," a few days after the Republic lay prostrate and the Marshal, between half-hourly injections of parathyroid hormone, decreed the death of Liberty, Equality, and Fraternity at the behest of Hitler, Mussolini, and Franco.

The military-clerical reaction, backed by big business, the banks, and the *grande presse*, seized upon the Spanish revolt as the most effective instrument to hamper and obstruct and finally bring to a fall the Popular Front government in their own country. It gave the government to understand that opposition to aid for Spain would not remain confined to verbal protests. Militant Fascist organizations led by army officers, one of them the Croix de Feu under the direction of Colonel de La Rocque, a personal friend of Weygand and his fellow member on the board of directors of the Paris gas and electricity trust, began to carry out "mobilization maneuvers" which sometimes assumed quite large and threatening proportions. Day after day, in the course of 1937, the Fascist press announced the "technical occupation" of such and such a community or of this or that strategic point. The occupations took place in the middle of the night, and one that I witnessed at Sartrouville on the night of October 27 involved long strings of motorcycles, trucks, ambulances, and a camouflaged machine-gun section. The maneuver, which I had first looked upon as a mere stunt and nothing to be alarmed about, surprised me with its military precision and efficiency. Of course, just as soon as the tocsin began to ring in that little Socialist town, La Rocque's bravi vanished. But the demonstration had been an indication of what was in the wind. Such paramilitary movements reminded one too vividly of the nocturnal street battles in Wedding and Berlin-Osten in 1931 and 1932 between trade unionists and individuals dressed in brown shirts.

At the same time the army command grew more and more insolent. It issued an order forbidding soldiers to read newspapers which supported the Popular Front. On two or three occasions leading generals refused to attend conferences on aviation matters with Pierre Cot, the Air Minister, whom the reaction held in particular detestation, probably because he insisted upon creating for France an air force that would be a match for Goering's fleet. At St. Cyr, the West Point of France, the commandant disregarded the government's request to fly the flag at half-mast on the morning when the death of the Minister of the Interior became known. The cadets, who were assembled on the parade ground prior to attending Mass, cheered the commandant when he ordered the flag up "higher than ever," for now France counted "at least one scoundrel less." The dead official, Roger Salengro, had been one of the strongest protagonists of intervention in Spain.

The entire air-force personnel was known to be Fascistic in sentiment, and hints were frequently given in the reactionary press that the bombers would know their duty in the event Blum ordered them to fly to the support of the loyalists. Rumors of insubordination in the army were in fact flying thick and fast. Soldiers of socialistic tendencies told you amazing incidents of their officers threatening them with death if they should be loyal to the government at a certain critical moment which was frankly foreseen. And not only soldiers: I came across an officer, the lieutenant colonel commanding the garrison of Montpellier, who told me without hesitation that his propaganda for Fascism had cost him his command in the Southern city. "But I was transferred to Metz," he added laughingly. "In Metz I am in charge of the arsenal. I think the arsenal and what it contains will, when the hour strikes, be worth a thousand times more to La Rocque and Weygand than the rotten Socialist garrison in Montpellier. In Metz too," he went on, "we have every soldier listed according to his political views. We figure that we will have to eliminate about a thousand of them when the signal comes."

These minor incidents are cited merely to show the existence in the reactionary camp of a state of mind foreboding evil for the Popular Front and for the continuance of social peace in France. It was but natural that in these circumstances the most advanced sections of the working class should have begun preparations for the formation of an anti-Fascist or workers' militia. But therewith appeared also the specter of civil war. The prospect of an armed struggle Blum dared not face, because he knew that under the circumstances, i.e., with the army command arrayed on the opposite side, it would be a futile struggle for the workers as well as a virtual invitation to Hitler to invade France. "I know the strength of the workers' movement in France," he said to me once, "but I also know its weakness. If we throw ourselves into battle now, we would lose our allies amongst the liberals at once. I even doubt if the Communists would be with us, for a revolutionary struggle in France is certainly something Moscow would oppose with all its might. And then," he added, "can we be sure that our reactionary opponents will not call on Hitler, the man they admire so much, to establish order? Did Thiers not call on Bismarck in 1871 to crush the Commune?"

It was on the rock of the class consciousness of the Radical-Socialists that the Popular Front finally was wrecked. The liberals deserted the proletarian parties. They feared that their continued association with Blum would lead the country too far in the direction of Socialism. That was a road they did not wish to travel. Blum sought to preserve the coalition by proclaiming a "pause" in the program of social reform. But that concession did not suffice. Daladier broke the pact, but managed to stay in the premiership by securing support in the Center and on the Right for a program which "more equitably distributed" the burden of financing the huge armament campaign; that is to say, the load was shifted back to the shoulders of the workers and the petty *bourgeoisie*. The new Daladier administration whittled down the achievements of the Popular Front to such an extent that the advantages gained by the submerged classes were soon completely wiped out. In order to do this he had to rule by decree, by order in council. The mandate for this authoritarian procedure was furnished him by the Center and Right. Daladier was no longer obliged to consult parliament.

He thus saved himself and his fellow liberals the embarrassment of having to debate and vote on measures which undid the work they had but a few months earlier accomplished together with the Socialists. They went back on democracy when they discovered that democracy cannot remain static, that it cannot, if it is to live, leave one class forever in a position of exclusive privilege, but that it must raise the submerged elements to equality in opportunity or die.

Then came the period which may come to be known to future generations as the Era of the Great Confusion. One will search in vain the records for another hour in the history of France when anxiety over the future of the nation was so general and disquietude so deep. In the place of that exceptionally high degree of patriotic sentiment and that intensity of national feeling which had been manifest during the first year of the Popular Front, when hope and idealism and courage had run on a truly heroic scale, there had come an immense lassitude, a weariness of spirit such as had not been seen even in the darkest days of the first world war.

The masses were in a state of angry and sullen despondency, almost unparalleled in history. Men shrugged their shoulders. They expressed themselves in terms of uncertainty and fear. Every one you met, total strangers sometimes, felt that the country was drifting along aimlessly and abandoned and that doom might lie around the next bend in the road. The spirit which would have made France invincible, and which had once been aroused by her New Deal, had departed. Had it departed? No, it had been undermined, vitiated, and chased into limbo by the very men who were later to charge others with responsibility for the national disaster. In 1939 the sense of frustration and disillusion among the people had produced an attitude of total indifference and of cynical *je-m'en-foutisme*. With that state of mind prevailing, all the optimistic forecasts of a French victory in the event of a war with the Reich, with which our press was inundated at the time, sounded, to those who had really felt the pulse of the French nation, like so much idle bragging and futile endeavor to bolster up a morale that was virtually nonexistent. Under the circumstances the best military equipment could not have saved France. In the presence of a political situation rapidly evolving in the direction of authoritarianism, paralysis had gripped the nation and its military genius had turned sterile. The fighting spirit was lacking because the people did not trust a government or a high command whose ideology did not differ one whit from that of the Fascist enemy.

In order that France might defend herself adequately, the people were told, their democratic and civil rights had to be drastically curtailed. Wages had to come down. The army needed tanks and airplanes and motorized material, hence the masses must needs follow the example of the Germans, and do without butter. Sacrifices, it was repeated over and over again, must be made by all alike, by Monsieur Richepain as well as by the family of Jean Vanupieds, the tenants on his estate. And if the poor by chance did not consent to this program and showed inclinations to oppose the government's Fascist methods—well, there were Daladier's Pretorians, the black-helmeted *gardes civiles,* who came to be quartered in every community where the population included a heavy percentage of workers. These *gardes civiles* were not quite a new corps, but their effectiveness was enormously strengthened as the crisis deepened. They were highly trained troops, well-paid men of perfect physique, who were strictly kept from fraternizing and even mixing with the people. The *gardes civiles* were not a combatant unit of the army— the army was not fed and housed a tenth part as well as they; they were placed under the administration of the Ministry of the Interior, a super police force, like the Ovra in Italy or the Gestapo in the Reich. The French masses and the regular troops knew full well what task the government had in mind for the *gardes civiles.* They were the storm troopers of a nascent authoritarian regime. Their presence in the working-class communes and in the large cities was to serve as a perpetual reminder that there was to be no return to Popular Front governments under any circumstances. The *gardes civiles* were to see to it that the sullen discontent of the people did not flare up into popular manifestations and insistence on a return to democratic procedure. In the event of war there was to be a battalion of *gardes civiles,* better armed, behind every regiment in the line. And indeed, right up the line they went, those elite guards of Fascism, when the war finally did break out—they and the coal-black legions from Senegal—to keep the French troops in position. Two important British periodicals, *The New Statesman* and *The Manchester Guardian,* have reported that more French soldiers were executed by the *gardes civiles* during the first eight months of the war than were killed by the enemy. I do not know how true this is, but if it is true, the *gardes civiles* in 1940 did precisely what their predecessors had done in the last war, when, as Jean Giono, who was an eyewitness and a participant in that war, reports in *Les Carnets de Moleskine*, they forced endless lines of soldiers to pass between two rows of sandbags and there blew their brains out "one by one, hour after hour, day after day." It was for making this revelation, incidentally that Giono was immediately arrested when war broke out in 1939—he and the men of the *Patrie humaine* movement.

And why should the French troops have shown a hesitation to fight with all their might? Because they were desperate. Because they did not care who sent the fatal bullet through their hearts, the German Fascists or the henchmen of the clique behind their backs which was intent on installing Fascism in France. They had no hope; they had lost all qualities to contain hope. They had been told that German Fascism was the enemy, but their own leaders had suspended democratic institutions; they had sacrificed Czechoslovakia and the Soviet alliance to the enemy and then asked them to die for Poland, which had just shared in the rape of Czechoslovakia. Mussolini was a potential foe, his blackshirts were clamoring for Corsica and Nice and the Savoy *départements*, but that same Mussolini had been helped to grab Ethiopia and to defeat the loyalists of Spain, France's best friends.

So long as Hitler delayed his attack on Poland, the Daladiers, Bonnets, and Lavals, as representatives of the French ruling class, persisted in their policy of appeasement, in the hope that a bargain might yet be struck with Adolf Hitler which would preclude a recourse to arms. All during the summer of 1939 emissaries from the French Foreign Office, Reynaud and Baudouin amongst them, were traveling to Berlin to consult with Hitler, Goering, Hess, and Ribbentrop, while François Poncet and Pierre Laval were in Rome in constant deliberation with Ciano and the Duce. The conditions of the Axis were simply a breach with England and an abandonment of the guarantee of aid to Poland. The last condition offered no insuperable obstacle; the French statesmen were not only prepared to sacrifice Poland as lightly as they had sacrificed Czechoslovakia, but they set to work persuading the British appeasement government of Chamberlain and Halifax to act conjointly with them in this matter. We know from Nevile Henderson's memoirs that, had Hitler restrained himself another week, the deal over Poland might have been consummated without bringing the Reich and the Western Allies face to face in an armed struggle.

Breaking off the British alliance, however, was a much more difficult undertaking. It would require time and a pretext, and the preparation of public opinion in France. Moreover, in return for leaving England in the lurch and therewith giving democracy a mortal blow, the French statesmen were asking a *quid pro quo* from Herr Hitler. In return for so enormous a service, which amounted virtually to the isolation of the British Empire and possibly its destruction, the French were asking the Fuehrer to leave France the status of an independent partner in the Fascist-controlled Europe of the future.

Herr Hitler procrastinated in giving satisfaction to these French overtures and demands because he clearly saw the danger that an eventual integration of France as an independent member in the Fascist constellation would present to the Reich. For the French, as was their secret plan once they would be taken into the combination, would almost surely seek to subvert Mussolini's loyalty to his Axis partner. Knowing how the Duce's personal pride and the pride of the Italian high command smarted under the Nazi lash, and how the Italian chief of state looked for a chance to liberate himself from Hitler's bondage, the French were willing to come into the Fascist alliance for the purpose of setting up a Franco-Italian bloc against Berlin. The British appeasers were, of course, fully conversant with this scheme, and on their side were quite ready to sacrifice Poland but only as a means to gain time. It would, they figured, take the Germans some time to absorb and consolidate their prospective gains in eastern Europe. In the meantime French diplomatic pressure on Mussolini might have its effect, and a totally different alignment might be set up in Europe.

Hitler struck at Poland before the Franco-Italian diplomatic fruit had time to ripen. Rather than have France as a partner, he launched his campaign in eastern Europe, which rendered the Franco-British pact with Poland operative, however reluctant Paris and London were to go to war over a question that could have been easily solved and that had already been virtually eliminated by diplomatic negotiation. To show Hitler that his attack on Poland did not greatly concern them and that it need not necessarily lead to a war *à outrance*, the Franco-British allies, both under the leadership of ap-

peasers, did not lift a finger, created not the least diversion in the
West to delay or frustrate Hitler's brutal intervention in the East.

Once he had overrun Poland, the Fuehrer waited eight months
for the French to break with Britain. That breach did not materialize because the French *bourgeoisie* had no stomach to tackle the
working classes and institute the outright Fascistic regime which
would have been the necessary preliminary to a change in the
international alignment away from England and towards Germany.
He did his utmost to facilitate the maneuver by repeating in every
speech that he had no quarrel with the French people—but saw
French diplomacy redouble its efforts in Rome and at the same time
keep the entente with Britain alive.

The Fuehrer began by overrunning Denmark and Norway and
capturing the Scandinavian coast in order to protect his rear and
his right flank in a forthcoming attack against the Low Countries
and France.

This all-revealing move on the Fuehrer's part produced nothing
less than a social revolution in England.

Winston Churchill stepped to the fore, and the policy of appeasement was at last definitely abandoned. The new Prime Minister
showed that he understood both the nature of the war Germany
was waging and the motives, the mental reservations, the lack of
drive and the complacency which had animated and characterized
his Tory predecessors in office in their half-hearted and downright
obstructionist conduct of the war. He called to his side the leaders
of what was potentially the most powerful anti-Fascist force left in
Europe: British labor. Whereas the French reaction had proven itself
the deadly enemy of democracy by scuttling it, and had thereby
deprived the country of France—even as Dollfuss six years earlier,
when he crushed the labor organizations in Austria, had stripped the
social-democracy of Vienna—of the most valuable if not the only
instrument with which to defend itself against foreign Fascist aggres-
sion, Winston Churchill, knowing that democracy can be defended
only through a democratic program executed by the people's leaders, deliberately moved in the direction opposite to the course
theretofore followed by both the French and the British ruling
classes. He adopted the program and policy once pursued by Léon
Blum in France: he called into existence a Government of the Popular Front. Instead of an interruption of trade union activity or a
curtailment of social reforms, these were extended and intensified as

soon as Churchill took over from Neville Chamberlain. The censorship was lifted insofar as discussion of non-military subjects was concerned. A great liberty of speaking and writing was allowed. Throughout the land positions of control and authority were entrusted to socialists, liberals and progressives. The government of national concentration which Churchill set up differed in this respect from the usual sacred union which the bourgeoisie adopts for the sake of window-dressing in critical situations, in that Labor was placed in effective control of the war effort and of the social transformation that went with it. Ernest Bevin, president of the Transport Workers' Union, who had led the General Strike back in 1926 and who had resorted to direct action in setting up shop-committees under the slogan "Hands off Russia!" in order to frustrate the plans of the Tories to wage an interventionist war against the Soviet Union, became Minister of Labor. Hugh Dalton, the great realist of Labor's foreign policy and the author of *Practical Socialism for Britain,* who had been held up to contempt by the Conservative press as "just a Bolshevik," took charge of the surpassingly important Ministry of Economic Warfare. With them came Arthur Greenwood, Clement Atlee, Parliamentary leader of the Labor Party, and Herbert Morrison, *bête noire* of the plutocratic tax-payers, extreme Left-winger, chairman of the London County Council, builder of schools and hospitals and creator of the famous Green Belt in the slum-infested imperial city.

Churchill raised the war from a quarrel between the rival ruling classes of Britain and Germany—in which light many socialists had seen the struggle up to that time—to a national issue for the entire British nation and to an international social issue for all men of good faith. The struggle became an anti-Fascist war, a battle of life and death against the men and the ideology whose vital concern it is to uproot, destroy and obliterate democratic institutions wherever they may still be found in the world. It became above all a war of liberation, for the war program of the Labor Party not only aimed at averting the danger of a Nazi conquest of Britain, but envisaged the reconquest of their independence and freedom for the peoples of Czechoslovakia, Poland, the Scandinavian countries, the Netherlands, Belgium and France, as well as "lifting the curse of Hitler from the brows" of German men and women. By Churchill's acceptance of labor's program the opportunity presented itself at last for the anti-Fascist forces in the world to proceed from mere words of protest and indignation against Fascism to deeds that may yet lead to an overthrow of Hitlerism and "to transforming British imperialism into the socialist ideal of a fellowship of free peoples."

The British people responded at once to Churchill's radical changes in the personnel of government and in the restatement of the Empire's war aims. They were galvanized into action. Labor went to work with a new sense of responsibility. They had something to defend and fight for. The English people knew that those henceforth in charge of the war's conduct were men whose hearts and minds were set on victory because they aimed at the overthrow of Nazism. They knew that it was no longer a question of re-arranging the world in such a way as to give Nazi Germany a sort of condominium with Britain in the economic sphere, but that it was Churchill's clear purpose to defeat Hitler and remove him forever, that there was to be no compromise, no appeasement, no patched-up peace, but that the issue was now victory or enslavement. On that issue the English people rallied around Churchill. They became imbued with a spirit which Chamberlain could never have aroused, nor other reactionaries at any time anywhere. The political and religious enthusiasm which inspired the pikemen of Cromwell, the ragged colonists of America and the hungry hordes of the French Revolution, electrified the English people to stand up in that hour and fight, no matter what the odds.

If Churchill's radical transformation of the social order in Great Britain did not come too late, it is to that New Deal, that hope of preserving democracy and enlarging it under Labor's aegis, that the final victory over Fascism in the world shall have to be attributed.

The elimination of the appeasers in Britain, and the social transformation which had brought the liberal and socialistic forces to the fore, produced a most painful impression in France. What had happened in England? In spite of the military disasters in Scandinavia, responsibility for the conduct of foreign affairs, including the war with Germany, had been transferred from the unreliable Tory class to the people, and the British masses were imbued with a new determination to resist the Fascist onslaught from whatever direction it might come, and in the end to conquer. It was clear enough that under the circumstances, and once the war was brought to a victorious conclusion, British labor would have a say, the preponderant influence, in the rebuilding of Europe, in a juster redistribution of the world's markets and in a new, more brotherly approach to the colonial peoples.

These prospects filled the French reaction with consternation. Churchill clearly had indicated the road to victory. Was France to follow suit? Was she too to revive her New Deal? Events in England might prove contagious. The spirit bloweth where it listeth, and ideas cross the seas quicker than pursuit planes. If the army of the French people could be given back its ideals of democracy and liberty, even then, in that moment of supreme distress, it could be counted on to fight in some preternatural outburst of national sentiment, on and on, behind the Meuse, in the streets of Paris, behind the Loire and in the stone labyrinths of Auvergne, to the last ditch, to the death.... Falling back under the blows which Hitler had begun to administer in the Netherlands and in Belgium, the men in the line might yet recover that demonic spirit of their predecessors who hurled back "the Brunswick Saint Bartholomew" and later the legions of von Kluck. But that could happen only if the war were proclaimed of revolutionary character, if Hitler's allies and spiritual kinsmen in the government and in the high command were without a moment's delay removed from positions of control. Was France to sit still and become as Poland, and her Rights of Man a Nazi concentration camp? Churchill's ambassador was on the way to Moscow. The British Prime Minister had chosen a Left-wing Socialist for that mission. Was France to follow suit there too? If she did, Russia might yet heed the call, for the voice of the French masses was sure to carry more weight in Moscow than what might be interpreted in that city as the desperate maneuvers of a converted Tory statesman. But that would also have required, as the least token of good faith, setting free the working-class organizations from the chains of censorship and constraint, a complete change of direction from pre-Fascism towards democracy.

Rather than entrust the destinies of France and of Europe to the democratic forces, the French reaction deliberately chose to accept defeat at the hands of German Fascism. Long ago a man said: "Where your treasure is, there your heart will be also." Germany's triumph alone, it was thought, would assure, for a time at least, the survival in Europe of a social order of which Adolf Hitler is the representative in Germany, Mussolini in Italy, Franco in Spain, and Pierre Laval and Philippe Pétain in France.

No attempt was made to bolster up the resistance of the French army. Generals abandoned important defense works and lines without so much as an attempt to halt the invaders. Trains loaded with munitions were purposely sent in the wrong direction. Scores of military chiefs left their troops to shift for themselves as best they could, without plans of either defense or attack. There were no battles. The story of the Battle of France is a myth, which is proved to be such by the Nazi casualty list. Of the three or four thousand planes no more than a thousand were thrown into battle. The Germans drove through the French lines on motorcycles, in many places in single file. In ten days' time the finest army in Europe was turned into a chaotic, panic-stricken multitude, streaming back before it had even made contact with the German main forces, which were never engaged except to smash at the British Expeditionary Force abandoned by its allies.

When it was clear that no power on earth could stem the rout, when everything was confusion and panic, the frightened Daladier turned the reins of office over to Reynaud, who in turn called in Pétain and Weygand to carry out the task that the reaction could never have accomplished in normal circumstances—that is to say, slip the straitjacket of Fascism over the head of the bewildered and dazed French people.

Thierry Maulnier, a clerical-Fascist writer, frankly and brutally indicated the fundamental motives of the *bourgeoisie*, the clericals, and the high command in their enterprise to lead the French people into servitude when he wrote, in justification of the Munich surrender: "A victory of French arms would not have been so much a victory for France as a victory of the principles rightly regarded as leading straight to the ruin of France and of civilization itself."

He meant democratic principles!

CHAPTER THIRTEEN

In the Shadow of Tomorrow

THERE WAS AN OLD STORY, still current in my boyhood days amongst the people of the Low Countries by the Sea, which told of what happens in the night when the month of May is born. No sooner, said the legend, have the singing towers ceased tolling the hour of twelve and the last silvery vibrations of the bells fled away across the darkened fields, than a strange, mystic light slowly overspreads that world of brooding silence. I have been told by old men, who had kept a vigil to watch the wondrous spectacle, that the sheenlike radiance which impregnates the whole universe on that night of Saint Walpurgis is really not a true light at all, but rather a pale, nebulous glimmer seemingly emanating from the earth itself not unlike those ghostly wraiths of mist that we see rising from the woodland streams on a morning in early autumn. No direct or apparent source of this spectral crepuscule is discernible, for the moon remains hidden, the stars have sailed off far into the ether, and the sun is at rest in the underworld. But even as the hours of night lengthen, the astonishing phosphorescent diffusion gradually turns into a glow of lurid and frightening immensity, an aurora of doomsday hues: crimson and mauve and violet, with a lambent flame of purple rising menacingly in the background. The sky reflects the smolder of cinders, of smoking lava and of hellish, red-hot sulphur. One man said to me that looking at the eerie spectacle had given him the impression that the Milky Way had run out of its appointed track that night and was falling towards the earth in flames. What happened in truth was that the face of the night was mirroring itself in a dark glass. The universe had become a book, but a book without letters. An enormous blank page of awesome apocalyptic mys-

553

tery, luminous and at the same time black, was spread across the horizon's expanse.

Blind is he who would read, murmur the peasants of Flanders on such nights, and fool who would seek to understand!

The name day of Walpurgis, the saint who comes with balsam for the wounded heart, replaced—we do not know when—an earlier festival which was a monstrous sabbath of unclean spirits cavorting in obscene revelry on the mountaintops. It is the echo of that distant heathen wassail which is heard by the old people who say that witches and gnomes and hag-faced vampires ride forth in that hour on the wings of the storm to sing their sacrilegious canticles by the ruddy glare of the fires which are lit from the smoking ruins of Sodom's temples. The storm that comes up in the night is the ribald screaming of lost souls haunted by the lust of blood. The thunder that rolls through the hills marks the passage of the god of all the Teutonic tribes, whistle-blowing Wotan, in the act of hurling from his chariot fiery thunderbolts to frighten away the innumerable host of disembodied spirits who follow him with their curses for having lost the sun and life in the senseless wars fought for his glory alone.

Long is that night of travail. The eternal lamps are extinguished and the earth seems doomed to darkness forever. Erect in the chaos of the elements the mountains quiver as the storm lashes their flanks with torrents of swishing rain. The earth trembles and the heavens flap like a sail. All creation groaneth together as a woman in labor of birth.

It is God who is reading His book tonight, say the people in awe, and the thunderclaps mark the turning of the pages.

When the orgy of debauch is at its height, so the legend goes, the silence rushes back for a brief moment and a voice full of sorrow, which seems to call from the deepest abyss, is heard to ask: "How long, how long till the light?" A crash of thunder smothers the voice. Livid darts flash through the Egyptian blackness, and the ghoulish sabbath on the mountain resumes with still intenser fury and abandon. Ocher-tinted bolts of lightning reveal vultures blinking over carrion, hyenas feasting at a graveside, giant boas lasciviously coiling themselves around the red-stained breasts of Paphia, the mother of harlots, and goats and satyrs and nude men and women cling together in one endless lecherous saraband, dancing as they wallow in blood and dregs and sperm. . . .

When at last the first feeble rays of the rising sun touch the tips of the sacred oaks—the *danse macabre* comes to a sudden end. Now a soft, sighing moan can be heard in the branches. The leaves stir with the murmur of silken robes. The music of the water is like the tinkle of small glass lamps tenderly brushed by a woman's hand. From the soil comes the insistent tap of moles digging their artful tunnels. In the shrubbery the low, strident whistle of beetles and roaches is heard. But their cry is yet distant and hushed, as if life were still buried or held captive in its chrysalis. A note of plaintive longing, the longing of a new creation to be born, creeps into the whisper of growing things.

But now a curtain splits in the heavens, and the voice is heard to speak again: "Who is it that bringeth the light?" And the answer, as compelling as the still, small voice that Elijah heard that day when he despaired in Horeb, comes with a soft stirring of the leaves: "It is I, the human spirit, who bring the light!"

Then the sky is suddenly aglow with a flood of sunshine, and a lark flies upward to heaven's doors to be the first to greet "the tranquil eye that knoweth no envy." A chickadee and a robin intone a Te Deum. Between the freshly colored reseda and jasmine a pair of thrushes recite their gurgling prayer, and a climber picks the pearl of morning from the ciborium of the white-cupped leaves of thyme. The meadows awaken and the young grass waves gently in the perfumed breeze. All life bursts into song. For May is there, the Queen of Flowers, the month of Mary, full of grace....

That is the legend and the way it symbolizes the triumph of the spirit over nature. All night long the watchmen—the visionaries, the idealists, and the dreamers of the ages—have interrogated the heavens and scanned their blackened canopy for a sign, for a ray of light to pierce the dismal gloom, sensing, knowing by instinct, as it were, that somewhere in the dense obscurity the dawn was wandering about awaiting its hour, impatient to appear and disperse the phantoms that torment humanity. When the light has come at last the birds are the first to wing their way into its beneficent splendor. In untutored song they cry out their hymns of joy. Those birds, which do not allow themselves to be caught, are the ideals and the dreams man has dreamed of the future, of life and light and freedom. The morning breeze stirs the leaves, and man opens the gates and windows of his house, which he had bolted and barred so anxiously in the hours when darkness was upon the earth. He lets in the free winds of the spirit. He steps out upon the threshold, inhaling deeply of the pure air while contemplating the scene of an awakening universe. And in the luminous clarity of morning he dares laugh at last at the infantile fears that haunted him in the dark. He feels himself lifted above all those natural brutalities which raged in the night that has gone. He has escaped the thralldom of nature, the servitude of hatred, ferocity, and blood, and finds himself at one with a world of beauty and goodness.

In latter days men and women have remembered that legend from the infancy of their race. In their memories lingered the sound of revelry on the Goat Mountain of life, that howling and untamed abandon of the elementary gods, the wild play of brute instincts. In the darkness they had bent their heads in a feeling of fear and shame, scarcely daring to look up. But the sun always rose again and it was May, the month of the spirit. And although the old world was still there and the echo of the witches' sabbath still went screaming through the distant mountains, there was something changed, too. For one moment the ideal stood out clearer than ever before, beckoning them onward. The dream did not seem altogether impossible of realization. The environment of misery and slavery was forgotten in the clear beauty of that morning in May. Internationalism had triumphed in human thought.

Then the flags were raised aloft, the scarlet banner of the Cross and of the weary and heavy-laden. Men and women adorned themselves with purple flowers, and in long, passionate processions they marched singing of their ideal: one people, one hope, one human race, one kingdom of knowledge and light. In that sacred hour they felt that, in spite of their division and the pain and the remorse of it, there was a link, a bond between them and all living creatures, that there was a sense in their striving, that they had a common goal, that they were *socii*, comrades, brothers. Together they had come up out of the primordial, antemundane, bloodsoaked past. Hand in hand, together, they would advance into the future, to fill that unstilled hunger in their hearts, to grasp the beckoning dream and build together the temple of humanity, the Kingdom of God.

With the destruction of that hearthstone of human freedom which was France, dark night has again come over Europe. Its gloom, which numbs the heart with apprehension, is deepening by the hour as it threatens to envelop one nation after the other and the entire human race. From the mountaintops comes again the sound of that obscene witches' sabbath. All the efforts of the past, the hope of the future, of democracy, of socialism, of peace and a new civilization, have been dissipated like clouds before the wind and seem condemned to utter sterility. In vain have the watchmen stood guard, in vain have the dreamers dreamed, in vain have love and goodness been poured out by the prophets of the ideal. What we witness in our time is a great and growing desolation of the life of the spirit and the progressive withering of a civilization which was bound up with mechanicalism, soulless brutality, and demons. It has in fact become downright absurd to speak of civilization at all, for each day sees us sinking deeper into the general barbarism. The still, small voice is silenced, and we are all learning to speak the language of the enemy. What announces itself is the dictatorship of Mammon and Moloch, of violence, of seething egoism and impious brutality.

There is no denying it: we stand on the threshold of one of the major transformations of history. A civilization is passing, a world is going under. But for that reason it may also be said that a new world is in genesis. For history never contents itself with radical ruptures followed by definite cessations. Like signals from the future, faint glimmers of the coming dispensation already dart across the blackened horizon. Scientific progress has increased the interdependence, the interpenetration, and the interrelation of peoples and races to such an extent that men in the remotest corners of the world begin to think alike and react alike to the problems confronting them. Whether we like it or not, history is moving in the direction of one single unified world economy. Imperialists, bankers, big businessmen, and the intellectuals in their service are shortening distances, opening up continents, preparing world statistics and inventories—in short, technically a new life on earth is in preparation.

The time of the small independent state is over. Modern technique and the perfection of the means of transportation are eliminating the infinite number of nationally independent cubicles which were set up at a time when railways were not yet in existence and electricity, radio, and the automobile had not been dreamed of. Mankind is being turned into one single organism. The pity of it is that the so-called democracies, for reasons of particularist interest, are not speeding this process of unification by making it dependent on the free will of the peoples, but instead are struggling against the very sense of history by leaving it to the dictatorships to accomplish by force. Yet, because mankind is growing into one organism, disasters and interruptions inherent in this biogenetical process of unification no longer bear a partial character, leaving certain parts of the world unaffected while throwing certain others into turmoil. The process is one involving hundreds of millions of people, it takes in entire continents, it is universal. Before its impact the remaining Chinese walls of isolationism, however thick and high they may be, will melt like snow, and every nation under the sun will ultimately be drawn into the vortex.

Because mankind is drawing together both technically and in consciousness of belonging together, it may also be said that when the new day dawns, as it surely will, not only one or two peoples will greet the springtime, but all. . . .

That new day, however, has not come yet. The world is still in commotion; a chaos of contradictory and conflicting interests and forces. It is impossible to see what lies immediately ahead. There is but one thought to which we may hold fast as to an Ariadne's thread in the labyrinth: that the history of mankind is not a series of coincidences and accidents, but a unit and a steady process of evolution; that everything goes its appointed way and that this way, according to the word of Hegel, leads to freedom indeed. Whoever knows this also knows that out of the chaos will emerge a new order and that upheaval and war and all destined events, those full of pain not excepted, are contributing factors to the final good.

Seeing human life as one, and seeing it thus as one sees one's own life, man also knows that life is governed and motivated from the inside, from the heart "from which are the issues of life." And even as he in respect to his own life, when he wants to cast a look into the future, wisely does not pay too much attention to exteriors but seeks in his soul what hopes rise there and what aspirations come up out of his subconscious self, even so will he, in order to know something of the future of mankind, now in an era of transition, seek to discover what goes on in the deeper consciousness of man and what aspects the general psyche reveals. He will, having done this, seek analogies in history. He will discover that more than once humanity has been like "a man marching under a somber cloud," but also that at all times there were connection and continuity even across sudden breaks and interruptions in the process of evolution.

What the prophets of Israel elaborated, without the slightest hope of materialization, and before the national catastrophe intervened, was the future. It was to their work and their vision that the post-exilic seers attached themselves until from the almost withered root of Jesse blossomed the branch which was to become the salvation of the world. Later, when the classic world with all its glory descended into the grave, Saint Augustine, at a moment when the Vandals were plundering his city and church, wrote his *City of God*, which across the ruins of the times opened the way for the world that was to come.

And earlier again: was there ever, before or afterwards, a more crushing defeat of the divine order, a more complete victory of evil than at Calvary? What hope could His disciples still cherish for the establishment of the Kingdom after Jesus had expired on the cross and had been laid in the grave? Nothing remained of the dream but a sacred memory. Yet a great earthquake took place, and with it came the angel who rolled away the stone from the tomb—an event forever symbolical of the manner in which the living God intervenes in history.

It happens frequently that the forces of evil accumulate and weigh on human life to the point where they seem about to crush it. The faith, the hope, and the charity of the best, the ardent supplications of the pious, the tribulations of the just—all these do not seem capable of averting the final disaster. The days of Golgotha return with inconceivable triumphs of evil and inconceivable defeats of goodness. Anguish, iniquity, vice, dynamic and demoniacal idolatries, impious and inhuman situations of all sorts take on the appearance of invincible fatality. Evil lies on the souls of men with the suffocating weight of a mountain. There is no escape, and the cry *"Who shall roll away the stone?"* seems uttered in an unresponding void. Human forces are impotent. Man can do nothing more.

But then always and again comes the Angel of the Lord and produces a great earthquake which rolls the stone away from the tomb.

The advent of the Kingdom was itself an earthquake of that sort. For it liberated man from the burden of sin, of distress and death. It rolled away the stone of belief in fatality, which, resting ineluctably on the ancients, kept the classic world fixed and rigid in the established order, that is to say, in a state of human degradation and slavery. With the return of a belief in the living God as the builder of His Kingdom there was released that ardent stream of hope from which flowed all the revolutions of the East and of the West, the most profound ones that changed the course of history as well as those which but superficially affected the social life. And each time when the open grave seemed about to close, the earthquake repeated itself. When Christendom's breath was nearly cut off by the contrast between the factual situation of the cause of Christ and the truth of Christ, there came the shock of the Reformation, which set in motion an impetuous current of freedom and truth that nourished the life of the succeeding centuries. When that current had in turn saturated humanity to the point where a new freedom could sprout forth, the peoples threw off the yoke of feudalism and absolutism in the violent gesture of liberation known as the French Revolution. And the Russian revolution, considered as a whole—was that not a seismic upheaval of colossal dimensions—a judgment of God, and, in spite of everything, like the rolling away of the gravestone under which had lain imprisoned as in death a tenth part of the human race? Was it not a gateway to the resurrection of peoples and tribes of uncounted multitude?

And Socialism—what was that but the announcement of a coming resurrection? It is but a few decades ago that the proletariat languished under the ban of a quasi-irreductible excommunication. The new industrialism ground the working classes down into the dust and the mire, with labor laws that permitted, nay, ordered a twelve and sixteen-hour day, with children in sweatshops and in machine-roaring factories, with millions living in squalor and misery, disease-ridden, destined to early death or penurious old age, seeking a poor consolation for distress in sordid joys and alcohol, working, slaving, always producing more wealth and yet starving in the midst of plenty, without a share in culture and education and only one hope: to forget, to drown one's sorrow. Socialism was the earthquake which brought a new hope and a new vision to the world's weary and heavy-laden.

In this sense it may well be that the new world upheaval which stands before the door is a divine instrument to sweep away a civilization that was unworthy of survival. Nothing positive is gained by a mere rejection of National Socialism, Fascism, and Communism. We must learn to understand that these movements in reality are attempting to pay off, in their own way, the immense and criminal debt incurred by democracy in allowing vast numbers of mankind to sink into ever deeper misery and in not being able to seize hold of them and inspire them with an ideal. It is both useless and inhuman to pass over with contempt the raucous cry for a new concept of life which goes up from the Fascist and Communist camps. For liberal-democratic society and the bourgeois period are things of the past. A struggle has begun for an attitude of life, a way of life that will be adapted to a collectivist society. Democracy, which to many has no more intrinsic significance than the well-being enjoyed in the *status quo ante*, a nostalgia for the security of the past, has not been able to formulate a clear and consistent, grandly conceived and bold policy understandable to the masses. For that reason it has not been able and will not be able to lead the peoples, nationally and internationally, into a movement, born of a strong will and of a great moral ideal, for peace. It will not be able to lead them against the tyranny of Fascism and break the terror by which it maintains itself; nor, on the other hand, will democracy succeed in breaking the attraction that Bolshevism exercises on strong fighting natures, on the youth and the unschooled workers.

Only a radicalism which grows out of a principled opposition to capitalism and which acts according to its own scale of values can lead to victory over Fascism and imperialism, over poverty and war and ignorance.

Fascism and Communism have shown that they are capable of organizing the masses and of inspiring them. The question of decisive significance is on what basis the masses are to be bound together: on a basis of social confidence or of social fear. Dictatorship and terror, it need scarcely be said, are built on fear. It is quite true that Hitler, Mussolini, and Stalin are acclaimed by millions and that they are the object of a veneration which, seen from a distance, almost approaches deification. But there is a good deal of illusion in that worship. Clever stage managership can produce what seem to be miracles of popularity. What counts in the final analysis is what state of mind is fostered in the masses by a system of terror, intimidation, spies, secret police, and eavesdropping. That state of mind is mass fear, which sometimes manifests itself as mass enthusiasm, even as individual fear—as every soldier who ever went over the top knows well—may appear as individual courage. A system of mass control through fear must use force. The greater the fear, the mightier the military apparatus. But the greater the confidence of the masses, the less force, the less compulsion is necessary.

The fact that the masses in the course of the nineteenth and the twentieth century have passed from the passive state to the active does not in itself constitute a menace to culture, although it places society before great new tasks of a pedagogical and a moral nature. Henri de Man has pointed out the possibility of growth towards a consciousness of belonging together, on condition that the masses find their spiritual leaders and that democracy produce its aristocracy. The chief condition for this growth he considers the disappearance of fear on the part of both the masses and the leaders. We are moving towards a society, he says, "wherein—since leadership is to be on the aristocratic principle and the leadership comes up out of a democracy which has cast off the last vestiges of feudalism—an ideal human type steps to the fore, a type which shall combine in itself the feudal and bourgeois virtues of our cultural past: a brave man, but a cultured man; a man with a social conscience sharpened by knowledge, but without fear of any power on earth that stands away from the commands of this conscience.... In this social order a new scale of positive values will come to fruition in the place of the exercise of power based on fear." For there are two types amongst the leaders who have no fear of the masses: first, those whose courage rests on the fact that they despise man, and secondly, those who have no fear because, while knowing man, they nevertheless love him.

However dark the immediate future, all is not lost. Humanity will live by the faith and the hope, the love and the suffering, of a small number of men, who are to be found in all camps, dispersed through all parties and through all nations, the men who say: "Nevertheless and in spite of everything, and whatever may come, I believe." They are the "sacred root," the saving remnant. In their hearts lies the force of the resurrection which will come after the night. The world does not stand or fall with discoveries or inventions, nor with the trample of armed hosts and the thunder of bombing planes. The world stands or falls with the laws of life which Heaven has written in the human conscience. Not what man does but how he does it is decisive. In whatever direction the future moves, whether the earthquake is long in coming or not, we must from now onward learn to live and act in the knowledge that we are all responsible to and for one another, because we have one common eternal destiny and because we are dependent on the one Father, who made brothers of us all.

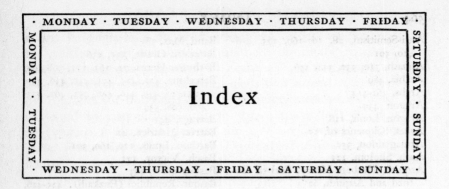

Index

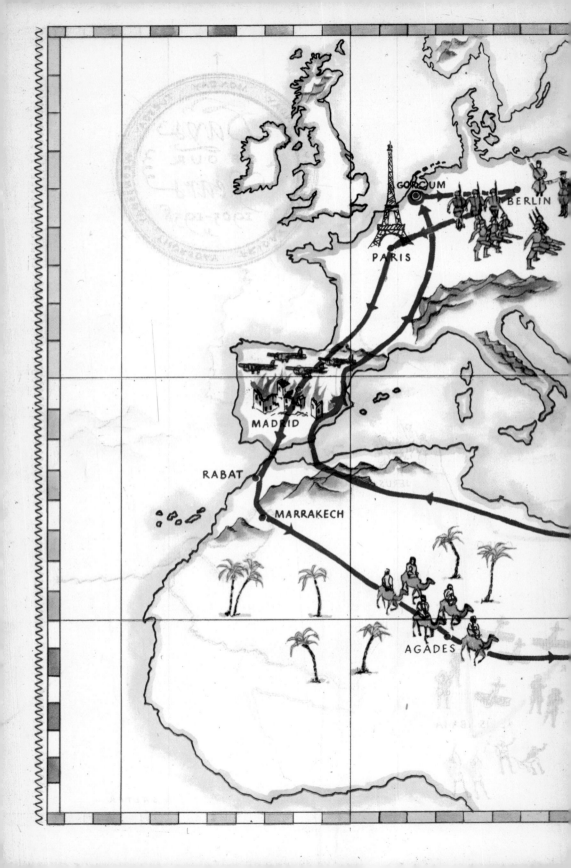